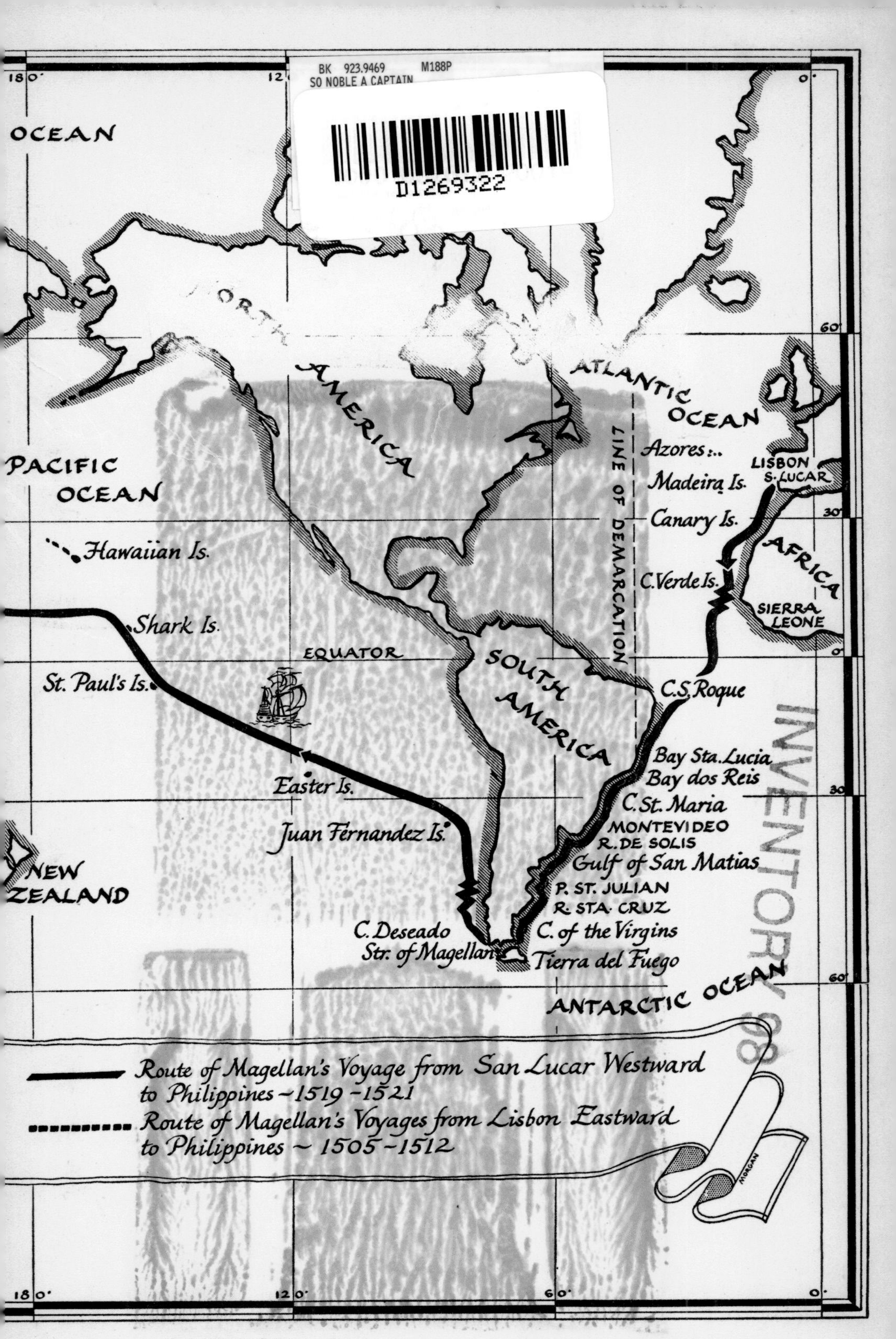
OCEAN
PACIFIC
OCEAN
AMERICA
ATLANTIC
OCEAN
LINE OF DEMARCATION
Azores
LISBON
S. LUCAR
Madeira Is.
Canary Is.
AFRICA
Hawaiian Is.
C. Verde Is.
SIERRA
LEONE
Shark Is.
EQUATOR
St. Paul's Is.
SOUTH
AMERICA
C. S. Roque
Bay Sta. Lucia
Bay dos Reis
Easter Is.
C. St. Maria
MONTEVIDEO
R. DE SOLIS
Juan Fernandez Is.
Gulf of San Matias
NEW
ZEALAND
P. ST. JULIAN
R. STA. CRUZ
C. Deseado
C. of the Virgins
Str. of Magellan
Tierra del Fuego
ANTARCTIC OCEAN
Route of Magellan's Voyage from San Lucar Westward to Philippines – 1519 – 1521
Route of Magellan's Voyages from Lisbon Eastward to Philippines ~ 1505 – 1512
MORGAN
180°
120°
60°
0°
60°
30°
0°
30°
60°

SO NOBLE A CAPTAIN

Engraving from "Ultimo Viage al Estrecho de Magallanes," 1788

FERDINAND MAGELLAN

CHARLES McKEW PARR

SO NOBLE A CAPTAIN

The Life and Times of Ferdinand Magellan

NEW YORK THOMAS Y. CROWELL COMPANY

Manufactured in the United States of America by the Vail-Ballou Press, Inc., Binghamton, New York.

LIBRARY OF CONGRESS CATALOG CARD NO. 53-7525

Designed by Dorris Janowitz Huth

To Elizabeth

PREFACE

THIS BIOGRAPHY has been written in compliance with a plea to do justice to the memory of Ferdinand Magellan which was uttered over four centuries ago by a shipmate of the great circumnavigator.

In 1525, Ser Antonio Francesco Pigafetta, Patrician of Venice and Knight of Rhodes, complained by implication that the unworthy men who had betrayed Ferdinand Magellan were persons of such influence at the court of the Emperor that he, Magellan's comrade, had not dared raise his voice to expose them and to defend his dead commander's honor. Therefore, the Venetian knight in despair made supplication in favor of Magellan's renown to his superior, "the Most Illustrious and Very Excellent Seignior Phillippe de l'Isle Adam, Renowned Grand Master of Rhodes."

He described the heroic death of the circumnavigator in moving phrases. "When they wounded him, he turned back many times to see whether we were all in the boats . . . Thus the natives killed our mirror, our light, our comfort, and our true guide . . . Had it not been for that unfortunate Captain, not a single one of us would have been saved, for while he was fighting, the others retired to the boats, which were already pulling off . . . When the Christian King learned that the Captain was dead, he wept . . . Among the other virtues which he possessed, he was more constant than ever anyone else in the greatest adversity. He endured hunger better than all the others, and more accurately than any man in the world did he understand sea charts and navigation. And that this was the truth was seen openly, for no other had so much natural talent nor the boldness to learn how to circumnavigate the world . . . I hope that through the efforts of your most illustrious lordship the fame of so noble a Captain will not be effaced in our time."

When I first ran across the words of this petition for justice to Magellan's memory, they had a strong appeal for me, for I had just read, in a volume published in 1911, a reference to Ferdinand Magellan by a scholarly English author who, misled by the false testimony of Magellan's detractors, had represented him in an odious light.

I read this slighting reference to Magellan in 1940, when I happened to be grounded on Guam as a result of a mishap to a Pacific Clipper, en route to Hong Kong. Although I had long been a student of Spanish colonial history, I knew practically nothing of Magellan, and my attention was then attracted to him because Guam had been his landfall in his historic voyage across the Pacific.

In the Philippines, I found a Spanish version of Pigafetta's Journal and encountered, to my surprise, the laudatory passages quoted above. My curiosity aroused, I finally spent a decade in study of the journals, logs, court records, and the many fabrications and forgeries which pertain to Magellan's life. I found it necessary to search many archives in several countries in order to learn the backgrounds and the records not only of Ferdinand Magellan and of his defender, Antonio Pigafetta, but also of his enemies, Cristóbal de Haro and Bishop Juan Rodríguez de Fonseca. I learned that, in the past fifty years, several writers have expressed a more sympathetic view of Magellan, but I retained my first impression that full justice yet remained to be done him.

Therefore I now present my evidence, in the hope that I may have been able to help carry out the mandate of Antonio Pigafetta, and that "the fame of so noble a Captain will not be effaced in our time."

ACKNOWLEDGMENTS

THIS VOLUME would hardly be complete without recording my appreciation and thanks for the help I have received from many quarters. Portuguese and Spanish historians made me most welcome and accorded me every assistance. In Lisbon I was substantially helped by the late Colonel Lopes Galvão, Perpetual Secretary of the Sociedade de Geografia, and by Dr. José Maria de Queiroz Velloso, Professor Jubilado da Universidade de Lisboa, author of *A Naturalidade de Fernão de Magalhãis.*

I am particularly indebted to my friend the Vicomte de Lagôa, who most generously offered me free use of the material published in his monumental *Fernão de Magalhãis.*

Also I am indebted to Senhor Antonio Machada de Faria of the Academia Portuguesa da Historia in Lisbon, and to Senhor José Gaspar de Almeida, Conservador do Arquivo Nacional da Torre do Tombo, as well as to Senhor Frazão de Vasconcellos, Primeiro Oficial da Biblioteca de Marinha. From Senhorita Luiza de Fonseca, of the Arquivo Histórico Colonial, I received valuable information concerning the Fonseca genealogy.

In Porto I was aided in many practical ways by Dom Antonio Pinto Machado, Director do Palácio de Cristal of Porto. The late Dr. Vasco Valente, Director de Museu Nacional de Soares dos Reis, and author of *O Vidro em Portugal,* supplied me with important genealogical information regarding his Magellan ancestors, as did Dr. Pedro Magalhães e Menezes van Zeller. The Conde de Alvellos, head of the Clan Magellan, and author of *O Brazão dos Magalhães,* was extremely generous with his assistance.

Dr. Gaspar de Abreu e Lima, who resides in the Magellan manor of Paço Vedro, in Ponte da Barca, was hospitality itself. The historic donjon keep of the *Torre de Magalhães* is on his estate. He took me about the countryside and supplied me with legendary accounts of the family at the *Quinta de Magalhães.*

I likewise am indebted for genealogical information and data regarding the boyhood of Magellan to the Reverend Avelino de Jesus da Costa, now of the University of Coimbra and formerly Professor do Seminário de Braga, historian, and author of *S. Martinho de Dume.*

In Sabrosa, Dom Antonio de Castro, Marques Marinho, helped me investigate the traces of the Magellans and da Sousas there.

In Madrid, the illustrious colonial historian, the Reverend Constantino Bayle, S.J., author of *El Descubrimiento del Estrecho de Magallanes,* was most kind, as was Señor Miguel Bordonau Mas, Director General de Archivos y Bibliotecas, who extended to me all the facilities under his jurisdiction.

In the Archivo General de Indias, Seville, I received cordial assistance from Dr. Cristóbal Bermúdez Plata, Director, as well as from the Secretary of the Archivo, Señor Diego Bermúdez Camacho, and from Dr. José de la Pena, Vice Director. Several of the professors and instructors of the University of Seville and of the Hispanic-American School gave me advice and assistance. The American Consul in Seville, Mr. Terry Bentley Sanders, Jr., was of material help.

Professor Manuel Hidalgo Nieto, Professor of History of the University of Seville, has continuously supplied me with notes and documentation for several years.

It is impossible for me to express my obligation to the eminent American paleographer, Dr. Adele Kibre, who, after a brilliant career at the Vatican, has in recent years been conducting research in Spain for the Library of Congress of the United States and for the Bancroft Library of the University of California. She enlisted in my aid the services of many scholars in Seville. Dr. Kibre for the past three years, in collaboration with Professor Hidalgo, has edited and transmitted to me a great number of copies of documents pertaining to the Magellanic enterprise, and particularly relating to the operations of Cristóbal de Haro, the financial backer of Magellan. A schedule of these documents is given in the Bibliography.

At the National Archives at the Castle of Simancas, Valladolid, I was given the wholehearted assistance of Dr. Alice Bache Gould, the foremost authority on the history of the Columbian expeditions. Dr. Gould graciously turned over to me her invaluable notes pertaining to Bishop Fonseca, sponsor of Magellan's expedition, which she had accumulated over a period of forty years of research in the Archives.

In Simancas I also was helped by Dr. Filemón Arribas, Deputy Director of the Archivo Nacional, and by his two able assistants, Señorita Asunción de Mendoza and Señorita Amalia Prieto.

In Coca I was aided in my researches by Don Arturo Acosta Garcia, Alcalde y Procurador en Cortes. In Alaejos I was much helped by the

Reverendo Isidoro Gonzales Frutos, and in Toro by Don Mariano Diez Vázquez, Secretario del Ayuntamiento, and in Haro by Don Enrique Hermosilla Diez, Oficial Mayor del Ayuntamiento. I also owe thanks to Don Miguel Gallardo, Dipl-Ing., of Puerto-Real.

I am indebted to Dr. Sidney R. Welch of Capetown, South Africa, author of *Europe's Discovery of South Africa* and *South Africa under King Manuel,* for much information.

I am grateful to Mrs. Frances Boyesen for the research which she did for me in Antwerp concerning the activities of Cristóbal de Haro and of Diego, his brother, in that sixteenth century emporium, and to Professor Manuel Hidalgo Nieto for conducting a similar search in the Archives at Coruña for me concerning the activities of Cristóbal de Haro in the Galician capital when it was the seat of the Casa de Especieria. Miss Isabel Ely Lord was of great help in the checking of details in the early stages.

I wish to thank the Right Reverend Henry J. O'Brien, Bishop of Hartford, Mr. James Brewster, State Librarian of Connecticut, and Lieutenant Colonel W. J. Morton, Librarian, U.S. Military Academy, for providing me with credentials that were to be so useful in my researches in Iberian libraries and archives.

I am obligated also to the Reverend Dr. Horacio de la Costa, S.J., of Manila, author of *Development of Native Clergy in the Philippines,* who was of help in the early stages of the manuscript.

The writing of this history was first suggested to me by Miss Elizabeth M. Riley, who had edited a former book of mine, and who has during the past ten years given me counsel and untiring assistance in the preparation of my manuscript.

I also want to thank Mrs. Frances Stillman not only for the sympathetic editing of the manuscript but also for the zeal and enthusiasm which she lent to the undertaking. My thanks go to Ruth Lapham Butler, curator of the Ayer and Greenlee Collections of the Newberry Library, Chicago, for help with the illustrations and for the preparation of the index.

My sister, Mary Parr, has patiently acted as my amanuensis and librarian and has been untiring in her devotion not only to the author but also to the subject of this book.

CHARLES MCKEW PARR

CONTENTS

ILLUSTRATIONS

SO NOBLE A CAPTAIN

INTRODUCTION

PORTUGAL AND THE MAGELLANS

FERDINAND MAGELLAN'S earliest ancestor in Portugal is a legendary figure who was probably a French adventurer from Burgundy named de Magalhais. He apparently established an estate at Ponte da Barca near Braga, in northern Portugal, about 1095 A.D. At that time he built, as a defense against the Moors, a rude stronghold whose vestiges are still called the *Torre de Magalhais;* there his descendant, Ferdinand, was to be born. This earliest Magellan was one of the followers of that fortune-seeking Henry of Burgundy who became Count of Portucalensis (the Roman name from which Porto was derived) in 1097 A.D. and who founded the modern kingdom of Portugal.

That the first Magellan found himself in Portugal with Henry of Burgundy was because their liege lord, the Gallo-Flemish Duke Eudes, had been led by the trend of the times to go adventuring abroad to expand his realm. Both Norman Duke William (who had just made himself King of England) and Burgundian Duke Eudes decided, almost simultaneously, that the Iberian Peninsula afforded them a field for exploitation. However, the Burgundian established himself in Spain a year ahead of the Norman and checkmated him.

It happened at that time that the Hispano-Gothic King of Leon, in northwest Spain, had been carrying on the reconquest of the Iberian Peninsula from the Moors. His wife was a Burgundian princess, and he had appealed to her relatives to aid him in his crusade; therefore in 1087 A.D. Duke Eudes of Burgundy led an expedition of French knights to Spain. The Burgundian Duke proceeded subtly to take possession of the Kingdom of Leon. Within a few years his brother had married the crown princess and become heir apparent to the throne. His cousin, Count Henry, married the other daughter of the King of Leon, a bastard princess, and acquired as a fief the former Roman province of Portucalensis, then a practically unpopulated no man's land between the warring Christian and Moslem principalities.

The earliest Magellan must have stood high in the favor of the ruling Burgundian clique, for the fief of Ponte da Barca which was bestowed upon him was in one of the most fertile and delightful tracts of farmland to be found in all Europe. This the pioneer Magellan subdivided into farmsteads, and he persuaded his men-at-arms to settle down and become his feudal tenants. He also offered free land, tax favors, and other inducements to the Christian groups called *Mozarabes* who had recently been liberated from serfdom in reconquered Moorish Castile, if they would immigrate to neighboring Portucalensis and become part of the colony that clustered about the walls of his stronghold. The community grew rapidly and became the town of Ponte da Barca; in 1125 A.D., it was granted a municipal charter by Countess Teresa, the widow of Henry of Burgundy, Count of Portucalensis.

The Magellan estate lay near the capital city of Braga, which became the seat of the Archbishop Primate of Portugal; and as the pioneer's descendants advanced in favor at the archepiscopal court, they made themselves secure in their feudal heritage and even became distantly connected by marriage with the reigning family itself. Hence the later Magellans were privileged to show as quarterings on their coat of arms the five bezants or *quinas* from the royal blazon.

For two centuries their history, although unknown in detail, must have been frequently punctuated by ambuscades, sieges, and pillage, for such was the life of a noble family in Portugal. During the early years the land was frequently raided by Vikings, who not only harried the coast but marched inland to attack Braga itself. The Norse pirates were succeeded by Moslem freebooters from North Africa, who sacked the churches, burned the villages, and abducted for their harems the nuns and young women. In these troubles, it was the feudal duty of the landed gentry, such as the Magellans, to furnish their lord, the Archbishop of Braga, with fighting galleys manned by their own farm tenants to patrol the coast.

Portugal now had become an isolated land, for a hostile Spain shut it off. Its only avenue of contact with the European world was the sea. Thus the Portuguese became perforce a race of sailors, and before long had established touch with those other amphibians, the men of the British Isles. French monks from Cluny, with the international power of the Church, supplied the clerical element in Portugal, but the nation was otherwise walled off by Spain from reaching Burgundy, France, and Italy.

Although the ancestors of Ferdinand Magellan were agrarian, nevertheless they were influenced by the nearby maritime city of Porto. Every spring the Venetian and Genoan caravans, as they were called, would put in for stores and water at Porto on their biennial voyages to and from Southampton, England, and Bruges, Flanders. Then the aristocratic commanders of the war galleys which convoyed the merchant fleets would visit with the rural gentry and would retail to them the news of the Adriatic, Mediterranean, and Baltic worlds.

Meanwhile the Archbishop of Braga under Genoese tutelage developed a native merchant marine, and his ships, with Portuguese crews and Genoese commanders, began to go north each spring across the Bay of Biscay to England. Possibly the Magellans participated in these ventures. In the year 1226, over one hundred safe-conducts against privateers were granted by the King of England to Portuguese merchant captains to visit England for trading.

As the Moors were progressively expelled from Portugal, substantially by the aid of English crusaders, the nation expanded southward to the land's end. The country became unified, and Lisbon, the capital, began to rival Porto as the metropolis. However, the naval leadership continued to center in the Archbishopric of Braga. In 1300, King Dinis planted along the sandy seacoast many thousands of coniferous seedlings, which grew into a great coastal pine forest; he wished to provide an unfailing source of timbers, spars, and resin for the ships.

The King also made of boat building an aristocratic calling, and had the Archbishop of Braga encourage his vassals, such as the Magellans, to build and operate local shipyards. The sheltered shores of the little Lima River, north of Ponte da Barca, provided a suitable location for upriver shipyards, for there the hulls were safe from Atlantic gales and from the torch of hostile sea raiders. These small dockyards lacked expert carpenters and riggers, and the Archbishop arranged with the labor guilds in Genoa to provide shipwrights in consideration of free homes for the immigrants in the villages near the plants, with exemptions from taxes and from military service. This program was a success, and the Magellans probably had their share in it. Before long, numerous squat, single-masted, square-sailed *naos,* of one hundred tons and more, were sailing north from Porto to England during the favorable summer season, with cargoes of port wine, cork, sardines, salt fish, hides, salt, and dried fruits; the next summer they would bring back wool, tin, and various Hanseatic products in exchange. The Moslem naval raids had now diminished, but this did not bring peace to the Magellans and their neighbors. They still had to maintain an alert naval patrol against the galleys from Spanish Galicia which continued to harry the Portuguese coast around Porto.

During these two hundred turbulent years, the Magellan family continued to cling closely to its fertile acres near Ponte da Barca as members of the minor nobility of the Province of Minho. To the head of the clan there descended by primogeniture the titles of *Senhor de Ponte da Barca, Senhor de Torre de Nobrega,* and *Senhor da Quinta e Torre de Magalhanes.* They still clustered about the original crude stronghold, too small to be called a castle, which had been built by the legendary crusader who came with Henry of Burgundy.

Families such as the Magellans of the later medieval period gave no thought to preserving for posterity any account of their personal lives. They were far too busy with practical affairs. Some scanty traces can be uncovered in terse municipal charters, feudal grants, and crabbed monkish archives, couched in a dog Latin that shows little learning. The parchment title deeds which have survived in the coffers of the military orders of the Knights Templars and the Knights of Avis sometimes yield an inkling to an important man's career.

Life in those times was chronicled not so much in parchments as in ecclesiastical architecture. The cathedrals and abbeys were built not like churches, but like castles, little more than square, unadorned donjon keeps, erected to give sanctuary to the families of the countryside when the Castilians made a foray, or when the Portuguese men-at-arms from a neighboring barony made a raid upon the region. At a time when contemporary Europe was being graced by exquisite Gothic structures, the Portuguese erected only castellated churches which symbolized the saddle and lance of the medieval freebooter, and unceasing civil war.

The only literary contribution of medieval Portugal was the great tale of chivalry *Amadis of Gaul,* which was translated into many languages. The unlettered common people expressed themselves in popular songs with a romantic or plaintive appeal. These were carried across the borders by strolling singers to be translated into the Provence dialects and sung by troubadours in the castle halls of Western Europe. Such little clerkly learning as existed was of French origin and was confined to the several monasteries of the Cistercian monks who first had been brought to Portugal by Count Henry, the Burgundian. Braga, as the seat of the Primate of Portugal, had its pretensions to a share of this primitive scholarship, and the Magellans, although only country gentry, probably participated to some extent in the provincial culture of the Archbishop's court. But there is no evidence upon this point.

The unceasing war with Castile so enfeebled the little nation, after many generations, that it finally made a desperate appeal to England for military help to keep from losing its independence. Therefore, in July, 1372, a formal British embassy arrived at the Archbishop's court at Braga and was met there by King Ferdinand of Portugal, who signed a treaty of alliance with England against Castile and France. However, the war went badly with Portugal both by land and by sea, and all contact with their English ally was cut off. At this point disaster was averted by an epidemic in the forces of Castile, and Portugal was able to negotiate a truce, although on harsh and humiliating terms. It looked as though the end of the nation was near.

But during the several years of confusion and struggle that followed, the Archbishop adopted a maritime policy that saved the country. Somehow, by hook or crook and immense hard work on the part of his vassals, he built up a small fleet. And when, in 1381, the Spaniards suddenly broke the truce and swarmed upon the little kingdom, hoping to subjugate it once and for all, the Archbishop was ready for them. His little fleet made a dash for England to appeal for help. The English, with Edmund, Duke of York, as their commander, answered the appeal. Under immense difficulties the siege of Lisbon was lifted, the enemy were driven back behind their borders, and a peace which saved the independence of Portugal was arranged.

The name of the first of the Magellans of Minho province whom we can reasonably identify as an ancestor of the Circumnavigator now emerges. He was Affonso Rodrigues de Magalhanes, the great-great-grandfather of Ferdinand Magellan. We have neither the date of his birth nor of his death, but we do know that he was married to a Donha Sancha de Novaes. Because of the political activity of his liege lord, Dom Lorenzo Vicente, Archbishop of Braga, it is likely that Dom Affonso Rodrigues de Magellan took an important part in the stirring events of his day. In 1383, the Archbishop did more than follow the high tradition of his office in fostering the growth of Portugal as a maritime power and as the ally of seafaring Britain. He now also assumed the role of king-maker, and through his efforts he aroused the burghers and lower classes to acclaim John of Avis, an obscure military monk, bastard half-brother of the late king, as King John the First of Portugal.

The King of Castile was the legitimate claimant to the throne, and most of the Portuguese nobility supported him; the Archbishop confiscated the estates of these nobles. He then pledged this wealth to the Jewish moneylenders of London, and used it to raise a mercenary army of unemployed English knights and archers to make good the usurpation.

The Archbishop had by now expanded his personal navy to comprise twelve oared galleys, seven galeasses propelled by both oars and sails, and seven square-rigged sailing *naos,* twenty-six fighting ships in all. With this force he kept open his sea lane to England, and in March, 1385, in "two *naos,* a *barca,* and a transport," as a contemporary document records it, he freighted the band of English mercenaries for Porto. A storm scattered the expedition. The two *naos* became separated from their consorts and were blown south past their destination at Porto; on April 6, 1385, they saved themselves by running into Lisbon harbor, which then was being blockaded by the navy of Castile. The Castilian war galleys eagerly dashed out to capture the two seemingly storm-wracked and helpless merchant craft thus delivered into their hands. When the galleys came alongside, ready to board, their decks were swept by a deadly flight of English cloth-yard arrows. The Castilian squadron, taken by surprise, sheered off in panic, and the English disembarked amid the cheers of the jubilant townspeople who had crowded the walls to watch the sea fight.

On August 14, 1385, at Aljubarrota, one of the decisive battles of Portuguese history was fought. The army of Castile was greatly superior in numbers, and at first, although the Portuguese fought desperately, the massive charge of the Castilian knights almost overwhelmed them. The Archbishop, who had donned armor and rode at the head of his contingent from Braga, was unhorsed and wounded in the face, and the group of knights fighting around John of Avis was surrounded. Then, suddenly, the English archers on the flanks of the Portuguese position came into their own, and with their deadly archery they mowed down the Spanish who had advanced only in the center of the line. Thus victory was snatched from defeat, and it was the story of Crecy and Poitiers all over again. In a few moments the astonished bodyguard of John of Avis found themselves in excited pursuit of a panic-stricken mob of fleeing Spaniards. In the rout, the royal standard of Castile itself sank down, and on the stricken field there were slaughtered not only the Castilian knights but also most of the ancient nobility of Portugal who had been fighting for Castile against the usurping Bastard of Avis.

After the victory of Aljubarrota, the restless Archbishop of Braga, although not yet recovered from his wound, decided to try to annex for his newly made King a goodly portion of defeated Castile. To do this, he again had recourse to his English allies, and in the name of John of Avis he made an agreement to share Castile with the heir to the English throne. This was Prince John of Gaunt, brother of the Black Prince, whom Shakespeare calls "time honored Lancaster," and who did not lack a good pretext for his claim to the crown of Castile. Once again the war galleys of the Archbishop of Braga left Porto to escort English troops to the Peninsula. The date was July 9, 1386. John of Gaunt embarked at Plymouth and sailed directly to Coruña, Spain, with his superb army of twenty thousand Englishmen. He captured the city easily and raised over the city's castle his heraldic ensign bearing the lilies of France, the leopards of England, and now the lions and castles of Castile. Thus he proclaimed himself King of Castile.

Philippa of Lancaster

This landing at Coruña was an event of lasting moment, for with John of Gaunt there came ashore his daughter, a plain-featured, brown-haired, Anglo-Flemish spinster whose destiny was to influence the course of Portuguese history. Like her grandniece, Queen Isabella the Catholic, and like her red-haired, great-great-grandniece, Queen Elizabeth Tudor, this unobtrusive woman named Philippa of Lancaster was to become the mother of a great empire.

It was part of the agreement made by John of Gaunt with the Archbishop of Braga that his daughter, Philippa, was to be married to King John of Avis. The Archbishop knew she was ugly and older than John by some years, for John was only 28, and her hand had in the past been refused by several other royal bachelors, notably by King Charles VI of France and Albert, Duke of Bavaria. However, the Archbishop's bargain had committed the King, and John of Gaunt now held them to it. John of Avis tried his best to get out of the arrangement. He went off to the country for two months with his mistress and their two illegitimate children, and sent back protestations that his monastic oath would prevent his ever contracting a marriage. John of Gaunt promptly produced a letter from the Pope absolving the bastard king of his vows of celibacy. John of Avis still temporized. On February 2, 1387, the Englishman sent a peremptory demand to John of Avis that he marry his daughter at once. He backed his ultimatum by an army of the best troops in Europe and threatened to withhold from Portugal a loan of which the country stood in desperate need. That did it.

In February of the same year, on Candlemas Day, the Archbishop of Braga, with his face still hidden in bandages to conceal his unhealed wounds of Aljubarrota, united the sullen King with the mortified princess in a resplendent ceremony. The royal couple played their part before the brilliant assemblage, but in private John of Avis treated his sensitive bride with churlish asperity, and after the festivities he left her at once for the camp of his army and plunged into the campaign against the Spanish.

Philippa had received a remarkable education. As a girl and young woman she had been the pupil of the Flemish poet Froissart, the foremost chronicler of medieval courts, who for years was a guest at her father's house. Another of her tutors was the learned Friar John, the great pioneer in physics and chemistry, who presumably developed in her a sense of critical inquiry that was to become one of her outstanding characteristics. Her dearest teacher, however, was Geoffrey Chaucer, her father's intimate friend, who did much to mold her gifted young mind.

Philippa was in, but not of, the English court, at that time the most dissolute and extravagant in Europe. From this fashionable society, where conjugal fidelity was derided, Philippa held aloof. Her father confessor was the reformer John Wycliffe, Professor of Philosophy at Oxford and first translator of the Bible into English. He passed on to Philippa his own philosophy, which was so free of superstition, and this helped to make her a tolerant and enlightened leader.

John of Avis, although he had been forced to go through a legal ceremony that made Philippa his Queen, was reluctant to accept her as his wife. He felt nothing for her but a sense of repulsion. So he avoided her and continued to seek solace, between campaigns, with his mistress in Lisbon. Philippa remembered with bitterness that her childhood home had been openly dominated by her governess, who was her father's mistress, and she was determined not to go through the same humiliating experience in the household she had set up in a foreign land. She awaited her time patiently; while the King was at the front, she sent a group of clerics and knights to the house where he kept his mistress. That lady was then immured in the ancient convent of Santos, where she would not be accessible; but Philippa saw to it that her discomfited rival was treated with every respect and given a dignified establishment with an ample allowance. Philippa adopted the King's two illegitimate children, the elder of whom was a boy of nine, and reared them with her own children as they were born. Thus she not only gave to Portugal her own sons, who became the great princes of the House of Avis, but she also conscientiously reared, in her husband's illegitimate offspring, the founders of the bastard House of Braganza.

Gradually Philippa's qualities of heart and mind, combined with her force of character, gained the respect and affection of her husband. In time she bore him ten children and made of him a devoted husband and father. She restrained his excesses, encouraged his taste for study, and brought out his literary ability, which had hitherto been unnoticed.

It was in this generation that the affairs of the Magellan family took a prosperous turn. Now that the Archbishop had become so influential politically, it followed that the noble families of Minho who were his vassals were advanced to important positions at court. Although we have no record of any high honors bestowed upon the contemporary Dom Affonso Rodrigues Magellan, we do know that, when King John assembled his knights to give welcome to John of Gaunt, he designated the Magellan manor of Ponte da Barca as the rendezvous for his suite. To have his home selected as the temporary abode of the King meant that Dom Affonso Rodrigues Magellan stood high in royal favor.

Drawing after a sixteenth-century illuminated manuscript

PHILIPPA OF LANCASTER, QUEEN OF PORTUGAL
Mother of the Portuguese Empire

Gil Affonso Magellan, the second child and heir of Dom Affonso Rodrigues Magellan, appears to have become a comrade and favorite of John of Avis, and probably also of Queen Philippa. In 1387, the year of the marriage of John of Avis and Philippa, there was also solemnized the wedding of Dom Gil Affonso Magellan with one of the ladies in waiting of Queen Philippa. She was Donha Ines Vasques do Urro, heiress of Don Antonio Gil do Urro and of Donha Leonor Vasques. At that time, a lady in waiting was treated as a ward of the royal family; her match must have been arranged by the Queen herself.

Gil Affonso Magellan was endowed with the estate and poetic title of *Senhor de Fonte Arcada,* one of the rich manors confiscated by the crown from a partisan of Castile. The old book of the peerage expressly refers to the bestowal as *por mercé de dom Joam,* by the grace of King John, so it is quite probable that he had distinguished himself by some feat at arms. Some time later, Gil Affonso Magellan lost his first wife, Donha Ines, in the epidemic of plague that decimated the court, and in due time he made another advantageous marriage with the daughter of Dom Gonzalo Rodrigues de Sousa. He evidently continued to enjoy royal favor, and eventually attained the title of Lord of the Village and Valley of Larim. With his inherited family estates and those which he acquired, he was now a nobleman of substance, and during his lifetime the fortunes of the Magellan family appear to have reached their peak. We do not know any further details of his life, nor is there a record of his death. After his successful career, the court influence of the Magellans seems to have diminished with the decline of the power of the Archbishopric of Braga, to which they were attached, and there is little more known of the family during the next two generations.

It was during this time that King John delegated the administration of civil affairs to Philippa. While he guarded the frontiers, Philippa established a more orderly state of affairs at home than Portugal had known since the days of the Romans. She became the balance wheel of the kingdom, and quietly introduced many enlightened customs from Flanders and England. Diplomatic and commercial bonds between Portugal and England were made permanent under a reciprocal treaty signed on May 9, 1396, a treaty which, in modified form, has continued in force between the two nations for over five centuries. In these pacific labors she was helped not only by the burghers and the sober new aristocracy which John of Avis had created from his middle class supporters, but also by the Jews, to whom she gave help and who in turn supported her aims. Clearsightedly, and with a deep devotion to duty, she ruled in the name of her husband.

By the year 1410, John of Avis and Philippa of Lancaster had ruled for a quarter of a century, and during all that time the nation had been at war with Spain or the Berbers. The entire economy was adjusted to a state of hostilities. All trade, finance, and taxation were on a war basis, and a goodly part of the male population was kept under arms. An index to the unsettled times is the law that compelled every able-bodied man not serving in the armed forces to labor for a certain number of days per year upon the walls and defenses of his home town. Besides this, all male noncombatants were required to serve for some weeks annually in the watchtowers and observation posts which had been set up at close intervals on the inland borders and along the seacoast to give warning of Castilian and Berber raids.

This unceasing border warfare, coupled with the expense of maintaining a strong navy, was exhausting the kingdom's economy. Despite Philippa's carefulness, the royal treasury finally lacked currency even to pay current expenses. The deficit grew until a metallic basis of payments was no longer possible. Philippa could not even buy copper for coinage from the Fugger Trust, and she was driven to issue as legal tender a bizarre fiat money, in the form of circular tokens blanked out of sole leather and stamped with the royal effigy and insignia. This desperate expedient naturally drove all the existing hard money out of circulation, and the nation was actually reduced to primitive barter to carry on its trade.

In 1411, national bankruptcy seemed imminent. This would, of course, have meant the end of the dynasty of John of Avis. But a political change in enemy Spain brought about a sudden cessation of hostilities. The abrupt change from war to peace disrupted all trade and completed the upset of a society that for a whole generation had been organized on a war footing. Thousands of soldiers, sailors, mechanics, and shipyard workers were thrown into unemployment, and distress and hunger were universal. Unless the government could devise a solution, revolution was inevitable. The royal councilors agreed that, since warfare had become the normal state of the nation, the crown would have to choose between a disastrous civil war, in which Castile would again undoubtedly intervene, or a diversionary foreign war. Some councilors suggested an alliance with Castile against the Moorish kingdom of Granada, but the Spaniards rejected the proposal. Others urged an immediate resumption of hostilities against Castile; an attempt to annex Spanish Galicia was always popular. It also was proposed that an army be sent to help the Emperor of Austria against the Turks, but King John vetoed sending the nation's defenders so far away.

It was Philippa who calmly proposed an armed expedition to penetrate the Moslem Kingdom of Fez, in order to reach the land of Prester John, the fabled African Christian ruler who now has been identified as the Negus of Abyssinia. An alliance with him, she maintained, would open up for Portugal the Indian sources of spices and oriental products now monopolized by Egypt and Venice.

To her astounded auditors the proposal of the Queen was preposterous. Most of the narrow prelates and unlettered nobles who comprised the royal council were incapable even of comprehending the scope of the suggestion. From a military and naval point of view it appeared suicidal to consider invading the Berber kingdom in Africa. Since the failure of the crusades no one had thought of such a thing. All Christendom was on the defensive against the Moslems, and Portugal itself was having difficulty in protecting its southern coast from the Berber raiders who were based on the citadel of Ceuta, opposite Gibraltar on the African shore, just across the Straits. The idea of going through the Kingdom of Fez in Morocco, thus by-passing Egypt, and reaching India via the fabulous Kingdom of Prester John appeared a fantasy. Most of the council believed that Fez represented the limit of the livable zone, and that beyond its borders the heat of the sun in the torrid desert was so intense that it not only turned men black, but if one had the temerity to persist in journeying onward, the solar rays would burn the rash traveler to a crisp.

When the Queen said that one might proceed south by sea, the objectors claimed that the final limit of safe navigation was at a promontory on the coast of Fez called Cape Non, beyond which was the Green Sea of Darkness, shrouded in mephitic vapors and said to be peopled by huge serpents and sea monsters. Moreover, any unlucky ship that might venture around Cape Non would be sure to be sucked down by whirlpools in the near-boiling Ocean Sea, or swept into the fall of a thundering cataract.

Some of the prelates who held these views were men of erudition on other subjects, but their minds were closed on geographic matters because the doctors of the Church had adopted the theories of a Greek cosmographer named Ptolemy, who in A.D. 130 had issued in Alexandria a comprehensive atlas of Europe and the Orient in which he had completely ignored the southwest coast of Africa below the Kingdom of Fez. In the East he had shown the Indian Ocean as a landlocked sea that had no communication with the South Atlantic, which indeed he suggested was quite unnavigable. Yet Ptolemy's atlas was still considered valid some twelve hundred years or so later.

The assurance and conviction with which Philippa pushed her proposal make it seem probable that her wide reading had made her familiar with the account written by the Greek historian Herodotus of a voyage around Africa from the Red Sea, south through the Indian Ocean, and north up the Atlantic to Gibraltar, said to have been made centuries before Christ by Phoenician galleys at the command of the Egyptian Pharaoh Necho. She also, no doubt, had pondered over the narrative written by the Roman historian Pliny of a southerly cruise along the southwestern African coast by a Carthaginian named Hanno. Most scholars of her day had read Herodotus and Pliny, but many, unlike Philippa, were influenced by the prevailing geographic theories and rejected as fables these stories of an earlier age of maritime enterprise. With her Hanseatic background, Philippa could not have failed to have heard of the voyages of Lief Ericson across the Atlantic to Greenland, and she could therefore be certain that the Ocean Sea could be traversed safely, despite the terrifying legends to the contrary.

Moreover, Philippa very probably had analyzed the description by Marco Polo of the oriental world, and perhaps she had been given an opportunity to read the reports in the Vatican of several overland visits to the Orient by monkish travelers who had materially corroborated the evidence of the classical historians. There were at that time in Europe some hundreds of Genoese, Venetians, and Byzantines, not to mention Jews, as well as Moors from Granada, who had personally voyaged to the Malabar coast of India and along the eastern coast of Africa as far south as Madagascar. They knew the bazaars of Calicut as well as they knew the Rialto at Venice. The Negus of Abyssinia had sent emissaries to the Pope at Rome, and there was on record at the Vatican so much information regarding that fabulous African kingdom, that Philippa would surely have known that the legend of the Kingdom of Prester John had some basis in fact.

Whatever may have been the sources of her knowledge and the extent of her information, the fact is that the Queen not only conceived the bold plan of an invasion of North Africa, but set about in a practical manner to win support for it among her opponents. She proposed that, instead of arguing further, the council send a spy into the Moorish emporium of Ceuta, the center of all North African activities, to report back concerning the feasibility of her plan. The scout selected for the mission was a Genoese named Antonio Malfonte, who had been a captive in Morocco, could speak Arabic, and knew Moslem customs. He was an employee of the crown's bankers, the Florentine House of Centuroni. After a period of ominous silence, the council sent a second secret agent named Benedetto Dei, who had previously gone openly to Morocco for the Florentine House of Portinari to negotiate for the ransom of Christian prisoners. He got into Ceuta from Algeria disguised as an Arab dealer in salt and was able to convey his consignment of salt in a caravan to Timbuktu, south of the Sahara Desert. He brought back to Lisbon the story of the detection and murder of his predecessor, Malfonte, and gave to the council a detailed description of the great south-central African market of which Timbuktu was the metropolis. He had no news regarding the Kingdom of Prester John, but he did bring news of the large importation of virgin gold into Morocco from Southern Africa. He described to the council the arrival at Ceuta's marketplace of a caravan from Timbuktu of two hundred camel loads of gold dust escorted by four hundred mounted Bedouins. This was the first the Portuguese knew of the source of the plentiful gold supply of the Arabs. Until then they had believed it was brought to North Africa from India. The Barbary States were almost the sole center of supply for gold-starved Europe, and the bankers of Florence and Genoa had to bid frantically for it in the extortionate money markets of Tunis and Tripoli, under humiliating restrictions. Now here was the report of a great depot of gold which, if it could be captured, would save Portugal.

This report solved the Queen's greatest perplexity, which had been how to finance her proposed invasion of Morocco. She decided that the Florentines could now be induced to advance the funds, so she called in the bankers and laid her plan before them. She represented the immense outlay for her scheme not as an expense, but as a brilliant speculation which promised substantial returns. She dangled before them the glittering lure of the hoard of African gold stored at Ceuta, and the moneylenders rose to the bait. The Portinari and the Centuroni banking firms agreed to form a syndicate, along with King John's Florentine friend, Nicolo Cambini, to supply all the money needed for an amphibious undertaking against Ceuta.

Now that the financial support of the expedition was settled, the Queen wanted the good will of the clergy in order to win popular support. She therefore turned to the leading prelates of her realm, the archbishops of Braga, of Lisbon, and of Evora, to plead with them to get the Pope's approval to engage in this as a holy war. The good men were reluctant, for many generations had passed since any Christian prince had dared to contemplate taking the initiative against the Mohammedans in their own domain. Previous popes had tried in vain to rekindle such a spirit in Christendom. Now this ardent Queen, who was over sixty years old, strove to infuse a crusading spirit into the cautious and conservative prelates. She eloquently appealed to their compassion for the thousands of Christian captives who were maltreated as slaves or were suffering in the dungeons of Ceuta, and the prelates finally secured the blessing of Rome upon the crusading attempt.

The hardest task of all for Philippa was to get her husband to authorize the undertaking. Dom John had had his fill of wars. He was a tired old soldier, he shrank from the foolhardy idea of attempting to storm the almost impregnable stronghold of Ceuta, and he said flatly he would have none of it. He remained unmoved even when the Queen tantalized him with the prospect of the gold so easily to be gained by a swift dash across the Straits, gold which would save the dynasty from bankruptcy. She painted the martial renown and the religious glories that would be his, but he still refused. For John, the experienced old campaigner, correctly recognized the military and naval risk to be extreme.

Philippa then slyly broached the plan to her three older sons, who were eager to win the spurs of knighthood. They embraced it wholeheartedly and at once descended exuberantly upon their father while he was holding council, interrupting the formal meeting. Dom John resisted their importunities at first, but when he found that his old comrades in arms on the council, and even the archbishops, had become convinced by the Queen of the feasibility of the plan, he yielded. It must have been a moving scene in the council chamber that day.

The few dozen people who knew of the proposal were aware that, if the secret leaked out and the Berbers were warned, the undertaking would end in disaster. A smoke screen of misleading rumors was released, and it was whispered that a punitive expedition was being formed against Moorish Granada, whose corsairs had been inflicting severe injury upon Portuguese commerce.

It took three years of active preparation before the army and fleet were ready for the mammoth amphibious expedition. Philippa, although the guiding spirit of the enterprise, subordinated her part, as usual, and worked through her husband and sons. She was now old, and had become worn out by the intensity and strain of her task.

At last the expedition was mobilized in Lisbon harbor. There the transports, loaded with forty-five thousand soldiers and mariners, lay at anchor awaiting a sustained seasonal breeze from the north to carry them on the fortnight's sail to Ceuta. The Queen had not forgotten she was of the House of Lancaster; at the masthead of some of the largest of the ships floated the leopard banner of England, and along their bulwarks were displayed the armorial bearings of over seven hundred and fifty of the leading knights of her homeland who had volunteered at the call of their great countrywoman.

With the task of financing and assembling the expedition completed, the exhausted woman collapsed. In her weakened condition she contracted the plague, and she failed to rally. When she knew her end was near, she called her children to her. Upon her deathbed she made a solemn request to her four oldest children, three sons and a daughter, to carry out her cherished dream, to try to gain the Kingdom of Prester John as an ally, and through it to attain the road to the Indies. They each swore upon a piece of the true cross to obey her dying request. The nature of Philippa's companionship with her children was such that it was natural for her to pass on her quest to them. As we shall see, this filial pledge was scrupulously honored; her third son, Henry, later had the duty of carrying out its provisions with the support of the other three.

When Philippa had finished this solemn deathbed conversation, she remarked that a strong breeze was shaking the casement of her bedchamber. Her sons told her that the steady northern gale had set in for which the fleet had been waiting. This was important news, for the clumsy *naos* could not tack or come about at sea and could go forward only with a fair wind.

No time was to be lost, and the dying Queen urged that they set sail at once. On July 25, 1415, the fleet of two hundred vessels dropped down the Tagus into the Atlantic Ocean and steered south; Philippa was dead, but they were carrying out her command.

The Conquest of Ceuta

The unwieldly *naos,* being able to sail only before the wind, failed to make the harbor of Ceuta on the African shore, and were swept through the Straits into the Mediterranean. This misadventure proved to be a blessing, for when Ceuta's defenders saw the Christian armada disappear to the east they thought that it was really aiming at Granada, as had been proclaimed, and they consequently relaxed their vigilance. They dispersed their galleys, dismissed the army of desert tribesmen they had mobilized, and retained only a small garrison. Dom John managed to catch a contrary night wind with a few of his clumsy sailing transports and, ignoring the rest of his fleet, guided these and his oar-propelled galleys back to Ceuta in a successful surprise attack. The fortress was a strong one, but the demoralized defenders streamed out the rear gates with their wives and their portable treasures as the impetuous Christians stormed and captured the citadel. The Moslems later made persistent efforts to regain the city, but it defiantly remained a Christian outpost, a thorn in the side of all Islam.

King John secured at once the immense store of Guinea gold so urgently needed for the royal mint. This was important to the treasury, but the emancipation of thousands of Christian prisoners by so small a band was a matter of even greater psychological importance to the national pride. With only a few casualties, Portugal had struck a resounding blow for Christendom, and its people felt a righteous and holy glow. The victory imparted to the little nation an elated sense of importance which stimulated its industrial and commercial expansion and gave it courage and self-confidence.

The conquest of Ceuta was an event with far-reaching political results in fifteenth-century Europe. The news of the capture of the supposedly impregnable Moslem naval base and chief commercial entrepot sent a wave of discouragement throughout Islam and greatly heartened all Christian nations. It held out hope that the initiative which had been lost with the crusades might again pass to the Christians. It greatly enhanced the reputation of Portugal, which became a power of importance in the concert of Europe.

Great as were its political and economic results, the real consequences of the victory were those envisaged, even though dimly, by the farsighted Queen. Ceuta proved to be the key which unlocked the Ocean gates for the Age of Discovery.

Prince Henry the Navigator

After the capture of Ceuta, a council of the royal family was held. It was decided that Henry, Duke of Viseu, third son of the King, should take the responsibility of carrying out the last wishes of his mother, and that the project should be adopted as the program of the dynasty. Duke Henry, who is known to history as Prince Henry the Navigator, was Grand Master of the military order of the Knights of Christ, was Governor of Southern Portugal and of Ceuta, and had command of the southern fleet. A young man of character, he already had shown talent as a statesman and as a military commander, and he early filled important roles in both fields. His contributions to naval science were considerable, and in discharging his pledge to the late Queen he helped usher in the Era of Discovery.

Prince Henry, half Portuguese, half Anglo-Flemish, was the favorite of both his gifted parents. He was a blonde, burly, medieval monk, as redoubtable in combat as his father, the exuberant, ax-wielding giant, John of Avis, and he had his father's power of inspiring his retainers and driving them to devoted self-sacrifice. A messianic ascetic, fired by his mother's mysticism, he nevertheless was also a realistic analyst. Perhaps Philippa had transmitted something to him from the great physicist and chemist, Friar John of England. Henry's monumental contributions to celestial navigation, to cartography, and to naval architecture still stand as milestones after five hundred years. Philippa's other sons were talented as linguists, poets, and authors, but they lacked the mathematical and experimental bent of Henry.

Until the death of John of Avis in 1433, Henry was kept busy as administrative aide to the aged King. During this period, he attempted to carry out his promise to Philippa by waging land war with the Moors, but he was unable to penetrate far into the Moslem barrier that separated him from his oriental goal. At a later date he made a further unsuccessful effort to win his way by land. In the meantime, he had learned from Arab prisoners that it would perhaps be possible to by-pass the military might of Morocco and reach the gold-producing country to the south of Timbuktu by sailing southward in the Atlantic down the coast of West Africa, and he determined to try to carry out the dynasty's program by sea.

The West African coast was entirely unknown to the Portuguese, and, although Henry had both galleasses and sailing *naos* at his disposal, he soon found it safer to explore it by means of small, light-draft, twenty-five ton fishing boats, called *barcas.* He employed adventurous young squires of his knightly order to officer the *barcas,* each of which carried a crew of but a dozen men. For several years the exploring *barca* sent out annually brought back only reports of sandy, barren shores, without population or signs of life.

Each spring, the young explorers managed to creep a little farther south along the coast before returning, but the results were still negative. At last one year they reached faraway Cape Bojador, on the northwest shoulder of Africa, and then for several successive voyages the *barcas,* when their supplies were exhausted, came back dejectedly with a report of spending weeks in trying unsuccessfully to pass that cape, whose sand shoals extended far out to sea. A prevailing wind to landward created thunderous breakers over the shoals, while the set of a strong northward current was at variance with the wind, thus making for a tumultuous sea beyond the promontory. Had a *barca* managed to clear the point of Cape Bojador, it could never have returned north against the wind, and probably would have been driven against the coast. It is true that Prince Henry owned galleasses propelled by sail and oar which could have disregarded the unfavorable elements and rowed around the Cape, but it was impossible to bring such a galley as far as Bojador. The long trip of fifteen hundred miles along the arid African coast from Portugal to Cape Bojador, with no harbors available for revictualling and rewatering, made the use of such heavily manned craft impracticable. That was because, built with a narrow beam and low freeboard in order to give play to the oars, the cubic capacity of their undecked hulls was too limited for the storage of the considerable supply of food, water, and firewood needed for such a long voyage.

In 1425, however, the stalemate was broken. The *barca* that had been sent out that year reappeared unexpectedly at port with electrifying news. The commander reported that he had been trying to get around Cape Bojador when he had been caught by a westward gale and had been driven seaward. After several days of prayer, just when his helpless crew had given up hope, they had miraculously found a safe harbor on an

Engraving from "Histoire des descouvertes et conquestes des Portugais," 1733

PRINCE HENRY THE NAVIGATOR

He ushered in the Age of Discovery

uninhabited island far out in the Ocean Sea, and they piously named it Porto Santo. The discovery of this fertile island lifted the veil of fearful mystery which had shrouded the dreaded Ocean Sea, and men wondered hopefully what lay beyond. Porto Santo was described by the captain as a garden, for it had no hostile aborigines, no savage animals, no climatic rigors. Its temperature was balmy, its rainfall abundant, and its soil amazingly fertile.

The elated Prince immediately sent colonists there, and shortly afterwards they discovered the big adjacent island of Madeira. The Prince divided up Madeira among his followers in feudal fiefs which he called captaincies. The captains subdivided their holdings to immigrant farmer tenants along the familiar lines of the feudal system, but retained for themselves control of navigable streams, harbors, water power sites, and certain monopolies such as the sole right to operate grist or sawmills and to collect salt from the coastal marshes. One of the captains introduced grape vines from Sicily, and these grew so well that before long there was a large production of what is now known as Madeira wine, which at once found a market in Portugal. Another enterprising captain brought in some stalks of sugar cane, and soon Madeira was exporting sugar of a superior quality at an attractive price. At that time sugar was considered a spice and was imported through Venice from the Orient. It was in very short supply and sold at extremely high prices.

The virgin soil of Madeira yielded a first crop of wheat which was ten times greater than normal, and it bore other grains with prodigal abundance. Cattle throve in the favorable climate, and meat and hides were exported in volume to the mainland. But Madeira's greatest source of income was from its bountiful forests of hardwood. Timber had long been scarce in Portugal and was of an unsatisfactory quality for building purposes, but now first-class lumber could be imported at a low cost. A building boom swept the country, and the lower-income groups could for the first time afford to build two-story wooden houses. Not only the architectural but the economic aspects of Portugal underwent a noticeable change.

In 1431, another *barca,* held up at Bojador, was swept to sea by a storm and made a lucky landfall in the Azores, a thousand miles out in the ocean. The Prince's staff was so burdened with the problems of administering the mushrooming economy of Madeira that he could not undertake to develop this new discovery, and he asked his sister Isabel, Duchess of Burgundy, to help him. She responded loyally and encouraged a number of Flemish landowners to migrate with their tenants, cattle, and farm gear to the Azores. The energetic daughter of Philippa pushed the project so wholeheartedly that the Azores became settled largely by Dutch farmers, and for a long time these Atlantic islands, a thousand miles west of the European coast, were identified on all maps as *The Flemish Isles.* Thus once again distant Burgundy participated in the affairs of Portugal.

These two discoveries by Prince Henry, Madeira and the Azores, were the earliest acquisition of new lands by Portugal. They represented the dawn of the Age of Discovery, and provided the first fields in which a modern colonial system was tried.

For almost two decades Prince Henry had persistently spent money and effort. Not only had he failed to find the Guinea Gold Coast, or Prester John, or India, but he had not even discovered any African lands that were inhabited. He had achieved no practical results on the African mainland from his steady expenditures, except the development for Portugal of new and abundant fishing grounds off the coast of Morocco and the establishment of a small import volume in seal skins and seal oil from some African islets.

Yet the old chronicles of these fifteen years of endeavor pulse with a sense of thrill and adventure, of the heroism of those resolute lads who overcame their own fears and those of their superstitious and exhausted crews. They subsisted on scanty rations and putrid drinking water in their crowded craft, and, exposed to tropic rain and sun, sometimes becalmed for weeks, and tormented by insects and fever, they patiently charted and sounded the coast. Because of their short cables they had to anchor close to shore, ready to run out to the unknown sea in case of a shoreward gale. The African coast was very hazardous, with its sandy shallows, hidden reefs, cavernous surfs, and unpredictable, capricious squalls, and called for seamanship of a high order.

The successful by-passing of Cape Bojador by an angular voyage via the Canaries to the lower coast of Africa was achieved in 1433, the year of the death of the old King. Until then Henry had had to stay in Lisbon and could not carry on more actively his astronomical and geographic experiments, although he did show his scholarly interest by founding a school of mathematics in the University of Lisbon. After the death of John of Avis, he was relieved of his routine governmental duties by his brothers and by his bastard half-brother of Braganza, so that he might concentrate on opening up the sea-road to India via the Kingdom of Prester John.

There is no record to show that any of the ancestors of Ferdinand Magellan were associated with Prince Henry, but Gil Annes de Magellan, the grandfather of Ferdinand, was a contemporary of the Prince and probably of about the same age. Gil Annes Magellan was a younger son of the successful courtier, Dom Gil Affonso, apparently by his second wife. He was hence a de Sousa on his mother's side, and he himself also married a de Sousa. This influential family made it a policy to advance its members politically, so it is likely that Gil Annes may have held a position at court.

We can in any event assume that he was in the service of Prince Henry in 1412, when the Prince was mobilizing the army to use against Ceuta. The Prince had been born in Porto and, by virtue of being Lord of Covilham, he was liege lord of the areas which embraced the Province of Minho, where the Magellans had their fief. Henry must, therefore, have drawn all the Magellans into his feudal service for the Ceuta campaign. The personal relationship of Dom Gil Affonso Magellan with John of Avis, Prince Henry's father, also lends weight to the conjecture that his son Gil Annes must have been among Prince Henry's circle, possibly even a member of the princely household. Henry maintained a lavish, almost regal establishment, but there is no extant list of the courtiers of his household. The only names of his entourage which have been preserved are those identified with his nautical, exploring, and colonizing activities, and the name of Gil Annes Magellan is not so mentioned.

Prince Henry was well provided with funds for his projects of exploration. In order to be closer to his field of operations in Africa, the Prince left Lisbon and established his administrative base at the convenient southern port of Lagos. He set up his own headquarters nearby and constructed a walled community known as *Vila do Infante,* or Village of the Prince, which subsequently became world renowned as a center of geographical and astronomical research.

As Portugal then lacked any experts in the theory of nautical and geographic sciences, Henry offered large salaries to qualified foreign specialists. He soon had enlisted a group of accomplished astrologers and cartographers which he called his junta, or council. These included a Christianized Jewish astrologer who became Henry's personal physician and close counselor, an erudite Spanish Jew who had learned astronomy from the Arabs, and an Italian astronomer, Padre Egidio, from the University of Bologna, whose intimate friendship with the scholarly Pope Martin V probably saved Henry from indictment for heretical theories. A Catalonian Jewish convert, Jehuda Crespes of Barcelona, descendant of a line of erudite Balearic makers of medieval charts, also joined the junta. Each captain of the Prince's exploring craft was required to record every shift in the current, every steady wind, and every area of continuous calm, as well as to sketch in his log all the indentations and capes, together with all sorts of identifying characteristics of the shoreline. The data supplied by each returning expedition enabled Crespes to make his charts more detailed and explicit.

Among the innovations which Prince Henry brought to the science of navigation were the wind-rose compass, the crude forerunner of our present-day mariner's compass; the astrolabe, already used by the Arab pilots in the Indian Ocean, which enabled them to find their bearings when far from land, at least as far as their latitude, or north-south position was concerned; and the immense improvement of his sailing craft by the revolutionary innovation of the type of ship which he called the caravel.

The early caravels were about thirty-five feet long and were undecked except for the high poop, which was housed. They had keels, but were of shallow draft. They were not limited to using a fair wind, as were the square-sailed European ships in previous use, but with their fore-and-aft, two-masted rig of triangular lateen sails could sail with a side wind and, to a certain degree, obliquely into the wind itself, as well as make headway against the wind by tacking. They were modelled on a type of felucca which the Arabs of the western Mediterranean had imported from the Indian Ocean, and were vastly superior to the *barinels,* galleys, and *naos* in maneuverability, speed, carrying capacity, and seaworthy qualities.

The problem of keeping an adequate supply of fresh water had long plagued the expeditions. Prince Henry now learned from a Jewish traveler from Arabia that in the Orient the Arabs kept water sweet on long voyages by sealing it in airtight casks. The Prince adopted the idea, and the cruising range of his caravels was thereby much extended. The size of a caravel was thereafter designated by the number of water casks, or *toneis,* which could be stored aboard. A vessel came to be described by all nations in terms of its *toneis* capacity or burden. The modern nautical concept of tonnage stems from this usage.

When Henry's exploring caravels finally passed beyond the uninhabited desert shores of North Africa and reached the populated coast of the jungle region, his captains, in accordance with the practice of the times, seized as many natives as could be crowded into the cramped holds of the caravels. There was such a shortage of agrarian labor in Portugal, due to the Black Death, that Prince Henry had offered convicted felons freedom if they would do farm work for him, and had even sent galleys on raids along the Barbary Coast to capture Moorish civilians to labor as slaves on his agricultural projects in Madeira and the Azores. There was still a great demand for slaves, and they brought very high prices.

When the first consignment of about two hundred and thirty Negroes arrived in Lagos, there was general rejoicing, and the nobility, the clergy, and the merchants all clamored for as many of the captives as they could get. The auction was made a gala occasion, and the Prince himself, mounted on a handsome charger, took part in it. He even presided over the distribution and saw to it that the churchmen got their fair share. Prince Henry gave a handsome reward to the captain of the caravel and created him a Knight for his service, at the same time piously rejoicing that the slaves were saved from paganism and would receive baptism as Christians.

After the arrival of the first cargo of Negro captives, there no longer was any difficulty in getting explorers to go south down the coast. All the merchants of Lagos were anxious to send caravels to Africa for the Prince at their own expense. The result was a series of barbaric slave raids which depopulated the African coastal villages, alienated the Negroes, and destroyed any chance of proselyting the Christian religion or of carrying on any trade in merchandise. The captains were interested only in capturing a cargo of Negroes and bringing them quickly to the market at Lagos. The situation soon became intolerable, and the Prince decided to do away with the excesses, put the slave trade upon a supervised and licensed basis, and insist that its operations be conducted in an orderly manner. He chose as his model the slave trade of Venice, which was one of the best organized branches of Venetian commerce. Most of the Venetian slaves were Slavs (hence the English word *slave*) who were imported from the Baltic region and from the Crimea, although the Venetians also got many Asian and African slaves from the great market at Alexandria. The Arabs had for centuries conducted in North Africa an efficiently administered trade whereby thousands of Negroes were procured each year from the jungle area of Central Africa and transported overland in caravans, along with other valuable commodities, to the Alexandrian market.

The slave trade was profitable and seemed as ancient as time itself. The native kings and chiefs of Central Africa supported their jungle harems from the proceeds of the sale of their prisoners of war. Arab merchants maintained their luxurious establishments in the cool uplands upon the resale of slaves purchased from these Negro chiefs. The cultured Sultan of Fez sustained the elegance of his sumptuous court from the tariff on this commerce. The courtly Venetian patrician embellished his imposing palace upon the Grand Canal because of his steady African business. These respectable pillars of society made pious donations and left ample bequests to their Islamic mosques or Christian churches from the fortunes thus gained. And now Prince Henry began to draw much of his own revenue from this same traffic. He licensed an association of slave importers in the port of Lagos, with the title of the Lagos Corporation, and extended to it a monopoly of the slave trade with West Africa, in consideration of fixed fees per capita to be paid to him upon every slave imported. He then issued a decree prohibiting, under penalty of death, any unlicensed raids for slaves on the African coast.

A traffic of a thousand slaves per annum at once began to flow into Lagos from the West African coast, and henceforth the Lagos caravels, bearing the Cross of the Knights of Christ upon their sails and flying the Prince's standard, sailed peacefully into West African ports and engaged in barter. The Negroes bought from the native chiefs of the ports were not indigenous to the coast, but were prisoners taken by Arab slavers in surprise forays upon villages hundreds of miles inland. The Arabs used these captives as bearers of ivory tusks, sacks of gold dust, and bales of hides, which they thus economically freighted to the seaports. The Negro chiefs who controlled the coastal harbors and acted as middlemen then bought both the native bearers and their burdens from the Arab merchants and bartered humans, gold, and ivory to the captains of the caravels in exchange for Barbary horses, brass basins, steel manacles, colored cloth, and, oddly enough, supplies of the cowrie shells which served as local currency.

The partners of the Lagos Corporation became rich in this traffic and praised the Prince's Christian spirit, his acumen, and his sound mercantile judgment. The new, sea-borne commerce diverted to the markets of the West African coast the rich trade in gold, ivory, and slaves formerly carried by caravan from Central Africa to Timbuktu. This weakened the Moslem Kingdom of Fez and enriched the Christian realm of Portugal; Queen Philippa's plan to gain for Portugal the gold production of Central Africa was now fulfilled. Prince Henry and a few zealots among the churchmen rejoiced in the conversion of the savages to Christianity, but many of the clergy expressed doubts as to the propriety of the slave trade and showed sympathy for the Negroes. History later proved their misgivings sound, but that was not for several centuries.

Another contribution to nautical science made by Henry must be mentioned, the discovery of the Sargasso Loop. As we have seen, Henry's earliest navigators had invariably crept south alongshore, hugging the coast of West Africa. Prince Henry developed a new round-trip route from the Azores to the Central African coast which greatly cut the time of a voyage to Africa and, by keeping out to sea and away from the coast, eliminated the risks of reefs, sandbanks, and shoreward currents. He discovered that there was a sustained trade wind blowing southward from the Azores, and that farther westward in the Ocean Sea was another trade wind blowing northward. All a caravel had to do was to spread its sails before these favorable breezes to be driven south or north as it desired. There was thus evolved the route called the Sargasso Loop, a wide-swinging round-trip to southern Africa which from then on was used by all Portuguese pilots, but which was kept a secret from competing maritime nations for over a century. During all this time the Portuguese navigators pretended that they continued to follow the African coast, with all its risks and delays, and thereby they defensively discouraged other maritime powers from intruding in their territory.

By the time of his death, in 1460, Prince Henry had discovered the Cape Verde Islands and had reached as far south as Sierra Leone. Although he was disappointed in not witnessing the ultimate attainment of Philippa's goal, the passage to India, he must have been aware that it was only a question of time before the end would be achieved.

It is worth noting that not only the genesis of the epochal voyages of da Gama and Magellan, but also in an indirect manner, the inspiration of the voyage of Columbus as well, came through Henry. This came about in 1459, the year before his death, when Henry, heavily in debt because of extensive campaigns against the Berbers in North Africa, sent a financial mission to Florence to float a loan. The crown of Portugal was endorser of the proposed loan, and the head of the mission was Henry's nephew, James, Cardinal of Portugal, grandson of Queen Philippa. One of the assets offered as collateral by Prince Henry was his patent of monopoly of trade to India, which had been extended to him by the Pope. The skeptical Florentine bankers doubted the value of this asset, and called in as their expert the renowned geographer, Dr. Paolo Toscanelli.

Dr. Toscanelli questioned the arguments advanced by Philippa's grandson, the Cardinal, in favor of the geographic theory sponsored by Prince Henry. He did not completely reject the possibility of an eastern route to India through African waters, but suggested that the quickest way to get to India would be to sail due west across the Atlantic. The western route had already been successfully followed by the Scandinavians, he pointed out, and Lief Ericson, the Viking, had centuries before even colonized the lands which lay westward over the Ocean Sea. The eleventh-century Pope had established bishoprics in the Danish overseas settlements of Markland and Vineland which, he assumed, lay in Western Asia. Toscanelli also cited a recent voyage in the path of the early Viking explorers, from Denmark to Greenland, made in 1430 by the Danish navigator Claudius Clarus Swart.

The great geographer's calm assurance captured the belief of several of the Portuguese mission, and the group divided into two factions of theorists who called themselves the "Eastists" and the "Westists." James, Cardinal of Portugal, inheritor and advocate of Philippa's theory of an eastern route to India, himself became captivated by Toscanelli's theory, and upon his return to Lisbon joined the Westists. Toscanelli was venerated in both Spanish and Portuguese university circles, and his westist ideas were not denounced in Lisbon, but were considered attractive geographic speculations. Several proponents of the westist route appear to have fitted out caravels and tried to put Toscanelli's plan to active test. However, the routes they chose were quite impracticable because, in the seasons in which they made their trials, the prevailing winds blew steadily eastward and balked any attempt to sail west. Consequently, the mariners of Portugal abandoned the ideas of Toscanelli as impractical, and they restricted their attention to the familiar African route, which had been started for them by the enterprise of Prince Henry and reserved for their exclusive use by the favor of the popes.

With the death of Prince Henry in 1460, there died also the obligation to carry out the pledge to Philippa, herself now dead nearly half a century. The crusading scientific urge to seek the land of Prester John and to find the sea route to India was dead. The technical research junta at *Vila do Infante* was dissolved, the village itself abandoned, and African scientific exploration ceased. Only the profitable slave caravels continued their voyages from Lagos to the depot at Arguim on the African coast, where, in huge barracks, the Arab slavers delivered the Negro captives to await transport to market.

Commercial Exploration

Ten years later, in 1470, exploration again was resumed, but in a commercial spirit and as an adjunct of the slave trade. Ferdinand Gomes, a wealthy merchant of Lisbon, used his political influence to secure an absolute monopoly for himself of the African slave trade and thus shut out all his competitors of the Lagos Corporation. One of the terms of the contract was that he would explore for the crown, at his own expense, three hundred miles farther down the West Coast annually, beginning from Sierra Leone, the farthest point south which had been reached by Prince Henry.

Gomes's franchise was at a high rental to the crown, with virtually exclusive import-export trade rights, not only on slaves but on all other commodities, except that all ivory imported by him was to be delivered to the royal treasury at a fixed rate per pound. Ivory was in great demand for decorative purposes, and the smallest slivers were eagerly sought by European craftsmen. Gomes commenced to import it in quantity, and its sale resulted in a substantial profit to the King. It had been sparingly doled out to the European market by the Venetians and therefore commanded a very high price. A curious clause in the contract restricted Gomes to the importation of a single civet cat each year. These rare creatures then sold for a fabulous sum because their liquid secretion was used commercially as a base for costly perfumes. It became a fashionable fad for great ladies at court to own a civet cat, and Gomes was besieged with applications from European politicians who wished to purchase his annual cat at almost any price as a gift to some royal favorite or mistress.

Gomes's contractual obligation to explore farther south worked to his immense profit when one of his caravels at last reached the Guinea Gold Coast. The resulting influx of gold strengthened Portugal's armed might, while it correspondingly weakened the Moroccan kingdom with which Portugal was at war. The treasury soon accumulated a gold reserve and issued a new goldpiece known as the *cruzado,* which enhanced the country's credit standing in the money markets of Florence, Venice, Augsburg, and Bruges. The discovery of a way by sea to the fabulous Guinea mines at last brought about stabilization of the currency, stimulated trade, and acted as a tonic to society, just as Philippa had predicted so many years before.

When the news got around the money centers that Portugal was actually importing large amounts of Guinea Gold, the French and British privateers whose cruising grounds had been the English Channel and the North Sea moved purposefully southward. Expeditions slipped out from Bristol and from Dieppe, and their booty was weighed not in ounces but in tons of gold. These fabulous hauls of the early smugglers so excited the greed of the respectable merchants who were the silent partners of the pirates that they fitted out numerous fast, well armed corsairs to harry the caravel route. Ferdinand Gomes had to convert his caravels into warships, send them out in strongly convoyed squadrons, and fortify and garrison his trading posts against landing parties of sea robbers. In 1476, war broke out between Castile and Portugal, and the hungry Spanish war galleys darted for the Guinea coast, causing Gomes such losses that he petitioned the government to relieve him of his African contract.

In 1479, a peace treaty was signed whereby Castile, in consideration of sovereignty of the Canary Islands, recognized Portugal's ownership of the other North Atlantic islands and agreed to Portugal's exclusive right to colonize and to trade on the West African coast. The Portuguese King declared the African trade to be a state monopoly and gave the administration of it to Crown Prince John, who was then twenty-one years old. He withdrew the crown from the slave traffic, and gave to the reactivated Lagos Corporation the exclusive right to deal in slaves and to do general trading. The King retained the monopoly of gold and of ivory and proceeded again to send scientific exploring expeditions down the Atlantic coast of West Africa with express orders to seek the route to India.

PART I

CHILDHOOD AND EARLY VOYAGES

CHAPTER I

CHILDHOOD AND BACKGROUND

FERDINAND MAGELLAN was born about 1480 in the township of Ponte da Barca in the Province of Minho, in north Portugal, the younger son of the junior branch of the noble family of Magellan. Dom Ruy Magellan and Donha Alda de Mesquita were his parents, and theirs must have been a devoted family. Throughout his life Ferdinand showed an abiding solicitude for his sister Isabel, the oldest of the three children, and consistently displayed an attachment to Diogo, his elder brother and comrade in adventure.

Diogo, although heir to the Magellan patrimony, did not bear the name of Magellan, but that of de Sousa, the great family to which his paternal grandmother belonged; this adoption of the de Sousa name enabled him to inherit part of his grandmother's estate. Ferdinand Magellan, too, proudly bore the quarterings of the renowned de Sousas on his Magellan coat of arms.

Because their father was of the cadet branch of the Magellan family, the children were raised not in the grand manor house known as *Paço Vedro* in Ponte da Barca, but in the more humble *Torre de Magalhais,* or Magellan Tower. This was a farmhouse which had evolved from a tumble-down fortress that, three centuries earlier, had been built as a defense against the Moors. It had been the stronghold of that pioneer Magellan, the crusader, upon whom the land was first bestowed in fief by Count Henry of Burgundy. The obsolete tower had later been partly razed, and its truncated base of cyclopean boulders had become the walls of a rude two story farm dwelling. The human members of Ferdinand's family occupied the upper floor; the lower level had been converted into a capacious stable for the farm cattle by utilizing the granite blocks from the high part of the former tower. The original castle courtyard had become the barnyard, through which ran the overflow of the bubbling spring about which the fortress first had been constructed. Although the comfortless farmstead reflected the Spartan crudity of the donjon-keep from which it had developed, nevertheless it is probable that nowhere in his long wanderings did Ferdinand Magellan ever gaze upon natural surroundings more lovely than those about his paternal home.

Behind the farmhouse ascended a series of sheltering hills covered with a close growth of pine, oak, and chestnut, while beneath it, to the west, one looked upon the fertile, well-watered valley that constituted the ancestral acres of the *Quinta de Magalhaes,* or Magellan Farm. Here was pastured the herd of large, seal-brown cattle, with wide, branching horns, which found a ready market at the great semi-annual cattle fairs at nearby Braga, where buyers came from all Portugal. Many brown sheep and goats browsed in mixed herds on the hillsides, and droves of scrawny hogs subsisted upon the chestnuts, acorns, and pine nuts in the forests. Amid the fields of wheat and rye were extensive patches of tasseled *milho,* or maize, rare elsewhere in Europe, but early brought by the Arabs into this region from Asia. The Magellans ground the *milho* into cornmeal to make the closely kneaded dark bread for which the Province of Minho is famous, and which along with *caldo verde,* or green cabbage soup, still forms the staple diet of Ponte da Barca.

They propagated in their vineyards a special variety of the clambering vines which bore the green, bitter grapes peculiar to this northern locality, as contrasted to the purple, sweet grapes which grew on low bushes in all other parts of Portugal. At the season of the vintage, the Magellan children had to work long hours to help the tenants pick these sour grapes before they ripened, and to bring the heaping baskets in ox carts to the vats. There they joined in trampling out, barefooted, the juice from which was made the farm's incomparable light wine known as *vinho verde.* This was consumed in generous quantities by the household throughout the year and commanded a high price at the vintner's in Braga.

In the fall the three children doubtless ranged the hills with groups of peasant families to collect baskets of the long, edible acorns and chestnuts which the forest yielded in profusion, the winter provender for both man and beast. As Diogo and Ferdinand grew older, they and their playmates hunted squirrel and rabbits in the woods with dog and crossbow, in noisy imitation of their seniors who chased the deer, wolf, and wild boar. The three children delighted to be taken by the household servants to the frequent *romarias* (or festivals) indigenous to this countryside. The tenants, garbed in their holiday best, marched in choral procession to one of the nearby churches to render homage to the saint whose feast day it might be. Then they trooped on to a grove or to the bank of a stream to picnic and to have games, dances, and frolics, which they continued by torchlight after the children had been conducted reluctantly back to the farmhouse and bed.

This childhood life at Magellan Farm must have seemed wonderfully simple and secure to Ferdinand in later years. However, this was the end of the fifteenth century, the renaissance period was in full flood, and it was not to be expected or desired that these promising boys should remain long at home upon their father's country estate while the whole great world with its expanding horizons beckoned to them.

King John II

Shortly after the time of Ferdinand Magellan's birth, in 1481, the Crown Prince had ascended the throne as King John II, and had decided to nationalize all colonial trade. He cancelled the charter of the Lagos Corporation and moved both its organization and the contents of its warehouses from Lagos to Lisbon, giving to the newly organized colonial office the name of Mina House. To prevent smuggling, he declared all trade with West Africa, Madeira, the Azores, and the Cape Verdes to be a crown monopoly, requiring a license, and he formally decreed a penalty of death to all interlopers, whether domestic or foreign.

Dom John rebuilt Prince Henry's old African fort at Arguim, halfway to the Guinea Gold Coast. He then built a stone castle at El Mina, the shipping port for gold, named it Fort St. George, and made it the advance seat of colonial government as well as the naval base and trading emporium for the West African coast.

A fleet of ten large *naos* had been employed to freight the construction materials and the artillery from Lisbon to El Mina for the fort. After the cargoes had been unloaded, the commander had all ten of the craft ostentatiously beached and burned. The King circulated a report in Lisbon that, although the cargo *naos* had easily sailed southward with a fair following wind to El Mina, they had been helpless to make the return voyage in the face of the steady southerly gales, and therefore they had been burned. He thus spread the belief that the round trip voyage from Europe to El Mina could be made only in caravels. The other European maritime powers had no caravels, and the crafty destruction of the fleet of *naos* at El Mina effectively deterred the King's European rivals from intruding upon his trading preserves.

Although the navigators of the burned *naos* knew that they could easily have made the return trip to Lisbon via the secret Sargasso route, nevertheless they discreetly kept silence; hearty King John, who resembled in appearance and in autocratic rule his cousins, the Tudors of England, was not a man whose command was to be taken lightly.

Christopher Columbus

One of Dom John's merchant captains was a handsome, red-haired Italian captain named Christopher Columbus. He is supposed by some Iberian historians to have been a *converso,* or Christianized Jew, although in the view of Dr. Madariaga and others he was only of part-Jewish descent. At all events, he had been brought up in Genoa, ostensibly as a member of the family of weavers, cheese merchants, and wine dealers whose name he bore, and who apparently were *converso* refugees of Spanish extraction. Columbus often stated to his intimates that he was of distinguished ancestry on the paternal side and that one of his immediate forebears was a Genoan admiral. He let it be presumed that, in accordance with the common practice of the times, his aristocratic parent had placed his illegitimate son in the home of a respectable, lower-class family. It actually seems that some hidden naval influence in Genoa was always at work in his favor.

Christopher Columbus had passed his boyhood in that tumultuous period of Genoese history when the city was engulfed in civil war, largely maritime, between factions fighting under the opposing banners of Aragon and France. He had served an apprenticeship as a lad on a Genoese vessel under charter to the English merchants of Bristol, trading to the Shetland Islands and among the foggy northern seas as far as Iceland. He was advanced rapidly and, when only twenty-one, was sent in command of a ship to bring to Genoa a cargo of medicinal gum mastic from the Isle of Chios, in the Aegean Sea. Then he became captain of a privateer under French letters of marque from the ruler of Genoa, Duke Renée of Anjou; thereafter he cruised in the Mediterranean to prey upon Moslem merchant ships, part of a corsair squadron under a French commander, significantly named Admiral Colombo, who later was hanged as a pirate in Genoa. In an attack with Colombo's piratical flotilla upon a convoy of peaceful merchantmen flying the banner of his native Genoa, his vessel was damaged by enemy broadsides and went down off Cape St. Vincent, Portugal. Columbus saved his life by clinging to an oar for many hours, and finally managed to swim ashore near *Vila do Infante.* Due to the efforts of a

Genoese banking firm in Lisbon who acted for his presumed parent in Genoa, Columbus obtained a command in the Portuguese marine service; he married the daughter of one of Prince Henry's former navigators. His wife's late father had been a captain donatory of Porto Santo, the first Atlantic island discovered by the Portuguese, and his mother-in-law's family was one of the most distinguished among the ancient Portuguese nobility. Iberian historians insist that, in order to have been acceptable to his wife's aristocratic family, Columbus must have been able to provide evidence concerning his noble birth. Bastardy, provided it was of a noble strain, was no barrier to marriage into the Portuguese upper classes.

Columbus for a time assisted his brothers-in-law in administering the estate on Porto Santo, but soon returned to the sea and secured command of a ship carrying cargoes of Madeira sugar to Portugal. About this time his mother-in-law turned over to him a collection of logs and charts found among the papers of her late husband, and Columbus deciphered secret notes that indicated the existence of islands many leagues to the west in the Atlantic. This discovery kindled his imagination, and he became enthralled by the idea of reaching Marco Polo's Cipango (Japan) and Cathay (China) by sailing westward. Printing was then in its infancy, and scientific works were rare and costly, but Columbus eagerly collected and read all available works about geography and travel in the Orient. Some of these books still survive, with marginal notes and comments in Columbus's handwriting which disclose interest in the possibility of a westward route to India, as well as his frank aim to secure the fortune in jewels and gold which he believed could be had there.

In order to be free to study, to meet other proponents of westward navigation, and perhaps because of a mercantile bent, Columbus forsook the sea and opened a shop in Lisbon with his younger brother Bartholomew where they sold charts and globes of their own design. The two brothers also manufactured and marketed astrolabes, compasses, hour glasses, and other nautical instruments. Columbus had learned during his earlier voyage to Iceland of the old Scandinavian voyages to Greenland, and he consequently was able to contribute information about the North Atlantic to the Jewish *converso* group of Westists with whom he now became identified. Soon he became the most vocal proponent of the westist nautical doctrine in Portugal. The subject became a monomania, and, as he was a devout Catholic, he commenced to imagine himself the chosen instrument of Providence to carry the gospel to Cipango.

When King John sent ten *naos,* in December, 1481, to carry construction materials to El Mina for the new fort, Christopher Columbus left his shop in charge of his brother and took command of one of them. This gave him an opportunity to study the southern skies and to observe the course of the trade winds and the currents of the restricted waters off

Africa, knowledge which would shortly be useful to him in preparing for his own great voyage of discovery.

Diogo Cam

King John had to employ commoners and foreigners like Columbus as his navigators, for the aristocratic Order of the Knights of Christ, which under Prince Henry had been the pioneer in African exploration, had become an appanage of Dom John's foes, the bastard Braganza branch of the royal family; consequently these veteran sea-knights were hostile to Dom John. He therefore promoted mariners of humble birth who would otherwise have been kept in subordinate posts. One of them, Diogo Cam, in 1482 reached new territory far down the African coast. In 1485, Dom John sent Cam on a second successful voyage, during which he checked a series of experimental calculations on latitude of Dom John's junta of astrologers in Lisbon through which the position of a ship at sea could be ascertained by observing the sun's height above the horizon at noon, instead of calculating the altitude of the North Star at night.

One of the great advantages of the new system of solar observation was that it was used in daylight. Whereas the polar star, a dim star of second magnitude, is not visible from anywhere south of the equator, the sun, of course, is in sight from any position on the globe. The report of the pilots sent with Cam was favorable, and the modern solar method of celestial observation was adopted instead of the earlier polar-star system developed by Prince Henry.

Captain Diogo Cam initiated the practice of setting up official monuments at suitable points in newly discovered areas. In the early days, the discoverers had marked Prince Henry's claims to sovereignty by carving his coat of arms on large trees. Later, the commercial captains of Fernando Gomes had established Portugal's rights by setting up suitably engraved official wooden crosses. Dom John now wanted more formal and durable markers, for he had secured by diplomatic negotiation, not only from the Pope, but also from the Kings of Castile, of France, and of England, acknowledgment of his exclusive right to colonize the West Coast of Africa. Therefore he had stone masons cut several marble pillars, about six feet high, surmounted by a cross and bearing the royal arms, on which were chiseled triple legends in Portuguese, Arabic, and Latin, giving the name of King John, the name of Diogo Cam, and the date of discovery. Cam ceremoniously erected these in appropriate locations, sounding trumpets and letting off broadsides, and made a careful notarized record of their exact geographic positions. This system was thereafter followed by Portugal in all its exploratory expeditions.

Ruy Magellan

The member of the Magellan clan contemporary to these events was Ruy Magellan, the father of Ferdinand Magellan. He was the younger son of Gil Annes Magellan and was, we conjecture, born at Ponte da Barca about 1425. He was married to Donha Alda de Mesquita, the daughter of Martin Gonsalves Pimental and of Donha Inez de Mesquita. The only other fact that we know of him is that he was High Sheriff of the city and district of Aveiro, on the Atlantic coast south of the city of Porto. This detail is, however, a significant one and indicates that he was an important and trusted officer of King John II. Dom John, constantly on the alert against plots, appointed only his own loyal vassals to the important posts of command throughout the country.

Many attempts were made by the Braganzas to kill King John; he lived the life of a hunted man, kept a strong bodyguard, and constantly shifted his abode. He always hovered warily near his stronghold of Palmela, where he had stored his substantial war chest of Guinea gold, for he was haunted by the fear that his foes might seize this treasure, upon which his power depended. The port of Aveiro was of strategic importance, and Ruy Magellan doubtless had a strong force under his command as High Sheriff to prevent any subversive activities there.

Bartholomew Dias

Ruy Magellan, in order to strengthen his political position locally, probably made it a practice to give preference in employment in the royal establishment to loyal residents of his shrievalty of Aveiro. Therefore, when King John decided to found an African trading post and slave market in the newly discovered agricultural area of Benin, just north of the equator, it perhaps was Ruy who put a fellow-townsman, John Affonso of Aveiro, in charge of the project. If so, he thereby unwittingly made his neighbor the richest captain in the royal service, for John Affonso of Aveiro returned to Lisbon in 1485 with his caravel loaded to the waterline with an enormously valuable cargo of pepper, which no one had thought grew in West

Africa; he had secured it from the native king in exchange for a few trinkets.

The discovery of African pepper led the Pepper Trust to send their Spanish agent, Cristóbal de Haro, to Lisbon as their manager. In order to ingratiate himself with King John, de Haro divulged to him the closely held secret of the enormous profits now enjoyed by Venice from its imports of spices, dyes, and drugs from India. This disclosure stimulated Dom John's intention to outfit another African exploring expedition to try to reach India. His favorite navigator, Diogo Cam, had died on his last voyage, and he appointed as his successor another self-made captain, Bartholomew Dias, with orders to do everything possible to reach India. In August, 1487, Bartholomew Dias crossed the bar of the Tagus with two fifty-ton caravels and vowed to return only if successful in reaching India. With him as a pilot went Bartholomew Columbus, the young brother of Christopher.

Previous expeditions to find the route to India had turned back because of their provisions giving out, and Mina House sent with Dias a square-sailed cargo *nao* loaded with supplies. When the squadron reached the farthest point which Cam had attained on the South African coast, Dias stocked up the caravels from the supply ship, which he left anchored in Walvis Bay with a well armed guard aboard it. He no sooner had set out to sea than he was caught in a tempest which, for almost a month, whirled the caravels under bare masts southward toward the antarctic. The sailors, fresh from the tropics and dressed in unsuitable clothing, suffered acutely from the cold gales and the icy waters which continually washed over the low waist of the caravels. They dared not light fires for cooking, and they slept in their sodden clothing, huddled together for warmth. At last the storm subsided, and Dias, who had no idea of his position, steered a northerly course, seeking the coast to get his bearings. When he made his landfall he observed, to his puzzlement, that the sun now set behind the land instead of rising behind it as previously. The next day, when he saw that the sun rose across the water instead of behind the shore, he realized that during the gale he must somehow have crossed from the west side of the continent of Africa to the east of it. By rounding the Cape in a wide sweep during the storm, he had achieved the long sought water passage to the Orient. He landed and formally set up a stone pillar to mark Dom John's sovereignty over the land he had discovered. He followed the Southeast Coast of Africa northward for some days, but his tired crew mutinied and refused to continue the voyage. Several were dead and more were dying of scurvy. Provisions were almost exhausted, and the frail caravels were so battered that the pumps had to be kept continuously going. The rigging and tackle were badly frayed, and the crew rightly feared to trust the ships in another storm. Dias wept, knelt to the men, and implored them not to dishonor him, making them promises of wealth if they would only continue. He had almost won their adherence when his second-in-command, an aristocrat who was jealous of the low born Dias, threw his support to the mutineers. It was perhaps just as well that Dias was forced to give in and turn back, for it would have been impossible for him to overcome the many obstacles that lay ahead.

On the return voyage, Dias sighted for the first time the majestic Cape; in memory of his struggle he called it Stormy Cape, but later, at the instance of King John, he rechristened it the Cape of Good Hope.

When at last the caravels got back to the supply ship in Walvis Bay, nine months had passed, and Dias found only three frightened men alive on the anchored *nao*. One of them dropped dead of a heart attack in his joy at being rescued. Six of the guards had disregarded orders and gone hunting ashore, where they were ambushed and killed by the natives. The three survivors led a life of terror on the desolate hulk until the squadron returned.

Instead of hurrying straight back to report to the King, Dias stopped to pick up passengers at various West African settlements and took aboard a consignment of gold dust at Fort George for Mina House. He finally reached Lisbon in December, 1488, after an amazing voyage of seventeen months.

Dom John was afire with enthusiasm, and so fearful lest Castile might steal a march on him and get to India first that he drove his maritime department hard to complete the task. Any public mention of the discovery of the eastward passage was suppressed, and Dias was given no public recognition of his achievement. It was many years later, and then by accident, that it was known outside Portugal that Bartholomew Dias had made such an epochal voyage.

During the eight years following Dias's discovery, King John concealed all news of further expeditions. It seems incredible that he could have suppressed every log and diary written in those eight years, but none has as yet been found. There are some scattered clues here and there which suggest that, in the succeeding biennium of 1489–1490, King John sent out as many as fifty exploring expeditions from Lisbon. Although some were experimental cruises to report on winds and currents in the South Atlantic, at least two carefully equipped armadas apparently were launched. There also are baffling references to another attempt made by Bartholomew Dias himself, and it would have been natural for the King to give him such an opportunity; however, the venture must have been unsuccessful.

Some of the caravels sent out at this time apparently went westward to test out the theories expressed by Christopher Columbus. These attempts, like earlier efforts to cross the Atlantic on a westerly course, were undertaken in unfavorable seasons of the year in latitudes where strong eastward winds blew steadily and made progress impossible. One reason why Christopher Columbus later succeeded where the Portuguese navigators failed was that he had learned from their trials; he sailed from the Canary Islands at the time of the year when there was a steady trade wind from the northeast which carried him westward across the Atlantic.

King John and Columbus

Columbus had tried to persuade the King to supply him with a caravel in which to attempt to make the western passage, but Dom John considered the Genoese captain boastful and vain and was cold to his proposition. Columbus had lost his wife and was heavily in debt, and, being much discouraged, he left Portugal in 1484 to try to interest the Spanish Crown in his project. He returned to Lisbon in 1488 to meet his brother Bartholomew upon his return with Dias, and learned from him the secret details of the discovery of the Cape. Columbus had another unsatisfactory audience with Dom John, and then went back to Castile to push his fortunes there.

Portuguese historians claim primacy for Portugal in the discovery of America. Early in 1492, the same year as the first voyage of Columbus, one of King John's captains, a Portuguese named John Fernandes, nicknamed Labrador, sailed from the Azores westward across the Atlantic, ahead of Columbus. He rediscovered Greenland and also that part of North America which is still called Labrador after him. However, he did not get back to Portugal for three years, and by that time his exploit had been eclipsed by that of Christopher Columbus. Hence he has received little credit in history.

Before the discovery by Bartholomew Dias that there was a sea route around the southern end of Africa, the King decided to send spies overland through the Moslem territory to try to locate the Kingdom of Prester John and to secure data concerning the oriental regions beyond the point of Dias's farthest penetration. He inspired two of his vassals who could speak Arabic to make the effort to reach India by land. One of them, Pedro de Covilham, an adventurous squire of the royal bodyguard, managed to visit all the great markets which lay about the Indian Ocean and the Persian Gulf and to send a detailed report to Dom John describing this entire area, until then unknown to the King in detail. He also sent comprehensive maps and assured the King of the feasibility of sailing from the Atlantic around the Cape to India. Covilham then went on to Abyssinia, the Kingdom of Prester John so long sought by Queen Philippa and Prince Henry, and was well received there. He was given rank and a rich estate by the Negus of Abyssinia, married, and had a large family, but he never could secure permission to leave the country and return to Portugal.

The King had been intoxicated by Covilham's letters describing the wealth and magnitude of the Indian markets, and he raged frantically at the failure of his captains to repeat the exploit of Bartholomew Dias. Once at Mina House, when he was giving vent to a stormy outburst, one of the navigators, probably Dias himself, made bold to suggest a solution of the dilemma. The angry King paid little attention, but the suggestion attracted the notice of his intimate friend Admiral Estevan da Gama, Comptroller of the royal household, who later supported it. The proposal was to abandon the use of caravels in the passage of the southern seas and to substitute a new type of ship designed by Bartholomew Dias to overcome the antarctic tempests south of the Cape of Good Hope. This was a cross between the *nao* of the Hanseatic cities and the traditional caravel developed by Prince Henry. It had very high, bluff bows, surmounted by a forecastle which was fully as large as the sterncastle of the caravel, which was to be retained. It had a much higher freeboard and higher bulwarks than the caravel and was completely decked. Dias contended that this hull would protect the ship against the antarctic waves. He proposed to provide the new ship with a large, square foresail, while retaining the fore-and-aft lateen mainsails and mizzen, and he suggested mounting a small, square spritsail upon the high bowsprit. King John became enthusiastic about the proposed new craft and himself worked out an improvement. This was nothing less than to build a lower halfdeck inside the hull, like a shelf running along the two sides of the ship. On this shelf he planned to mount some newly invented breech-loading cannon, pointing the muzzles through apertures pierced in the side of the hull, called *puertas,* or portholes, with flat doors which could be closed against the sea. Until that time all marine artillery was muzzle-loading and had been emplaced on ships' decks or on the fighting tops. The King's idea was adopted later and led to an improvement in the effectiveness of marine gunnery which was to prove of decisive value to the Portuguese navy.

Although Estevan da Gama, who himself had had considerable experience in the North Atlantic, had recognized the theoretical advantages of the proposed new ship, the proposition was received as heresy by many older captains. The great prestige of the caravel, the fact that it was essentially a Portuguese craft, and its proud record of performance, all were obstacles to consideration of the new type. Although King John constantly studied the model and dubbed it a *caravela redonda,* or rounded caravel, he was swayed by the opposition and finally announced that he would not undertake the expense of building a trial ship.

However, his attitude changed when, in March, 1493, he interviewed Christopher Columbus when the explorer stopped in Portugal on his return from his first voyage of discovery. The Admiral apparently convinced the Portuguese King that Dias was right and that, although the old type of caravel was best for African coastal and river navigation, a heavier square rigger had advantages for deep water cruising. Columbus had made his historic first voyage with a *nao* and two partly decked caravels, and although he had lost the *nao* while coasting offshore and had come back in a caravel, he presumably advocated to the King the use of the larger ship.

King John, much shaken by the success of Columbus, now determined to overcome all obstacles to reach India by his own eastern route. He therefore gave orders that the proposed *caravela redonda* be adopted and that two sister ships be constructed at once.

In the meantime, King John sent a truculent protest to Ferdinand and Isabella against the invasion of his territorial seas by Christopher Columbus, and he belligerently threatened war if the trespass were repeated. The Spanish sovereigns temporized and suggested arbitration by the Pope. The Supreme Pontiff, Alexander VI, pretended to weigh the case impartially and to rule on it judicially. In reality he rendered a decision which took away rights which had been many times confirmed to Portugal by bulls of his predecessors and which he brazenly transferred to Spain in accordance with a secret agreement he had made with his friend, King Ferdinand. The Pope, born Rodrigo Borgia of Aragon, was as much a Spaniard as was King Ferdinand himself. Spanish was the language of the Papal court, all his attendants and bodyguards were Spanish, and his policies and his acts were Spanish too.

Dom John was not the man to be defrauded, pope or no pope, and he openly prepared for war. The Spanish rulers persuaded him to send delegates to a geographic conference at Tordesillas, in Spain, and there a compromise was worked out and agreed upon by both nations. A solemn pact was signed in 1494 which was known as the Treaty of Tordesillas, in which the entire globe was peaceably divided into two exclusive fields of exploration and colonization. Portugal was to keep the East, in which it had made its discoveries, and Spain the West, where lay its new-found lands. This was known as the Treaty of Demarcation.

Once the treaty was signed, King John felt safe from Spanish invasion of his eastern route to India, and he openly prepared to make an effort to reach India via the East before King Ferdinand could forestall him from the West.

It was in the atmosphere of these stirring events that young Ferdinand passed his childhood. While he could not yet be aware of their many ramifications, such were the influences which reached even Magellan Tower, and were to play ever more strongly upon the imagination of the adventurous boy.

CHAPTER II

BOYHOOD AND PREPARATION

AT THE age of seven Ferdinand joined his brother at school, probably at the neighboring monastery of *Vila nova de Muia,* a local dependency of the great cloister of *Santa Cruz de Coimbra,* the first center of medieval culture in Portugal. Here he learned his catechism and the rudiments of Latin and arithmetic. When Diogo was twelve and Ferdinand ten years old, their father secured for Diogo an appointment as page to Queen Leonora, at her court in Lisbon, so that he would be educated at the cost of the state. The heir of every noble family had the right to receive such an education by a pact between the crown and the nobility, and this privilege was soon extended to Ferdinand, despite the fact that he was a younger son. The appointment of both boys as court pages was a mark of unusual grace from King John to their father, and indicates that Ruy Magellan may have had either high standing in his own right at court or influential connections. Perhaps, however, the exception merely was made because Dom John had exiled so many of the nobles that there were unfilled places in the school, and it was to his interest to bring up as his partisans all the sons of families that had remained loyal to him.

The school for pages to which young Ferdinand was now appointed mirrored the unsettled times. It was not maintained at Dom John's personal court, for this was virtually an armed bivouac which was shifted constantly as a precaution against attempts to assassinate the King. The pages were domiciled at the Queen's separate court, which was not much more stable, for the Queen frequently left her permanent residence in Lisbon to escape contagion from the plague, which was then endemic in

Portugal. From time to time she would move with her personal suite to some castle or monastery in a plague-free area, and the perambulating aggregation known as the court, which included the school for pages, would straggle after her, sojourning as best it might in the neighborhood until another outbreak of the plague caused yet another move.

Portugal in those days was a personal despotism in which both the King and his Queen had governmental functions. Dom John exercised at his own court the command of the armed forces, the direction of foreign affairs, and the administration of the colonies. The major part of Portuguese officialdom, including the law courts, the fiscal department, and the ecclesiastical establishment, was left to cluster about Queen Leonora.

The curriculum of the pages' school embraced music, dancing, and the science of venery, or hunting with hawk and hound. The future cavaliers were taught horsemanship and jousting, and were expected to become ambidextrous in handling sword and lance. Ferdinand Magellan must have been one of the most promising of the pupils in the tiltyard, for in his later career he won renown as a cavalry leader and as a formidable contender in close combat.

In addition to attending classes and receiving training at arms, each boy also had to perform his work as a page, that is, to serve as a messenger, usher, or attendant in the palace. This daily service in the Queen's anterooms and audience chamber was considered part of their polite education. The discipline of this court employment was stern; the aristocratic lads were required to perform humble domestic work in the royal household and to assist in such menial tasks as making up the huge state beds then used by dignitaries.

Apart from the acquisition of courtly accomplishments, the pages were required to study map-making, the rudiments of astronomy, and celestial navigation. In no other country at this time were such courses given. The King himself saw to it that these subjects were taught by experienced navigators and that the boys were thoroughly grounded in the practical elements of maritime science, for he foresaw the future need for well trained commanders. It was here that Ferdinand Magellan acquired the foundation of his later mastery of astronomy and of navigation. Dom John entrusted the supervision of the study of nautical science to his brother-in-law, Duke Manuel. He was the Queen's brother, only eight years older than Diogo de Sousa, and was in a position of authority over the pages. Duke Manuel was interested in astronomy and had been encouraged by the King to pursue advanced studies in practical celestial navigation. In recognition of his proficiency, the King added to Manuel's armorial escutcheon the design of a globe or sphere, formerly the insignia of Prince Henry, and the Duke was very proud of this distinction.

Duke Manuel was tall and spare, and his brown hair and green eyes showed his part English ancestry, for he was descended not only from the bastard Braganza, but from Anglo-Flemish Queen Philippa as well. He was the youngest of five brothers, all of whom predeceased him, had spent most of his boyhood in Spain in semi-confinement as a hostage, and had been educated at the court of Castile. He devoted himself much to games and hunting. Being fond of dancing and music, he was the center of the gay life of the court, and indulged in many pranks and practical jokes with the Queen's clowns and jesters. He was exceptionally good at athletic games because of his unusually long arms; it is said that when he stood at ease, arms straight down, his hands came to below his knees. Although Duke Manuel was made much of by his sister, Queen Leonora, he enjoyed no political favors from his cousin, King John. Taking to heart the lesson of the fate of his older brother, who had been stabbed to death by Dom John because of complicity in Braganza plots, he affected frivolity and pretended not to care for politics; he carefully refrained from becoming identified with the conspiracies against the King which were continually being hatched by his mother, the irrepressible and vengeful Donha Beatrice de Braganza.

When, in 1492, young Ferdinand left the sheltered surroundings of the family homestead at Ponte da Barca to join his older brother Diogo as a page at the Queen's court, he was immediately plunged into an environment most unsuited for a boy of twelve, fresh from the farm. During the previous two years, while his brother Diogo had been a page, the situation of the pages who were scions of families like the Magellans, devoted to the cause of the King, had sharply deteriorated. They had become the victims of hazing and of sly nagging. This was because the attitude of the courtiers about Queen Leonora reflected a sharp change which had occurred in Portuguese politics.

When Diogo first had entered the page's school, he had as a junior schoolfellow a boy a year younger than his own brother Ferdinand. His name was George, and he was a bastard son of King John who had been sent to the pages' school for his education. Queen Leonora was naturally cool in her treatment of this intruder, who was something of a thorn in her side and a possible rival to her only child, Affonso, the heir apparent. Little George was of course conscious of the unfriendly attitude of the attendants about the Queen and sought companionship with the sympathetic group of his schoolmates whose families were adherents of the Queen's aloof husband.

He was a lovable, manly little fellow, while his fortunate half-brother, Affonso, the Crown Prince, five years his senior, was effeminate and gave disturbing evidences of abnormality. King John kept the Crown Prince away from his mother and in his own company. He tried in vain to instill in him a liking for hunting and martial practices to take the place of his love of finery and self-adornment.

Ambitious King John had won a great diplomatic victory by bringing about the marriage of fifteen-year-old Prince Affonso to the heiress of Ferdinand and Isabella of Spain. The degenerate and frivolous youth thereby became heir apparent to the crowns of the other four Christian kingdoms of the Hispanic Peninsula, and he would eventually be the monarch of all Iberia. He therefore was one of the most important political personages of Europe, and his mother struggled against his being kept away from her influence and resented having the bastard George foisted upon her in his stead. But this situation was altered suddenly and tragically.

In June, 1491, at the age of sixteen, Crown Prince Affonso was killed under mysterious circumstances which have never been cleared up; it is generally thought that he was slain by the Braganzas. His death was officially reported to be the result of a fall from a horse; he was last seen riding alone at dusk to join his father, who was bathing at the beach. When he did not arrive at the shore, the alarm was sounded and the whole court searched all night for him. It was not until the following noon that a disfigured and battered body was found lying in a fisherman's hut and with difficulty identified as that of the missing prince. The death of Crown Prince Affonso at once changed the situation at court of page Diogo de Sousa and of his companions, who now found themselves isolated in an environment hostile to all loyal retainers of the King and subject to persecution by the officials of the school. Perhaps it was because of this situation that King John then decided to recruit a stronger force of future adherents by adding a number of new pages to the school. At all events, it was at this juncture that Ferdinand Magellan got the coveted palace appointment and was enrolled, along with a cousin of his own age, Francisco Serrano. The two boys came under the tutelage of Ferdinand's brother, Diogo de Sousa, now a senior page, and the three became inseparable companions. The intimacy thus established between the two brothers and their cousin was to continue throughout their lives.

Queen Leonora, having lost her only son, the Crown Prince, no longer had any interest in common with Dom John, her estranged husband. Therefore she apparently joined her kin, the Braganza family, in plotting the King's death, in order to place her brother, Duke Manuel, on the throne of Portugal. Evidently she, at least, did not hold Manuel responsible for the death of her son. The King was at first prostrated by the blow dealt to his soaring dynastic plans because of the death of the Crown Prince. He soon rallied his energies and summoned the new heir, Duke Manuel, to join him at court and assume his responsibilities as Crown Prince. But

Manuel was wary of trusting himself within dagger's reach of formidable Dom John, and prudently kept under the protection of his sister the Queen.

King John then called for his illegitimate son, Prince George, but Leonora endeavored to keep him with her by claiming to be devoted to the child and reluctant to part with him. She made a great outcry when Dom John finally took him from her.

Once the King had his illegitimate son with him, he proclaimed him heir to the throne, began to train him in the responsibilities and offices of Crown Prince, and undertook to have him legitimatized by the Pope. He gave eleven-year-old George the rank of Duke of Coimbra and made him Master of the Knights of Santiago and also Master of the Knights of Avis. This was to offset the rank and privileges of the legitimate heir, Duke Manuel, who was hereditary Grand Master of the Order of Christ. The King transferred the dignities and privileges of Duke Manuel's Order of Christ to Dom George's two orders, forbade the Order of Christ the use of its symbols and insignia, and virtually suppressed it.

Duke Manuel dissembled his feeling of rebellion, but reacted to the King's persecution by eliminating from the Queen's court on various pretexts any persons who were pronounced adherents of Dom John. He did not, and in fact dared not, eject from the pages' school the boys who had been friendly to Dom George, but he did impose severe discipline upon them.

When Ferdinand Magellan became a student in 1492, Duke Manuel took a dislike to him from the very start. Whether his unfriendliness to Ferdinand was caused by some prank of the young page, was based on political factionalism, or was a simple case of two incompatible personalities, the details are unknown, but the existence of an enduring grudge is affirmed by contemporary historians. This antipathy was to continue into their years of maturity and to intensify into a feeling of vindictive hostility on the part of the prince which played no small part in determining the course of Ferdinand Magellan's life.

Ferdinand began to devote himself seriously to his lessons and particularly to his studies of maritime science. He looked forward eagerly to the time when he could escape his painfully unhappy position under Duke Manuel and graduate into the King's maritime service. King John's own devotion to navigation and to the expansion of Portugal's overseas activities had inspired him, as well as his brother and his cousin, with nautical ambitions.

In March, 1493, Ferdinand Magellan was thirteen and was looking forward to early advancement. It was in this month that Christopher Columbus, storm driven, made port in Portugal on his return from his first voyage of discovery. Everyone, including the ambitious thirteen year old scholar, was electrified by the news. The announcement of his discovery of a westward route to Cathay and Cipango dumfounded King John, who at first was skeptical of the assertions of the exultant Genoese adventurer. However, the Portuguese King finally became convinced by the Asian appearance of the brown-skinned, long-haired, native captives, who were strikingly unlike the black, curly-pated slaves brought back from the African coast by his own explorers.

Although King John had been chagrined by the exploit of Columbus, whose previous offers to sail westward in his service he had rejected, Ferdinand Magellan and his comrades were very naturally exhilarated by it. They saw before them widening possibilities of adventure. Almost at the same time, rumors began to be whispered throughout the school regarding the amazing accomplishments of an overland mission sent to India by King John. Ferdinand and his brother had always dreamed of the sea and of the naval careers ahead of them. They and Francisco Serrano belonged to the favored faction of Dom John, who was ever seeking further discoveries. His heir and their future leader had been their own schoolmate, and despite their temporary subjection to the tyranny of the jealous Duke Manuel, their future in the royal service seemed secure.

Everyone now was talking of the King's orders to Captain General Francisco de Almeida to defend by force Portugal's claim (based upon earlier and somewhat vague papal rulings) to the lands discovered in the West by Columbus. King Ferdinand and Queen Isabella's efforts to avoid war by a conciliatory treaty were scornfully viewed by the pages, who were excited at the prospect of raiding the ocean lanes of Spain's vulnerable West Indian convoys. Consequently they were much dejected when King John let the pro-Spanish Pope intervene in the quarrel and impose an armed truce. However, by his superior diplomacy, and by judicious bribery of the Spanish envoys, King John emerged in 1494 from a bizarre conference of geographers, pilots, and explorers with the very favorable Treaty of Tordesillas as his prize. This treaty awarded to Portugal an immense area of the western Atlantic for its exclusive colonial development, and its terms gave promise of activity to the adventure-loving pages. The way for expansion now seemed clear, and the victorious King ordered Captain General Francisco de Almeida to prepare a fleet to sail westward across the Atlantic in competition with Columbus in the race for India. Meanwhile, he rushed the construction of two specially designed ships in which Admiral Estevan da Gama was to steer southeast for the same goal, around the Cape of Good Hope, recently discovered by King John's caravels. The pages were afire with expectancy. Diogo de Sousa was then seventeen and Francisco Serrano and Ferdinand Magellan were fifteen, so they could reasonably anticipate early employment in the great fleets now being outfitted. They waited impatiently to be relieved of their palace jobs and go to sea.

Then their young ambitions suffered a heavy blow. Their king-hero, Dom John, who was only forty years old, was poisoned; in October, 1495, their enemy, Duke Manuel, ascended the throne. The promise of any naval careers whatsoever for them seemed blotted out. The influential friends of their family who were to have secured seagoing appointments for them now suddenly found themselves not only out of office, but also homeless and penniless, and many of them fled into exile in Spain. The thoroughgoing Braganza faction not only repossessed themselves of the estates formerly confiscated by King John, but also seized every office that had been filled by the followers of the late King. We do not know the fate of Ferdinand's father, Ruy Magellan, but presume that he retired to obscurity at Ponte da Barca, glad to be allowed to live unmolested on his little farm, and content to have his two sons still provided for at court, even though with diminished prospects. The three insignificant pages from the Province of Minho were fortunate enough to be retained in their palace employment, even though without indulgence or hope of preferment.

The Braganza order of the Knights of Christ now triumphantly came into its own. King Manuel not only restored to it the banners, arms, and symbols which had been proscribed by the late Dom John, but aggrandized it in every way. When he ascended the throne there were sixty chapters of the order; at the end of his reign there were four hundred and fifty. As Grand Master, he allowed the Knights to revoke their oath of celibacy and to marry, as well as to forsake their vow of poverty. They now acquired wealth, and their outward appearance changed greatly, for they abandoned their former obligatory crusader's garb and dressed fashionably in costly silks. The King not only advanced the Knights of Christ to become the dominant nobility of Portugal, but he also appointed its members to the leading prelacies of the realm. In fact, as Grand Master of the Order, Dom Manuel used it as a means to make himself the ecclesiastical as well as the temporal head of the country.

After the death of their patron, not only did the pages lose their opportunities for nautical careers, but the nation itself abruptly withdrew from all the maritime undertakings into which it had been plunged by the late ruler. Dom Manuel himself had formerly appeared to approve of King John's scientific advances at sea. However, now that he had become ruler, he showed no interest in the maintenance of Portugal's leadership as a maritime and colonial power. This was largely due to the fact that his own political party, the Braganza faction, was controlled by the conservative and agricultural element of the aristocracy which was opposed to maritime expansion. Almost all his advisers in the Royal Council were hostile to any proposal to revive the naval plans of Dom John. Another political development unfavorable to a continuance of maritime expansion was the loss of influence by the Jewish bankers and traders who had so strongly supported King John's expansionist program.

The influx of Jewish refugees from Spain at this time had been detrimental to the interests of the Portuguese Jews and had created a social and fiscal situation with which Dom Manuel was unable to cope. His predecessor had given the Spanish Jews shelter in return for a substantial immigration fee, but, as the number of the newcomers increased, their orderly assimilation became more difficult, and Manuel's policy toward them changed from benevolence to repression. After a year of indecision, Dom Manuel, under pressure from Ferdinand and Isabella of Spain, in December, 1496, decreed the expulsion of all unbaptized Jews from Portugal. Besides having long been a major intellectual and scientific force, the native Jews had also been a dominant financial element in the country, so that this drastic change of policy created a chaotic economic condition. The Knights of Christ seized the privileges which had formerly been granted to the Jewish business houses. However, since they were not a mercantile body, they then leased their monopolies to the Florentine traders who were rivals of the Jews throughout Europe and who were eager to profit by their discomfiture in Portugal. Once the Florentines had got control of the Portuguese shipbuilding and shipping trades, they were not slow to recognize their possibilities; they now urged Dom Manuel to revive Dom John's dormant program of exploration. They were backed in this by their rivals, the German bankers, led by Cristóbal de Haro, the representative of the pepper trust in Portugal, whose knowledge of Venetian and Hanseatic sea trade made him avid to exploit the obvious overseas opportunities that now lay open to the foreign traders at Lisbon. Business influence, from whatever quarter, was eager to exploit the trend toward exploration and expansion.

The Florentines soon won over to their side the King's uncle and most influential adviser, Dom Alvaro Braganza, who began to form a pro-maritime group in the King's Council. Then they saw to it that Dom Manuel should discover, in the private files of the late King, a hidden casket containing the secret reports of foreign spies concerning the encouragingly rich prospect for Portugal in the development of the sea route to the Indies. His interest once enlisted, and dreading being forestalled by Castile in reaching India, Manuel developed an anxiety to follow up the discoveries which Bartholomew Dias had made eight years previously. He overruled the objections of the Royal Council, with the support of Dom Alvaro Braganza, and ordered the squadron of the late Estevan da Gama to be recommissioned. The Florentine financiers at once provided him with funds for the expensive undertaking and were permitted to become his active associates in the enterprise, supplying one of the four ships for the expedition. The dormant colonial and maritime organization which King John had called Mina House was revived, and the neglected water front again resounded with shipbuilding activities. Manuel enthusiastically created a new maritime staff which he installed in offices convenient to himself in the palace. Under the impetus of the King's new mood, the court began to take on the bureaucratic aspect of a colonial and naval office.

The school for pages had been moved to the King's court several months after he ascended the throne, and marine activity was resumed about six months later, in mid-1496. This development at last gave an opportunity to Ferdinand Magellan and his comrades; Ferdinand had reached maturity. Now, with his brother and cousin, he was transferred to a post as clerical worker in the newly established marine department in the palace. In due course he advanced from the rank of page to the rank and pay of squire in the royal household. Thus he presumably was employed in the fitting out of the new fleet which was to try to complete the unfinished task of Bartholomew Dias; and no doubt he was present at the ceremony at Restello on July 8, 1497, when Dom Manuel formally invested twenty-eight-year-old Vasco da Gama as leader of the expedition to India which his late father, Admiral Estevan da Gama, had initiated. Da Gama's departure is dramatically described by Camoens in the Lusiads.

The resolute da Gama returned with a cargo of spices twenty-six months later, in September, 1499. He had put down mutinies, passed through cyclones and calms in unknown waters, and outwitted and beaten off Arab and Hindu attempts to capture his armada. He had lost two of his four ships and two-thirds of his men, among them his brother, but he had succeeded in finding the sea road to India. One of the two ships that returned flew the private house flag of the Florentine House of Marchioni.

After da Gama's return, Magellan and the other squires were engulfed in the excited swirl of the court in which little else was thought of than the good fortune which had made Portugal claimant to the wealth and influence hitherto enjoyed by Venice and Egypt. The state of mind of the King himself can be seen by the private letter which he hurriedly wrote in 1499 to his wife's parents, Ferdinand and Isabella of Spain. "We learn that our captains did reach and discover India and other Kingdoms and lordships bordering upon it; that they entered and navigated its seas, finding large cities, large edifices and rivers, and great populations, among whom is carried on all the trade in spices and precious stones which are forwarded in ships to Mecca and then to Cairo, whence they are dispersed throughout the world. We hope, with the help of God, that the great trade shall be diverted, in consequence of our regulations, to the natives and ships of our kingdom, so that henceforth all Christendom in this part of Europe shall be able in a large measure to provide itself with these spices and precious stones."

Although Vasco da Gama did not bring back many spices, nevertheless the profit on his small cargo more than paid expenses, and the financial credit of King Manuel was as much enhanced by it as though the ships had returned laden with gold. Da Gama brought back with him to Lisbon from India two competent international merchants, a Moor named Moncaide and a Jew called Gaspar da Gama, both of whom had had extensive trade experience in the Venetian and Egyptian markets. These two men divulged to the financiers of Lisbon the details of oriental trade with Europe. Their facts and figures were confirmed by the Florentine merchants who had gone on the caravel *Berrio,* privately owned by the Florentine banker Marchioni, which was the first of da Gama's ships to reach Lisbon on the return trip. Cristóbal de Haro was not slow to compete with Marchioni in offering credit facilities to the King. However, Dom Manuel favored the Florentines and, with their financial backing and the participation of Florentine ships, prepared a strong fleet to follow up da Gama's discovery. On March 19, 1500, a second expedition was dispatched to India under command of a court favorite, Pedro Alvares Cabral; the obscure Ferdinand Magellan tried but was unable to enlist in its complement. There were thirteen ships in this fleet, one of which, the *Annunciada,* was owned by Bartholomew Marchioni, the Florentine, who thus again scored on de Haro, for the Germans were not allowed to participate. Less than half of Cabral's ships returned safely, but the *Annunciada* brought back such valuable jewels, Chinese works of art, fine textiles, drugs, dyes, and spices that the manifest of its cargo appeared like a fantastic tale of magic to its owner.

Everyone at court now wanted to sail to India to make a fortune, and Ferdinand Magellan and his two comrades were no exception. However, it required political influence to be allowed to enlist in one of the expeditions, and the three squires were given no such opportunity. Instead they were forced to work hard in the outfitting of squadrons for the lucky ones who were to set forth. They ate their hearts out when each year a returning fleet discharged the home-coming adventurers covered with nautical distinction and laden with incredible gains.

We presume that Ferdinand Magellan continued to be employed in a clerical capacity in the maritime division of Mina House, and we can visualize his being sent daily through the narrow, hilly downtown streets to the nautical shops in which were prepared maps, globes, and instruments such as compasses, hourglasses, and astrolabes. Along the water front of the Tagus he had to visit the private warehouses of the Florentine and German traders, and the ship chandlers and suppliers, only a few of whom were of native Portuguese stock. Before him in the stream lay anchored hundreds of merchant ships from all Christendom, come to Lisbon to trade for the oriental wares formerly sold by Venice. All along both shores of the river were the shipyards, teeming with activity as they tried to meet the urgent demand for delivery of new ships.

Ferdinand Magellan's personal interest was not wholly in the East, for all his life he seems to have clung to the westist theories of Toscanelli which had been so strikingly vindicated by the discoveries of Christopher Columbus. He may indeed have been employed in the work of the Western Atlantic division of Mina House. For Dom Manuel, even after da Gama's sea route eastward to India had been firmly established, did not neglect the possibility of finding a western route across the Atlantic to India. On March 15, 1501, he sent a fleet of four ships under the command of Juan da Nova to explore along the coast of Brazil en route to India. With this fleet Dom Alvaro Braganza sent along, as captain of a caravel, Dom Diogo Barbosa, who became an advocate of a western route to India, and who years later initiated the westward expedition commanded by his son-in-law, Ferdinand Magellan. Cristóbal de Haro also was a believer in the possibilities of a westward route, and he persuaded Dom Manuel to let him send, on May 3, 1501, Captain Cristóbal Jacques with three caravels to explore the southern Brazilian coast. On May 13, 1501, Dom Manuel himself dispatched the Florentine, Amerigo Vespucci, on a similar voyage to northern Brazil to try to find a passage to India. These pioneers did not discover the westward route nor find the wealth in gold and diamonds that lay hidden in Brazil, but they did make satisfactory profits from their cargoes of brazil dyewood, Indian slaves, and bright-plumaged parrots, which found a ready sale. Besides being continually pressed by the rival bankers, Marchioni and de Haro, to continue to probe to the West, the King was eager to flank the Spanish western colonies, and therefore he also sent several northwest expeditions to explore the coasts of Greenland and Labrador. They found no northwest passage to India nor did they bring back any gold, but they did establish valuable fisheries off the Newfoundland banks; though less spectacular, over the years these proved to be as much of an asset as gold mines. The riches of the Orient were the constant goal, however, and the speculative foreign bankers even persuaded the King to devote an heroic Portuguese expedition to the task of trying to reach India by sailing northeast of Scandinavia through the Arctic Sea. This expedition gave the name it still bears to the frozen land of Novaya Zemlya and, after great hardships, brought back to Lisbon only furs and unicorn horns (walrus tusks) as its spoils.

The main effort continued to the East, however, and in 1502 a strong expedition of twenty vessels set out to India under Dom Vasco da Gama. Although a numerous personnel made up the expedition, Ferdinand

Magellan again could not get permission to enroll with the adventurers. In 1502 also the newly elected Doge Loredano of Venice turned to Jakob Fugger, of Augsburg, for financial assistance. In that same year, a papal bull proclaimed that henceforth "Our beloved son Manuel" would by signal approval of His Holiness the Pope style himself "King of Portugal and of the Algarve on this side and beyond the sea in Africa, Lord of Guinea, and of the Conquest, Navigation and Commerce of Ethiopia, Arabia and India."

In 1503 the King changed the name of Mina House to India House, to indicate that its administration no longer was restricted to the West African coast, but now embraced the entire field of overseas colonization. De Haro still persisted in his westward ideas, and in 1503 the King permitted him to send Captain Gonçalo Coelho with six *naos* to thrust far down the southern coast of South America. This large, well organized fleet carefully explored the Patagonian coast and may have discovered the mouth of the strait which later was penetrated by Magellan. It is indeed quite possible that Ferdinand Magellan himself may have been so placed, in the colonial bureau in which he was employed, as to have learned of it. Upon the return of this expedition to Lisbon, all reports of its findings were suppressed. If it did discover the westward strait, the King probably decided it was not to his interest to disclose its existence, since it would be advantageous to Spanish commerce. At all events, on November 15th, 1504, Dom Manuel issued a decree that ordered complete secrecy, under pain of death, of all maps, logs, reports, and any other details of southeastern or northeastern navigation. He evidently thought he would eventually have Spanish competition in the Orient via the western route, and hence, in 1505, he determined to desist from further efforts westward and to entrench himself in the possession of the eastward route. At that time he commenced the establishment of a chain of fortified naval bases down the Atlantic coast of Morocco to prevent Spain from using its Canary Islands as a base to raid his line of eastern communications around the Cape of Good Hope.

During all this period, which in Lisbon seemed to be devoted to the preparation of outgoing adventurers and the reception of enriched returning veterans, Ferdinand Magellan was kept busy in his shore-bound work while he vainly tried to get the coveted license to enroll in one of the expeditions, either to East or West.

However, the adventurers returning exultantly with their spoils by no means did as well as some of the stay-at-homes among the Knights of Christ. This was because Dom Manuel kept in his own hands all the richest patronage connected with the Indian service, and he gave it not to his returning soldiers and sailors, but to the courtiers and prelates about him. He maintained a rigid monopoly of the means of transport, and no one was allowed to import anything from the Orient for his own account. Every cargo had to be consigned to India House, which took title to all incoming goods and reimbursed the owner for their value as assessed by the bureaucrats, less the forty per cent duty due the crown. Even Cristóbal de Haro and Bartholomeo Marchioni could not sell the imports which arrived in their own ships, but had to deliver their merchandise to India House and to accept warehouse receipts for it. It became necessary to pay bribes to the officials even to procure one's own property, once it was in the hands of the government, and many a returned veteran without political influence was defrauded of the rewards of his work and sacrifice.

The tonnage capacity of the returning royal ships was divided officially into many small units of cargo space which theoretically represented cubic room for freight having the weight of a single *quintal* (four *arrobas*, or a gross of 128 pounds). Under this method, each member of the crew, including even the cabin boy, was given a negotiable certificate called a *quintalada*, which conveyed the privilege of importing for his own account one or more *bultos*, or bundles of merchandise of standard limits in weight and dimensions. The number of *bultos* which each individual could import varied in accordance with his rank in the crew. Sometimes additional *bultos* were allotted to the crew as incentive bonuses. The *quintalada* system had first been used by Prince Henry to insure an equitable distribution of profits among the crew of his caravels, and also to provide a fair measure of participation by the merchant adventurers of Lagos. It had worked in a satisfactory manner, and when the water route to India was established by Vasco da Gama, it was adopted as a basis of compensation for his returning crew.

Under such a system it followed that the most desirable commodities were valueless unless they could be supplemented by a *quintalada*. The courtiers soon learned, for example, that a sack of pepper purchased in India for two *cruzados* could be sold in Lisbon for twenty *cruzados*, but only if the owner had a *quintalada*. The King therefore was deluged with requests for the issuance of *quintaladas* to his favorites. The result was that soldiers and mariners ready to return from India found that the *quintiladas* issued to them by the government in India were of no use, due to the fact that the entire cargo capacity of the vessel on which they were given passage home had been allocated in royal priorities to courtiers even before the ship had sailed eastward from Lisbon. Thus the veterans' goods would be left in India on the piers, or auctioned off for a pittance, in favor of cargo consigned to some stay-at-home prelate or lady of the court at Lisbon to whom a royal *quintalada* had been issued.

Moreover, when a veteran got his gains safely back to Portugal, he discovered to his consternation that his property might be subject to sequestration or even confiscation while in the warehouse of India House. This was because the King gave legal monopolies to his favorites for the importation into Portugal of specific commodities. The courtiers scorned to engage in trade themselves, but leased their monopolies to the trader who would bid the highest. These lessees, generally foreigners, took legal steps to force the returning veterans to sell their goods cheaply to them. These monopolies, or patents, so capriciously created at the whim of the monarch, applied not only to rare articles, but also to general trade goods and materials that were imported in bulk, such as the many drugs of oriental extraction which formed the basis of the European pharmacoepia, and the lacquer work and rattan-ware which soon became popular.

An example of these arbitrary trade monopolies is afforded by the control of dyestuffs by a clique of noblemen. One favored Knight of Christ commanded the market on two vegetable products called woad and indigo, which produced the popular blue colors, another was master of the dried crocus flowers from which saffron was derived, and a third noble huckster controlled brazilwood, a reddish forest product. Thus likewise were allocated the imported dried roots of the madder plant, which was used for turkey-red, and the dessicated bodies of millions of cactus bugs called cochineal, and of tree lice known as *kermes* which produced a shade of scarlet. Even bundles of a rock lichen called *orseille* were traded by the aristocratic profiteers. The largest dye importations in bulk, and the cheapest in price, were tons of gall nuts and bales of sumac berries, which formed the base of other dyes; but the palace favorite to whom was assigned the patent for the least plentiful of all dyestuffs, royal purple, was the most richly rewarded of all. This rare tint had to be obtained by collecting the juice produced by pricking a tiny sac in the body of a sea mollusk. Its use was largely restricted to dyeing the fine garments of high functionaries, and it therefore commanded a fabulous price in the Lisbon market.

In this shortsighted distribution of favors, the King and his advisers wilfully neglected the lesson he might have learned from the example of Venice, which had used its control of dye imports to set up a native textile manufacturing, converting, and finishing industry. However, the genius of the Portuguese race was neither financial nor mercantile, and indeed the country quite lacked the skilled workers that would have been necessary to build up a textile industry. Therefore, it eventually happened that political arrangements were made to buy off the noble patentees, and the dyes were bid in by Cristóbal de Haro to be shipped to the textile makers in Venice, Flanders, and Germany, or were secured by Marchioni for the textile makers of Florence.

As was to be expected after the return of Cabral's fleet in 1501 with its cargo of Asian riches, the country had become the Mecca of German,

Flemish, and Florentine merchants; before long its entire domestic economy was controlled by the activities of the newly arrived alien traders. Buyers from every part of Europe settled in Lisbon, which became the metropolis of Europe. The Portuguese people themselves were infatuated by the chimera of the Orient; they abandoned not only the shops and market places, but the farms as well, and rushed pell-mell to try to enrich themselves in the East. Within the quarter-century following da Gama's discovery of the route to India, it was estimated that eighty thousand able-bodied men had gone abroad to seek their fortunes, only a fraction of whom ever returned home. As the total population of the country at the start was less than a million, it may be seen that almost all its younger men were being drained away. The resulting scarcity of all kinds of skilled personnel was not favorably offset by the importation of thousands of jungle savages from Africa, who were useful only as common laborers. An incredible wave of wealth poured into the country from India, but most of it was spent abroad, not only for imported luxuries, but for necessities that should have been produced at home. Much of the new capital, instead of being invested in productive enterprises, actually was sent abroad to buy foodstuffs that in past times had been raised in Portugal.

The increase in the personal wealth of the Knights of Christ, of the King's own circle, was prodigious. Palaces and mansions sprang up on every side. The streets were filled with fashionable equipages, and the women of Lisbon wore more costly silks, furs, and jewels than were to be seen at the court of Caesar Borgia in Rome or in the brilliant group at the palace of the Medici in Florence. It became the mode to copy the architecture, furnishings, costumes, and styles of the Orient, to employ Hindu slaves as household servants, and to serve Indian dishes at table. Before this time the aristocracy and even the royalty of Portugal had had but meager incomes, and the national economy had with difficulty sustained itself on a subsistence level. The rents of the aristocratic landholder had been received mostly in kind, and the gentry had lived modestly upon their estates, their comfort not much greater than that of their more prosperous tenants. Moreover, most of these suddenly opulent notables of King Manuel's court had, up to a few years ago, been penniless political exiles. The transition from poverty had been so rapid and their enrichment so enormous that few were able to adjust themselves to their bewildering good fortune, and consequently grotesque extravagance and prodigality were displayed on all sides.

Ferdinand Magellan shared in none of this, but labored in obscurity in the glittering environment of a court intoxicated by sudden wealth. He was proud of his lineage, ambitious, and consumed with military ardor; but like many others of the former faction of King John, he had no choice but to work in the prosaic and ill-paid routine of palace employment, while favored but less able contemporaries were allowed to sail to India and to return in a few years with honors and wealth.

Six years passed before, in 1505, Ferdinand finally got his opportunity. This was not by royal favor, for when the King at last gave his reluctant permission to the three restless squires to seek their fortunes in India it was no doubt against the wishes of his administrative staff at India House. Diogo was now twenty-six years old, Ferdinand and Francisco twenty-four, and they had been trained for a dozen years to help carry on the departmental work of Dom Manuel's imperialistic program. The operations of India House were hampered by a real manpower shortage which had been caused by the plague as well as by the exodus to India of most of the younger men, and the overworked officials naturally did all in their power to keep competent aides from leaving. Increased maritime activity had meant increased work for the staff of India House, who had to provide everything for the year-long voyages of the King's fleets. India House had expanded its operations to include huge bakeries for ship's biscuit, large barrel factories, and great slaughtering and packing houses, as well as foundries, machine shops, armories, arsenals and shipyards. The three squires, who had grown up with this mushrooming, sprawling organization and discharged essential duties in it, would have had small chance of being freed from their desks and sent to India had not Dom Francisco de Almeida made a requisition upon India House to supply his expedition with men trained in its system.

The King had now decided to strengthen his grip upon the commerce of the Afro-Indian basin by establishing permanent shore stations for his fleets, so as to maintain Portugal's shakily held trade relations. Up to this time, he had relied upon annual naval expeditions which had been timed to arrive in India with the easterly monsoon and had to depart hurriedly with the westerly one. He now named as Viceroy the able naval commander, Dom Francisco de Almeida, and instructed him to establish trading depots and naval bases upon the east coast of Africa and the west coast of India. Dom Manuel nominated individual Knights of Christ as port captains at each land station, and also appointed selected functionaries from India House to be factors in charge of fiscal and mercantile operations. They had to be accompanied by experienced subordinates called scriveners, or writers, and this was probably the sort of opportunity that opened to Ferdinand Magellan.

Ferdinand was accepted to go with Almeida along with his brother Diogo and his cousin Francisco Serrano, and since the three squires belonged to the noble class, they were rated as supernumeraries. They did not have to relinquish their seniority in the royal household, but in accordance with custom obtained a leave of absence for the term of three years, or for the duration, if longer, of their service in India. Francisco Serrano's older brother, John, a veteran of the Indian service, and Ferdinand's future companion on his great expedition, sailed with the armada as a senior naval officer. The roster is replete with the resounding titles of now forgotten Knights of Christ who commanded the sixteen *naos* and six caravels of the armada, but barely mentions the squire from Ponte da Barca who was to make more history than any of them.

CHAPTER III

THE ATLANTIC

ON MARCH 25, 1505, the fleet of Dom Francisco de Almeida was to sail from Lisbon. The *Caes da Ribeira* was crowded with the adventurers' heavy-hearted relatives, who had been waiting there since daybreak. At dawn a High Mass had been solemnized at which the members of the expedition and their families had joined in receiving holy communion and in asking God's blessing upon the enterprise. After the Mass, those who were to depart had been conveyed in boats to the waiting fleet of twenty-two ships, in all fifteen hundred soldiers, four hundred artillerymen, and a group of civil service employees from India House. Among the latter were Ferdinand Magellan, his brother, Diogo de Sousa, and his cousin, Francisco Serrano. The extant roster of the fleet does not show the name of the ship to which they were assigned, but discloses that they shipped as gentlemen adventurers of the household of the King. They were classified on the rolls as supernumeraries, and were to serve without pay, but to be given their subsistence aboard ship. They were not regular members of the crew, but would be assigned certain duties and in an emergency would be called upon to lend a hand.

Across the water from the ships came the brave music of cymbals, trumpets, and drums as the royal standard was unfurled and the richly brocaded banners of the various knights were displayed, but the throng at the waterfront made no pretense of cheerfulness. The wives and mothers who were left behind had been given six months of the seamen's pay in advance, but they knew they could look forward to a long and dismal period of straitened circumstances. All the members of the expedition had signed for three years' service in the Orient, and all knew that many would never return. Apart from maritime risks, the mortality of the previous expeditions from scurvy, cholera and tropical diseases, as well as hostile action, had been enormous. The Lisbon astrologers had cast gloomy horoscopes for the voyagers. None could know that neither Captain General Almeida, nor his son, Dom Lorenzo, nor many of the distinguished fidalgos who accompanied him, were ever to return, but it seemed that a pall of foreboding hung over the shore. All were aware that in the earliest voyage to India of Vasco da Gama, only a few years before, only two of his four ships had returned, bringing back an enfeebled third of those who had gone out with him. On the second expedition to India, that of Cabral, in 1500, four caravels had been lost with all hands in a sudden storm in the South Atlantic. Such disasters to the frail Portuguese ships were to continue for many years.

But young Ferdinand Magellan was at long last embarked on the sea route to India.

Now the tide in the river had turned and was rushing seaward. A last boat cast off from the flagship and rowed landward. The sailors on the *capitana*, or flagship, the Sam Miguel, chanted the customary pious hymn as they tramped about the four-barred capstan, noisily drawing up the anchor cable through the hawse hole in the bows. The *trinquete*, or foresail, was hoisted, the trumpets blew a flourish, a salvo was fired from the ship's twenty guns, and the Sam Miguel glided on the ebb tide down the Tagus, followed by the other ships in single file, under foresails only.

The Sam Miguel crossed the bar first, and then lay to in the Atlantic until the last vessel had crossed as well. With the whole fleet now out at sea, the flagship hoisted all three sails and took the lead, which it was thereafter to maintain throughout the voyage. It was the established procedure, as set forth by the maritime regulations of India House, that the *capitana* should invariably lead the way.

The Captain General's orders had detailed the system of signals by which he proposed to control the navigation of the fleet, and he had required each captain individually to swear at the altar to obey his orders and to follow the *capitana*. During daylight, each vessel was to copy the example of the *capitana* as to sails and course, and at every dusk, each ship of the fleet was in turn to run up alongside to make a verbal report and receive orders. The signals were given at night by means of combinations of *faroles*, or torchlights, and were to be acknowledged by repetition to show they were understood. By this means the Captain General could order sails set, reduced, or furled, or the course changed. A number of lights or the discharge of a mortar from the *capitana* were emergency warnings that land was sighted or that shoals or reefs were ahead.

Remarkable seamanship was exercised by Almeida in keeping together so large a flotilla of craft so difficult to steer. The average rate of progress of the fleet was from four to six knots. If a vessel was missing when a fog lifted or day broke, the fleet spread out and proceeded under shortened canvas until the sails of the laggard could be discerned on the horizon. When we realize how low was the freeboard of Almeida's ships, and how near to the sea's surface were not only the decks, but also the lookouts atop the stubby masts, and when we consider that in addition to these handicaps, they had only the naked eye with which to take their sights, we marvel that in a voyage of so many months the group of ships was kept so well in hand.

The caravels all had painted upon their sails the crusader's cross of the Knights of Christ, but some of the *naos* did not show this insignia; these were foreign merchant craft, belonging to private individuals. The three largest of these merchantmen, the Sam Jeronimo, the Sam Raefael, and the Sam Leonardo, flew the house flags of the three foreign banking firms of Fugger, Welser, and Marchioni. Another *nao,* the Sam Christopher, carried the flag of the Jewish *converso,* Ferdinand de Lorenha, who was the concessionaire of the monopoly of trade with Brazil, while a fifth ship bore the standard of another wealthy *converso,* Lorenzo Fernandes.

The royal revenues from India had not yet made Dom Manuel financially independent of the alien bankers, and he still needed to finance his costly expeditions by their loans. Therefore he had to let them participate for their own private account in his undertakings. There were ten such private merchant ships out of the total of twenty-two which made up the fleet.

The other twelve vessels were ships of the King's Navy, and were to remain on station in the Orient. Dom Francisco de Almeida's orders were to seize six selected ports along the East African and Indian coasts and to convert them into fortified naval bases. The royal ships were laden with lumber and prefabricated masonry for the swift construction of strongholds in the captured ports similar to those which defended harbors in Portugal.

It had been planned to include many heavy cannon for the new fortresses in the fleet's cargo. The ordnance had been delayed in arrival from the gun foundry, and Captain General Almeida had had to sail without it; however, he arranged to have a reserve squadron of five large *naos* follow him with this artillery within a fortnight. He himself could not delay his departure, because ships bound for India had to leave Lisbon by early April in order to round the Cape of Good Hope in time to catch the favorable eastward-blowing monsoon in the Indian Ocean; this would bring them to the Malabar Coast of India about the first of September. Leaving earlier would have been pointless, for it was impossible for merchant ships to enter the ports in southern India during the months of June, July, and

August because of the heavy surf at the river bars at the entrance to the harbors. When the *naos* arrived there, early in September, they would have to discharge their cargoes and load very quickly, in order to catch the favorable westerly monsoon which would insure them a rapid homeward passage across the Indian Ocean. This was an exigent schedule, and it must be followed or the spice ships would lose a whole year before getting back to Lisbon. The royal treasury was dependent upon the proceeds of the sale of the spice importations; therefore the timing of the departure of these *naos* was a matter of first consideration.

We do not know the ship on which Ferdinand Magellan and his two comrades were billeted. Francisco Serrano's older brother, John Serrano, commanded a caravel in the fleet, probably a small one, and the three young supernumeraries may have been on it. We do not know which ship Serrano commanded, but we may sketch their probable environment by describing the conditions aboard a caravel about which we have full details, the Sam Miguel, which was of the latest type of *caravela de armada,* built for service in the Orient. It was a compact ship of a hundred tons burden, with almost no keel, and of a shallow draft to permit navigation in the shoal waters of the East African and Indian coasts. Its beam, or width of hull, was almost half the length of its keel, and its chunky hull was clinker-built, that is, the oaken planks overlapped. They were reinforced on the outside by strong vertical wooden ridges, or wales, across which were nailed horizontal wooden strips, or strakes, to prevent injury when grinding against other ships in boarding or similar operations.

The Sam Miguel carried three masts. The mainmast was as tall as the overall length of the ship. It was planted in the center of the ship and rose from the low waist, or *combes*. It bore the square mainsail called the *papahigo,* which was made of stout hand-woven canvas, doubled at right angles, and suspended from a single yardarm at the top. The flax cordage then in use, with which this heavy main yard was fastened to the mast, was so weak that in a storm it was customary to reinforce the rope by a steel chain to hold the yardarm in place. The *papahigo* could be enlarged by the addition of an extension piece called a bonnet sail, which was a rectangular strip of canvas that could be looped to eyelets on the lower edge of the mainsail for use with a fair wind.

The foremast rose out of the high forecastle and had a single square sail called a *trinquete,* which had a top yard only. The mizzenmast rose from the towering sterncastle and carried the familiar lateen sail called a *messana,* borne on a diagonal yard such as was used on the traditional caravels.

In addition to these three sails there also was a small square spritsail, called a *cebadura,* mounted with a yardarm on a small mast that rose vertically from the bowsprit. This was very useful for maneuvering the ship, but could not be used in a heavy head sea. The bowsprit was as large as the foremast itself and rose at a very sharp angle from the prow. At its tip there dangled on a chain a many-fluked small anchor, to grapple an enemy ship in boarding operations.

There were no topmasts, and each mast was of a single piece of timber, topped by an ungainly platform. These platforms were designed to accommodate archers and slingers, and had wooden walls to protect the occupants against the missiles of the enemy. They were reached by large rope ladders and were in continuous use for navigating purposes, for a lookout was necessary to keep watch for shoals and reefs, as there were as yet no dependable charts.

The weakest feature in the design of the Sam Miguel was in its steering apparatus. It had a heavy stern rudder which still was something of an innovation, having superceded the two broad steering oars which had been relied upon in the previous generation. The tiller was a long horizontal beam, mortised into the upright rudder post under the poop, outside the hull, and instead of being above the deck, the tiller was brought into the hull about four feet below the deck. Consequently, a narrow horizontal opening had to traverse the stern to allow the tiller to be moved from port to starboard. This was a very hazardous arrangement, because the slot was open and, being near the water line, it exposed the vessel to being swamped by a heavy following wave in a fair wind.

This rudimentary tiller was operated by the steersman, who stood below decks on the little steerage platform. His head was beneath an open hatch just forward of the quarter-deck, which was the lower of the two poop decks in the sterncastle. He could not see to steer his course, could not watch the sails or the sea, nor gauge the wind, but was directed by an officer who conned the compass in the binnacle on the quarter-deck and shouted steering instructions down the open hatch to him. The helmsman needed considerable muscular strength to hold the caravel to its course in a gale, for the high forecastle and towering poop presented large surfaces to the wind.

The Sam Miguel had only a single main deck. There was a lower deck, but it had such a large central aperture, or hatch, that it was little more than a broad shelf about the interior of the hull. The height of the ceiling of this lower deck barely permitted the stacking of two wine casks. On it were mounted the carronades, which could be fired only in fair weather through ports closed by hinged flap doors near the water line. There also was a large, square port in the ship's side, with a door which opened upon this lower or gun deck, which was used for loading cargo when in port.

The hold below the gun deck was less than eight feet deep and had bilge water sloshing about in it at all times. The men had a slovenly habit of discharging fecal matter down the hatch into the bilge water. The toilet facilities were primitive at best, being reached by a small, railed outside gallery at the exterior of the stern; there were two enclosed privies jutting out at the back of the ship which emptied into the wake. In rough weather nobody could get to these toilets, and then there was no option but to make use of the ship's hatch. The noisome accumulation caused an almost insupportable stench and harbored a host of rats and cockroaches which swarmed over the waist-deck at night. In a heavy storm, the sediment of the bilge would be stirred up and the resulting effluvia would be so overpowering as to make even the most hardened seamen seasick.

The personal baggage of a supernumerary like Ferdinand Magellan was limited to a small sea chest for his belongings and a blanket roll to serve as bedding. He likewise brought his arms and a complete suit of armor. He needed lightweight clothing for use in the equatorial zones and heavy woolen clothing for the antarctic climate which he would encounter at the Cape. The only accommodation that would be assigned to Magellan and his two companions, as supernumeraries, was a small area of the open waist-deck where they might stow their chests and arms. These had to be lashed down, since the deck had a curved surface because of the arched beams on which it was laid. This sloping deck was inconvenient, for any loose gear was easily dislodged by the roll of the ship and would slip down the inclined surface into the scuppers.

Their belongings were continually damp, for the low freeboard gave no protection against the spray and occasional waves that soaked everything. Much of the area of the deck was taken up by the foot of the mainmast, by the hatch, and by the batel, the ship's heavy longboat, which was lashed to the mainmast. This cramped space on the deck between the forecastle and aftercastle represented the sole living quarters for almost all the ship's complement, and there was no protection from the elements and no privacy for anyone.

While the forecastle had no living quarters, it did offer a refuge of sorts to the supernumeraries. It had a small central compartment known as the *panol,* or sail locker, where spare canvas, gear, and cordage were stored; it was into this cramped, cheerless, damp space that the young supernumeraries crept, grateful for shelter in bad weather.

On the port side of the forecastle was the closed bread-room, where the hardtack was kept to protect it from moisture, and on its starboard side was the cook's galley for the *fogon,* or fire box, a sanded, enclosed hearth, where in good weather a fire was kindled to cook the one hot meal of the day.

The lofty aftercastle had several cabins in it for the captain and the aristocratic passengers, and there also was a little hut called a *todillo* on the quarter-deck of the aftercastle which had cubicles for several higher officers of the ship.

In the poop, just off the quarter-deck, was the stateroom of the Captain General. Dom Francisco was the Viceroy, and since it was expected he would receive state visitors in his cabin, it was a splendid apartment, with carved and gilded wainscoting, and hung with Flemish tapestries. The furnishings were of regal magnificence, but a grim, naval note was struck by the three brass carronades which were mounted on gun carriages at the cabin windows to provide a stern battery.

The lower officers had to eat, sleep, make their toilet, and keep their belongings on the *combes,* or waist-deck, along with the supernumeraries, the soldiers, and the crew.

Limited as were the accommodations, it must be remembered that a fully-decked Portuguese caravel such as the Sam Miguel represented a great and comparatively recent advance in marine architecture. When Christopher Columbus had made his first voyage, a dozen years previously, only his flagship, the Santa Maria, was fully decked. The Niña and the Pinta, the only two of his craft to return safely to Spain, were but partially decked caravels, and their crews had practically no shelter.

Ferdinand Magellan and the other supernumeraries, as well as the petty officers, partook of the same rations as the crew, which were served in heavy wooden bowls or trenchers. Forks were not then in use, and the members of the mess dipped their fingers into the food and used their own daggers to cut the meat. The quantity served was more generous than many of the crew had been accustomed to at home. The midday meal consisted of tough salted beef or pork, which was made palatable by being soaked in a so-called steep tub, a large hogshead lashed outside the bulwarks, abaft on the port side. Every morning the day's ration of salt pork or beef was put into the tub. A few buckets of sea water were added, and a *grumete,* or common sailor, was assigned the job of trampling upon the meat in his bare feet for an hour to tread out the brine and make the meat tender. On fast days, rice, cheese, or salt fish were served instead of meat. Generous issues of dried figs, raisins, hardtack, olive oil, and vinegar completed the rations; a pint and a half of claret and two and a half pints of water were issued daily to each man. The food usually had to be eaten cold, since during windy weather no fires were allowed, and it was often windy. There was no grumbling about this rule, for all hands recognized the extreme risk of even a small ember in the wooden caravel when the wind was brisk.

The supernumeraries were required to serve their turn in the three watches, or *guardias,* of the night. The first *guardia* was under the captain and lasted from sunset until midnight, the second, the *modorra,* was under command of the pilot, and lasted from midnight until just before dawn, and the third, under the *contramaestre,* or boatswain, was called the *diane,* or *guardia* of the morning star. He who stood the first watch on one day stood the second watch the day following, while he who stood second, stood third the next day, and so on; thus the service on watch continued to change progressively.

Although there was no chaplain in the ship's company all hands turned out daily for prayers at dawn and at dusk which were led by the captain.

Throughout the day and night, every half hour, when the *ampolletas,* or sand glasses, were reversed, the ship's boy who performed this task sang a prescribed sacred ditty; so did the lad who lighted the binnacle lantern at dusk. Religious chanteys were sung by the men as they hauled upon the halyards or tramped about the capstan to bring up the anchor. They sang pious songs to the rhythm of the thumping pump's double wooden handles, as the *tonelero,* or cooper, and his crew pumped out the bilge seepage twice daily, and there were hymns to be chanted every four hours when the *guardias* were changed.

Prayers were addressed to the ship's patron, the Archangel Michael, whose carved likeness they carried on the prow as figurehead. St. Vincent, the guardian of Lisbon, was a favorite of the crew, while St. George was the patron of the officers. One and all, however, sought the protection of Mary, Queen of the Sea, and each night at dusk the entire complement, headed by the Captain General, intoned the *Salve Regina.*

Officers and seamen alike believed that only by constant devotional exercises could the dangers about them be escaped, and since the achievements of the Portuguese mariners were little short of miraculous, it was not strange that the sailors constantly invoked the help of supernatural agencies.

Upon leaving Lisbon the Sam Miguel led the armada south-southwest with a favorable wind. Four days after leaving port the supernumeraries were able to see at dawn the hazy silhouette of the mountainous Isle of Madeira, and the Sam Miguel soon was sailing close enough to the shore to permit Ferdinand Magellan to make out the white façades of the Portuguese houses which spotted the forest-covered hillsides, and to watch the white sheets of spray which rose, wavered, and fell in rhythm with the cadenced onslaught of the great Atlantic rollers, perpetually shattering themselves against the rocky coast. At dusk the next day, they saw the triangular shadow cast on the ocean's surface by the great peak of Tenerife, and at the following dawn they beheld the perfect triangle of the peak itself, with its base so obscured by clouds that it appeared to be a detached cone floating in the ether. That evening they watched the cloudlike outline of the distant Island of Palma in the Canaries.

Then, for a fortnight, driven steadily southwestward by the trade wind, they found each dawn more balmy than its predecessor. Blown about by the breezes, there danced on the water like irridescent bubbles the little bladderlike jelly fish which later were called "Portuguese men-of-war." From the Sam Miguel's deck Ferdinand could see flocks of terns and petrels, schools of leaping dolphins, and swarms of flying fish. Beyond that was only the intensely blue ocean, with its floating patches of orange saragossa weed.

Then, it seemed of a sudden, a high volcanic peak appeared at latitude 15° North, and the whole flotilla of twenty-two vessels, like a flock of homing birds, sailed toward it and cast anchor in the Cape Verde Islands.

The expedition stayed a week, refilling the water casks. The supernumeraries had no duties while in port, and could spend their time ashore, relaxing on the sandy beach. They consumed all the fresh fruits and vegetables they could hold, and feasted upon seafood and fresh meat.

The Captain General now issued orders to divide the armada into two sections according to their speed. He placed the faster caravels in the advance squadron, of which he took personal command. The merchant *naos* formed a second and slower fleet, with separate orders. After rounding the Cape of Good Hope, the first squadron had been instructed to sail north along the Mozambique Channel, between the East Coast of Africa and the Island of Madagascar. The second fleet was to have no concern at all with Africa, but was to strike out on a new and adventurous route. Their course was to be northeast by north; they were to pass to the outside of Madagascar, traverse the Indian Ocean at an oblique angle, and steer directly for the Angedive Islands, off the Indian coast near the hostile Mohammedan city of Goa. They were to anchor in an isolated, landlocked bay in the Angedives, and there await the arrival of the Viceroy and the fighting ships before exposing themselves to the risk of attack by Arab warships on the Indian coast.

On leaving the Cape Verde Islands, the course of the Sam Miguel was laid south-southwest so as to get the benefit of the trade winds, and swing far enough west to avoid the area of deadly calms of the Gulf of Guinea at the equator. Now that the caravels had been relieved of the drag of the slower *naos,* they struck a faster pace. Soon the Cape Verde Islands were left behind them, and the mutton birds of Cape Verde which escorted the fleet for a day were no longer to be seen.

When they reached the latitude of Sierra Leone on the African coast, they encountered head winds against which they could make no progress for a whole week. Then the winds suddenly died. They were becalmed, and for two weeks the sails hung limp. Rain fell almost continuously. The moisture permeated every cranny of the ship, and mildew appeared on all personal effects. The frequent heavy thunderclaps had no cooling effect upon the humid tropical atmosphere. The stifling, depressing air, the almost insupportable heat, and the clammy discomfort of the rain made the men so irritable that knives were used in several senseless disputes. Ferdinand and the other supernumeraries, usually so energetic and active, were enervated by sleeplessness and prickly heat and prayed for a breeze to end their sense of physical prostration.

One day when the men lay naked on the deck in the teeming downpour, too dispirited to raise their heads, Ferdinand saw the yawl of Captain Pero Fogaza came alongside. He climbed aboard and reported to the Captain General that his *nao,* the Bela, was taking water faster than the pumps could eject it, and that his *calafate,* or calker, could not stop the leak. The Bela's crew had shifted its guns and its cargo to one side so that the vessel was canted at an acute angle to bring any opening in the hull above the water line. One point of leakage was located, and it was calked. Lead strips were laid over the seams and a blanket of rawhide fastened over them. Nevertheless, when the ship was again righted, the water continued to pour into the hull. Bits of oakum began to appear floating in the bilge, and it was evident that the seams had opened.

The Captain General decided to salvage the cargo and abandon the ship. The cursing mariners unleashed the longboat of the Sam Miguel and with great effort got it overside. With the help of other boats, the lighter items of cargo, the casks of powder, and the belongings of the crew were transferred to other vessels before the Bela went down. The portable altar of the Captain General and his chest of silver table utensils were among the items that were saved.

It was fortunate for the men aboard the Bela that the leak had occurred during a calm, for if there had been a brisk breeze the other ships in the fleet would not have been able to send their boats to save them. Ordinarily, there was little its consorts could do to rescue the crew of a ship in distress, because of the inability of the caravels to come about in a wind and reverse their course; it was impossible to maneuver a ship to go back, whatever the purpose. A ship would not dare drop off its longboat to perform a rescue unless the weather was so calm that the rescuing craft could take in all sail and lay to. If it continued moving, the ship could never get back to pick up its own boat. The longboat and the small yawl carried by a Portuguese ship could accommodate only a fraction of its crew. Hence there was little chance of being saved if your ship went down, even though there were other ships at hand.

Despite the calm, the pilots were uneasily conscious of strong unseen currents which swept them along, although they could not calculate their force or direction. It was what sailors called a rolling calm because, although there was no wind, and the surface was unrippled, the sea heaved continually with great subsurface rollers; the Sam Miguel plunged and wallowed, her timbers creaked, and her spars banged as noisily as though she were in a storm. When they first became becalmed, the crew expectantly cast baited fish lines over the side, but they caught nothing. It seemed the deep black depths contained no living thing. There were no sea birds to be seen, and they saw only the tiny creatures that swam and crawled in the floating masses of sargasso weed.

The squadron drifted eventually into range of the welcome southeasterly winds, and for several days sailed along merrily on the port tack, making more westward progress, however, than was desired. Then they suddenly were struck by a terrible tempest. The Sam Miguel lay over so sharply that her yardarms touched the sea, and the Captain General ordered the *contramaestre* and the carpenter to stand by with axes to cut the mainmast at his signal. Many of the sailors gave themselves up for lost. They were praying loudly, and weeping in despair, when suddenly brilliant, sputtering balls of fire appeared at each masthead, blinding in their brightness. The superstitious mariners shouted for joy and fell upon their knees in thanksgiving, believing this was an apparition sent in answer to their prayers by the saints from heaven to save them from the storm. The violent wind immediately abated, and the men were confirmed in their conviction that a miracle had been performed in their behalf. Actually, they had seen a natural electric phenomenon common in these regions which is known as St. Elmo's fire.

In pursuing this southwest course, Chief Pilot Pero Anes was uneasy for fear he might be approaching dangerously close to the coast of Brazil, about which there was but scanty knowledge, so the pilot was relieved when the squadron was picked up by northwest gales and was driven steadily southward. Soon there was a chill in the air which was keenly felt after the prolonged sweltering in the tropics, and woolen clothing and blankets were brought out from the sea chests.

The surface of the ocean now was covered by a floating seaweed called kelp, in which there were numerous schools of fish. Many sharks appeared, and there were spouting whales on every side. The pilots avoided coming too near the whales, fearful of the damage they might do the ship.

Before long, ice began to form from the spray on the decks and rigging, and there were flurries of snow and sudden fierce gusts of stinging hail. Ferdinand, Francisco, and Diogo, like all the men, suffered severely from the cold. Their sodden clothing froze on them, and sleeping on the exposed deck became a nightmare. Their hands were raw from tugging on the stiff, icy ropes when called to aid the crew, and their bodies were covered with sores caused by the constant salt water wetting and aggravated by the friction of their frozen apparel. Because of the high gales, the *contramaestre* forbade the cook to have a fire in the *foganza,* and for some weeks they had no warm food. The three comrades, when not at work, huddled miserably together under the lee of the forecastle, trying to avoid the screeching blasts and gazing with apprehension at the gray billows, half-shrouded in mist and snow.

During a wildly howling gale, a great gray albatross suddenly appeared out of the mist. Without apparent effort it hovered almost motionless over the Sam Miguel's wake, causing shivers of superstitious fear in all. No one aboard had ever before seen such a creature, and when it circled in the air about the ship without moving its pinions or flapping its wings, its supernatural character was confirmed. It soon was joined by two others, one of which was black, and this the terrified sailors believed was surely an evil genius of the polar sea.

About this time the men of the Sam Miguel managed to snag a hook into the neck of a giant turtle, and Ferdinand Magellan watched with interest as, using a rope pulley over the mainyard, they hoisted it aboard. The entrails provided effective bait, not only on the fishing lines, but also for numerous water fowl such as Mother Cary's chickens, noddies, skuas, and penguins, which were caught by fish hooks in the floating lures trailed astern. Among these were a species which Pero Anes recognized as the Cape Pigeon, indigenous to the Cape of Good Hope; this confirmed the pilot's calculation of their being off the Cape. While some of the men managed to stomach the uncooked flesh of the turtle and of the seafowl, most of the meat was salted and held for the time when the galley fire might again be kindled.

Although his observations now showed their position on the chart to be at latitude 35° S., well below the Cape, the Master Pilot nevertheless continued to hold his southerly course; he announced his intention of reaching 40° S. latitude, or some hundreds of miles beyond the Cape, before attempting to double it and reach the Indian Ocean.

This course is an index to the hazards for the Portuguese pioneers of the passage about the Cape, for thus they not only traveled hundreds of miles out of the way, but exposed the ill-protected members of the expedition to all the rigors of the frigid zone. The bafflement of the Portuguese navigators led them to carry caution to extreme lengths. Since the first successful passage by Bartholomew Dias, two decades previously, several Portuguese squadrons had attempted to repeat the feat before Vasco da Gama was successful in doing so. Da Gama had to quell a mutiny, put his defiant pilots in irons, and navigate the fleet himself with the aid of his brother and his personal feudal retainers in order to succeed. Since his day, there had only been half a dozen successful passages. Pero Anes held the title of Pilot Major of the Indian and Persian Seas and was the most experienced navigator of these southern waters. Later, when the course of the currents and the direction of the winds were accurately recorded and plotted, the voyage about the Cape became less terrifying; but it is hazardous even for modern vessels, and when the Sam Miguel rounded it, in 1505, the pilots were groping blindly against unknown elements.

It was now June, or midwinter in the Antarctic. The enormous waves, the suddenly shifting winds, and the howling tempests that struck without warning made every moment perilous. Ferdinand was relieved when Pero Anes at last announced that they had reached the 40th parallel and gave orders to change the course. The Sam Miguel, on June 20th, three months after leaving Lisbon, finally rounded the Cape of Good Hope. The course then was changed to north-northeast, through a smother of breaking seas. The atmospheric unsettlement caused by the conflict of the five-knot, warm Agulhas current with the frigid Antarctic stream causes violent disturbances of the weather in that region, and there were sudden hurricanes with alternating rain, hail, and snow, and violent seas that tossed the caravels about with terrific force. On July 2nd the storm reached its peak. It was of such frightful intensity that the surface of the sea was a chaos of tossing waves that leaped above the mastheads. It was necessary to carry sail to attempt to escape out of the maelstrom. One caravel, that of Diego Correa, lost all its canvas and was spun like a cork in the whirling sea. The waves swept its decks, and three members of the crew were washed overboard; at daybreak, by some miracle, one man was seen swimming in the icy water, and he was able to catch a rope and be saved.

After another terrible day, the weather became milder and soon they were in the relatively calm waters of the Indian Ocean. The prow of the Sam Miguel now turned northeastward toward the Mozambique Channel.

Ferdinand Magellan was later, in another hemisphere, to call upon the experience which he had acquired at the Cape of Good Hope, as he set an example of fortitude to his men off the far colder and more tempestuous coast of Patagonia. But all this was still far in the future.

CHAPTER IV

THE INDIAN OCEAN

THE Sam Miguel led the way northward in the Mozambique Channel between the African East Coast and the great Island of Madagascar, the veteran pilot proceeding with utmost caution. So numerous were the uncharted shoals and reefs, and so treacherous the unpredictable currents, that Pero Anes had the fleet sail in single file and drop anchor at night. All the preceding expeditions had pursued this same route, but their experiences had been so harrowing that the Pilot Major navigated as though the passage were an unknown one; therefore he had the lead cast constantly from the bows, and kept lookouts at the mastheads.

The slow, cautious passage of the Mozambique Channel must have been very tedious, particularly as the winds were fickle and the ship had to combat the strong southward-flowing Agulhas Current. Nevertheless, the balmy air and the relatively peaceful waters were a relief to the tired crews after their antarctic experiences. At last the uninhabited Primieras Islands, their destination off the African coast, were sighted, and soon the entire fleet cast anchor in a landlocked bay.

In the four months since they had sailed from Lisbon, the hulls had become foul with barnacles and seaweed, and the ships were sluggish and hard to steer; it was imperative that they be cleared of the impeding growth. Orders now were issued to careen the ships for scraping and to repair several which were leaking. Their cargoes were hoisted out of the hatches and placed ashore under tarpaulins. Thatched shelters were made with palm leaves to provide shade for the many who were ill of scurvy, and a palisaded battery was constructed at the entrance to the bay as a defense against any raid by Arabs or pirates.

Ferdinand Magellan was now to observe the marine operation called careening, which he was later to employ many times and was to describe in an extant letter as a particularly hazardous engineering performance. Each of the affected vessels was towed at high tide to the sandy beach and fastened both head and stern by its anchors, of which every caravel carried six. Then enough of its cannon were shifted so that their weight would cant the ship upon its side. Timbers were inserted as props beneath the hull, to bear the stress that would ensue after the tide receded. A scaffolding then was built upon the high side of the ship, and the barnacles and marine growth were scraped away. The planks were tested, in case they had been damaged by sea worms, and any that were weakened were replaced with ready-made ship timbers which were carried in reserve.

After the hull had been cleaned and repaired, the seams were recalked and boiling tar was applied to the entire exposed surface to destroy any remaining worms and to give a protective coating to the hull. Half of the ship being thus put in condition, at high tide the guns and other weights again were shifted and the ship carefully laid upon the other side, so that the other half could be treated. While the mariners were engaged under the *calafate* and the carpenter on the outside of a careened ship, the *contramaestre* took advantage of the removal of the cargo to employ the *grumetes* in the filthy task of pumping and bailing out the bilge and scrubbing the interior of the hold.

Ferdinand Magellan and the other supernumeraries had a holiday during their stay in the Primieras, and advisedly drank citrous juices and coconut milk to cure themselves of the scurvy that already had affected their joints and gums. The short stay at the Primieras was as much designed to restore the scurvy-stricken men to health as to put the ailing ships into navigating condition.

Once his fleet was reconditioned, the water casks refilled, and the sick members of the crew recovered, the Captain General proceeded to carry out his mission. He planned to drive the Arabs out of the Indian Ocean and to blockade the straits from the Red Sea and the Persian Gulf into the Arabian Sea; these moves would force all freight and commerce between Europe and India to be carried to Europe in Portuguese bottoms, via the Atlantic to Lisbon.

King Manuel had not arrived at a constructive policy in regard to the treatment of the East African city republics, and the threatened invasion of the Indian Ocean by the Venetian-Egyptian armada made a decision necessary. Unless favorable alliances were offered by Portugal, the East African sheiks would undoubtedly welcome the Egyptians as deliverers and would give them naval bases athwart the line of communication between Portugal and India. Moreover, in Lisbon the merchants had come to recognize the East African trade as a very valuable one. They had learned that the Arab merchants at the seaports had a widespread marketing network throughout Central Africa which it would be folly to destroy. Consequently, the King gave Dom Francisco de Almeida instructions to set up a fortified trading post in the important metropolis of Kilwa, at about 8° S. latitude, which appeared best suited to serve as the point of control for the East African Coast.

The fleet now numbered eight vessels. They left the Primieras Islands on July 18, 1505, picked up a very brisk fair wind and therefore did not stop at the port of Mozambique, but steered directly for Kilwa, which they reached in the remarkably fast time of four days. Kilwa had become the most important city on the coast because it had managed to establish control over numerous smaller coastal trading points, and hence its sheik claimed jurisdiction over a much greater area than in reality fully recognized his authority. He held sovereignty over the southern port of Sofala, from which was shipped the South African output not only of gold, but also of silver, which was worth almost as much. Sofala also sent to Kilwa a large tonnage of copper, which was in intense demand from India for coinage, as well as for making rice bowls for the populace. Because of its control of these metal exports, Kilwa had made itself the marketplace for Arabian traders coming to East Africa from Egypt, Persia and India. It also exported ivory, honey, wax, hides, and great numbers of slaves gathered from the rich hinterland which it dominated. It was a mercantile rather than an industrial center, with only a few factories, but it imported from India a large volume of manufactured goods which it distributed down the coast and throughout Central Africa.

Vasco da Gama, on his second voyage to Africa, had forced the Sheik of Kilwa to swear fealty to King Manuel and to agree to pay an annual tribute in gold. Subsequently the sheik had defaulted in his payments and had not shown a friendly attitude to such Portuguese ships as had entered his waters. Dom Francisco de Almeida's orders were to endeavor to bring the sheik back into the fold by diplomatic means if possible. If he failed to cooperate, Almeida was to depose him and to install as the new ruler a plotter who had been in secret correspondence with the Portuguese.

The Sam Miguel led the fleet into the crowded harbor of Kilwa in a peaceable manner, with all flags flying, and with the guns shooting blank charges in the prescribed royal salute to a friendly power. This should have elicited the conventional welcome, a return of the salute by the guns of the fortified palace which faced the harbor, and the sheik should have run up on his own flagstaff the royal standard of Portugal which he had accepted from Vasco da Gama in vassalage to King Manuel. Instead, no notice was taken of the fleet's arrival; in the ominous quiet which ensued, the armada anchored with its broadsides trained upon the palace.

Ferdinand Magellan, from the masthead, saw before him on its island a city which he knew had some twelve thousand inhabitants; surrounded by a wall surmounted by high towers, it quite resembled a city of southern Portugal. An Arab geographer wrote in the 14th century that Kilwa was the most nobly built city in the Moslem world. Its stone houses were of three and four stories, with high windows and flat roofs, and were laid out along streets and squares. On the waterfront were warehouses and wharves where many large Arabian dhows were discharging or loading merchandise. Two mosques with minarets and many public edifices were in view, and in the center was a public square lined with tall palm trees. The larger houses were surrounded by gardens and had an air of opulence and grandeur. The fleet was so close that he could see people who were fair in complexion going about their business on shore. The cultivated countryside about the harbor, well watered and wooded, contained the estates of many wealthy merchants. Herds of cattle and flocks of fat sheep in the fields, the well-kept orchards of bananas, lemons, and oranges, and the extensive acreage of sugar cane, all presented a far more civilized picture of equatorial Africa than Magellan had expected to see.

Not entirely surprised at the lack of any welcome, the Captain General sent ashore an officer who had previously enjoyed friendly relations with the Sheik of Kilwa to request an interview. The ruler, Sheik Ibrahim, was the forty-fifth occupant of the throne, which had been established by his ancestor, a Persian nobleman, more than seven centuries previously. He grudgingly agreed to meet Dom Francisco de Almeida at the seashore, stipulating that their conference be unarmed, and belatedly sent aboard some fresh fruits and meat as a gift. The sheik's present included several live sheep, and Ferdinand, familiar with the spare, rugged, brown animals of his homeland, was impressed by the size and plumpness of these African sheep, and particularly by their fat, heavy tails.

The Captain General went ceremoniously to the proposed meeting place, but found no one there to meet him. He sent a dignified protest, again requested an audience, and once more was humiliated by the nonappearance of the sheik. Almeida then sent a sharp remonstrance and was blandly informed that Ibrahim had started out to meet him, but a black cat had crossed his path; since this was an augury of ill luck, the sheik had desisted. Dom Francisco realized he was being trifled with and decided to make himself respected. At dawn on July 24th, when the

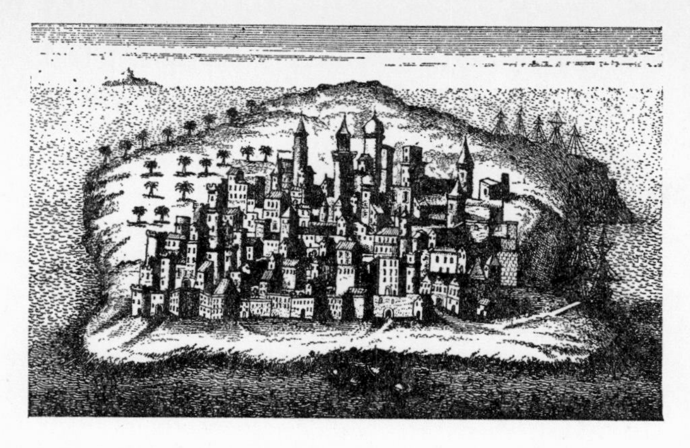

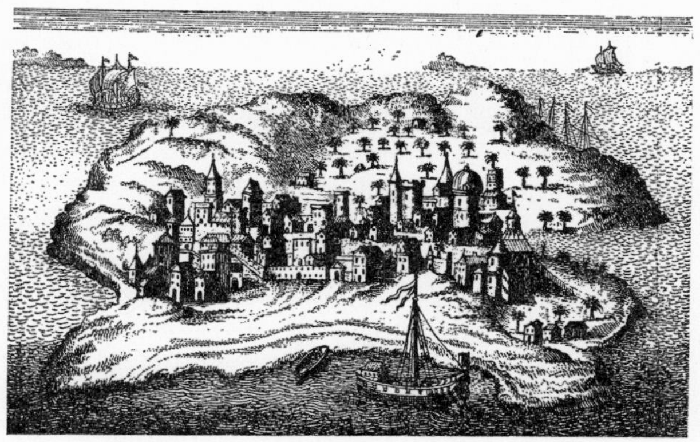

Engravings from "Conquestes des Portugais," 1733

THE AFRICAN FORTRESSES OF MOMBASSA, KILWA, AND ST. GEORGE OF THE MINES

high tide washed the city's walls, a trumpet sounded and the eight Portuguese longboats dashed for the shore, carrying an attacking force of five hundred.

Ferdinand Magellan and his two companions were permitted to accompany the landing party. Being gentlemen of the royal household, they naturally expected this consideration from Dom Francisco de Almeida, who was the personification of punctilious knighthood. The fact that each of the supernumeraries possessed a complete suit of steel armor was additional reason to include them, for the Portuguese used no small firearms, but depended upon crossbow, lance, sword, and buckler to win their battles. The Arabs employed trained Swahili, or half-breed soldiers called Askari, officered by white Saracens; they were brave fighters, but they had little defensive armor, so an armored Portuguese knight had considerable advantage.

Captain Lorenzo de Almeida led the advance body of two hundred. Despite the arrows and spears of the garrison, the Portuguese scaled the walls and fought their way through the narrow streets. Ascending to the flat roofs, they struggled from house to house until they reached the central square of the city. Then the sheik and many of his men fled across the narrow moat to the mainland.

The royal Portuguese banner was raised over the palace, and the town was plundered systematically and under strict discipline. All the booty was piled in the central square for a fair division among the landing force. Only one palace was spared, that which belonged to Mohammed, the leader of the political faction that opposed Ibrahim.

The deposed Sheik Ibrahim, in fleeing from Kilwa, had led with him a considerable proportion of the garrison. This formidable body retained its discipline, and the sheik at once divided it into detachments. These he ordered to march overland to seize and put into defensible condition the several centuries-old subsidiary ports at the mouths of the parallel rivers which emptied into the sea along the coast both to the north and south of Kilwa.

The Captain General decided to prevent the enemy from organizing these ports as points of future harassment and immediately dispatched caravels to each town with orders to destroy them before they could be reached overland by the troops of Ibrahim.

This group of related ports were export staging points for the Central African slave trade. The princelings of the area lived in palaces which were maintained by the revenues derived not only from the general slave trade which they conducted, but also from their profitable specialty of converting young African boys into eunuchs who were exported at high prices to all parts of the Mohammedan world. Their most remunerative traffic was, however, creating and rearing the so-called sealed African virgins, who were in great demand in the Indian market. The method of sealing, or infibulation, guaranteed the maidenhood of the girl to her purchaser. It was accomplished by sewing up the vaginal lips of the child at the age of four, so that when she attained puberty the skin of the walls of the orifice would have grown together and would have to be incised with a knife to permit entrance.

The Portuguese adventurers swooped swiftly upon the subsidiary ports. The caravels appeared suddenly in the harbors and sent boats ashore; the men indulged in an all-out orgy of rape and plunder. The Arabs were slaughtered, their harems were overrun, and the army of female slaves in the barracks were enjoyed by the voyagers who for half a year had seen no women. When after several days the caravels were recalled to the fleet at Kilwa, the entire coast had been desolated, its towns were a heap of ashes, and the only Arab survivors were the few who had managed to flee into the jungle.

Meanwhile at Kilwa the Portuguese victors quickly set about building a strong fort of mangrove logs at the waterside, whose batteries would command both the harbor and the city. Dom Francisco himself labored at this construction from dawn until dusk, and the entire Portuguese force threw itself into the undertaking. The captains and the Knights of Christ were inspired by the Captain General's example and worked energetically alongside the soldiers and mariners. In twenty days a stronghold was constructed which was judged to be impregnable to assault by native troops. Almeida christened it Castle Santiago.

The Captain General, in the name of King Manuel, now offered the throne to Mohammed, the political rival of the sheik, who accepted with alacrity. Mohammed was escorted into the fort on a superbly caparisoned Arab horse with ceremonious pomp. A solid gold crown was placed upon his head and he was hailed as Sheik of Kilwa. He swore allegiance to Dom Manuel at a solemn high mass, signed a trade treaty, and agreed to pay an annual tribute and to permit the Portuguese to garrison Castle Santiago. Dom Francisco then selected a garrison of five hundred and fifty picked soldiers and named two priests as their chaplains. He announced, as Captain of Kilwa, Dom Pero Fogaza, whose ship Bela, it will be remembered, had sunk in the Atlantic.

Having firmly established Portuguese rule in Kilwa, Dom Francisco de Almeida sailed north five hundred miles to the important Arab city-state of Mombassa, which on August 15, 1505, he captured, sacked, and burned after a desperate resistance. With his caravels loaded with booty, including a rich haul in pig copper and two hundred selected prisoners as slaves, he then sailed across the Indian ocean to the rendezvous of all his ships at the Angedive Islands near Calicut.

Ferdinand Magellan did not take part in the capture of Mombassa, but was among the staff that was left with Captain Pero Fogaza. Kilwa's importance as an export market for the products of Central Africa was increased by the destruction of the rival port of Mombassa, and Captain Pero Fogaza's plan was to foster and develop its trade and make it the metropolis of East Africa. He needed, in order to maintain Kilwa's well-being, to encourage the continuance of its export to India and Persia of all indigenous products other than gold and ivory, such as copper, honey, wax, hides, and of course, slaves. He desired that these commodities should continue to be called for at Kilwa by Arabian dhows, and he established a licensing system to try to insure that they would not be diverted from their approved Persian and Indian destinations and carried to the forbidden markets of blockaded Egypt. Although he had several factors from India House to administer these controls, it is possible that he employed the experienced Ferdinand Magellan as an assistant in this work.

In addition to supervising commercial operations, Dom Pero Fogaza had heavy political responsibilities for which he was untrained, and he may have employed young Magellan also to help in these activities. Viceroy Almeida had delegated all local government to the sheik, but had left the police powers and the control of the port in the hands of the Captain. Fogaza continually had to mediate in bitter factional disputes between his puppet ruler, the upstart Sheik Mohammed, and the opposing political elements in Kilwa who were loyal to the exiled Ibrahim. The sturdy Captain was often at a loss to cope with the duplicity of the subtle Arabs. He also had to help his Portuguese lieutenants maintain a semblance of internal peace in the small neighboring Arab ports under his jurisdiction, and to make executive decisions concerning the conduct of affairs in the Portuguese garrisons at the distant southern port of Mozambique and at the gold-exporting city of Sofala.

The harassed Portuguese captains in these subordinate areas themselves had similar fractious local sheiks and unruly Portuguese adventurers with whom to deal, and there was much official correspondence between them and Fogaza. The captains at Mozambique and at Sofala did not willingly accept his decisions and complained aggressively to Viceroy Almeida of Fogaza's incompetence and lack of judgment. They appealed against so many of his orders that the Viceroy finally wrote Dom Manuel for permission to relieve Fogaza of his authority. However, the King refused to let Fogaza, his old courtier and a Knight of Christ, be supplanted. Fogaza no doubt relied heavily upon such energetic lieutenants as Magellan, but the problem was insoluble. He had only a handful of fever-ridden, unhappy Portuguese adventurers, themselves half besieged in their coastal fortresses, to administer the vast country and to control the populous, savage interior. After a long struggle, he finally found it best to make his peace with the deposed Sheik Ibrahim, who thereupon accepted King Manuel's lordship and proceeded to rule the coast in the manner his ancestors had done before him. Years later, on his death bed, the old sheik sagaciously advised his heirs always to remain loyal to the wise and benevolent King of Portugal.

The Portuguese had to abandon their early plans to proselytize the pagan or Moslem natives. Any missionaries they sent into the bush country were murdered, and it was impossible to send armed forces to protect them. Neither could they establish trading posts or operate the gold and silver mines of the interior. They could not impose the European system upon the inscrutable, unchanging land that through the centuries had seen come and go the Egyptians, Persians, Greeks, and Romans.

Captain Pero Fogaza soon found that he needed the energy and fidelity of Ferdinand Magellan not only in the countinghouse of the fortress at Kilwa, but even more vitally at sea. Along the low shore, fringed by mangrove swamps, and in the numerous estuaries and hidden, shallow bays, wily Arab smugglers were diverting from Kilwa a great volume of native products and running the blockade to take them to Egypt. The commerce of the hinterland was controlled by half-breed Mohammedan chiefs, partisans of the deposed Sheik Ibrahim, who zestfully conspired to outwit and boycott the Christian Captain at Kilwa, and surreptitiously continued to trade with their co-religionists in Egypt. Consequently, Captain Fogaza found it necessary to establish a naval patrol of the coast. For this work he had a small, fast caravel of very light draft and a flat-bottomed, oar-propelled, half-decked barge, like a heavy galley of broad beam, known as a *bergantym.* It would have been a clumsy, slow craft, if rowed by ordinary sailors, but a complement of muscular Kaffir slaves, rowing in relays, could, under the lash, drive it along at a sustained rate of high speed. This formidable guard ship carried several carronades, accommodated a number of crossbowmen and armored men-at-arms, and was invincible in combat against the Arab dhows.

Sometime during late 1505, Ferdinand Magellan was assigned by Captain Pero Fogaza to duty on this *bergantym.* That he must have won outstanding distinction in this service is evidenced by a report sent to Dom Manuel by Viceroy Francisco de Almeida on December 25, 1506, concerning affairs on the East African Coast. In this dispatch he advised the King that a civil war had broken out in Kilwa which Captain Fogaza had been unable to quell, and that he therefore had sent adequate reinforcements to Fogaza under command of the Knight of Christ, Dom Nuno Vaz Pereira, one of his most able captains, with Dom Luiz Mendes de Vasconcellos as second-in-command and Ferdinand Magellan as his assistant. Magellan was then but twenty-six years old and had been on the African coast for only eighteen months. In this report to the King, Dom Francisco added that his instructions to Pereira were, once he had helped Captain Pero

Fogaza re-establish the royal authority in Kilwa, to proceed to the relief of the besieged garrison at Sofala, a thousand miles farther south.

The mere arrival of Pereira's squadron in Kilwa calmed civil conflict and restored the authority of Captain Pero Fogaza. Pereira then lost no time in setting his course for Sofala. He was accompanied by Ferdinand Magellan, perhaps in his *bergantym*, for with the southward-flowing Agulhas current, his Kaffir oarsmen would not have found the row of a thousand miles too arduous. If the winds were light, they probably outdistanced the caravel on the way.

At Sofala, a dozen broadsides from the ships of Pereira sufficed to raise the siege and to relieve the three dozen human scarecrows who had held the little log stockade against six thousand savage attackers. Their captain had been killed, and Nuno Vaz Pereira now took over the captaincy of Sofala, with Ferdinand Magellan as his lieutenant. Sofala lies at about latitude 20° South. Although the temperature is mild, the location of the Portuguese fort was swampy and unsalubrious, and the mortality of the garrison from fever was very high. Sofala enjoyed a large import business of textiles and general merchandise from Northern India, and had a notable export of ivory and of hippopotamus teeth, but the main commodity which caused its harbor to be crowded with Arab dhows was the gold dust from the South African gold fields. The city was identified by the Portuguese as the Ophir of the Bible, from which Solomon got his gold; and there are massive ruins in the interior which are known as King Solomon's mines.

At the end of January, 1507, Pereira, taking Ferdinand Magellan with him, sailed to Mozambique to meet the small squadron due from Portugal under command of Affonso de Albuquerque. Young Ferdinand's first contact with Albuquerque, the future dictator of India, was an unfortunate one. The hard-bitten veteran of North African wars of an earlier generation, who had been a personal bodyguard to the late King John, was of the court faction hostile to Dom Francisco de Almeida and already had in his pocket secret instructions to supplant him. Apparently Pereira produced an unwelcome order from Viceroy Almeida to Albuquerque to turn over, for patrol duty in Africa, a knocked-down, prefabricated light caravel which was in his cargo. Albuquerque had intended to use this ship in his own operations about the Gulf of Aden, and he therefore parted with it reluctantly and with very ill grace. His imperious, vindictive nature is well known, and he may well then have first taken the dislike to Magellan which was to become evident in their later relations.

The work of assembling the prefabricated caravel was assigned to John Serrano. It was christened the *Espera* and, when it was launched, was given to Captain Duarte de Mello, a Knight of Christ, who picked Ferdinand Magellan as one of his officers. While awaiting completion of the

Espera, Magellan remained at Mozambique with his *bergantym.* This port is at about the 15th parallel South. It was an important Arab city where the Portuguese had built a fort and naval repair base, and it already was the principal port of call for the Indiamen. There are several references to Ferdinand Magellan in the naval payroll records at Mozambique in 1507, as well as at Sofala and Kilwa, for he patrolled the entire coast. After the *Espera* was finished, John Serrano was ordered to build two war galleys at Mozambique, and he later was commended by the Viceroy for his brilliant command of these galleys in actions against the Mecca ships on the African coast.

During all the twenty-seven months in which Ferdinand Magellan served in East Africa under Captains Pero Fogaza, Nuno Vaz Pereira, and Duarte de Mello, we have encountered no reference to his brother, Diogo de Sousa, and his cousin, Francisco Serrano. But in September, 1507, when Pereira was called back to India by Viceroy Almeida to help prepare a defense against the threatened Venetian-Egyptian naval invasion, he returned in command of the *nao* Sam Simon, and on the ship's roster of officers appears not only the name of Ferdinand Magellan, but likewise that of Francisco Serrano. It is quite possible that, during his adventurous career in East Africa, Magellan had both his cousin and his brother at his side, for Diogo de Sousa sailed from Mozambique for Lisbon on the *Santa Marta de Lagos,* commanded by Antonio Saldanha, which reached Portugal in August, 1507. It is more than probable that Ferdinand Magellan took with him from Africa to India a substantial fortune, for his share of the spoils of many captured Mecca ships could hardly have failed to amount to a considerable sum.

Magellan fortunately possessed the strength of character to withstand the powerful temptations and influences of tropical life upon the foreign conqueror. The allurements of the licentious Afro-Indian underworld of the seaports of East Africa proved irresistible to many of the Portuguese. After months at sea, the crews were delighted to find the women of these ports complacent and adept in the arts of love. The half-breed Arab women readily won their lovers' trust by becoming Christians, but their conversion had no inhibiting effect on their conduct. They were accustomed to the use of aphrodisiacs and stupefying narcotics such as Datura, and from them the Portuguese learned the habit. It is no wonder that, under these circumstances, there was a loss of morale in the Portuguese armed forces there.

CHAPTER V

THE ARABIAN SEA

FERDINAND MAGELLAN arrived in India from Mozambique with his cousin, Francisco Serrano, in October, 1507. They disembarked from the *nao* Sam Simon at the city of Cochin, which lies on the northern Malabar coast of India below the 10th parallel south latitude. Events had developed rapidly in Cochin in the two years from the autumn of 1505 to that of 1507, during the time Magellan had been serving in the westward Indian Ocean.

The Rajah of Cochin had been friendly to the Europeans from the beginning, and in 1505 he swore fealty to Dom Manuel. Although treated with royal honors, he gradually was reduced to the status of a hereditary native governor under Portuguese rule, rather than an independent allied sovereign. Dom Francisco de Almeida had made Cochin his official headquarters. He expanded and reinforced Fort Manuel, constructing an arsenal and dockyard in which he built galleys and light caravels and made repairs to his ships. A hospital, a church, and many government buildings were erected, and when Magellan arrived in 1507, Cochin already had assumed the status of a colonial capital.

Ten years had elapsed since Vasco da Gama had first appeared with three little ships at the city of Calicut on the Malabar coast and had petitioned the mighty Zamorin there for the right to trade in spices. The spice trade with Europe was then concentrated in the hands of Saracen traders at Calicut. Each August, from time immemorial, the eastward-blowing monsoon had brought from Aden, Arabia, to Calicut a fleet of a dozen large Mecca ships bearing Venetian and Syrian wares; these the Arab importers of Calicut redistributed throughout the Orient. The Mecca ships were reloaded in Calicut harbor in an unhurried manner with spices, drugs, dyes, textiles, and Chinese goods, while comfortably awaiting the westward turn of the monsoon. Then they sailed back to Jidda, the port of Mecca, in the Red Sea, which was the terminal of the Arabian camel caravans which carried spice cargoes overland to Alexandria in Egypt.

The Portuguese newcomers at Calicut had brusquely intruded in this Arabian monopoly and aggressively demanded the right to participate. The Saracen merchants had fiercely resented the attempted invasion of their market and had driven da Gama away from Calicut. He had managed, before returning to Portugal, to secure some spices from the minor rival ports of Cananor and Cochin and to establish the possibility of future commerce there. Since then the Portuguese had struggled to share in the spice trade with India. During the decade, they had precariously maintained fortified trading posts at the friendly ports of Cananor and Cochin, and had barely withstood the vigorous attempts of the Zamorin of Calicut to drive them out.

During this first pioneering epoch of the Portuguese invasion of India, young Ferdinand Magellan had been a squire in the King's household, working in India House in Lisbon, and soliciting an opportunity to enlist in one of the annual fleets to India. His participation in the great adventure in India was to begin in the second phase of the Indian undertaking, in which Dom Francisco de Almeida was embarked. The Viceroy no longer sought the mere right to share the traffic in spices, but was attempting to evict the Arabs altogether and to make the trade between Europe and the Orient a monopoly for Portugal. The discomfited Arab traders and their Hindu allies were put on the defensive, and called upon Egypt and Venice to help them combat the increased Portuguese effort. The overt war between Christian Portugal and Moslem Egypt, supported covertly by Christian Venice, was about to be fought out, not in the Mediterranean, but in the faraway Arabian Sea.

The Arabian Sea is an inverted, semicircular gulf of the Indian Ocean, with Arabia as its base and East Africa and India as its sides. The Portuguese under Almeida had secured footholds on both edges of this inverted bowl by establishing bases at Sofala and Kilwa on the coast of East Africa, and at Cananor and Cochin on the southern Malabar coast of India. The Saracens, besides being entrenched in Arabia, retained strong bases in East Africa at points north of Kilwa and in India at points north of Cananor.

The war fleets of the hostile Indian sovereigns, the Zamorin of Calicut, the Rajah of Goa, and the King of Cambaya, greatly exceeded the squadrons of the Portuguese in tonnage and in personnel, but their ships were much weaker in combat efficiency. The Arab shipwrights had followed a traditional pattern in designing their dhows, using wooden pegs to hold their timbers together. Only in the construction of their largest ships did they employ even a few iron spikes and nails. Their carpentry was very skillful, for they fitted matched planks so accurately that, after they were joined, they were permanently held in place, without nails, by expert lashings of twisted coconut fiber ropes which passed through holes in each piece of timber.

The smaller Arab dhows were undecked, but the larger Mecca ships were fully decked and had commodious deck houses for passengers and capacious covered holds for cargo. Their square sails were made of matting. These ships, despite their shortcomings, were in reality well suited to the service in the Arabian Sea and Indian Ocean for which they were designed, and had gradually supplanted the seaworthy and time-tested Chinese junks along the Malabar coast.

Navigation in the Arabian Sea was practicable only during the summer season, from September until March; during this period, the seas were placid, and there were dependable trade winds, or monsoons, which blew steadily, first southeastward, then veering to northwestward, so that by timing the voyage correctly an Arab vessel would have a strong fair wind behind it from Arabia to India and back.

Much of the carrying trade of the Arabs called for more expert seamanship than did the voyages of the Mecca spice fleet. The Arab pilots had as good a knowledge of celestial navigation as had the Portuguese pilots, and they had the advantage of operating in a limited geographic area for which they had accumulated accurate maritime data. They not only used the astrolabe, but could take observations of both the stars and the sun to calculate the position of their vessels by the ingenious use of a small, flat piece of wood in connection with the employment of knotted cords.

Good seamen and resourceful navigators though they were, the Arab sailors found it difficult to use their dhows for coastwise navigation. The clumsy, heavy hulks, efficient enough in a fair following gale at sea, were helpless to cope with the fickle shifting winds, the prolonged calms, strong currents, and rushing tides that were encountered all along the Indian shores of the Arabian Sea. The Arabs, therefore, had developed for coastal navigation a long, broad-beamed, oar-propelled barge of about fifty tons capacity called a *zambuco*. It was upon their hundreds of *zambucos* as well as upon their large, square-sailed dhows that the Arabs and their Hindu allies relied to defeat the Portuguese caravels at sea.

During all the year 1506 no ships at all arrived from Portugal; therefore, the Viceroy received no advices from Lisbon. Even before he sailed in March, 1505, he knew that sooner or later in the Arabian Sea he would have to meet the strong Egyptian-Venetian fleet which was being constructed at Cairo; he therefore was very desirous of disposing of the formidable sea forces of the three native allied sovereigns of Calicut, Goa, and Cambaya before they could be reinforced by Egypt. For this reason he maintained his caravels at fighting strength and placed his son, Captain Lorenzo de Almeida, in command of a task force to destroy the Malabar potential at sea. Dom Lorenzo was reasonably successful in this, but the numbers of the enemy craft were so great and their harbors and ports of refuge so numerous that the little fleet of caravels was hard put to it to patrol the entire coast line effectively. When Pereira arrived at Cochin from the African coast, in October, 1507, the Viceroy immediately put him in command of the small caravel *Santo Espirito* and sent him to the assistance of Captain Lorenzo. Ferdinand Magellan accompanied his commander.

The tactics of Dom Lorenzo were to trust to the superior maneuverability of his caravels, keeping just beyond bowshot of the dhows and *zambucos* so that he could use his artillery against them. The enemy, on the other hand, always tried to catch the caravels in narrow waters, trapped behind some headland or becalmed; then, with a tremendous spurt of oars, they would come alongside and attempt to board the Portuguese. Several times when it appeared that the Portuguese were cornered, they called upon God and the saints for aid, and a breeze sprang up. The well-handled caravels easily managed to break away by sailing well into the wind, leaving the baffled Asiatics far behind.

The Indian fleet used a few stone-throwing and arrow-throwing catapults, but in general depended upon arrows and hand-flung missiles. Once they grappled, they rained ignited flax and burning arrows upon the Portuguese sails and rigging before sending their boarding parties swarming onto the deck.

The Portuguese navy in Europe had not hitherto demonstrated any great superiority in combat over the Turkish, Berber, or Spanish warships. Their triumph over the Saracens in the Orient was mainly due to the inferiority in combat of the Mecca ships to the European war craft which had been strongly built to carry artillery in accordance with the latest naval tactics. The flimsy hull of an Arab dhow could not even withstand the shock of recoil of any guns mounted on its own decks, much less the crashing impact of the Portuguese broadsides against its flanks. The Arabs were defeated because their tradition-bound naval architects were a full century behind the times. They had not learned to copy the fore and aft rig of the lateen sails which permitted the caravels to sail into the wind, nor had they developed a lower gun deck with port holes piercing the hull, as in a caravel.

The Zamorin of Calicut had, in 1503, secured through Venice the service of two ordnance experts, Pero Antonia and Joam Maria, who had set up a fully equipped foundry at Calicut for the casting of cannon. These men also trained a body of cannoneers for the Zamorin and were themselves in command of his artillery. They attempted to equip some of the larger Arab dhows with guns, having the decks reinforced and cannon installed from the extensive land artillery of the Zamorin. However, in battle the concussion of their own broadsides broke or loosened the rope lashings which held the timbers, and the Arab ships literally disintegrated before the eyes of the astonished Portuguese.

Magellan's experience in naval warfare had, up to that time, been limited to the coastal actions between his *bergantym* and the Arab blockade runners on the East African coast. He now learned from Pereira the technique of handling a caravel in combat so as to get and maintain a windward position and, while keeping just beyond reach of enemy fire, to shatter his rudder and foremast, thus rendering him helpless. Then the Arab hull was pounded with heavy stone cannon balls until the rope-fastened timbers fell apart. If in a light wind the oar-propelled enemy gained upon the *Santo Espirito,* Pereira would hold his fire until the attackers were within a few yards, then discharge a broadside of gravel, scrap iron, broken stone, and small pellets, slaughtering the fighting men massed upon the deck for boarding.

In his anxiety about the Egyptians, the Viceroy sent his fleet far north to cruise toward the Arab coast. There Dom Lorenzo encountered a strong Indian squadron which was sailing to join the Egyptians. Dom Lorenzo showed hesitancy in engaging the enemy and allowed them to escape to safety under the guns of the hostile stronghold of Dabul. The Viceroy, who had himself been an intrepid naval commander, was infuriated at his son's failure to dispatch this Indian fleet. He angrily accused Dom Lorenzo of cowardice and ordered him court-martialed. It was proved at the inquiry that Dom Lorenzo had acted on the advice of his captains in a council of war. Therefore he was acquitted, but his Spartan father at once sternly deprived the responsible captains of their commands. Fortunately Pereira had found it necessary to take the *Santo Espirito* to Cochin for repairs; and he and Ferdinand Magellan were not involved in this misadventure.

Dom Lorenzo continued northward in a dispirited manner, with considerable loss of morale in his crews. His fleet was off a lee shore, at a river bar near the enemy port of Chaul, when the lookouts reported a squadron of vessels of European rig on the horizon to the north. Dom Lorenzo negligently assumed these to be the caravels from Ormuz under the command of Albuquerque, who had been ordered by the Viceroy to reinforce him. Consequently he took no defensive steps until the newcomers were almost upon him, when he awakened to the fact that this was the Red Sea fleet of the Soldan of Egypt.

This Egyptian force, backed by the Venetians, who were desperately trying to avoid having their spice trade entirely wrested from them by

Portugal, consisted of thirteen Egyptian ships, of which eight were equipped and armed by Venice, reinforced by over a hundred Arabian and Indian ships. It would have been a much stronger fleet had not the Venetian supply ships, attacked en route to Alexandria by the Knights of Rhodes under the command of their Chancellor, Andrew de Amiral, a Portuguese, suffered the loss of fifteen of their twenty-five ships. The supplies which reached Alexandria then had to be carried by camel back across the desert to the Red Sea, where shipyards were set up by Venetian technicians. The Egyptian fleet had finally been launched and sent down the Red Sea with orders to break the Portuguese blockade. Doge Loredano and the Venetian notables anxiously awaited news of the decisive action they hoped for against the upstart Portuguese.

The Portuguese were surprised by the accuracy of firing from the enemy artillery, which was served by Venetian gunners. Contrary to their usual tactics, the Portuguese attempted to board the enemy, but were driven back with heavy losses before they could grapple. They had been accustomed to such easy victories over the Arabs that their mercenary German and Flemish gunners had become lax in the training and drill of the Portuguese cannoneers, who as a consequence had lost their efficiency. After two days of long-distance cannonading in which they were much worsted, the Portuguese fleet broke off the engagement and sailed south in headlong flight, despite the entreaties of Dom Lorenzo, who begged his captains to stand with him and die rather than retreat.

The enemy concentrated their fire upon the flagship; Dom Lorenzo was wounded four times and finally was slain. The Portuguese lost one hundred and forty killed, including thirteen fidalgos of rank, and one hundred and twenty-four were wounded. Sixteen survivors were held captive by Malik Ayyaz, Governor of Diu.

The news of this defeat spread quickly throughout East Africa and the Malabar coast and caused an immediate decline of Portuguese prestige. Their volatile native allies forsook them on every side. The tidings were carried by camel courier to the Soldan at Cairo, who communicated them by fast galley to Venice, where there was great rejoicing. Stocks on the Rialto in Venice and on the Bourse in Antwerp reflected the elation of the Venetian and German merchants.

Dom Francisco de Almeida was momentarily prostrated by the news, since he blamed his own harsh condemnation of his son as the cause of the disaster. From then on he became a changed man, vindictive, hard, and cruel, and he vowed to devote himself and all the resources under his command to revenge upon the slayers of his son. The Viceroy now drew upon the garrisons of the fortresses in East Africa and India to assemble more Portuguese resources at Cochin in order to deliver his counter attack. The winter season, which lasted from April through August, had set in, and it was impossible for either the Red Sea fleet or the Portuguese fleet to go to sea.

Magellan was busily engaged in preparing the *Santo Espirito* for the coming campaign when he was detached from Pereira's command. He had been chosen for a special service for which he was recommended by his commander because of his past record in the *bergantym* on the African coast.

The Viceroy, who was stripping his harbors of almost all means of defense in order to equip his fleet for the campaign, was uneasy to realize the number of corsairs and rovers that might prey upon his defenseless settlements. It was characteristic that he determined to anticipate their attack and to destroy them first.

All the ports on the Malabar coast were located at or near the mouth of a river, and consequently a sand bar had to be crossed to obtain access to them. During the winter season, when the eastward monsoons blew, the surf upon these river bars was so furious that it was almost impossible for a ship to sail through the broken water. All Indian shipping then stayed in port, and the Portuguese caravels in India followed this custom. However, Dom Francisco de Almeida decided that, since all the Arabian pirates and smugglers who had in the past managed to elude Dom Lorenzo's patrols were locked in their harbors during the stormy period, this was the time for him to invade their winter quarters and destroy their ships before they could emerge and scatter at sea. Consequently he constructed a number of heavy, oar-propelled galleys and *bergantyms* which he called his *armada de remo*, or fleet of oars. He manned these coastguard cutters with slave oarsmen and boldly sent them out over the boiling bar at Cochin into the wintry seas to struggle through the monsoon. They made sudden dashes into the pirate harbors, caught them unawares, burned their ships, and seized their strongholds. Ferdinand Magellan was gratified to be assigned to duty with one of the *bergantyms* on raids against the corsairs, for these forays broke the tedium of winter inaction and also offered an opportunity to capture valuable loot.

After this assignment, Ferdinand had been back in Cochin only a short time when he was called by Captain Pereira to sail with him on a new adventure.

A Chinese junk from Malacca had brought the news to the Viceroy at Cochin that a fleet of Calicut ships had reached the Spice Islands to take advantage of the withdrawal of Portuguese patrols to run the blockade to the Red Sea. The Viceroy determined to try to intercept them, and he ordered Captain Pereira to sail in the *Santo Espirito* to the Maldive Islands, where it was expected that the blockade runners would rendezvous and refit before making their dash across the Arabian Sea to the Gulf of Aden.

Ferdinand Magellan accompanied Pereira on this voyage. The *Santo*

Espirito was caught in a storm in the Laccadive Sea en route to the Maldive Islands, was driven eastward and almost wrecked on the coast of Ceylon, and managed to make port at the city of Colombo. Ferdinand Magellan was therefore one of the earliest Europeans to land at this rich island. The Portuguese had heard much of the fertility of Ceylon, its production of sugar, fruits, and cinnamon, and its general prosperity. It was reputed to be the principal source of the great flow of rubies, sapphires, and pearls which came annually into the Indian market from the farther Orient. Ceylon had been briefly visited for the first time in 1505 by Captain Lorenzo de Almeida, who, like Captain Nuno Vaz Pereira, had been driven there by a storm.

Ferdinand Magellan did not have an opportunity to become well acquainted with Ceylon, for as soon as the weather permitted, Captain Pereira hurriedly left Colombo and made all haste to reach the Maldives. He could find no trace of the Arabian spice fleet there, and in accordance with his orders at once sailed to join the Viceroy in Cananor early in December. On December 12, without fanfare or display, the war fleet grimly left the harbor of Cananor and sailed northward.

Dom Francisco de Almeida had gathered together almost every Portuguese capable of bearing arms, including the factors, clerks, and scriveners, and had managed to recruit a full force of thirteen hundred men. He also had inducted into his ranks four hundred selected Hindus from the friendly forces of the Rajahs of Cochin and Cananor. The naval force comprised nineteen vessels in all, of which some were armed merchant *naos,* some were sailing galleys, and some the oar-propelled *bergantyms* which he had created for coastwise work against the pirates. The royal caravels constituted the core of the fighting fleet. Dom Nuno Vaz Pereira, as senior Captain, was second-in-command under the Viceroy, who was himself the most experienced fleet commander of the Portuguese service. Prior to coming to the Orient, he had been the Admiral at Sea in charge of the entire Portuguese navy. On the voyage north from Cananor he established a system of signals and drilled the captains of his nondescript fleet in the maneuvers which he expected to employ against the Red Sea armada. The formerly genial Viceroy was now a dour, somber, harsh commander, and he communicated to his small force his personal sense of desperate determination. When he came opposite the strong city of Dabul, which was associated in his mind with the memory of his unjust rebuke to his son, the bitter, brooding Admiral suddenly directed his force to cross the bar and sail into Dabul harbor.

The Portuguese bombardment quickly drove the surprised defenders from the walls, and Dom Francisco de Almeida led his force in person to scale the ramparts, put the garrison to the sword, and slaughtered every living person within the city. The walls and towers were blown up, and the town was completely razed by fire. So savage and pitiless was the massacre that the Arabs derived from it a proverbial malediction long in use, "May the wrath of the Portuguese fall upon you as it did upon Dabul." We may assume that Ferdinand Magellan took part in this bloody action.

Again at sea, they were not long in sighting the enemy, who had wintered in the harbor of Diu, which was the headquarters of the fleet of the great Indian King of Cambaya. These Cambayan war vessels, together with the large fleets of the Zamorin of Calicut and the Rajah of Goa, acted as auxiliaries to the modern Egyptian *naos* commanded by the Turkish Emir Husayn, whom the Portuguese called Mir Hocem.

The encounter took place on February 2nd. Almeida gained and maintained the windward position and inflicted heavy damage upon the Egyptians during a long-distance artillery battle. Shortly after midday, the range was shortened and the fleets closed. Captain Pereira led his men onto the deck of the Egyptian *capitana,* while Almeida's flagship grappled the ship on the opposite side and poured its contingent aboard. The Egyptian flagship was defended by eight hundred Mamelukes clad in chain mail, the flower of the personal bodyguard of the Soldan of Egypt. Ferdinand fought beside his Captain, and after five hours of desperate hand-to-hand combat the final group of grimly fighting Mamelukes was cut down. Mir Hocem leapt into a fast-rowing yawl and escaped. When the royal standard of Portugal was raised upon the Egyptian *capitana's* masthead, Captain Pereira lay dead upon the deck, and across his body, in the jumbled mass of slain, lay Ferdinand Magellan, wounded almost to death.

Disheartened by the loss of the flagship, by the flight of their leader, and by the defection of the Cambayan fleet, which had been bribed by Almeida, the Egyptians gave way; several of their ships managed to escape during the night and were able to reach the safe harbor of the Moslem city of Goa in southern India, but most of their *naos* were captured or sunk.

For the Portuguese, the date of February 2, 1509, is one of the most eventful in their history. The battle insured Portuguese control of Asian waters and brought about the collapse of the Mameluke Empire of Egypt and the mighty Venetian Commonwealth. Had Almeida lost at Diu, Christian Europe might have returned to economic subjection to Islam, and the history of the Italian Renaissance might have been considerably different. The Doge of Venice would not give up the struggle, but his further efforts to circumvent the Portuguese, first by trying to reach the Atlantic and sail westward, and second by promoting the restoration of ancient canals connecting the Nile with the Red Sea, were doomed to failure.

Dom Francisco de Almeida revenged the death of his son by inhumanly torturing the Venetian officers and gunners whom he captured, giving no consideration to the fact that they were fellow Christians, and then executed all of them by blowing them to pieces at the mouths of his cannon.

Ferdinand Magellan lay at death's door in Diu for many days. He was so badly wounded that it was six weeks before he could be transported to the hospital at Cochin. In addition to his physical wounds, he had suffered a great loss in the death of his patron, Captain Nuno Vaz Pereira, whose high personal qualities and military abilities had made him the foremost of the Portuguese captains in India. The pattern of ill luck which dogged Magellan was now beginning. The course of his life was to be influenced several times by the loss at a crucial moment of a chieftain to whom he could have looked for favor and support.

The wounded Magellan reached Cochin on March 8th, 1509. He was still there on July 30, 1509, for the record of the King's treasurer shows there was issued to Ferdinand Magellan, at Cochin, a number of measures of wheat which were due him from the treasury in lieu of subsistence.

At this time he appears to have abandoned the navy and perhaps to have used some of his prize money in the purchase of a horse, in order to enter the elite corps of mounted knights which the Viceroy then created. To the modern reader it may appear strange for Ferdinand Magellan, who had served for four years as a naval officer in the Indian Ocean and in the Arabian Sea, suddenly to be metamorphosed into a cavalryman. This amphibious form of service was common to the Portuguese fidalgos of the time. It can best be illustrated by the history of Dom Francisco de Almeida, who had a most distinguished career as a cavalry commander against the Moors in Spain, and who also was the leading naval commander of Portugal. His successor, Dom Affonso de Albuquerque, fought for many years as a mounted knight in North Africa before becoming a captain and later an admiral in the Portuguese navy.

Portuguese military tactics had always been built around the use of cavalry, particularly in their campaigns in North Africa. In their land engagements in India they had hitherto been very much handicapped by the lack of mounted troops. The Malabar *nayres,* or knights, were skilled horsemen who had spent their days in the tiltyard, on the polo field, or galloping across country after the wild boar, and they made excellent light cavalrymen.

The climate of the Malabar coast was unfavorable for horses, and the Indian cavaliers had to secure frequent replacements for their mounts from Arabia. Arabian horses were the most important items of export from Ormuz, and the great horse market was the city of Goa. After the victory of Diu, when the Portuguese caravels blockaded Ormuz, Goa, and Calicut, the importation of horses was cut off, and the quality of the Indian cavalry began to deteriorate. At the same time, the Portuguese knights could get as many choice Arabian chargers as they needed. The Portuguese heavily armored horsemen thereafter easily rode down the light-armed, poorly mounted Indians, and they were even effective against the armored elephants which generally formed the first line of the Malabar offensive. However, they never ventured far from the protection of the guns of the fleet or the batteries of the fortresses, since they dared not risk becoming engulfed by the greatly superior number of Asiatic attackers.

The Viceroy offered special privileges and grants of land to those of his veterans who would maintain a horse for military service. It was whispered that Almeida was preparing the cavalry corps in order to regain favor at court. It had long been a dream of Dom Manuel to capture the tomb of Mohammed in Mecca, seize the body of the prophet, and hold it for ransom in exchange for the sepulcher at Jerusalem. Almeida now saw a chance to carry out this dream. The victory at Diu had opened up the entrance to the Red Sea, and he planned to form a force of four hundred well-mounted knights to land suddenly near Mecca, dash inland, and seize the prize.

Ferdinand Magellan, being at loose ends because of the death of his captain, Dom Nuno Vaz Pereira, embraced this opportunity, along with his comrade, Francisco Serrano. Shortly after they became mounted men-at-arms, they again entered upon a maritime adventure, but this time in their capacity as mounted knights. This came about in a most unexpected fashion. Ferdinand Magellan was now to leave behind him Africa and India, to enter the far eastern zone in which lay the Spice Islands, his lifelong goal.

CHAPTER VI

THE STRAIT OF MALACCA

FERDINAND MAGELLAN and Francisco Serrano now enlisted in the service of a new patron who had just arrived in Cochin from Lisbon, Captain Diogo Lopes de Sequeira, fidalgo of the royal household, Knight of Christ, and one of the most trusted of Dom Manuel's personal circle. This knight had first won the King's favorable attention by the able manner in which he had served as judge in the courts of law, and as a result he was appointed to the key political position of comptroller of the household of the Crown Prince. The group about the heir presumptive intrigued to alienate him from the King, but Sequeira checked their schemes and gained the King's grateful confidence.

In 1509, Dom Manuel was disturbed by reports concerning discord between the captains at the gold port of Sofala, the naval base at Mozambique, and the headquarters at Kilwa. He therefore sent Dom Diogo Lopes de Sequeira as his personal representative, with broad powers to sift out the conflicting charges and to re-establish a stable form of government in East Africa.

The King did not realize it, but the dissension in East Africa was largely due to his own unwise policy in not supporting his Viceroy's authority. Instead, he listened to every malcontent who brought complaints from the provinces. Consequently there was disorganization not only in East Africa, but throughout Portuguese Asia, and sending an emissary with plenary powers to interfere was not the way to correct it. He should have supported his present Viceroy or have replaced him if necessary, but the essential thing was to have a unified authority rather than a divided one.

Sequeira was an able executive, but was quite ignorant of the situation in the area to which he was sent as inspector general. After investigating conditions in the island of Madagascar and in the colonies along the East African coast and reconciling the differences of the disputing captains, he sailed across the China Sea to Cochin, the viceregal capital, to discuss East African matters with the Viceroy, Francisco de Almeida, and to inform him of his decisions. His authority did not extend to India itself, so his position at Cochin was delicate.

The Viceroy had not been informed by Lisbon of Sequeira's mission. When, in July, 1509, a fleet of three caravels entered Cochin and proved to be a wholly independent squadron under command of Sequeira, instead of the badly needed reinforcements for which he had been pleading, the Viceroy was surprised and displeased; and when he learned that the newcomer had entered into his own province of East Africa, had countermanded his personal orders, and had supplanted his own appointees, he was furiously indignant. However, Sequeira showed him such courteous consideration that his anger soon calmed, and he found it politic to accept his proffer of friendship. It was bitter to recognize that his own standing at court was on the wane, but Sequeira could be of help to him. When Almeida was first appointed Viceroy, in 1505, his political star had been high. His father, Count d'Abrantes, in whose veins royal blood flowed, was then one of the most influential statesmen of the realm, and three of his brothers filled posts which in the past had at times been filled by members of the ruling family. One brother was Master of Avis, another was Prior of Crato, and the third was Bishop of Coimbra. Yet King Manuel had no sooner elevated Dom Francisco to the viceregal position than he began, as usual, to undermine the authority and hamper the freedom of his appointee. The Almeida family tried to support him at court, and his brother, the Master of Avis, even engaged in a public altercation with the King in his defense. But Dom Manuel brooked no opposition, and the fortunes of the Viceroy were only injured by the attempt of his relatives to help him. Before long the Almeida faction at court had gone into complete political eclipse, and the rival group who succeeded them were scheming to have Almeida supplanted in Asia by their colleague, Captain Affonso de Albuquerque. That was why Viceroy Almeida circumspectly swallowed his resentment and accepted the olive branch extended to him by Sequeira; he even agreed later to try to turn over the viceroyship to him, thinking it better than that Albuquerque should have it.

Sequeira now reluctantly delivered another blow. He tactfully divulged to the Viceroy that he had not only been commissioned to inspect the East African establishment, but also was directed by the King to lead his squadron on an exploring voyage two thousand miles farther eastward, as far as the great oriental emporium of Malacca, which lay in the zone for which Almeida was responsible. This the Viceroy rightly construed as a final mark of withdrawal of the King's favor.

Four years earlier, at his farewell audience before sailing, Dom Francisco de Almeida had been explicitly instructed by the King that he was not to assume the title of Viceroy until he had conquered the far eastern city of Malacca and had erected a fortress there. But Almeida had assumed the rank of viceroy as soon as he arrived in India in 1505, relying upon Dom Manuel's sympathetic comprehension of an altered situation in India, submitting the problem to his council, and securing its unanimous approval. Indeed, conditions in India were so disturbed that he had not even been able to carry out the King's mandate to conquer Ceylon, and to make that island rather than the city of Cochin the viceregal headquarters.

From then on, Dom Manuel kept prodding Almeida to send at least a probing detachment to Malacca, but the distracted Viceroy, fighting to retain the Portuguese foothold in Asia, had been quite unable to do more.

King Manuel had secret reports that Bishop Fonseca, head of the maritime department of Spain, was preparing an expedition, under the Portuguese renegade Captain John de Solis, to sail westward across the Atlantic seeking a new route to Malacca and planning to claim the city for the crown of Castile. Dom Manuel had become feverishly impatient to forestall this attempt by establishing himself immediately in Malacca. It was typical of the King's methods to send an independent expedition into the Viceroy's area of authority.

Almeida rightly saw in the King's action an intent to break up the viceregal authority and to make of it three separate provincial governments under direct control from Lisbon. The three provinces would be East Africa, the Malabar coast of India, and Malacca and the Spice Islands. This would give to Lisbon all the revenues from Africa's gold fields and the Spice Islands and Malaya, and would reduce India to minor importance. By offering to transfer the viceroyalty to Sequeira, Almeida hoped to preserve the present system of viceregal rule and to retain for his own loyal subordinates and lieutenants the posts they now filled.

Almeida was not a man to do things by halves. He agreed to help Sequeira discover and conquer Malacca and generously put all his own resources at his command. Before the naval disaster at Chaul, in 1507, the Viceroy had tentatively prepared to carry out the deferred invasion of Malacca. Although he had sent no Portuguese scout ships east of Ceylon, he had acquired native charts showing the reefs and shoals to be avoided and the courses to be laid in the voyage between the Malabar coast and Malacca. He also had collected logs and *rutters* of Hindu and Chinese pilots giving astronomical guidance and navigational details concerning the winds and currents at various seasons of the year. Not the least useful of this data was the information regarding the patrol areas of Chinese pirates, whose depredations in the Malay seas constituted an element of risk which even the armed Portuguese caravels would have to face.

Besides giving Sequeira these exceedingly valuable navigational aids and selecting dependable Hindu pilots for him, the Viceroy gave him provisions and ammunition and also sent along some of his own best fighters. Sequeira entirely lacked soldiers skilled in land fighting against Orientals, and Almeida therefore added to the expedition a contingent drawn from the elite corps of mounted men-at-arms which he had recently formed. This reinforcement consisted of seventy of his veteran troopers, among whom were Ferdinand Magellan and Francisco Serrano. We may assume that this troop was sent with their own cavalry mounts, because they were transported in a *taforeia,* which was a heavy *nao* especially constructed to carry war horses. Since the voyage to Malacca at that season of the year would take no more than a month, it was quite feasible for the men-at-arms to carry their mounts by sea. The command of the *taforeia* was given to Captain Garcia de Sousa, who had in the past shown some hostility to the Viceroy; it is not known why he was chosen for so important a post. His selection proved a good one, however, and he discharged his duties with loyalty and ability.

As the *taforeia* would be the slowest and weakest combat element of the squadron, the Viceroy sent to protect it one of his own fast and well-armed caravels, commanded by Captain Geronimo Teixeira. The expedition was now so strongly manned and equipped that its success appeared assured. Ferdinand Magellan felt confident that he was being given not only an opportunity to attain distinction, but also to win the worldly fortune that so far had eluded him.

The monsoon had abated early at Cochin that season, and hence the four caravels, accompanied by the square-sailed, bluff-bowed *taforeia,* were able safely to cross the bar and enter the Laccadive Sea on August 18, 1509. The Hindu pilots steered the same southeasterly course between the Maldive Islands and the Isle of Ceylon which Ferdinand Magellan had followed in the *Santo Espirito* the previous year. Then they proceeded due east for a fortnight through the Indian Ocean, until they sighted the Nicobar Islands. Veering southeast, they sailed down the Strait of Malacca, stopping ashore briefly to make friends with the local Rajah at Pedir, on the north coast of Sumatra; then they erected a *padroan,* or official monumental stone, formally asserting the sovereignty of Dom Manuel over that immense and prosperous island.

Then, after an easy voyage of only three weeks, they reached their destination. At dawn on September 11, 1509, with flags flying, trumpets sounding, and bombards thundering, the five European vessels nosed their way into the bustling harbor of Malacca, crowded with Chinese junks, Arab dhows, and Malay sampans. The medieval banner of Christian Portugal, bearing its five enigmatic *quinas,* was unfurled there for the first time, to flutter proudly over the waters of the fabled Golden Chersonese.

The harbor authorities at once came aboard the *capitana,* and the Captain General assured them of his peaceful intent, asserting that the fleet had merely come on a commercial visit. He asked for permission to come ashore to offer gifts and friendly greetings to Sultan Mohammed from the King, his master. He also solicited a license to trade copper, Venetian glass, and ambergris in exchange for spices, dyes and drugs. On the same afternoon, a majestic state galley, bedecked with pennons and draped with Chinese rugs, rowing to the rhythm of drums and cymbals, came alongside with a delegation of court officials. They brought a gracious welcome from the Sultan, gifts of silk and perfumes for the Captain General, and fresh provisions for the fleet. An audience at the palace was arranged for the next morning.

When the Captain General went ashore next day, none of the fidalgos sent by the Viceroy from Cochin was included in his landing cortege. For although Sequeira had gratefully accepted the pilots, charts, and supplies given him by the Viceroy, his own staff jealously resented the intrusion of the Cochin men into their undertaking. Secure in their own political standing at Lisbon, and aware of the disfavor into which Dom Francisco de Almeida had fallen with the King, the haughty Knights of Christ who were Sequeira's captains had from the very beginning been supercilious toward the Viceroy's men. Even though Almeida's men had been snubbed and held at arms' length during the cruise, they were startled and disturbed when Sequeira ignored them in making up his landing party, and they thus realized the degree of unfriendliness with which they were regarded. Therefore Ferdinand Magellan and Francisco Serrano watched from the maintop of the anchored *taforeia* as the longboat put out from the *capitana* bearing the Captain General and his officers, resplendent in their gorgeous court regalia and carrying the gold brocaded silken royal standard. They saw them land at the customhouse wharf and then lost sight of them as they were surrounded by a glittering group of functionaries and ceremoniously conducted through the sally port into the harbor fortress.

From the maintop, Malacca presented an alluring spectacle. It was not surrounded by walls, and seemed to spread endlessly along the shore. The harbor front itself was castellated with high, brown ramparts, from which a great number of brass cannon pointed at the harbor, but both Ferdinand and his friend had scaled too many forbidding fortifications to be dismayed by them. Behind the battlements, embowered in groves of palms, they saw the minarets and domes of temples and mosques, and the gardens and pleasances of rich mansions, while on the acropolis, crowning the panorama, rose the glistening marble pile of the Sultan's palace.

During the anxious day no word came from the city. Captain Garcia de Sousa kept his men alerted and a number of them under arms. Neither he nor Captain Teixeira, commander of the caravel anchored alongside the *taforeia,* would permit Malay venders of fruit, fish, and fowls to come aboard, although the harbor sampans were clustered thickly about the three Lisbon caravels. Magellan, at the masthead, could see the crowd of Malay peddlers on their decks, chaffering and bargaining with the Portuguese.

Night fell without any word from the shore party, and the Cochin men became very disturbed. The crews were armed, the gun ports opened, and every preparation was made to defend the ships. They loosened the sails and prepared to cut the cables and run for it at the first sign of attack. They waited tensely. At last they saw torches at the pier and lights moving across the harbor toward the caravels, accompanied by the sound of tipsy singing and merry laughter. They could relax.

While still maintaining the *taforeia* in a state of defense, Captain Garcia de Sousa eagerly went aboard the *capitana* to learn of the result of the visit to the palace. The Captain General was much elated at the success of his mission. Sultan Mohammed had received him cordially, had presented all his retinue with handsome presents, and had feasted them sumptuously. He had given him magnificent gifts for King Manuel and had hinted at a willingness not only to enter into a treaty, but even to consider paying an annual tribute to Portugal.

The next day, a delegation came aboard the *capitana* to begin drawing up a commercial agreement. Negotiations went on rapidly, and the Malays seemed eager to enter into a close alliance with Portugal. The Sultan gave permission for any of the Christian visitors to go freely about the city, only stipulating that they return to their ships at nightfall. The Captain General gave shore liberty to his Lisbon men, and they flocked to the bazaars and to the seraglios. Cautious Captains Garcia de Sousa and Geronimo Teixeira, however, would only allow small shore parties of the Cochin crews to leave at a time. Although it went against the grain, they felt it necessary to ferry the sea-weary, cramped horses from the *taforeia* to a compound near the piers.

As Francisco Serrano could speak the Malabar dialect, Captain de Sousa sent him ashore daily to try to ascertain the true situation, giving him money to spend in shops, in taverns, and upon courtesans, in order to secure information. Ferdinand Magellan also was sent on pretended buying trips to seek any signs of treachery in the city. There was a quarter devoted to Indian merchants with warehouses full of silk, calico, muslin, cashmere, and other Indian fabrics. In another quarter, Chinese traders offered silk, porcelain, lacquer and brassware. There also was a prosperous commercial colony from Java, another from Sumatra, and a great open-air market, where country produce was massed in profusion. He made purchases in the street of the jewelers and goldsmiths, where fat Cingalese gem dealers displayed pearls, rubies, turquoises, sapphires, and diamonds. Malacca was the world center of trading in precious stones, and gorgeous jewels could be had in its bazaars for a fraction of their European value. The factors of the fleet who had visited many markets said that Malacca exceeded Antwerp, Venice, Nuremberg, and Alexandria in the wealth, diversity, and volume of its transactions.

Magellan and Serrano thought it significant that all the stocks of pepper, cinnamon, cloves, ginger, rhubarb, camphor, and nutmeg were in the hands of Arab monopolists, who also controlled the sale of imported Venetian and Hanseatic wares. The Arabs evidently had become dominant, with large, handsome mosques much in evidence; most of the officers of the garrison were Arabs. As these armored Saracen cavaliers rode by on their Arabian chargers, they scowled and spat in fierce hatred. The entire populace was armed; even the peaceable, portly Cingalese goldsmiths had murderous-looking krisses thrust into the silken scarves that wrapped their protuberant middles. To men like Ferdinand Magellan and Francisco Serrano, who had experienced the treachery of the Saracens in East Africa and in India, the air held an intangible malevolence. Each night they returned to the *taforeia* more apprehensive and disturbed. Serrano had established an intimacy with a Chinese prostitute who had connections at the palace, and he showered her with gifts and attention. He disguised himself and stayed in the city with her for several nights.

He learned that Sultan Mohammed had for a long time been in contact with Portugal's archenemy in India, the Zamorin of Calicut, and his spies at Cochin had reported to him every detail of the outfitting of this fleet. He had been informed of the sailing long before they reached Malacca and had been on the lookout for them. Their reception had been carefully staged, and he was now cozening Dom Diogo until he could lure him into the prepared trap.

The Sultan intended to capture the entire Portuguese expedition alive and to seize their ships intact. He already had cajoled Sequeira into sending all his merchandise ashore by turning over to the factors an entire customhouse building and a pier to use as a market. He planned, at the proper time, to entice the officers of the fleet into the city, get most of the crew ashore, and then to take over. This coup against the hitherto irresistible Portuguese would ensure his leadership of all Moslems and his prestige in the Asiatic world.

Everything was now ready. Mohammed had so completely deceived the

Portuguese that they had abandoned all precautions. He had secretly brought troops and war elephants from the interior and had hidden a strong amphibious force of sampans in a cove near the harbor. The assault would take place when he gave the signal from the palace at about noon the next day.

Upon hearing this report from Serrano, which confirmed his worst suspicions, Captain Garcia de Sousa rowed to the *capitana,* but found all the principal officers ashore. That evening, he finally was able to talk privately to the Captain General, but his warning was taken lightly. When he returned to the *taforeia,* he wasted little breath railing against such stupidity, but prepared to save his men from the coming debacle.

The developments next morning increased the uneasiness aboard both Cochin ships. The shore authorities had, during the night, piled up a great number of sacks of pepper, worth a fortune in any market, and they invited the Portuguese to send to the pier for them. The factors eagerly went ashore with all the ships' longboats to take possession of this tempting cargo. Word also came from one of the Cingalese jewel merchants who had been very friendly to the Portuguese that a consignment of unusually fine jewels had just arrived, and he would be willing to barter them for copper at an extraordinarily good rate of exchange. This news excited the cupidity of Sequeira, and he ordered a party of fidalgos to the city to negotiate for the stones. Once they went ashore, and with almost all the crew busy at the pier loading the ships' boats with spices, the caravels lay unguarded in the harbor.

Ferdinand Magellan climbed to the maintop to watch for developments. First he looked for Francisco Serrano, who had been detailed, with other Cochin men-at-arms, to act as guard on the pier; he noted with the experienced eye of an old soldier that Serrano had selected a spot on the wharf near the water's edge where he could not easily be taken by surprise. Serrano caught sight of him, and signalled significantly; Magellan knew his friend was tensely on the alert. He saw with concern that the ships' boats were half filled with sacks of pepper and were moored unguarded at the pier; the sailors had been drawn away from them to the far end of the customhouse and were mingling with a crowd of stevedores and coolies. When he looked toward the fleet, he saw an unusual concentration of venders' sampans about the caravels and noted numerous Malays upon the decks. He descended hastily and hurried to report his fears to Captain Garcia de Sousa, whereupon the captain sent him in the skiff to the flagship again to warn the Captain General.

Dom Diogo was lolling half naked in the tropical heat, good-humoredly playing chess with a high Malay dignitary; looking on at the game was a group of Malay *datus,* or nobles. Magellan sauntered up to the Commander, and, since none of the Malays understood Portuguese, he pretended to make a routine report; in casual tones, he advised the Captain General of the danger. Dom Diogo proved equal to the occasion. Pretending to be annoyed at Magellan's intrusion, and bored at the distraction, without lifting his head or averting his gaze from the chess board, he negligently called the *contramaestre*. In a matter-of-fact voice, he ordered him to pretend to tighten up the ships' yards, but in reality, to gather the crew and prepare to clear the deck of visitors. The *contramaestre,* with great presence of mind, sent a sailor aloft to call a warning to the other four ships. He himself rallied his own crew, while pretending to bawl orders for routine operations. The Captain General saw from the corner of his eye that one of the *datus* was preparing to draw his kriss. He jumped up, upset the chess board, unsheathed his dagger in the same motion, and stabbed the Malay leader. The natives, who had been awaiting the signal from the palace, were taken by surprise and were easily driven from the decks.

During the general melee, the lombardiers rushed below, threw open the gun ports, depressed their already loaded cannon, and fired a devastating broadside into the sampans clustered against the hull. At the sound of firing from the ships, the Christians ashore were at once attacked in overwhelming force. Some barricaded themselves in the customhouse and were made prisoners, and many were massacred running for the boats. Serrano's vigilance saved many; rallying the Cochin men, he held the mob at bay while others cut their way to the boats.

Ferdinand, with great presence of mind, broke away from the fracas on the deck of the flagship and, with two comrades, hurriedly seized the one available skiff and rowed to the pier in time to take off Serrano and several others. Loyalty to a blood-brother was one of his strongest emotions, for which he readily risked his life.

Thirty Portuguese were killed on the pier and thirty were made prisoners, while forty men, mainly Cochin veterans, escaped in the boats. The officers who had gone to the goldsmith's shop were taken captive without a chance to resist.

A fleet of Malay boats that had been awaiting the signal, crowded with armed men, suddenly raced to attack the squadron. Before they could come alongside, the caravels cut their anchor cables, hurriedly hoisted sail, and the brisk breeze aided them to evade the onslaught. They came about smartly in the wind and bore down in battle formation upon the mass of sampans. With guns blazing, they crushed and sank many of the smaller craft. The Portuguese fleet then withdrew and anchored in the roadstead outside the harbor, while the Captain General sent a boat with a flag of truce in an attempt to ransom the prisoners. His Hindu emissaries were unable to make any contact with responsible officials at the palace, and were warned to return to the caravels. The Sultan made no further attempt to molest the Portuguese ships. He was appalled at the fiasco of his plot and realized that he had blundered. Henceforth he lived in terror of retribution and made preparations to strengthen his defenses against the counterblow which was now inevitable.

However, the Portuguese fleet was too weak to attempt immediate reprisals and was itself in a vulnerable position. The Captain General reluctantly decided to abandon further attempts to negotiate a release of his compatriots and to sail to safety.

As soon as the squadron left the Strait of Malacca and turned westward in the turbulent open sea, the *taforeia* found it difficult to keep up with the caravels. No ballast had been taken aboard to offset the loss of its cargo of seventy-five war horses, and the empty transport rode high in the water and was difficult to steer. The Captain General, furious at his own errors, was resentful toward Captain Garcia de Sousa, whose warning he had scorned, and was in no mood to shorten sail of the entire squadron to help his ship. Gradually the caravels drew ahead, and by nightfall of the second day Ferdinand could barely make them out, hull down on the horizon.

The next day, off Great Nicobar Island, the wallowing transport was sighted by a four-masted Chinese junk, which bore down rapidly upon it. The *taforeia,* being a fleet auxiliary, carried little artillery; it had only a few carronades on the deck and several culverins and serpentines on the main top. Some of the veterans aboard were excellent artillerymen, and they tried to halt the oncoming junk by aiming at its foremast and its rudder. The *taforeia* was plunging so wildly in the heavy sea that, although the Portuguese made a few hits, almost all the shots went wild. The junk, being to windward, blanketed the sails of the transport, crashed heavily alongside, and grappled. The yelling pirates tumbled aboard, but the armored men-at-arms faced them boldly, cut many of them down, and drove the survivors pell-mell back to their ship. The frightened Chinese then cut the lashings, and the two ships separated. Captain Garcia de Sousa saw that a small group of his men, under Francisco Serrano, had followed the pirates aboard the junk and, with their backs to the mainmast, were defending themselves against the swarming Chinese. He tried desperately to bring the *taforeia* alongside again, but found himself helpless to do so.

At this juncture Ferdinand Magellan, with four others, put the skiff overboard, and, although it seemed impossible, the heavily armored men boldly rowed through the heavy sea and clambered aboard the junk. They took the pirates in the rear and slashed into them so effectively that they threw down their arms and gave up the ship. Magellan's amazing presence of mind, coupled with his complete fearlessness, were never better demonstrated. It was he, practically single-handed, who captured the junk.

The captors were overjoyed to find a very valuable cargo of plunder, including spices and silks, on the large and serviceable vessel. Captain Garcia de Sousa decided to transfer all his men and supplies to it and to abandon the almost unmanageable *taforeia.* The junk proved to be fast, and on the second day caught up with the Portuguese fleet. The Captain General received them churlishly and showed no feeling of relief at their safe return. He left a prize crew of twenty-eight Cochin men on the junk and distributed the others among his ships. Francisco Serrano had been badly wounded in the arm and was brought upon the *capitana* for treatment by the surgeon. Magellan accompanied him to act as nurse.

The junk easily kept up with the caravels until its rudder, which had been weakened by the Portuguese gun fire, suddenly gave way and dropped into the sea. The big hulk then broached to and lost its headway. The Captain General had a towline put aboard from the *capitana,* meaning to tow the prize to a nearby island and salvage its cargo, but a gale arose and the junk began to yaw and tug dangerously upon the towing caravel. The master of the flagship protested against the risk of damage to his vessel, and so the Captain General called a conference of his officers. They, being Knights of Christ of the Lisbon faction, cynically voted to cut the tow rope and abandon the helpless junk.

Ferdinand Magellan did not know of this pitiless decision until he saw the *contramaestre* with uplifted axe, about to sever the tow rope. With his usual decisiveness of action, he stopped the man from carrying out the order. Then he protested so vehemently that the Captain General grudgingly gave orders for the caravel to steer alongside the rolling junk and try to take off the twenty-eight members of the prize crew. The junk and its valuable cargo could probably have been saved, had the Lisbon men felt any interest in aiding the fortunes of the men from Cochin, so the resentment of the prize crew can be understood when they had to abandon the junk and watch it lost in the storm. The Lisbon men, for their part, wished the prize crew might have gone down with the junk.

A few days later, a typhoon struck the squadron. One of the Lisbon ships went down with all hands, and the Cochin caravel could be kept afloat only long enough to reach an island where it was beached, dismantled, and burned. The Cochin men were taken aboard the other caravels and the rest of the voyage was a miserable one. The Cochin men were bitter and mutinous, and the dispirited Lisbon men, dejected at their defeat and losses, quarrelled angrily among themselves. The atmosphere of the caravels was one of rancor.

They finally made port at Travancore on the Malabar coast, and here learned that Albuquerque had succeeded to the rule of India. The discomfited Sequeira, fearing to expose himself to the enmity of the new Governor, decided not to go to Cochin but to sail directly back to Portugal. He therefore refitted the two caravels, took aboard what spices and treasure had been procured at Malacca, and, abandoning the Cochin men, set sail for home. He was thus the first to carry to Dom Manuel the report of his expedition. He covered up his blunders, put a good face on the fiasco, and presented to the King a glowing account of his discovery of Malacca.

Ferdinand Magellan and Francisco Serrano finally got back safely to Cochin, but their costly war horses had been lost, they had been deprived of their prize money, and they were burning with resentment. They expected that the Viceroy would assemble a fleet and send them back to Malacca, not only to rescue their fellows and punish the perfidious Sultan, but also to reap the spoils of the opulent metropolis. Their expectations were dashed, however, when they found that Dom Francisco de Almeida had gone home, most of his important aides had vacated their commands, and men who were no friends of theirs now held all the posts of authority. However, they were well received by the new Governor, for Captain Garcia de Sousa had done justice to their fortitude and bravery in his report. He gave special credit to Ferdinand Magellan for his acts of personal heroism, and the Governor transmitted this commendation in his dispatches to Lisbon. In recognition of their services, Albuquerque promoted both Magellan and Francisco Serrano to the rank of captain, and gave each the command of a caravel.

The Governor's recognition of Magellan and Serrano was not entirely disinterested, for he intended to make good use of them. He shared the disquiet of the entire Indian administration at the action of Dom Manuel in sending Diogo Lopes de Sequeira directly from Lisbon to Malacca and by-passing the authority of India. If he expected to retain his proconsular power over the entire Far East, it was evident to Governor Albuquerque that he would have to conquer Malacca quickly. He expected the experience of Captain Garcia de Sousa's veterans would soon be very useful to him, and he took pains to attach them to him. Ferdinand Magellan was well aware that he had no real chance of future consideration from Albuquerque's faction. As a partisan of the fallen Viceroy, he knew he was a marked man; the hatred between the two groups had been too extreme for him to expect favorable treatment from his former enemies.

Moreover, Magellan's feeling for the great fallen Viceroy was sincerely loyal, and it cut him deeply to hear him derided by the sycophants who surrounded his successor. He was saddened to learn that when his hero had given up his office, he went aboard the second-rate ship that was to take him to Portugal and refused to come ashore again until the ship sailed, remaining in his cabin for an entire month. The supplanted Viceroy had only sailed on November 19, 1509, and Magellan reached Cochin in December. Many of the leading officials had accompanied Almeida when he left, and there is no doubt that Ferdinand Magellan would have been one of that company had he then been in Cochin.

Although Magellan first was encouraged by his promotion in rank and the prospect of returning to Malacca, he soon concluded that Governor

Albuquerque would be unable to carry out his plans for an expedition, since he dared not leave Cochin and Cananor unprotected. Several ships of the Egyptian-Venetian Red Sea fleet had escaped after their defeat at Diu and found shelter in the port of Goa, where their Venetian and Turkish technicians had enlisted in the service of Sabayo, Rajah of Goa. Along with a group of Portuguese renegades, they had helped the Rajah build a modern navy, armed with effective artillery, which was a constant threat to the Portuguese.

Once Magellan had deduced that there was no chance of another expedition from Cochin to Malacca, restlessness overtook him, and he decided to follow Almeida and his group to Portugal. Captain Sebastian de Sousa, with whom he had once served in East Africa, was due to sail for home in his caravel on January 1, 1510, and Magellan asked for permission to accompany him. He hoped that with fair weather, he might even be able to catch up with Dom Francisco de Almeida at Mozambique, where he was known to be delayed. Magellan had already served in the Orient for five years, although the usual term of service was limited to three. He had fought with distinction in Africa, India, and Malaya, and had probably accumulated a substantial fortune in prize money and plunder. His record entitled him to an ample amount of *quintalada* space on the caravel, and he arranged to take with him as many sacks as his quota would permit of "Malabar money," as pepper was called. In Lisbon, he could sell it for six times what it cost him at Cochin. If he dreamed, it was that then he would be in easy circumstances, and if the opportunity to return East did not present itself, he could return to the old family homestead in Ponte da Barca. He could marry an heiress of one of the Minho County clans, rear a family, and settle down to bucolic life, raising brown, wide-horned oxen to sell at Braga fair. Or he might visit his sister Isabel and her husband at the distant little mountain town of Sabrosa, invest in one of the port-wine vineyards there, and perhaps make a matrimonial alliance with one of the many aristocratic families of that district. If he did not care for a life of ease, he was a moneyed man, he could buy shares in a trading ship and sail back to the East.

Whatever were his plans, he was forced to defer them. Late in December, 1509, just when he was ready to sail with the westerly monsoon, Governor Albuquerque suddenly forbade the sailing of any ships to Portugal and requisitioned not only the vessels, but the military passengers and crews as well. He had decided to make a surprise attack on the City of Calicut while its ruler, the Zamorin, was away with most of his forces on an inland campaign. Therefore, on January 3, 1510, Ferdinand Magellan found himself on the beach of Calicut in a landing party. They fought their way inland, stormed the city's defenses, and rushed to sack the richly furnished palace of its ruler. While the victorious soldiers were scattered through the royal grounds thinking only of plunder, the *Nayres*, or Knights of Calicut, suddenly counterattacked. They drove the disorganized, booty-laden Portuguese back to the sea in demoralized rout, massacring hundreds of them as they tried to escape, still burdened with treasure that they stubbornly retained. More than seventy of the most prominent Knights of Christ were killed, and only a small group, which included both Governor Albuquerque and Magellan, managed to return to the ships. Magellan was badly wounded, and Albuquerque, almost fatally hurt, was unconscious for some days.

This was the most humiliating disaster ever suffered by Portugal in the Orient. The fleet hastily returned to Cochin, and the requisitioned merchant ships were surrendered to their owners. When Captain Sebastian de Sousa was released from the royal service, he lost no time in leaving Cochin. Among his passengers was Ferdinand Magellan, who, although convalescing from his recent wound, had insisted upon being taken along. He left behind him his friend, Francisco Serrano, who had managed to win the good will of the Governor and had chosen to remain in India.

Captain Sebastian de Sousa's ship and another commanded by Captain Francisco de Sa were delayed in getting clearance, but the third of the homeward bound caravels did not wait for them and hence got a day's start. The two captains, to make up for the delay and in order to catch up with the leader, decided to take a short cut in the Indian Ocean. A strong wind came up during the night, and the ships bowled along easily. Then suddenly on Magellan's ship there was a crushing thud, and the caravel shivered and heeled over at an angle, tumbling the rudely awakened passengers and their belongings helter-skelter. All three masts snapped off simultaneously and crashed heavily with sails and cordage athwart the hull. The rollers pounded upon the hulk, making it budge and tremble with each blow. Amid the shrieks, curses, and prayers, some of the crewmen managed to launch the ship's skiff, but it quickly became overloaded and sank. The heavy longboat was buried beneath the clutter of spars and could not be moved. Some of the officers tried to light a signal to inform the other caravel of their distress, but they could not get it lighted. Most of the seamen and pasengers simply clung to whatever piece of the ship they could and waited for the end.

When dawn broke, they saw their sister ship not far away, in a similar distressing situation; both ships had run aground on the Shoals of Padua, and near them, encircled by crawling white surf, was a bare, treeless, sandy atoll. In the daylight it was possible to get the batel over the side, and everyone from both caravels was ferried safely to the islet, along with a supply of food and water. During the terrifying pandemonium of the night, Ferdinand Magellan, like the rest, had expected imminent death by drowning. Now that his life had been saved, he realized he had emerged

Engraving from "Conquestes des Portugais," 1733

AFFONSO DE ALBUQUERQUE, FOUNDER OF PORTUGUESE INDIA

Engraving from "Conquestes des Portugais," 1733

CALICUT, METROPOLIS OF THE SPICE TRADE

from the shipwreck with little else; he was a ruined man, his dreams of a triumphant return to Portugal were at an end. Before abandoning the ship he had managed to get hold of his chest from the wreckage and had salvaged a few gold coins and his arms; but his precious pepper in the hold was already ruined by salt water.

Once the survivors were safe on the atoll, Sebastian de Sousa, as senior captain, took command. The pilots estimated they were about a week's rowing distance from Cochin, and Captain de Sousa at once stationed a guard of Knights of Christ upon the two batels and provisioned them for the trip. There was not space enough for all, and he ruled that only the fidalgos should go, but as soon as they reached Cochin he would send back for the rest of the personnel. Ferdinand Magellan, as a fidalgo, was entitled to a seat in one of the boats, but one of his blood-brothers, either Nuno Vaz or Martin Gadis, was excluded as not being of that rank; therefore Magellan, in accordance with the code of the Portuguese pioneers, refused to forsake his sworn brother-in-arms and declined to utilize his privilege. The sailors and common *soldados* were in the majority, and they soon reached a pitch of desperation in which they proposed to attack the smaller group and attempt to take the longboats from them. As a first step, they surrounded the water casks and refused to let a supply of water be put aboard the boats. Knives and swords were already drawn, when Magellan intervened to act as mediator. The better armed Knights of Christ could probably have won the fight, and Magellan feared it would become a slaughter of the crew. He expressed confidence in the good faith of Captain de Sousa and pointed out to the marooned majority that he was voluntarily throwing in his lot with them with full trust that they would all eventually be saved. In this way he managed to pacify the mutinous sailors, and they permitted the boats to be prepared. As the fidalgos were about to push off, Magellan had occasion to go aboard a boat to speak to one of the occupants. Immediately a cry was set up from the beach, for those left behind suspected he was abandoning them.

The chronicler quotes one of the common seamen as crying out, "Senhor, did you not promise to stay with us?" Magellan's reassuring answer came, "Yes I did, and here I am!" He leapt to the strand and the confidence of the marooned and unhappy crewmen was restored. Although Ferdinand Magellan maintained a confident front and a serene manner, in order to hearten his mates, his own heart was heavy. He was only thirty years old, but his five years of hardship, the difficult Indian climate, and his wound at Diu had aged him, and this last misfortune had struck just as he was recovering from his recent wound at Calicut. With his fortune swept away in the shipwreck, it would be folly to return home, for nowhere else in Europe did the possession of wealth mean so much as it did in Portugal. He felt friendless and without influence, and whatever direction he looked, he could see no promise of a successful future.

It is likely that during those grim weeks as a castaway he suffered deeply and introspectively, and his character underwent a decisive change. Up to this time, his youthful thirst for military distinction and zest for knightly adventure had been at least equal to any worldly desire to accumulate a fortune. From now on, however, the acquisition of an estate was to become his constant objective.

All day the equatorial sun beat down relentlessly on the bare, uninhabited atoll, and life was a purgatory. It was three weeks before the shipwrecked watchers saw on the horizon the lateen sails of a caravel. The rescue ship soon was anchored beyond the shoals, and its boats took the shipwrecked mariners aboard. The captain of the caravel, Dom Antonio Pacheco, sent salvage crews to try to save what they could from the two hulks, which still lay upon the sand banks. They managed to salvage some of the less destructible cargo, such as tusks of ivory and casks of Chinese porcelain. But the fabrics, dyes, and drugs were ruined, as well as the sugar and spices, including Magellan's precious pepper.

When Ferdinand landed again at Cochin, he found the capital deserted by his old naval and military associates. All, including Captains Francisco Serrano, Geronimo Teixeira, and Garcia de Sousa, had left in a large armada with Governor Albuquerque to attack Ormuz, far north on the Persian Gulf. Even the fidalgos from the wrecked caravels, who had arrived at Cochin a fortnight ahead of him, had already pushed on to join the Governor. Ferdinand felt no urge to follow them. Weakened by his recent wound and by the privations following the shipwreck, and dejected by his financial loss, he was relieved not to have his prosperous friends witness his return.

Shortly thereafter came the news of the death of Dom Francisco de Almeida. On March 1, 1515, the great Viceroy, along with twelve of his most distinguished captains and a number of his civil officials who were accompanying him to Lisbon, were murdered by an excited mob of Hottentots, for they had landed unarmed to inspect a squalid South African village on the seacoast. This disaster meant that Magellan's own last hope of influential political support from Almeida was gone.

Society in Cochin normally reflected the pattern of Portuguese Asia, in which there were three invariable elements, the priest, the factor, and the soldier. Now, however, since the Governor had drawn off all the fighting men in his armada, Ferdinand found Cochin peopled by the clerical colony, clustered about the archepiscopal palace, and the merchants, scriveners, and accountants whose lives revolved about the counting room of the King's factor.

It suited Magellan's temperament and experience to seek the companionship of the men of money, rather than of the clerics. Thus it came about that he became acquainted with a man of great charm of personality, Duarte Barbosa, Scrivener of the King. Their friendship was frequently to influence Magellan's thoughts and acts, and the lives of the two men were to become closely intertwined.

CHAPTER VII

THE CHINA SEA

FERDINAND MAGELLAN had never been on close terms with the financial and commercial men in the Cochin Colony. Probably they had looked upon him merely as a typical military man, intent on winning martial distinction and fired by a crusading zeal against the Moslems; such a figure would not be of much interest to them. Ferdinand, since his involuntary apprenticeship in India House, appears to have looked on mercantile employment as drudgery, and had gladly escaped from it to become a man-at-arms. He had probably avoided any association with the counting rooms and factors in the Eastern ports in which he had served. It was a fact that up to this period a *soldado* had had a better chance of making his fortune by pillage than had a scrivener in a factor's office. Now, however, a change had occurred, and just at the time when he had become impoverished, the road whereby he had previously made a fortune was blocked by Albuquerque. Anxious as never before to gain riches, Ferdinand sought out the company of Duarte Barbosa, who was a close friend of his cousin John Serrano.

Barbosa's first interest in Ferdinand Magellan was probably more scholarly than commercial. He had by then largely completed his manuscript concerning the countries lying about the Arabian Sea and wished to learn more of the peoples and customs of that far eastern zone from which Magellan had just returned. However, when he had listened to Magellan's account of the fabulous wealth of Malacca, doubtless the man of business in Duarte Barbosa triumphed over the geographer.

The change in Magellan's aim in life can perhaps be measured by a pecuniary transaction in which he engaged at this time. When he disembarked in Cochin, he had on his person all he had been able to salvage from the shipwreck. This was the small sum of gold which he had taken from his chest before abandoning the ship, ten gold coins called *portugueses,* each worth ten silver cruzados, and having a total modern value of about fifteen hundred dollars. This was his cash reserve, which he had held out for expenses in Lisbon while awaiting from India House the proceeds of his investment in pepper. Since he would have no use for it in Cochin, he decided to forward it for safekeeping to his brother, Diogo de Sousa, in Portugal. An opportunity soon presented itself for him to transmit the funds and to double his capital while doing so. Perhaps with the advice of Duarte Barbosa, he laid out his hundred cruzados in a loan to a Jewish merchant named Pedro Anes Abraldez, who was about to return to Lisbon. The interest on the loan was to be one hundred per cent for the first year and ten per cent per annum thereafter. This was not an unusual rate of interest in Cochin, for gold was scarce, and a borrower could make about four hundred per cent on it, after duties, by taking pepper back to Lisbon. However, the law against usury in Portugal limited the legal rate of interest to ten per cent per annum, and Ferdinand laid himself open to the risk of prosecution for usury. If Abraldez wished to act in bad faith, he could repudiate the contract, and it would be unenforceable in court. Magellan used a device, doubtless customary, by which two separate documents were recorded and notarized. One was a formal promissory note by which Abraldez acknowledged the receipt of the loan of one hundred cruzados and agreed to pay the legal interest of ten per cent. This note was secured in the usual manner by a lien at India House upon Abraldez's importation of pepper. The second document was a separate contract whereby Magellan agreed to insure Abraldez against marine risks on an imaginary cargo of pepper which Abraldez was supposedly shipping to Portugal on the *nao* Santa Cruz. For this pretended insurance, Abraldez agreed to pay Magellan a premium of 100 cruzados. Payment of this premium was guaranteed by a lien against any spices belonging to Abraldez which might be in the warehouses of India House in Lisbon.

Thus the rate of interest was camouflaged by Magellan's business advisers in Cochin. The net result of this legal fiction was that Abraldez bound himself firmly to pay to Magellan's brother in Portugal the sum of two hundred cruzados for the loan of one hundred for one year. The benefit to Magellan was not only the doubling of his capital, but also the safe transmission of his money to Portugal, through the usual medium of foreign exchange, "Malabar money," i.e., pepper.

Although Ferdinand could see no prospect of attaining a fortune in East Africa or in India, no one was more aware than he that one last frontier for exploitation remained. This was the opulent metropolis of Malacca, and he was uniquely qualified to profit in that field. If he could get command of a merchant ship for the German or Florentine bankers whom the Cochin factors represented, he might utilize his knowledge and skill to realize immense gains, working on shares with the owners of the ship.

Duarte Barbosa drew Ferdinand Magellan into the group which was headed by Dom Antonio Real and Dom Lorenzo Moreno, the two Royal Factors of India House in Cochin, who were the local arbiters in all trade matters between India and Europe. They were the King's men in that they were officially the trade representatives of the crown, yet Antonio Real was backed by the Fuggers and the Welsers, and Lorenzo Moreno had the support of the Florentine bankers in Lisbon. Both men thus had important allies at court; however, since both had supported the late Viceroy Almeida against Dom Affonso de Albuquerque, they now shared the apprehension of Duarte Barbosa as to their prospects under the new regime. Soon they found there were grounds for their misgivings, for word came to Cochin that Governor Albuquerque, who had captured the important Arab seaport of Goa by a surprise attack on February 17, 1510, had announced his decision to make it the capital of Portuguese Asia. This meant that the local headquarters of India House, together with the Arsenal and Navy Yard which now were based on Cochin, would be removed to Goa, and that the Archbishop would probably also move there. It was obvious that the commercial men with Governor Albuquerque at Goa would be put in charge of all the Malabar spice trade, displacing Duarte Barbosa, Antonio Real, Lorenzo Moreno, and the other officials who had administered trade affairs from the fortress at Cochin. The blow would be a particularly heavy one to the Brahman Rajah of Cochin, who had been a faithful ally of Dom Manuel from the first day of the arrival of Vasco da Gama's fleet a dozen years before.

As soon as the two Royal Factors learned of the proclamation making Goa the capital of Portuguese India, they prepared a counterstroke. Their plan was to return to Lisbon, abandoning both Albuquerque and the Rajah of Cochin, and institute direct trade between Portugal and Indonesia. An experienced navigator like Magellan could take their ships to Sumatra for gold, to Banka for tin, to Pegu for rubies, pick up such spices, sandalwood, camphor and pearls as might be available from Chinese traders, and catch the westerly monsoon back, so that the whole round trip from Lisbon could be made within a year. The profits of such a trip would be prodigious. The connections and resources of Antonio Real and Lorenzo Moreno made the project feasible, and Ferdinand Magellan was ready and willing to undertake it, for it would merely mean navigating along the same route he had already pioneered with Sequeira.

However, this plan never was carried out, for to the astonishment of all, Governor Albuquerque brought his badly battered fleet of twenty-three ships laden with wounded men back to the harbor of Cochin. Rajah Sabayo of Goa had counterattacked and, after a savage struggle, had forced the Portuguese to evacuate the recently captured city. Albuquerque did not, however, intend to abandon his plans to make Goa his capital. He proceeded at once to enlist all the ships and men available at Cochin for an expedition to recapture the island city.

The preparations for the expedition extended throughout the winter season and were not completed until the latter part of November, when spring was well advanced. Ferdinand Magellan was placed in command of a caravel, and perhaps he hoped to make a lucky haul in Goa if the attack was successful. Although Governor Albuquerque had honored him with the command of one of his three dozen ships, this was not to be construed as a mark of special favor. The assault would be a desperate one, and the Governor needed leaders like Magellan to overcome the tremendous odds in favor of the defense.

An unfortunate incident now occurred in which Ferdinand Magellan was forced to oppose the Governor, and which placed him irrevocably in the black books of Albuquerque, who was notoriously of an unforgiving and vindictive nature.

Four large *naos* belonging to the Fuggers and the Welsers arrived at Cochin with the monsoon in September. The modern, heavily constructed, and well-armed vessels were to load and return with the westward monsoon early in January. However, the Governor General coveted them. He was fearful of the naval strength of the Rajah Sabayo, who had been reinforced, it will be remembered, by the Venetian and Egyptian ships that had survived the battle of Diu. He argued that the four spice ships could sail with him to Goa, help him capture the city, and then come back to Cochin and load by the first of February, which was their deadline for sailing. If they did not get away from Cochin by then, the winds would make it impossible for them to sail back to Portugal until the following year. All the shipping men realized that this plan could not be carried out by February, but the Governor was vehement in denouncing anyone who questioned his program.

The commander of the spice fleet was John da Empoli, a member of a noble Florentine family, who had learned the spice business in Flanders as a representative of Florentine bankers. He had sailed with Governor Albuquerque to India in 1503; on that voyage he had made a great fortune in spices for his Florentine principals and for himself. He had visited Brazil and South Africa, and was a man of such eminence that, although a Florentine, he had been honored by being invited to lecture in Venice before the Council of Ten and the Signori. Pope Leo X, in a letter to King Manuel, referred to him as "our friend and yours."

Da Empoli strongly resisted having his fleet commandeered by the

Governor General and cleverly based his objections upon the fact that Dom Manuel's exchequer would rely on the taxes on his spice cargoes to balance the royal budget for the forthcoming year. His resistance was strongly supported by the Royal Factors, Antonio Real and Lorenzo Moreno, and by Duarte Barbosa. Governor Albuquerque's authority over the Factors was restricted by law, and he dared not use his naval power to ride roughshod over their opposition, particularly as they had such powerful backers at Lisbon. He therefore decided to shield himself behind a decision of a Council of War, and on October 10, 1510, he summoned his sixteen senior captains, among whom were Ferdinand Magellan and Garcia de Sousa. Captain Francisco Serrano, with his wonted political dexterity, had managed to take his caravel on a cruise up the coast at this time and was not called upon to take part in the Council. The minutes record that most of the captains supported the imperious Governor General, yet there was enough opposition to send the peremptory Albuquerque into one of his frenzied rages, which frightened a few more into agreement. Ferdinand Magellan, however, was not to be browbeaten, and in his usual courageous manner, supported by Captain Garcia de Sousa and two others, he stood up against his chief. He stated his opinion that the limited aid which the four merchant ships could lend the fleet would not compensate for the loss to them of a year's time, the consequent upsetting of the European spice market, and the loss of governmental revenues which would ensue. Albuquerque scowled and said he would sail with as many ships and men as he could get together. He would go and take Goa, and he trusted in our Saviour's passion that He would aid him. Raving and threatening to write the King to report the names of the mercenary men who preferred sordid mercantile profit to the honor of attacking the Moslems, Albuquerque frightened the Council into voting for commandeering the four ships.

From that time on, although the Governor continued Magellan as one of his captains, he never again would show him any favor. In a later letter to the King, he accused Magellan of insubordination and even insinuated that he was perhaps one of the captains whom the Portuguese Government suspected to be secretly in the pay of the King of Spain. Dom Manuel, who had members of the Royal Council of Spain secretly in his pay, had learned that there were in fact certain Portuguese captains in Asia who were accepting money from the Spanish Crown. He therefore had written to put Albuquerque on his guard, and although the Governor General was never able to identify the traitors with certainty, he gave the King the names of those captains, like Magellan, whom he did not fully trust. Ferdinand Magellan's close relationship with Duarte Barbosa, whose family connections with Castile were known, contributed to the suspicion.

The four spice ships were incorporated in the fleet as a squadron under the command of John da Empoli, and, on November 24, 1510, the Governor General arrived off Goa with thirty-four ships of war carrying fifteen hundred Portuguese troops. The Rajah of Cochin had been made to contribute to the undermining of his own fortunes by sending three hundred of the best Malabar soldiers, although he knew, if Albuquerque captured Goa, it would mean the ruin of Cochin. After a valiant defense, the Rajah Sabayo was driven from the city, and Albuquerque turned it over to his army for sack and pillage.

In order to enhance the terror of his name among the Moslems, Albuquerque always separated the Arabs from the other inhabitants of a captured city and cut off the right hands of the men and the noses and ears of the women. He spared only the comeliest of the girls, whom he reserved as personal gifts for men of influence. At Goa he outdid himself, ordering massacred every Arab man, woman, and child, from doddering ancient to newborn babe. It took the Portuguese soldiers three full days of systematic search and slaughter, during which they slew over eight thousand Saracens, or about six for each Portuguese soldier engaged. The Governor General wrote gloatingly of this exploit to King Manuel in his official report, in which he gave pious thanks to the Almighty for His aid.

No mention is made in Albuquerque's dispatches of the activity of Captain Ferdinand Magellan in the assault upon Goa, nor in the subsequent sack of the city. We can, perhaps, judge his revulsion from the barbarities committed upon the Moslem civil population by the fact that he personally got no booty worth mentioning from the plundering of "Goa the Golden," although the loot was so enormous that Albuquerque sent to Dom Manuel the equivalent of three million dollars as the King's share of the plunder. Magellan at this time was certainly eager to gain some material reward for all his hardships and risks, but he was a man for whom principle outweighed interest when the two were in conflict. Therefore he remained a poor man while a poltroon retired on his riches.

John da Empoli, who had been so unwillingly conscripted to fight at Goa, distinguished himself by his valor and was knighted upon the field of battle by the Governor General. This dramatic act may well have been actuated by diplomatic considerations, for as Magellan had predicted, the spice ships missed their deadline and had to stay over in the Orient for a whole year.

The Governor General immediately started to carry out his plan transferring the seat of government from Cochin to Goa. The Rajah of Cochin, as well as Duarte Barbosa and all Ferdinand Magellan's other friends opposed the move. Antonio Real and Lorenzo Moreno took ship for Lisbon and there became a focal point in the antagonism against Albuquerque. They at once took a leading position in Lisbon financial circles, harassed unmercifully the operations of the Governor General in India, and did not scruple to use slander and perjury against him. This further harmed the already precarious standing of Duarte Barbosa and Ferdinand Magellan with the Governor.

Once established in Goa, Albuquerque decided to carry out Dom Manuel's wishes and to attack Malacca. The Sultan of Malacca, greatly perturbed by the fall of Goa, realized that he would probably be the next victim, so he took every precaution, maintaining spies around Albuquerque and at the same time strengthening his defenses at home. However, Albuquerque pretended, very plausibly, to be preparing an expedition against the northern Arab city of Aden, at the mouth of the Red Sea.

Captain Diogo Mendez Vasconsellos now appeared at Goa with four caravels from Lisbon, under royal orders to conduct an expedition against Malacca. Albuquerque received Vasconsellos with pretended friendliness, and managed to absorb his independent squadron in his own armada.

For public consumption, Albuquerque continued his pretense of aiming at Aden, and when he sailed from Goa with his fleet of nineteen warships and transports on March 31, 1511, he took a northerly course. Once beyond sight of the spies, the expedition reversed its direction and sailed southward.

Ferdinand Magellan commanded one of the caravels. The passage was unusually slow because of storms, and one of the ships was lost. In the Indian Ocean, the fleet captured five Indian merchant ships carrying textiles to Malacca from the industrial Kingdom of Cambaya, in Northern India. In the Bay of Bengal they made prizes of two pirate junks and a pirate caravel. They reached Malacca on July 1, 1511.

During the two years since Magellan had seen Malacca, the fortifications had been strengthened and many new batteries erected. Albuquerque had eight hundred Portuguese *soldados* and six hundred Malabar archers to attack a fortified city defended by twenty thousand soldiers and protected by three thousand pieces of first-class artillery. A strong fleet of Chinese junks and Malay parangs was reported to be on the way to help defend the city.

Albuquerque immediately demanded the release of the prisoners from the expedition of Diogo Lopes de Sequeira two years before. Sultan Mohammed made several attempts to establish a truce and agreed to give up the captives and make amends for past misdeeds; but he did not carry out his promises, and it seemed he was playing for time to allow the naval reinforcements to arrive. Albuquerque sent him an ultimatum and, when that was disregarded, he burned all the shipping in the harbor and bombarded the city. Mohammed again attempted to arrange a truce, and this time actually sent the prisoners aboard the fleet, but the negotiations fell through.

After prolonged bombardment of the shore batteries, on July 24th the Portuguese penetrated the outlying defenses and entered the city. They were driven out again, but on August 10th returned to the offensive and step by step fought their way through the streets. The Malays were well entrenched in the Mosques and about the bridges over the river that traversed the town; under the personal command of Mohammed, they put up an able defense. The Portuguese followed the course of the river and used as their center of offense a large junk with heavy teakwood sides. They mounted gun batteries on this floating fortress and inched it up the channel with every high tide, while the defenders tried to prevent its advance and set it afire. As the junk advanced, the fortified bridges one by one were captured. At last the Portuguese stormed the palace, but the wounded Sultan eluded capture, fleeing on an elephant. He meant to organize another army and retake the city.

The name of Ferdinand Magellan is not included in the list of those commended by the Captain General for meritorious service, which is not surprising. However, one extant report of the siege mentions him by name and says he gave a good account of himself.

Many prisoners were taken during the sack of the city, and as a special mark of grace Governor Albuquerque permitted each of his captains to select a captive for his own personal body servant. Ferdinand Magellan thereby acquired a Malay slave boy to whom he gave the name of Enrique de Malacca.

Malacca contained many palaces of Malay and Chinese magnates, and its sack yielded spoils greater than ever before taken by the Portuguese. If there had been an equitable division of the booty, Ferdinand could hardly have failed to recoup his fortunes. The enormous plunder accumulated and reserved for the King and for the captains of the fleet was so bulky that it presented a problem to handle and to safeguard. Therefore it was sequestered by the Captain General and held under guard in his headquarters, to be taken by him personally to Goa for later allocation and distribution. Magellan's heart must have sunk, for he had previously seen deserving combatants defrauded in this manner.

Before order could be completely restored in Malacca, the Governor General received an urgent call to return to Goa, which was being besieged by land and sea. He hurriedly sailed for India with four ships and three hundred Portuguese men-at-arms, carrying with him on his flagship all the plunder of Malacca. This he promised to divide equitably among his captains as soon as he arrived in India. However, one night his ship struck a reef during a storm off the coast of Java and sank. Albuquerque saved himself by clinging all night to a small raft, but many of his aides were drowned. The immense treasure was lost, and with it any chance Ferdinand Magellan might have had for his share. The official estimate of the King's loss in this ship was two hundred thousand ducats. As the King was entitled to one fifth of the value of the captured treasure, the total must have been a million ducats, or about fifteen million dollars, though comparisons with modern money are almost impossible. Magellan was one of two dozen sea captains, and his share would have been substantial. However, without riches, he remained on patrol duty at Malacca in command of his caravel and accompanied the fleet in several raids upon nearby pirate strongholds.

Albuquerque had acted in his usual rapid and decisive manner to establish a government and to restore order in Malacca, but was called away too soon to have everything fully organized. John da Empoli, whom he appointed King's Factor, dominated the other officials and became *de facto* governor of the faction-torn colony.

Before leaving Malacca for India, Albuquerque had organized an expedition to sail to Maluco, which so far had never been visited by any European. He selected the personnel, laid out the route, and wrote detailed orders for the commanders. He named Captain Antonio d'Abreu commander of the fleet of three caravels and one junk, the other captains being Simon Affonso and Francisco Serrano. The junk was commanded by a trusted Hindu named Nakoda Ismael who had often made the voyage of two thousand miles from Malacca to Maluco and who was familiar with the twisting route through the maze of archipelagoes, its unpredictable winds, its capricious currents, and its uncharted reefs and sandbanks.

The Governor ordered that the junk should lead the way, and that the experienced Hindu pilots whom he sent on the caravels should invariably follow the lead of Nakoda Ismael and defer to his judgment. The caravels were well armed and were manned with selected crews. Each one was supplied with muscular negro slaves to man the pumps, in order to keep the holds dry and protect the cargoes of spices which they were expected to bring back. In case the Moslem rulers of the spiceries proved inhospitable, the Governor sent one hundred and twenty veteran *soldados* along to act as assault troops. He preferred, however, to avoid hostilities if possible, and his instructions on this point were specific.

He charged the officers of the fleet to treat the local rulers with justice and liberality and to pay the market price for any merchandise or supplies they might purchase, so as to establish cordial relations along the waterways to the Spice Islands. The captains were forbidden to stop en route except for water and supplies, or to attack any merchant ships they might encounter. Governor Albuquerque sent one of his own pursers on each caravel to see that his instructions were followed.

In December, 1511, the expedition left Malacca, sailed through Singapore Strait, and, without once dropping anchor, passed the harbors and stately cities which they saw along the coasts of the populous islands of Sumatra and Java.

The little squadron soon was reduced by the loss of the caravel of Simon Affonso during a storm off the coast of Java, and at the same time the caravel of Francisco Serrano became separated from the others, perhaps intentionally, and never again rejoined them.

Captain Antonio d'Abreu never reached Maluco. He got to the Island of Banda with his caravel and the junk and was held there for four months by a delay of the monsoon. In Banda he was able to purchase for both vessels full cargoes of cloves brought in from Maluco by native traders, and he sailed back to Malacca with a profitable consignment, but without having accomplished the object of his mission.

In the meantime, Serrano was on his own with a first-class, well-armed ship, manned by a picked crew. It was such a command as he had dreamed of, and he probably planned to make his fortune.

At this point, his high spirits were dashed by disaster. His stout ship burned, and he and his men were lucky to escape with their lives. In the narrow waters, he was able to beach the flaming vessel and get his men away under arms before the magazines exploded. They found themselves upon a barren island which they later identified as one of the little Lucipara Islands, in the Banda Sea.

They were desperately trying to improvise some sort of craft to take them back to Malacca when Serrano's luck turned again. A large junk was bearing down upon the island; the smoldering hulk on the beach had doubtless attracted the attention of its commander. With great presence of mind, Serrano quickly hid the traces of his crew's activity and concealed his men in the dense growth near the beach. The seamen waited in their hiding place, sending up prayers to their favorite saints that the junk should not pass on. It dropped its sails, came to anchor, and sent two boats ashore whose occupants disembarked to inspect the wreck. After they had gone past the hiding place of Serrano's men, down the beach, the Portuguese quickly emerged from ambush, seized the boats, boarded the junk, threw its few occupants over the side, drew up the anchor and hoisted sail. The marooned Chinese knelt on the beach and begged piteously not to be abandoned, and Serrano, confident of the superior strength of his armed veterans, took them aboard. They proved useful as interpreters, as well as pilots and navigators for the captured vessel. The junk thus providentially at their disposal proved to be a well-found Chinese pirate ship, a passable substitute for the burned caravel except for the lack of artillery. To be sure, Serrano no longer had the valuable cargo of trade goods with which the lost caravel had been provided, goods which were known to be in demand in the Isles of Spice. However, there was plenty of worth-while merchandise in the junk which could be used for trading, and therefore Ser-

Engraving from de Bry's "Peregrinationes," 1594

THE SAM MIGUEL IN THE ATLANTIC

Engraving from de Bry's "Peregrinationes," 1599

EARLY REPRESENTATION OF A CHINESE JUNK

rano decided not to rejoin Antonio d'Abreu at once, but to make an independent trading cruise and see what profit he could pick up. The junk cruised from island to island, bartering its merchandise for local products where none of the natives had ever seen a European before, nor had any realization of the value of the spices and other products which they offered freely to the strangers. The Chinese pilots were familiar with the islands, and they followed a desultory course, sailing always in the general direction of Maluco with the intention of eventually rejoining the squadron there.

When the junk reached the large and well populated island of Amboina, Serrano found a civil war in progress. He decided to throw his weight on the side of the reigning rajah, and his disciplined, armored Portuguese veterans easily brought their protegé victory. The grateful ruler made much of Serrano, gave him costly presents, and persuaded him to stay some weeks with him.

The news of the coming of the Christians spread through the archipelago, and while Serrano was still visiting the rajah at Amboina, a mission of a thousand soldiers arrived in ten parangs from the Datu Boleyse, the Moslem ruler of Ternate, asking him to come to his aid in a war against the Datu Almanzor, of the neighboring island of Tidore. Since he knew that Tidore and Ternate were two of the most important spice islands of Maluco, the goal of his ambitions, Francisco Serrano agreed to visit Ternate and to discuss the offer of alliance. He sailed from Amboina to Ternate, escorted by the Datu's flotilla.

An ancient prophecy had predicted that, at about that time, there would come to Ternate a group of Men of Iron who would extend the glory and the dominion of its people. Hence when Serrano and his compatriots stepped ashore in shining steel breastplates and glittering helmets, the natives believed the fulfillment of the prophecy had come, and reverenced them accordingly.

Serrano was royally received by the Datu Boleyse. He accepted the command of the army of Ternate and, after a single engagement, managed to effect a truce and compromise the differences between the two rival Moslem rulers. In order to cement the peace and to strengthen his own position, he married the young daughter of the Datu Almanzor of Tidore. He now assumed the post of Grand Vizier of Ternate, and by diplomatic negotiation with the rulers of the other islands of the Spiceries he soon established himself as arbiter of all Maluco. He formed a regular military and naval regime under the direction of his Portuguese officers and subordinates, all of whom were installed in polygamous South Sea establishments of their own.

Francisco Serrano remained in supreme control of Ternate for a period of eight years, maintaining a harem and living in royal splendor. Once he was firmly seated on his bizarre throne, whenever possible he sent messages to Albuquerque at Goa assuring him of his loyalty and asking that he be confirmed as governor and supplied with reinforcements. He had secured formal permission from the Datu Boleyse for Portugal to erect a fortress on Ternate, from which to dominate all Maluco, and he again and again begged that a caravel be sent to him. But Malacca was short of ships and men, and could not or would not send him help. Albuquerque himself was friendly to Francisco Serrano, but his aides were intensely jealous, and the Knights of Christ at Goa used every weapon in the arsenal of bureaucracy to prevent his getting official recognition.

There is extant a letter from Dom Affonso de Albuquerque, at Goa, to Dom Manuel in Lisbon, dated September 22, 1515, or four years after he had sent Serrano to the Spiceries from Malacca, which reads: "I have received news of Francisco Serrano, who is alive and is in control of the Isles of Spice and is ruling the king and the entire territory."

It is a matter of record that Francisco Serrano sent letters by every available channel to Ferdinand Magellan, at Malacca, telling him that all he had to do to become enormously rich was to secure a caravel and come to Ternate, and urging him to come to his aid. However, Magellan could not do this, for Ternate was months away, and the royal caravel that he commanded was continually needed in Malacca, which was constantly beset by foes.

Ferdinand Magellan's activities during the eighteen months he spent in Malacca are only vaguely recorded, but such details as are available permit us to sketch with confidence his probable employment. Apart from his routine command of a patrol ship guarding Singapore Strait from pirates and perhaps convoying junks bearing tin from the nearby islands of Banka and Billiton, he was intermittently engaged in sea battles and amphibious operations. The foes who encircled the Portuguese in Malacca kept its defenders continually on the alert. While he was on duty at Malacca, Magellan seems to have gone off with his caravel on an unauthorized exploring expedition which extended six hundred leagues, or about two thousand miles, to the eastward. This illicit voyage was doubtless instigated by John da Empoli, who was interested in using Ferdinand Magellan to discover what lay to the east of the Spice Islands. Now that Maluco had definitely been located upon the chart, it was logical for the enterprising John da Empoli to wish to push eastward across the Great South Sea, hoping to reach the west coast of South America, already discovered by Spain. Perhaps the navigator, Magellan, could supply the one link yet missing in his chain.

When Magellan's caravel suddenly disappeared and was not heard of for a long period, it was asserted he had gone in search of the Isle of Gold. Malacca was agog with a fable that there was in the southeast an island where gold in quantity was to be picked up freely on the beach. Legend had it that the simple blacks who inhabited the island had no idea of the value of gold. The tale probably embroiders on a casual contact with what we now call Northern Australia. The recital grew in the taverns of Malacca into the exciting legend of the Golden Isle, and stern measures had to be taken to prevent adventurous members of the garrison from deserting to seek their fortunes there.

When Magellan's caravel suddenly reappeared, much the worse for wear, there was a wave of hostile criticism in official circles. Ferdinand was very mysterious in public as to his discoveries, but he eagerly sought official authorization to take a cargo of trade goods and pursue his explorations further. In the light of modern nautical knowledge, we can assume from the evidence we have that he had cruised from two thousand to twenty-five hundred miles to the northeast, through the South China Sea. He may have visited the Chinese settlement of Paria on the Island of Luzon, and he probably coasted about the Philippine Archipelago, which he later was to discover officially for Spain while sailing westward across the Pacific. Since there was then much gold mined on the Island of Luzon, and there was a great market in pearls on the large southern island of Mindanao, it is quite likely that Magellan, in his private report to John da Empoli and to his naval chief, Dom Ferdinand Petre Andrade, gave very good reasons why he should be allowed to return at once with a suitable cargo of trade goods.

However, in writing his formal report for transmittal to headquarters at Goa, the astronomer in him could not refrain from riding his hobby. He appended to his report the disturbing suggestion that careful solar observations and the deductions of experienced Chinese navigators had convinced him that not only the newly discovered archipelago, but also by inference the coveted Spice Islands themselves, lay to the east of the longitudinal line bounding the area of the globe reserved to Portugal by the treaty of Tordesillas. A flat refusal of any license for further trips and an acrimonious retort concerning his geographic surmises came from Goa. Ferdinand Magellan, wounded in his scientific *amour propre,* tactlessly engaged in controversy not only with his superiors in Goa and Malacca, but before long even with the astronomers and savants at Lisbon as well. This, of course, wrote finis to his career at Malacca and sowed the seeds for his disgrace at Lisbon.

One chronicler gives a variant record, saying that after the four ships had been sent by Albuquerque to the Spice Islands, Ferdinand Magellan managed to secure command of another caravel with orders to proceed to the Spiceries and join Francisco Serrano. However, before reaching Ternate, "seeking fame and glory," as the chronicler puts it, he disregarded his instructions and boldly went on an unauthorized voyage into the unknown eastern seas. The chronicler duly records that he encountered a number of islands six hundred leagues beyond Malacca.

It was characteristic of Magellan to choose the scientific rather than the lucrative goal, and despite his hunger for riches deliberately to have risked official displeasure in order to prove the geographic theory that had become his monomania. His loyalty to Francisco Serrano also was sacrificed to his zeal for astronomic and geographic research. In this connection, we may conjecture that Serrano's reports of his fabulously voluptuous way of life at Ternate probably repelled rather than attracted the austere Ferdinand Magellan.

The chronicler also relates that Magellan, immediately upon his return, sent a letter to Serrano at Ternate describing his exploit. Serrano did not take this in good part, but complained bitterly in his letters to Magellan and others that his old comrade had deserted him in his time of need by going off on a cruise of his own instead of coming to his aid at Ternate.

It seemed that Ferdinand Magellan's voyage pleased no one. John da Empoli was disappointed that the explorer brought back only confirmatory information about the Philippines, concerning which he felt he already had authentic data. Serrano was indignant and resentful toward his old comrade, and Dom Ferdinand Petre Andrade, Magellan's immediate superior in Malacca, was angry and mortified because he had to bear the brunt of the furious criticism from Goa, where the incident was looked upon as evidence of insubordination.

John da Empoli apparently was unable to protect Magellan and became apprehensive for himself. Therefore he quietly loaded his three caravels with spices and oriental goods and slipped away to Europe without apprising anyone of his intention. He thoughtfully visited his powerful friend, Pope Leo X, and got his unqualified support before exposing himself to any criticism in Lisbon.

At Goa, the Knights of Christ now apparently determined to discipline Magellan, but because of his eminent military services they decided not to make a public example of him, but merely to deprive him of his ship and send him home, writing directly to the King of their reasons.

None of the details of this action are preserved, but Magellan apparently was quietly relieved of his command and, in January, 1513, sailed for India, reaching Cochin on February 10, 1513. There he found his friend, Duarte Barbosa, as a last resort preparing a letter of protest against the discriminatory tactics of the Goa group. This letter he proposed to send directly to Dom Manuel by the hand of Captain John Serrano.

Ferdinand Magellan's orders apparently were that he should immediately leave India for Portugal; but there is no official record of his arrival in Lisbon. For to that rich and heedless capital, Ferdinand Magellan was at that time a person of no consequence whatever.

PART II

PRINCES, PRELATES, AND PROFITS

CHAPTER VIII

HOME IS THE SAILOR

AFTER eight arduous years in the Orient, Ferdinand Magellan was home again. The caravel Santa Cruz, from Cochin, crossed the bar with the tide at dawn, and Ferdinand Magellan stood on the quarter-deck with Captain George Lopez to view the changes in the harbor and city he had left eight years before. The roads now were so crowded with anchored craft that the homecoming Indiaman had to proceed carefully, using only its foresail, to avoid running afoul of any of the hundreds of foreign merchant ships of diversified rig that filled the river. Captain George Lopez pointed out along both shores of the Tagus the prosperous suburban communities with mansions, municipal buildings, and churches where Magellan remembered only straggling fishing villages. He viewed the new, compactly exquisite Tower of Belem, which rose out of the water to command the entrance to the harbor, with an appreciation heightened by an acquaintance with the architecture of the Orient. Nearby, on the shore, a screen of scaffolding hid the unfinished church of the Jeronymos which Dom Manuel was erecting to commemorate da Gama's achievement.

The ship dropped anchor off Restello. In accordance with Captain Lopez's vow, all the company rowed ashore and marched barefoot, bearing candles, to the little sailors' chapel to render thanks for their safe return.

The Santa Cruz then anchored well up the river, opposite the pier known as the *Caes de Sodre.* Beyond, Ferdinand Magellan could see a line of busy wharves, stretching for miles, and behind them stood the arsenals, shipyards, and warehouses of a once sleepy city that had awakened to become the busiest seaport in Europe. The waterfront had been cleared for a space to give way to a handsome public plaza where stood the new royal palace; a broad, sweeping stairway led directly up to it from the river. About the palace were grouped many large stone buildings which housed the departments of India House, the vast bureaucracy that administered Portugal's far-flung empire.

The Santa Cruz was bedecked with all its pennons and the standards of the fidalgos aboard, including a family banner of the Magellans which Ferdinand had had the sailmaker sew up for the occasion. As the anchor was let go, the broadsides of the ship thundered the news to Lisbon that mail, spices, and returning adventurers had arrived safely home from the Orient. A number of shore boats immediately put out for the caravel, but it was some hours before the official barge came alongside to give the voyagers clearance to go ashore. The commander of the barge explained apologetically to the indignant Captain that a number of ships had entered with the tide of the preceding evening. These had required the attention of the harbor police earlier that day. He grumbled at his heavy duties, cataloging the craft he had already had to inspect that morning. There had been a large *nao* from North Africa, a squadron of Venetian galleys from Southampton, England, a slaving caravel from El Mina in West Africa, and ships from Palermo and Genoa.

No relatives or friends awaited the homecomers on the dock, for there could be no advance news at Lisbon of their arrival. The only person who could ever forecast the time of a ship's homecoming was shrewd Cristóbal de Haro. Often, as soon as the pepper fleet left Mozambique in East Africa on its long return voyage around the Cape, the financier's agent sent word to him surreptitiously, using a fast Arab dhow as far as Mecca and camel messenger overland to Alexandria. The couriers brought de Haro a detailed schedule of the pepper and spices the ship carried. His advance knowledge of the supply of pepper for the next year's market could be used with profit for speculating in pepper futures on the Antwerp Bourse and the Venetian Rialto. Such news was jealously guarded by the close-mouthed banker and ordinarily not divulged even to the King himself.

Once ashore, the officers and fidalgos left their hand baggage at a waterside tavern and went at once to the new palace to report their arrival. Ferdinand Magellan was still a member of the royal household, or *Casa de ElRei,* though he had been on leave of absence for foreign service since 1505; it was his first duty to report his return.

The vast royal palace had halberdiers on guard at every passageway and formal ushers and footmen at every door. Ferdinand found it a chilling contrast to the old Moorish castle he had known so well as a student and page during the old days when Dom Manuel first was a king; he now felt himself to be an alien at the court. He wandered uncertainly about the unfamiliar halls of the new palace, but at last found the proper court officer with whom to register. This functionary obviously had never heard of him, and when he finally located his name upon the rolls, he muttered disdainfully that he had not expected a man of his bearing to be classed as a junior squire. Stung by this ungracious official welcome, Magellan stifled a retort and grimly signed the register, hoping that this experience was not a foretaste of what he might expect. The courtier patronizingly remarked, as he returned the roll to its receptacle, that in due course Ferdinand Magellan would probably receive a promotion to the rank of usher or gentleman in waiting, which would be appropriate to his years. The hardbitten veteran replied that he expected immediate advancement to the status of *Cavaleiro fidalgo da casa de ElRei,* or cavalier of the household. The official looked surprised and said, in an icy tone, "You will be lucky to be advanced at all, for you have been absent from your post for many years." The implication that time-serving in the palace was better than the manner in which he had employed his absence infuriated the choleric Magellan, and he shouted hoarsely, almost incoherently, that during those years of absence he had fought continuously for his King, had been wounded at Diu and at Calicut, and now bore the rank of Captain in the armada of His Highness. The supercilious, silken Knight of Christ bowed low and said sardonically, "No doubt when His Highness learns of all this, he will hasten to create you not a *cavaleiro fidalgo* but a *fidalgo cavaleiro.*" In the formal nomenclature of the court, the simple transposition of the order of the two words had a world of significance, as the latter title, borne only by members of the highest nobility, indicated supreme rank in the royal household.

Ferdinand Magellan, had he still been in Malacca or Cochin, would have taken his dagger to the insolent popinjay, but now he choked down his indignation and turned away. As he hurried from the building, he muttered rebelliously to himself that he would never return except as a *cavaleiro fidalgo.*

He emerged in a temper from the palace and, seeking to meet some old acquaintance, crossed the square and entered the imposing *Casa de India.* No friendly face greeted him there. As he walked down the long corridors and read the titles and classifications of the innumerable departments, he realized with a sinking heart how much things had changed since the days when he and Francisco Serrano had known the occupant of every desk and had been familiar with the contents of every file. He smiled grimly as he remembered that in those days there had been only five porters attached to the warehouse, and he had known each of them by name.

He passed through a veritable maze of departments, sections, and bureaus. The *Casa de India,* which corresponded to a modern Ministry of Colonies, had been split up into some dozens of subordinate divisions. Some of these sections were so extensive as likewise to be called *Casas,* such, for instance, as the *Casa* of the Slave Trade, of Dyes and Drugs, of Textiles and Jewels, of Pepper and Spices, of the Atlantic Isles, of Guinea, of Brazil, and of the Maritime Service, each of which in turn had many subdivisions. There also were numerous bureaus for the exercise of legal functions, as well as courts of assessment and inferior and superior courts of appeal.

Ferdinand Magellan, a sailor and man of direct action, was appalled by the number of jurists and legalistic boards which he saw pyramided upon the administrative organization. He knew, of course, that all merchandise and property entering Portugal, other than personal belongings, had to be consigned to India House at Lisbon, and that everything had to pass through tedious processes of evaluation and taxation before reaching the importer. He also knew that incoming shipments had often been impounded and held up for long periods because of jurisdictional disputes between departments. When he saw how confused and complicated the organization had become, he understood better why such needless delays took place.

That afternoon as Ferdinand walked through the halls, the crush of litigants was very great because of the news that mail had arrived from India. Since it took at least a year to get any evidence from India, the anterooms of India House filled with anxious petitioners whenever there was a chance that documents or testimony might at last have come.

Ferdinand Magellan read on several doors the names of some with whom he had served in the old days; but when he peered in and saw the numerous personnel in the anterooms and the crowd of waiting petitioners, he did not enter. At last he ran into an old comrade and greeted him with enthusiasm, but his one-time friend maintained a guarded and distant manner. He realized then that his outmoded provincial apparel looked far from impressive and that most courtiers would be chary about being seen with him.

He saw how the organization had grown fat upon the fruits of the hardship and danger of the soldiers of the East, and he felt a warm wave of friendship and homesickness for his old comrades, even for Albuquerque, whom he could now pity with the rest as the victim of palace drones. On the long homeward voyage he had more than once thought that, in case his plans for a return to Malacca were delayed, he could, at a pinch, obtain a good post in India House, provided he were willing to tie himself to a desk. Now he realized he had been wrong. He had sensed at once, even during his brief survey, the rivalries and jealousies of the cliques that ruled this bureaucracy, in which any returned veteran would need strong political backing to obtain recognition, or indeed even justice.

Although he had only been in Lisbon two days, Ferdinand Magellan was glad to get passage on a caravel bound for the coastal port of *Vianna do Castello,* whence he took horse for his brother Diogo's home at Ponte da Barca. After a few days' stay there, he rode to neighboring Ponte de Lima to see his debtor, Pedro Anes Abraldez, to collect the two hundred ducats due him. He found to his dismay that Pedro was dead, and that his father, Abraham, who had inherited his son's estate, was absent in Galicia. This was a serious financial setback, for he was quite out of funds, even for personal expenses.

Ferdinand was discontented and restless at his brother's house. His homecoming was far different from what he had dreamed during many vigils on the deck of his rolling caravel, in unknown waters under the Southern Cross. More than once when he was in extreme peril, his struggle to survive was animated by the wish to see his beloved homeland again. Now he found Ponte da Barca itself unchanged; the verdant countryside, with its lovely valleys and forested hills, was more restful to his tired gaze than any vista he had looked upon in half the world. His heart was gladdened by the familiar sights of his childhood, the well-tilled cornfields and vineyards, the huge, brown, slow-moving oxen with their wide-branching horns, the flocks of sheep and goats which continually blocked the road, and the smiling shepherds who saluted him as he rode past, as well as the benevolently friendly priest of a little chapel at which he dismounted one day.

At his old home, the *Torre de Magalhanes,* his brother Diogo was unchanged in his affection, yet the atmosphere of the crowded old farmhouse seemed less than hospitable. His sister-in-law evidently feared having her husband's taciturn, unemployed brother as a permanent visitor in her cramped household. He went with Diogo to call upon his cousin, John de Magalhanes, now Lord of Ponte da Barca and occupant of Paço Vedro, the hereditary manor house of the Magalhanes. John had married one of their wealthy and fashionable relatives, Isabel de Sousa, and now was lord of two other estates; he had become a county magnate of importance. No doubt had Ferdinand returned from India with a substantial fortune, an eligible bachelor of thirty-eight, he would have received a cordial welcome at Paço Vedro. Ferdinand the crippled, impoverished, discharged sea captain, out of favor at Goa and at Lisbon, was given no encouragement to call again. Diogo himself was not on very cordial terms with his rich relatives, since he had only brought back from East Africa a modest amount of prize money and had not made a good match. Although he was head of the junior branch of the family and occupied the old tower and the farmstead, he was a person of little importance among the county gentry.

The neighboring society had changed much during Ferdinand Magellan's absence. Wealthy Knights of Christ and successful members of the Braganza clan had moved into Braga and the Province of Minho and now occupied all the old mansions and estates. The old country homes, reconstructed and renovated, had become fashionable establishments in the Lisbon style. Penniless Ferdinand was made to feel his unimportance by his worldly relatives, yet their indifference did not gall him as much as the snubs of the Lisbon flunkeys and the pompous African slaves who manned their households. That these base creatures should judge him by his unfashionable clothes and his possession of only one outlandish body servant, that they should look down their noses upon him as the family's poor relation, that they should make him feel his inferior position, was the final indignity.

In reality Ferdinand Magellan was deeply conscious of the exploits which had made him a man of mark in India. He felt scornful of the shortsighted viewpoint of the stay-at-homes, who had been absorbed in amassing wealth and squabbling for petty privileges while he had taken part in great events that had shaken the fabric of Asia and changed the course of empires.

Yet it was not fashionable to mention India. People had already heard too many breath-taking accounts of returned travelers. Society in Minho province was interested only in the gossip and politics of the county, and in the rivalries and scandals of the court at Lisbon. Worse, the report had been whispered around that Ferdinand had been sent home by Governor Albuquerque for cause, so he himself was made a subject of gossip. There was nothing for him to do but remain on the farm while awaiting his orders to rejoin the royal household. He hoped then to ask a royal audience, and to have a chance to present his plan to take reinforcements to Ternate, build a Portuguese fort, make Francisco Serrano governor, and send to Lisbon the immensely valuable spices that Serrano had accumulated. It had been Serrano's idea to tempt Dom Manuel by offering him personally almost all the spices.

Weeks passed, and no orders came from the palace. Ferdinand grew restless at the monotony of life at the homestead and went to visit his sister Isabel, who had moved beyond the mountains to Sabrosa after her marriage to Dom John da Silva Telles, Lord of the *Casa Pereira de Sabrosa*. Ferdinand had inherited a small vineyard there which he also wished to visit. However, his stay in the aristocratic little provincial center of Sabrosa proved even less pleasant than at Ponte da Barca, for his brother-in-law proved to be anything but congenial. So he settled accounts with the tenant of his vineyard and found an excuse to return to Ponte da Barca.

Once more he rode to Ponte de Lima to collect the sum due him from the estate of Abraldez. He not only found his debtor still away, but learned to his dismay that this absence was no doubt in order to evade payment of his son's obligations. This was a blow, for the loan and the accumulated interest now amounted to two hundred and fifty ducats, a substantial sum in itself and his sole capital. If he could invest this sum in copper, it would easily be worth twenty-five hundred ducats in Maluco, and Francisco Serrano could help him make that worth twenty-five thousand by the profits of one voyage back from Maluco to Lisbon. He at once engaged a lawyer, who laid an attachment upon any spices in India House to which the Abraldez estate had title.

Upon his return to Ponte da Barca, he found an order re-establishing him in the *Casa de ElRei* in the capacity of an usher, or gentleman in waiting. This put him in a dilemma, for while it would be mortifying for a man of his years of overseas service and his rank of Captain to act in this secondary capacity, yet his membership in the royal household was in itself a valuable privilege which he did not wish to jeopardize. He realized that this place, however unsatisfactory, nevertheless gave him an official foothold in the palace, and that the next step would be to enlist the assistance of some one of influence in the court so that he might gain promotion to the rank of *cavaleiro fidalgo da casa de ElRei.* His recent social experience both at Ponte da Barca and at Sabrosa had convinced him that his own relatives and neighbors would not be willing to make any effort for him, even if they possessed the proper connections. He bethought himself of the Archbishop of Braga, who for so many generations had been the feudal lord of the Magellan family, and rode to Braga to solicit archepiscopal assistance. However, he found that conditions in this provincial capital reflected those of Lisbon. The Archbishop of Braga was titular Primate of Portugal, but in actuality the archbishopric of Lisbon had superseded the more ancient see. Dom Manuel had become an intimate friend of Giovanni de Medici, who ruled in Rome as Pope Leo X, and had gradually gained control of ecclesiastical as well as political authority. As Master of the Knights of Christ, he had first seized control of the prelacies in the overseas dominions; this he could do because, years before, a Pope had delegated to Prince Henry authority over all churchly establishments in the lands which he was to discover. But Dom Manuel wished to be autocrat of the Church in Portugal as well. He persuaded the reluctant Pope to bestow the red hat of the cardinalate upon his sixth child, Alonso, then a little boy seven years old. As the immature Cardinal grew up and various episcopal sees became vacant, Dom Manuel nominated Alonso to these seats. Thus his young son became Cardinal of Portugal, Archbishop of Lisbon, Archbishop of Evora, and Abbot of the important Abbey of Alcobaça.

Ferdinand Magellan did not realize that the Archbishop Primate of Braga no longer held his influential political position. Therefore he waited as patiently as he could in the anterooms for several days of interrogation by self-important monks before he learned that the Archbishop was not even in Braga, but was in attendance upon the King at a royal hunting lodge. It was evident that all roads in Portugal led to Lisbon, and Ferdinand returned to the capital.

Had Ferdinand Magellan been a member of either the Knights of Christ or the Knights of Santiago, he could have found channels of influence. Had he belonged to one of the monkish military orders, there would have been some member of the fraternity to help him past official barriers. But he could find no sponsor. His former superiors in India had either perished in action or were as out of favor as he was. A few of them, to be sure, had followed the intended plan of Viceroy Almeida and had gone into the service of Spain, where any able Portuguese navigator or soldier was sure of a welcome.

While he was anxiously looking for an advocate at court, Ferdinand was overjoyed by the return from Cananor of Captain John Serrano, but if he hoped for assistance from him, he was soon disillusioned. Serrano, who counted upon the favor previously shown him by the King, had been given an early audience. He did not know that disparaging reports from Governor Albuquerque had preceded him. He boldly presented a strong letter from Duarte Barbosa protesting the discrimination in India in favor of Goa and against the interest of the ports of Cochin and of Cananor, at which the King showed immediate displeasure. This destroyed any chance of advancement for John Serrano. After some months of fruitless solicitation, he awakened to the hopelessness of his situation and, embittered and indignant, quietly crossed the border into Spain and secured a commission as pilot in the royal navy.

The friendship of John Serrano therefore could not help Ferdinand Magellan at the Portuguese court, though John's experience might have taught him a lesson had he heeded it. Next he turned to his former Commander, Dom Diogo Lopes de Sequeira, who once again stood high in the circle about the throne, but who would do nothing for him. John da Empoli, who might have helped, was at Rome, and Ferdinand's only hope lay with the two returned factors from Cochin, Antonio Real and Lorenzo Moreno, who had been friends of Duarte Barbosa and himself. They were in a good political position, but were engaged, along with Cristóbal de Haro, in a factional battle at court against the group favoring Governor General Affonso de Albuquerque. Neither of them showed any inclination to become his advocate. On the other hand, they were willing to revive the project to send him to Maluco in command of one of the caravels of Cristóbal de Haro. This, if it were arranged, might mean the reunion of Magellan and Francisco Serrano. However, various political barriers had to be overcome by Ferdinand himself, for Cristóbal de Haro could not give him command of one of his caravels unless he received a license from India House, which required the approval of the King. Moreover, they pointed out that Francisco Serrano was being pinned down at Ternate by the lieutenants of Governor General Albuquerque at Goa. His position was precarious and his foes were only biding their time until they could unseat him at Ternate or beguile him into falling into their power. It did not seem probable that the officials at Goa would permit Magellan to carry Francisco Serrano's treasure away. Unless some sort of safe-conduct were first secured from the King, both Real and Moreno feared that, even if Ferdinand Magellan were able to bring back Serrano's hoard from Ternate to Lisbon, Cristóbal de Haro would not be able to take title to it. They felt sure that it would be confiscated by India House as soon as it arrived, and they would only become involved in one of the interminable legal battles in which the lawyers of India House delighted to engage. It was obvious that Ferdinand Magellan must establish himself personally in the good graces of the monarch in order to get back to the East, or indeed to get any employment where his experience and talents could be used. Without the approval of Dom Manuel, nobody could be of help to him. As a member of the *Casa de ElRei,* Ferdinand Magellan now drew up, in formal documentary form, an humble petition to the King begging submissively that he be promoted to the post of *cavaleiro fidalgo.* He outlined modestly his long overseas services in Africa, India, and Malaya, mentioned the victories in which he had taken part, the wounds he had suffered, and the two official commendations which had been given him. He also claimed as an exploit worthy of reward his unauthorized exploration of the eastern waters beyond Malacca. He limited his supplication to asking for promotion, without mentioning his hope of another oriental command, but he solicited an audience by begging, in the court jargon to which autocratic Manuel best responded, the gracious boon of kissing the royal hand.

The recital of his many claims and the minor nature of the promotion requested made the granting of the petition appear probable, and Ferdinand's hopes rose. Several weeks passed without any word from the palace, and his advisers lost hope for him, although he himself still clung to the illusion that the silence was not ominous. Accordingly he remained in readiness for the summons to an audience.

Magellan's financial situation was becoming increasingly embarrassing, and his lawyer reported that Abraham Albradez had denied the legitimacy of his claim for repayment of his loan. It would be necessary to bring suit to obtain payment, and his lawyer advised him that, even were he successful, it would take at least a year to collect the money, and the court costs and legal fees would be heavy.

In this situation only one means of livelihood remained available for Ferdinand Magellan, his sword. Fortunately, an opportunity had arisen not only to find remunerative employment, but also to utilize his exceptional military talents to gain recognition. The approbation of *ElRei* was necessary to all his future projects, and military distinction would provide the best means to achieve this.

The rebel Berber chief, Muley Zeyam, Sheik of the tributory Moroccan state of Azamor on the North Atlantic seaboard of Africa, having made careful preparations to throw off the Portuguese yoke, had withheld his annual tribute and defied King Manuel to collect it. Dom Manuel therefore proceeded to raise a force large enough to crush the rebel and teach others an object lesson. The nobility were called upon to furnish their hereditary contingents, and the summons went out to the feudatory landholders of the Province of Minho, including Ferdinand's brother, Diogo de Sousa. The royal recruiting officer for the area about Ponte da Barca was Captain Ayres Teles, and Ferdinand Magellan joined his command as a volunteer. The high cost of obtaining a suitable charger must have presented a financial problem, and it is probable that Diogo provided one for him.

The great expedition against Muley Zeyam was under the titular command of the King's nephew, Jayme, Duke of Braganza. It comprised eighteen thousand infantry, two thousand cavalry, and a number of auxiliary troops. The armada was the largest ever despatched by Portugal and was made up of over four hundred vessels. John of Lisbon, then considered the leading navigator of Europe, had just been named as chief pilot. He had been engaged in secretly preparing a flotilla which Cristóbal de Haro proposed to send under his command to try to find a strait from the Atlantic Ocean through the American land mass westward to Maluco. The undertaking had Dom Manuel's tacit approval, but as it was illicit, in that it would trespass upon the zone reserved by treaty exclusively to Spain, he pretended ignorance and used de Haro to hide his participation. It was made to appear merely a profit-seeking, commercial venture. Actually it was to be an attempt by Portugal to control all routes from Europe to the Spiceries and, by discovery of a westward approach, to bolster its claim to the sole right to Maluco. Dom Manuel had had numerous conferences with John of Lisbon concerning the navigational and astronomic aspects of the adventure and had developed a liking for him and great confidence in his abilities. While John of Lisbon continued busily engaged in getting Cristóbal de Haro's squadron ready to sail, the King suddenly became apprehensive concerning the possibility of disaster to the large armada which was to carry his expedition down the coast of Africa. Perhaps some evidence of ineptitude in the management of the fleet alarmed the King and made him distrustful of the pomp and pageantry of the young Duke. At all events, he borrowed John of Lisbon's services from Cristóbal de Haro and gave him supreme responsibility for conveying the Duke and his army safely to Morocco.

John of Lisbon put little trust in the group of armored court dandies who made up the military and naval staff of the Duke, and chose as his own unofficial coadjutor and fellow pilot his old comrade, Captain Ferdinand Magellan, on whose expert judgment and professional skill he could rely. Ferdinand shared the cabin of John of Lisbon and acted as his aide throughout the voyage. The fleet cleared from Lisbon on August 13, 1513, and reached its destination without incident within a fortnight.

Once the army was disembarked, John of Lisbon gave up his post and hurried back to Portugal to resume work upon his own undertaking. Before leaving Morocco, he apparently called Ferdinand Magellan's abilities to the attention of the African proconsul, Count John de Meneses, who, with his veteran cavalry leader, John Soares, now had to take over the actual responsiblity of command from the Duke. Dom John Soares at once perceived how useful Ferdinand Magellan would be to him, appointed him to his staff, and employed him in important commands. Although the details of his service in Morocco are unknown, it is evident that Magellan's outstanding qualities of leadership brought him substantial promotion and won high commendation from his superiors. When he had gained advancement in the Orient by headlong valor and cool sagacity, he had been only twenty-five years old, but now he was over thirty-five and could offer experience as well as intrepidity. That he did not spare himself in Morocco is evidenced by the loss of his charger in a melee under the walls of Azamor, even before the main force had disembarked. He took part in the storming of the city, and when, in March, 1514, the Moors tried to retake it, he received a serious lance wound in the knee which lamed him for life.

Ferdinand Magellan then received a promotion from the General in Chief, Count John de Meneses, a reward that could only have been given to an officer of rank who had rendered unusually distinguished services. He was named one of the two *Quadrilheiro Mors* of the army. This was a combination of Provost Marshal, Captain of the Guard, and Master of the Horse. The *Quadrilheiro Mor* was responsible for the safekeeping of the prisoners of war and of the booty captured from the Moors. This position was an army plum, and its bestowal upon him must have been doubly welcome to Magellan, since the appointment was not only a mark of commendation for military merit, but also represented a chance to acquire financial independence and to aid his friends by privilege and favoritism. Undoubtedly it was the intention of Count de Meneses to have Magellan handle the spoils so as to foster the fortunes of those favored by the General in Chief, for this was the usual practice.

The possibilities of profit for Magellan may be appreciated when it is realized that every Moorish prisoner in his custody had a substantial monetary value, either for ransom or to be sold as a slave. An even more lucrative lot of plunder under his control were two-hundred thousand head of cattle and some three thousand camels and horses. These animals were the chief evidence of wealth in the peacetime economy of North Africa, and had great military utility in the mobile warfare of the desert. They could readily be disposed of anywhere for cash. Since there were no accurate official records of the exact number of human prisoners nor of captured animals, the opportunity and temptation to sell for personal profit were great.

As usual when fortune seemed to smile upon him, Ferdinand Magellan lost his patron. Count John de Meneses died suddenly on May 15, 1514, and Magellan was left at the mercy of his envious rivals.

The appointment of Magellan, who prior to the campaign had been virtually unknown in Europe and who was not even a member of the Order of Christ, to a position of such authority and financial possibilities had caused great discontent among the politicians who surrounded the Duke of Braganza. Now his foes officially preferred charges against him for malfeasance in office. This would not have been too serious an allegation, but they also accused him of collusion with the enemy and, specifically, of having delivered four hundred horses to the Moors by prearrangement during an alleged mock night raid. Magellan's superior, Dom John Soares, tried hard to defend him, but he could not prevail over Dom Pedro de Sousa, who had succeeded Meneses in the chief command, and who was hostile to Magellan. De Sousa dismissed Magellan from his post and ordered him tried by court-martial. Ferdinand Magellan unwisely treated the charges against him with disdain. The war now was over, he held only a volunteer's commission, and had been relieved of his post. Not asking Dom Pedro de Sousa for a formal discharge and angrily ignoring the court-martial pending against him, he left the army and returned to Portugal.

Ferdinand's thoughts were again all in the Orient, for in Morocco he had received another letter from Francisco Serrano, dilating upon the enormous value of his hoard of spices and urging his friend to come quickly, both to rescue him and to bring the treasure to Portugal.

Upon his arrival in Lisbon, Ferdinand was reimbursed for the loss of his horse, as is evidenced by the record of a claim against the crown notarized in Morocco on March 29, 1514. His lawyer also now informed him that he had secured a court order dated September 4, 1514, attaching a quantity of spices in the warehouse of India House belonging to the Albradez estate, and he felt reassured that he would have some capital to invest in copper to barter for spices in Ternate. He was anxious to complete his arrangements to get a ship from Lorenzo Morena and Antonio Real, and he seems to have become hopeful that he could get royal permission to return to the Orient. His confidence in this respect no doubt was based upon the favorable reports of his military exploits which had been sent to the King by Count John de Meneses and Dom John Soares.

He was quite oblivious to the fact that his departure from the army in Morocco was unauthorized, and that he had thereby infuriated his already antagonistic superior. Dom Pedro de Sousa no doubt thought that Magellan's sudden departure for Portugal evidenced an intention to appeal to the King and perhaps denounce his accusers. Therefore, he at once sent a letter to the King complaining of Magellan's desertion.

When Dom Manuel received a request from Ferdinand Magellan for a private audience, he probably assumed that it concerned his situation in the Moroccan Campaign. Dom Manuel granted the audience and apparently was surprised when Ferdinand Magellan did not speak of recent events in Morocco, but presented his proposal to sail east either for the King or for Cristóbal de Haro, to establish for the King a fort in Maluco, and to hold it for him, despite his own frankly expressed belief that the Spiceries lay on the Spanish side of the line of demarcation. Dom Manuel had no inclination to give Ferdinand Magellan any such favorable appointment, nor would he have trusted him in such a capacity. However, he dissembled his personal hostility and, instead of expressing himself upon it, changed the subject, took a serious view of Magellan's departure from the army without leave, rebuked him for desertion, and sternly ordered him back to face the charges against him.

Magellan at once returned to Morocco and reported to his commander for trial. His foes, since they had succeeded in having him discredited and ousted from his post, had not bothered to press the case, but had left it pending. Magellan now insisted that he be formally tried.

The testimony presented in the trial is not available, but in the factional quarrels in Dom Manuel's armed forces the use of calumny was a common weapon, and cabals of officers did not hesitate to use perjury and forgery to oust the holder of a coveted post. Magellan's real offense had been his display of military genius and his rapid rise in rank. It is probable that his enemies had not troubled themselves to make more than unsupported allegations. These they had to let drop when Ferdinand Magellan, awakened to the seriousness of his case by the King's censure, began to present a spirited defense. One of the two counts of the indictment was that he had used his office to line his own pockets. It was then the custom for paymasters, quartermasters, and sutlers to enrich themselves by lucrative perquisites without anyone protesting, but Ferdinand Magellan could not have profited in such a manner, for when he was discharged he was entirely without funds. Indeed Count de Meneses may have appointed him in the expectation that he would prove to be that rarity, an honest quartermaster. If so, the attack upon him by the politicians can well be understood.

The second count, that of selling captured horses to the enemy, appears preposterous, in view of the character of Magellan. Had the accusation been seriously believed, Magellan would have been subjected to torture and, if found guilty, put to death. His enemies obviously failed entirely to establish their case.

The defendant was unable to secure a clear-cut acquittal, and the indeterminate verdict of "not proved" was later to cause embarrassment to him. However, three years later, when the factor of India House in Seville made inquiry by letter of Diego de Haro, the banker at Lisbon, concerning the reliability and reputation of Ferdinand Magellan, he was informed by return of post that Magellan was entitled to full confidence. Had there been any credence given in Lisbon to the Moroccan charges, it is certain that Diego de Haro would not have endorsed Magellan's character as he did.

Upon his unsatisfactory and qualified acquittal, Ferdinand secured his formal discharge from the army and returned again to Lisbon with the expectation of hastening back to the East.

When he reported for duty at the palace and resumed his post as gentleman in waiting, Magellan again made official application for an audience. Anxious weeks passed, but he received no acknowledgment of his request. There was nothing he could do to expedite his application. It was already late in the year, and unless he could make his preparations and set sail before the end of March, he would have to wait nine months before the weather would again permit a voyage to Maluco. Francisco Serrano's great political power in Ternate was like ruling over a volcano; and Magellan knew, from his long experience in the Far East, how dangerous another year's delay could be for him.

At last he decided to risk everything by audaciously accosting *ElRei* without formal permission. He had no tactful friend at court to warn him how ill-advised was this resolution. His opportunity soon arose, for Dom Manuel held one of the periodic public audiences in which petitions were laid at his feet. On such occasions, access could not be obtained to the steps of the throne without prior examination of each petitioner by the ushers, even though as a matter of public policy the traditional right of supplication to the ruler was open to all. Those who approached the Monarch in such a manner were usually humble subjects who lacked the political influence to obtain a private audience. The subject matter of these public appeals often had human interest, and consequently the King's favorites gathered about the royal seat as spectators and the hall itself was filled with courtiers. It was before such an assembly that Ferdinand Magellan, driven to desperation by the snubs and rebuffs he had received, decided to play his part. He contrived to be on duty in the hall; by an appropriate bribe, he had his name inserted at the last moment on the list, and by gifts to his fellow ushers he insured himself against their possible interference. He had carefully rehearsed his petition, and, when his moment arrived, he steeled himself for the ordeal as if for battle.

When the herald called out the name of Ferdinand Magellan, it attracted no attention, but when the figure of the lame usher appeared and knelt at the steps of the dais, there was a murmur of surprise from the audience;

Drawing after the portrait by Blas del Prado, 1519, Museo de S. Roque, Lisbon

MANUEL THE FORTUNATE, KING OF PORTUGAL

the Monarch frowned in perceptible annoyance. In the abject posture which etiquette required, Ferdinand begged that his *moradia,* or monthly subsistence allowance in the *Casa de ElRei,* be raised by a few *maravedis.* This was the ancient formula whereby a member of the household attained advancement to the rank of *fidalgo da casa de ElRei.* The increase in token pay meant the high honor of advancement in rank. After making his request, Ferdinand Magellan, without pausing, supported his plea with a modest statement of his twenty years service in the household of the King's sister and of *ElRei* himself. He mentioned the battles in which he had taken part and the three wounds which he had suffered.

As Magellan concluded, Dom Manuel's face hardened, and he brusquely responded that the request for the increased *moradia* was denied. The cold rebuff shook Magellan's confidence, for he had not expected a flat refusal. However, he remained kneeling and stammered a request that he again he allowed to serve *ElRei* as he had done hitherto, in command of a caravel to Maluco, citing his experience in the Far East. He made this request, although he knew it would be rejected, as a preliminary to asking for a leave of absence from the royal household and a license to go to the Orient in a privately owned merchant ship, which he was confident would be granted.

Dom Manuel answered his petition for the command of a royal caravel with a sharp and emphatic negative, and then, to Magellan's consternation, he added in a tone of flat finality that he had no opening anywhere for his services. Magellan could hardly believe his ears at the vindictiveness of the last remark. He now forced himself to ask his last boon, the license to sail on a private ship, and felt completely hopeless when the King muttered a peevish no.

There was nothing more to be said. Stunned and confused, he knew he should now retire as quickly as possible. Yet the contempt in the King's last words, together with a great sense of indignation at the injustice with which he was being treated, aroused his pugnacity. He doggedly held his place. As though in a dream, he heard himself cry out, almost defiantly, asking whether he might enter the service of another lord. His hoarse cry of protest seemed to sting the despot. Dom Manuel rose from his chair and towered over the suppliant, whose small stature was accentuated by his kneeling posture on the step of the dais. He paused a moment, apparently attempting to keep his composure and to give an indifferent answer, but his exasperation and dislike got the better of him, and he shouted venomously that he did not care what Magellan did nor where he went.

The nightmarish humiliation was more terrible than he had ever imagined possible, but Magellan, confusedly following the inherited instinct of generations of loyal fidalgos, begged in a low voice that he be allowed to kiss the royal hand in farewell. The aroused King, instead of conceding this pitiful favor, spitefully withdrew his hand and turned his back upon him. Magellan could have received no greater disgrace. He gazed uncomprehendingly for a moment at Dom Manuel's back before he painfully rose and, with bent head, backed awkwardly from the royal presence. His lameness hampered him, and he stumbled. One of the courtiers called out to abandon his bogus limp, and there was a storm of derisive laughter. Ferdinand crept from the audience chamber and fled, an outcast from the palace.

This unusual incident created a sensation in court circles, and almost all their contemporaries upheld the King and condemned Ferdinand Magellan; they would hardly have dared do otherwise. Garcia da Orta, in his book published some years later, described Ferdinand Magellan as "the Devil entered into the body of a Portuguese." Vasco da Gama echoed the chorus of the court against Magellan by saying, "When Ferdinand Magellan complained at the rejection of his request for an advancement in the royal household, had Dom Manuel then ordered him beheaded, he could not later have done against the King what he did." This obvious statement carefully avoids expressing an opinion, although it seems to do so. Da Gama himself was so frantic at Dom Manuel's failure to reward him according to his deserts that in 1518, the year after Magellan had left Portugal for Spain, he petitioned King Manuel for permission to do likewise. It was only by this overt threat that he was able at last to obtain the rewards long promised him by the King. Dom Manuel wielded despotic power, and it is easy to understand why all the court historians joined in a chorus against Magellan.

Dom Manuel no doubt felt justified in his refusal to give Magellan a promotion, and he found ample reason for the rejection of his application to return to the East. It will be remembered that both Governor General Albuquerque, in India, and General Pedro de Sousa, in Morocco, had written the King complaining of Magellan. He was identified with the two Serranos and with the group headed by Duarte Barbosa, who were suspected of secret Spanish relations. Moreover, Magellan had embarrassed the King by his persistence in averring that Maluco lay in the zone of Castile.

However, the King's manner in rebuffing Magellan disclosed a real personal animosity toward him. One chronicler states that Dom Manuel "detested Magellan from the beginning." This rancor may, as we have noted, have stemmed from some incident of their youth, when Ferdinand belonged to the group favored by King John II, while Manuel was in a somewhat precarious position, under the protection of his sister, Queen Eleanor. Whatever may have been the grudge nursed by that unforgiving autocrat, Magellan's ill-advised public appeal gave him a perfect occasion to vent it. No one could henceforth be in any doubt where Magellan stood in the estimation of his monarch.

After Ferdinand had bolted from the scene of his disgrace, his sole desire was to get away from the capital as soon as possible. He gathered up his books and belongings and managed to get passage that same night on an English merchantman bound for Porto, where he sought obscurity in a small mariners' tavern near the waterfront. He found sympathizers for his grievances in an insignificant group of unfortunate returned veterans like himself, who met unnoticed in modest taverns in Porto. Even here, Magellan knew he must be careful, for Dom Manuel's spies were everywhere.

In Porto he was ostracized by the members of good society. His public repudiation by the King led his former acquaintances to assume he must have been guilty of disgraceful crimes in the Orient. There were only a few carefree sea captains and navigators who, sailor-like, were independent of courts and conventions, who cared to see him. It was humiliating, too, to be so freely accepted as one of their own by discredited former comrades in the Orient, many of them with dubious records.

By his resignation from the army Magellan had relinquished his military pay and subsistence, and by his dismissal from the royal household he was deprived of his salary as a gentleman usher. The rents from his small estate at Sabrosa were inadequate to support him, and he undoubtedly had to borrow from his brother until he could collect the sum due him from Albradez. It had even become a burden for him to support his slave, Enrique, who in his extremity had become his sole confidant and whose devotion offered him what solace he had.

Night after night he sat in the noisy, torch-lit taproom of the tavern, feeling a man apart. In imagination he was far away from Porto, steering his caravel once more through Malayan archipelagoes teeming with ginger, mace, sandalwood, and camphor. Perhaps he thought of the storms of the Indian Ocean, or the rushing currents of the hazardous Indonesian straits. Then he would come back to the present abruptly, drain his tankard, and limp off into the darkness, knowing himself to be a master mariner without a ship, a disarmed cavalier without a mount.

The proceedings against Albradez at last began to make some progress, and Magellan pushed the matter energetically. The record shows that on September 4, 1514, the Crown sequestered a quantity of pepper belonging to the Abraldez estate which was located in the warehouse of the spice department of the *Casa de India.* On December 4th, a formal court action was entered against the Albradez estate. On June 5, 1515, the suit was decided against Albradez, and judgment was rendered. On July 4th, Magellan executed a power of attorney in favor of Duarte de Sousa, apparently his lawyer and presumably a relative, to receive payment of the proceeds. On November 24th, the sum of two hundred cruzados, plus the interest due, was paid in Ponte de Lima to Duarte de Sousa for the account of Ferdinand Magellan.

Magellan had thus been living in Porto almost a year before he again came into possesion of his capital. He did not dare draw freely upon it for his maintenance, for it was practically all he had; but, with the lawsuit settled and his capital in hand, he could turn his mind to the problem of what to do next. It was hopeless, he realized, to expect to get employment on a Portuguese ship, and there were very few other markets for his services. He ruled out both Genoa and Venice, since their merchants were no longer in a position to employ sailors to poach upon Portuguese waters. For different reasons, he also felt that both England and France were out of the question. In England, the major interest was in finding a northwest passage to India, and he knew nothing about the North. To sail for France in Portuguese waters would mean becoming a corsair, outside the law, which he did not wish to do.

There was only one place where he could possibly expect to find employment, the Court of Spain. Captain John Serrano was now in the service of the Spanish India House, and the uncle of his friend, Duarte Barbosa, was head of the arsenal in Seville; they might provide him with a few introductions to Spanish authorities.

Some years previously, John Dias de Solis, a refugee from Portuguese justice who had risen to high favor in Spain, had convinced King Ferdinand that Maluco lay in the Spanish zone. Don Ferdinand therefore became interested in finding the westward passage rumored to exist through the American land mass. From then on, Bishop Fonseca, who was at the head of Don Ferdinand's maritime establishment, sent various expeditions to probe along the American coast for the strait. Bishop Fonseca had finally assured the Spanish Regent, Cardinal Ximenes, after Don Ferdinand's death, that Maluco was certainly in the Spanish zone, and moreover that the westward route from Spain to the Orient did not trespass in the area assigned to Portugal. The Regent therefore ignored the protest of the Portuguese Ambassador and authorized Bishop Fonseca to prepare a royal expedition to Maluco, utilizing whatever ocean passageway could be found in the West.

The Bishop thought it best to find a Portuguese commander for the expedition, since the Portuguese were well acquainted with navigation south of the Equator. Captains Estevan Gomes, Juan Diaz Golez, and John Dias de Solis competed for the post. De Solis received the appointment, and his expedition of three caravels sailed on October 8, 1515.

At first this news seemed a terrible blow to Ferdinand Magellan, who might have hoped for such a command himself. However, he soon realized that, if de Solis succeeded in establishing a route to Maluco across the

Atlantic, an active traffic would ensue in which he would have a good chance. He might well hope to secure a command from Bishop Fonseca and establish the contact he had long desired with Francisco Serrano in Ternate.

At about this time, Magellan met Ruy de Faleiro, another impoverished outcast from the court and from the world of action, whom he had known slightly as a boy. These two men, each of gentle birth, each educated in the pages' school of the *Casa de ElRei,* each of considerable earlier distinction, soon became close friends. Magellan, an intellectual man of action, and Faleiro, an active man of reflection, were both profoundly versed in astronomy and geography. To each of them it meant a great deal to find a friend to whom he could unburden himself.

Ruy de Faleiro was recognized as one of the leading Portuguese astronomers of his day. He and his brother Francisco had been school-fellows of Magellan years before, in the King's household; they had distinguished themselves at the pages' school by their proficiency in the study of celestial navigation. Although they later became the leaders in this science in Portugal, they failed to win the favor of King Manuel. When Ruy de Faleiro sought appointment to the vacant post of Astronomer Royal, he was passed over in favor of a less erudite but more courtly savant. Both brothers then retired from court. Francisco left Portugal for Spain and became an associate in Barcelona of the scholarly brothers Reinel, the Portuguese geographers who had been persuaded by Bishop Fonseca to enter the Spanish service as hydrographers and nautical advisers. Here Francisco de Faleiro attained high renown and became the author of the first book on navigation to be published in Spain.

Ruy de Faleiro, however, did not go to Spain with his brother, but retired from Lisbon to Porto. After a long period of study, he produced a set of navigational tables so simple in form that even an unlettered pilot could easily calculate his position on the chart of the Atlantic Ocean; he seems to have evolved his tables empirically by studying the logbooks of many Portuguese pilots. Since they were based upon observations almost exclusively from the part of the Atlantic which surrounded the Azores, his formulas could be used effectively only in the area between the 30th and 40th degrees North latitude. Although in reality his empirical longitudinal theory was one of very limited application, at that time it was accepted with respect by both navigators and students.

It will be recalled that, after leaving Magellan in Morocco, in the spring of 1514, John of Lisbon had departed on his clandestine search for the westward passage to Maluco under the auspices of Cristóbal de Haro. He now returned to Portugal and was distressed to learn of Magellan's disgrace at court. He soon found a pretext to go to Porto to look up his old comrade.

John of Lisbon pronounced Magellan's plans for Spanish service quite feasible, and proceeded to divulge to him the secret information which he had secured for Cristóbal de Haro. On October 12, 1514, he had discovered Cape Santa Maria, which he did not know, of course, was at the mouth of the La Plata River. He sailed some distance up the broad estuary and became convinced that it was the long-sought strait to the West. Since his orders from Cristóbal de Haro had explicitly prohibited lingering in the Spanish area, for fear of complications, he took his observations as quickly as possible, locating the strait at the 20th parallel, and sailed back into Portuguese waters off the coast of Brazil.

He returned from the Antilles not only with a profitable cargo of Indian slaves, dye wood, and multicolored macaws, but also a number of silver ornaments procured from the Indians on the shore of the estuary. These Indians had excited him with a story of a mountain of silver to the west, information we now know to have been correct, except that the Indians failed to tell him how far west. Actually, their silver mountain at Potosi was thousands of miles away.

John of Lisbon, in his anxiety to help his old comrade, gave him full information from his own logs and charts, together with data on the course, including the bearings, soundings, anchorages, shoals, currents, and landmarks. He also told Magellan that Cristóbal de Haro had accumulated considerable navigational data concerning the American coast from several previous voyages of exploration and discovery, and this was now on deposit in the King's chartroom in Lisbon. These secret expeditions, he said, had gone much farther south along the continent and had reported a sharp westward trend of the coast. Its contours had reminded him of the line of the eastern coast of Africa below the equator, with which both he and Magellan were thoroughly familiar. John of Lisbon therefore thought it probable that, if the strait at Cape Santa Maria should not prove navigable, he could navigate around the unknown extremity of the continent, just as Bartholomew Dias had sailed around the southern tip of Africa. Magellan agreed it was likely that the land mass of the western hemisphere would be found, if followed far enough south, to taper off to a point, just as did the African continent.

Apparently there was a secret sympathy on the part of the veteran pilots of Lisbon for their maltreated colleague, and some one, probably John of Lisbon, was able to arrange for Magellan to have access to the royal chartroom, where he could inspect the logs, rutters, and charts describing the winds and currents of the Southwest Atlantic. These secrets were closely guarded by Dom George de Vasconcelos, custodian of the chartroom where, since November 13, 1504, a royal decree had concentrated all maps, globes, and log books pertaining to navigation south of the equator.

Ferdinand Magellan was overjoyed to find in the chartroom a sphere made by the Bohemian cartographer, Martin Behaim, which definitely showed a strait cutting across the southern part of South America, joining the Atlantic to the Great South Sea just about where John of Lisbon had described it, at the 20th parallel. The globe was not explicit, showing a blank place where the strait was, but there was a secret key in cipher which gave the details. Magellan may have made an exact copy of this globe, but in view of his resentment of Dom Manuel's treatment, he would probably not have hesitated to purloin the original, which he later used to good effect in his negotiations with the Spanish authorities.

When Magellan returned to Porto, he told Ruy de Faleiro the results of his investigation, and the two partners began to build up the case they meant to present to Spain. Early in 1516, they learned that Captain General John de Solis had been killed by natives while exploring the very strait of Santa Maria which John of Lisbon had discovered in the preceding year, and that his fleet had returned to Seville. Although Magellan and Faleiro were disappointed to learn that the secret of the location of the strait was already in the possession of Spain, Magellan felt that there would be an opening for him in its exploration.

Ferdinand was pondering the best means of getting in touch with Bishop Fonseca, the head of India House in Spain, when the question was answered for him in a very satisfactory manner. His old friend, Duarte Barbosa, paid him a secret visit in Porto. Barbosa had finally completed the monumental book on the geography of the Far East to which he had devoted so many years. At the same time, disheartened by the defeat of his party there, he had resigned his writership in the factor's office at Cananor and returned to Portugal. In Lisbon he had met the same frigid reception as John Serrano, Magellan, and the others of his faction, and had realized that he had no future in the Portuguese service.

He left Lisbon for a visit with his family at Seville. His uncle, Diogo Barbosa, told him of Bishop Fonseca's desire to renew the effort begun with John de Solis to reach Maluco. Diogo Barbosa had married an heiress of one of the most prominent aristocratic families in Andalusia and had himself accumulated a vast fortune; as Governor of the Castle and of the Arsenal in Seville, he occupied a position of influence. There was no one in Europe better acquainted with oriental conditions than he or his nephew Duarte, and they both realized the feasibility of the westward project proposed by Bishop Fonseca, provided it were captained by a mariner of boldness and ability. Duarte first thought of Captain John Serrano, who already was a pilot in the Spanish service, and he drew him into the consultations. John, however, suggested that his cousin, Ferdinand Magellan, next to his own brother Francisco Serrano, was the pilot best qualified to navigate the waters east of Malacca. Although John Serrano had managed to keep in close touch with Ferdinand in Porto, it would have been dangerous for him to cross the border. Duarte Barbosa was still free to do so, and it was decided that he should be the intermediary with Ferdinand Magellan and attempt to enlist him in their plans.

Diogo Barbosa was well aware that Dom Manuel would resent Spain's employment of Ferdinand Magellan. Therefore he laid the idea before Bishop Fonseca, who in turn secured the approval of Cardinal Regent Ximenes. Fonseca then authorized Duarte Barbosa to offer the command of such an expedition to Magellan on general terms, the details to be worked out after his arrival in Spain.

When Duarte Barbosa made the proposal to Ferdinand Magellan in Porto, his friend informed him that he would make no contract with India House in Spain unless his comrade, Faleiro, could participate as an equal partner. Duarte Barbosa had been impressed by the astronomical attainments of Faleiro and felt that he would prove a valuable acquisition to India House; therefore, he agreed to Ferdinand Magellan's terms and offered employment of a high nature in the proposed expedition to both of them.

While he was in Porto, Magellan introduced several other well-qualified, veteran Indian pilots, including his cousin, Alvaro de Mesquita, to Barbosa. Barbosa must have communicated with his uncle in Seville by messenger, for he soon authorized Magellan to employ several pilots with promises of attractive compensation.

Dom Manuel's spies were everywhere, but the arrangements were carried out with all the secrecy necessary to a conspiracy. Magellan bade farewell to Duarte Barbosa in private when his friend left Porto. They both felt satisfied at the tentative agreements they had made.

Ruy Faleiro suddenly informed Ferdinand that he could not leave Porto immediately, and for a moment Magellan's confidence was almost shaken. However, he kept to his determination, arranged with Ruy that he should follow later, and completed his plans. He had hired several Portuguese pilots for the adventure that lay ahead, and he and these men boarded a ship singly, so as to avoid notice.

As the ship left the harbor, Ferdinand breathed freely again. His men joined him on the small deck, and they exchanged a few words in loud voices, for the first time careless of eavesdroppers.

At last Magellan felt he had made the break with Portugal and the past. He was on his way to Seville to enter the service of Spain, and his explorations would henceforth be for the benefit of that country.

CHAPTER IX

JAKOB FUGGER, BANKER OF THE EMPIRE

FERDINAND MAGELLAN, in going to Seville, came to one of those punctuation points in a man's life which put a full stop to one epoch and leave him ready to begin another. In this pause, it will be well to take stock of the background of the next great undertaking, and in particular of some of the leading members of the *dramatis personae* who stand behind the curtain which is about to go up. A picture of these men will set the broad scene and explain the causes that put the events in motion. The first of these Titans whose influence formed Magellan's world was a little German banker from Augsburg who was already a man in his prime when Ferdinand was born in Portugal.

Jakob Fugger's personal and fiscal interest in the expedition of Magellan was brought about by a chain of economic developments that began around 1453, when Constantinople fell to the Turks, and coincided with the beginning of the Renaissance period and of modern history. Jakob's life span encompassed the transition of European finance from medieval usury to modern industrial capitalism and international banking. With supreme dexterity, he steered through the series of economic storms that engulfed his contemporaries and availed himself of changing business tides and shifting political winds to accelerate the advancement of his own amazing schemes. These eventually made him master of the finances of Europe and its colonies.

Fugger subtly initiated and dominated Magellan's undertaking through his lieutenant, Cristóbal de Haro. How he did this can best be shown by first sketching the preliminary happenings. It was imperative for the

Drawing after Hans Holbein, original in Staatsbesitz, Berlin

JAKOB FUGGER, INTERNATIONAL BANKER

House of Fugger to maintain a continuous flow of its imports of pepper, spices, and dyestuffs. Fugger consistently supported Venice, his long-time partner in the spice trade, in her heroic struggle against Florence for control of this commerce with the Orient.

In 1459, when Jakob Fugger was born in Augsburg, in what is now Germany, it might be said that the great civilized powers of the world were the four vast empires of the Orient, which took but dim cognizance of the huddled cluster of Christian nations in Europe. The leading European powers were the petty commonwealths of Venice, Florence, and Genoa, all three drawing their strength from Asia. Southeastern Europe was on the defensive against invasion by Asia, which had already annexed the Balkans. In the southwest, Europe was trying to free itself from the inroads of Africa, which was so strongly entrenched at Granada in Spain. Within Jakob's lifetime the discoveries of printing, papermaking, gunpowder, and the science of navigation were to transform European civilization and commerce and to give it domination over Africa and Asia. In this great awakening of Europe, Jakob Fugger, the financier, was to play his part.

Jakob was of the third Augsburg generation of a burgher clan that had been made wealthy and influential by Venetian patronage. In 1350, more than a century before Jakob's birth, the farsighted Signory of Venice, disturbed by the constant interruption to its industry caused by incessant wars in northern Italy, decided to transfer some of its manufacturing activities to more stable areas which were accessible through Alpine passes. The enlightened Venetians encouraged the establishment of locally owned textile industries in South Germany, taught the Swabians their manufacturing secrets, and extended credit to them.

As the Swabian industry expanded, it fell under control of an unprogressive group of business leaders who attempted to limit the growth of the area for their own private enrichment. Not only the Venetians but also the guilds of workers resented this throttling of commerce; about 1375, an ambitious demagogue named Johannes Fugger organized the workers, overthrew the oligarchs, gained the confidence of the sympathetic Venetian overlords, and thereby managed to assume industrial leadership. He had come to Augsburg, the capital of Swabia, as a poor country weaver, but by his political acumen and his organizing ability he gradually won the trust of his fellows.

Egypt had a monopoly of European trade with the Orient, and through a long-standing treaty had restricted its sales of spices to the Republic of Venice. The stream of spices flowed in a single channel from Egypt to Venice, whence it branched out in all directions by galley or sailing cog, river boat, packsaddle, or creaking wain, to be distributed by the spice trust of the Hanseatic League of Free Cities to the fairs and markets of all Europe.

The demand for spices dominated the economy of Europe. The term spices covered not only Arabic condiments, but also other rare Eastern commodities. It described those imported drugs, narcotics, and simples which formed the basis of the European pharmacopoeia. It also covered all those aromatic ingredients of strong scents then used as perfume by both sexes, and also such indispensable industrial items for manufacturers as bleaches, dyes, pigments, gums, resins, and the embalming preservatives used by all undertakers.

The call for pepper and other piquant preservatives was constant because there was never an adequate supply of winter forage in Northern Europe and hence most meat animals had to be slaughtered in the autumn. It became general practice to preserve the great autumn surplus of meat by the use of pepper and other spices, particularly as the seasoning disguised the partially spoiled condition of much of the meat. Pepper was in reality not a luxury for the rich, but a necessity for the well-being of all classes. Strong flavors moreover became customary in good cookery and also in wines and beer, and since the palates of Europeans called for increasingly liberal use of imported spices to offset the unpalatibility and sameness of the poor food then obtainable, the market demand for them appeared insatiable.

Initially, spices were only dried berries, nuts, roots, leaves, and pieces of peeled bark; these grew wild in such profusion in the Moluccas, called the Spice Islands, that they were gathered, baled, and sold for the trivial cost of native labor in picking them. The Malay merchants who bought them so cheaply from the local rulers in the Spiceries had to risk both their sailing vessels and their lives, in the narrow seas infested with Chinese pirate junks, in transporting them to market at Malacca, on the Malay Peninsula.

At Malacca, visiting Hindu traders from India purchased the spices from the Malays, paid a heavy tax to the Sultan of Malacca, and then ran a gauntlet of Malay marauders with bases in the islands in the Bay of Bengal and the Indian Ocean. The cargoes that got safely through from Malacca to the emporium of Calicut, on the Malabar Coast of India, were sold there by the Hindus at a good profit to Arab traders, who also paid a substantial tariff to the local potentate, the Zamorin of Calicut.

The Arabs, with their cargoes of spices from Calicut, sailed for Egypt in fleets in order to beat off the squadrons of Hindu raiders that swept the Arabian Sea. Once safe in the Red Sea, the merchandise, if destined for Alexandria, could be landed at the port of Massaua, Abyssinia, and in consideration of payments for protection to the local chiefs would be escorted by black spearmen carrying shields of hippopotamus hide through Ethiopia to the Egyptian border, and thence to Alexandria by camel and by river dhow. If consigned to Beirut, Syria, the cargo would be discharged at the Arabian port of Jidda and conveyed by caravan across the desert, successive tributes being paid to the sheiks and emirs of the fortified oases along the way.

The loss by Arab merchants in both overland passages was considerable. Caravans were composed of numerous units of fifty camels fastened head to tail by ropes, each string led by an ass that slowly picked the way. The grunting, swaying beasts, plodding along at two miles an hour, could make at best no more than twenty-four miles a day, for although the serpentine line got under way before dawn, it had to make several halts for rest before making camp at dusk. Even though it was accompanied by a rabble of motley guards, it was impossible to defend by foot soldiers such a crawling, strung-out column against ambush by bold, well mounted Bedouins. The many gullies and ridges of the desert favored surprise attacks by raiding bands concentrating against a weak section of the extended line, and the Arab traders often saw their rich cargoes snatched from them, and deemed themselves fortunate to escape slavery or death.

When the dusty caravans reached the ports of Alexandria, on the Nile, or Beirut, in Syria, the Sultan of Egypt collected a full third of the highly inflated value of the merchandise from the Venetians who came to convey their treasure over the Mediterranean. This final convoy across the inland sea was menaced not only by blockading galleys of the Turkish navy, but also by Salee rovers, who lay in wait for any lagging ship. If the convoy was unlucky enough to be scattered by storm or attack, not only the ships and their cargoes, but also their owners and crews were seized as slaves by the corsairs, to be auctioned off in the markets of Tripoli or Tunis. Even in the well patrolled Adriatic, which was considered a Venetian lake, there were losses of vessels to Albanian raiders who crept out in small boats at night to board stragglers from the convoys.

The pyramiding of transportation costs and taxes, of gabelle, cumshaw, squeeze, and baksheesh, added to the multiplicity of profits on as many as twenty separate resales between the spiceries and the European markets, so increased the value of spices that it has been calculated that a bale of dried leaves which had originally cost one ducat in the isles of Amboina or Ternate would sell in London or Bruges for one hundred ducats, or 10,000 per cent of the original price.

At the Rialto in Venice, importers from all Europe gathered at the great yearly fair to welcome the arrival of the spice fleet. The supply of Oriental stuffs was far below demand, so that avid speculators competed fiercely for the goods. It was then that the Venetian importers reaped their harvest.

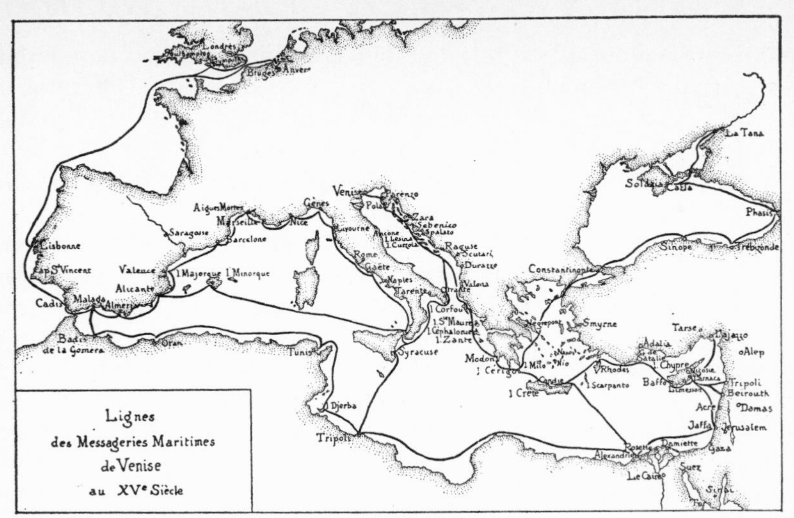

From "Messageries maritimes de Venise," 1938

SEA ROUTES OF THE VENETIAN GALLEYS

Engraving from de Bry's "Peregrinationes," 1599

SPICE CARAVAN ON THE WAY TO ALEPPO

The Venetians let Johannes Fugger make allocation to the Swabian plants of the wool, cotton, alum, and dyes which they needed. By this control of raw materials, he was able to extort from the manufacturers a monopoly of the sale of the finished products. He then built up a large weaving and finishing business of his own and established a profitable chain of distributing outlets in the Hanseatic counters, as the Hanseatic markets were called. When he died in 1407, his sons and grandsons continued to follow his strict rules, one of which was to retain all earnings in the partnership, and to continue it as a close-knit but expansive family enterprise.

Jakob, a grandson of old Johannes, was given every educational advantage that an opulent and cultured family could command. Since his older brothers intended to enter the firm, his parents planned to have him become a priest. The Church offered a promising career for a youth with Jakob's connections, and a brilliant ecclesiastical future undoubtedly lay ahead of him.

At the age of fourteen, when he had already taken minor holy orders, Jakob was called upon to withdraw from the divinity school to devote his talents to the counting room. His father and uncles had all died in the prime of life, and had left the burden of directing the family business to his brother Ulrich, eighteen years his senior. Ulrich summoned Jakob to come to his assistance. It was vital that he learn the business as quickly as possible, and Ulrich decided that he could best do so in Venice. Consequently, in 1473 Jakob was installed as an apprentice in the Venetian branch of the Fuggers, located in the palatial House of the Teutons, on the Grand Canal, just east of the Bridge of the Rialto.

Venice at that time was not only Europe's chief market place, but also its greatest shipbuilding center, its foremost transport agent, and one of the leading manufacturing communities, rivaling Ghent and surpassing Florence, Nuremberg, and Lyon in the diversity and the volume of industrial production. Over thirty thousand persons worked in the wool industry, six thousand in silk weaving and dyeing, and many thousands in the manufacture of laces, brocades, velvet and satin. The Venetians were foremost in the manufacture of gilt leather, used for clothing, household hangings, and horse furniture; they also virtually monopolized glassmaking.

Venetian manufacturers had a great competitive advantage since Venice controlled the importation of dyes and raw materials for all Europe. Domestic tranquillity and satisfactory living conditions for the masses characterized the internal economy of Venice for centuries, and its workers had never suffered the periodic crises of unemployment that caused bloody riots in other manufacturing towns. No provision of an armed guard for the Doge or for the municipal buildings and rich palaces was necessary, and the buildings were in marked contrast to the castle-like public edifices and fortified private mansions of the Florentines, who feared sack by the turbulent populace.

Although this prosperity was not to last long, in the face of Portugal's success in wresting the spice trade for itself, the Republic of Venice at the end of the fifteenth century occupied a position of primacy in world commerce similar to that of Great Britain in later days. It owed its influence to preponderant sea power and to the possession of a system of strategically placed naval bases and overseas trading depots that gave it mastery of trade with the Orient. Disruption and unemployment in its industries lay ahead as a result of its imminent loss of trade preeminence, but for the present Venice still was supreme.

Into this complicated and cut-throat world, young Jakob was plunged. He started from the bottom as an office boy and rapidly worked up through the textile department, the metals division, and the money changing department. After becoming familiar with the complicated world currencies and learning the rudiments of banking, Jakob was transferred to the spice division of the firm. This was subdivided into two branches, known as the grocers' department and the mercers' department. Earlier, the official name of the merchants had been pepperers, but this was changed to grocers, or dealers in gross lots, indicating that the merchants of the guild were wholesalers, rather than retail dealers, in pepper. Although the coat of arms of the Grocers' Guild showed a camel bearing a bale of spices on its back, the grocers handled only pepper, and were not allowed by their charter to deal in other spices. Pepper represented over seventy per cent of the total volume of the spice trade. Other spices were marketed in smaller lots and in a less speculative manner by the Worshipful Company of Mercers.

The Grocers' and the Mercers' guilds had impressive guild halls in all the cities of Europe, and drew up minute regulations controlling the sale of spices at fixed prices and terms. They allocated supplies to territories, had their own courts for settlement of disputes, established standards of quality and weights, and regulated trademarks. Their memberships were exclusive and their discipline severe. Annual dues were high, and an additional source of revenue was the system of fines assessed on member concerns for any infringements of the rules.

The spice department of the Fuggers was by far the most profitable part of the business. Jakob was initiated into its jealously guarded secrets, which were called the "mystery or art of the Grocers' Guild."

Pepper was the first fungible commodity to be traded in by European speculators, that is to say, the first of such uniform grade and character that any unit of it could be exchanged for a similar quantity in any market. Since the peppercorns had a value equal to their weight in gold, did not readily deteriorate, and were always in short supply and hence immediately salable, and since bags of pepper were easily stored and transported, pepper became the favorite medium for market gambling. Its price was volatile, and soared and plunged on the Rialto. Frankly a speculative medium, it was driven up and down by every trick and artifice of unrestricted manipulation.

The pepper trust, headed by the Fuggers, maintained a strategic reserve, and could squeeze out the shorts by pretending to have no free pepper available, or could bring down a top-heavy market with a crash by suddenly flooding it with offers of spot pepper. The banking department of the Fuggers made large profits from short-term loans to the pepper gamblers on the Rialto; they co-operated with the other Venetian banks to maintain a corner on the scanty available supply of gold and silver specie, which the outside speculators had to borrow in order to pay cash in settlement of their contracts.

Despite speculation, most of the pepper transactions of the Fugger firm at Venice were bona fide mercantile sales, in exchange for other goods. European commerce was still one of barter, and great merchant princes from all countries came to Venice to exchange or to purchase merchandise at the time of the arrival of the annual Caravan of the Levant. Therefore, during the years of his Venetian apprenticeship, the heir of the Fuggers formed international friendships that were useful in his later career. He was welcomed in the homes of the patrician leaders of Venice and established lifelong intimacies with them. After completing his course in the Italian metropolis, we may assume he was sent to Bruges, in Flanders, a city which was then the principal counter of the Hanseatic League. Here he was employed in the Fugger branch on the Public Square, known as the Bourse. He also probably worked for a while in the firm's offices in Lübeck, Bremen, Hamburg, and Antwerp, in order to learn the viewpoints and methods of its customers, the grocers of the Hanseatic League.

Although the Fugger family had acquired a coat of arms and acceptance by the gentry, Jakob was careful on this trip to identify himself with the burgher class and to give the nobility a wide berth. There was bitter feeling between the impoverished nobleman, still clinging to a feudal age, and the prosperous burghers; and Jakob's interests all lay with the men of business. The up-and-coming burghers, although at odds politically with the patricians, aped their social manners and dreamed of becoming members of the gentry. The men of business had more luxurious homes and more comforts than the nobility, kept better tables, and their wives wore finer clothes and richer jewelry; they were greater patrons of art, literature, and music, and since they were more traveled, had a broader general outlook than the nobles. Their lives were apt to be more peaceful, as they lived in the towns, whose courts had developed equitable processes of law and favored arbitration, while the aristocracy still ordinarily appealed to trial by arms for settlement of disputes. A burgher, protected by the ramparts of the city, could safely construct a spacious mansion. A nobleman, living outside the walls in the open country, had to raise his family in a dreary, comfortless donjon-keep, garrisoned by rough men-at-arms and kept constantly on the alert against surprise assault. There was danger of attack not only by rival barons, but sometimes by mobs of starving peasants and outlaws.

Jakob learned much from his burgher hosts. The grocers and weavers in whose homes he was a guest were men of responsibility and experience, not only in commerce but also in politics and legislation. Each of the cities he visited was a completely independent and self-sufficient republic, ruled in local affairs by a burgomaster and a city council chosen entirely from the ranks of businessmen. Each was a separate nation in miniature, with its own flag, coinage, ships, and armed militia. In foreign affairs they were all governed by the parliament of the Hanseatic League, which determined foreign policies and to which each city sent its deputies to debate and vote.

The League used its armed forces only for defense of trade. It had a strict rule not to engage in religious or political rivalries, confining its interests to the mercantile field. In contrast to the nobility, whose sole calling was war, the shrewd Hanse munitions makers were peace-loving, because they knew that war was bad for their international trade. Their motto was, "A good trade gained is better than a war won." "A good distance is better than a steel shirt," they said sagely, meaning that it's better to keep away from trouble than to wear armor.

Jakob accompanied the Fugger representatives to the more important annual fairs in several of the outlying trading centers of the Hanseatic League. All mercantile and financial transactions in Europe were still made in the traditional medieval manner, at established meeting places called fairs. The partners of merchant firms traveled in person from fair to fair, conveying their merchandise and carrying the currency needed to finance their trading.

Jakob probably accompanied the contingent of grocers who went, in the usual armed caravan, to the Russian fair at Novgorod, which was held for six weeks every summer. This annual counter in faraway Muscovy was not a free and open fair such as those of France, Germany, or Spain. It was precariously conducted in an isolated trading outpost where the merchants had to be on the watch at all times. The Hanse in Novgorod had its own fortified enclosure, including a church and barracks. Members of the staff were forbidden to mingle with the uncouth Slavs and were not permitted to marry Russian women.

The Fuggers exchanged Venetian commodities not only for ermine, sables, and other furs, but also for beeswax for the candles of the Church and caviar for the tables of the rich. There, too, Cossack traders brought to them rare Chinese tea and costly silks which came from a distant fair in southern Russia, at Nishnii Novgorod, the terminus of a camel caravan route from distant Mongolia.

Upon Jakob's return from Novgorod, he left Bruges with a company of grocers carrying a consignment of pepper for the great annual fair at Bergen, in Norway. Here the Fuggers traded for salt fish, amber, forest products, and grain. There were no women allowed at the walled Hanse trading post, and the staff were vowed to celibacy for their ten-year term of service. All barter was under armed watch, and there were few amenities exchanged with the crude Norse traders.

Among the unexpected commodities sold to the Norse at this Bergen fair were oil paintings from Flanders for the castles of the Scandinavian nobility. Bergen, with its long winter nights, was also a hungry market for the printed books produced by the recently invented printing presses that had been installed at Lübeck, in Germany.

Jakob next, no doubt, accompanied the Fugger merchant train to England, where they conveyed their pepper to the London counter of the Hanseatic League. At that time England was convulsed by the War of the Roses, and as yet had developed no industries. It was, however, the greatest wool-producing country of Europe, and everywhere in the island were great flocks of sheep belonging to the monasteries, which exchanged wool for pepper and malmsey wine from the Mediterranean. The London counter was called Easterlings' Hall, and it had to be manned by alert guards, for the jealous English merchants had several times incited London mobs to attack it.

In London, Jakob received a letter from his brother Ulrich calling him home to Augsburg to become a partner of the firm. He took a Venetian ship from the port of Bristol and arrived in Bruges just in time to join a caravan going from Flanders to South Germany, organized by a group of grocers who were carrying specie south to purchase spices at Venice. The company was augmented by churchmen traveling to Rome and by a group of pilgrims on their way to Jerusalem. Merchants carrying wool and tin from England, grain from Scandinavia, and furs from Muscovy swelled the ranks of the caravan. By thus banding together, travelers were able to reduce the prorata cost to each of a military escort. The escort was very necessary, for highwaymen lay in wait for unprotected travelers, and the rule of the road was, "Let him take who hath the might, and let him keep who can."

Since there were no common carriers, nowhere was there an organized, continuous movement of merchandise. Each merchant house convoyed its own bales and fardels, and a member of the firm accompanied the consignment in person. All bundles had to be of small enough compass to be transported by packsaddle and loaded so that they could be easily opened, inspected, and measured at any toll gate. Much of the merchandise, as well as the treasure, was carried in four-wheeled covered wagons drawn by four horses, with the horses generally in tandem, since they could not be driven abreast through narrow town gates and across flimsy bridges. The roads were so rough that they could not cover more than ten or twelve miles a day. The master, apprentices, and clerks traveled on horseback, but had to proceed at the slow rate of the wagons in order to guard their property, and there was much singing and storytelling to enliven the tedious progress. Each night they lodged at a roadside hostel of the monks of Cluny, innkeepers for all Europe.

Jakob, not being hampered with any merchandise, was able to ride freely up and down the line and enjoy the sociability of the caravan. To him, impatient to get home to Augsburg, the most exasperating form of delay was presented by the many toll gates that were set up along the highways and rivers. The caravan encountered a toll barrier about every ten miles.

The successive taxes imposed upon spices in their passage through Asia have already been noted, but the extortion from commercial travelers was even greater in Europe. The merchants rarely paid their toll in coin, but almost always in kind, which caused much haggling at the toll gates. Merchants who were transporting bulk goods of small value would, because of this continuous attrition, arrive at their journey's end with many fewer pack animals than they had at the start.

Jakob left the Rhine at Heidelberg, along with those of the caravan whose destinations were in Bavaria, and rode overland to Augsburg. There, at the age of twenty-one, he was accepted as a junior partner by his brothers and installed as deputy director of the grocers' and mercers' departments. His years of apprenticeship in Venice and Flanders had prepared him for his new duties, which were largely routine, for the efficiently organized Fugger spice monopoly had attained great precision of functioning. Never before had the pepper trust carried out its operations so smoothly and so profitably.

In 1485, after five years of expansion under Jakob's energetic direction, the marketing machinery of the grocers' department suddenly sustained an unexpected jolt from a surprising quarter. The Fugger representative at Seville, Spain, sent a dispatch to Augsburg that agitated the pepper trust. Jakob, now in charge of pepper sales, apparently had to hurry to Portugal. He crossed the Alps to Venice with his attendant staff, riding hard and changing horses at every posting station. From Venice a fast galley with a double contingent of rowers carried him speedily down the Adriatic and through the Mediterranean to the sleepy little Atlantic seaport of Lisbon.

For the past half-century, the Kingdom of Portugal had been quietly developing into a maritime and colonizing power. The expansion had been in Morocco and along the Atlantic coast of Africa, partly in the form of a religious crusade against the Moslems and of religious missions among the blacks of the Congo region. Until about 1470, the Portuguese explorations had brought them additional Atlantic fisheries off the North African coast, as well as some importations of sealskins and seal oil from Northwest Africa, but the principal profit from the African enterprises had been from Negro slaves, in which a steady traffic had been developed. Sugar, wine, and lumber from the recently colonized Atlantic isles, the Azores, the Madeiras, and the Cape Verdes, had created a boom in Portugal. Then the Grain Coast was reached, and shortly afterward the Gold Coast, and now the Pepper Coast.

The spectacular news that called Jakob to Lisbon was the arrival there of a cargo of pepper from a new source. In their slow southerly progress along the desert and jungle shores of the Atlantic, the Portuguese had reached a prosperous agrarian littoral that they dubbed the Grain Coast. The captain of the first caravel to arrive there was astonished to be offered forty tons of wild malaguetta pepper by a native chief. He filled his ship with the precious spice and brought it to the port of Lisbon. The value of even this small quantity of standard Indian black pepper would have been around four million dollars, and the cost to the Portuguese captain in trade goods was probably a few hundred, so the cargo was fantastically profitable. It had an electrifying effect upon the market at Lisbon.

Up to that time, malaguetta pepper had been such a great rarity in Europe that on the Rialto in Venice such peppercorns were termed "grains of Paradise" and were sold at a handsome premium over ordinary pepper. Malaguetta was more pungent than the regular Malabar and Ceylon black peppercorns, and it had a tang that made it prized as a novelty by European epicures. The costly grains were served only at special banquets and with great ostentation. Heretofore the Venetians had received a trickle of malaguetta each year from Alexandria, but they had never known its source.

When the shipload of malaguetta reached Lisbon, the House of Medici recognized this as an opportunity to liberate themselves from purchasing their pepper at their rivals' extortionate rates and to enter into competition with them. The local representative of the Fuggers quickly reported to his chief in Seville, who sent to Augsburg the dispatch that brought Jakob hurrying to Lisbon to repair the break in the dam of the Fugger pepper trust.

His sudden arrival in a state galley no doubt created a sensation in Lisbon. King John not only gave Jakob a courtly reception, but admitted him to his private circle and soon dealt frankly with him. Jakob easily secured exclusive rights from the Crown to all the wild malaguetta pepper that was imported. With true German efficiency, he set up for the King a colonial agricultural department that was to lay out extensive plantations in Southwest Africa. This was an economic step of great importance to European commerce, since it thus became partially independent of the Soldan of Egypt and secured malaguetta or Guinea pepper at much less than the cost of Sumatra pepper, although it was still resold at the same lofty prices.

Jakob at once opened a Fugger countinghouse in Lisbon to make immediate cash payments to the royal treasury for all pepper entering the port. This businesslike arrangement ensured King John a revenue nearly as substantial as that derived from his Guinea gold mines. Jakob, now having completed his mission, was about to leave Lisbon and go to visit his Spanish branch in Seville when he was sent for in haste and secrecy by Dom John.

In his private cabinet the King confided to Jakob a secret report he had just received from two monks, Antonio of Lisbon and Pedro of Monterroyo, whom he had sent as spies to Asia to try to confirm rumors regarding the source of spices in India. In Jerusalem the two friars had met some Indian and Christian pilgrims and had extracted from them the information that the continent of Africa ended in a southerly cape, around which one could sail from the Atlantic to the sea that washed the shores of India.

The next day Jakob attended a quiet conference held in the private residence of Master Rodrigo, the King's Jewish physician, to elude Venetian espionage. Besides Dom John, Master Rodrigo, and Jakob Fugger, there were present the royal chaplain, Bishop Diogo Ortiz, a geographer of note, Martin Behaim, the famed German cartographer, and two Jewish astrologers, leading authorities on celestial navigation in Europe, Master Abraham Zacuto and Master Joseph Vizinho.

After some hours of deliberation, King John decided to send out two exploring missions, one to go disguised across Egypt to India, and another by water along the unknown Southeast African coast.

Jakob Fugger encouraged the King in his resolution and offered to contribute to the project financially. He saw in this an opportunity to have Christian Portugal take the place of Moslem Egypt as the source of spices and dyes for Venice. If Portugal could open a water route to India, then the extortionate tolls paid by Venice to the Soldan of Egypt could be saved. Pepper could reach Europe in greater bulk and at less cost.

Farsighted Jakob saw but one unfavorable sign, the growing influence at Lisbon of the Florentine merchants. Until recently the Jewish merchants had monopolized trade in Portugal as well as in Spain, and the Fuggers had co-operated with them. Now a strong anti-Semitic movement was sweeping Spain and influencing Portugal. This was fostered by the Florentines, traditional enemies of the Jews as well as of the Fuggers. Already Bartolomeo Marchioni, the Florentine leader, had usurped the influential position of the Jews at the Portuguese court and had attempted to seize the malaguetta pepper trade. If Portugal became a direct importer of Indian spices, then the Florentines would no doubt try to wrest that prize from the Fuggers.

The risk caused Jakob to defer his departure for Seville until he could arrange to introduce at the Portuguese court a deputy of sufficient caliber to act decisively in the event of a sudden Florentine attack. He sent to Spain for his able lieutenant, Cristóbal de Haro, and installed him at Lisbon. As agent for the Fugger trust, de Haro soon became the financial backer of colonial expansion in both hemispheres.

In the life of Ferdinand Magellan, Jakob Fugger was important in the background, supporting the activities of Cristóbal de Haro. It is fitting to complete here the account of Jakob's personal relationship with Magellan's voyage. After he had installed Cristóbal de Haro in Lisbon with plenary powers, he probably rode overland to inspect his Spanish headquarters in Seville, then took passage homeward in a Venetian galley, and thence went from Venice through the mountain passes to Augsburg.

Jakob Fugger was now twenty-eight, and had become a full partner in the firm. From this time on, his multifarious responsibilities were such that he was no longer able to devote exclusive attention to the details of the spice trade, important though it was. He looked to Cristóbal de Haro to foster the expanding political interests of the pepper and dye trust in the Iberian Peninsula, and to Doge Leonardo Loredano to defend its fortunes in Egypt. He was prepared for a possible conflict between Portugal and Egypt, but felt confident that, no matter who won, Venice would benefit. Until the death of his elder brothers, George in 1506 and Ulrich in 1510, Jakob worked with them to direct the sprawling Fugger empire of factories, mines, banks, wholesale houses, and transportation lines. At Ulrich's death, he became head of the family partnership, and he decided it had grown too diversified for efficient operation. He discontinued many of the firm's activities and turned others over to friendly competitors, such as the great house of Jakob Welser and Sons of Nuremberg. He formed a simplified new partnership called Jakob Fugger and Nephews, to function largely as bankers. Through subsidiaries he retained control of the spice and dye trade, of the copper and silver industry, and also of the weaving of fustian. This last was a coarse cloth made of hemp and cotton that had an enormous sale throughout Europe and Asia.

The total family wealth of the Fuggers at that time has been estimated at sixty-three million florins, which, in purchasing power, would be in excess of a billion dollars. During the sixteen ensuing years, in which Jakob was at the head of the firm, its annual profits averaged over fifty per cent on the working capital.

The efficiency of this complicated international organization was amazing. All ledgers from every branch throughout Europe were sent to Augsburg for audit each year, and a budgeted control over expenses was effected. All the strands of the intricate and far-reaching web centered in the private office of Jakob Fugger in the monumental headquarters building in Augsburg known as the Golden Counting House. Here Jakob Fugger exercised his uncanny mastery, seated at a magnificent carved desk with many pigeonholes, over each of whose compartments was painted, for identification, a view of a city in which was located a Fugger branch. Current correspondence and accounts with the branches was filed in them. The managers of every foreign office regularly sent confidential reports not only of mercantile but also of political and social happenings. These went to Jakob personally, and hence he kept in touch with significant occurrences and trends in every market and at every court.

Jakob found time to indulge in his hobby of architecture, to travel widely, and to devote attention to art and literature, of which he was a munificent patron. He not only conducted an immense industrial enterprise, but was also a moving factor in the politics of empire. There is extant in the official chronicles of Augsburg an entry that reads: "The name of Jakob Fugger is known in all kingdoms and lands; yea, among the heathen, also. Emperors, Kings, princes and lords have sent to treat with him. The Pope has greeted him as his well-beloved son and embraced him, and the Cardinals have risen up before him. He is the glory of all Germany." And we have the bold letter that Jakob wrote to the Emperor Charles V, whose dominions then exceeded those once ruled by Caesar Augustus or by Charlemagne: "It is well known that Your Imperial Majesty could not have gained the Roman Crown save with mine aid." Testimony likewise is borne by the querulous protests of the Emperor Charles himself, who grumbled when signing an Imperial charter for Jakob: "I have never granted such favors to any other man and am not minded to repeat them in the future."

Furthermore, there are the words of Martin Luther, who before he launched the Protestant Reformation was engaged in a passionate campaign of social reform against Jakob in which he said, and repeated many times: "See now what greed can and dares do. The Fuggers raise or lower prices at their pleasure, and depress and destroy all small merchants just as the carp devours the small fish, just as though they were lords over all God's creatures and free from all laws of faith and love. Is it any wonder they are become Kings and we beggars?"

The old lexicons list the verb "to fugger" as meaning to charge extortionate interest, to practice usury.

And yet, Jakob Fugger was a man of probity who led an exemplary private life. A revealing glimpse of his modest character was afforded by a memento which hung framed in the sumptuous private office of the Golden Counting House. Monarchs came there as petitioners for loans, but on the wall in a place of honor was displayed a piece of coarse fustian cloth, woven in 1375 by the hands of old Johannes Fugger when he was a country weaver working his own cottage loom.

Jakob was not unaware of his obligations to society, and contributed immense sums to hospitals and orphanages. One of his social experiments was in low-priced housing; he built a model village one can still see in Augsburg, called the *Fuggerei,* where one hundred poor families were lodged at nominal rents.

Although the Doge of Venice, the King of France, and the Pope himself were clients of Jakob Fugger, his principal debtor was Maximilian Hapsburg, Holy Roman Emperor. He, like all the Hapsburgs, was a politician of ability, but he was contemptuous of economy and heedless of expense. It was said, "Gold falls on the hands of a Hapsburg like water on a hot stone." The spendthrift Emperor became so impoverished that toward the end of his reign Jakob was actually furnishing him cash to cover his petty household expenses. During the last year of Maximilian's life, in 1518, Jakob advanced to him personally, in small sums, a total of three thousand florins. He explains in his private notes that he made the loans because otherwise His Imperial Majesty would literally have had "nothing to eat."

After the death of Maximilian, Archduke Philip the Handsome, his son, succeeded him as the ruler of Austria, Burgundy, and Flanders. He found the treasury empty, so he naturally turned for aid to his father's unfailing source of financial support, Jakob Fugger. When the Archduke later became King Philip I of Castile, Jakob Fugger met the cost of his great expedition to Spain to be crowned and his heavy expenses while there. After Philip's death, when his small son Charles of Ghent in turn became Archduke of Austria and Count of Flanders, it was Jakob Fugger who financed his rule. In 1517 Charles of Ghent ascended the Spanish throne, and it was Jakob Fugger who supplied funds for his costly voyage with a resplendent train from Flanders to Spain.

Fiscal relations between King Charles and Jakob Fugger became even closer in 1519. The King, in accordance with the dying wish of his grandfather, became in that year a candidate for the office of Emperor. The title of Holy Roman Emperor was largely one of honor, as the constituent states of the empire were all self-governing. The Holy Roman Empire was founded in 800 A.D., on Christmas at midnight Mass in St. Peter's Church at Rome, when Charlemagne, King of the Franks, was anointed and crowned by Pope Leo III as successor to the Caesars and saluted by the Pope as *Imperator Augustus Romanorum.*

At the death of Emperor Maximilian, the empire was comprised of Austria, part of Lombardy, part of Switzerland, the Kingdom of Bohemia, the French-speaking territory along the west bank of the Rhine, the German kingdoms of Bavaria, Saxony, Cleves, and Nassau, and the princely archbishoprics of Trier, Mainz, Cologne, Metz, and Strasbourg. A number of Hanseatic city-states such as Hamburg, Lübeck, and Bremen also owed allegiance to the Emperor.

The succession to the imperial throne was elective. There were seven electors, of whom the four hereditary lay electors were the King of Bohemia, the Duke of Saxony, the Duke Palatine of the Rhine, and the Margrave of Brandenberg. The three ecclesiastical electors were the Archbishops of Trier, Mainz, and Cologne. A newly elected candidate could call himself King of the Romans after being crowned at Aix la Chapelle, where Charlemagne lies entombed. He could assume the title of Emperor only after he had been anointed and crowned by the Pope.

Upon the death of Maximilian, the votes of the electors were frankly put up for sale to the highest bidder. The late Emperor had, through Jakob Fugger, already bought five of the seven votes for his grandson, Charles, for six hundred thousand florins (about nine million dollars), but upon his death the electors cynically withdrew their pledges. They did not return the bribes, but announced their votes were again on the market.

Now the banker had to provide more money to save his investment. To outbid the King of France, Jakob Fugger was forced to lend Don Charles an additional five hundred forty-three thousand florins, and this not sufficing in the mad auction, he had to call upon the Nuremberg banking firm of Welser for help, and also had recourse to a syndicate of Genoese and Florentine moneylenders. In all, it was eight hundred and fifty thousand florins, or over twelve million dollars, which Jakob was forced to borrow at usurious terms and lend to King Charles in order to win the election for him.

The purchase of the crown for Don Charles had seemed to Jakob Fugger at the start to be a good speculation. Before long, however, the speculation went sour, and it turned out to have been a costly extravagance. Though Jakob made frantic efforts to regain his capital, he had to advance more and more money to Don Charles for expenses to maintain his Imperial throne, and thus in fact became the prisoner of his own loans. It was far too late to cut his losses. He had already become the unwilling creditor of the Doge of Venice for immense unpaid advances. Now that Don Charles was also a delinquent debtor, Jakob was at his wit's end. It was, among other reasons, partly to help these debtors become solvent and thereby to get some return upon his immense investment in the Imperial crown that he accepted the proposal of Cristóbal de Haro to employ the maritime might of Spain and the genius of Ferdinand Magellan to invade the lucrative Indian monopoly of Portugal.

CHAPTER X

CRISTOBAL DE HARO, MASTER GROCER

CRISTOBAL DE HARO, who came to the court of King John in Lisbon as agent of Jakob Fugger, was the son of Juan Alonso de Baera, a native of the vicinity of Burgos, Spain. The family probably came from the provincial capital of Haro, a center of the northern Spanish wine industry, where for some centuries there had been a Jewish colony of moneylenders and goldsmiths. In the fourteenth century this group was dispersed, after a murderous sack of the ghetto during a civil war, and many of the refugees from Haro settled in Burgos and became Christianized. That Cristóbal had a Jewish background is indicated by the fact that he was never able to obtain the coat of arms that any man in his influential position would otherwise have acquired. The great Constable de Haro was perhaps his protector during the persecutions of the Christianized Jews that occurred during his boyhood, and he probably changed his patronym to that of his benefactor then or later.

By 1486, when he was summoned to Lisbon, Cristóbal had already made his mark in the Fugger organization, and Jakob Fugger made an effort to establish him with the King in the favored personal relationship to which he himself had been admitted. In this he was not successful.

Cristóbal de Haro was essentially a promoter and speculator. A bold, enterprising man of attractive address and considerable tact, he used bribery when other means failed to secure both business and political preferment. His mercantile vision was wide-ranging, his grasp of commercial affairs phenomenal. He had great driving power and was ubiquitous in his activities. Backed by the name and resources of the Fuggers, he became a dynamic influence in the maritime and colonial world.

His younger brother, Diego de Haro, joined him in Portugal, dividing his time between the branches in Antwerp and Seville and the main office in Lisbon. Because they traded in pepper, spices, and dyes, they were at once attracted to the maritime operations of the King.

Although the King would not accept de Haro socially, he invited the trader, soon after his arrival in Lisbon, to accompany him on an inspection tour of Mina House, with its stores from all over the world. The warehouses were filled with imported ivory and Guinea gold, and there were mountains of cheap merchandise to be used by the trading caravels. With apparent carelessness, the King let Cristóbal view the great accumulation of sulphur, saltpeter, lead, and copper that indicated his preparedness for war.

Dom John permitted the de Haro firm to participate in several profitable transactions with Mina House, since he wanted to have competition between the Medici and the Fuggers, so as to play one group against the other. At Cristóbal's suggestion, Jakob Fugger soon advised his ally, the Welser Company of Nuremberg, that it also might profitably open an office in Portugal. Thus Lisbon became the field of battle between the warring Florentine and German cartels.

The tension between the rival groups was accentuated when the King began to implement his ambitious plan to reach India. Cristóbal de Haro contracted close friendships with Bartholomew Dias and other navigators and soon was admitted to the maritime circle about King John. The King secretly dispatched other fleets to follow up the discoveries of Dias in the Southeastern Atlantic, but they failed to repeat his achievement and were unable to round the Cape of Good Hope. They did, however, bring back much useful information about the currents and winds of the South Atlantic.

He also sent several squadrons across the Atlantic to sail along the coasts of Greenland, Newfoundland, and Labrador, to try to find a western passage to India far to the northwest of the route of Columbus. He even arranged for a fleet to go to the north of Europe eastward, past North Cape and Novaya Zemlya, to attempt to get to China through the Arctic Ocean. Meanwhile, his scouting expeditions also surreptitiously probed for a westward passage along the coasts of Venezuela and Colombia, in the Caribbean waters claimed by Spain.

As a result of King John's strictly maintained policy of secrecy about these expeditions, it is now next to impossible to find official records of these early Portuguese voyages. All charts, logs, and journals were confiscated and suppressed by the Crown, and their publication was prohibited under pain of death. There now survive only tantalizing but convincing traces of the manifold activities of this dynamic Portuguese ruler.

In 1495, Dom John died. During the bitter factional struggle that preceded the King's death, Cristóbal de Haro had circumspectly attempted to keep friends with both sides, but his competitor, Marchioni of Florence, forestalled him. After Dom Manuel ascended the throne at twenty-six, it is quite evident that he favored the Florentine rather than the German group of local financiers, and the affairs of Cristóbal de Haro and the House of Fugger in Lisbon received a serious setback.

In fact, within a year after Manuel's accession Cristóbal found himself so much out of grace at court that he deemed it wise to absent himself from Portugal, and announced that he intended to visit his branch at Antwerp. Actually, however, he had decided he would fight the Florentines and King Manuel through an alliance with King Henry VII of England. He sailed ostentatiously for Antwerp in one of his own ships, but quietly went ashore at Bristol, England, where there was a colony of Portuguese merchants friendly to his interests. He was met there by a Fugger associate, John Cabot, a Genoese who had been a sea captain in the service of Venice in the oriental spice trade.

De Haro knew that Cabot had for some time been petitioning the King of England for a royal ship in which to sail by a northwest passage to China, and he determined to investigate his proposition. After a conference with his Hanseatic advisers in London, he decided that Cabot's expedition would be a good speculation and might turn the tables on his Florentine enemies at the Portuguese court. He easily persuaded King Henry VII to give a charter of exploration to John Cabot when he explained that the Fuggers, through de Haro, would defray the cost of the undertaking. The Tudor King had known Dom John well, and was aware of the value the late King had placed on de Haro's knowledge and experience.

Jakob Fugger and de Haro had considered the matter carefully. The Fuggers at that time, through the Hanseatic League, were in control of English commerce, and they realized the advantages of having England import spices and dyes directly from the Orient. De Haro knew that Captain John Cabot had had vast experience in the spice trade and had traveled as a Venetian agent to Arabia. He also knew, from the secret explorations made by King John, that there appeared to be a Canadian passage to the northwest through Davis Strait and Hudson Bay. Cabot's plans seemed quite practicable, and if he was successful, the enormous returns would make the outlay well worth the gamble. It would mean that London would take the place of Alexandria and Lisbon as the depot for spices.

Cristóbal proceeded to Antwerp from England, then in 1497 returned to Lisbon to await the report of Cabot's voyage. When he learned its negative results, he withdrew his financial support of the plan. With unerring judgment, he concluded that there must be an impassable continental barrier in the Northern Hemisphere; he decided that it would be more profitable to follow the Southeastern Atlantic route of Dias. The Portuguese merchants in Bristol did not, however, accept de Haro's advice, and between 1501 and 1505 they financed four costly expeditions to Newfoundland, Greenland, and Labrador, seeking the northwest passage.

Cristóbal now resolved to gain the good graces of Dom Manuel, cost what it might. He made lavish presents to members of the King's intimate circle and paid handsome retainers to members of the Royal Council and other officials, but this bribery had no effect. De Haro was rigidly excluded from any part in the expedition of Vasco da Gama, and, to his chagrin, his enemy, Bartolomeo Marchioni, was allowed to send along a caravel of his own as the fourth ship of the fleet. His mortification can well be imagined when, in July, 1499, he watched the Marchioni caravel, the Berrio, return with flags aflutter and bombards banging, laden with spices, and when he heard that the da Gamas had discovered the route by sea to India.

However, Cristóbal soon learned that Marchioni's victory had been a costly one, and he found the King more receptive to his overtures. Despite the fact that the caravel had returned gloriously, the voyage represented a staggering loss. The squadron had barely escaped annihilation by the Arabs. Only two of da Gama's four ships came back, and out of one hundred and sixty picked men of the crews, only fifty-five had survived. Among the dead was heroic Paul da Gama, to whom much of the success of his brother Vasco was due.

Dom Manuel had financed the da Gama undertaking on a loan from Marchioni. Now that he was without funds and found it difficult to interest the local moneylenders in any further ventures, he was open to friendly approaches by Cristóbal de Haro. When a second expedition was sent out under Pedro Alvares Cabral in March, 1500, among its thirteen ships there were two sent by Cristóbal, one flying the standard of the Fuggers and the other that of the Welsers. Unfortunately this expedition failed to defray its expense and brought back few spices. Many of its important members were massacred by the Arabs, and a number of others were lost at sea, including the great navigator Bartholomew Dias and the King's Jewish astronomer, Master John. Of the thirteen original ships, only six badly battered craft straggled back into Lisbon Harbor. Despite the storm of criticism now raised, Dom Manuel determined to send still another fleet. His council and all conservative elements in the realm opposed further expenditures, but backed by a Fugger loan and participation, the persistent King sent a third small squadron of four ships to India under John da Nova.

Although Dom Manuel and his uncle, Dom Alvaro Braganza, who was his chief moral support in his oriental ventures, hungered for profits, they did not actually taste them in full until the return of Vasco da Gama from his second voyage in 1503. The total expense of this voyage amounted to two hundred thousand ducats, and they brought back a cargo that sold for over a million ducats, a clear net of four hundred per cent. However, the King was so much in debt to the foreign bankers that he had to apply most of this profit to paying back their loans to him. He consequently still lacked the cash to send out the annual spice fleets and for some years still found it necessary to speculate on borrowed money. Both the Florentines and the Germans were well content to advance him the funds. Dom Manuel also followed the policy of letting the foreigners send their own fleets under their own house flags, assuming all expenses and risks and paying him forty per cent of the gross profits.

The wide-awake Cristóbal de Haro made the most of this situation. By dipping into the bottomless purse of Jakob Fugger, he was soon able to push the Florentine Marchioni entirely out of his earlier favorable position. Bartolomeo Marchioni sent an appeal to Florence for assistance which was answered by his fellow countryman, Amerigo Vespucci, who held the power of attorney for the Medici in Spain. Vespucci hurried to Lisbon to offset de Haro, and the weight of Medici gold brought the local lending market back into equilibrium. The Florentines and the Germans then largely underwrote for Dom Manuel the fiscal risk of Portuguese spice importations. For a dozen years these competent entrepreneurs reaped a harvest richer than any European financier had previously imagined.

Meanwhile, the Signory of Venice was alert to help its spice traders meet the competition of the Florentine merchants who were marketing Portuguese spice imports. Small executive committees, under the Council of Ten, were set up in 1502 and 1506 to study the spice trade and meet the Florentine threat. They had plenary powers to meet the crisis, but the tide of history was against them.

The rivalry developed into a stalemate, with the Florentines monopolizing the Italian, French, and Iberian markets, while the Germans controlled through Antwerp the British, Scandinavian, Flemish, German, and Bohemian fields. After 1500, Dom Manuel had followed the policy of his predecessor King John, and divided his favors so that both groups bid for them. In August, 1501, he made two import contracts for spices and for dyewood, one with Anton Welser of Nuremberg, and one with Cazano Negro of Genoa. The Florentines were persistent in their sales inroads into Cristóbal de Haro's own markets and invaded them through various channels. A thorn in his side was the firm of Frescobaldi and Gualterrati in the Hanse counter of Bruges, in the very center of his own territory. Another annoying intrusion was that of Benedict Morelli, a cousin of Bartolomeo Marchioni, who opened an office in Venice itself and spied from there on the Fugger activities.

An even more aggressive and disturbing competitor was a converted

Portuguese Jew named Francis Mendes, who established himself in Antwerp, the inner stronghold of the Fuggers. He also opened an active branch in London, where the Fuggers up to then had a monopoly. To cap it all, he finally was able to found another office in Constantinople and to win the support of the Turkish government. Francis Mendes worried the Florentines as well as de Haro, for they also had been catering to the Turkish trade, and they insinuated to Dom Manuel that Mendes was anti-Christian and pro-Islam. The wily international trader, however, managed to keep his foothold in Lisbon and became a very important factor in the spice trade.

Dom Manuel became restless when he realized that, while he was getting forty per cent of the gross return to Cristóbal de Haro on his spice imports in Lisbon, de Haro at once reimbursed himself for this expense by adding it to his resale markup in the markets of Northern Europe where he had a monopoly. Dom Manuel's discontent was spurred by the envious Florentines, who, while retaining strict control of their own exclusive resale markets in France, Italy, and the Iberian Peninsula, urged him to use the facilities of a small office of the Portuguese government in Antwerp, an office which King John had established for the import-export trade of Portugal with the Hanse cities. The King decided to make the full resale profit for himself, and he therefore in 1503 sent Tomas Lopes of India House to Antwerp as his agent. Lopes expanded the former small establishment there, rented a substantial mansion in a suburb called Kipdorf, and named it Portuguese House. There were only ten Portuguese merchants then in Antwerp, and none was qualified to handle a large marketing operation. Therefore Lopes employed an experienced German spice wholesaler to act as director of sales and build up an organization which, by means of independent wholesalers, competed with the Fugger and Welser chains. The Fuggers countered by spreading the rumor that the Portuguese spices were adulterated and even dangerous, and this caused many spice retailers to refuse to buy them.

Cristóbal himself was not interested personally in reselling the spices from Antwerp, but left the domestic marketing details to his brother Diego. Cristóbal, however, devoted much time to building up a chain of procurement warehouses in East Africa, India, and Malacca, and developed an efficient overseas import-export organization of high caliber. He became the largest private shipowner and operator in the world by investing Fugger capital in a fleet of fifteen capacious, fast, square-rigged *naos* for the India trade. Yet even while they were bringing him enormous profits, canny Cristóbal, himself a Spaniard with a branch in Seville, was conscious of the ever present threat that Spain would someday carry further the plans of Columbus and discover a southwest passage to India.

Therefore, he asked the King's permission to test his idea that it might be possible to skirt the presumed southern extremity of South America, just as the Portuguese fleets now sailed around the southern tip of Africa. When the King grudgingly consented, Cristóbal quietly sent two caravels under Captain Gonsalvo Coelho and later three more under Captain Christopher Jacques in a quest along the far southern coast of South America. This territory was in the area reserved by treaty to Spain, so this action was beyond the law, and his interloping caravels would have been fired upon had the Spaniards detected them. Daring Captain Jacques reached South America, investigated the estuary of the River Plate, then continued far south, and possibly discovered the mouth of the strait that later was named for Magellan. He brought back charts and full navigational details of this route to de Haro.

Cristóbal informed Dom Manuel of Jacques's report, but they determined to keep the discovery a secret, since the development of such a route would be through the Spanish zone of the Atlantic and would destroy Portugal's monopoly.

Cristóbal de Haro, basking precariously in the royal favor, felt warily that things were going too well and could not last. The King's intimates all knew that Dom Manuel was of a jealous and ungrateful nature, and could not suffer having men of accomplishment about him. Although he showered wealth on his favorites, he starved the very overseas administrators who produced the revenue.

Dom Manuel, in his shortsighted niggardliness, not only failed to pay his heroic naval and military conquerors decent compensation, but was also penurious with his fiscal administrators. The factors, however, were able to outwit him for their own enrichment by becoming secret agents for Cristóbal de Haro. Thus many of the best jewels seized from the native princes and the richest treasures looted from oriental cities were smuggled to de Haro instead of being sent to the Royal Chancellor at India House.

According to his agreement with Dom Manuel, Cristóbal was paying to the Chancellor forty per cent of the gross value of spices and other goods brought into India House by the de Haro fleet. The customs on spices had become the principal source of income of the court at Lisbon, just as previously they had supported the throne of Cairo. Prodigal King Francis of France later jeered enviously at opulent King Manuel of Portugal by referring contemptuously to him as "the Grocer King."

As we have seen, Dom Manuel, although now the richest sovereign in Europe, began to envy Cristóbal de Haro the great resale profit he was making. He wanted all the immense income from the spice trade for himself, particularly as he was squandering his huge revenues faster than he received them. And the crafty Florentines were always at Dom Manuel's elbow, whispering details of Cristóbal's evasions of customs and of his bribing of factors.

The Florentines could safely denounce de Haro for the same corrupt practices in the spice trade which they also followed, because Dom Manuel needed Medici political support with the Vatican at Rome, and therefore was tolerant toward the Florentines in Lisbon. They now definitely set out to oust de Haro from royal favor, urging the King to confiscate his treasures for having been illegally and scandalously acquired at the expense of the Crown.

For over a decade the de Haro ships had been almost an independent merchant marine, using Portuguese harbors and enjoying special maritime privileges. They bore the standard of Portugal, but also flew the house flags of the alien de Haros, Fuggers, and Welsers, who were subjects not of King Manuel, but of the Emperor. The Florentines now aroused the covetous courtiers and had them point out to the King that a substantial part of all the imports brought in from India were handled by de Haro in direct competition with the Crown. Once this hostile trend became evident at the palace, the bureaucrats of India House joined with the Knights of Christ at court and with the Florentines in plotting against the de Haro organization. The atmosphere at the palace grew chilly for Cristóbal de Haro. Experienced courtiers began to snub him, and friends whispered caution to him.

An unequal struggle ensued between Cristóbal de Haro and the avid courtiers, but its issue could not be long in doubt. Dom Manuel was no longer dependent on the Fuggers, for in addition to his vast income from the spice trade, the King's revenues had been temporarily swelled by a recent flood of loot from the Orient. His predatory commanders had succeeded in confiscating the hoarded wealth of generations of Arab Sheiks on the east coast of Africa, of Hindu Rajahs in India, and of the rich Sultan of Malacca. Not since the days of Imperial Rome had there been such a wholesale transfer of wealth from East to West as came pouring into Lisbon in a veritable cascade in the decade between 1505 and 1515.

Dom Manuel could no longer tolerate the fact that Cristóbal de Haro was collecting his share of this loot. But Cristóbal, like all gamblers, was tempted to risk one or two more flings, in spite of many danger signals. He redoubled his bribes to highly placed friends who surrounded the King, and boldly hazarded his personal safety and the Fugger interests by continuing his enormously profitable operations.

At last, in 1516, the King made his first hostile move, and de Haro's annual squadron returned empty from India, the ships riding high in the water, without cargo. The commodore reported to Cristóbal that his argosies laden with spices and treasure had put in at a harbor in southern

India for water and supplies before sailing for Lisbon, and the governor of the port had seized all their cargo and sent the empty vessels home in ballast. Cristóbal knew that no local commander would have dared take such highhanded action without explicit orders from Dom Manuel, so he rushed in protest to the King. He could no longer obtain instant audience, and, when he was finally received, Dom Manuel professed incredulous surprise at his complaint and promised an investigation. This meant a two years' delay, since a reply from India would take that time. It was obvious that the King was toying with Cristóbal, for all the facts were available to him in the returned fleet. However, it was politic for de Haro to dissemble; he had to pretend to be relieved by Dom Manuel's bland assurance, and he expressed confidence that he would eventually be compensated for the immense loss he had suffered.

But even then Cristóbal failed to heed the warning; he deluded himself into thinking that there was still time for one last coup. Despite a sense of foreboding, he refitted a fine fleet of seven *naos* and dispatched it again to the East. His misgivings were soon confirmed, for news came that all seven of his ships had been sunk in the Atlantic off El Mina, the Portuguese naval base in West Africa, by the King's caravels under Dom Estevan Yusarte. His vessels had been halted on the high seas just as though they had been unlicensed intruders. Yusarte first transferred to the royal caravels the valuable consignment of brass, quicksilver, and cinnabar, all of which were Fugger monopolies that de Haro's ships had carried for exclusive trading. Yusarte then probably locked the hatches over the unfortunate crews and poured broadsides into the *naos,* sinking them without mercy. It is not known if there were any survivors, but it is possible that all were massacred, as this was the punishment set by royal proclamation to be meted out to interlopers in the Portuguese seas.

A disaffected government factor who was on de Haro's private pay roll at El Mina apparently sent him a warning by a slaving caravel which hastily slipped away and managed to outstrip the slower official report to the King. Cristóbal's brother Diego probably received the message at night at his quarters over the office at Lisbon. He hurriedly sent word to Cristóbal at his suburban villa, and within an hour we conjecture that Diego himself led a well-guarded mule train to the water front to be ferried before dawn across the Tagus. The selected pack animals, loaded with leather bags of gold and silver ducats, were lashed into a steady trot and were changed at short intervals by relays held in readiness all along the southeastern route to Spain. This plan to save their working capital in case of danger had no doubt been carefully worked out by the de Haro brothers. No expense had been spared to ensure readiness for a rapid flight through the quiet byways of the Algarve and safely across the border to Andalusia.

Meanwhile Cristóbal had at once taken horse and galloped with a retinue of servants through the darkness northeastward along the King's highway. They spurred their horses unmercifully, and scattered gold pieces at every post house to secure all the horses available, thus both providing for themselves and frustrating pursuit. It had been Cristóbal's policy to cultivate the good will of the royal postmasters, who were valuable sources of information. He now paid them richly for their connivance as he fled through the relay stations.

Although Cristóbal had taken precautions for flight in case the Florentine faction should prevail with the King, he had not expected any hostile step by Dom Manuel so soon. The King had dissembled with him, and no doubt had planned to effect a swift coup against all the Fugger interests at the same time that he attacked their fleet. However news of the stroke against his fleet had reached Cristóbal de Haro first, and instant flight was his only recourse.

The fugitive dared not stop for food or rest, for he knew only too well what his lot would be if he were taken. Torture could extort any confession the King desired, and confiscation of the de Haro possessions would then have been legally authorized. This indeed had been the fate of many rich Portuguese Jews at that time.

Though he was saddle-weary and exhausted, as Cristóbal turned again and again to look anxiously down the mountain road winding through pine and chestnut covered slopes far below, his restless mind was planning retaliation and recovery.

It had been over thirty years since Jakob Fugger had presented him to King John in Lisbon as his Portuguese agent. He had helped not a little to create Manuel's maritime empire. He had served the King well, and had been repaid by the destruction of his life's work. His captains had been murdered, his fine fleet sunk. He could foresee the looting of the depots and branches in Africa and Asia of which he had been so proud. The great spice trade that he had developed and which Jakob Fugger had entrusted to his keeping would now go to the Medici.

Cristóbal prayed fervently that his brother Diego would get their treasure safely to Spain. He took consolation in the thought that he still had his flourishing Spanish business and his branches and ships in the Spanish West Indies. He weighed the possibility of being able to carry on his East India trade from Seville. He had native goodwill and connections in every oriental port, and only needed the protection of a maritime flag to continue his trade. His buoyant nature and quick imagination reacted resiliently to the thought. Jakob Fugger would back him as always, and he could count on the help of his silent Spanish partner, the great Fonseca, Bishop of Burgos, head of Spain's *Casa de Antillas.* He knew that the Spaniards would welcome his disclosure of the existence of a western route to India through their own waters in the Southwest Atlantic.

The quiet household of the Lord Bishop of Burgos in Seville was startled in the early night by the clatter in the palace courtyard of a jangling cavalcade of armed Portuguese. In the dancing lights and shadows of torches, the unkempt riders looked like wild marauders from over the border. Their disheveled and dust-begrimed leader, unshaven and haggard, demanded instant audience on urgent business with the Lord Bishop. On giving his name, he was at once ushered in, and was closeted with Juan Rodriguez de Fonseca until dawn.

In the meantime, in Lisbon no official mention was made of the flight of de Haro and the sinking of his fleet, though all Europe buzzed with the story, and it was looked upon as a signal defeat of Jakob Fugger by the House of Medici. Diego de Haro courageously reappeared there and, quite unmolested, stayed on quietly for some months, closing out the firm's commerce and liquidating its contracts. He was a citizen of the Free City of Antwerp and a leading member of its governing body, and his personal activities in Lisbon had been wholly mercantile, not political like those of his brother Cristóbal. Once Cristóbal had escaped, King Manuel scorned to concern himself with the fiscal operations of Diego. He let him leave Portugal openly for the company's branch at Antwerp, where he thereafter made his personal residence. From Antwerp he succeeded in having a formal but amicable protest, in Latin, addressed by the City Council of Antwerp to Dom Manuel, complaining of the unjustified sinking of seven out of the fifteen ships belonging to Diego de Haro and employed by him in the spice trade. It is not known what response, if any, was made by the King of Portugal.

Arrogant Dom Manuel had, with rude defiance, attacked and worsted Jakob Fugger through Cristóbal de Haro. But he would have done better to follow the wise policy of his predecessor, Dom John, and to have encouraged the two alien financial groups of Florence and Augsburg to compete for his favor. Now he had let the Florentines beguile him into breaking with the Germans and giving the Medici the monopoly of Portuguese trade, Dom Manuel was to learn that vindictive Jakob Fugger had a long arm. By using as weapons Cristóbal de Haro and Ferdinand Magellan, the Fuggers would retaliate halfway across the world in the Spiceries, where the papal shield of the Medici would be of no avail.

CHAPTER XI

JUAN RODRIGUEZ DE FONSECA, BISHOP, BUREAUCRAT AND BUSINESSMAN

THE protector to whom Cristóbal de Haro fled in Seville was the Very Reverend Father Juan Rodríguez de Fonseca, Archbishop of Rosano, Lord Bishop of Burgos, Count of Pernia, Prince President of the Supreme Council of the Indies, member of the Royal Council, and the wealthiest and most influential politician in the realm. This powerful prelate had already exploited Christopher Columbus and Vasco Nuñez de Balboa, and had not scrupled to ruin their careers for his own personal aggrandizement. It therefore required little argument on the part of Cristóbal to secure his acquiescence to becoming the patron of still another expedition of discovery. For the past three decades the churchman had urged Spain to pursue the original idea of Columbus and tap the riches of Asia by a western route to Cipango and Cathay. He listened with interest to Cristóbal's revelations about the Portuguese discovery of a southwest passage.

The Fonseca family had been established for generations as feudal lords in a rich, well-watered valley of northern Spain whose beauty and fertility were praised by Lope de Vega. They had castles in the important towns of Toro, Alaejos, Ulloa, and Coca, and their hereditary title was Lord of Alaejos and Coca. This part of Old Castile was then the most highly industrialized and thickly populated portion of the country, and the wealth and influence of the Fonsecas were correspondingly important. They were patrons of the university at nearby Salamanca, which was then the cultural center of Spain.

Juan's father, Fernando, died of wounds after the Battle of Olmedo in the civil war of 1467, and Antonio, the oldest son, succeeded to the title.

Juan was then sixteen, a student at Salamanca. After his ordination he followed his brother Antonio to war under the banner of Queen Isabella, and when she was established on her throne by the victory over the Portuguese at Toro in 1476, Juan, as a young priest, entered the household of Ferdinand and Isabella in Valladolid. One of his aunts was an influential lady-in-waiting to the Queen, and as he also was connected by marriage to Don Pedro of Castile, cousin to Isabella, he and Antonio were treated by the royal family as relatives. He was of the same age as the ruling couple and was admitted to their private circle.

Juan immediately looked for a source of income from some of the remunerative clerical livings reserved for the family. The younger sons of the Fonsecas, as a matter of right, expected to inherit the bishoprics and abbacies in Old Castile. Juan's grandmother, the Marquesa de Canete, once boasted that she was the sister of a Cardinal, the mother of an Archbishop, and the grandmother of a Bishop. His uncle, Alonso de Fonseca, now Archbishop of Toledo, had been successively Bishop of Avila, Bishop of Asuna, Bishop of Cuenca, Archbishop of Santiago, and Archbishop of Seville. As Archbishop of Toledo he was, next to the Pope, the richest prelate in Christendom. He had more vassals owing allegiance to him than any lay grandee in Spain, commanded a private army, and exercised sovereignty as feudal lord over fifteen populous towns and innumerable smaller communities. His archepiscopal revenue amounted to a million five hundred thousand ducats a year.

Juan's uncle and cousins then in the hierarchy saw to it that their newly ordained young relative was given early opportunity to exercise his promising talents. They soon had him made Archdeacon of Olmedo in the Bishopric of Avila and Abbot of *San Zoil de Carrion y de Parraces*. He apparently drew the revenues of the abbey for life without ever performing the duties of abbot. Later he was given the desirable post of Provisor of Granada under Archbishop Ferdinand de Talavera.

Although he was appointed to these clerical offices and collected the revenues, he continued in attendance at Court.

When Juan had served in the royal household as chaplain for half a dozen years, he found that, as his responsibilities increased, his expenditures at Court exceeded his means. Therefore he pressed his relatives to get him some additional appointment, and, at the age of thirty-two, with his family's help, he seized an opportunity not merely to earn an increased income, but to acquire a very substantial fortune. He was named as special judicial assistant to the Archbishop of Seville, a political plum of the first order.

Seville was, during the 1470's, the flourishing financial capital of all the Jewish world, and in no other city, either Christian or Mohammedan, except perhaps in Rome, did the Jews enjoy such civic and economic freedom. The Jewish merchants had been driven from the markets of the rest of Europe by the various guilds, and had found a mercantile haven only in Spain, where their race enjoyed royal favor and protection. During ten centuries the Sephardic Jews, native to Spain, had become an integral part of the Spanish people and not only dominated Spanish trade and finance, but also were leaders in the field of medicine and active in law and in parliament. Their influence in the Church had become so great that one out of every four Spanish bishops had Jewish blood. Many of the daughters of wealthy Jews had married into impoverished aristocratic families, and there was a notable Jewish strain in the nobility. The army, largely made up of the four monastic military orders, was without discernible Jewish influence, except that the quartermaster's department was conducted by Jews.

Eighty-five per cent of the Jews in Spain were in Seville, which they had made a thriving metropolis and a growing rival of Florence and Venice. They were quite unmolested in the practice of their religion and openly taught the Hebrew language in their own schools, just as the Moorish population of Seville were permitted to worship in their mosques and to give lessons from the Koran to their children.

Both the sovereigns were tolerant toward the Jewish people and markedly favorable toward the *conversos*, or Christianized Jews. The confessor of both Their Majesties was Bishop Ferdinand de Talavera, who was of Jewish blood. The royal family physician was a *converso*, as were also the three trusted secretaries of Queen Isabella who handled her most confidential correspondence. King Ferdinand's fiscal adviser, Louis Santangelo, Treasurer of the Kingdom of Aragon, was the political leader of the *converso* group at Court, and was a member of the personal circle of the sovereigns.

In 1478, the Jews of Seville were plunged from their political and fiscal pre-eminence into disaster. The author of the Jewish downfall was Tomas de Torquemada, a fanatical Dominican monk of incorruptible but perverted zeal. He, almost single handed, created in Seville the inquisitorial body known as the Holy Office, which revived long dormant anti-Semitic laws and usurped police and judicial authority over the Jews.

In 1478, Torquemada commenced his persecution of the Jews in Seville, but for five years the Andalusian upper classes managed to protect many of them from him. Both the orthodox and the *converso* groups formed defensive organizations, assessed their members, and collected large legal defense funds. They appealed to the Pope against Torquemada's most flagrant sentences of death and confiscation, and in many instances secured at Rome a reversal of his judgments.

However, in 1483, Torquemada was appointed by the sovereigns, with papal sanction, Grand Inquisitor of Castile and Leon. This made him independent of the local Catholic authorities, who up until then had shielded many of his intended victims. To a large degree this also made him independent of Rome. The original purpose of the crown in establishing the Inquisition, which was to ferret out treason in Seville, was now quite lost, and Torquemada made of the organization an instrument of anti-Semitic persecution. Unchecked by higher authority and supported by the mob that he had excited to frenzy, Torquemada, now became a madman, loosed his terrible police force, the so-called familiars of the Holy Office, upon the defenseless orthodox Jews.

All the better-class Christians, including most of the Catholic clergy in Seville, and headed by the great feudal lords of Andalusia, vigorously protested to the sovereigns, demanding that some control be exercised and that a judicial review be made of Torquemada's convictions. The sovereigns, therefore, confirmed the general authority over Torquemada of the Archbishop of Seville, to whom they gave broad powers of judicial review of the sentences of the Inquisition. They named Juan de Fonseca as his judicial assistant, with the rank of a Dean of the Cathedral of Seville.

The venerable and ailing Archbishop much needed a deputy, for he had become quite eccentric. He always went about accompanied by a pet Nubian lion, without teeth or claws, which even lay on the steps of the altar while he read his Mass. He was reluctant to accept the new judicial office and had neither the strength nor the qualifications to discharge its responsibilities. Everyone recognized that he would be a figurehead, and that his responsible functions would have to be carried out by a competent deputy. Juan de Fonseca had early perceived the importance of this office, and managed to secure the appointment. He immediately established friendly relations with the Grand Inquisitor, whose aristocratic background was similar to his own, for he also was the nephew of a prominent churchman.

As soon as the Court of Appeals was set up, the relatives of the condemned Jews crept trembling to implore Dean Juan de Fonseca to save them, and it may be assumed that he extracted large fees under pretense of using the funds to help them. Neither Juan nor the other officials were often able to get the Inquisition to release any of the petitioners, who confessed under torture and then either disappeared into life imprisonment or met death at the stake.

If Juan took advantage of this opportunity to enrich himself, he was not alone. Since the estate of a convicted man would be confiscated, half going to the Inquisition and half to the Crown, the court officials had little scruple in trying to divert as much as possible to their own pockets. There is no evidence to convict Juan Rodríguez de Fonseca of judicial corruption, but soon after his assumption of office in Seville, he became a wealthy prelate, and the deduction is inevitable.

The King and Queen were persuaded, in 1492, to sign a decree expelling all orthodox Jews who would not accept Christian baptism. They thought this would bring about a mass conversion and make for religious uniformity and racial cohesion in the realm. But after the expulsion of the orthodox Jews, the Holy Inquisition turned upon the *conversos* and proceeded to ruin them wholesale, regardless of their profession of Christianity.

In interrogating the frightened *conversos,* to whom he posed as savior, Juan de Fonseca extracted from them valuable secret information about the Arab caravan routes and markets in the African interior, of which the great city of Timbuktu was the metropolis. He learned much about the Arab Red Sea traffic to the Malabar Coast of India and to the eastern ports of Africa. This stimulated his interest in the possibility of direct trade by Spain with the East.

The Moors, too, unsettled by the intolerant atmosphere aroused by Torquemada, sought exit permits from Juan de Fonseca for their families and possessions. From them he also doubtless gathered information about the oriental trading areas. The Castilians feared reprisals against Christian captives in North Africa, and hence permitted the Moors to leave without confiscating their property.

Up to this time there had been no definite knowledge on the part of Christians in Spain regarding either the Arab trade in Central and Western Africa or the Egyptian and Venetian commerce in the Red Sea, Persian Gulf, and Arabian Sea. Fonseca was apparently one of the first Spaniards to penetrate this secret. When he interrogated the would-be emigrants, both Moorish and Jewish, he was impressed by the bold theories of celestial navigation and cartography held by some. From Moslem astrologers in Egypt and Persia and from Arab navigators in the Indian Ocean, they had acquired ideas of which the ecclesiastical professors at Salamanca had not even an inkling. The *conversos* made reference to the theories of a *converso* cartographer from Lisbon named Christopher Columbus, and Juan learned that he had for a long time been cooling his heels in the anterooms of the Spanish Court in the hope of securing royal support for a project to sail westward to Cipango, across the Green Sea of Darkness. To Juan's amazement, these *converso* scholars did not find this idea preposterous. On the contrary, the influential *converso* group surrounding the Catholic sovereigns had been quietly advocating it, but they had not dared come out for it openly for fear that Torquemada might decide it was heretical. Columbus had circumspectly avoided any public personal identification with the Spanish *converso* courtiers, who privately regarded him as one of their own. The mother of his natural son, Ferdinand, appears to have been a Jewess of Cordoba. Christopher Columbus was devoted to her and was on intimate terms with her relatives.

Juan de Fonseca arranged to have Columbus brought to him and was captivated by his magnetic personality. Once Juan became convinced of the feasibility of the proposal that was so congenial to him, he adopted it and exercised his political talents in its favor.

He introduced Columbus to Diego de Deza, a *converso* who had become Archbishop of Seville, and won his ardent support. The cause of Columbus began to prosper, and a royal commission investigated his proposal. However, despite the fact that the Archbishop was a member of this committee, the majority report was unfavorable. Columbus was disheartened, but Fonseca merely prodded Archbishop de Deza to form a second junta of investigation, to be composed of scientists selected from his own University of Salamanca. This committee obligingly rendered an approving verdict. Armed with this document, the Archbishop and Juan de Fonseca pushed the project vigorously. The influential *conversos* at Court headed by Louis Santangelo, Treasurer of Aragon, backed the intrigue and secured a contract and an appropriation for Columbus from the Crown of Castile.

Fonseca pulled wires to have himself appointed royal comptroller of the expedition, and Isabella, always partial to him, gave him sweeping powers. She made him virtually a copartner with Columbus. The extent of his participation is evidenced by the extant royal orders in which the names of Fonseca and Columbus are coupled as being jointly responsible for the enterprise. Fonseca embraced his new duties with enthusiasm, worked cordially with Columbus, and fitted out, manned and dispatched the squadron. Isabella, as a mark of her appreciation, made him Archdeacon of Seville.

When the second expedition of Columbus was decided upon, there was no question as to who should be given charge of its preparation. In March, 1493, Fonseca sent it to sea, fully equipped in record time. Yet he did not work so well with Columbus in preparing the second voyage. He had no tolerance for the great navigator's confused administrative processes, and furthermore, he was irked that this alien had become His Magnificence, Admiral of the Ocean Sea, Viceroy of the Indies, and Governor General of Hispaniola. The title of Admiral had hitherto been one of the proudest in Spain, and Fonseca, the aristocrat, was enraged that it should be bestowed upon one suspected of being an Italian Jew. Flamboyant Columbus was in such favor that he was permitted to keep his hat on his head in royal audience, the privilege only of grandees, and was even once allowed the unique honor of seating himself in the presence of the sovereigns.

Fonseca became Columbus's unrelenting foe and did all he could to check and hamper the hero. He opposed Columbus when he insisted upon the fulfillment of his contract with the Crown. Columbus claimed to hold all the land in fief as feudal lord, under the King, with the sole right to parcel it out. But he could not enforce his authority, because the prizes were too rich. Columbus played into the hands of his archenemy by a number of blunders, and Fonseca took advantage of his errors to trick, entangle, and eventually to overthrow him.

Isabella depended on Fonseca to build a merchant marine which, in the delirium of colonization of 1493, was needed almost overnight. Juan was helped in this by Captain Diogo Barbosa, a Portuguese exile with experience in maritime administration. Diogo Barbosa brought in naval architects and shipwrights from Portugal, and Juan soon was launching seaworthy caravels. He also recruited artillerists from Germany to teach naval gunnery to his captains, and persuaded Jewish astronomers and map makers to come from Lisbon, under his protection, to improve the charts and nautical instruments for his navigators. He then opened a royal school of navigation in Seville under the direction of his Florentine friend, Amerigo Vespucci, with authority to examine the qualifications of all pilots and to withhold or to grant licenses to them.

It was so rare for an aristocrat to have commercial ability that it was a matter of comment by Fonseca's peers, who could not fail to see that his capacity for administrative detail was prodigious. This extraordinary priest found himself called upon by his sovereigns to shoulder many fiscal burdens, and before long he became virtually the Army and Navy Quartermaster for the Crown.

Juan was helped in this work by the versatile Florentine, Amerigo Vespucci, who was not only the preceptor of his pilots but also agent of the Medici bank. Juan gave him many trade privileges, always taking care to share privately in his gains. Many of the caravels that plied to the Spanish colonial ports flew Florentine house flags, and in the colonies the banks and warehouses were largely theirs. So extortionate were their prices in the West Indian stores for farm tools and necessities that a Spanish wit quipped that the Castilian colonists robbed the Indians and then the Florentines robbed the Castilians.

After the first founding of settlements in the West Indies in 1493, the work of Juan's department was hampered by the probability of war with Portugal. However, the Supreme Pontiff intervened and established a truce, and in 1494 the Treaty of Tordesillas established the demarcation of zones of exploration. It was under the controversial terms of this treaty that Fonseca later justified sending Magellan's fleet into the Indian waters over which Portugal claimed sovereignty.

In 1497, Fonseca sent Amerigo Vespucci on an expedition down the South American coast to probe for a passage to India, and in 1499 he also dispatched Alonso de Ojeda to Venezuela to find the strait. The Crown delegated its colonial governing powers to a Supreme Council of the Indies, of which Fonseca was appointed Prince President. In 1502 he set up the *Casa de Antillas* as a subordinate operating department. This administrative bureau eventually operated an arsenal, shipyard, ammunition factory, bank, bakery, and packing house. It issued all passports, licensed the clearance of ships, supervised colonial exports and imports, collected customs, imposed fines, and controlled the courts and the police in the overseas dependencies. The colonial government, from top to bottom, was autocratically dominated by Fonseca, through the *Casa de Antillas.* He administered the organization effectively, but never overlooked his private interests. Because the *Casa* operated what corresponded to a colonial post office, he was able to censor the mail, suppressing all criticism of himself and delaying or diverting any official orders he pleased, even from the Crown.

In 1503, Juan de Fonseca permitted Christopher Columbus to sail on his fourth voyage with a wretchedly equipped squadron, having secured the Crown's reluctant permission to try once more to find the Westward Passage to Cathay. The Magnificent Admiral of the Ocean Sea came back frustrated, discredited, and broken-hearted. In 1506, having become a Franciscan monk, he died in obscurity at Valladolid, impoverished and forgotten.

On December 24, 1507, at Burgos, King Ferdinand signed an order which read: Everything concerning India is to be in the hands of Juan Rodríguez de Fonseca, the Bishop of Palencia, our Chief Chaplain, and of Lope Conchillos, our Secretary. In 1511, a royal order appointed Fonseca Chancellor of the Indies and Keeper of the Seal, thus confirming his absolute command of fiscal and judicial matters. He retained this authority not only during Don Ferdinand's life and during the regency of Cardinal Ximenes, but also during the early part of the reign of King Charles.

Fonseca curbed the lawless adventurers who made up the advance guard of Spain's penetration of the New World. Only an administrator of his implacable type could have maintained the royal authority over those audacious and defiant pioneers. In 1513, he brought about the execution of Vasco Nuñez de Balboa, who, after discovering the Pacific Ocean, had set up his own government in Panama. In 1519, during the time he was busied with Magellan's project, Fonseca sent an armed expedition to Mexico against the upstart Hernando Cortes. When this failed, he attempted to have him assassinated.

A conquistador might brave incredible dangers, and after victory beg the King to confirm him as Governor of his conquered territory, accompanying his petition by a gift to the monarch of gold, silver, or pearls. Needless to say, the message and the tribute were sent through the *Casa de Antillas*. The letter of petition, however, would be suppressed by Juan de Fonseca en route and a new one substituted bearing the signature of one of Juan's partisans. The rich gift would also go to the King in the name of Fonseca's candidate for office, and Juan would then press the King to give the governorship to him. Once the royal commission was signed, they would get rid of the original conquistador by condemning him as a rebel and outlaw. Fonseca's strategic position made it impossible for the friends of the defrauded to bring their complaint to the attention of the King.

The religious orders to which were entrusted the conversion of the Indians were independent of Fonseca's administration, and they provided a channel of protest. Some of the friars had access to the King and endeavored to have reforms introduced in the corrupt overseas governments, but Fonseca always managed to overcome such attempts to interfere in his domain. It was not until the Holy Father himself intervened to expose to the Emperor the rascalities of the hypocritical prelate that his malpractices were curbed.

King Ferdinand gave Fonseca the title of Archbishop, appointing him to the nominal see of Rosano in Sicily, and Fonseca then tried, in his capacity as Archbishop, to assume authority over the ecclesiastical as well as the secular departments in America. King Ferdinand was favorable to this scheme and applied to the Pope for Fonseca's appointment as Patriarch of the Indies. The prospect of his elevation was so promising that he was prematurely addressed by the title, but the missionary friars prevented his investiture, and King Ferdinand died before Fonseca could obtain a Cardinal's hat.

The most favored beneficiary of Juan's partiality was the fashionable young courtier Juan de Cartagena, whom he called his nephew. The records of the Fonseca family show no such legitimate nephew, and it is probable, therefore, that he was Juan's natural son. It was customary politely to designate the favored illegitimate children of churchmen as nephews and nieces.

Although Fonseca proved himself to be a competent administrator of the *Casa de Antillas* and established a brilliant record as an executive, he never deluded himself as to the real reason for his retention for three decades in his post as head of the Supreme Council of the Indies. He was well aware that his favored position was due to his own continuous cultivation of close relations with the members of the royal family. He made this a paramount consideration. He never hesitated to drop any employment at the *Casa de Antillas,* no matter how important, if some royal personage desired his services or his company.

Histories of the reign of Ferdinand and Isabella contain little recognition of the important but unobtrusive part he played in the dynastic plans to which the Queen devoted her life. During all the period in which he was presumably enriching himself in Seville by spoliation of the Jews and later, when entrenching himself as founder of the *Casa de Antillas* and as autocrat of the Supreme Council of the Indies, he occupied a position of decisive influence with the royal family. He was admitted to the private cabinets of both Ferdinand and Isabella, and likewise had access to the nursery and study room of the Prince of the Asturias and of his sisters, the Infantas, who successively became heirs to the throne. He was Head Chaplain of the royal household.

The foreign policy of the "Catholic Kings," as Ferdinand and Isabella were styled, was directed primarily to unifying the Iberian Peninsula by bringing Spain and Portugal beneath the rule of a single scepter, and they tried to accomplish this through the marriage of the princesses. Their second object was to isolate their rivals, the Valois, who ruled hostile France. Strategic marriages of the princesses to the heirs of the reigning families of Hapsburg in Flanders and Germany and of Tudor in England would, they hoped, achieve this as well. In bringing about these results, the reigning family mades free use of the diplomatic talents of Fonseca. He was sent on many diplomatic missions by his sovereign, and to him was delegated the honor of escorting the Infantas Isabella, Catherine, and Joanna as they departed to marry, respectively, scions of the royal families of Portugal, England, and Austria. In January, 1506, he paid his fourth diplomatic visit to Flanders, where Archduke Philip of Austria, the Infanta Joanna's husband, ruled. The powerful Spanish Bishop found Queen Joanna much changed from the carefree, gay princess he had known in her girlhood. Now she was a violently possessive woman, jealous of anyone to whom her husband showed favor.

Fonseca's visits to Flanders had played an important part, commercially as well as diplomatically, in the orientation of Spanish power, for he formed a business alliance with the Fuggers which displaced the Medici from their favored position in Spain, doubtless not without profit to himself. Jakob Fugger himself may have made the journey to Antwerp in order to confer with him.

Queen Isabella had died, at the age of fifty-three, in November, 1504. She had been ruler of Castile in her own right, and her union with Ferdinand of Aragon had united the two great kingdoms of Spain in their two persons. Now she was dead and her daughter, Joanna, had become Queen of Castile. The primary aim of this fourth visit of Bishop Fonseca to Flanders was to bring Philip, Joanna's husband, into closer understanding with Don Ferdinand, Joanna's father, and thereby retain the close links binding Aragon and Castile.

Despite his misgivings and contrary to all predictions, Juan's mission to Flanders for King Ferdinand was successful. This was due to the support given him by Joanna, now Queen of Castile, by his old-time friend, the Archduchess Margaret, sister to Archduke Philip, and by his new secret partner, Jakob Fugger. He outgeneraled the opposing French diplomats and Spanish exiles and succeeded in preventing an open break between

Archduke Philip and Don Ferdinand. The Archduke was furious at the terms of Queen Isabella's will, which favored Don Ferdinand, and asserted his own right to the throne of Castile as Consort to Queen Joanna, but Fonseca persuaded him to promise to come to Castile and to meet his father-in-law amicably.

In April, 1506, Philip and Joanna landed in Castile, but Philip brought with him a strong army of German mercenaries. Don Ferdinand came to see Philip unescorted and suavely recognized him as King of Castile. However, he lured Queen Joanna away from her husband and secretly ordered Fonseca to keep her in his custody. Fonseca was entertaining her in La Mota Castle, at Medina del Campo, when Philip sent her a note bidding her come to him "in any way she could." The Bishop tried to keep her from going, but Joanna was regally insistent, and Juan, who had only a handful of guards, thought it wise to let her go.

The Archduke was now recognized as King Philip I of Castile, joint ruler with his wife Joanna. He dismissed Ferdinand's friends from office, reversed his policies, and made overtures to the King of France, his mortal enemy. Philip virtually assumed sole sovereignty; he kept Joanna secluded and would not allow her father to visit her.

Juan de Fonseca and his brother Antonio, as grandees of Castile, did homage to their new king, but they were uneasy and kept secretly in touch with Don Ferdinand in Aragon. Ferdinand meanwhile hid his resentment and bided his time. It had been traditional for his ancestors to settle family feuds by the judicious administration of poison, and, in his Kingdom of Naples, the Renaissance art of poisoning had long been discreetly practiced as a weapon in political warfare. It was not long before boisterous, overweening, Teutonic King Philip died suddenly, having eaten a rich Spanish stew at dinner. Mosen Ferrer, a groom of the bedchamber, is suspected of having acted for King Ferdinand in this matter. The ill-starred Philip was only twenty-eight years old, and had been King a short three months.

Both Antonio and Juan de Fonseca had unobtrusively come to Burgos just before the King's death, and it is significant that they had met there the Italian physician of Don Ferdinand. In retrospect few of the sophisticated believed this to be by coincidence. After Philip had expired, and during the indescribable confusion at the palace, Bishop Fonseca smoothly took command of the scene in the royal bedchamber, called in the Italian doctor together with a medical collaborator, and had them make a formal diagnosis, after which they hastily issued a notarized medical certificate of natural death from indigestion. Juan immediately submitted this evidence to the hurriedly summoned Cortes of Castile and quickly dispatched it to the important European chancellories.

The adherents of the late King were taken by surprise, and before they could pull themselves together, Juan and Antonio de Fonseca decisively carried out their plans and took the distraught Queen Joanna into protective custody. They already had mobilized formidable forces at their castles at Alaejos and Coca, and they now seized possession of Burgos. The partisans of Don Ferdinand in the Cortes proclaimed him to be Regent of Castile, in accordance with the will of the late Queen Isabella, while Philip's adherents fled. The *coup d'etat* was supported by the influential Cardinal Ximenes. Fonseca now was in a stronger political position than ever, and his influence in Castile was second only to that of the Cardinal himself.

Don Ferdinand returned from Italy, where he had conspicuously absented himself, to accept the Regency of Castile from the Cortes. He rewarded Juan and Antonio de Fonseca munificently from the confiscated estates of the Castilian grandees who had proved his enemies and who had now fled to Flanders.

Don Ferdinand ordered Bishop Fonseca to assume permanent custody of Queen Joanna, which meant he would have the sole responsibility for safeguarding her. This was a very important charge, for many of the Castilian nobles were still hostile to Don Ferdinand and were continually plotting to get possession of the Queen's person. Because of Juan's long, affectionate association with her, no one could have been better suited to care for the afflicted Queen, who had lost her wits entirely in her grief. She had the embalmed body of Philip kept in her bed, and she would brook no other female near it. When she was in labor with her fourth child, shortly after Philip's death, she would not permit even an ancient midwife, selected because of her advanced age, to come into the royal bedchamber. Rather than allow any woman, no matter how old, to approach Philip, she lay there alone beside her husband's body and gave birth to her baby unaided. She refused to give up the body of her husband and stubbornly carried it with her as she journeyed through Spain to Granada, pathetically addressing the lifeless corpse as though it were still alive.

The grief-stricken, mad Joanna was Queen of Castile in her own right. She made a weird passage through Spain, unkempt and unwashed, her thoughts and attention centered on the wagon, drawn by four horses, which carried Philip's coffin. She was accompanied not only by Bishop Juan Rodríguez de Fonseca, her custodian, but by ladies in waiting, grandees, prelates, and the whole ceremonious train of household dignitaries required by rigid Spanish etiquette. At one stage, Fonseca had arranged to have the cortege spend the night at a convent en route. However, when they arrived, the Queen in her jealousy refused to allow Philip's corpse to lie under the same roof with any other woman, holy or otherwise. Fonseca and the train of disgruntled dignitaries had to pass an uncomfortable night in the open, beside the highway.

After Philip's body was at last buried in Granada, Juan cajoled the Queen into accompanying him back to Old Castile. He installed her cere-

Engraving from "Memorias de las Reynas Católicas," 1770

JOANNA, MAD QUEEN OF CASTILE,
Daughter of Ferdinand and Isabella, mother of Charles V

moniously as guest in his brother Antonio's well-guarded establishment at Toro, and while treating the poor Queen with all deference, he kept her confined to the premises. Joanna's mental lapses made it impossible for her to reign. Later the mad queen was transferred to the great tower of the castle at Medina del Campo, where she lived on for half a century in closely guarded captivity.

In 1507, as a splendid reward for his loyal services, Don Ferdinand created Juan Rodríguez de Fonseca Bishop of Burgos, an office with an annual income of twenty thousand ducats, or about three hundred thousand dollars. Because of the Bishop's feudal privileges over the thriving industrial city, this was the most lucrative see in Spain next to that of the Archbishopric of Toledo.

King Ferdinand died in 1516, and Fonseca transferred his allegiance to Cardinal Ximenes, who ruled Spain as regent for Ferdinand's grandson, young Charles, who was absent in Flanders. When Charles, after a year's delay, finally arrived in Spain, Bishop Fonseca betrayed Cardinal Ximenes and probably was implicated in his sudden death. At the time of Magellan's arrival in Spain from Portugal, Juan de Fonseca had made himself the power behind the Spanish throne by his control of the mind and person of the isolated and alien young ruler.

After Fonseca had attained supreme power in the kingdom, he made a mistake which often has caused the downfall of successful politicans. He became so absorbed in his new and broader responsibilities that he relaxed his control of the political organization which he had used in reaching his exalted post. When, confident in his new and lofty authority, he began to neglect the administrative details of the *Casa de Antillas,* there were others who immediately moved in to take advantage of his inattention.

It had been Fonseca's policy in building up the staff of the Colonial office to fill the executive positions with men of limited capacity and restricted ambition, men he was sure neither could nor would usurp his powers while he was abroad on his frequent absences for the royal family. This system insured his continued domination of the far-flung organization, as long as he continued to watch for any incipient rebellion in the lower ranks and to stamp it out immediately. However, as virtual head of the Spanish government in a particularly difficult time of rebellious turmoil, he could no longer give thought to the unruly elements in the colonies who constantly had to be checked and brought to heel. He relied upon his puppet directors to maintain discipline, but forgot that he had selected them precisely because of that lack of initiative and ability which meant they were unable to fill his place.

Consequently, while Juan had been preoccupied with his absorbing cabinet tasks as virtual Prime Minister and Minister of the Interior, his enemies, sensing their opportunity, had formed an alliance with the colonial malcontents under Hernando Cortes. The autocratic bureaucracy that Juan had entrenched in control at Seville, in Cuba, and in Hispaniola during his three decades of rule was now demoralized and breaking up; it was imperative that he take personal command at once of his badly shaken forces. His foes were attacking in his most vulnerable spot, his overseas possessions where his vast fortune was invested.

Overworked and exhausted as he was, Juan had to abandon temporarily his vital post beside the King, leave unfinished the overwhelming mass of pressing business in Valladolid, and hurry south to Seville.

He left his brother to guard the precious persons of the two royal prisoners. For indeed the young Charles, for all his regalia of kingship, was almost as much a captive of the Fonsecas as was his mother, Queen Joanna. The Bishop was now sixty-seven, and had grown portly and soft with the years, but he took horse and rode hard for Seville, for he felt that time was now against him.

Upon his arrival in Seville, he was appalled at the mediocrity in the *Casa de Antillas* in face of the blazing colonial rebellion. Taking hold, he struggled masterfully to inspire and revitalize his disorganized machine, but after a fortnight of effort, he was finding it uphill work. His rich plantations, his slaves, and his monopolies and special privileges in the West Indies, all might be swept away from him by the rebels. It was essential quickly to assemble and dispatch a well-found armada, but he encountered only bureaucratic fumbling and ineptitude. For the first time Juan de Fonseca, hitherto so resilient and tireless, became aware of exhaustion in his fatigued and aching body, and sat dismayed and despondent in his apartment where he had retired for the night.

It was at this moment that touseled, travel-stained Cristóbal de Haro was ushered into his presence, a refugee from Portugal, blasphemously indignant and vibrant with the energy of his discontent. When it dawned upon Juan that King Manuel had in so timely a manner driven this man of resolution, swift action, and sure accomplishment into his arms, he crossed himself in a moment of humble thankfulness and relief.

He heard Cristóbal plead for employment, make an offer of his talents and experience. The Bishop's momentary weakness vanished, and he was once again the forceful director of empire. With de Haro as a lieutenant, he could immediately enlist in his colonial faction the strong Fugger and de Haro overseas organization. He also could put this competent administrator in charge at Seville at once to send reinforcements to protect his jeopardized Caribbean estates.

Cristóbal lost no time in unrolling the project of reprisal against King Manuel which he had worked out during his flight. He had known for years that it was Fonseca's aim to establish for Spain a southwest passage to India, and he had helped King Manuel to block such an enterprise. Now, however, he freely disclosed to Juan de Fonseca secrets that the Spanish spies had never been able to uncover. Cristóbal thus planned to get revenge on Dom Manuel by helping Spain find the Southwest Passage to the Indies.

The two men were open with each other. Fonseca was grateful for the information that de Haro brought, and in return disclosed the state of his plans of exploration. He informed de Haro that after the death of his explorer, the Portuguese renegade Juan de Solis, at the hands of the Indians at Rio de la Plata, that he had decided to employ Estevan Gomes, another Portuguese refugee, to command a second expedition to seek a westward route to Maluco, and Gomes had practically been confirmed in the post and had commenced quietly to assemble a squadron. However, Fonseca's nautical adviser in Seville, the former Portuguese, Dom Diogo Barbosa, had learned that Gomes had been in secret communication with the local agent of Dom Manuel in Seville. When Cardinal Ximenes was informed of this suspicious incident, he declined to issue a commission to Gomes, and the plan had to be postponed until another Portuguese pilot familiar with the South Atlantic could be secured.

Fonseca now told how Diogo Barbosa, after secret negotiations in Portugal, had proposed to him that he make use of the talents of an unemployed captain named Ferdinand Magellan. Barbosa described him as of noble birth, a wounded veteran of Indian and Moroccan wars with a distinguished record, a sound knowledge of navigation, and an acquaintance with the waters about the spiceries. He reported that Magellan was out of favor with Dom Manuel and was disaffected and resentful in consequence. With the approval of Cardinal Ximenes, he had had Diogo Barbosa get Magellan over the Portuguese border to Seville, along with another gifted malcontent, Magellan's associate, Ruy Faleiro, an astronomer of scientific renown, and several other competent Portuguese navigators.

Juan de Fonseca told de Haro that he had not yet interviewed Magellan, for, since the landing of King Charles and the death of Cardinal Ximenes, he had been too preoccupied with matters of state.

Cristóbal de Haro said that he himself would be reluctant to employ Magellan to lead such an enterprise. He did not dislike Magellan personally, but had observed that he had been at loggerheads with all his former superiors and that his subordinates had found him hard to get along with. He described Magellan as very ambitious and headstrong, and deemed that, once given power, he would be difficult to control. He thought him grasping and feared he would demand an inordinate share of any treasures or spices the expedition might secure. Cristóbal therefore recommended that Estevan Gomes again be considered, rather than Magellan, as commander of the proposed expedition. He said he felt sure that Gomes had been wrongly judged by Diogo Barbosa, that he personally had found him trustworthy and thought Gomes equal in professional ability to Magellan, both as a navigator and as a commander. He knew him to be tractable and was certain he would carry out instructions to the letter. He remarked that Gomes always had got on well with his lieutenants, and he thought he would be modest in his expectations of participation in the financial returns if the expedition was successful.

Fonseca agreed to accept de Haro's endorsement of Gomes, and incidentally informed him that he intended to appoint his heir, Juan de Cartagena, as co-commander. He wished to be sure that young Cartagena, who lacked experience, would have a reliable and co-operative staff and would not be hampered by a jealous associate. He felt no personal responsibility for Magellan and his companions, whom Diogo Barbosa had brought over into Spain at his request, for he was sure he could find suitable employment for them in the fleets of the *Casa de Antillas*.

Cristóbal de Haro remarked dryly that he would probably not have to worry about Magellan long, for he believed that Dom Manuel would have him and his group kidnapped and brought back to Portugal to be executed, in order to deter any other pilots from deserting and betraying Portuguese secrets to Spain. Dom Manuel had already issued an order forbidding any Portuguese sailor to enter a foreign service and denouncing such action as high treason, and threatened any offender with the confiscation of all his goods and exile to the penal colony on the Island of St. Helena.

Juan de Fonseca frankly disclosed to de Haro his need for assistance in sending an armed squadron at once to the West Indies. De Haro promptly agreed to turn over the needed ships and armament from the ample Fugger marine establishment. Juan, his mind more at ease, delegated this task to his new friend with confidence that it would be executed speedily and efficiently.

Fonseca promised de Haro to lose no time in putting into effect their project to establish a westward route to India, for he recognized that Dom Manuel would soon learn of it and oppose it. The first step would be to get approval by the King's Council. He thought there would be no great difficulty in persuading his fellow members, Chancellor Chièvres, Treasurer Sauvage, and Cardinal Adrian, to accept the plan, with his endorsement, in which case they could count on the King's acquiescence. He himself now had to hurry back to Valladolid in response to a desperate summons from his brother Antonio; and he assured de Haro he would initiate the proposal there, immediately upon his arrival. The two men, so dissimilar in background and training, yet bound by their need for one another's services, parted well satisfied with their understanding. Each expected the other to be invaluable to him in his own selfish aims. For the present, those aims happened to be compatible, and that was enough.

CHAPTER XII

CHARLES OF GHENT

LITTLE Prince Charles did not inherit the crown of Castile at the death of his father, King Philip I, for his father had been king only as the consort to Joanna. The mad Queen, as we have seen, was kept in seclusion by her guardian, Juan Rodríguez de Fonseca; and her father, Ferdinand, King of Aragon, ruled Castile in her name as Regent. Joanna's place as Charles's mother was ably filled by his Hapsburg aunt, Margaret of Austria, the friend of Bishop de Fonseca.

At the age of six, Charles became Archduke of Austria, Duke of Württemberg, Duke of Burgundy, Duke of Brabant, Duke of Luxemburg, Count of Flanders, Count of Holland, Lord of the Western Isles, and King of Jerusalem. Since he could not legally govern until the age of fifteen, his foster mother, Margaret, acted as Vice-Regent under his grandfather, the Emperor Maximilian, and ruled the Low Countries for him.

Charles Hapsburg was born in February, 1500. He was first known as Charles of Ghent, from his birthplace in Flanders, and later was called Charles of Luxemburg from the duchy that was one of his hereditary holdings. He was saluted in Spain as Don Carlos Primero, or Charles the First, and was later designated as Carolus Quint, in the official Latin of diplomacy, after his election as Holy Roman Emperor.

Charles, growing up in the old family castle in Mechlin, gradually assumed to the highly individualistic towns and factions of Flanders a symbolic significance as the personification of centralized authority. Because he had been born a Flemish prince, and because he was bereft of his parents' care, the sympathetic Lowlanders conceived a paternal affection for the royal boy. Even as a very small child, he was made the central figure in the gorgeous pageants in which the Renaissance populace took such delight. Little Charles endeared himself to the burghers by the instinctive dignity and natural courtesy with which he carried off his public appearances. The crowds were enraptured when the small Archduke, dressed in Flemish brocades or encased in a miniature suit of damascened Nuremberg armor, rode beside the Vice-Regent, gravely perched on the war saddle of a great Belgian charger.

Charles's subjects were intensely interested in palace gossip about his daily life and eager for details about his education and training. The will of his father had named a Flemish nobleman, William du Croy, Lord of Chièvres, to be his tutor. He early impressed upon the boy a sense of the responsibilities to which he had been born and instilled in him a liking for governmental affairs. The child was not afraid to work and had a Dutch persistence in handling details.

Charles was heir presumptive to all the crowns of his maternal grandfather, King Ferdinand of Aragon, Navarre, and Sicily, but his paternal grandfather, the Emperor Maximilian, had control of the child and jealously kept him from Ferdinand. The colony of Spanish exiles in Flanders also persistently tried to alienate him from his Spanish grandfather. Don Ferdinand was therefore at a loss to keep in contact with his grandson and heir and, as in so many matters, turned to Bishop Fonseca, whose friendship with the Archduchess Margaret might be useful in reaching the boy.

Fonseca reported from Flanders that he found Charles to be a serious, silent little fellow, friendly to other children and fond of animals, birds, and flowers. He liked to play quietly alone with clocks, mechanical inventions, and even with scientific instruments; and he loved to study maps. Small things like mice or spiders frightened him. Unfortunately he had had more than one fit of epilepsy.

In addition to his aunt and his tutor, Charles was fortunate in his third preceptor. This was the Dutch priest Adrian Dedel, Dean of the University of Louvain, who had taught at the University of Utrecht and was author of a book on philosophy. He was a man of simple honesty, uncompromising in his hatred of laxity in the clergy. He therefore always held aloof from Bishop Fonseca, resisted his advances, and more than once rebuked him for hypocrisy. Years later, when Adrian became Pope, he intervened to rescue the victims of Juan's tyranny and caused his political downfall. In religion Dean Adrian was a fundamentalist, but his placid piety was congenial to the phlegmatic nature of Charles. As spiritual adviser he was dutifully listened to by the boy, but as schoolmaster he was given little heed. Charles would not study, and Dean Adrian could not do anything about it.

All well-educated boys were then expected to know some Greek and much Latin. The latter was still the common European tongue of diplomacy, of letters, and of jurisprudence. But Charles would have none of Greek and never learned to be more than a passable Latinist. Neither would he study Spanish, Dutch, Flemish, German or Italian, each of which was spoken by people whom he was being trained to govern. All those about him in Mechlin spoke French, and what was good enough for them was good enough for Charles.

The only books Charles liked were on the history of government, for his inclination was toward statesmanship. Therefore Dean Adrian employed his friend, the great Dutch scholar Erasmus, to compose for Charles a book of advice on Christian kingcraft. This might be compared with Machiavelli's contemporary handbook *The Prince,* which it resembled only in general topic, as Erasmus's advice was quite different from that of the worldly Italian.

Chièvres' aim was to make not a scholar but a great captain out of his young charge. The pale, red-haired boy, of slight, short stature, was not a martial figure like burly Henry Tudor of England or stalwart Francis Valois of France, but he had considerable muscular strength and co-ordination. Under careful schooling by the best masters he became a competent swordsman. In manhood, he dared challenge long-armed Francis the First of France to meet him in a duel to the death with rapiers. He used to delight the Flemish populace by winning tournaments in competition with the best knights of Europe, riding Moorish style with a lance at a series of suspended rings, and it was later said that a first-class cavalry general had been spoiled when he became a king. Fonseca hunted with him during his stay in Flanders. The Emperor Maximilian, his grandfather, wrote, "We are surely happy that our boy Charles gets so much enjoyment out of hunting, as otherwise we are afraid people would suspect him to be a bastard."

Don Ferdinand was, however, much perturbed about Fonseca's reports of the nervous condition of his heir apparent. Because of his distressing experience with Charles's mother, Joanna, he was apprehensive that the boy might have inherited a strain of madness. He had Juan suggest to Chièvres that female companionship might be of benefit to the lad, and that his epilepsy could perhaps be corrected by cohabitation. The Emperor Maximilian concurred in this and authorized Chièvres to make the experiment. The lad, wrapped up in the details of government, much occupied with hunting and with jousting in the tiltyard, had so far paid no attention to women. Chièvres selected an amiable and personable young woman of the burgher class, purchased her parents' consent, and artfully introduced her into the adolescent Archduke's society. He at once developed an affection for her and in due time became father to a daughter. The little girl, christened Margaret for Charles's aunt, was taken away from the middle-class mother and educated as a Hapsburg princess. Later known everywhere as Ma Donna (My Lady), she played a brilliant role as aide to her father in the affairs of Empire. The only other known illegitimate child of Charles was the renowned admiral, Don Juan of Austria, victor against the Turks at Lepanto, who likewise was the child of a Flemish mother of the burgher class.

Neither love nor concupiscence was an important motivation in Charles's life, and at no time in his career could he be influenced in his policies by courtiers or favorites working upon him through mistresses. The only women to whom he ever listened for any political advice were his illegitimate daughter, Ma Donna, his aunt, Margaret of Austria, his sister, Mary of Hungary, and his wife, Isabella of Portugal.

Charles was the most eligible matrimonial catch in Christendom, and therefore the child was surrounded by intrigue concerning his eventual marriage. While still in the nursery he was engaged successively to four daughters of the Valois family. Later he was affianced to Mary Tudor, the sister of Henry VIII of England, and subsequently to another Mary Tudor, her niece. None of these engagements ended in marriage, having been merely moves in the game of international politics.

The basic foreign policy of Don Ferdinand was to build up a coalition against the King of France. In this he conflicted with the Emperor Maximilian, who followed a pro-French policy. Chièvres, a Walloon, was wholly French in his sympathies and hence opposed to Don Ferdinand. Margaret, though she had been raised at the French court, hated the reigning Valois family of France for having jilted her. Fonseca encouraged Margaret's resentment toward France and nurtured her friendliness for Don Ferdinand, whom she knew well, as she was his son's widow.

Fonseca used his intimacy with Margaret to gain the confidence of young Charles. He commiserated with him over being treated as a pawn by the Emperor Maximilian in matchmaking negotiations. Charles had been meek about these arrangements, even though they involved him so deeply; but he lost his tractable resignation and displayed very human feeling when he was suddenly denied his fiancée, young Mary Tudor. Henry VIII of England, her brother, summarily broke off her engagement to Charles and, to the fury of the Emperor Maximilian, married her to the scrofulous, aged, and dying King of France.

When the news was broken to Charles he was sitting on a window seat playing with a young hunting falcon, perched hooded upon his wrist. The boy said nothing, but almost beside himself, began feverishly to pluck the feathers from the hawk. A courtier, standing by him, impulsively remonstrated at the cruelty of his act. At his words, Charles burst into protest, comparing himself to the young creature who, like him, was blindfolded, shackled, and defenseless under torture.

On New Year's Day, 1515, Charles, Archduke of Austria, became by proclamation ruler of the Low Countries. The great cities vied with one another in showing their loyalty to him as he made a triumphal procession about his realm. Each town tried to outdo its neighbor in the extravagance of its parades and ceremonies of welcome. When he made his *joyeuse entrée* into Antwerp, fourteen cities of Flanders sent deputations in carnival costume to pass in review before the Archduke. So extensive were the festivities that all business in that great port city stopped for a whole month's holiday.

Although Charles was the favorite of his Flemish subjects and of his paternal grandfather, the Emperor Maximilian, he inevitably fell into disfavor with his maternal grandfather, Don Ferdinand. Bishop Fonseca was now in a difficult position in the Spanish court. Don Ferdinand had encouraged him to maintain close relations with the Hapsburgs and to be his liaison lieutenant between Flanders and Spain. Now, however, the aged king had grown to hate his grandson, Charles, and his former daughter-in-law, Margaret Hapsburg. Once when Fonseca attempted to defend Margaret to him against an absurd charge, the old man flew into a rage, denounced him as a turncoat, and ordered him out of his presence. The Bishop discreetly remained away from court for a short time, but meanwhile assiduously cultivated Cardinal Ximenes, who now had the greatest influence with the aging monarch. Before long Juan was back in favor.

Don Ferdinand considered that his grandson had been alienated from him by the Hapsburgs, and he did all he could to prevent Charles from becoming King of Aragon. The vigorous septuagenarian even married a young French princess and surprised the court by having a son, but the baby died in the cradle, and Charles again became heir to all the crowns of Spain. Don Ferdinand then named Charles's younger brother, Prince Ferdinand, as his heir in Aragon. He also decreed in his will that young Ferdinand should succeed him as Regent of Castile for incompetent Queen Joanna. Cardinal Ximenes, however, persuaded Don Ferdinand on his deathbed to revoke his will and reconfirm his older grandson, Charles of Ghent, as heir to Aragon. The dying King recognized Ximenes's patriotism and therefore made him Regent of Castile.

Upon Don Ferdinand's death, Ximenes naturally expected Charles to set out at once for Spain to assume the rule, and sent dispatches arranging for his immediate entry. Charles owed his Spanish throne entirely to Ximenes, but he was kept in ignorance of the Cardinal's intervention in his favor by his tutor and adviser, Chièvres, who feared that his own influence might be weakened.

Cardinal Ximenes also persuaded the Pope and the Emperor to decree that Queen Joanna was unfit to rule Castile alone. He thereupon prevailed upon the Cortes of Castile to proclaim Charles co-ruler. Charles had governed the Lowlands as Archduke for only a year when, at the age of sixteen, he thus entered upon his second splendid inheritance. He became the first sovereign to rule both Castile and Aragon, which embraced the five kingdoms of Spain.

The realm was in such a condition of unrest that it was urgent that the new king, who had never even been seen by the Spanish people, take office at once. Abroad there was a state of active hostilities with the Berbers of North Africa, and even more serious, at home there was danger of rebellion by a league of grandees who had already mobilized their armed retainers. Yet despite the need for the new King's presence, Chièvres did not wish Charles to go to Spain and therefore found every pretext to delay his departure for over a year. The lad respected Chièvres like a father, and worked with him in all administrative matters as a submissive junior partner.

At that age Charles seemed to be dazed and apathetic, and it has been suspected that Chièvres administered drugs to keep his protégé in a torpid state, for the unscrupulous tutor's appetite for power and wealth made him stop at nothing. On the other hand, however, perhaps Charles was passing through a period of delayed adolescence that retarded his natural vigor. In a contemporary woodcut showing his profile, he looked dull and stupid, almost a cretin. The pallid, red-haired boy suffered from adenoids, which affected his respiration so that he generally kept his mouth open to breathe, and that gave him an imbecilic look. He had the undershot lower jaw and pendulous, moist lower lip of the Hapsburgs, which made him drool, and a vacuous expression that, coupled with the known insanity of his mother, made foreign ambassadors mistrust his comprehension. It is no wonder that all who came on official business preferred to deal privately with the competent Chièvres.

Yet Chièvres himself knew full well it was not an oaf he kept in captivity, but a youth of dormant talent and incipient greatness, and was careful to treat him with deference and consideration. However, when Archduke Charles was prematurely elevated to the thrones of Spain, Chièvres by no means rejoiced, but looked on the event as a calamity for his own private interests. He had discharged his duties in an upright manner during Charles's childhood, but as his ward began to grow self-reliant, Chièvres foresaw that the period of his tutelage was nearing its end and hurriedly began to enrich himself at the expense of the state.

Chièvres now plotted with Bishop Fonseca to undermine the Regent, Cardinal Ximenes, and to strip Spain of all the wealth they could. They permitted no disinterested person to reach the King and thus managed to keep Charles in ignorance of the enormous flow of stolen Spanish ducats into the Fugger bank at Antwerp. The urgent pleas from Regent Ximenes that Charles come at once to Spain were also hidden from him. Knowing that the Cardinal's lofty character would undoubtedly captivate the candid young King and turn him against their cabal, Chièvres put every possible barrier between the Regent and the King. The only Spanish dispatches that he let reach Charles in Flanders were those of Fonseca, whom Chièvres represented to him as his loyal lieutenant in the conduct of Spanish affairs. Since it took a month or more to get state documents from the Spanish court at Valladolid to the Archducal court at Brussels, so long as Charles remained in Flanders there was bound to be great inefficiency and confusion in the handling of official business. Juan de Fonseca and other political buccaneers there made the most of the chaos to increase their wholesale pilferings, despite a chorus of outraged complaints from every class in Spain.

Late in 1517, Charles at last sailed with an entourage of Flemish courtiers and a very strong force of German mercenaries equipped as though for an invasion. The pilots of the royal fleet lost their bearings in the Bay of Biscay and made their landfall unexpectedly at a little fishing village in the province of Asturias. There was no one to welcome the new ruler when he disembarked, for the villagers were terrified at the spectacle of an unknown armada and had fled to the interior.

The fear of the villagers was prophetic, for the landing of an invading foe could hardly have been more sinister to the future of the country than was this entry of hungry foreign office seekers who bore the inexperienced young King with them, a virtual prisoner in their midst.

Bishop Fonseca had long been secretly hostile to Cardinal Ximenes, who as his ecclesiastical superior had rebuked him for unchurchly conduct as a bishop. As Regent of Spain, Ximenes had protected some of the victims of the machinations of India House and had begun to look into abuses in its administration. High-minded Ximenes had little in common with self-seeking Fonseca, but he was so burdened by his duties as Regent that he left him temporarily undisturbed in his offices.

Fonseca consequently was in a position to plot secretly with his ally Chièvres and a disaffected group in the Spanish aristocracy and Church against the preoccupied Cardinal. He now followed the tactics that he had already found successful in *Casa de Antillas* in appropriating the fruits of another's work. When the young King landed in Spain in 1518, Fonseca, who alone had early knowledge of his debarkation, hurried to be first to greet him and officially welcome him to his new realm. Kneeling reverently, the Bishop delivered to Charles the last will and testament of his grandfather, Don Ferdinand, which had made him his heir.

Chièvres led the King to believe that his gratitude was due solely to Fonseca for his succession. Charles, who had looked up to the Bishop on his visits to Flanders as a statesmanlike churchman, accepted this fable and at once appointed the Bishop as the only Spaniard on the Royal Council. The other three councilors were Chièvres, one of his henchmen, Sauvage, and Dean Adrian, now Cardinal of Flanders.

When the news of the King's armed entry belatedly reached Cardinal Ximenes, he immediately sent a fearless letter to Charles urging him to dismiss his martial foreign followers and avoid the mistake made by Philip, who had likewise come to Castile with a strong Flemish contingent and thereby offended Castilian pride. He begged Charles to enter Castile as a true Spaniard coming to his homeland, having faith in the welcome of his loyal subjects.

Much to the alarm and uneasiness of Chièvres, Ximenes started out at once to meet the King and to render an account of his stewardship. Chièvres and Fonseca were determined at all costs to prevent the meeting, and therefore decided to eliminate Ximenes from the scene. When the Cardinal Regent neared the halting place of Charles, he was suddenly taken violently ill, with every symptom of poisoning. He became so weak that he was unable to proceed even in a litter. In spite of his pain, he wrote the King a detailed letter of advice as to his procedure in Spain. A reply soon came. It was a cold, brief note, signed by Charles, in which the boy, after dryly thanking him for his letter, reminded the eminent Cardinal of his years and infirmities, dismissed him from his service, and recommended that he retire to his diocese and make his peace with God. The heartlessness of this letter broke the sick, aged Cardinal's heart. He collapsed and died a few hours after reading the letter. With his last breath he spoke of the King's ungratefulness toward him.

Charles was at the time only seventeen, and he had been kept in ignorance of all the Cardinal had done for him. Little more than a cipher, he did what he was told, and when the fatal letter was subtly laid before him by Bishop Fonseca, his trusted counselor, he initialed it without at all realizing its malevolent significance.

Bishop Juan Rodríguez de Fonseca virtually became ruler of Castile and Aragon upon the death of the Cardinal. The Walloon Chièvres, as Chancellor, was head of the government, but he knew nothing of the peculiar and complicated Spanish political structure or of its traditions and unique practices. He was interested in making as much money as possible for himself by bribery, confiscation, and the sale of offices and privileges. As Juan was the only Spaniard in the ruling junta of four, domestic political questions were referred solely to him for decision.

The succession of materialistic Bishop Fonseca to the position of arbiter on Spanish affairs was a calamity. Charles, a boy unacquainted with Spain and not even speaking Spanish, needed an honest counselor to advise him. Had his mentor been Ximenes, his reign might have been a better one.

Spain was still technically subdivided into five historic kingdoms, having five separate parliaments vested with the power of the purse. Juan de Fonseca, in his way, was unusually well qualified to deal for the new King with the diverse and conglomerate elements which constituted the government of Spain. He had served in the inherited Fonseca posts of Mayor of the city of Badajoz and Councilman of the town of Toro and understood how to manipulate for corrupt ends the municipal governments which Ximenes had helped make autonomous. He also had been a member of the Cortes of Castile and had been President of the Cortes of Aragon. He was a past master in parliamentary lobbying, vote-buying, and manipulating parliamentary cleavages. The individualistic legislative bodies already were vociferously announcing their determination to wrest reforms and guarantees from the Crown before confirming Charles in his inheritance, levying taxes, voting subsidies, or passing any appropriation bills. The stability of the throne was by no means assured. A strong faction favored the crowning of Charles's pro-Spanish brother, Ferdinand, but Fonseca kept Prince Ferdinand out of contact with his adherents and had him guarded by his grandfather, the Emperor Maximilian, in an Austrian fortress. Another group of influential Castilians was loyal to mad Queen Joanna, and therefore Fonseca took every care to keep her safely in La Mota Castle at Medina del Campo.

So imminent did Bishop Fonseca judge the danger of a rebellion that he commenced to accumulate a supply of munitions and to concentrate the artillery at strategic points. He ferried over trusted forces from Sicily and had his brother Antonio de Fonseca appointed Commander in Chief of the army.

The haughty Spanish people were nationalistic and antiforeign, and their sense of racial superiority had recently been stimulated by a series of military triumphs over France. They became furiously indignant at being exploited by the mercantile Flemings whom they considered boors and peddlers. The grandees were mortally offended when their hereditary offices and ancient perquisites were sold by Chièvres to Flemings, and the clergy was equally displeased when he appointed his callow nephew to the Archbishopric of Toledo, thereby making him Primate of Spain.

In the meantime, Chièvres was intoxicated by the ease with which he could pillage the rich and seemingly supine nation. He neglected his state duties, but still kept the King wholly isolated from all Spaniards except the two Fonsecas, while he and his cronies redoubled their depredations upon the half-stunned state. During the first year of his office as Chancellor,

Chièvres smuggled over one million stolen ducats (about fifteen million dollars) in actual cash out of Spain to Flanders. The clandestine shipments were made on Fugger ships, and the specie was hidden in bundles of hides, bales of wool, and casks of wine and olive oil, consigned as merchandise to the Fugger bank in Antwerp. The two ailing, avaricious old men, Chancellor Chièvres and Treasurer Sauvage, both of whom were to die within a year, were so preoccupied with their own aggrandizement that Juan de Fonseca was able to seize the reins of state. Feudal aristocrat that he was, he hated democracy and representative government. He now used his influence with the King to bring about the destruction of the historic civic liberty of Spain and the inauguration of a royal despotism in its stead. The young King, under his inspiration, developed into the implacable enemy of the ancient freedoms of Castile and Aragon, and his autocratic reign became baneful to the true interests of Spain.

Juan de Fonseca was mustering his forces to suppress the outbreaks of protest of the exasperated Spanish people when he was unexpectedly distracted by dispatches from Seville urging his immediate attendance at the *Casa de Antillas.* There he encountered Cristóbal de Haro, and they entered into plans for the westward voyage to the Spice Islands which Magellan was to command.

CHAPTER XIII

FERNAO MAGALHAIS BECOMES FERNANDO MAGALLANES

FERDINAND MAGELLAN landed in Seville on October 20, 1517. Ruy Faleiro, his comrade in Porto, planned to join him in Spain by the middle of December. Several Portuguese pilots who had also been engaged by the Spanish *Casa de Antillas* came with Magellan; among them were John Rodrigues de Mafra and Vasco Gomes Gallego, who later accompanied him on his great voyage.

Duarte Barbosa took the newcomer to the magnificent Alcazar, the palatial residence of his uncle, the Governor of the Castle of Seville, where he presented him not only to Knight Commander Diogo Barbosa, but to Beatriz Barbosa as well. As part of their agreement, Duarte had already arranged the engagement of Magellan to his cousin, the daughter of the Knight Commander. While no description of Beatriz survives, it is clear that the penniless Magellan was fortunate in executing this marriage contract. Beatriz was a great heiress, for in the marriage contract her dowry was set at six hundred thousand *maravedis,* besides which her future inheritance would be substantial. She was of good ancestry on both sides, and through her mother was related to many prominent families of the Andalusian aristocracy. As her father had enjoyed high favor in both the Portuguese and the Spanish courts, she probably had been given the thorough education and taught the accomplishments which characterized the upbringing of young ladies of that period of the Renaissance.

The fact that the marriage ceremony was formally celebrated a few weeks after Ferdinand Magellan's arrival in Seville shows that Duarte Barbosa must already have made most of the arrangements in Porto, or at the very least must have cleared up the preliminaries, subject to Dom Diogo's approval after he had had the opportunity of becoming acquainted with Magellan in Seville. It is convincing evidence of the estimation in which Duarte Barbosa held Ferdinand that, empty-handed as he was, his personal qualities were considered to counterbalance the wealth and the political and social prestige which the daughter of Knight Commander Diogo Barbosa brought to their marriage. The subsequent achievement of Ferdinand Magellan vindicated the shrewdness of the old knight, who must have recognized the extraordinary capability of the man whom he bound to his own family by a marriage contract.

Dom Diogo Barbosa had made a great fortune in the spice trade and was himself a veteran navigator. He had been one of the earliest explorers of the coast of Brazil and was one of the pioneers in East Africa and in India. In 1501, he had sailed as captain of one of the four caravels sent by Dom Manuel to India under John de Nova. Later he became business manager for Dom Alvaro Braganza, Dom Manuel's uncle, who had extensive trading interests in West Africa, East Africa, and India. Dom Diogo married a Spanish lady, became a subject of Spain, was made maritime adviser to Bishop Fonseca, and was himself one of the principal backers of the ill-fated Spanish expedition of Juan Dias de Solis. Although now in the Spanish service, he always had been kept informed as to the details of the Portuguese spice trade through his brother Gonzalo, who was King's Factor in Cananor, and through his nephew (or possibly his natural son) Duarte, who was King's Scrivener in Cochin.

He apparently decided, after the return of the survivors of the de Solis adventure, to send another fleet to seek Maluco through a westward strait which he believed to be at Cape Santa Maria, at the mouth of the Rio de la Plata. He had the secret consent of Cardinal Ximenes, Regent of Castile, and his silent partners in the speculation were to be Juan de Aranda, Factor of the *Casa de Antillas,* and Bishop Fonseca, President of the Council of the Indies.

Soon after Ferdinand Magellan's arrival in Seville, Diogo Barbosa had him make formal application to the *Casa de Antillas* for state employment in command of a Spanish fleet to sail to the Spice Islands by a secret westward route. The proposal was rejected by the *Casa,* as Barbosa had foreseen, and this left the way open for Magellan to go ahead with Barbosa's plan of a private undertaking, for which a crown charter or franchise would be needed. Ferdinand Magellan therefore commenced to work with Juan de Aranda to organize an expedition, ostensibly to be financed and directed by himself and by Ruy Faleiro, but under the auspices of the Supreme Council of the Indies.

Ruy Faleiro arrived in Seville with his brother, Francisco, in time to be present at the formal ratifying of the marriage contract of Ferdinand and

Beatriz. He did not, however, enter into the festive spirit of the occasion. He was jealous of having to share Ferdinand's friendship with any one else and at once began to display tempermental characteristics which caused distress to his partner.

To Magellan's consternation, Ruy Faleiro attacked him for having taken Juan de Aranda into his confidence and for having disclosed to him the plans which they had discussed in Porto. His objections were quite irrational, and Magellan was unable to placate him, even by pointing out that Aranda, one of the highest functionaries in the Spanish Colonial Service, was an intimate associate of the Barbosas and was fully acquainted with every secret of the spice trade. Their contract would be worthless without his support, for he was their sole possible intermediary with the otherwise quite inaccessible Bishop Fonseca, from whom their franchise would have to come.

Faleiro abruptly cancelled his agreement with Magellan and refused to have anything at all to do with Juan de Aranda. Magellan, partly because of his characteristic loyalty to a comrade, and perhaps partly still blinded by his overvaluation of Faleiro's qualities, was disturbed at the situation and called on Dom Diogo Barbosa to intervene.

Don Juan de Aranda's support and co-operation had now become even more important to them, because of a sudden change in the political situation which threatened to destroy their prospects. On September 13, 1517, at just about the time when Ferdinand Magellan was taking ship from Porto to come to Seville, there had appeared unexpectedly at Villa Viciosa, a fishing village in northern Spain, a squadron of strange vessels from which disembarked Charles, Duke of Austria, King of Aragon and heir to Castile, with a large contingent of Flemish and German troops. Ferdinand's misgivings mounted when he learned that Cardinal Regent Ximenes had died on November 3rd, apparently by poisoning. It seemed to him that the same fatal misfortune had struck again at his career. Whenever he had gained the favor of a powerful patron, his prospects were suddenly destroyed by the patron's death.

The reassuring news soon arrived, however, that Bishop Fonseca, who had spent much time in Flanders and had established good relations there, was the sole Spanish leader who was admitted to the Flemish circle about the King, and that he was in high standing with the influential foreigners who were the advisers of young Charles. The prospects for Magellan again appeared favorable. Diogo Barbosa decided it was time for the marriage to take place, and accordingly, in December, 1517, Beatriz Barbosa became the bride of Ferdinand Magellan.

Knight Commander Barbosa now tried to bring about a cordial working arrangement between Ruy Faleiro and Don Juan de Aranda. Although Ruy's brother, Francisco Faleiro, tried to help, the scowling, dark Ruy could hardly be persuaded to be civil to Don Juan de Aranda. Dom Diogo Barbosa pointed out that he had arranged with Don Juan de Aranda to present their proposal to Bishop Fonseca, whom ordinary petitioners found it impossible to reach; in fact, Aranda was even prepared to take them with him to see the Bishop, who was in attendance upon the new King at Valladolid. Ruy Faleiro confessed that neither he nor his brother had funds to make the long and expensive trip to Valladolid, and Don Juan de Aranda generously offered to defray his expenses from his own pocket. Nevertheless, although Ruy Faleiro was willing to accept the money from Don Juan de Aranda, he refused to go to Valladolid with him. Neither Ferdinand Magellan nor Francisco Faleiro could persuade the self-important astrologer to alter his stand. The situation was saved by the patience of Aranda, who good-humoredly ignored Faleiro's rudeness and arranged to have him and Magellan go forward without him. He generously supplied Francisco Faleiro with horses for the journey and even with pocket money for their necessities. For their safety against footpads and highwaymen, he got permission for them to accompany the armored cavalcade of the Duchess of Arcos, who was traveling from Seville to the court.

The two partners set out on January 20, 1518. Travelers in those days used to while away the tedium of the road with song and story; and since Ferdinand Magellan had with him his accomplished bride, Beatriz, and as Francisco Faleiro, a polished man of the world, accompanied his brother, Ruy, they no doubt made their contribution to the entertainment furnished by various members of the party. They traveled through the Province of La Mancha, along the rolling road later to be made familiar to countless readers of *Don Quixote,* and the journey must have been a pleasant one to Ferdinand Magellan, accompanied by his young wife and buoyed up by bright prospects. Beatriz, who was pregnant, traveled in a comfortable palanquin slung on poles between two ambling mules, as did the Duchess and several of the other ladies, although some of them rode horseback. The old Roman road was a good one, although winding and hilly. It was heavily traveled, not only by cavalcades such as theirs, but by transport carts, trains of pack animals, mules, burros, flocks of sheep and goats, and herds of swine; all raised clouds of dust in their passage. The countryside was intensively cultivated and well irrigated, and each farm had its own pump operated by a horse or mule, traveling wearily in a circle. While crossing the Sierra de Guadarrama they were overtaken by a mounted messenger who brought a note from Juan de Aranda. He wrote he had heard that there had been new developments, and it would be necessary for him to be at court; he was so encouraged by the prospects that he personally would present them to Bishop de Fonseca and press their case for them. He was leaving immediately and meant to take a shorter mountain route; he asked them to wait for him at a certain inn in the city of Medina del Campo.

Ferdinand and Beatriz passed on the highway from the orchards of figs, oranges, and olives of the south to the region of cork trees and oaks farther north, and everywhere there were vineyards with their low, bushy grapevines. The party rarely stayed overnight at an inn; they usually sent a servant ahead to notify friends among the country gentry of their passage, and they were hospitably entertained at private homes all along the route. One of the ladies had a relative at the royal quicksilver mines at Almaden. There they were guests at a lavish luncheon given them by the German agent of the House of Fugger, which operated the mines under lease from the crown. Beatriz had previously made the journey and was a delightful guide to Ferdinand, conducting him through the old Mosque at Cordoba and showing him the cathedrals, churches, and Roman ruins in Toledo and Segovia.

They arrived in Medina del Campo during the great annual fair, which was attended by merchants from all over Europe. While waiting there for word from Don Juan de Aranda, Beatriz and her attendants spent several days wandering through its lanes of booths, in which were displayed all sorts of alluring merchandise: silks, furs, laces, jewels, weapons, and many rare examples of the Eastern workmanship with which Ferdinand was familiar.

When Juan de Aranda joined them, Ruy Faleiro proved as belligerent as ever toward him, despite the efforts of his brother and Ferdinand and Beatriz Magellan to calm him. Juan de Aranda was at the moment paying Ruy Faleiro's expenses and was his sole hope of attaining even an interview at court, but nevertheless he was treated with disdain by the irrational astronomer.

Juan de Aranda's attitude also had changed, and he was much less conciliatory toward them. He told them frankly that another new development at court might make it more difficult to carry out their program. Much more work and expense would now be necessary, and he felt he should have some assurance of compensation for himself. He suggested that, in view of the substantial assistance he already had rendered them and in consideration of the valuable aid he now was prepared to supply, he be given a share in the profits. He asked for one-fifth of any benefits which might accrue to the two adventurers. Ferdinand had confidence in the good faith of Don Juan de Aranda and was willing to negotiate with him, but Ruy Faleiro furiously refused even to talk to him. Therefore they separated, and the Magellans and the Faleiros rode to Simancas, where they stayed three days, while Aranda went on to Valladolid, where Bishop Fonseca was at court.

In Simancas they were guests of a relative of Beatriz in the old castle. They then went to Valladolid, but as it was impossible to get accommodations at any inn because of the presence of King Charles and his court, Beatriz had lodgings in a convent in the outskirts of the town, where a family friend from Seville was abbess.

Aranda came back much disturbed and said that his worst fears had been confirmed. He had not been able to reach the Bishop, who was in constant attendance on the King, but had managed to learn that he and the renowned banker, Cristóbal de Haro, recently come from Lisbon, were sponsoring another project to the King's Council. This was a plan of maritime exploration which had been proposed by the Portuguese navigator, Estevan Gomes, who had been one of de Haro's pilots in Portugal. Aranda knew very well the unscrupulous character of the crafty Bishop. He feared that Fonseca had decided to abandon his Seville partners in favor of an alliance with Cristóbal de Haro, who could be infinitely more helpful to him in putting into effect the plans he had already worked up with Aranda and Barbosa. Aranda reported that a royal commission, dated February 10, 1518, had already been made out to Estevan Gomes as pilot of the *Casa de Antillas*. The seriousness of this threat brought Ruy Faleiro to his senses, and, after some days of wrangling, he finally agreed to concede to Juan de Aranda a one-eighth share of their profits. On February 23rd, a formal legal contract was drawn up to this effect which is still preserved in the records. Ferdinand's signature to this contract appears not as Fernão Magalhãis, the Portuguese form of his name, but Fernando Magallanes, the Spanish form, indicating that his nationality now was Spanish, and that he no longer was a subject of Dom Manuel of Portugal.

Don Juan de Aranda's action in demanding a contract for a share in their profits from the two Portuguese was apparently unpremeditated. Until then he had been quite content with the partnership arrangement with Knight Commander Barbosa and Bishop Fonseca which had insured him a fair share of the gains if the proposed voyage were successful.

Now that the Bishop was discarding Magellan and Faleiro in favor of Estevan Gomes, he would, of course, recognize no obligation to Don Juan de Aranda. Therefore that prudent politician decided he had best look out for his own interests. He had had many years experience in court intrigue and knew that half a loaf was better than none. On his long journey to Medina del Campo from Seville, he had had time to weigh all possibilities, and he had decided that, even if the original plan was not carried out, he could utilize Ferdinand Magellan and Ruy Faleiro as pawns and derive a good profit for himself. Magellan's knowledge and attainments would still make him very useful to Estevan Gomes, either as a pilot or as the commander of a ship. He and Dom Diogo Barbosa could make a private deal with Bishop Fonseca to let them finance Ferdinand Magellan with a consignment of copper for Francisco Serrano in Ternate, and they could realize a splendid return on their investment.

After he arrived at Valladolid with his two clients, Juan de Aranda found it difficult to secure an audience with Bishop Fonseca and was uneasily aware of what was transpiring behind the scenes. The Bishop and his new partner were losing no time and had already had several conferences with Chancellor Chièvres. De Haro had formerly maintained close relations in Antwerp with Chancellor Chièvres and Treasurer Sauvage, and, being aware of their cupidity, he enlarged to them upon the fantastic fortunes which had been acquired by numerous Portuguese officials as their share of the loot of the Orient. He assured them that similar opportunities still were available. All they needed to do was to authorize the sending of a Spanish fleet to the spiceries.

Unaware that death would claim both of them before the fleet should sail, the avaricious Flemings at once entered eagerly into a compact with Fonseca and de Haro to put the project into execution. The Bishop, an experienced promoter of such expeditions, assured them that the cost to the crown of a fully equipped fleet would be repaid many times over by the returns from a single voyage. He emphasized that the importation of dyestuffs and fabrics would aid Spain's expanding textile industry, and the distribution through Europe of spices and drugs would be beneficial to Spanish commerce. On the political side, the King's popularity would be strengthened by so sensational an achievement as the discovery of the long-sought southwest passage to India. In all the twenty-five years since Bishop Fonseca had helped Columbus discover the West Indies, nothing further of moment had been achieved by Spain, while Portugal, a petty, backward country, had conquered great empires and gained high prestige and fabulous wealth.

Chièvres undoubtedly recognized that success along these lines would divert attention from his peculations, which were now receiving critical scrutiny by the lawmakers. The imagination of Charles would doubtless be captured, and with his interest focused in another direction he would not be likely to interfere in their fiscal operations.

Before seeking royal approval of the plan, Chièvres set about getting the acquiescence of the remaining member of the Royal Council, Cardinal Adrian. To his chagrin, he was unable to win over the Dutch priest. Adrian refused to approve a scheme which was in flagrant defiance of the recent bull of Pope Leo X, who had assigned to Portugal the exclusive right to Christianize, and incidentally to colonize, the pagan islands of the East, including, of course, the spice islands. Chièvres called upon Treasurer Sauvage to help him, but their worldly arguments could not move the scrupulous churchman. They and Fonseca took advantage of the next absence of the Cardinal from a meeting of the Royal Council to fetch Cristóbal de Haro to an audience with the King. Charles already, through his family bankers, the Fuggers, had known de Haro in Flanders and could be expected to be favorable toward him as a petitioner.

Cristóbal de Haro proposed to the Chancellor that they also bring the Portuguese pilot, Estevan Gomes, to the audience, suggesting that they could have Gomes advocate their plan to Charles as his own idea. This was approved by Chièvres, who knew that the young King's support would have to be attracted by the romantic rather than by the mercenary side of the proposal. Charles, since his exciting voyage from Flanders to Spain, had shown an awakened interest in maritime matters, and Chièvres hoped that Gomes, a seasoned sailor and salty character, would appeal to his boyish sense of adventure. This turned out to be a mistake, for Gomes, although well-born and a competent seaman, possessed a commonplace personality, was devoid of magnetism, and quite failed to capture the imagination of young Charles. He had to present his proposal through an interpreter, became abashed by the presence of royalty, and began to stumble in his delivery. Cristóbal tried to save the situation. He took the initiative from the floundering navigator and, in French, tactfully outlined to Charles the advantages to Spanish industry and commerce which would follow the seizure of the spice trade by Spain. This emphasis upon the profits to be gained by what had been so awkwardly presented by Gomes as virtually a commercial raid upon Portugal not only failed to win King Charles, but aroused him to hostility. Nor did the King receive at all favorably the assurance from Cristóbal de Haro, as a Fugger partner, that a strong Venetian fleet would be willing to co-operate with a Spanish armada, for he resented the implication that Spain could not cope with Portugal unaided at sea. Moreover, Don Charles showed a solicitude not to offend Dom Manuel, his prospective brother-in-law. Tractable though Charles generally was to management by Chièvres, he could not be brought even to consider such a palpably anti-Portuguese plot. It had been presented solely as the scheme of Gomes, upon whom he now began to look with obvious dislike. Once the King began to express his disapproval, Cristóbal de Haro, fearful of losing favor, quickly disassociated himself with Gomes and hurriedly shepherded the crestfallen petitioner from the council room.

Once more Bishop Fonseca's hope to establish the western passage to Maluco was frustrated by the fear of offending the King of Portugal. He was busily engaged otherwise, and the setback was not at the moment too important to him, but to Cristóbal de Haro the blow was catastrophic. Although dejected by this reverse, he was not a man easily to accept defeat. Not only did he ache to be personally avenged on Dom Manuel, but for the House of Fugger the stakes were too great to warrant dropping the proposal. De Haro's whole rehabilitation, personal, financial, and political, depended upon his regaining his position in the spice trade. The Fugger prestige itself had suffered from the way Dom Manuel had treated him, and it was imperative that a counterblow be struck.

De Haro therefore canvassed every possible means to find a method of gaining Charles's consent. He noted in a letter from his brother, Diego de Haro, who was still in Lisbon, that he had received in the previous month a confidential inquiry from Don Juan de Aranda, Factor of the *Casa de Antillas* in Seville, asking about the character and ability of Ferdinand Magellan, who was reported to be in Seville seeking employment from Spain.

Cristóbal then remembered that Bishop Fonseca had first proposed Ferdinand Magellan to him as a candidate for command of a spice fleet, and that he had rejected him for Gomes. Therefore he at once asked the Bishop why his lieutenant, Aranda, should be inquiring in Portugal about Ferdinand Magellan. The Bishop informed him that Juan de Aranda was then in Valladolid with Magellan, trying to get Fonseca to sponsor him in place of Estevan Gomes as a successor to the late Juan Dias de Solis. He also remarked to de Haro that Magellan had shown initiative and energy by coming to Valladolid, and that perhaps he would have made a better case for them with King Charles than Gomes had done. Cristóbal de Haro, who had as yet had no success in devising a way to further his plan, at once admitted that no doubt he had made a mistake in disagreeing with Fonseca's early suggestion, and that the ambitious and aggressive Magellan might perhaps have been a better choice.

The Bishop and de Haro submitted the idea of utilizing Magellan to Chancellor Chièvres, who, being avidly impatient for the spoils of India, had been fretting at the King's unexpected stubbornness toward their scheme. He recognized that they had selected the wrong instrument in appealing to the King through Gomes and conceded that Magellan, as described by Cristóbal de Haro, might arouse a favorable interest in the King. Bishop Fonseca was impressed also by the experienced Juan de Aranda's enthusiasm for Magellan. He knew, of course, that Aranda had been haunting his anteroom, petitioning for an audience, and he now sent word to him to bring Ferdinand Magellan to see him.

The next day, Ferdinand Magellan and Ruy Faleiro were ushered by Juan de Aranda into the presence of the august Archbishop Juan Rodríguez de Fonseca, Bishop of Burgos and Prince President of the Council of the Indies, who gave them his attentive interest, listened to their arguments, and graciously agreed to study them. On the very next day they were granted another interview by the omnipotent prelate, who, to Magellan's elation, seemingly was won over, for he at once took them with him to a meeting of the Royal Council. There the Bishop called upon Magellan to present his proposal to Chancellor Chièvres, who at first appeared to oppose the idea, arguing against the evidence, but finally appeared to give in and to be convinced of the feasibility of the plan. He then joined Bishop Fonseca to try to convert their colleague, the learned Cardinal Adrian, to Magellan's thesis that the spice islands did not lie within the zone reserved by His Holiness to Portugal but, on the contrary, lay in the Spanish area. Chièvres skillfully cajoled the scholarly cleric and overcame his conscientious objections with the aid of Magellan's maps and globe and of the longitudinal calculations of the astronomer, Ruy Faleiro, as well as by quoting the logs of Portuguese pilots, which had been supplied by Cristóbal de Haro. Magellan's own straightforward personality tipped the balance with the Cardinal, for the Portuguese veteran was undeniably a devout son of the Church who would never violate a papal command and who obviously believed fervently that he had a divine mission to fulfill in carrying the cross to the heathen idolators of the South Seas.

The Bishop and his two associates, the Chancellor and the Treasurer, jubilant at having at their first session gained the acceptance of Magellan by the Dutch Cardinal, now felt encouraged to hope to secure approval by the King. They decided that Magellan, who spoke Spanish, would prove to be his own best advocate, even though he might have to address His Highness partly through a French interpreter. Charles had been getting increasingly restive at having decisions made for him in advance by Chièvres and was obviously determined to assert his independence. Therefore, Chièvres thought it prudent not to suggest acceptance of Magellan's petition, but merely to present Magellan to the King and let him speak for himself.

Realizing why the drab Gomes had aroused no response in the King, Chièvres, whose art it was to read and interpret his mind, personally coached Magellan.

It was customary for the secretary of the Royal Council to prepare for the King's perusal an advance summary in French of the details of any petition to be presented. Chièvres took personal pains to edit the secretary's preliminary report on Ferdinand Magellan. It was deftly composed to create in Charles's mind a favorable impression of Magellan as a gallant knight, a Christian crusader, and a navigator of scientific competence. In composing this précis, Chièvres brought out Magellan's noble ancestry, his personal participation in the earlier, heroic Portuguese battles in India which already had begun to assume legendary proportions, the exciting shipwrecks which he had experienced, and the fact that Magellan had returned to Portugal a poor man after seven years of continuous warfare, while most of his fellows had amassed fortunes. That he had been severely wounded three times while fighting the Mohammedans and that he had recent experience in Morocco were also recorded.

Before Ferdinand Magellan entered the royal presence, Chièvres stressed to him that he should at the very outset of the audience state humbly that he had received permission from his Sovereign Lord, the King of Portugal, to seek employment abroad. He also was to affirm that he had for some years publicly expressed in Portugal his positive conviction that Maluco lay east of the line of demarcation, and that hence it was definitely in the territory of the King of Spain. By boldly making these preliminary assertions, Magellan would avoid the judgment the King had made against the previous petitioner, Gomes, who had appeared a renegade proposing to poach upon the preserves of his rightful lord.

Briefed by Chièvres, Magellan made his appearance before Charles. The pale, slight boy at once addressed the seamed, crippled veteran with the blunt camaraderie of one soldier to another. Waving the interpreter aside, he deigned to speak in halting Spanish and to listen attentively to Magellan's soldierly answers to his questions about Moorish tactics in North Africa and the behavior in battle of their troops. Charles's mind was full of plans for campaigns against the Moslems in Morocco, and he was impressed by Magellan's observations.

Encouraged by this promising start, Magellan presented his petition. He set forth his facts simply, supported by Faleiro's scientific testimony, and was endorsed at each step by Chièvres, Sauvage, and Fonseca, and unopposed by the Cardinal. Ferdinand convinced the King that he personally would not dream of trespassing in Portuguese territory, that Dom Manuel could have no just cause for complaint, and that, on the contrary, Don Charles was the aggrieved party who had been imposed upon by the Portuguese administrators in India. He then showed King Charles the letters from Francisco Serrano giving a firsthand description of the islands of Amboina, Tidor, and Ternate, and also describing the other islands in the spiceries group which made up Maluco. The Italian traveler Varthema's account of Maluco, written some twenty years earlier, was submitted, as well as the sphere of Pedro Reynal on which the position of Maluco was shown within the Spanish zone.

He then showed the King another very handsome sphere, beautifully made of leather, and hand-painted, on which the position of Maluco was also shown well to the east of the line of demarcation. On this same globe there was an enigmatic reference to a strait passing westward from the Atlantic to the Great South Sea, with the explanation in cipher that it had been left blank on the map so as not to divulge its location. Apparently this sphere was the one made by Martin Behaim, which Magellan is supposed to have purloined from the royal chartroom in Lisbon. In any event, it was effective in impressing upon the King the fact that Maluco lay well within the sphere of Spanish influence.

To add a human touch to his carefully rehearsed presentation, Magellan now presented to Don Charles his body servant, Enrique, who was a native of Sumatra. He had him carry on a short, rehearsed colloquy in Malayan with a slave-girl from Sumatra, dressed in native costume, who seems to have been Enrique's wife, and probably had been given to Beatriz as a maid by Magellan.

The emphasis which Ferdinand Magellan and Cristóbal de Haro placed upon their assurance to the King that Maluco lay within the Spanish zone is set forth in the account of King Charles's secretary, Maximilianus Transylvanus, and is of sufficient importance to quote:

"They (Magellan and de Haro) both showed Caesar that though it was not yet quite sure whether the city of Malacca was within the confines of the Spaniards or of the Portuguese, because, as yet, nothing of the longitude had been clearly proved, yet it was quite plain that the Great Gulf (of China) and the people of Sinae lay within the Spanish boundary. This too was held to be most certain, that the islands which they call the Moluccas, in which all spices are produced, and are thence exported to the city of Malacca, lay within the Spanish western division, and that it was posible to sail there; and that spices could be brought thence to Spain more easily, at less expense, and cheaper, as they come direct from their native place."

Another eyewitness, Bishop Las Casas, the historian of the Indies, was present in Valladolid when Magellan presented his plan to the King, and he also has recorded his recollection of the event. "Magellan," he writes, "had a well painted globe on which the whole world was depicted, and on it he indicated the route he proposed to take, saying that the strait was left purposely blank so that no one should anticipate him. And on that day and at that hour I was in the office of the High Chancellor (Chièvres) when the Bishop of Burgos brought the globe and showed the High Chancellor the voyage which was proposed; and, speaking with Magellan, I asked him what way he planned to take, and he answered that he intended to go by Cape Saint Mary, which we call the Rio de la Plata, and from thence to follow up the coast until he hit upon the strait. But suppose you do not find any strait by which you can go into the other sea? I asked. He replied that, if he did not find any strait, he would go the way the Portuguese took. . . . This Fernando de Magalhanes must have been a man of courage, valiant in both his thoughts and in undertaking great things, although he was not of imposing presence, since he was small in stature and did not appear to be much."

Don Charles's royal assent was won in this single audience. Such celerity was due to the fact that Chièvres had made an unusual effort to prepare Charles's mind in advance to favor the proposal. Sauvage and Bishop Fonseca had also painstakingly co-operated with him to support Magellan, and even the Cardinal had beamed assent at his words and had endorsed

Ruy Faleiro's scientific presentation. Chièvres had stimulated Don Charles's youthful yearning for adventure. He encouraged the excited young King to enlist Magellan on the spot and to accept the general terms of a contract of employment which he proffered, without much scrutiny as to its details.

Cristóbal de Haro, recognized by all as the best informed authority on trade and navigation with the spiceries, had been brought by Bishop Fonseca into the council chamber to endorse Magellan's statements to Charles. He had, of course, nothing to do with the terms of the agreement, but was present merely as a testifying expert. He listened in silent disapproval to Magellan's proposition whereby, if successful, the navigator was to receive lordly feudal benefits. De Haro had been accustomed to looking upon fleets and fleet commanders merely as pawns in his operations. He had always been generous in his compensation to his captains, for he was a keen judge of ability and was willing to bid high to get able navigators into his service. However, although he paid his mariners very well, he paid them only a flat sum out of hand, without giving them any claim to a share in his own and Jakob Fugger's monumental profits. Therefore Magellan's fiscal stipulations seemed absurdly pretentious to him. He could not see why the Portuguese adventurer should be given more than a handsome salary with a promise of a generous bonus if successful.

Cristóbal de Haro looked with approval upon the theatrical presentation of Magellan's plan to the King, which had been prepared and rehearsed under the skillful stage managership of Chièvres. He co-operated in supporting the showmanship, but, although he was satisfied to have young Charles favorably impressed, he was by no means to be expected to swallow any part of it himself. He considered the whole thing a hoax, based upon Magellan's swollen pretensions. His case was predicated largely upon the secret knowledge which he claimed of a strait through the American land mass, but de Haro was aware that Magellan had never been in the Western Atlantic. He knew his information regarding the supposed strait had been received from John of Lisbon, who had made the exploration in the employ and at the expense of de Haro, and that therefore Magellan must be basing his assertions upon mere hearsay, concerning which de Haro had his doubts. He also identified at once the cunningly painted globe which had made such an impression upon Charles as one which he had himself handled in meetings of the Junta of Dom Manuel. De Haro already had an unfavorable impression of Ferdinand Magellan, which he had gathered from Dom Manuel. Now he thought he detected a strain of charlatanism, on which this story of the hidden strait was based. Magellan's prestige as an explorer was built upon his record of having been in early expeditions to Ceylon and to Malacca, as well as upon his own cryptic account of the mysterious archipelago which he claimed to have discovered six hundred leagues east of Malacca. De Haro was inclined to discount all such claims to special knowledge, for his own secret intelligence service in the Orient was of the best. Whereas Magellan had been only a subordinate in the exploratory expeditions to the east of India, de Haro had had access to the confidential reports of the Viceroys and Governors themselves. He considered it impossible that Magellan should have any information which he, de Haro, did not have.

It can readily be seen, therefore, that when he endorsed Magellan's attainments, achievements, and knowledge while testifying in the royal audience, he did so as a courtier, with his tongue in his cheek. When it came to entrusting his own interest and the Fugger capital to Ferdinand Magellan and Ruy Faleiro, his attitude was more than skeptical. He had no confidence at all in Faleiro's ability, and, with his usual penetration, immediately saw that the man had crazy pretensions and would be impossible to work with. Accordingly, he expressed to Bishop Fonseca his emphatic conviction that the authority and scope of the two commanders should be circumscribed and counterbalanced by a co-commander of equal authority, whose nomination he requested should be subject to his approval.

Cristóbal de Haro silently resented Magellan's demanding a reward greater than that paid by Portugal to Bartholomew Dias, who had discovered the way around the Cape of Good Hope, greater than to Vasco da Gama, who had established the lucrative contact with the Indian spice market, and greater than to Albuquerque, the founder of the Portuguese Indian Empire. He knew only too well that he and Fugger would, in the long run, be the only ones to split their gains. They would not only be required to finance a great part of the cost of the proposed expedition, but would have to take all the financial risks involved and then give to the exorbitant Chièvres, Sauvage, and Fonseca the lion's share of any returns. He could not avoid paying the politicians, but he swore to himself he would not be mulcted by the two Portuguese upstarts as well.

Had Cristóbal de Haro had his way, he would have bartered with Magellan to whittle down his demands before letting him have any contract whatsoever. However, when Fonseca saw that the King was willing to agree to the contract immediately, he felt it wisest to get the royal seal on the charter before Dom Manuel's ambassador could dissuade the King.

One of the clauses of the contract to which de Haro objected stipulated that the crown would give no one else permission to follow the route or sail in the regions discovered by Magellan for a period of ten years. This would have shut out de Haro and the Fuggers. Another clause was that Magellan and Ruy Faleiro should each receive, as a reward, one-twentieth of the proceeds from all the lands and islands discovered, together with the title of Joint Viceroys of those lands and islands for their sons and heirs for all time. There was another clause permitting them to make a yearly investment of a thousand ducats in any ships which might be sent to the islands. They were also given, as an additional prize, the tax revenue from any two of the islands which they might discover after the first six; if they discovered six or less, of course they would get nothing from this provision. They were to get twenty per cent of the net proceeds of the first voyage.

The plan originally had been drawn up with the intention of having Ferdinand Magellan's nominal share subdivided into equal parts for himself, Fonseca, Aranda, Diogo Barbosa, and possibly John Serrano and Duarte Barbosa. When Ruy Faleiro forced himself into the contract, he demanded an equal share with Magellan and was willing to split with no one. Juan de Aranda later testified in court, under oath, that at the start the unbalanced Ruy Faleiro, who was making no real contribution to the undertaking, had demanded an even greater share of the profits for himself. When the King suddenly and unexpectedly accepted the contract as it stood, neither de Haro nor Fonseca had time to insure an equitable distribution of the profits among the promoters nor to relax the unrealistic grip of Magellan and Faleiro upon the results of the voyage.

The Portuguese spies of Ambassador Dom Alvaro da Costa immediately apprised him of Magellan's and Faleiro's audience, and he at once called upon each of the royal councilors, trying urgent appeals, cajolery, offers of bribes, and even veiled threats in order to influence them. Since the project was in reality secretly their own, Chièvres, Sauvage, and Fonseca, the three councilors other than the Cardinal, all deceived him with promises of aid and beguiled him with misinformation in order to gain time for the sealing of the contract. Cardinal Adrian, sensing the rascality behind the interest of Chièvres in the project, and having good reason to mistrust the integrity of the other clerical councilor, Bishop Fonseca, was inclined to counsel delay in closing the contract, in order to investigate Magellan's and Faleiro's statement that Maluco lay in the Spanish zone. The Portuguese Ambassador wrote Dom Manuel that their best hope lay in the Cardinal, and that Bishop Fonseca was the chief supporter of Magellan.

Dom Manuel instructed Ambassador da Costa to see the King privately, to remonstrate with him on his behalf in the spirit of their close family relationship, and to use every personal plea to get him to delay signing the contract, even if for only a year. Da Costa replied that stupid Charles was only a puppet in the hands of his councilors, that he thought it a waste of time to talk to him personally, but that nevertheless he would, of course, obey Dom Manuel's command.

He was right, as it turned out, in thinking his appeal to Charles would be futile, but not for the reason given. It happened that Charles, whose age was one third that of da Costa, quite outwitted the self-satisfied diplomat.

Da Costa also called on his compatriot, Magellan, and again showed the arrogance that alienated those whom he should have conciliated. Surprisingly enough, however, he himself gathered a very favorable impression of Magellan. He wrote Dom Manuel that Magellan was a navigator of high professional attainments and a man of spirit, and he urged the King to attempt to win him back to his service by offering him honorable employment. He also commented that Ruy Faleiro was a person of no importance or ability. Da Costa's frankness in praising Magellan to Dom Manuel required some courage, since he must have known it would be unpalatable to Dom Manuel. However, the Portuguese king submitted da Costa's recommendation to his council, which disapproved of the advice to induce Magellan to come back to Portugal by giving him high employment. It was feared that such a policy of conciliation would encourage other discontented navigators to follow his example.

Paradoxically enough, it was due to da Costa's excited activity that the formal contract with Magellan was rushed through in record time. Chièvres feared either that Dom Manuel might issue an ultimatum or that he might procure from his friend the Pope an interdict which would paralyze the program. For this reason, Chièvres and Fonseca verbally accepted, in the name of the Royal Council, the excessively high terms of Ruy Faleiro, and had the document formally cast into legal form, signed, notarized, and sealed in short order.

Although Chièvres, Sauvage, and Fonseca would no doubt have played fair with the modest Gomes had he been invested with the command and would have paid him handsomely, they accepted Magellan's terms in bad faith and agreed with Cristóbal de Haro in his criticism. This resentment on the part of the backers of the voyage, themselves quite unscrupulous, was to seal Magellan's death warrant before he even hoisted the admiral's flag for his new command. Charles intended honorably to carry out the agreement he ratified, but Chièvres, Fonseca, and de Haro had no expectation whatsoever that Magellan would ever enjoy any of the benefits they solemnly promised.

On March 22, 1518, King Charles signed the contract exactly as presented by the two adventurers. It was not the prolix proposal which they originally had submitted for Cardinal Ximenes, providing that Magellan and Ruy Faleiro would defray all the costs of supplying, fitting out, and arming the fleet, would furnish the necessary trade goods, and would supply the personnel, all in return for exclusive rights to trade with Maluco. Such a formal proposal by two absolutely penniless aliens would have been absurd indeed had not Cardinal Ximenes known that Knight Commander

Diogo Barbosa would supply the funds and furnish the expert experience to make good the contract. The contract as submitted to King Charles embodied an alternative offer, providing that the crown should supply and man the fleet, and would give the stipulated hereditary privileges and a share of the profits to Ferdinand Magellan and to Ruy Faleiro. That the second proposal was accepted in the final contract signed by the King was because Fonseca wanted to eliminate Dom Diogo Barbosa from control and get everything in his own hands as head of the Maritime and Colonial Ministries. His complete command of all phases of the undertaking would, under this arrangement, be subject only to the tenuous contingent liens of Magellan and Faleiro.

Don Charles's good faith toward his brother-in-law, Dom Manuel, is emphasized in the following explicit clauses in the contract: "Inasmuch as you bind yourself to discover islands and mainlands and rich spiceries, etc., in the dominions which belong to us and are ours, in the Ocean Sea within the limits of our demarcation, etc., you are strictly enjoined not to discover or do anything within the demarcation and limits of the Most Serene King of Portugal."

Don Charles gave the title of Captain to both Ferdinand Magellan and Ruy Faleiro, and delegated to them as commanders the full power of life and death or, as it was termed, of the knife and of the rope, which then was legally exercised by naval commanders while operating beyond the physical confines of the King's authority.

Once Bishop Fonseca had made sure that the contract was signed, he set about arousing some uneasiness in the King's mind as to the wisdom of entrusting the entire armada to the control of two aliens. He craftily had the King initial, on April 10, 1518, a royal memorandum to the *Casa de Antillas* suggesting that Juan de Cartagena be made a third commander, having equal rights with Ferdinand Magellan and Ruy Faleiro, so as to insure participation in control by a man of Spanish birth. Cartagena, it will be remembered, was Fonseca's natural son, known as his nephew.

Although the King approved of this plan in principle, some instinct of caution kept him from signing the official order which Fonseca had prepared for him. As Don Charles's trust in Magellan grew, he refrained from thus crippling his authority, and consequently Bishop Fonseca never was able to cajole the monarch into granting these sweeping powers to Juan de Cartagena.

On April 17, 1518, a royal order was issued at Aranda del Duero, where the King was staying, insuring that the heirs and assigns of Ferdinand Magellan and Ruy Faleiro should be given the privileges of the contract in case of the death of the principals. At the same time another order was issued fixing the salaries of each of the captains at fifty thousand *maravedis* during the time they actually were in command at sea. The King subsequently increased Magellan's annual salary to one hundred and forty-six thousand *maravedis.*

On the same day, the King signed an order to the *Casa de Antillas* instructing them to pay the Chief Pilot of the fleet an annual salary of twenty thousand *maravedis,* plus three thousand *maravedis* per month during the voyage. The *Casa de Antillas* was to nominate as Chief Pilot whatever person Magellan might select. This order was in reality slyly arranged by Fonseca in order to permit Cristóbal de Haro to carry out his promise to the disgruntled Estevan Gomes. Bishop Fonseca then used his influence with Magellan to have Gomes appointed. It is probable that Magellan was in no position to refuse to nominate Gomes, and no doubt he felt it would tend to conciliate him for his loss of the post of Captain General. However, it was a decision which he was later to regret and which bore almost fatal results to his own fortunes.

Estevan Gomes was a distant relative of Ferdinand's and at that time was outwardly on very friendly terms with him and his wife. In fact, when the fleet sailed Gomes left some of his personal belongings at the Barbosa mansion, in the custody of Beatriz. Gomes had had a distinguished maritime career in Portugal and enjoyed a high professional reputation as a navigator, but he lacked Magellan's character and breadth of vision and was intensely jealous of him. Therefore he lent a favorable ear to the subversive suggestions of Cristóbal de Haro, and before long was a secret enemy of the man whom he felt had usurped the command to which he was entitled. The experienced Portuguese pilot was indispensable to Cristóbal de Haro and Bishop Fonseca in their plot to oust Ferdinand Magellan once the fleet was on the high seas.

On May 15, 1518, King Charles made his entry into Saragossa, the capital of the Kingdom of Aragon, and Ferdinand Magellan and Ruy Faleiro followed, along with all the other petitioners and clients who had business at the court. At this time the King inquired as to when Magellan would be ready to sail on his expedition and received the optimistic assurance that the fleet could sail in three months' time. Consequently the King named August 25, 1518, as the official date on which the expedition should get under way. Juan de Aranda and Bishop Fonseca, both speaking from experience with the slow processes of the *Casa de Antillas,* objected, and, on May 21, 1518, a royal order extended the date of sailing to some time in December, 1518, thus allowing four months extra time, which should have been ample.

Both Magellan and Faleiro returned to Seville with all speed in order to work on the preparations so that the expedition could sail in accordance with the royal mandate. Don Juan de Aranda immediately was sent by the *Casa de Antillas* to Cadiz to purchase such ships as might be suitable for the voyage. He selected five old merchant *naos* and had them brought up the river to Seville for refitting. Duarte Barbosa was sent to Bilbao, the iron-making city in Northern Spain, to contract for cannon, arms and armor for the fleet. From there he set sail in company with Don Antonio Semeño, of the technical staff of the *Casa de Antillas*, for Flanders, where they bought ship's stores, rigging, and marine supplies. Another official, Captain Artieta, was dispatched to Vizcaya to pick up ship's stores from the ship chandlers there. At last Magellan could feel that the great enterprise was actually under way.

In the meantime, Cristóbal de Haro and Bishop Fonseca laid plans to eliminate Dom Diogo Barbosa, Juan de Aranda, and Ruy Faleiro from any share in the undertaking. It did not take long for the wise old Knight Commander, veteran as he was of a hundred fights with court cliques and political factions, to sense what was going on. He immediately took counsel with his nephew and his son-in-law as to the defensive measures to be taken against Fonseca and de Haro in the undercover warfare between them for control of the expedition.

Indeed Dom Diogo knew Bishop Fonseca too well not to have expected that the predatory prelate would now plot to eliminate him and Aranda from any part in the undertaking. The Bishop's first step had been to acquire ownership of the expedition by the crown, thus destroying the keystone of Dom Diogo's plan, which had been to be owner of the fleet and its cargo himself. The next step had been the appointment, ostensibly by Ferdinand Magellan, of Dom Diogo's personal enemy, Estevan Gomes, as Pilot Royal of the fleet. Dom Diogo countered this step by organizing a protest to the King by all the royal pilots at Seville as well as by the board of the *Casa de Antillas* because they had not been consulted in the matter. They objected that Estevan Gomes had only recently been made a royal pilot, and they asked the King not to confirm his nomination.

Bishop Fonseca recognized that Knight Commander Barbosa was attempting to organize a revolt against him in his own political bailiwick, the *Casa de Antillas*. Therefore, he tactfully composed a mollifying letter which he had Don Charles sign on April 18, 1518, addressed to the Board of Directors of the *Casa de Antillas*, asking them to explain to the pilots his royal reason for having acted with such dispatch and assuring them of his appreciation of their loyalty and high qualifications. In this letter the King stated that he had commanded the Grand Chancellor Chièvres and the Bishop of Burgos officially to present, in his name, to the pilots Sebastian Cabot, Andre Niño, Andres de San Martin, Juan Rodríguez Serrano, and Juan de Mafra, his personal thanks for their loyal services.

At the same time Bishop Fonseca composed another letter to be signed by the King addressed to the officials and Board of the *Casa de Antillas*. In this letter the King excused himself for not having consulted them in making several recent appointments and offered, as a placatory gesture, to permit them to select the Spanish officer to go along with Magellan as the third Captain General in command, referring to a former memorandum on this subject regarding Juan de Cartagena. He also promised to let the Board fill the vacancies that remained, namely the positions of Treasurer, Scrivener, and Vedor. The latter was the inspector who, representing the crown, accompanied a fleet and noted any irregularities or other acts which he thought were subject to criticism. This offer to permit the board of the *Casa de Antillas* to make these appointments was in reality an empty gesture since, although all the nominations would be made in the royal name, they would be suggested to the King by Bishop Fonseca.

This clever counterstroke by Fonseca weakened the position of Knight Commander Barbosa. The unrest of the pilots was much appeased by the frank apology and the flattering mention of their individual names by the new Monarch. A vague letter of the same date to the bureaucrats, informing them that the King would communicate his wishes to them through Bishop Fonseca, was an implicit warning against any opposition to the Bishop; this effectively cowed any nascent insubordination of the board of directors of the maritime ministry.

The Board of the *Casa de Antillas* was composed of Juan de Aranda, the Factor or General Manager, Dr. Sancho de Matienzo, Abbot of Jamaica and Canon of Seville, the Treasurer, and Pedro de Isasaga, the Comptroller. The only other board member, Sebastian Cabot, who held the title of Chief Pilot and Superintendent of Geographic Works, had gone to London early in the year and had been detained there on business. Although he very probably had a part in the initial plan of Knight Commander Diogo Barbosa, Cabot had been absent during these developments. Doctor Matienzo and Don Pedro Isasaga were both old friends of Dom Diogo Barbosa, but the ominous royal letter frightened them into submission to their real master, the Bishop of Burgos.

Bishop Fonseca had, by demonstrating his position in relation to the throne, quite neutralized any further action on the part of Dom Diogo. The Knight Commander was too experienced a politician not to realize how vulnerable he was to punitive measures, not only against his office in the Arsenal, but also in regard to his personal estate. A new administration was now in control of the nation, and none of his formerly influential friends, the grandees of Spain, had any political power at court. Therefore he henceforth limited his activity to advising his nephew, Duarte, and his son-in-law, Ferdinand Magellan.

Having effectively disposed of Dom Diogo Barbosa, the Bishop then proceeded to punish his unruly henchman, Juan de Aranda, making an example of him and breaking his career. Cristóbal de Haro and Bishop Fonseca had been much disturbed to learn that Juan de Aranda had a binding legal claim to one-eighth of the joint profits of the two Captains

General, according to the contract executed at Simancas on February 23, 1518. The Bishop therefore had one of his creatures in the *Casa de Antillas* pretend to discover the existence of this clandestine contract and denounce Aranda, the Chief Factor, for it, claiming he had made a corrupt arrangement with Magellan and Faleiro while he himself was acting as head of the board which had to pass upon their petition. The Bishop saw to it that the complaint was given official attention, and the culprit was, in October, 1518, temporarily suspended from his high office for allegedly utilizing his position to make an illegal private profit.

The case was pushed to a conclusion. On June 15, 1519, Juan de Aranda was called before the Supreme Council of the Indies, sitting in full conclave in Barcelona, and subjected to a pitiless public grilling. Ferdinand Magellan was summoned from Seville as a witness and gave full testimony concerning the arrangement made in Simancas between Juan de Aranda, Ruy Faleiro, and himself. The record still survives, and most of it was favorable to Juan de Aranda, who appears to have been quite zealous for the royal interest in dealing with the two Portuguese adventurers and to have merely followed the custom of the day in combining public service with private profit. Ordinarily Juan de Aranda would doubtless have been exonerated, but on this occasion the Supreme Council issued a hypocritical report which vigorously censured his venality. The finding of the Council was signed by its President, who had presided at the hearing, none other than the Very Reverend in Christ, Father Archbishop of Rosano, and Lord Bishop of Burgos, Don Juan Rodríguez de Fonseca.

On July 2, 1519, the King's fiscal secretary issued a royal order formally censuring Juan de Aranda and legally cancelling his contract with Ferdinand Magellan and Ruy Faleiro as against the public interest. He was not fined nor imprisoned, but his career was ruined. From the record of the trial, we gather that Juan de Aranda spent, for the expenses of Ferdinand Magellan and Ruy Faleiro, the very substantial sum of fifteen hundred ducats from his own pocket, and that he felt himself lucky to have got off at that price. In ruining Juan de Aranda, Bishop Fonseca rid himself of Aranda's claim to an eighth of the profit of the expedition and set a salutary example for any other of his placemen who might be tempted to work against him.

The next step of Bishop Fonseca was to eliminate Ruy Faleiro as an equal participant with Magellan in the proceeds of the expedition. Juan de Fonseca, who three decades earlier had encompassed the fall of the Magnificent Admiral of the Ocean Sea, Don Christopher Columbus, knew it would be an easy task for him to entrap and destroy the Portuguese astronomer. By then the executive incompetence of Ruy Faleiro had been recognized by all, and even Magellan had awakened to the extent of his delusion as to Ruy Faleiro's abilities. The Bishop adroitly played upon

Faleiro's vanity and egotism, thus helping increase his already swollen estimate of his own importance. Loyal though Ferdinand tried to be to his friend, he found it impossible to employ him in practical matters, and much of his valuable time and energy was taken up by senseless squabbles caused by Faleiro's touchy insistence upon having a voice in all decisions. Fonseca now artfully had it suggested to Faleiro to demand that he be made sole custodian of the royal banner which was to be carried by the fleet and which, in accordance with tradition, would be entrusted to the Captain General of the armada as a symbolic mark of command. Faleiro was encouraged to be adamant in his preposterous claim, and the two partners were soon embroiled in a bitter quarrel. Fonseca, with his Machiavellian genius for intrigue, now actually persuaded the sorely tried Magellan to write to the King asking that Ruy Faleiro be relieved of his post as co-commander of the fleet, and also that Faleiro's captaincy of a ship be transferred to Juan de Cartagena. Although Ruy Faleiro was thus relieved of his naval authority, he still had his contract for a share of the profits, and Bishop Fonseca then set about having him voluntarily relinquish this most valuable privilege. He coaxed the befuddled Faleiro into agreeing to a cancellation of his contract by getting him a formal royal promise that he would have sole and supreme command of a second fleet, which was to follow that of Magellan to the Orient. Ruy Faleiro was at once put to work at the fictitious task of preparing such a supplementary expedition, and his brother, Francisco Faleiro, was persuaded to approve of the arrangement by a royal promise that he would be second-in-command in such a fleet. To lend this promise some illusion of reality, Bishop Fonseca finally had a royal order issued on April 30, 1519, confirming Francisco Faleiro's duties in assisting to prepare a second fleet and assigning him a residence in Seville and a salary of thirty-five thousand maravedis per annum.

The scientific prestige of Ruy Faleiro as an astronomer had been so high that his sudden resignation as co-commander of the expedition created a sensation in Seville. It was rumored that he had cast the horoscope of the undertaking and had foreseen fatal consequences for himself if he went. Others, jealous fellow-astronomers, alleged that he realized the inaccuracy and unreliability of his own system of calculating longitude and was afraid to put it to the test on the proposed voyage.

Ferdinand Magellan, however, still believed in the practicability of Ruy Faleiro's system, and he therefore arranged with Bishop Fonseca that Faleiro not be given his appointment as Commander of the second fleet until a certain book in manuscript form, illustrating his method of calculating longitude, was turned over to Magellan for navigational use on the voyage.

Now that the monopolists had successfully cancelled the legal liens upon the profits of the voyage held by Barbosa, Aranda, and Faleiro, they audaciously turned their energies to voiding the right of the crown itself to any mercantile gains the expedition might make. The contract signed by the King had required the crown to invest four thousand ducats in trade merchandise. Now the Bishop of Burgos had the *Casa de Antillas* call upon the royal treasurer, Sauvage, for these funds. The royal treasurer reported that there were no funds available for this purpose. Spain was then the richest country in Europe and was at the peak of its industrial and commercial prosperity, but Sauvage and Chièvres were jointly stealing over a hundred thousand ducats monthly from the royal treasury and frequently found it difficult to leave enough money for the running expenses of the government. Therefore, Treasurer Sauvage was quite willing to carry out the quiet suggestion of the Bishop of Burgos and certify that he could not supply the money from the royal treasury as requested by Treasurer Matienzo of the *Casa de Antillas*. When this news was brought to the King, what disturbed him about it was that the sailing of the fleet would be indefinitely delayed. Some one of his advisers then discreetly suggested that perhaps Cristóbal de Haro might be willing to advance the funds. Don Charles at once sent for de Haro, who proved quite willing to serve His Majesty and to provide the trade goods for the account of himself and his associates. As a consequence, on March 10, 1519, a royal order was issued stating that, although the crown had agreed to invest four thousand ducats in trade goods to be exchanged for spices in Maluco, because of other heavy expenses the funds were not available and the Royal Treasury would be unable to carry out the commitment. Consequently, permission was given to Cristóbal de Haro to raise the cash and Bishop Fonseca was authorized to participate in the underwriting. He permitted a close financial associate, Don Alfonso Gutierrez, a member of the City Council of Seville, to subscribe four hundred and twenty ducats, and entered a subscription for Juan de Cartagena for about fifty thousand *maravedis*. For some reason, perhaps because of his special qualifications as an expert in oriental trading, Duarte Barbosa was allowed to become one of the underwriters, but the extent of his investment is not known. Cristóbal de Haro also secured a subscription by the House of Fugger for the imposing sum of ten thousand ducats, in addition to his own substantial personal contribution. It is not now clear why the original estimate of four thousand ducats was tripled. Cristóbal de Haro, in soliciting contributions, stated that he conservatively anticipated the net profit would be at least two hundred and fifty per cent, but that the bankers of Seville calculated the figure to be at least four hundred per cent. In order to stimulate subscriptions, the King issued a royal order giving subscribers extraordinary privileges for participation in the following three hypothetical royal voyages to Maluco. To such investment in these subsequent voyages he extended the same exemptions from all taxes, port charges, and customs as for this first voyage, and he guaranteed the many trade privileges and preferences which Cristóbal de Haro had carefully inserted in the current royal agreement.

Cristóbal de Haro now moved to Seville and practically took charge of all the details of preparing the expedition. The Portuguese Consul at Seville, Dom Sebastian Alvarez, wrote to Dom Manuel that de Haro was in fact directing matters as though the enterprise was his own private affair, and that he gave orders to the officials of the *Casa de Antillas* as though they were his own employees.

Control of the fiscal details of the expedition was now taken away from Doctor Matienzo, the Treasurer of the *Casa de Antillas,* who was a friend of Dom Diogo Barbosa. Bishop Fonseca, on March 30, 1519, had a royal order issued from Barcelona appointing Don Luis de Mendoza, a retainer and friend of the Archbishop of Seville, treasurer of the fleet at a salary of sixty thousand *maravedis* per annum. On the same day, another royal order appointed Juan de Cartagena to the important post of Vedor General. He shortly thereafter also was confirmed in the commission of captain previously held by Ruy Faleiro and was assigned a salary of one hundred ten thousand *maravedis* annually, which was larger than the pay of any other officer of the fleet, not excluding that of Magellan himself. The order conceded to him the privilege of retaining, during his absence on the voyage, all the posts which he enjoyed in the royal household, with the usual proviso that his full emoluments "are to accrue to his account during his absence." It is easily seen that Bishop Fonseca took good care of the interest of his so-called nephew.

On April 6, 1519, a royal order from Barcelona appointed Gaspar de Quesada captain of the fourth ship. It is known that he was a nobleman and a close friend of Cartagena, and his subsequent actions indicate he was selected by Bishop Fonseca to help carry out the plot which he and Cristóbal de Haro had concocted.

On April 19, 1519, Gonzalo Gomez de Espinosa was named *Alguacil Mayor,* or chief sergeant at arms of the fleet, at eighteen hundred *maravedis* a year. This man was selected by Bishop Fonseca to be the police officer and to control the marines on the ships, and against him the Captain General would be helpless. Ferdinand Magellan saw through this plan and, realizing the importance of having the chief police officer on his side, treated Espinosa with great consideration and did all he could to wean him from the plotters. On April 30th, Antonio de Coca, apparently a bastard of the Fonseca family, perhaps of Don Antonio, the Bishop's brother, or even of the Bishop himself, was named comptroller of the fleet at a salary of forty thousand *maravedis.* Another appointment was that of Geronimo Guerra, who was styled the nephew and adopted son of Cristóbal de Haro. De Haro was supposedly a bachelor, and Jeronimo may well have been his natural son. With the nepotism that seemed the order of the day, he was appointed an accountant of the armada at a salary of thirty thousand *maravedis* a year.

Bishop Fonseca thus had put his own satellites in all the key posts of the fleet, and he now proceeded to control the Board of the *Casa de Antillas* so as to strip Dom Diogo Barbosa of any support in that quarter. Having already had Juan de Aranda removed from office, he next relieved Don Pedro de Isasaga and appointed Don Lopes de Rescalde as factor, or general manager of the *Casa de Antillas.* Although Dr. Sancho de Matienzo was continued as treasurer, his authority was neutralized by the new Factor, who had the full support of the Bishop and directed all the resources of the Ministry.

The enemies of Ferdinand Magellan had by now succeeded in driving out of positions of authority all those to whom he could look for support and had surrounded him with those pledged to his destruction. Magellan countered by striving to build up a protective organization through enlisting his own compatriots in the key operating posts in his ships. In this strange jockeying for position, the only powerful support he could rely upon was that of the King himself.

CHAPTER XIV

YO EL REY

PROBABLY the happiest period of Ferdinand's whole life was the year dating from March, 1518. From the time of his first audience with King Charles, everything seemed to work out for him as never before. He naturally ascribed his success to the influence of his distinguished father-in-law and gave him credit not only for obtaining his appointment in command of the expedition, but also for the honors and latitude which were granted him. Straightforward man of action that he was, the farthest thing from his thoughts was that he and Ruy Faleiro were in reality the dupes of that Machiavellian schemer, Bishop Fonseca. It was not to them, but to the office of Captain General which they jointly held, that every privilege and perquisite which could be wheedled from the King was being granted. When later they were dispossessed of their post, the Bishop would garner the benefits; meanwhile, they were the decoys attracting the benevolence of the King to the offices they held. To the Bishop, their exercise of the supreme command was quite temporary. He used them merely as stand-ins in the role which he designed for his favorite, Juan de Cartagena. At the start, however, everything seemed felicitous.

Magellan was given unhampered authority and support in superintending the local preparations. He at once established his shipyard at the Dock of the Mules, upon the opposite river bank in the industrial Triana quarter of Seville. With his cousin, Captain John Serrano, an experienced shipbuilder, as his lieutenant, he had ways built and all five of the hulls shored up; soon the yards were swarming with busy shipwrights. The five vessels all had seen hard service before Juan de Aranda bought them second-hand in Cadiz harbor and would need extensive reconditioning. The Portuguese consul, Sebastian Alvarez, writing to King Manuel, said they were rotten and that "their ribs were as soft as butter." He personally would not like to venture on them "even as far as the Canary Islands."

This may, however, have been only the kind of wishful thinking that a politic agent would report as fact to a distant employer to whom such predictions of disaster would be welcome. His estimate of unseaworthiness must have been an exaggeration, since all the vessels later withstood the pounding seas of the South Atlantic gales. The ships had been built in Spanish yards and lacked many of the structural advantages which the Portuguese naval architects had learned to provide. The Castilian shipwrights had had no experience in designing hulls to withstand the crushing blows of the massive Antarctic rollers which all Portuguese Indiamen had to encounter. They did not know how to compensate for the effect upon timbers of the acute climatic changes experienced in sailing from the equatorial to the polar zones. Consequently, every plank and rib had to be inspected, tested, and in many cases replaced by Magellan's experienced shipbuilders.

Inasmuch as the artillery would be unusually heavy, for the ships must be ready to engage in combat against the Portuguese, Magellan ordered the gun decks to be reinforced and the walls of the hull to be strengthened in vulnerable parts of the ships.

To the Captain General the task of fitting out his fleet was a labor of love, and he was wholly wrapped up in his work. The only thorn in his side during this period had been the irrational attitude of Ruy Faleiro, which strained his friend's loyalty and indulgence to the utmost. Although the scholar had had no practical experience in maritime construction, he demanded to be consulted about every detail and asserted his authority over the conduct of operations concerning which he was wholly ignorant.

It was at the day's close that Ferdinand Magellan must have found contentment. Comfortably housed in the sumptuous quarters of Knight Commander Diogo Barbosa, in the regal Alcazar, for the first time in his turbulent and straitened life he enjoyed surroundings of elegance, as well as what seems to have been a happy marriage. The charms of the Lady Beatriz, in the midst of the lovely gardens, fountained courts, and exquisitely embellished, tiled chambers of the Alcazar, must have satisfied his pent-up longing for the beautiful side of life. One rejoices that he had that springtime of 1518 in Seville.

The local notables vied with one another to pay social attentions to the distinguished veteran of oriental wars, upon whom had been conferred such high and lucrative honors. Moreover, he had become one of them by his marriage to their cousin, the Lady Beatriz Caldeira Barbosa. The noble

Drawing from a polychromed terra-cotta bust in the Gruuthuse, Bruges, of about 1518, attributed to Conrad Meyt

CHARLES V IN HIS BOYHOOD

families of Andalusia then were at the apogee of their opulence, for the victories of Spanish arms in Italy, Morocco, and Navarre had been won under the leadership of Andalusians, and they claimed credit for Spain's triumphs in the New World as well. Ferdinand Magellan now held out an opportunity for Andalusia to parallel the achievements of Portugal in the Orient. He would bring to Seville the riches of Maluco, and the Andalusian magnates acclaimed his ambitious project.

The recently married couple no doubt were showered with invitations to attend house parties at the castles and mansions throughout the province. Art and literature were the mode in fashionable Seville, which was proud of its newly founded University, and the hostesses vied with one another in honoring the latest artistic or intellectual celebrity. Someone gave a garden party at which a scholar from Florence read aloud to an appreciative and understanding audience a translation from Homer or from Virgil. A painter, just arrived from Rome, unveiled a masterpiece at a reception in his honor. The artist Raphael had currently aroused an interest in antiquities in the Roman court of his Holiness, so at Seville there must be a picnic in the ruined amphitheatre of ancient Italica nearby, and Ferdinand and the Lady Beatriz might wander off, as did the others, to search for old Roman coins or bits of bright mosaic washed out of the eroded site by recent rains.

In July, 1518, the King raised Magellan to the rank of Knight Commander of the military brotherhood of Saint James of the Sword, known as the Order of Santiago, which much enhanced his prestige in Seville. At the same time Don Charles wrote the directors of the *Casa de Antillas* that he was personally supporting the expedition of Ferdinand Magellan, and that he expected them to co-operate with his Captain General in every way. On August 15, 1518, the Board dutifully responded to the royal admonition that it could be counted upon to do its best. All the directors of the *Casa* at that time were friends of Dom Diogo Barbosa and had a true interest in quickly and effectively fitting out the armada.

Ferdinand Magellan's happiness was supreme when, in early September, the Lady Beatriz safely brought forth an heir who was christened Rodrigo, after Ferdinand's father. Ferdinand already confidently dreamed of Rodrigo as an opulent grandee of Castile, and foresaw the blazon of the Magellans carried by his son in the proud ranks of the hidalgos of Andalusia.

Meanwhile Dom Manual, even as the plans for the consummation of his marriage to Eleanor Hapsburg, King Charles's sister, were being pushed forward, himself directed the undercover activities against his future brother-in-law. He inspired the efforts at sabotage of his consul at Seville, Dom Sebastian Alvarez, and supplied him with ample funds and a numerous staff. Alvarez was an energetic, competent diplomat, and as the local representative of Dom Manuel was accepted in the highest circles of Seville, as well as having complete immunity from police interference with any of his activities, including those against the Spanish state. Of pleasing personality, insinuating address, and a boldness verging on effrontery, he made every effort to ingratiate himself with the Portuguese colony in Seville and particularly cultivated the society of the officers of Magellan's ships. He professed a feeling of friendship and sympathy for the Captain General, attempted to treat him with familiarity, and pretended to be solicitous of his personal interests.

On October 22, 1518, Dom Sebastian Alvarez almost achieved a triumph of sabotage. The day had opened most auspiciously for Ferdinand Magellan, for he was to celebrate getting his squadron afloat. The Trinidad, his flagship, had been careened, its hull reconditioned, and the initial work of refitting it completed; now, on this proud morning, he proposed to launch the vessel from the ways. On the previous day he had secured from the *Casa de Antillas* an extra force of eighteen laborers to help drag the ship into position, and all was ready. The tide would reach its height at three in the morning, and the Captain General not only summoned his entire dockyard force to carry out the task of floating the hull, but also added twenty-two recruits from the *Casa's* marine forces. He had planned a ceremonious celebration, providing that the royal Spanish standard be hoisted on the mainmast and that the individual flag of the Trinidad, which showed the symbol of the Holy Trinity, should show at the foremast. As the ship's Captain, he also had ordered that his own banner be hoisted on each of the four capstans of the ship, as was the custom in the Spanish navy. Unfortunately, the royal standard and the Trinidad's ensign had been sent back to the flagmaker for repainting and through oversight had not been delivered on time. Therefore the only standards shown on the ship were the four small ones bearing the Magellan coat of arms, which were mounted fore and aft.

A large crowd of the idle dwellers on the Triana waterfront surrounded the ship in the later morning to watch the delicate operation being completed, and the agents of the Portuguese Consul were present in the crowd. One of these paid disturbers became aware that not only was no royal Spanish banner shown on the vessel, but that the *quinas* of the King of Portugal were displayed upon the windlasses of this Spanish flagship, for Magellan's family standard showed the *quinas* as a quartering on its coat of arms. He began to circulate in the crowd saying that Magellan was now showing his true colors in displaying the banner of his homeland in place of that of Spain. The onlookers all recognized the hated insignia, became excited, and began to yell abuse. A self-important official of the port bustled up to the Captain General and began to upbraid him. The hot-blooded Magellan lost his temper at the stupid accusation, whereupon the officer, urged on by the crowd, tried to take down Magellan's standard. The Captain General and several of his staff prevented this, and the interloper called upon the bystanders for assistance. At this juncture, Dr. Sancho de Matienzo, Dean of the Cathedral and Treasurer of the *Casa de Antillas,* came riding by; he hastily intervened and prevailed upon Magellan to take down his banners in order to pacify the crowd. All would have become quiet had not the blustering policeman now attempted to arrest Magellan. The ship-workers tried to defend the Captain General, but they were set upon by the excited mob and took to their heels, abandoning their superior officer. Ferdinand Magellan was severely mauled in the melee and received a knife cut in the hand. Even the dignified Dr. Matienzo, who was in clericals, was struck. Magellan loudly and formally called out to all present to witness that the official, who had the rank of port lieutenant, was endangering His Majesty's warship and would be held responsible by the King. The police then released him, but, since all his workers had fled, he himself stalked off the pier, leaving the ship half afloat and in imminent danger of capsizing. The sobered port lieutenant suddenly found himself officially in charge of the ship and personally accountable for it. He had Dr. Matienzo hurry after Magellan to persuade him to return, to recall his dispersed workmen, and save the Trinidad from destruction.

Magellan recognized the part the Portuguese agents had played in the incident and felt that the outrage should not be allowed to pass unreported. Therefore, two days later he wrote a detailed account of it to the King, blaming the Consul of Portugal as its instigator. He explained that he was protesting not because of any injury done him as an individual, but because of the indignity offered to him as the King's Captain. On November 21, 1518, Don Charles replied in a sympathetic letter, saying that he had sent orders to Don Sancho Martinez de Leyva, his lieutenant in Seville, to apprehend the culprits, had directed him to punish the port official for his temerity, and also to discipline the local police authorities for neither quelling the riot nor defending His Majesty's property. He added that he was writing Dr. Matienzo thanking him for his courageous stand and expressing his regrets at the treatment accorded him. This decisive disciplinary action of Don Charles deterred any further public interference with the operations of the shipyard and much strengthened Magellan's authority on the Triana water front.

However, during all the autumn of 1518, Ferdinand Magellan found himself more and more hampered by sly sabotage, and progress became increasingly difficult. Every imaginable obstacle was encountered by his staff, and even what was done often was done wrong. It was obvious that the unlucky fleet would never get away by the end of the year as planned. Bishop Fonseca and his staff at the *Casa* had many times launched and outfitted similar squadrons in much less time than the nine months officially allotted to the preparation of Magellan's armada. Never before had there occurred so many mishaps, mistakes, and delays.

In November, 1518, the royal marriage ceremony was carried out with great pomp and splendor. Dom Manuel married Eleanor, the shrinking Hapsburg princess thirty years his junior, who loathed him and was deeply in love with his son, to whom she had formerly been affianced. The marriage gave Dom Manuel little increase of political influence over young Don Charles, for Eleanor did not hide her scorn of her husband from her brother.

Don Charles was sincerely resolved to respect the rights of Dom Manuel to the exclusive colonial exploitation of the area assigned to Portugal by treaty, but he was equally determined to assert his own rights. On February 20, 1519, he sent Dom Manuel an amicable personal letter assuring him that Ferdinand Magellan's armada would continuously remain in Spanish waters and would in no manner trespass in the Portuguese zone. This ingenuous communication from his candid brother-in-law made Dom Manuel furious because of its calm assumption that Maluco lay on the Spanish side of the division line.

International conditions had changed, and Dom Manuel did not hold the diplomatic whip hand over this exasperating boy as he had held it over his grandfather, Don Ferdinand of Aragon. The French war was over, and both Sicily and Navarre now were safely Spanish; hence Portugal could no longer play France against Spain. Ambassador Alvaro da Costa had little means of applying pressure upon Don Charles, whom he now belatedly realized was wholeheartedly in favor of the expedition. Its adventure appealed to the King's youthful, action-starved spirit, but he also was well aware that its success would make his rule popular with the Spanish people, and its financial returns would help pay off the heavy debts he was incurring in the electoral campaign for the crown of the Holy Roman Empire.

The Portuguese ambassador no longer could pay bribes to Chancellor Chièvres and to Treasurer Sauvage, for both were too ill to be interested in the question, and indeed, soon passed away. Cardinal Adrian, on whom Dom Alvaro had pinned his hopes, could not be of help because he had become otherwise engaged. He was at this time wholly concerned with what was a virtual rebellion of the Spanish prelacy, which resented the scandalous appointment of Chièvres' nephew, the callow William of Croy, to be successor to Cardinal Ximenes as Archbishop of Toledo and Primate of Spain. Bishop Fonseca, of course, was coldly unreceptive to da Costa's approaches, for to him the undertaking promised glory for Juan de Cartagena and was to be the first step in the creation of a Fonseca family empire in the Orient.

Ambassador da Costa now informed Dom Manuel that Don Juan Rodríguez de Fonseca, Bishop of Burgos, had become the power behind the throne in Spain. When the Cortes of Castile, resenting the abuses committed by the Flemish counselors of Don Charles, had hesitated to confirm him as their King, it was Fonseca who, by lobbying, bribery, and consummate political jockeying, had finally secured a favorable vote and appropriation from the reluctant legislators. He had been equally indispensable in Saragossa, when the Cortes of Aragon had proved even more reluctant to acknowledge Don Charles as their sovereign. After winning the consent of the Aragonians, together with tax concessions from them, he journeyed with the King to Lérida, and thence to Barcelona, where he arrived on February 15, 1519, prepared to face the rebellious legislators of Catalonia.

The sickness of the King's two principal Flemish mentors and the preoccupation of the fourth member of the oligarchy, Cardinal Adrian, who, as we have seen, was trying to cope with the Spanish ecclesiastical revolution, gave Fonseca the opportunity to monopolize the King's attention as far as Spanish affairs were concerned. He hovered over him, surrounded him with his own adherents, and had his brother, Don Antonio de Fonseca, Lord of Alaejos and Coca, made commander of the armed forces. The two Fonsecas kept at arm's length all the other grandees of Spain who previously had enjoyed hereditary access to the throne.

The strength and attention of Don Charles were at the moment almost exclusively devoted to his rivalry with Francis of France for the crown of the Holy Roman Empire, and therefore he left Spanish matters almost entirely to Bishop Fonseca, in whom he had considerable confidence. Fonseca had by now become wholly captivated by de Haro's portrayal of the rich prospects of a Spanish dominion in Maluco and had determined to seize this golden opportunity for himself. As we have seen, he proceeded to take over from Diogo Barbosa and his associates the control of the fleet of Ferdinand Magellan, planning also to eliminate Magellan himself. Consequently he gradually built up his mastery of the undertaking, preparing suitable royal orders which he from time to time artfully put before the King for signature, along with a mass of other official documents.

The Bishop found that Don Charles had taken a strong liking to Ferdinand Magellan, and that he had given his trust to the alien adventurer. Consequently he was very discreet in his scheme to displace Magellan and plotted first to deprive him of his supporters, so that he might later deal with him more easily. Therefore, whenever the navigator was goaded to protest to the King against some adverse action at the *Casa de Antillas*, the Bishop skillfully concealed his machinations and hypocritically pretended, for the King's benefit, to support Magellan, adroitly criticising the activity which he himself had initiated. His position was paradoxical in that, while undermining Magellan personally, he was as anxious as Magellan himself to have the armada well-found, well-manned, and under sail as quickly as possible. But try as he might, even assisted by the experienced staff of the *Casa de Antillas,* by the strenuous efforts of Magellan, and by all the Barbosa faction, the Bishop was unable to offset the Portuguese machinations and lavish bribery in Seville. The fleet should reasonably have cleared by the end of 1518, and yet by March 1, 1519, it was not half ready to go to sea. Fonseca itched to be in Seville and get things started, but he dared not leave the King unguarded for a single day. Don Charles was even more impatient than he to have the expedition sail, and the Bishop cleverly took advantage of the King's discontent to get the entire control of the enterprise for himself. He did this first, as we have seen, by creating a financial crisis at the *Casa de Antillas* which paralyzed all operations on the ships, and then by suggesting to the King that Cristóbal de Haro be allowed to furnish the funds to carry on the work. He also proposed that the great practical experience of de Haro in preparing maritime undertakings be utilized. The King, sensing no hostility to his Captain General in this proposition, but considering it rather as helpful to him, gave his consent. On March 10, 1519, he signed a contract put before him by the Bishop which virtually turned over not only the financing, but the administration of the armada as well, to Cristóbal de Haro.

Now Fonseca proceeded, as we saw in the last chapter, to have his satellites appointed to key positions in the armada, all at very rich salaries. On April 6, 1519, Cristóbal de Haro came to Seville and brought with him Don Juan de Cartagena, who served as his lieutenant. As soon as this occurred, Ferdinand Magellan apparently embarked on a fast lugger for Barcelona to see the King and inquire what his status actually was to be. In the meantime, Don Charles had become so disturbed at the interminable delay that, on April 15, 1519, not knowing that Ferdinand Magellan was on his way to see him, he sent positive orders to him to sail at once, whether the fleet was ready or not. Three days later, the King, perhaps perturbed by some diplomatic pressure by Portugal to cancel the undertaking, and being extremely anxious for action, wrote directly to the *Casa de Antillas* and again ordered the fleet to sail at once. The very next day he repeated the order to the *Casa,* insisting that the fleet must clear immediately. In this reiterated command to the *Casa,* the King continued, however, to display his unwavering devotion to his Captain General and took occasion to state explicitly in the order to the *Casa* that the armada was to be under the absolute command of Ferdinand Magellan.

But royal orders, no matter how peremptory, did not produce sailors for the ships. Of aristocratic officers, with their luxuries, valets, and pages, the armada now had a plentitude, but of able seamen, of men before the mast, there were not enough to work the ships. Magellan was furious at the selfish pomp of the noble Spanish captains who enlisted their own retainers in the crew to wait on them, but not to haul the ropes or swab the decks.

The frustration and helplessness of the hard-bitten veteran commander may be guessed from a survey of the personnel. This discloses that the number of body servants of the three Spanish captains amounted to one sixth of the active personnel. Captain Juan de Cartagena brought aboard his ship, the San Antonio, a suite of ten retainers, all coming from the Fonseca estate in Old Castile. One was a crossbowman who had been his ceremonial bodyguard at court, whom he continued in this useless employment. The proposed full roll of the San Antonio added up to forty-four men, including officers and supernumeraries, and hence one fifth of that ship's company would be drones carried as servitors to the pampered favorite of the Bishop.

On the Concepcion, Captain Gaspar Quesada had four personal servants, or ten per cent of a crew of forty-four, and on the Victoria, Captain Luis de Mendoza had four personal servants out of a total complement of forty-eight.

On the other hand, on the Santiago, with a crew of thirty-two, the Portuguese captain, John Serrano, had only Juan, his own Negro slave whom he had brought from Mozambique, to serve him.

On the Trinidad itself, the *capitana* of the armada, where official pomp and pageantry were appropriate, the spartan Captain General had only two pages besides his own body servant, Enrique, who, had he been a freeman, would have been signed up as a Malayan interpreter. One page was an African dwarf called George the Moor, who had belonged to the Sheik of Azamor and had been captured by Ferdinand Magellan in the sack of that city. Cristóbal Rabelo was the other, a lad from Oporto who apparently was related to Magellan and of whom he was very fond.

Ferdinand Magellan knew the rigorous trials and hardships which lay ahead. He knew it was preposterous to have the crowded little ships, crammed with armament and merchandise, and averaging less than a hundred tons of cargo space apiece, so overburdened with unnecessary flunkies, who pre-empted the most desirable quarters from the crew and would consume an undue share of the precious ship's stores.

Cristóbal de Haro, who was personally footing the bill, may have grimaced wryly in private to Magellan at this extravagance of the dandies who had been imposed on them as captains, but he was doubtless much too politic to utter any objection. The discreet banker knew that his surest path to favor with grim Bishop Fonseca was through Don Juan de Cartagena. Consequently, he made much of the pompous King's Vedor, obsequiously sought his company, and flattered him as though he were royalty itself. Indeed de Haro was ever mindful of the Bishop's plan to let Juan de Cartagena not only reap the full glory of the expedition if it was successful, but to install him thereafter as the head of the proposed *Casa del Oriente* in Coruña. He also had promised to make Cristóbal de Haro the Factor and Treasurer of the new *Casa,* which would be a situation of immense satisfaction and profit both to him and to the House of Fugger and was well worth any preliminary inconveniences. Ferdinand Magellan was unable, without the aid of de Haro, to put a stop to the nonsense, and he could only grit his teeth and promise himself that once at sea he would set his fine passengers to work.

In the meantime, however, the fleet could not find enough hands to make up its crews. There was a great shortage not only of mariners but of every kind of labor, for the plague which had swept through Spain had carried away such vast numbers of workers that the survivors could be independent about taking a job. The pay offered by the crown for an able seaman was much less than a man could earn by staying safely at home with his family, even if he figured on finally collecting the rich profit-sharing *quintalada,* or bonus, which was to be distributed among the seamen upon the return of the fleet.

The King's recruiting officer had stood with banner unfurled in the squares and on the piers of Seville, and the flourish of drums had helped the public crier call for recruits. "Join the armada and see the wonders of an unknown world!" was the cry. He cunningly painted a picture of easily acquired riches, of pearls and rubies to be had for the asking, and of languorous South Sea virgins awaiting the embraces of a bold Western mariner; there were almost no takers. These blandishments no longer were bait to the sophisticated seafaring men of Seville. Glamorous overseas adventure the seamen translated into sickness, hardship, and unending toil. They had seen too many leave that port to seek riches in the Indies only to return home impoverished, diseased, and broken men, if indeed they returned at all. In sum, only seventeen native Sevillians signed up, not experienced sailors, but adventurous young men of good family who enrolled as supernumeraries and a few inexperienced striplings who had been inveigled into seeking fame and fortune in the Orient.

Cristóbal de Haro had now been in the *Casa de Antillas* for some time, working at Seville in close co-operation not only with Ferdinand Magellan, but also with Don Luis de Mendoza as Fleet Treasurer and Don Juan de Cartagena as Fleet Inspector. He therefore had an opportunity to observe closely their personalities and to compare their relative abilities. As an experienced man of the world, de Haro no doubt soon concluded that the two foppish captains upon whom the Bishop was depending in due time to overthrow Ferdinand Magellan could never prevail against him unless given overwhelming odds in their favor. He recognized that the decisive Captain General could be a resolute and resourceful fighter, whom it would be very difficult to overcome, even by treachery. Ferdinand Magellan already had entrenched himself by placing his compatriots in the positions of pilots and *maestres* on all the ships and by enlisting a block of Portuguese in the crew. It seems reasonably certain that de Haro now conferred with the Bishop as to how best to weaken the position of Magellan and at the same time strengthen the hand of their partisans. To carry out their plot they would have to eliminate Magellan's adherents from their strong positions about his person. They must replace them with their own accomplices, such as the Portuguese navigator Estevan Gomes, who at the proper juncture could fall upon Ferdinand Magellan and dispose of him. It seems that the Bishop now undertook the task of displacing all Ferdinand Magellan's lieutenants. His method of effecting this was to implant in the mind of the King a distrust of Magellan's loyalty and a suspicion that he had been won over by Portugal to betray the undertaking. The Bishop seems to have persuaded the King to have the Portuguese officers replaced by dependable Spaniards. He no doubt tactfully proposed Magellan's continued employment because of his special knowledge and his talents, but under prudent safeguards for the interests of Spain.

A series of confusing orders, emanating from the *Casa* or from the King, mark the development of the Bishop's plot. The Bishop first apparently inspired his accomplice Lopes de Rescalde, whom he had made Factor of the *Casa,* officially to demand from Magellan the full details of his proposed route and the location of the mysterious strait of which he claimed to have certain knowledge. Ferdinand Magellan declined to furnish this information to Rescalde, and therefore the Bishop had a royal order issued from Barcelona, on May 5, 1519, requiring the Captain General to deposit with the officials of the *Casa de Antillas* a chart showing his proposed route to Maluco. This royal order was coolly ignored by Magellan, and, although it was signed "Yo, el Rey," it probably did not have the King's personal support. In this same royal order, each of the four captains was also ordered to indicate to the *Casa,* in writing, the course which he individually thought should be followed and the manner in which he thought the fleet should be guided and directed. This, if put into effect, would have destroyed the Captain General's authority and put the captains on a parity of command with him. This is one of the several illogical and contradictory orders which the King now signed and which are an indication of the control the Bishop was acquiring either over the royal mind or over the royal secretaries, who were in a position to prepare such an order, slip it in with a sheaf of hundreds of official forms, and have it signed without close scrutiny. Don Charles was at this time in the very thick of his struggle for election as Holy Roman Emperor, and it is possible that he was so busy that he gave but perfunctory attention to minor details in Spanish domestic affairs. Besides, he necessarily trusted his secretaries to give him a correct précis of the documents put before him.

The next surprising step in the complicated web of intrigue resulted in what was essentially a mutiny on the part of the Portuguese pilots and *maestres*. It is difficult to trace the cause of this, but since the Bishop could use it to convince the King that the Portuguese pilots should be replaced by native Spaniards, one can hazard a guess that he fomented it. No doubt it was also stimulated by Sebastian Alvarez, to whom it must have been a welcome happening. The incident was initiated by the disclosure to the pilots of the generous salaries being paid to their compatriots Ferdinand Magellan and Ruy Faleiro, together with the fabulous contingent profits which had been promised them. Human nature being what it is, the pilots held an indignation meeting and voiced their discontent at their own salary level, threatening to refuse to go with the fleet. The Captain General was, of course, most disturbed at this turn of events, and he appeared before the board of the *Casa de Antillas* to sustain the reasonableness of the pilots' claim for better pay, emphasizing how necessary their services were for the safety of the armada. Evidently the *Casa* concurred in this view and communicated their recommendations to the King. The Bishop then, it seems, skillfully intervened; he had the King ignore the request for higher pay and send instead a placatory letter containing vague pledges of liberal rewards to the pilots and the *maestres* upon their return from the voyage. They were naturally not satisfied by these glowing promises, which were not at all what they had asked; after another indignation meeting, they sent an ultimatum to the *Casa* demanding an immediate increase in salary of three thousand *marevedis* per annum for both pilots and *maestres*. It is not known whether this request was granted, but since the *Casa de Antillas* about that time made public the appointment of the three Spanish captains at very handsome salaries, it seems probable that they gave in to the pilots and *maestres*.

This unrest among his principal navigating aides, who were his fellow countrymen and friends, must have greatly disturbed Magellan. He seems to have won over the King to his views, as he always did when he could reach him personally. Indeed he made such vigorous representations to Don Charles that in May, 1519, a royal order was issued giving each of the Portuguese pilots the right to bear his individual coat of arms as a gentleman. This was a much coveted honor and a mark of very high favor that was most sparingly bestowed. This act of royal regard fully restored the morale of Magellan's operating staff, and represented a resounding personal victory for him.

Ferdinand Magellan's triumph, however, was not of long duration, for Fonseca cancelled it by a crushing blow which he dealt in return. On June 17, 1519, he managed to get a royal order issued at Barcelona prohibiting more than five persons of Portuguese nationality to enroll in the fleet's complement, and limiting these five to the category of pages or servants. At one stroke he thus had removed all Ferdinand Magellan's supporters from employment in the fleet. Incredibly enough, the royal order actually discharged all the Portuguese pilots to whom Don Charles himself had just promised rich inducements to consent to serve. The Bishop must have made preliminary arrangements with Lopes de Rescalde, Factor of the *Casa de Antillas,* for as soon as the royal order was issued this official at once cancelled all the commissions of the Portuguese officers already on duty and ordered the Capain General to discharge them immediately. In order to force this action, Rescalde withheld the salaries due them for past services.

Ferdinand Magellan must have protested hotly to Don Charles, for eighteen days later, on July 5th, a revised royal order was issued at Barcelona. Magellan was still restricted to taking only five Portuguese with him in the fleet, but instead of being limited to servants, they could be of any rank. This restored employment only to Duarte Barbosa, Estevan Gomes, John Serrano, Magellan's nephew, Alvaro de Mesquita, who had now come from Portugal to join him, and his page Cristóbal Rabelo. It eliminated several of the indispensable Portuguese pilots such as Juan Rodríguez de Mafra and Vasco Gomes Gallego, who had originally arrived from Porto with Magellan to serve as navigators, and who were essential to the accomplishment of his plans. Although Magellan protested to the *Casa* against this damaging order, he was unable to get any satisfaction.

Ruy Faleiro then complicated matters further by petitioning the King that his brother Francisco be commissioned for sea duty and be allowed to go with the fleet. He received a response which no doubt was composed by the Bishop, but which was signed by the King, that his brother could go only as one of the maximum number of five Portuguese who were permitted to sail.

The effect of this was to increase Magellan's perplexities, for when he declined to replace one of his indispensable lieutenants with Francisco Faleiro, he further antagonized the bellicose Ruy. The astronomer furiously insisted that his brother be given preference over the other Portuguese officers, veteran Indian navigators though they were. Although Magellan no doubt would have been glad to have Francisco Faleiro come along, had it been possible, he could not agree at the cost of one of his veterans.

Ferdinand Magellan seems to have felt it necessary to accept defeat, at least temporarily, in the matter of limitation of the nationality of his pilots. He now attempted to reinforce the few dependable officers that were left him by enlisting more alien common sailors, preferably Portuguese, in the crew. Consequently he pressed the *Casa* to supply him with men before the mast. He informed them that he could secure veteran sailors from Portugal, but since such were not to be permitted, he challenged the Spanish authorities to produce competent native seamen for him.

Castile was then a free country, in which the civil rights of the common man were jealously guarded, and so despite its desperate need, the *Casa de Antillas* dared not crimp or shanghai men for marine service, as was the practice in Tudor England. The *Casa*'s efforts were redoubled, and the recruiting officer made one good haul in the fishing villages on the Bay of Biscay. There a group of two dozen seagoing Basques signed up in a body under the leadership of their compatriot, Sebastian del Cano, a member of the petty nobility of Viscaya, who had had navigating experience and who shipped as a petty officer. Del Cano had a dubious record, and it is possible that he may even have been a secret agent of Dom Sebastian Alvarez.

When all the other likely harbors had been scoured without success, and the *Casa* seemed to have reached the limit of its possibilities, Magellan petitioned them to permit him to meet the shortage by enlisting Portuguese seamen. The *Casa* refused his request and stuck to the previous limitation set by royal order of five Portuguese for the entire fleet.

Magellan then boldly risked an open break with the *Casa* over this point. When summoned to a session of the Board, he defied their authority and boldly asserted his independence of them in the hiring of common seamen, claiming that the limitation of five did not apply to ordinary sailors. On August 9, 1519, he appealed directly to the King. He explained to Don Charles that recruiting parties had gone to Cadiz, Málaga, and other ports in an attempt to obtain Spanish sailors, but that the low rates of pay and the hazardous and mysterious nature of the expedition had deterred enlistments. He was sure he could get Portuguese sailors to go with him, and requested that the restrictive order be relaxed.

Don Charles, evidently on Fonseca's advice, supported the *Casa* and wrote that absolutely no more than five Portuguese would be allowed to sign up in any capacity. He followed up this decision by another letter saying he had learned that some of the common seamen were Portuguese, and he insisted that they be dismissed forthwith. Just how the King's fears had been so aroused as to take this stand cannot now be ascertained, but it is probable his signature was obtained by artifice.

Magellan delayed discharging his hard-won sailors and at once hurried to Barcelona, where the King gave him audience.

It is obvious that Don Charles found Ferdinand Magellan a man after his own heart. Reared by his aunt and grandmother, cloistered with his tutor and his chaplain, and now almost grown to manhood, the lad must have ached for martial comradeship. Trained to unusual expertness as a horseman, and master of fence, he no doubt had hoped for a bolder life in coming to Spain, of whose chivalry he had heard much. Instead, he found himself in an unfriendly land with the same old tutors around him. His only new companions had been the worldly, aging Bishop Fonseca and his brother, and the moneyed men who were engaging him in the auction for the imperial crown. Don Charles had no companionship, male or female, of his own age, and was in fact a prisoner of the Fonsecas.

When Magellan reached the King, his honesty and sincerity overcame whatever distrust had been implanted by Fonseca, and Don Charles showed his confidence by reversing himself, granting him permission to enroll twenty-four Portuguese, twelve to be nominated by the King and twelve by Ferdinand Magellan himself. The frank young King met the blunt sailor half way, and thus was formed the partnership in which Don Charles won Magellan's fervent loyalty.

Upon his return, encouraged by the King's trust and probably with his implied consent, the Captain General ignored the official limitation of twenty-four and at once hired thirty-seven of his fellow countrymen, experienced, able seamen whom even the Spanish commanders of the various ships, hungry for help, now accepted as satisfactory. Because Ferdinand Magellan had the reputation among Portuguese seafaring men of being considerate to his sailors and of sharing their privations and hardships, and since his navigating staff was made up of Portuguese officers of renown, he had no difficulty in attracting Portuguese seamen for his crews. Beyond the thirty-seven admitted Portuguese, he permitted additional sailors to sign up under assumed Spanish names. The authorities of the *Casa,* beaten in the struggle against his dogged persistence and Spanish indifference, wearily paid no further attention.

It had not been so difficult to get petty officers, and each ship had enrolled a chief steward, a caulker, a carpenter, a cooper, and a blacksmith. There was a chief armorer for the fleet, but every vessel had its own barber and its own notary. There was only one surgeon for the entire squadron, but at that time the ship's barber generally acted as physician as well.

The Spaniards had not yet developed first-class naval artillerymen, so the fifteen *lombarderos,* or gunners, were well-paid foreign mercenaries, experts of French, German, or Flemish nationality. They were distributed equally among the five vessels. The master gunner of the fleet, Master Andrew of Bristol, was the only Englishman in the expedition, but he counted as a Spaniard, since he had become a naturalized Spanish subject, married a lady of Seville, and raised a Spanish family.

Once the sizable quota of Portuguese seamen had been signed up, Ferdinand Magellan did not find it so difficult to round out the crew, and he picked up, on the docks and in the sailors' taverns, thirty Italians, nineteen Frenchmen, and a scattering of other nationalities, including Germans, Greeks, Flemings, Moors, and Negroes. It is quite likely that, in casting an appraising eye over his men, the Captain General felt these aliens would be inclined in a pinch to line up with the Portuguese group against the native Spaniards.

Magellan recognized that he commanded a war fleet rather than an exploring or trading one, and he took pains to see that his seamen would be able to take care of themselves if the ships were boarded by the Portuguese. He therefore persuaded the *Casa de Antillas* to supply him with a hundred steel plastrons or corselets, with armlets and shoulder plates, and a hundred morions, or pikemen's helmets. This heavy armor was suitable both for use on shipboard by the marines and for landing parties, but was too stiff to be worn by the sailors. They, during battle, needed mail light enough to permit them to spring to the rigging or work the oars, yet resistant enough to protect them from missiles and in hand-to-hand combat against boarding attacks. Therefore, for his seamen he procured a hundred lighter and more flexible cuirasses, or sailors' breast plates, complete with shoulder pieces. Every man, even the pages and cabin boys, was provided with a long wooden shield, called a pavis, which covered the fighter's person and would withstand the impact of a bolt from a crossbow. All hands therefore were as well armed as any Spanish infantryman. It was Magellan's intention to drill and train the entire personnel of his armada so as to create of them a formidable fighting unit, effective in combat afloat and ashore. The locker was well stored with offensive weapons of all sorts, including even a number of matchlock harquebuses, a new innovation. There was also a good store of light and heavy artillery and ammunition.

One item which bulked large in stowage space on the Trinidad was a sturdy *bergantym,* all knocked down, with its parts numbered so that it could be reconstructed by the carpenters. Such a boat, of light draft for river waters and shoals, mounted several serpentines and was spacious enough to accommodate a fair-sized landing party. This was the type of oar-propelled craft which Ferdinand Magellan and John Serrano both had commanded in East Africa and in India, and they appreciated its suitability for inshore work.

For repairs and refitting, there were provided all the tools that past experience could suggest: forges, grindstones, anvils, bellows, shipwright's and blacksmith's implements, as well as spades and pickaxes for throwing up fortifications to protect shore parties. Mason's and stone cutter's supplies were brought along to use in constructing the stronghold at Ternate, and some shaped blocks of granite which would be useful as keystones for arched doorways at the fort were distributed among the ships as ballast.

The usual supply of shipyard lumber, formed and wrought so as to replace planking and timbers damaged by marine worms and by mishaps at sea, was also stowed in the holds. On such a long voyage it was to be expected that the wooden hulls, unsheathed and held together by pegs, would need numerous repairs, and that the ships would have to be beached, careened, and recalked several times. Each vessel carried six sets of canvas, many extra spars, and a complete supply of all such replacements as would be needed for its own rerigging and refitting. All this is still recorded in the *Casa de Antillas*'s inventory, with the cost of each item meticulously added up in the books.

Although the old ledgers show the cost of the vessels and of their equipment, armament, and stores, there is no entry for clothing and bedding. It is probable that each mariner had to supply his own wearing apparel and sleeping equipment. Neither is there any inventory of medical supplies, and it is likely that the five barbers and the one surgeon all stocked their own medicine chests.

De Haro consigned, for the account of the House of Fugger, a valuable bulk cargo of copper in bars and of quicksilver in flasks, as these metals were the most profitable items of European export to the East, being in short supply and in avid demand by the coinage mints of many Oriental rulers. In textiles, an immense quantity of colored caps and handkerchiefs were shipped, and also ten thousand bolts of cheap yellow cloth, besides numerous bales of other cotton materials dyed in gay colors. Some really choice pieces of lace, brocade, velvet, satin, and scarlet cloth were carried as presents for such discriminating potentates as might appreciate them.

Cristóbal de Haro also supplied the fleet with a variety of other articles suitable for barter in the East Indies. The records show that he furnished as many as twenty thousand small bells of different kinds and grades, together with ten thousand fishhooks, and nine hundred small looking glasses and a hundred larger ones. He delivered to the ships five thousand cheap knives of German manufacture, as well as many hundred brass basins and thousands of brass and copper bracelets. One of the largest items which he contributed consisted of thousands of colored crystals cut to represent all types of precious stones. Another article which his experience led him to supply in great volume was an assortment of ornamental combs for the hair, made of bone and dyed in different colors.

Although these trade goods were of trashy quality and cheap price, they nevertheless had been most judiciously chosen. De Haro knew the tastes of the native buyers in Malaya and had learned to his cost how captious and suspicious they were. One had to know the market so as to avoid goods contrary to native taboos, superstitions, or ingrained distastes, no matter how fine their quality. The inexperienced competitors of de Haro had more than once had to abandon or bring back large consignments of merchandise with ruinous losses because goods sold in one trading area would be looked at with indifference or hostility in another market. It was his merchandising skill as well as his organizing and managerial ability which had let Cristóbal de Haro make immense profits in the very markets in which his Florentine and Portuguese rivals at times suffered disastrous setbacks. No doubt it was this demonstrated business competence which had gained for him the unquestioning financial support of Jakob Fugger.

Ferdinand Magellan stressed to the *Casa de Antillas* the importance of keeping the men well fed so as to maintain their health and spirits, and he urged the *Casa* not to stint on the supplies. Fonseca and the supply division of the *Casa de Antillas* had been accustomed to furnishing steward's stores only for the relatively short Atlantic voyages undertaken by the Castilians, and therefore did not fully appreciate the extreme importance of diversified and extensive rations for the men on a much longer cruise. De Haro realized, however, that the failure of many of the earlier Portuguese voyages had been due to the loss of morale and the mental and physical exhaustion produced by too monotonous and restricted a diet. Consequently he heartily supported Magellan in his demands for a well-stocked larder. He endorsed the guiding principle that Dom Manuel had established for the Portuguese marine, which was that the seamen's mess should be even more abundant than the fare to which the men had been accustomed at home. In this connection, it must be remembered that the diet of the ordinary workingman or farmer of those days would seem poor indeed by modern standards.

With de Haro's help, the Captain General won approval of his requisitions for steward's stores. The basic ration was to be ship's biscuit, or hard tack, salt beef, salt pork, cheese, dried codfish, and pickled anchovies. This was to be supplemented by ample issues of dried beans and chick peas, the staple Mediterranean peasant food. To these were added onions, garlic, marmalade, honey, raisins, currants, olives, figs, almonds, and other nuts. Some dependence was placed upon catching fish and shooting sea birds en route. Magellan planned to procure citrus fruits and coconuts wherever a landfall was made. He recognized that the greatest hazard to his voyage was the dreaded disease of scurvy, which had wrecked so many Portuguese maritime undertakings. He was fully aware that its cause was the lack of fresh fruits and vegetables, and he planned to make one of his principal concerns the procurement of frequent supplies of fruit and of fresh water. He and de Haro also saw to it that a sufficient number of casks of good native wine from the vineyards at neighboring Jerez were put aboard, so that a liberal daily issue of claret could supplement the ship's water supply, which could be expected in time to become less than palatable.

There was one interested person in Seville who was quite as well aware as was Magellan that the outcome of the undertaking could largely be affected by its supply of edibles. The Portuguese Consul, Sebastian Alvarez, knew that the most effective way to ruin Magellan was to create a shortage of food on his vessels. He therefore planned to create a hidden dearth of victuals which would be unsuspected until too late to be remedied.

Alvarez's scheme would work best if Magellan sailed with the comfortable confidence that his steward's stores were so abundant that he could afford to be liberal in supplying the seamen's mess. This false sense of plenty would accentuate the disastrous shock of the discovery of a scarcity when far along on the voyage. Alvarez craftily concealed his activity. He needed to do little more than to bribe the harbor police, because he had willing co-operation from the Sevillian purveyors of ship's stores. He consequently very quietly made them his unconscious agents and facilitated their pilferings and abstractions by the substantial bribes he gave all officials connected with the loading operations at the piers.

Both Magellan and de Haro were insistent in keeping watch against fraud and stayed on the piers early and late checking every detail of the lading of the steward's supplies. The strain was severe on both men, because the staff of the *Casa de Antillas* was corrupt from top to bottom. Ever since it had been founded, the ship's stores department of the organization had thrived on short weights and false counts and had learned to outwit even the most exacting sea captains. Neither Magellan nor de Haro was aware that Sebastian Alvarez was devoting his energies to nullifying their precautions against the stealing of their supplies. It was not until the ships had all been provisioned and were ready to cast off that Ferdinand Magellan appears to have become somewhat aware of some surreptitious abstraction of vital supplies. He then suspected two of his Portuguese seamen of doing the bidding of Sebastian Alvarez and summarily discharged them. He did not even then realize the grave extent to which his essential reserves had been sapped. Had the Bishop himself been able to oversee the lading of the ships, it is likely that, with his intimate knowledge of the devious ways of the land pirates at the Triana docks, he would have proved more than a match for the wily Portuguese Consul. However, both Ferdinand Magellan and Cristóbal de Haro were completely hoodwinked by Alvarez, and both obviously felt confident that the armada was sailing well-stocked and well-found.

In late June, 1519, there arrived in Seville from Malaga a young Venetian patrician named Ser Antonio Francesco Pigafetta, who bore a personal note of credentials to the Captain General from Don Charles himself. In it the King asked Ferdinand Magellan to accept the Venetian as a supernumerary in the expedition. The Captain General felt personally drawn to the newcomer, and at once invited him to serve upon his own ship, the Trinidad. His name was entered on the official muster of the *Casa de Antillas* as Don Antonio Lombardo, after the Spanish custom of identifying people with difficult foreign names by the name of their place of origin, in this case Lombardy. Don Antonio was probably sent by the Signory of Venice to report back to them on Magellan's expedition, for Venice, now in desperate straits, yet endeavored to keep pace with the rapid shifts of economic power. After being rebuffed by the Turks, in 1518, Doge Loredano had sent a delegation to Portugal to ask the privilege of acting as Portugal's middleman in the distribution of spices. The Portuguese temporized for over a year, while the industrial decay of Venice accelerated. Bankruptcy, unemployment, and want loomed over the Republic, but the Doge saw hope in Spain.

Don Antonio states in his journal that he brought letters of introduction to several of the nobility of Seville. Being a Venetian patrician, he was no doubt cordially received by Cristóbal de Haro, so that he at once took part in the social life of the city. He was acquainted with cosmopolitan society not only in Venice, but in Antwerp and in Rome, and his polished manners and cultured viewpoint must have made him popular with the group of friends of the Lady Beatriz and the Captain General who met in the Alcazar. His sound nautical knowledge, based upon his experience in navigating both the North Atlantic and the Mediterranean, made him congenial to Ferdinand Magellan, as did his acquaintance with the spice trade in its Egyptian and European aspects.

By July, 1519, Bishop Fonseca seems to have felt that he had succeeded in undermining Ferdinand Magellan's position with the King, and that he now dominated the situation. He apparently judged that it would be good strategy to commence to whittle down the Captain General's authority even before he assumed command at sea. Therefore, he appears to have encouraged Don Luis de Mendoza, the Treasurer, whom he had had appointed captain of the ship Victoria, to disregard an order of the Captain General. When checked, Mendoza became openly insubordinate toward Ferdinand Magellan and treated him with insolence. The Captain General did not let it pass, but at once complained of the affront in a personal letter to Don Charles, and Mendoza immediately received a rebuke from the King of a sufficiently minatory nature to frighten him and reduce him to a respectful attitude toward his superior. This warned the cautious Bishop that Magellan still had the trust of the ruler and at once made Fonseca more circumspect. Charles had now been elected Holy Roman Emperor, and the Bishop of Burgos obsequiously addressed him as Caesar Augustus Romanorum and took more care than ever to avoid crossing him.

Toward the end of the same month, as we have seen, the Bishop finally succeeded in disposing of Ruy Faleiro and having Don Juan de Cartagena made his successor as captain of the San Antonio.

Eighteen months had passed since the King had ordered Magellan to go to Seville and start assembling a squadron. At that time Don Charles had urgently written the *Casa* to support the undertaking in every way and to expedite its preparation. And yet the fleet was not ready. It had never before taken so long to launch an expedition, and the paralysis of this one had provided the court wits with a subject for many quips. The King, his patience exhausted, at last flatly ordered the fleet to leave Seville. He fixed the departure for August 10, 1519, whether or not all supplies had been received. The Captain General thereupon withdrew all shore leave and issued his sailing orders.

The entire personnel of the armada, with their families and friends, attended a solemn High Mass of farewell in the Church of Santa Maria de la Victoria in Triana, near the dockyard. After the benediction, the Corregidor of Seville, Don Sancho Martinez de Leyra, administered an oath to the kneeling Ferdinand Magellan that he, as a good subject of the King, would carry out the royal orders in conducting the enterprise. The Corregidor then ceremoniously entrusted to him the royal silken standard bearing the arms of the Kingdoms of Leon, Aragon and Castile.

The Captain General took his position at the steps of the altar with the symbolic banner in hand, and the four captains, the pilots, and the *maestres,* each in turn, knelt before him and took a solemn oath of allegiance to the King and vowed entire obedience to the orders of Ferdinand Magellan. They specifically swore "to follow the course ordered by him and to obey him in everything." Three of the commanders who took this solemn oath were already secretly committed to mutiny against him and to murder him as soon as the occasion might permit. Don Antonio wrote in his journal at this time, "The captains hated him exceedingly, I do not know why unless because he was Portuguese and they Spanish."

And then, at last, on Monday morning, August 10, 1519, the broadsides of all five ships thundered a loud farewell to Seville. The anchors were hoisted, and the vessels drifted one by one from their berths at the Dock of the Mules into the channel of the Guadalquiver River, gaining headway by the use of the long wooden sweeps manned by seamen in the waist. Once the current of the stream caught them, the foresails were hoisted and the ships sailed slowly in single file down the river.

Ser Antonio Pigafetta, who had become Don Antonio Lombardo, now commenced his diary of the voyage and, like any modern tourist, noted in his journal the sights they passed going downstream. He commented on two submerged piles of an ancient, destroyed Moorish bridge which presented obstacles to navigation; it required the aid of a high tide and the services of river pilots to get past them safely. After sailing slowly with the current for about seventy-five miles down the river, the five ships reached the ocean port of San Lucar de Barrameda and dropped anchor

Engraving from de Bry's "Peregrinationes," 1596

THE FONSECA CABAL: DE HARO, FONSECA, CARTAGENA

Engraving from de Bry's "Peregrinationes," 1592

DEPARTURE OF THE ARMADA FROM SAN LUCAR

opposite the castle of the Duke of Medina Sidonia, which protected the river's mouth.

The extent of the shortages of operating and deck supplies now began to be apparent. The ships lacked numerous essentials, and the fleet was in no shape to go to sea. Never before had the *Casa de Antillas* functioned so ineptly, and everyone was indignant at the bureau for what was in reality a masterpiece of artful sabotage by Dom Sebastian Alvarez, the Portuguese Consul. Strenuous efforts now were made by Cristóbal de Haro to locate and furnish all that still was needed, and the commander of each ship drove his staff hard in procurement. The Captain General and the captains made several trips in their ships' longboats to Seville to secure wanted items.

San Lucar was a flourishing little city which combined the characteristics of an ocean port and of a fishing village. It now was invaded by the wives and sweethearts of the crew, and also by many of the public women of the Seville waterfront. The Lady Beatriz, although again pregnant, came down with Dom Diogo Barbosa and her brothers and joined in the many festivities with which the wives attempted to mask their apprehensions. The guest chambers of the monastery, all the inns, and the spare rooms of many private homes in San Lucar were crowded with visitors. Quarters were also afforded at the comfortable hunting lodges of the nobility of Seville, who were accustomed to hunt and fish in the salt marshes about San Lucar. The Duke of Medina Sidonia made his castle the center of the social activities, and parties came by riverboat from the nearby city of Jerez. As most of the officers of the fleet had shore leave, there was a month of continuous gaiety, while ship's supplies were feverishly being obtained by the captains.

It was on one of his visits to Seville from San Lucar, less than a month before his final departure from Spain, that Ferdinand Magellan drew up his last will and testament. He apparently had not intended to make a will, expecting that under the Spanish laws of inheritance his wife, his son Rodrigo, and the unborn child which they expected would naturally inherit his estate at Sabrosa and any other fortune of which he might die possessed, including the benefits which might accrue from his contract with the Crown. His plans were changed, however, because on August 6, 1519, a royal order proclaimed that the proceeds from any contingent benefits acquired by members of the expedition who might die intestate on the voyage would accrue to the national religious fund dedicated to the ransom of Spanish captives among the Moslems. As most of Ferdinand Magellan's prospects for an estate were contingent upon his contract with the Crown, he hastened to make his will, which was dated in Seville on August 24, 1519.

Much of what we have learned of Ferdinand Magellan's character is confirmed by his will. His intensely religious nature is revealed throughout the document, as well as his meticulous carefulness in both past records and future plans. He wanted to be buried in the local Church of Santa Maria de Victoria, near the dockyard where he had worked for so many months in preparing his voyage, and one can imagine that the troubled knight had often sought solace in this church, although he attended Mass on Sundays at the Cathedral with his wife and family.

He made a number of religious and charitable bequests before turning to provisions for his family, and all were carefully thought out. The consideration he showed for his wife mirrors his true regard for her. His great hopes for his children are revealed even in the stilted, legal language, and he did not forget his dear sister Isabel in Portugal. His page, Cristóbal Rabelo, of whom he was very fond, was to receive a generous bequest, and Enrique, his faithful slave, was to be freed and to receive a sum of money.

That Magellan had great expectations of wealth coming to him through the success of the expedition is shown in detail. Apparently he never doubted for a moment that the contract he had made would be honored, even if he himself were not there to receive his due. He concluded his will by naming Knight Commander Diogo Barbosa and his friend, Dr. Sancho de Matienzo, Canon of the Cathedral at Seville, as executors.

The man disclosed in this will is a conscientious Christian, charitable and generous, a solicitous husband, parent, and brother, an appreciative master, and a prudent, scrupulous man of affairs. He shows a sense of loyalty to his adopted country and a great pride in the name and escutcheon he has inherited from his forebears.

In attempting to reincarnate Ferdinand Magellan from a study of the scanty records reflecting his personality, the interchange of correspondence between him and Don Charles is of first importance. From these letters one senses the intense, deep-seated devotion of the Portuguese adventurer for his liege. One may well assume that Don Charles reciprocated the personal regard and had not only great trust in his alien admiral, but also a deep affection for him.

From the start, the personalities of the future Emperor and the future circumnavigator, hampered and fettered though they both were by sordid, petty placemen, sensed each other's caliber and felt akin. The King not only gave his consent to Magellan's bold adventure, but wholeheartedly made it his own and devoted his interest to it. The later and more mature Charles, Emperor of the Holy Roman Empire, is rated in history as a modern man, but at the time he accepted the fealty of Ferdinand Magellan, perhaps no cavalier in Europe was more immersed in the spirit of knight-errantry than was young Charles of Ghent. He had passed his boyhood in the decades when the already outlived cult of romantic chivalry was yet accepted by society. He was a contemporary of Chevalier Bayard, the knight *sans peur et sans reproche* who shines in history as the beau ideal of chivalry. The era in which his ideals were molded was the same to which the mocking Cervantes was later to hold up a candid mirror.

Ferdinand Magellan, with his great talents hungry for appreciation, who in his whole life had been constantly disprized by a succession of commanders of his own race, had at last by great good luck found a foreign master able to understand him, to get the most out of him, and to call forth his passionate devotion and intense loyalty. Despite the medley of contradictory orders issued in his name, Charles was to Ferdinand Magellan always the trusting Prince who, unswerving and unperturbed, had confidence in his lieutenant, inspired his efforts, and supported him without stint.

The letters between Magellan and King Charles show that the expedition of discovery was the dream not only of Ferdinand, but of Don Charles as well. Frustrated by the early fumbling of the *Casa de Antillas,* Magellan had only to appeal to Don Charles to have the royal whip crack sharply over the heads of the bureaucrats. When the *Casa de Antillas* alleged that the gold resources allocated to the work were exhausted, Charles instantly threw the resources of the banker de Haro into the breach. When de Haro swung his support to the insubordinate Juan de Cartagena, a royal letter quickly brought Cartagena under Magellan's orders. When Luis de Mendoza, the influential hidalgo, was insolent, the royal word cowed him. When the port captain at Seville failed to restrain the mob that attacked Magellan, the punishment that followed was swift and severe. When the question arose as to the selection of the crew, Charles wrote, "Magellan is to choose his men." When the *Casa de Antillas* refused to pay the Portuguese sailors illicitly recruited by Magellan, Charles promptly reversed himself, astonished the *Casa,* and backed up Magellan by the extraordinary proposal that he, "*Yo el Rey,*" and Magellan will each choose twelve Portuguese to go. Nothing could better testify to the trust in which he held his lieutenant than this brushing aside of intermediaries, which took Magellan into partnership. The combination of "I and Magellan" was irresistible.

The extant royal order, dated May 8, 1519, is divided into seventy-four heads. One part gives detailed instructions about landing in strange lands, how to treat the native chiefs, and how to gain their amity. There is advice about trading and bartering with the aborigines. Women must not be maltreated, but the sailors are not expected to be too straight-laced with them. The crews must not swear, nor play cards, nor dice, "for from such often arise evil and scandal and strife." Great care must be taken not to have embers aboard ship when there is a gale, and precautions are suggested at all times in handling fires at sea. When camps or settlements are made ashore, they should be located on high ground and not in marshy or poorly ventilated spots. The captains are enjoined to visit their sick and disabled men each day, and to see that they are given full medical attention without charge to the patients. They are instructed to treat their men in a loving, paternal manner, and not only to insist that they get an ample daily ration, of which Charles gave the proportions, but are instructed to inspect and taste the food themselves. There is the canny Hapsburg note also: "If the Kings or seigniors of the land give any jewels or presents, they shall be ours, and the Inspector General or Accountant shall place them in charge of the Treasurer."

As one reads the carefully detailed nautical orders from the boy whose maritime experience was limited to a single trip by sea from Flanders to Spain, one recalls that Don Antonio Pigafetta wrote of the sea yarns of the old salts at Barcelona, and it is apparent that Don Charles himself must have been a rapt auditor to the veteran sea dogs who frequented his court, petitioning for a caravel and a license to explore.

However, Charles's instructions to Ferdinand Magellan constituted a practical set of rules for the conduct of any fleet, and were more than a collection of aphorisms. Many of the passages evidently are based on Portuguese instructions to naval commanders, but in its grasp of executive detail, and in its disclosure of the imaginative, adventurous nature of Don Charles, the document gives promise of the great leader he was to be. Ferdinand Magellan was the precursor of Cortes and of Pizarro, the first of the captains whom Don Charles was to send forth to bear his banner across unknown seas and plant it in faraway lands.

At last, despite the saboteurs, the essential supplies had all been secured and the provisioning of the fleet was completed. The Captain General and his four commanders had come down, each in his own ship's boat, from Seville, and had hoisted their pennants, taking over command. Don Antonio records that, during all the month of waiting, the crews had daily gone ashore at San Lucar to attend Mass at the Church of Our Lady of Barrameda, and now that the day of departure had arrived, the entire personnel went ashore to confession and received communion at a solemn High Mass.

The Captain General, accompanied by the captains, now made a full dress, ship-to-ship inspection to make certain that all was ready and that none of the distraught wives or sweethearts of the crew had stowed away for the voyage. Then the anchors were weighed, the foresails were raised, the guns fired, and on the day of Saint Eustacio, September 20, 1519, the five little vessels put out to sea.

At the very end, before he weighed anchor, the devoted retainer addressed his King for the last time. The lines voice a premonition that he will never return, and they betray, with the excuse of saying farewell, the affection which prompted them.

As a final legacy, he left for Don Charles personally a confidential memorandum of the latitudes and location of the Spice Islands with his evidence that they lay within Don Charles's rightful dominion, "because some time the Portuguese King may try to declare that the islands of Maluco are in his Kingdom." In farewell, he bade the young King keep this note carefully, for there may come a time when he will be in need of it. Had he ended the letter "Ave Caesar! we, who are about to die, salute you," it perhaps would not have been more revealing of his mood.

On leaving San Lucar, as he stood upon the quarter-deck of the Trinidad and saw in his wake the swelling canvas of the four ships, all bearing the Cross of Santiago, who may surmise where the thoughts of Ferdinand Magellan, Knight Commander of Santiago, turned? Perhaps he thought of the Lady Beatriz, his son Rodrigo, and his unborn child; perhaps of the magnificent opportunities for distinction and wealth that lay ahead of him, and of his comrade Francisco Serrano awaiting him in Ternate; but most certainly he thought of the youthful ruler in Barcelona who had shown trust in him and for whom he would achieve the best of which he was capable.

PART III

SO NOBLE A CAPTAIN

CHAPTER XV

SHORES OF BRAZIL

IT WAS a confident flotilla that, with bombards thundering farewell salvos and every banner displayed, spread its sails and went to sea on Tuesday, September 20, 1519. The women who were left behind at San Lucar wept as they watched the vessels sail so bravely away, and were full of foreboding, despite the promises and assurances they had received from sons and husbands before their departure. Men of power in Spain, Portugal, Italy, and as far north as Augsburg, having done all they could to foster or to wreck the expedition, now sat back to await developments.

Ser Antonio Pigafetta, or, as he appeared on the ship's roll, Don Antonio Lombardo, wrote, referring to the high spirits of the men: "The Captain General had omitted to disclose certain particulars of the voyage to the crew, to avoid their uneasiness in contemplation of the great impetuous reverses inherent in such an enterprise at sea." Ser Antonio Pigafetta was a Venetian gentleman who must have been about thirty years old at this time. His motive for accompanying Magellan is obscure; it may have been merely the love of adventure, but it seems more likely that he was there in order to be able to make a full report, later on, to the Signory of Venice. Whatever his reason for making the voyage was, later centuries have been grateful for it. His journal is not only a masterpiece of early travel recording, but is our chief source of information concerning this great expedition.

It is hard to understand how any member of the company could have been unaware of the dangers ahead, especially in view of the effort of the Portuguese agents to discourage enrollment in the fleet. Yet a number of the officers took young relatives with them as cabin boys, and the spirit of the enterprise was remarkably sanguine. Ferdinand Magellan himself had with him two young relatives, the lad Cristóbal Rabelo of Porto, whose exact relationship is unclear, and Martin Magellan, a cousin from Lisbon whose expenses he had defrayed. Francisco, the son of Captain Alvaro de Mesquita, and Juan de Torres and Francisco Paxe, the sons-in-law of Captain John Serrano, were also with him. The pilot of the Victoria, Vasco Gomes Gallego, brought his son Juan; the pilot of the Concepción, Juan Lopes Carvalho, was accompanied by his boy Juanillo; the pilot of the San Antonio, Juan Rodríguez de Mafra, had his son Diego; and the mariner Cristóbal Garcia of Palos enlisted his son Diego. In addition to these boys, whose parentage has been identified, there also were enrolled several Portuguese striplings of good family who presumably were relatives of the officers.

Another mark of confidence in the safety of the voyage was the number of personal servants the Spanish aristocrats brought with them. It is hard to believe that Juan de Cartagena, fop though he was, would have shipped a train of ten attendants had the perilous nature of the adventure been foreseen.

The first leg of the voyage, through the Sea of Mares, was in the nature of a shakedown cruise, and each man was absorbed in learning the sailing characteristics of his craft. The Captain General at once commenced to drill the squadron in fleet tactics, in accordance with the rules which he had given in writing to each of the commanders. These were based on the King's letter of instruction, and in general were the standard regulations of the *Casa de Antillas.* Like the Portuguese regulations under which Magellan had formerly sailed, they stipulated that the *capitana,* as the Trinidad was called, should always lead the armada and that during the hours of visibility the other craft should set their course and carry their canvas in imitation of the example set by the leader. At night the *farol,* or large lantern, on the high poop of the *capitana* was to be their guide. A series of signals by lighted torches would indicate whether the fleet's sails were to be furled or spread and whether the course was to be changed. In case reefs or shoals were sighted ahead, then many torches would be shown by the *capitana* and a warning gun would be fired. All signals were to be answered in kind by each ship.

From the beginning, Magellan permitted no laxity in the observance of this system, especially since there had been rumors in San Lucar that a fleet of Algerian galleys was cruising outside the harbor awaiting their emergence. It was said that the Moslem commander had been bribed by King Manuel to attack the Spanish vessels, hoping at least to cripple enough of them to force Magellan to return for refitting. The Spanish navy was at war with the Barbary pirates, and even if this rumor was untrue, some such encounter with corsairs was a possibility. Also it was known that a Portuguese fleet had been concentrated at Lisbon, mysteriously held in readiness for some undisclosed purpose. Consequently Magellan not only commenced at once to practice fleet maneuvers, but also ordered the foreign *lombarderos* on each ship to drill the gun crews for action. However, no hostile craft were encountered, and the lofty peak of Tenerife was sighted on schedule.

In the forenoon of September 26th, the squadron steered straight for what appeared to be merely a cleft in the rocky wall of Tenerife, the opening into the cliff-sheltered harbor of the city of Santa Cruz. There they were welcomed by the fleet treasurer, Don Luis de Mendoza, captain of the Victoria, who had preceded them to purchase supplies. Spanish ships for the West Indies then customarily made Tenerife a port of call, for provisions there were cheaper than at Seville or Cadiz.

These first days were happy ones for Ferdinand Magellan. At last he was at sea, emancipated from the drudgery of outfitting and the paper work demanded by the *Casa de Antillas*. From now on, his problems would be those of a sailor. He was firmly in command, and there was no longer anyone to challenge his authority. As he breathed the air of the sea and felt the familiar roll of the deck beneath him, with the distance widening between his fleet and the interference of the plotting Bishop, he felt that he and his captains would at last be able to co-operate as comrades for a common aim.

He was soon, however, to be jarred from his optimism. On the day after his arrival in Tenerife, a fast dispatch boat came into the harbor, having raced under press of sail from San Lucar to deliver a letter to him from Dom Diogo Barbosa. It had been written hurriedly and sent off with all speed to warn the Captain General that, as soon as the armada had sailed from San Lucar, and hence when the need for secrecy had passed, friends of the three Spanish captains had begun to boast publicly of the captains' intention, once well at sea, to form a triumvirate headed by Juan de Cartagena and take over the command of the expedition. They proposed to kill Magellan at once if he opposed their usurping his authority.

Magellan's reply was characteristic. Thanking Barbosa, he wrote, "I will work as a servant of the Emperor, and to this end I will offer my life." He did, however, assure his father-in-law that, in spite of this rumor, he would attempt to win the good will of the captains and would do his best to prevent any disruption of the undertaking. Diogo Barbosa conveyed this reassuring message to the board of directors of the *Casa de Antillas*, who were also much perturbed by the ominous talk, and the chronicler says they were relieved by it and praised Magellan's sagacity.

Until then, Magellan and Diogo Barbosa seem to have deluded themselves into believing that the hostility of Mendoza, Cartagena, and Quesada had subsided, and that the Bishop's plots would cease at the water's edge. Diogo Barbosa had been with Magellan within the week, and it seems somewhat extreme for him to go to the length of chartering a dispatch boat to send him this warning. However, although they were doubtless aware of some hostility on the part of the captains, the definiteness of the rumored plot was probably something new.

Tenerife was suited for the plot of which Dom Diogo warned Magellan, for the stay of the armada there gave the captains a chance to meet ashore and act in unison. The island, which had only been conquered and settled within the quarter-century, still had a frontier form of colonial government and was largely under the influence of Bishop Fonseca. Captain Luis de Mendoza had had an opportunity, through preceding the fleet to Tenerife, to insure the support of the local authorities, and may indeed have been sent ahead for this purpose.

We cannot doubt that the timely warning from his father-in-law saved Ferdinand Magellan's life. We assume that Juan de Cartagena proposed to him that, since the armada was now a fleet in being, it would be desirable to call a council of the captains and pilots to discuss their experiences with their ships and to confer concerning any other matters that had come up in the six days' initial run. Ferdinand Magellan, now on his guard, guessed what tactics were behind the proposal, and at once assented without challenging Cartagena's tacit assumption of coeval authority. He had seen too many conspiracies of captains in the Portuguese fleets during the anarchic early days in India not to recognize that Cartagena was taking the first step of a captains' cabal. He could foresee the probable program and no doubt decided that his course would be to dissemble, to keep his peace, and to acquiesce amicably in whatever was proposed. Time would be on his side, and he must at all costs avoid a crisis until he was ready to meet it.

The junta was held after supper in the cabin of the Trinidad. The Captain General took the chair at the head of the table and cordially made way for Captain Cartagena, the King's Vedor, to sit at his right. Captain Luis de Mendoza, his avowed enemy, sat at his left. He noted that his cousin, John Serrano, was maneuvered into the seat beyond Mendoza, and that John Lopes Carvalho, whom he distrusted, sat on the other side of Serrano. Magellan himself was farthest away from the door and cut off from any aid. He saw through the corner of his eye that each of the Spanish captains seemed tense. As he looked about the table he concluded that his foes were the three Spanish captains and the Portuguese pilots Gomes and Carvalho. The pilots Gallego, de Mafra, and San Martin evidently were oblivious of any impending action. His only friend present was John Serrano, who, however, was aging and slow. He sensed that they would use provocative tactics to try to arouse his well-known quick temper and to incite an altercation. Having been schooled in such machinations, he expected that a scuffle would be simulated and that, in the dim light of the cabin, John Serrano would be stabbed by the unscrupulous Carvalho, who sat beside him. The conspirators would then lay hold of Magellan, deprive him of his dagger, and accuse him of the accidental murder of his cousin in the melee. Their evidence would be irrefutable, and he would be apprehended and turned over to the local police. The fleet would not tarry, but would sail under command of Juan de Cartagena as Captain General and be navigated by Estevan Gomes, who already had the post of Chief Pilot.

By arrangement with Sebastian Alvarez, the Bishop could have Ferdinand Magellan removed by a Portuguese war caravel from whatever merchant ship might carry him in irons to Seville for trial. Neither the busy Emperor nor anyone else in Spain, expecting perhaps old Dom Diogo Barbosa, would be sufficiently interested even to consider trying to intervene with Dom Manuel for the unfortunate expatriate. Once Magellan was in the hands of Dom Manuel there would be no further trouble. The legal lien of Ferdinand Magellan upon the results of the expedition would automatically be cancelled, and Fonseca, de Haro, and Fugger would monopolize Spain's commerce with Maluco.

Magellan saw that a decisive moment had arrived. He was that rare type of man who is most relaxed and composed at a time of crisis, and when he glanced covertly at Cartagena and perceived how agitated he was, he realized his own superior strength and felt confident that he could outwit him. He resolved to keep cool at all costs and to stomach any affronts as he calmly awaited the first move. As he had anticipated, Cartagena brusquely ignored him as chairman and himself called the meeting to order. Instead of protesting, Magellan treated the procedure as being quite in order. Cartagena then pompously assumed direction of the meeting and asked each captain in turn for comments regarding the ship under his command. He did not question Magellan until last, and, when he did so, he received a deferential report in a mild manner. Then Cartagena arbitrarily announced that the route to be followed by the armada would be the course decided upon at the *Casa de Antillas* in Seville. It will be remembered that at the time Magellan had not been in accord with the decision of the council in Seville, but now he acquiesced without a murmur. Cartagena obviously was baffled by the Captain General's supine acceptance of this and looked in confusion to Mendoza for guidance, but saw that he also was nonplused. They had been keyed up for a dispute and could not adjust themselves to the deferential manner of Magellan. Cartagena's program had been based upon easily provoking a quarrel, and, being frustrated, he weakly decided to temporize, just as Magellan had hoped. Now that Magellan had obsequiously bowed to his assumption of the supreme command, he compromised with himself and ineptly decided to defer any drastic move. He promised himself that, after he had profited by Magellan's services and had fully exploited him, then he would dispose of him.

The other conspirators looked to their leader for their cue, and when they perceived that he had patronizingly accepted the subservience of his intended victim, they, of course fell in with him. The council broke up without further incident. While Magellan politely saw his visitors down the companionway of the *capitana,* he realized what a narrow escape he had had, and he determined to take forehanded steps to protect himself against the next subversive move.

Swaggering, self-satisfied Cartagena may have deemed his unopposed assumption of command to have constituted a victory, but his father, the Bishop, eagerly awaiting the news at Valladolid, recognized angrily that the opportunity had been fumbled and that once again he had been checkmated.

While Magellan was in Tenerife he figured in a mysterious episode that has yet to be clarified. There were at that time in the Canary Islands a number of Portuguese political refugees who had found sanctuary in that Spanish colony. One writer hints that Magellan secured a fabulous leather globe there, which had been smuggled out of Portugal and which disclosed the location of the *paso.* It is definitely known that a Portuguese of unknown antecedents who was reputed to have personal navigational knowledge regarding the *paso* was residing in Tenerife. Magellan sought out this mysterious person and tried to persuade him to accompany the armada, but failed to get him to volunteer. Thereupon he sent the *alguacil,* Espinosa, ashore with an armed squad, shanghaied this unknown person, kept him aboard, and sailed away with him. That this high-handed action was not at all in keeping with Magellan's general behavior and character heightens the enigma. The unknown man is identified in the Spanish records only as "Master Peter," and, after leaving Tenerife, he was entered on the armada's rolls under that name as a *sobresaliente* at the minimum salary of eight hundred *maravedis.* Don Antonio makes no mention of him, and the archives are contradictory. The unfortunate refugee was later captured and given short shrift by the Portuguese. The facts concerning him have never been uncovered.

After staying three days in Tenerife to load the stores of firewood, cheese, and salted meat purchased by Captain Mendoza, the fleet dropped down to Monte Rosso, at the south end of the island; here Mendoza had accumulated a supply of pitch for use on the hulls and of charcoal for the cooks' galleys. The stevedoring was completed in two days, and, after the last keg of tar had been stowed below decks, the *Armada de Maluco* cast off its final tie with Europe.

Ferdinand Magellan took the lead without challenge from Cartagena; at midnight on Monday, October 3rd, the *capitana* broke out its foresail and led the way out of the harbor on the ebb tide, followed by the rest of the squadron in single file. Once clear of the islands, the Trinidad hoisted all three sails, the others followed suit, and they picked up the steady wind called the sirocco which held them upon a straight southwest course.

At noon on October 4th, the Captain General took the sun and observed that the position was 27° N. and that they then had covered twelve leagues at the rate of four nautical miles per hour. At daybreak on the next morning, October 5th, the Trinidad altered its course, steering south-southwest. Signals were set for the fleet to follow. The consorts complied, but after a short while the San Antonio ran under the stern of the flagship. Captain Juan de Cartagena called in an authoritative tone to the pilot, Estevan Gomes, and asked the course. Gomes replied, "South by west." Cartagena questioned belligerently why it had been changed from southwest, which had been agreed upon previously. Magellan, who was standing on the quarter-deck with Gomes, here broke in to say sharply to Cartagena, "You are to follow me and ask no questions."

Cartagena was obviously astonished at Magellan's stern response. His face turned red and he was speechless for a moment. Then he furiously retorted to the Captain General that he should have consulted the other captains and not have thus arbitrarily reversed the decision made by the council at Tenerife. Magellan did not respond but maintained an expression of severity. Cartagena then asserted hotly that it was bad navigation to keep so close to the West African coast just off Cape Bojador. Ferdinand Magelland replied tersely that Cartagena had his orders, and that these were "to follow my flag by day and my lantern by night."

Juan de Cartagena was dumfounded at the reversal of Magellan's attitude toward him. From virtual obeisance it had changed to acerbity, and he was not prepared to cope with such defiance. In all his sheltered past, whenever he had encountered opposition he had only had to invoke the name of the terrible Bishop to see resistance fade. Now, here in the vast waste of the Atlantic, he suddenly experienced futility. In a flash he realized how Magellan had tricked him at Tenerife. He recalled too late the admonishing words of the Bishop regarding the cunning of the despised little adventurer, and was suddenly aware how he had let opportunity escape him.

One can well imagine the excitement this exhibition of disrespect for the fleet commander by his senior captain must have caused on the decks of the two ships, the other craft no doubt being out of earshot. One can see the two *naos* proceeding at about four knots in a fair wind, with the steersman of the San Antonio keeping it just abaft the beam of the Trinidad, and the elegantly clad Cartagena standing in the forecastle holding onto the foreshrouds, excitedly bawling his protest. The rustling of the waves, the slapping of the San Antonio's sails, the rattling of its yards, and the creaking of both wooden ships as, with a following sea, they slowly rose and fell in the strong southward current, must have made it difficult for the startled crews to hear all of Cartagena's tirade.

One also can see the small, tense figure of Magellan standing defiantly on his quarter-deck as his authority was thus flouted by his second-in-command, who claimed to be speaking in the name of the other captains. It was a humiliating moment for the Captain General, and he stood as if frozen, stoically refusing to reply to the storm of rebuke. Cartagena was frustrated by his impassiveness, and, after an incoherent repetition of the warning about danger, the sound of his voice trailed away as the San Antonio fell off and resumed its position behind its leader.

Magellan had adroitly reasserted his authority, but Cartagena's inexplicable paroxysm of fury over the change of course disturbed him. Why had he made so much of it? His resentment was understandable, but his insensate vehemence seemed to have a hidden significance, and Magellan sought for the motive. Behind shallow Cartagena lurked the shadow of the Bishop, and it dawned upon him that his enemies wanted very much to have him follow the course laid out at Seville. This intensified a suspicion over which Ferdinand Magellan had been brooding ever since he had received the letter of warning at Tenerife, a suspicion which had been heightened while the ships lay at Monte Rosso. While they were there, a caravel with a cargo of salt fish for the squadron came into port from the North African fishing grounds, and the fishermen reported having sighted a sizable fleet of large Portuguese *naos* sailing south. The destination of such an expedition could not have been the Orient, for it was the unfavorable Indian monsoon season, and Magellan realized that Dom Manuel must have sent this force to lie in wait for him. He resolved to make every effort to elude the Portuguese fleet. History has confirmed Magellan's analysis, for Dom Manuel had indeed sent a strong fleet out from Lisbon to intercept the *Armada de Maluco* south of the Canaries. If it failed to waylay Magellan early in the voyage, then it was directed to divide into two squadrons. One division was ordered to cruise in the Southeast Atlantic to prevent Magellan's armada from sailing eastward via the Cape of Good Hope. The other squadron was to patrol the Brazilian coast from Pernambuco down as far as the estuary of the Rio de la Plata, so as to halt the Spaniards if they attempted to find the *paso* and reach Maluco via the setting sun. Still a third squadron had been commanded by Dom Manuel to sail from Goa, India, to Maluco, but we are not yet concerned with that one.

Magellan realized now that Dom Manuel must have been informed as to the route of the expedition. It will be remembered that, before the departure from Seville, Magellan and all the other captains were ordered to submit in writing to the *Casa de Antillas* their suggestions as to the best course to be followed in the North Atlantic. Magellan stubbornly declined to disclose his views to the council, despite pressure to do so. Thereupon the *Casa de Antillas* officially selected a southwest course until latitude 24° N. should be reached, and this choice was confirmed by the captains at the meeting at Tenerife, with Magellan's concurrence.

Captain General Magellan therefore had deliberately disobeyed the orders of the *Casa*, and also had repudiated his own agreement of a few days before at the council in Tenerife. Captain Juan de Cartagena was quite within his rights, as King's Vedor of the Armada, in asking why the orders were being disregarded, and he even would have been justified in making a dignified protest to the commander-in-chief. It is important to note this, because one of the many official charges later laid against Ferdinand Magellan was based upon this deviation from his written instructions.

When Cartagena shouted the warning to Magellan that if he persisted on the new south-southwest course he would run aground on the Guinea Coast, he merely displayed the ignorance of West African waters which was common to Castilian navigators. This dispute between Cartagena and Magellan as to the course to be followed is not mentioned by Don Antonio in his journal, but the episode is given in detail in a report which Don Lopes de Rescalde, the Factor of the *Casa de Antillas,* later sent to his superior, Bishop Fonseca. By a bold misrepresentation of the facts, the charges later made against Ferdinand Magellan accuse him of altering the direction of the voyage because of complicity with the Portuguese. In reality his motives were the opposite.

The insistence of Cartagena upon maintaining the southwest route to Brazil convinced Magellan that a rendezvous had been arranged with the Portuguese in the waters somewhere east of Cape Roque. He knew very well that Bishop Fonseca was quite capable of making some such arrangement with Alvarez to let the Portuguese arrest him and some of the other Portuguese officers as deserters and carry them back to Lisbon, letting the Spaniards proceed under Captain Cartagena. As Magellan pondered over these possibilities, he resolved to watch Cartagena even more carefully.

For a fortnight the armada sailed steadily south with a fair wind and, aided by the Guinea Current, passed between the Cape Verde Islands and the African coast without sighting land and without being seen by any Portuguese craft. After reaching latitude 15° N., the Captain General commenced to hug the West African coast to the east of the route of any Portuguese ships sailing southward from Lisbon or northward from the Cape of Good Hope or El Mina.

On October 18, 1519, when opposite Sierra Leone, the armada was met by terrifying thunderstorms, with head winds that stopped all progress. These increased to gale force and so buffeted the high, castellated prows and poops that it looked as though the wallowing *naos,* with their rounded hulls and without deep keels, would certainly capsize; indeed, they rolled over so far that their yardarms touched the sea. The waves sluiced over the low waist decks, and the crews clung together on the forecastles and wept. Don Antonio says that at last, in answer to their prayers, the blessed lights of Saint Elmo appeared at the mastheads and the storm abated. Then, in a few days more, the wind died down completely, and the fleet lay becalmed. Magellan knew they were in that same stagnant area where, a quarter of a century earlier, Christopher Columbus was becalmed on his third voyage. The course he had deliberately taken was one he knew would be shunned by every Portuguese pilot, since it led directly into the paralyzing calms of the doldrums, or horse latitudes.

Magellan completely outmaneuvered the Portuguese Admiral by hiding in that blighted, windless sector. No experienced navigator would knowingly steer a fleet into such imprisonment, yet here Magellan brought his armada. If he had had a homogeneous, disciplined crew, he might have been candid about the strategy which he had followed, but unfortunately he had to keep his own counsel, knowing his taciturnity could only make him appear an incompetent commander.

There was no breeze whatsoever, but the sea was troubled by long rollers with steep troughs, and the five becalmed ships were never still, but spun and pitched continuously amid the groaning of the timbers and the rattling of the spars. The equatorial sun blazed down from a cloudless sky, and the heat seemed insupportable. The tar melted and oozed out, and the seams of the hulls opened. The men said the deck was like a stove, and in fact wheat parched and salt pork turned putrid when left in the sun. The hold was a furnace where the hoops of the casks burst so that the precious wine and water began to leak, but it was so stifling that the cooper and his helpers could not repair the barrels. The seamen sent below to man the pumps had to be relieved every five minutes. There were occasional clouds to obscure the sun, but these discharged only sticky showers which caused prickly heat. The nights were even more uncomfortable than the days. The sultry purgatory seemed endless, and did indeed last for a dreadful twenty days and nights.

During the calm the Spanish captains frequently visited one another, being rowed back and forth in their skiffs to their stationary but tossing ships. They conspicuously did not approach the *capitana,* and Magellan could take no overt notice of the ostracism. In the silent opprobrium with which he was surrounded, he no doubt found solace in the company of Don Antonio and of Cristóbal Rabelo. During his nightly vigils on the quarter-deck, he studied with them the equatorial skies and told them tales of the storied East or listened to Don Antonio's talk of Rome, Venice, and Cairo.

The two priests of the armada visited the units of the fleet and attempted to maintain the spirits of the disconsolate men. One of them, Father Pedro Sanchez de Reina, was a protégé of Juan de Cartagena. He continually circulated among all the crews and was very popular. Not only was he an indulgent confessor, but he amused the sailors with bawdy songs, accompanying himself on a guitar. He was a merry drinking companion, had a fund of droll stories, and was a good loser at dice. Magellan's chaplain, Padre Pedro Valderrama, a young Dominican, was scandalized by the lay priest's loose habits and remonstrated with him. He reported to the Captain General that behind Padre Reina's gay pose there was sedition, and that he was fomenting discontent among the seamen. No one knew anything about his background, or how and why he had been enrolled, and some suspected him of being an agent of Consul Sebastian Alvarez.

After a fortnight in the calm, Ferdinand Magellan began to worry at the steady dwindling of their provisions, and therefore he reluctantly ordered the daily issues of wine and bread to be reduced. Because of the leakage from the casks, he also cut the water ration to four pints daily. The panting, sweating men grumbled at being deprived of their already scanty dole of water. The frequent showers could have provided ample rain water, but the men lacked the energy to rig up contrivances to catch and preserve the precious liquid. Instead they lay in whatever shade was available and cursed the day they had enlisted under so inept a commander; and Padre Sanchez de Reina fanned their resentment by whispering that they were suffering because Magellan had disregarded the advice of the experienced Captain Juan de Cartagena.

On the twenty-first day of the calm, the unseen ocean current carried them out of the doldrums into the track of the trade winds that blew from the southeast. The sails filled, the ships heeled over and commenced to foam through the sea, and all ill-humors were temporarily blown away. No man in the armada was so relieved as was the Captain General, who, in addition to setting a serene example to all during the dreadful three weeks, also had to bear the weight of the curses that had been muttered against him. But while they were hidden in the doldrums the Portuguese caravels gave up the search, so that, despite the loss of time and waste of food, Magellan had saved the *Armada de Maluco*.

During the calm the armada had drifted westward across the Atlantic to a position about 15° west of Greenwich, and it now steered south-southwest and crossed the equator about November 20, 1519, just two months after having left San Lucar. Don Antonio writes: "Having passed the equinoctial line, we lost the Transmontana." This was the name given the North Polar Star by the Venetian navigators. From now on Magellan would have to rely upon the Southern Cross instead for celestial navigation by night.

In his account of the ten weeks' voyage fom San Lucar to Brazil, Don Antonio filled his journal with sailors' yarns about the marvels of aquatic and bird life and descriptions of marine novelties noted from the decks of the Trinidad. If he included any mention of the most dramatic happening of the trip, the struggle of Captain Juan de Cartagena to depose Ferdinand Magellan as Captain General, he had to excise it before publication for fear of offending Cartagena's influential relatives. But a written report made to Fonseca by one of the survivors supplies the narrative which Don Antonio discreetly suppressed.

As we have seen, the Spanish captains spent considerable time together during the period that the armada was becalmed. Evidently they then evolved a scheme to entrap Magellan. It was the rule of the *Casa de Antillas* that, when an armada was at sea, each vessel should sail alongside the *capitana* just before the evening hour of prayer, and the commander should then report to the Captain General the events of the day and ask for his instructions. Such verbal conferences were indispensable to the control of a fleet in those days, before the use of effective systems of signaling. It was not a difficult maneuver to hold a ship alongside the flagship in normal weather, for the speed of a fleet was rarely more than four knots, and the wind generally was a fair following one. In King Charles's letter of instructions to Magellan is the explicit command: "You will issue an order to the captains of the other ships that they will each evening give you their salutes, as it is customary to do to the Captain General in every armada." The official instructions issued before the *Armada de Maluco* left Seville provided that each vessel in turn should run alongside the *capitana* and that the Captain should then hail the Captain General with the formula: "God save you, Sir Captain General and Master and good Ship's company." All the four captains had conformed daily to this rule until, one day shortly after the equator had been crossed, Captain Cartagena deliberately disobeyed it.

Instead of performing this daily duty himself, as heretofore, Cartagena let the *contramaestre*, or boatswain, of the San Antonio hail the *capitana* and, in a disrespectful way, salute Ferdinand Magellan as Captain rather than as Captain General. Magellan sharply rebuked the man for the studied discourtesy. Cartagena, who had been watching for Magellan's reaction, immediately appeared on deck and shouted to him, "I sent the best man on this ship to salute you, but next time, if I wish, I'll have one of my cabin boys do it." Then the San Antonio sheered off without making the customary report. It is not clear what the King's Vedor expected to gain by this insubordinate act, but it evidently was a deliberately planned provocation calculated to lead to some interference in Magellan's command.

The prestige of Magellan in the armada, already low because of the loss of two months' time in crossing the Atlantic, was shattered by the contemptuous gesture of Cartagena. Everyone gossiped about it and conjectured what Magellan would do. When three days had passed without the

San Antonio's making the customary daily salute and Magellan still had taken no action, all men wondered that he could be so supine.

Although Cartagena abstained from making his daily report, the other three captains continued to conform to regulations. On the third evening, Captain Luis de Mendoza, in his routine report, told the Captain General that the *contramaestre* of the Victoria had been apprehended in the act of sodomy with a *grumete,* or common seaman. Under Spanish naval regulations this was a capital crime. Hence Captain Mendoza asked the Captain General, to whom alone the King had delegated the legal power of the "knife and the cord," for instructions as to administering the penalty. The offense was a rather common forecastle abuse, and was often punished by flogging rather than hanging. However, the morale of the seamen had deteriorated to such a degree and their behavior had become so lax that Magellan felt it necessary to make an example of the offenders in order to restore discipline. He therefore ordered a full-dress trial of the culprits as soon as possible. The next morning the wind died down, and the Captain General at once summoned all four captains to the Trinidad to hold a court-martial. He anticipated that Cartagena would soon take his next step, and he was determined to forestall him. He sensed that this court-martial would be a crucial test of strength.

The ships lay becalmed in a cluster as each of the four captains, in full regalia, was rowed to the Trinidad. The two prisoners were brought before the court, the trial was held, and capital sentence was passed with due formality. In order to deter other transgressors by making the punishment impressive, it was voted to perform the executions on shore after reaching Brazil.

When the court-martial was over and both prisoners and guards had left the cabin, Magellan and John Serrano were left alone with the three Spaniards. There were five men around the table, and Magellan divined that Cartagena intended to carry out the plan of simulating a fracas which he had failed to put into execution at Tenerife.

Captain Cartagena proceeded at once to catechize the Captain General in an aggravating tone regarding the recent route down the West African coast and the becalming of the armada. He taunted Magellan, obviously trying to goad him into making the first move. Magellan, however, followed the same tactics he had used at Tenerife and remained silent, apparently cowed, weakly reiterating that his orders as Captain General were to be obeyed without question. Juan de Cartagena, carried away by his excitement and misled by Magellan's seeming meekness, lost his head and impulsively shouted that he, for one, was no longer going to obey his fool commands. This was an incontestable act of open mutiny, committed in the presence of all the captains of the royal armada. Magellan's counter trap was sprung immediately. He gave a quiet signal, and Espinosa, the *alguacil*, in armor and with a file of marines, swiftly moved into the cabin, their halberds pointed at Juan de Cartagena. Captain John Serrano drew his dagger, and Duarte Barbosa and Cristóbal Rabelo rushed into the cabin with drawn swords and stood beside the Captain General. Magellan, throwing off his simulated meekness, rose, seized Cartagena by the shirt front, and held him firmly in his chair, crying triumphantly, "Rebel, this is mutiny! In the name of ElRey you are my prisoner!"

The dumfounded nobleman, not daring to lay hand on his poniard, shouted to the other two captains to strike Magellan down, but they did not dare move. He began to revile them for not helping him and, to their dismay, his hasty words gave away the plot to stab Magellan. Magellan nodded to the *alguacil*, who quickly gave an order; the men-at-arms dragged the elegantly dressed hidalgo from the cabin. They hustled him, yelling and cursing, across the quarter-deck, down the ladder, and along the waist deck to the pair of stocks on the forecastle which were used in the punishment of common seamen, and there they clamped his fashionably booted legs. This exalted cavalier of the King's household, the scion (though illegitimate) of the most powerful family in Spain, was thus left to the derision of the gaping crew.

For Ferdinand Magellan's purpose the trick had been turned perfectly. Machiavelli himself could have spun no more subtle entanglement than the summons to a court-martial to get the plotters in his grasp. Juan de Cartagena, at a formal naval court of the King's captains, had announced his resolution to disobey the order of King Charles's own representative, whom he had solemnly sworn to obey. Then, before witnesses, he had called upon the other commanders to join in his mutiny and to attack the Captain General. A more certain way for Cartagena to commit self-destruction could not have been devised.

Yet Juan de Cartagena, even though fallen and in irons, was still the favorite of the powerful politician who would hold Magellan's fate in his hands. His offense might later be viewed at court as a merely technical act of mutiny, a few excited words uttered unmeaningly during a hot dispute. He had been appointed by King Charles himself as Inspector of the Fleet, and somewhat ambiguously by the *Casa de Antillas* as *conjunta persona*, or co-commander with Magellan. Although the Captain General quite properly could remove him from command of the San Antonio and hold him prisoner as a mutineer, nevertheless the situation needed to be handled with the greatest discretion.

When Captains Luis de Mendoza and Gaspar Quesada submissively petitioned Magellan that Juan de Cartagena should not be kept in the stocks like a common seaman, Magellan saw a politic escape from his dilemma. He decided to entrust the prisoner, on parole, to Captain Mendoza's keeping, exacting an oath from the latter that he would be faithful to his trust.

Thus Cartagena, who that morning had had his own captain's cabin with ten servitors to wait upon him, was now conducted as a prisoner to the boat of Captain Mendoza where he would be isolated from his personal adherents.

Later in the day, a blare of trumpets from the *capitana* heralded a formal order which was hallooed to each of the ships; the Spanish nobleman, Antonio de Coca, was named as captain of the San Antonio. This appointment was designed to mollify Bishop Fonseca for the degradation of Cartagena, for Antonio de Coca was apparently a natural son of the Bishop's brother, Antonio de Fonseca, Señor de Coca.

The armada continued on its route without further incident, and each evening the Spanish captains reported obediently to the Captain General. Magellan now called John Lopes Carvalho to the Trinidad to act as chief pilot for the armada because of the special knowledge of the coastal waters of Brazil which he had gained during his Portuguese service.

When Carvalho judged the coast of Brazil to be near, the Captain General proceeded with the greatest caution, for John of Lisbon had warned him that very dangerous shelves, or flat reefs, extended as much as seventy miles eastward from this coast into the Atlantic, and the early Portuguese navigators had lost many caravels in these waters. He had no means of calculating longitude, or east-west distances, but had to speculate as to his westward position on the chart by using dead reckoning based on the same rule-of-thumb he had used in sailing with the Portuguese; to gauge the speed he was making, he measured the time it took to sail past a piece of wood tossed into the water at the bow of the ship. He was only vaguely aware of the great mid-ocean currents, and this factor alone made his dead reckoning an undependable guess. However, since it seemed they must be nearing land, he had a constant lookout kept from mastheads of all the ships, made frequent soundings, and carefully examined the sand or soil brought up from the sea's bottom on the lead used for soundings; all these he compared with the records of previous soundings given him by John of Lisbon. When the flight of land birds, the scent of tropical forests on eastward breezes, and the presence of floating vegetation were detected, Magellan doubled the number on watch and ordered all sails furled at night. One morning at sunrise they saw a forested coast in the distance. Magellan at once ordered the course changed to south-by-southwest, so that the fleet would follow the shore, but well out to sea, with land barely visible.

Magellan reached the Brazilian coast just where he had pointed for it, at about 8° S. latitude. Had he veered only a couple of hundred miles farther north and made his landfall above 5° S. latitude, he could not have sailed south, for the contrary winds and currents at Cape Roque would have blocked such a course. In that case he would have had to put back almost all the way to Spain, like many another European mariner of that time, wasting two months or more before he could try again for the right spot on the southern coast of Brazil.

Don Antonio reports simply: "We sailed south-southwest with a wind which blows between the south and the west, until we reached a land called the Land of Verzin, which lies in 23½° of the Antarctic Pole."

Although Magellan hoped that his withdrawal into the doldrums off the African coast had baffled Dom Manuel's fleet, he could not be sure he had shaken them off. He was anxious, therefore, not to have his ships seen from the land, and he kept so far out to sea that only the lookouts at the mastheads could descry the faint outline of the shore. Because of the dangers of coastal navigation, he felt this course doubly desirable. He was now not only in hostile waters, but in a dangerous and unknown sector of the Atlantic. Gun crews, therefore, were prepared for action if need be, and the pilots were ever on the alert for hidden reefs.

The weather was good, and with a fair wind and helpful current the armada made substantial progress southward. Each day, as they left the equator behind them and came nearer the temperate zone, the temper of the crews improved; they looked forward eagerly to the sensuous delights of a land which John Lopes Carvalho had painted to them as a garden of Eden.

The orders from King Charles forbade landing anywhere in the zone assigned to Portugal, and therefore Magellan got no water or fresh fruits ashore, but sailed steadily southward, keeping the coast barely in sight. It had been over two months since the last fresh provisions were taken on at Tenerife, and now the only rations were salt pork, salt fish, and sea biscuit. Their nearness to a land with an abundance of fruit and green vegetables exasperated the sailors, and their discontent led to several requests from the officers that the Captain General send a landing party ashore for provisions. He, however, thought only of escaping as soon as possible from this Portuguese area where his mere presence would be construed as an aggression, and he therefore exhorted his officers to bear their discomforts for a short time longer, promising them early rest and refreshment in a comfortable harbor just a few days' sail ahead. He knew that there were no Portuguese settlements as far south as the 20° S. parallel of latitude, so he decided to put into an unoccupied harbor which John of Lisbon had recommended as a safe anchorage and which is now known as Rio de Janeiro Bay.

On December 13, 1519, the Trinidad led the way through the channel, past the grotesque island peak now called Sugar Loaf, and came to rest in the beautiful harbor beneath the shadow of the contorted elevation which we know as the Corcovado. It was the feast day of St. Lucy, and consequently Ferdinand Magellan gave to the scenic bay the name of Santa

Engraving from de Bry's "Peregrinationes," 1592

MAGELLAN'S ARRIVAL AT BAY SANTA LUCIA (MODERN RIO DE JANEIRO)

Engraving from de Bry's "Peregrinationes," 1624

MAGELLAN'S ARMADA IN THE ANTARCTIC

Lucia. No sooner had the fleet dropped anchor than the vessels were surrounded by native canoes, each carrying thirty or forty paddlers. The pilot, John Lopes Carvalho, greeted them in the Guarani tongue and assured them of the friendly intentions of the white men.

The dwellers at Rio de Janeiro at the time of Magellan's arrival were a nomadic tribe which had only recently taken possession of the area and had had no previous acquaintance with Europeans. A prolonged drought had been causing distress, and Magellan was fortunate that his arrival coincided with the beginning of an abundant rainfall, for they therefore looked upon the white men as their benefactors. They not only believed the Spaniards to be supernatural beings, but at first they endowed the *naos* with life and considered the ships' boats as their young. When the boats returned to the ships from the shore and moored alongside the *naos*, the imaginative natives thought the parent ships were giving suck to their offspring. Through the good offices of Carvalho, a trading arrangement was initiated with the Indians, who soon brought aboard an abundant supply of fruits and other provisions.

During the long voyage, Carvalho had entertained the sailors with descriptions of the charms of the Indian women who would be available to them in Brazil. Throughout the monotony of the calms off the African coast and during the long watches of the night at sea, the talk of the sailors was largely of the pleasures which awaited them with the Brazilian landfall. The seamen, after eleven weeks of continence at sea, became much excited when the completely naked Indian women came aboard the *naos* with their husbands, and they began to make advances to the women. Carvalho warned them to take no liberties with these married women and cautioned them that, although the Indians used their wives as beasts of burden and made them perform the menial tasks of the household, nevertheless they were very jealous and had poisoned arrows for their bows. The seamen quieted down when he promised to procure unmarried women for them. Then he spoke in the vernacular to the chiefs and arranged that a number of young virgins should at once be made available to the Spaniards.

This was effected in an orderly manner, for it was the tribal custom that the sons of a family had the privilege of bestowal of their own sisters. The young warriors were accustomed to trading them off in exchange for weapons or other desired possessions, and Carvalho arranged that the sailors should carry on such a trade with the young men. Don Antonio states that for a knife or a hatchet a sailor could purchase one and sometimes two Indian virgins, and in no time at all every mariner was in possesion of a delectable mate, if not of a harem.

The Indians had no metal tools or weapons, and once they learned that an almost priceless steel jackknife could be had in exchange for a young girl, the supply of women began to exceed the demand, avid though the sailors had been at the beginning. When the Indian maidens learned that their more venturesome sisters had not been abused, and when they saw them return from the ships bedecked with glass beads and copper bracelets, Don Antonio writes, they began to make advances on their own account. Soon bevies of girls came aboard daily to offer themselves in exchange for trinkets.

Magellan had tolerantly intended to give the exhausted, scurvy-ridden men a few days of shore leave in which to satisfy their appetites. He had then expected to get on with the serious business of the armada, the filling of the water casks, the loading of provisions, and the care ashore of the seriously ill. He did not want to stay long at Santa Lucia Bay, for he feared that the Portuguese armada might suddenly descend upon him; therefore he kept some of the *lombarderos* and marines constantly on duty on each ship. The men did not demur, for once they had acquired the Indian maidens by barter, they could carry on their amours on the vessels. One day Don Antonio was standing talking with Magellan on the quarter-deck, he tells us, when they observed a young native girl come aboard. She happened to stumble upon a large iron nail lying upon the deck, and immediately bent over and seized it. Then, looking about to see if she was observed, she quickly inserted it for concealment in what Don Antonio calls her private parts. To the amusement of Magellan and himself, the girl awkwardly took herself off, crouching and walking bent over, got into a canoe, and paddled ashore with her prize.

Magellan, however, became gravely concerned over the morale of his crews, for the shore leaves had degenerated into one long orgy. Even some of the officers abandoned their responsibilities for the voluptuous pleasures of the tropics. The person who, above all others, should have helped Magellan in his attempt to preserve order was Duarte Barbosa, but that hedonistic officer had been as swept away as the rest. He lost all sense of decorum, abandoned his post beside Magellan, and gave himself up to nightlong revelries in the native village along with his boon companions, John Lopes Carvalho and the dissolute lay priest, Padre Pedro Sanchez de Reina. Magellan rebuked him, and appealed to him to set an example to the others, but to his dismay Duarte then deserted the Trinidad altogether and stayed ashore without leave for three days and nights. Magellan sent him several messages imploring him to return to duty, and the scandal spread throughout the ships. At last the Captain General had to send the sergeant ashore with a squad of marines to arrest Duarte Barbosa. He became insubordinate, and Magellan had no choice but to put him in irons until he should recover his senses. Magellan had come to rely upon the fidelity of his *alguacil,* Gonzalo Gomes Espinosa, who already had begun to display those qualities of leadership which later distinguished him, and who exercised such control over his little group of marines that he managed to keep them on duty during this crisis of unbridled license. It was well that Ferdinand Magellan was able to maintain this effective corps, for Captain Antonio de Coca, yielding to family ties and ignoring his oath, suddenly released Juan de Cartagena from custody and, with the other malcontents, attempted to seize command of the armada. The Captain General used his marines to put down the mutiny and to seize Cartagena and Coca. Once more he was faced with the problem of incurring the enmity of Bishop Fonseca by punishing the two Fonseca heirs, and again he dared not stain his hands with Fonseca blood. He listened to pleas for clemency presented by Captains Mendoza and Quesada, and, deeming it politic to be merciful, he again entrusted Cartagena to Mendoza upon the latter's solemn oath to hold him fast. He forgave Antonio de Coca for putting kinship above duty and punished him only by demoting him from his captaincy. This left him in a quandary to replace Coca in command of the San Antonio. The person entitled by qualification and seniority to the post would have been Duarte Barbosa, then in chains for insubordination. There were few others to whom Ferdinand Magellan dared entrust the ship, the largest in the armada, and he finally named his cousin, Alvaro de Mesquita. Although qualified by rank and experience for the post, Mesquita lacked the quality of leadership. However, he was loyal to Magellan and would carry out his orders to the best of his ability; Magellan persuaded himself that this was enough, and thus made a most unfortunate appointment.

During his stay in Santa Lucia Bay, Ferdinand Magellan and Andres de San Martin, the fleet astronomer, made an effort to calculate the longitude of the spot. A conjunction of the Moon with the planet Jupiter occurred at this time, and the Captain General assembled all the pilots in council on the *nao* Victoria to study the phenomenon. Their findings and observations were later transmitted to Europe and did, in fact, make a contribution to the studies then in progress on the subject of longitude.

An Indian woman with whom John Lopes Carvalho had lived during his long sojourn with the Guarani tribes now arrived at the settlement, bringing with her their seven-year-old child. Carvalho immediately acknowledged the young half-breed as his son and enrolled him as a cabin boy on the Concepción. This greatly pleased the Indians, gave Carvalho influence with them, and contributed to the maintenance of peace between the armada and the natives. Because he was intruding in forbidden Portuguese territory, Ferdinand Magellan took great pains to treat the Guarani scrupulously, to pay fairly for all goods, and to make no slaves. As they were an amiable, well-meaning people, the relationship between the races remained cordial.

The fleet stayed in Santa Lucia Bay until fully reprovisioned and repaired, which took two weeks, and on Christmas Eve, 1519, the order was issued to sail with the tide on the morning following Christmas Day. On the afternoon of the last day, as in San Lucar before departure, the *alguacil* and his police were sent through the ships to see that all women were sent ashore. Many of the sailors had become attached to their gentle brides, and when the anchors were lifted and the ships sailed out of the harbor, the lamentations of the abandoned Indian women could be heard far across the waters. One permanent result of that fortnight's stay at Santa Lucia no doubt was the birth in due course of several hundred Ibero-Indian infants, whose descendants may still be living in the locality.

As he led the armada southward, the Captain General was a harassed commander. Beside his responsibility in conducting his squadron through uncharted coastal waters and his fear of an encounter with a Portuguese squadron, he now had to face the fact that the Spanish captains would not be conciliated. This, coupled with the realization of the undependability of Captain Duarte Barbosa and of the inadequacy of Captain Alvaro de Mesquita, made him feel very much alone. Magellan throughout his adventurous life had always shared his trials with a comrade, in accordance with the custom of the Portuguese pioneers in the Orient to select a blood-brother with whom one teamed through thick and thin.

Now, however, as Captain General, isolated from his subordinates, he was a lonely man. Of those with him in the armada, there was none whom he could call comrade. His asceticism recoiled from the sensuality of Duarte Barbosa. John Serrano was old and negative, Alvaro de Mesquita was a mediocrity and a sluggard. Gonzalo Gomes Espinosa was a bold man, much after his own heart, but illiterate and of low birth. His only intimates seem to have been his cherished page, Cristóbal Rabelo, his beloved slave, Enrique of Malacca, who was a Malay, and the Negro dwarf named George.

Congenial friends were scholarly Don Antonio and high-minded Padre Valderrama, with both of whom Magellan shared a fanatical religious zeal. He shared their faith in the intervention of the saints, which touched hagiolatry. He relied upon the aid of the militant Saint James of the Sword, whose knightly habit he wore, and most of all upon Our Lady of Victory, to whom he had dedicated his voyage and before whose shrine in Triana he had made his vows. For Ferdinand Magellan, in his introverted isolation, was developing a Messianic sense of election for his mission.

In his serene confidence in divine protection, although aware of the ill will of his chief lieutenants, Magellan calmly received their verbal reports each dusk and gave them his instructions. He meant to sail inshore and search every navigable estuary on the South Brazilian coast that might prove the opening to the *paso*. Doubt as to the outcome did not trouble him, for would not the Lord guide his way and in due time lead him to his destined goal?

CHAPTER XVI

URUGUAY AND THE ARGENTINE

THE spirit of the *Armada de Maluco* had been lifted by the fortnight ashore. The water casks were refilled and the lockers stocked with fresh meat and greenstuffs; the men were no longer ill-nourished and grumbling. The season was pleasant and the sea quiet. With the favorable southerly current and southeastern breeze, the sailors had but little work and could spend their time boasting of amorous exploits with the Brazilian maidens and predicting future conquests in the Isles of Spice.

Magellan himself, however, was not so free of care. Relieved as he was at the improved temper of the crews, and reassured concerning the condition of his ships after their overhauling while in harbor, he still had much to disturb him in his relations with his staff. Although he had put down the incipient mutiny of Antonio de Coca at Santa Lucia Bay, he had to reckon with its results. It had been demonstrated that all four Spanish captains, two deposed and two still in command, were incorrigibly hostile, and he recognized that, with the covert support of the Portuguese pilots Estevan Gomes and John Lopes Carvalho, their resources were greater than his own. In particular he was uneasy about Geronimo Guerra, the so-called nephew and probably the son of Cristóbal de Haro, who had been the accountant for de Haro's fiscal interests. Guerra, the assistant to Antonio de Coca on the San Antonio, would ordinarily have been promoted to the captaincy when Coca was relieved of his position. Magellan, however, dared not trust him in so important a post. We have seen how, for lack of a more suitable candidate, Magellan had selected his Portuguese cousin, Alvaro de Mesquita, as captain of the San Antonio.

The new captain met with resentment from Geronimo Guerra and from those crewmen who were former retainers from the Fonseca estates, who were, of course, partisans of their lords, Cartagena and Coca. Magellan was seriously worried, for if the pursuing Portuguese fleet should suddenly make an appearance, and if the Concepción under Quesada and the Victoria under Mendoza should side with them, perhaps Mesquita would not be able to hold the San Antonio, the key ship of the fleet, in support of the Trinidad and the Santiago. Magellan strengthened his faction aboard the San Antonio by assuring for Mesquita the backing of Juan de Lloriaga, Basque master of the San Antonio, and of the ship's chief *lombardero,* the Italian, Simon de Aggio, both of whom were at loggerheads with Geronimo Guerra, but he still had misgivings as he led the way southward.

The armada sailed from Santa Lucia Bay on St. John's day, December 27, 1519, and swung west-southwest into the Atlantic Ocean. They kept near the shore until they reached a large bay; because it was the Feast Day of Kings, Magellan named it the Bay of Kings, or Baia dos Reis, which name it still bears. He spent the entire day searching this gulf for a possible inlet to the *paso.* It is most puzzling that, at a point so far north as latitude S. 23°, Magellan should have shown uncertainty as to the location of the *paso.* He had already expressed the conviction that the *paso* was at about latitude 35° S., or seven hundred and fifty miles farther down the coast. Both John of Lisbon and John Dias de Solis had previously explored the Brazilian coast along which he now was probing, and he had their complete navigating records for his guidance. After emerging from the Baia dos Reis, Magellan anchored each night and continued searching by day along the indented coast, with its many inlets, at an average rate of four knots. He does not seem to have stopped at the inviting harbor which is now the port of Santos, probably because John of Lisbon had found only a river there. On January 11, 1520, three hills appeared on the low coast which seemed at first to be three islands in the sea. This was the landmark for which he had been looking, and the pilot Carvalho immediately hailed it as marking Cape Santa Maria, as he had learned when he sailed with John of Lisbon six years earlier. Soon he pointed out the great cape projecting southward; the armada passed beyond it, and then the Captain General changed course in order to find a bay behind the cape which Carvalho recommended as an anchorage. The armada was now at 35° S. latitude, and near here the pilots expected to find the entrance to the *paso.* They shared the belief of the leading geographers of Europe that the coast of South America continued southerly in an unbroken line along the Atlantic from Cape Santa Maria at 35° S. latitude to about 75° S. latitude, at which point in the Antarctic this land-mass was believed to turn eastward so as to form a southern shore of the Atlantic and Indian Oceans, which it thus enclosed in a landlocked basin. This far-flung Antarctic land-rim had never been actually discovered, but was believed to constitute the legendary continent called Terra Australis.

Magellan appears to have accepted this orthodox belief, except that he thought a narrow strait separated the southern tip of Brazil at 35° S. (ending with Cape Santa Maria) from the extreme northern prolongation of the Antarctic continent of Terra Australis. He thought Cape Santa Maria to be the western counterpart of the Cape of Good Hope. It lay in the same latitude, and it was the terminus of the vast rounded hump we now call Uruguay, which resembles the southern tip of Africa. This plausible theory had been the belief of John de Solis and John of Lisbon, and was generally adopted in Spain, although Cristóbal de Haro himself seems to have subscribed to it with some reservations. Although Magellan appears to have felt convinced at this time that the entrance to a passage westward to the Great South Sea began at Cape Santa Maria, nevertheless he previously had considered an alternative theory, the possibility that the *paso* might be found at 50° S. latitude. However, now he was at Cape Santa Maria, and he wished very much to find the *paso* there.

A strong conviction now swept the entire armada and likewise took possession of Ferdinand Magellan's mind. Not only he, but all his navigators as well, acclaimed Cape Santa Maria as the goal toward which they had struggled. After he had scanned the wide westward and southward-reaching passage ahead of him (which we now know as the estuary of the Rio de la Plata), Magellan made no effort to dissemble his triumphant conviction that the first great objective had been attained. He was expansively communicative, asserting to the pilots that he had had certain foreknowledge that they would round the continent at just about this point, pricked off on the globe at 35° S. latitude. They would follow the strait westward and emerge into the Great South Sea, and then only a few weeks ahead lay Maluco and its spices, and rich new islands to be discovered for the Emperor. The buoyancy of the Captain General spread down through all ranks. All doubts vanished. The African doldrums, the storms of the Guinea Coast, the grumbling at the short rations, and the criticism of Magellan's competence as a navigator, all were forgotten. Don Antonio, who had never wavered in his faith in the commander's genius, marvelled at the certitude of his guidance.

The fleet kept to its sheltered anchorage while the Santiago, being of light draft, was sent forward on the exploratory errand. Ferdinand Magellan warned Captain John Serrano against the hostile natives, ordering him on no account to land, but to follow the passage westward for as much as fifty leagues, taking soundings and making observations, and then if he had not encountered the western outlet, to return and report without going farther toward the Great South Sea.

While Serrano went westward to explore the strait, Magellan decided also to search for the north shore of Terra Australis which he supposed lay somewhere to the south, although he could not see it across the wide mouth of the estuary. He resolved to conduct this exploration personally, probably with the ambition of being the first European to set foot on the unknown southern continent sketched by cartographers for a thousand years without having been seen by any Christian. He felt it would be unwise to sail there in the Trinidad and leave Captain Mesquita exposed to attack by Geronimo Guerra, aided by Captains Mendoza and Quesada. Once his back was turned and the guns of the Trinidad withdrawn, he feared what could happen. So he left the Trinidad behind, no doubt with instructions to Duarte Barbosa and Gonzalo Gomes Espinosa to watch the two disaffected captains. He personally took command of the San Antonio and sailed southward for Terra Australis. After crossing the broad estuary and finding the supposed north shore of Terra Australis, he followed it westward for several days, probably to where the Argentine city of La Plata now stands, and perhaps as far as the site of modern Buenos Aires. Then, perceiving that the strait narrowed and turned northwestward, as he expected, he sailed back to join the armada. He sighted an elevation on the shore ahead (now Uruguay) and called out "I see a mountain!" Thus it was dubbed *Montevideo*.

When the San Antonio rejoined the fleet, Magellan was startled to see the Santiago already had returned. Captain Serrano hurried aboard with somber face and dejected mien. He reported that he had followed the presumed strait westward until the channel had decreased to a depth of only three fathoms, when the pilots protested at the risk of running aground. He had water drawn up over the sides and it proved to be not salty, hardly even brackish. He noted that the flood tide had become feeble, while the ebb had remained vigorous, indicating the presence of an eastward current. The loudly hailed *paso* evidently was only a river. The infallible evidence from Dom Manuel's chart room must have been a hoax.

This was a stunning shock to Magellan, and for a short time he did not even try to conceal his despair. He managed to recover his self-control, but found the strain too great and abruptly withdrew into isolation in his cabin, leaving his officers to gossip about his reaction to this setback. Yet the next morning he surprised everyone by his serenity. He treated the survey of the river as having been incidental, and calmly ordered that the preliminary reconnaissance should now be followed by a systematic exploration by the five batels, or longboats, of the fleet. For three long weeks Magellan stubbornly stayed at Cape Santa Maria and kept all the ships' boats at a methodical search of every foot of both banks of the estuary, up to the point where it became a fresh-water river. Obviously he still hoped to find the entrance to the *paso* in some sector of the gulf, but after both banks of the river had been scoured without finding an outlet, and after the longboats had rowed up far beyond the tidal limits to where the water was sweet and fresh, Magellan reluctantly admitted defeat. He named the river Rio de Solis, in honor of his unfortunate predecessor who four years before had been killed there by the natives. Then he announced that the armada would sail forth and continue its southerly search down the coast. The Fonseca faction immediately opposed this program and provoked resistance from the sailors against it. The air had already begun to feel sharp to the Mediterranean sailors, and since they were in the same latitude as the Cape of Good Hope, many knew from experience what discomforts they could expect in navigating the frigid Antarctic seas in February and March. The men therefore clamored to return to Santa Lucia Bay, where the winter could be passed in comfort and safety.

On February 2, 1520, Magellan faced one of the crises of his career. The dissident captains had persuaded the entire personnel of the armada to meet in open convention to vote whether to go forward as ordered or return to Santa Lucia Bay for the winter. It was not a mutiny, but a democratic procedure which Spanish crews had a traditional right to invoke. Magellan now could not enforce his command, but it was still his privilege to convince and persuade. He faced a gathering in which the majority were in favor of hibernating in pleasant Santa Lucia Bay. Magellan opened his address by emphasizing that their Sovereign Lord, the King, had explicitly commanded the armada not to intrude upon the domain of the Portuguese monarch. He pointed out that for the armada to occupy Santa Lucia Bay for months would undoubtedly be construed by the Portuguese as a hostile act, and that they would undoubtedly attack.

He artfully won them to his proposal to continue to sail southward. Instead of rebuking the defiant seamen for yearning for languorous Santa Lucia Bay, he conceded that the toil of sustained navigation in the Antarctic winter was unthinkable. What he offered was the prospect of sailing westward through the *paso* into the Great South Sea and steering for the balmy clime of the Spice Islands. He assured them that the *paso* lay near. True, there had been a miscalculation as to its being exactly at the latitude of the Rio de Solis, but it assuredly lay just a few leagues ahead. The ocean was not yet wintry, and, if they took advantage of the opportunity, wealth and enjoyment were close. His cajolery was successful, and his proposal was accepted by the mariners. At dawn on February 3rd, the Trinidad led the armada out into the Atlantic on a southerly course.

The extant logs of the pilots permit us to follow the slow progress of the armada as it traveled southward, keeping close inshore and tracing every indentation in hope of finding the opening to the *paso*. The ships anchored at dusk and hoisted sail at dawn, and some days they were farther back at sundown than they had been at sunrise. Several times the whole armada was in peril from furious, sudden squalls. Twice the Trinidad, leading the others, barely escaped being wrecked, and once the Victoria ran upon a sandbank, but at high tide scraped off unhurt. In one storm the fleet was driven out to sea and dispersed, so that each vessel was alone in the tempest, without knowledge of the fate of the others. Once, when a detail was sent ashore to fill casks of drinking water, an offshore gale suddenly came up, blowing the ships out to sea and causing the abandonment of the landing party for several days. Another time a boat's crew landed upon an islet to kill seals and penguins for fresh meat, a storm made it impossible for them to get back to the fleet, and they had to bury themselves under the pile of carcasses to keep from freezing to death. One storm bottled up the whole flotilla in a little gulf for six days, during all of which time they could not anchor, but darted back and forth like frightened swallows trapped in a room. The entries of the pilots are eloquent in their terseness. Thus, "Feb. 24–25, 1520, Latitude 42°54′ South, entered Gulf which we named St. Matthias because it was his day. We searched for an outlet to Maluco, and there being no anchorage, sailed out again."

There could have been no more difficult undertaking than that now imposed upon Magellan. Under the regulations, his ship had to be in the van, and he was under the constant strain of piloting the course over an uncharted sea, around headlands, into bays, past sandbanks and hidden reefs. The four heavily laden *naos,* burdened with weighty armaments, wallowed and lurched in the wake of the *capitana,* but the responsibility was his alone. The clumsy, square-sailed, round-bottomed craft, with their high, castellated prows and poops, often were helpless against headwinds. In beating their way south they sometimes made only a few miles a day, and at times progressed backward. Even the captains of modern ships shrink from attempting the Cape Horn route against the winter storms, and of course they have full sea-room, while Magellan was obliged to take the much more difficult course of skirting the coast.

For sixty days Ferdinand Magellan neither had any real repose nor wore a dry garment. The shrieking Antarctic gales tore at the Trinidad continually as it worked along the unknown coast under storm canvas, the rigging covered with ice and the waist deck a sluice of great, green seas. The screaming winds bore hail and sleet, and the spray splashed into every corner of the ship. No fires could be lighted, and of course no warm food was served; a piece of uncooked dried fish or raw salt pork, a soggy biscuit, and an onion or a handful of raisins could be snatched only at long intervals in the labor. At night no lights could be used except the tiny binnacle lamp. Each man's water-soaked clothes were so frozen that they crackled whenever he made an unusual movement, the constant salt water in the men's garments caused sores on their chafed skin, and their feet were raw in their waterlogged shoes. Palms and fingers were cracked from clutching at frozen canvas and pulling on icy ropes, and almost everyone lost one or more fingernails. Their beards had icicles, and the tips of their noses, ears, and toes were frostbitten.

The perpetual screech of the wind and the rushing sound of the waves made speech difficult, and when it was necessary for Magellan to shout orders the tempest seemed to mock him as it swept the sound away. Don Antonio says that during all that aching period, Magellan took care to share the men's privations and to appear in good humor. When the shuddering Trinidad was thrown almost upon her beam-ends, and the mounting graybacks came tumbling over the side, he would sing a snatch of song, inaudible in the uproar, but nevertheless heartening in its pantomime. His conduct under stress won him the trust of his suffering shipmates.

All through February and half of March, Magellan had kept peering ashore through the spray for the opening to the *paso*, while the winter deepened and the cold increased. At last he realized that the limit of his men's endurance had been reached. He decided to seek a sheltered harbor and await the arrival of spring before continuing the quest for the *paso*. After that decision, for two more weeks the armada sought a place of refuge. The various bays that they inspected, one after another, all lacked something essential, such as shelter from gales or a good holding bottom for the anchors, or had excessive tides.

It seemed impossible for the buffeted ships to creep farther into the frigid seas. All the officers now urged him to turn back, but Magellan doggedly continued on his course. On Saturday, March 31, 1520, the lookout at the masthead reported a break in the coast. Magellan pointed the Trinidad for it and, proceeding cautiously and taking soundings constantly, they passed over a foaming bar through a narrow channel into a landlocked bay. There they found good holding bottom, and the landing parties reported good drinking water, favorable beaches for careening, and ample firewood. There were numerous edible shellfish, the shores were alive with waterfowl, and the bay evidently abounded in fish. Sheltered from storms, it constituted an ideal harbor. The only drawback was the tumultuous current caused by the thirty-seven foot tide which rushed through the narrow ocean entrance. This necessitated the use of several anchors for each ship and impeded ship-to-shore navigation.

The Captain General announced that this was to be their base for the balance of the winter and named it Port Saint Julian. Here at least no Portuguese ships would attack them, for it was at latitude 50° S., over a thousand miles south of Rio de Solis. In sixty days the armada had made about a thousand miles of tortured progress.

During all this time of travail, Magellan had been well aware that, trailing unhappily behind the Trinidad in their plunging craft, the Spanish captains had been daily cursing his leadership and aching to be rid of him. He recognized that, now they could again unite, the time might soon come for the long-deferred encounter. The anchors had barely splashed in the bay, he noted, before skiffs began to row back and forth between the Victoria and the Concepción. The conspirators did not have to wait long for an opportunity to foment a mutiny. On Palm Sunday, the day after their arrival, the Captain General issued an order that, because the armada would have to spend some months in winter quarters, it would be necessary to cut in half the daily ration of wine and ship's biscuit. The sailors reacted immediately, holding indignation meetings on each ship and asserting their right to petition the Captain General to restore the cuts; they elected delegates from each of the five crews to protest to him. The Fonseca faction took advantage of the excitement and worked the crews into a frenzy by suggesting that Magellan was in the pay of the Portuguese King and had plotted to destroy the fleet by bringing it into the frigid zone from which none would return. When Magellan learned of this, he invited the delegates from the crews to come aboard the *capitana.* He was fortunate that the caliber of the delegates was well above that of the average Mediterranean crew. Apart from many young men of good family, the armada had several warrant officers and able seamen whose unusual merit was later to be proved, and most of the men before the mast were adventurous spirits, of a higher type than usual. Magellan therefore felt able to answer their complaints on a reasonable plane. He himself had spent years in a subordinate capacity in the maritime service, and no man knew better how to gauge the temper of the disgruntled seamen who now aired their grievances. In his reply, he admitted their right to petition him and praised the fortitude which they had displayed in the past trying months. He mentioned the stoicism that had been shown by the Portuguese sailors under Vasco da Gama, who also combatted Antarctic seas, and he compared their heroism with the mutinous attitude of the Spanish crew of Columbus. He appealed to their Castilian pride to show the Portuguese King their mettle, and he dangled before them the hope of passage to Maluco as soon as spring came. As to the rations, he said that his only object was to conserve wine and biscuit which they would need later at sea. Now, at Port Saint Julian, they would have plenty of sweet water, seafowl, and fish. He would build barracks ashore to keep them snug, and there would be winter garments of downy bird and seal skins. Work would be restricted to careening the hulls and replacing the rigging, and there would be leisure for fishing and hunting. He ended with a stern reminder of duty, telling them he had given his oath to King Charles not to turn back until Maluco was reached; and he appealed to their loyalty to support him. The speech was well received. The men pressed close to assure him of their obedience, and the delegates returned to their ships to dispel the discontent.

Having quieted the men, it was necessary to face the officers, and he called a meeting on the Trinidad of Captains Serrano, Mesquita, Mendoza and Quesada, together with the five pilots. Since Antonio de Coca and Juan de Cartagena had been deposed from their captaincies, they did not attend the council, but their unofficial spokesman was Geronimo Guerra who, because of his prestige as a navigator and his link with de Haro, was also invited to the conference. Captain Mendoza began by criticizing Magellan for bringing the armada into the frigid zone in the stormy season and for his selection of such barren winter quarters. He was supported in this by Captain Gaspar Quesada, and less aggressively by the pilots Estevan Gomes and Carvalho. The others present appeared tacitly in agreement.

This was the fourth formal council of his officers which Ferdinand Magellan had held, and in all of them he had been on the defensive. In the three previous meetings, at Tenerife, off Sierra Leone, and at Rio de Solis, the attacks against him had been motivated by the Fonseca faction for political ends. He had always been able to count on support from those outside the Spanish captains' cabal, but now he found himself almost alone in arguing that they should keep their foothold here on the rim of the polar region and push farther southward as soon as the weather might permit. While the opposition of the Fonseca group was as vicious as ever, now they spoke for all the pilots. The navigators were frightened in this unknown polar region. The clumsy rig of their sails and the high prows and poops of their craft had made it difficult to cope with the shifting, sudden storms that tore at them ferociously from every point of the compass. The towering waves, the menacing icebergs, the floating ice fields, and the blinding fogs had terrified the pilots. They were exhausted, after the vigils of sixty days and nights, and were distrustful of Magellan's promise to wait out the winter at their new haven. They felt certain that their commander would drive them southward again too soon, in his eagerness to find the *paso*. As we know, their misgivings were true, he did not really want to hibernate for months of frozen inaction. He would rather continue to combat the rigors of the Antarctic Sea. Although none could know it, the strait was in fact within their very reach, only a few days' sail away.

The chronicle gives Magellan's spirited reply to their expressions of fear. The Scandinavians, he said, habitually navigated during similar arctic conditions; in the winter they sailed to Iceland, penetrating fogs and ice fields as far north as 65° N. latitude. Mendoza's answer was that the Norwegians were used to such conditions and well prepared for them, and their voyages were but a few hundred miles from their home bases. During the hot argument that followed, the Captain General was on the defensive.

Finally, Luis de Mendoza put the motion that the fleet avail itself of the prevailing northerly gales and return at once, not to Santa Lucia Bay, as previously proposed, but only to Rio de la Plata. The resolution was carried almost unanimously, probably opposed only by Magellan's cousins Serrano and Mesquita. The Captain General now had his back to the wall. He refused to accept the decision of the council, which he classified as merely advisory in its scope, and asserted his own supreme authority. He declared flatly that he would pass the winter where they were, at 50° S. latitude, and that in the spring he would lead the fleet southward even to 75° S. if need be. The meeting broke up in sullen disorder, the two Spanish captains in particular in an ugly mood. Next day the captains' yawls of the Concepción and the Victoria were seen visiting back and forth, and on Holy Saturday word was conveyed to Magellan that the Fonseca faction was conspiring to take action. He issued an order that all the crews were to attend divine services on Easter morning on a little islet where he had had a sheltered altar erected, and he sent a conciliatory message to all four captains inviting them to breakfast with him aboard the *capitana* after Mass. However, before leaving the Trinidad to attend Mass he announced to his own crew the rumor that an attack would be made upon him, and he ordered his men to go armed to the service.

The Mass passed off without incident, and of the captains only Luis de Mendoza was present. Magellan repeated his invitation to breakfast, but Mendoza courteously declined, alleging duties aboard ship. Captain Alvaro de Mesquita was the only guest at a gloomy meal, and Magellan ordered him to set a strong watch and to be on his guard against an outbreak on the San Antonio. Easter Sunday thus passed uneventfully, and the night was undisturbed.

The next morning the Trinidad's longboat was sent off with a shore party to cut wood. It was routine procedure for the batel to stop at each ship to pick up a detail of woodcutters from its crew. The first vessel to be approached was the San Antonio. Observers on the *capitana* immediately called the Captain General to the deck, for the longboat was seen to be held off at the San Antonio and then to sheer away and row hurriedly back toward the Trinidad. The *contramaestre* breathlessly reported that his boat-hook had been fended off the San Antonio by a halberd, and that, when he had protested and cited his orders, he had been told gruffly, "We are for Captain Gaspar Quesada, and obey only his orders." He said the gun ports of the San Antonio were open and the cannon ready for action, and that he had seen Captain Gaspar Quesada of the Concepción in armor on the quarter-deck of the San Antonio.

Magellan was amazed, for he had urged Captain Mesquita strongly to maintain vigilance during the past night. However, he could not stop to think of that, but at once armed the batel's crew and sent it on a round of visits to the other ships to find out how they stood. The Concepción and the Victoria harshly warned the boat away, and only the Santiago, under John Serrano, remained loyal. Magellan thereupon ordered the weapons locker of his own ship and Serrano's opened, had the men-at-arms put on their corselets, and the guns loaded. He then awaited the next move of the rebels.

In the early forenoon, the yawl of the San Antonio came alongside with a communication for Magellan. The boat's crew declined to answer the questions put them by the Captain General, replying tersely that they had been ordered not to talk. They refused to come aboard and kept out of reach while awaiting a response. The note was signed not only by the two Spanish captains, but also by Juan de Cartagena and Antonio de Coca, the commanders he had demoted but who still held royal commissions. It had obviously been composed for later evidence in the official record; in it Magellan was upbraided for not having consulted the captains as to courses and policy and rebuked for having disobeyed royal instructions and failing to carry out orders of the *Casa de Antillas.* The captains invited him to come at once aboard the San Antonio and confer with them, promising him safe conduct; they frankly proposed to treat him no longer as Captain General, nor as their superior, but as one of themselves, commanding a single ship. The signers promised to recognize him as the senior captain, and to follow his counsel, but not his commands. The whole concluded in a conciliatory tone in urging him to come to meet with them. Magellan answered in a stern note, sharply ordering Captains Mendoza and Quesada to report to him at once on the Trinidad, and ignoring the other two signers. No acknowledgment of this communication was made, and again Magellan waited.

About noontime, the longboat of the San Antonio, crowded with men, was seen to push off and row toward the Concepción. It was caught by the outrushing tide, which was unusually strong, and was swept toward the sea in spite of the efforts of the oarsmen, in danger of being borne through the swift raceway at the narrow mouth of the bay and of being plunged into the surf at the bar. The swirling current brought it near the Trinidad and the frightened men called for help. A rope was thrown them and the batel was with difficulty hauled alongside. There was only a petty officer in charge, and Magellan received him graciously, gave each man a good drink of wine, and made much of them. They were harmless seamen being shifted to the Concepción to replace active mutineers from that ship who were transferred to the San Antonio in preparation for battle. They were willing to talk freely, and Magellan then learned that the fatuous Mesquita had evidently considered his chief as overly apprehensive, had neglected his explicit warnings, had posted no guards on the San Antonio, and had turned in for the night without taking precautions to protect the key ship entrusted to him. During the first watch, Quesada, Cartagena, Coca, and Juan Sebastian del Cano, Master of the Concepción, silently came aboard with thirty armed men and were met by Geronimo Guerra with a group of his fellows among the San Antonio's crew. They fettered Mesquita, locked him in Guerra's cabin, and took possession. The Master, Juan de Lloriaga, denounced the intrusion, commanded them in the name of the King to leave the ship, and ordered his boatswain to arm the crew and hold the forecastle. Quesada cried out, "Shall we let this fool wreck our plans?" He thereupon stabbed the unarmed Basque six times and left him unconscious on the deck. Geronimo Guerra then had the *contramaestre*, the pilot, and half a dozen seamen who were loyal to Magellan locked up. The reluctant *lombarderos* were forced to man the ship's cannon, and all the weapons aboard were collected and locked in the cabin where Captain Mesquita lay bound. Quesada then took command of the San Antonio, and Juan de Cartagena assumed the captaincy of the Concepción.

Magellan elicited enough information from these seamen, thrown by chance into his hands, to guide him in his own strategy. Juan Sebastian del Cano evidently had transferred to the San Antonio to supplant Simon de Aggio, in charge of the batteries, and the men-at-arms from the other ships had been concentrated on the San Antonio under Captain Quesada. It was apparent that the court favorites, the bastards Cartagena, Coca, and Guerra, were making way for veteran men of combat, with Mendoza as directing head. Magellan deduced that the mutineers would not want to destroy the Santiago, which would be invaluable to them in later exploratory work because of its shallow draft, and that therefore Serrano's ship would not be attacked. The enemy would concentrate upon the *capitana.*

The best time for the assault would be in the evening at the slack tide, when the land breeze would be favorable to maneuvering in the bay. He expected that the Victoria and the Concepción would sail up to the Trinidad, use their batteries at short range to destroy its masts and rigging, and wreck its rudder. The San Antonio could several times rake the motionless flagship fore and aft, then grapple, and boarding parties would attack both stern castle and forecastle.

In analyzing the enemy's probable scheme of battle, Magellan recognized that the main objective would be to kill him, which Mendoza would attempt to do with as little damage to the armada as possible. Mendoza would realize that he was personally risking condemnation if, by his tactics, the armada suffered a heavy loss of ships and cargo. He must know that Bishop Fonseca would consider a knife thrust or a few drops of poison a better means of eliminating Magellan than a fleet action. Magellan, therefore, knowing Mendoza's temperament, surmised he would be anxious to avoid battle. He might be susceptible to a hint for a parley, and be accessible to a confidential proposal from him. It was upon this shrewd premise that Magellan based his first thrust.

He took from the men of the San Antonio such clothing as was distinctive, and had fifteen marines from his own ship assume their apparel. These marines noisily embarked in the San Antonio's longboat when the tide had abated, pretending to be the same sailors who had disembarked there earlier.

Magellan then sent the yawl of the Trinidad, bearing *Alguacil* Espinosa and four rowers, all unarmed, to the nearby Victoria with a letter to Captain Luis de Mendoza. The boat was halted by a challenge, but when Espinosa answered he had a confidential letter he was allowed on deck. The *alguacil* whispered to Mendoza that his message was secret, for his ear alone. The Captain, armored but unhelmeted, rashly took him to his own cabin, closed the door, and was so negligent as to let one of Espinosa's men accompany him. The note from Magellan was a ruse, for it merely ordered Mendoza to return to his duty. He read it, laughed scornfully, and crumpled it in his hand to throw it away. Espinosa, bowing ceremoniously, held out his hand as though to receive the rejected letter, but in a flashing movement, he grasped the beard of Mendoza, jerked back his head, and thrust his poniard through his unprotected throat, while Magellan's other man slashed him from behind on his unarmored legs. Mendoza expired without a cry, and Espinosa gave the prearranged signal, the waving of a cloth from the cabin window. The longboat of the San Antonio, with its disguised crew, was rowing very slowly past the Victoria; it now dashed alongside. The marines, led by Duarte Barbosa, swarmed over the bulwark before the crew even knew that Captain Mendoza was dead. Barbosa immediately disarmed them and put them to work at the capstan to raise the anchors. Then he had them put out the sweeps, raise the foresail, and move the Victoria toward the *capitana.*

When Gaspar Quesada, on the San Antonio, saw to his surprise that the Victoria was in motion, he hailed it and asked for Captain de Mendoza. A member of the crew whom Quesada knew replied, under duress, that the Captain was in his cabin writing a note to the Captain General. That seemed to satisfy Quesada for the moment, and before he could gather his wits to take any action, the vessel had passed out of the San Antonio's line of fire and had dropped anchor alongside the *capitana.* In a short time the Santiago likewise moved up and joined the Trinidad. Now the tables were turned, and the Captain General had three ships blocking the exit to the sea of the two rebels, who were thereby trapped.

When Quesada realized that he had been outwitted, he lost his courage and went to his prisoner, Captain Mesquita, abjectly begging him to intercede for him with the Captain General. Mesquita refused, saying it would be useless even to try to mollify Magellan. Then Quesada called the mutineers into council. He did not attempt to arouse them to join the Concepción and attack the *capitana,* but asked, "How can we escape the vengeance of Magellan?" The San Antonio and the Concepción should have been nearly a match for the three others, and one wonders that the rebels should not have hazarded everything in an attack. Yet all that the strong crew of the San Antonio could offer Quesada in this emergency was the advice to try to slip past Magellan in the night and escape to the open sea. However, they did promise to stand by him if he should have to fight his way out. He therefore decided to abandon his confederate, Cartagena, on the Concepción, and to make an attempt at flight. He ordered two of the anchor cables cut so that he could slip the remaining one noiselessly in the dark, for it would be necessary to desert the Concepción without any warning. All this is explicitly set down in the testimony of the pilot of the San Antonio.

Quesada went into his cabin to put on his armor, and the pilot says that then one of the men loyal to Magellan secretly cut the remaining cable. The San Antonio began to drift unnoticed toward the *capitana.* When Magellan saw the ship approaching he called his crew to quarters, and, just as Quesada came back on deck in full armor, the Trinidad loosed a broadside at point-blank range. The mutineers took cover below deck, and the men in the fighting tops of the Trinidad struck Quesada with several lances and some arrows which glanced off his armor. He stood alone on the quarter-deck, his shield protectively uplifted, trying to rally his crew, in a state of panicky confusion. The decisive Magellan leapt into his longboat and, with a boarding party, attained the waist-deck of the San Antonio without any resistance. He then walked up to Quesada on the quarter-deck and ordered him to surrender, which he did. The powerful ship with its reinforced crew was thus personally captured by Magellan without the loss of a man. Magellan did not delay a moment, but at once sent Espinosa with his marines to the Concepción. The *alguacil* rowed right under the menacing guns and hailed the ship, asking for whom it stood. Cartagena, attired in a magnificent suit of armor, replied abjectly from the quarter-deck, "We stand for King Charles and for Don Ferdinand Magellan as his Captain General." Espinosa boarded the Concepción and seized the fallen leader, and the mutiny was over.

The record of the mutiny gives us much insight into Magellan's remarkable character. The seeming ease with which he quelled the mutiny at Port Saint Julian obscures the mastery of his tactics. The initiative had been with the Fonseca faction. Their capture of the San Antonio, the largest ship in the fleet, was a telling stroke and made their ratio in fighting potential about two to one. Their plan to wait until slack tide and then converge with their three ships upon the *capitana* was a sound one, particularly as we now know that Estevan Gomes, the pilot of Magellan's ship, was their confederate. The truth is that Magellan out-thought them at every point. He not only could call the plays before they made them, he had the unhesitating decision to take action to prevent them and to turn the tables upon his enemies.

The only other casualty of the outbreak, beside Captain Mendoza, was Juan de Lloriaga, the loyal first officer of the San Antonio. Captain Quesada had stabbed him, and he languished from his wounds. The Captain General visited his sickbed daily and showed him every attention, but the faithful Basque died after two months of suffering. The loss of his influence with the crew of the San Antonio was sadly felt.

Magellan rewarded Gomes Gonzalo de Espinosa, the *Alguacil,* with a gift of money, well knowing his intrepidity was priceless, and put him in command of a reorganized, hand-picked guard of men-at-arms. The men of the guard were kept under discipline, relieved of all routine work aboard ship, and issued extra rations to conserve their strength and vigor. These favors aroused the hostility of the seamen and made them a group apart, but their isolation from their fellows intensified their dependability.

Although the rebels had been taken in avowed mutiny, Magellan circumspectly gave them a conventional court-martial, with the neutral pilots as judges; he carefully observed every naval formality in their trial, keeping a notarized written record of all testimony and evidence. At the court-martial, according to custom, the dead body of Captain Luis de Mendoza, still in its bloodstained armor, was propped up at the bar beside his living accomplices, and his name was included in all the charges against the defendants.

The Court found Cartagena, Quesada, Mendoza, Antonio de Coca, and Juan Sebastian del Cano guilty of treason, and also singled out Luis de Molina, confidential secretary to Quesada, who had been active in organizing the rebellion. Forty members of the crew were adjudged mutineers, as a result of the sworn testimony presented by witnesses. In accordance with custom, the body of the dead Mendoza was hanged, drawn, and quartered, just as though he were alive to be punished, and his remains were hung on four gibbets about the bay. Captain Gaspar Quesada was condemned to decapitation instead of hanging, but no member of the crews would agree to act as executioner. Luis de Molina was offered a pardon for consenting to sever the head of his master, and Quesada himself persuaded his vassal to accept the abhorrent commission. Molina steeled himself to do the deed, and his lord's members were suspended from the gibbets with those of Mendoza.

Although the two unfortunate captains, tools of the Bishop, received capital punishment, Magellan thought it impolitic to execute Cartagena and Coca, the heirs of the Fonsecas. He spared Geronimo Guerra because he feared to incur the enmity of Cristóbal de Haro. All the other conspirators were condemned to die, but Magellan's officers pleaded for them, not only in pity, but because the armada could not afford the loss of forty crewmen. He therefore commuted the death sentence to hard labor. For the ensuing three months, the wretched mutineers, including Antonio de Coca and Juan Sebastian del Cano, were forced to work in chains in the cruel weather, sometimes up to their waists in water, repairing the hulls, working at the pumps, and cutting wood. The fact that they were penalized by being kept on short rations made them feeble and less able to perform the heavy tasks at which they were set. Many of the mutineers were simple sailors who had followed the orders of their aristocratic captains and had been swept along by their leaders. The suffering of these unfortunates aroused the compassion of their shipmates who had been loyal to the Captain General, and alienated the attachment of some of his followers. The inclusion of del Cano among the castigated rebels, while Cartagena was exempted, particularly aroused the indignation of the group of Basques among the seamen, for del Cano belonged to the petty nobility of Vizcaya and was looked up to by his compatriots. Instead of putting the *alguacil,* Espinosa, in charge of the chain gang, the Captain General delegated this duty to his cousin Mesquita, who had been the victim of the mutineers. He proved an unfeeling taskmaster, and his obduracy toward the prisoners aroused their abiding resentment.

The members of the crew who had not been condemned for treason were spared the drudgery imposed upon the prisoners and were granted such privileges and comforts as the dismal port afforded. Not until the fleet was ready to sail were the mutineers finally pardoned and reinstated in their posts. Although Juan de Cartagena was spared hard labor and merely confined to his cabin, the Captain General's politic leniency toward him proved misplaced. He plotted with Padre Pedro Sanchez de Reina to attempt to stir up the exasperated prisoners to another mutiny, but his fumbling attempt was put down. Magellan convened a second court-martial, which condemned him and the priest to be marooned on the bleak shores of Patagonia. The clergyman deserved death, for he had been a troublemaker from the start, but Magellan wanted no later conflict with the church authorities. Marooning was then a common form of punishment, and was considered an act of clemency. In fact, Sebastian Cabot, the commander of the second *Armada de Maluco,* followed the example of Magellan and also marooned his second-in-command on an island off the Brazilian coast. It is a curious coincidence that, decades later, Sir Francis Drake, sailing also on a voyage of circumnavigation, likewise held a court-martial because of a mutiny at Saint Julian Bay and executed his second-in-command there under the very shadow of the old gibbets erected by Magellan.

The position of Saint Julian Bay corresponds to that of Newfoundland in the north latitude, though the winter temperature by thermometer is milder, being about like that of the British Isles. However, the frequent cold winds which sweep seaward from the Andes across the flat pampas, and the bitter sea gales blowing northward from Cape Horn, made it seem terrible to Mediterranean men. Snug barracks were quickly built on shore, warmed by large fires, and the men soon were clothed with seal pelts or with the skins of sea birds. These were easily tanned, sometimes with their soft down unplucked, and were sewed into warm garments, hoods, and boots; but in them the bearded, long-haired seamen must have presented a barbaric appearance.

During the first two months of the stay in Port Saint Julian, no natives at all were seen. Then, one day, a naked Indian of giant stature appeared. He proved to be friendly and before long brought others of his tribe to the fleet; Ferdinand Magellan gave them the name of Patagonians, or big feet. These natives were dressed in the skins of the llamas called guanacos and lived largely upon their meat. They had captive young guanacos with them, to be used as decoys in hunting the wild herds, and this was the first the Spaniards learned of the existence of game there. Don Antonio depicts the Patagonians as enormous beings, about eight feet in height, and describes their persons, customs, and language in minute detail. The report that there was a race of veritable giants in South America later created a sensation in Europe and became the subject of much discussion. Others of the early explorers confirmed Don Antonio's account, but later travelers disagreed.

There was excellent fishing in the shoal waters of the bay, and at low tide an extensive stretch of mud flats was exposed on which the men gathered crustaceans and mussels. Many of the sailors came from fishing villages and knew how to utilize every variety of sea food. The bay and its marshes abounded in flocks of ducks and geese, but the hunters who went inland to look for venison found no trace of large game. Despite the rich and plentiful fare, they lacked fresh fruits and vegetables, and the health of the men was affected.

The daily portions of wine and hard tack had already been cut, but Magellan now found, to his great dismay, that he would have to reduce these staple rations further. The discovery of an unforeseen shortage of provisions was made when all the contents of the ships, ammunition, cargo, and supplies, had been taken ashore and put in temporary sheds so that the hulls could be careened on the beach. After the stores were put on land, the Captain General ordered the accountants to make a careful inventory. They discovered that there was barely enough wine and biscuit to last six months. A recheck of the records disclosed that the armada had cleared from Seville with provisions for only about a year's voyage instead of for two years, as Magellan had believed. It hardly seemed possible. The auditors now discovered that many consignments had been receipted for twice at Seville, in accordance with a subtle system that had entirely deceived the ships' pursers and Magellan's checkers. The Captain General faced the disastrous fact that the armada would face starvation if he carried out his program of extensive exploration. He concealed the appalling discovery from the men and set about offsetting the shortage by having quantities of fish and sea fowl smoked, salted, and packed in barrels. From now on, his apprehensions as to supplies would outweigh any other worries with which he was confronted.

Because of the shortage of provisions, Magellan realized that he no longer could afford to wait, inactive, throughout the long Antarctic winter from April until September, but must push forward, regardless of risks. He felt sure that the *paso* could not be much farther south, and he determined to take up the search again without delay. Instead of risking the whole fleet and breaking his promise to the crews, he decided to send forward a single scouting vessel. The Santiago was safest for this inshore work, so Serrano was sent out to continue to look for the *paso* along the unknown coast.

Sixteen days of constant struggle brought the Santiago southward a mere sixty miles, or about four miles a day. Captain Serrano felt that he could go on no longer when, on the afternoon of the feast of Saint Gregory, he sighted a wide estuary with a sand bar at its mouth. He guided the ship across the bar and entered a river of considerable depth. The next day was the Feast of the Holy Cross, so Serrano gave the river the name it still bears, Rio Santa Cruz. It provided a sheltered harbor, a good bottom for anchoring, and a plentitude of wood for fuel, and fish, seal, and water fowl. He therefore determined to recommend to the Captain General that the winter quarters of the armada be transferred there from Saint Julian Bay, which he loathed because of its somber memories. As soon as he judged his crew to be rested, Serrano put out to sea again, but he had hardly emerged when a terrific easterly gale suddenly struck the Santiago, and a tremendous roller tore away the rudder. The ship was helpless, but by superb seamanship, utilizing his sails, Serrano drove the vessel upon a sandy spit, and the crew of thirty-seven men were able to drop from the bowsprit to the beach "without even getting wet," as Don Antonio says. Only one man was lost, Serrano's personal Negro slave, Juan, who mistimed his jump and was licked off the sand by a wave. The ship broke up in a few moments, was sucked off the beach, and disappeared with all its gear and cargo. No explorer ever had worse luck than Captain John Serrano, for, although he did not know it, the Santiago was wrecked within two days' sail to the *paso*.

Except for their knives, the survivors had no weapons, and beyond their scanty, soaked clothing, no protection against the piercing cold. Fortunately, John Serrano had a flint and steel, so that a fire could be made. Two of the castaways volunteered to try to get back to Saint Julian Bay for help. Without food or weapons, they managed to cross the wide Rio Santa Cruz on a log raft, and, waving to their three dozen miserable comrades on the far shore, they set out northward on foot.

They had planned to follow the shore line, where they could expect to find shellfish and other edibles, but their road along the sea was blocked by impassable swamps, and they had to strike into the interior. They traversed a gravelly, rolling prairie, covered with thorn bushes and cut by numerous dry gullies. They saw herds of guanacos, the camel-like llamas they had seen with the Indians at Saint Julian Bay and also some rheas, or South American ostriches, as well as foxes, rabbits, and some small, burrowing rodents; and flocks of sparrows alighted near them. Being unarmed and without means of making snares or traps, the starving men were unable to catch any of the abundant game and had to chew roots and leaves in order to satisfy their hunger. They found no water, but relied upon snow to quench their thirst. Their half-frozen, bare feet were bruised by the harsh gravel, and their clothes were torn away by brambles. The icy wind from the nearby Andes swept over the low pampas and never abated its numbing attack. At night, lacking blankets or a fire, they sought a hollow, filled it with leaves, and slept huddled together for warmth. They were fortunate in not being discovered by some of the nomadic Patagonians whose hunting grounds they had invaded.

After eleven days of stumbling forward, the pair crawled over the crest of a ridge and saw below them the smoking fires of Magellan's encampment. They uttered feeble shouts and waved to the sentries at the stockade. The guards thought them to be natives, and an armed patrol was sent to investigate. So emaciated were the two forlorn figures that at first they were not recognized as Spaniards. Even then their mates could hardly identify the two scarecrows as the stalwart seamen they had previously known.

As soon as the exhausted messengers had regained enough strength to act as guides, Magellan sent a rescue force with all needed supplies. After another month of privations, John Serrano and all his men were brought back safely.

Serrano convinced the Captain General that the Santa Cruz anchorage offered a haven preferable to Saint Julian Bay for the balance of the winter, and Magellan decided to abandon the dismal place with its gibbets and unhappy atmosphere. The prisoners were now released from chains and restored to their ships, but, in accordance with the sentence of the court-martial, Juan de Cartagena and Padre Sanchez de Reina were left on land with a supply of provisions, wine and weapons. They last were seen kneeling and weeping, hands raised in piteous supplication, as the vessels crossed the bar and swung south-southwest in the wake of the *capitana.*

It was August 24, 1520. The squadron made the passage southward without mishap, despite the heavy weather, and safely crossed the bar at Rio de la Cruz. They went into winter quarters there and waited for the ocean gales to subside. Many of the men were kept occupied salvaging the artillery and stores of the Santiago, for, by great good fortune, the whole wrecked hull had been found far down the coast. A valuable consignment of copper ingots and iron bars belonging to Cristóbal de Haro was recovered in its entirety.

A team was organized to kill seals, tan the skins, and salt the meat. Don Antonio was astonished at the size of the seals and says that the dressed carcass of one old bull weighed five hundred pounds. Other teams were kept busy catching fish in seines and salting them away in casks, while another group shot sea birds, preserved the skins, and smoked the carcasses.

At last, after two months, it was evident that winter was near an end, and the armada could soon go to sea. A secret meeting was called, probably by Estevan Gomes, Chief Pilot of the armada, which was attended by a number of the officers. He suggested, since the *paso* had not been found, their supply of provisions was so scanty, and the health of the men affected by scurvy, that they abandon further search. He did not advocate an immediate return to Spain, but proposed instead that they sail at once, eastward rather than westward, to Maluco. Here they could get fresh fruits and vegetables and could stock up on meat and provisions. They would get in touch with Francisco Serrano at Ternate and exchange their valuable cargo of copper, iron and trade goods for the rich hoard of spices he had accumulated. They could establish a fortified trading post there for Spain and assuredly bring back home as much as half a million ducats worth of spices, drugs, and precious stones.

This was an entirely new approach to the problem. The previous mutinous suggestions had involved merely the return to comfort at Brazil, but this latest proposal had much greater appeal. The officers who were acquainted with conditions in the East Indies pronounced the plan to be feasible and said that by sailing east along the latitude of 50° S., where they now were, they could reach Maluco without encountering any Portuguese ships. Don Charles had formally claimed Maluco to lie within his own area of colonization, and, under the terms of the Treaty of Tordesillas, his ships had a technical right to trade there. The proposal was not rejected even by the officers who had been loyal to Magellan, and it was agreed to present the plan to him.

They took their scheme to the Captain General, but he firmly resisted the suggestion, although he finally agreed that, if the *paso* was not found by the time they reached the 75th south parallel, he would give up the search for the southwest passage and order a course directly east to Maluco, there to keep his rendezvous with Francisco Serrano. He candidly admitted that he did not positively know just where the *paso* was to be found, but that he expected to locate it before they reached 55° S. latitude. If he was disappointed there, he would still keep on for another two months, until they reached either Terra Australis or until they got to 75° S. latitude, where he presumed the ice would stop them. His frankness was not at all well received. Estevan Gomes emphasized to the other officers that Magellan had told the King that he had positive knowledge of the location of the *paso,* and now he was confessing he had misled him. He denounced him as a self-confessed impostor who had obtained his command under false pretences by deceiving the King, the very accusation which had been voiced again and again by Juan de Cartagena. He urged that Magellan be put in irons, that the armada sail back to Saint Julian Bay, rescue Juan de Cartagena, put him in command, and then sail east for Maluco. He argued that if the armada returned to Spain with a cargo of spices and with the politically powerful Juan de Cartagena in command, they would surely receive a royal welcome.

Gomes's suggestion that Cartagena be put in command was what saved the day for the Captain General. Even John Serrano, who now had the Concepción, and Duarte Barbosa, who had been made Captain of the Victoria, had been tempted by the proposal to abandon the search for the elusive *paso* and to grasp the sure gains of an eastern voyage to Maluco. However, when Gomes proposed to put the ex-mutineers back in charge, all the Portuguese and many of the Spaniards such as Espinosa recognized that their own safety depended upon the continuance of Magellan in command.

All the captains therefore reluctantly accepted the plan of the Captain General, and the arrangements for abandoning winter quarters were actively pushed to completion. In preparation for what might lie ahead, most of the men confessed to Padre Valderrama and went to Communion at a last solemn High Mass. On October 18, 1520, the four ships left the Rio de Santa Cruz.

CHAPTER XVII

THE STRAIT OF MAGELLAN

ONCE clear of the estuary of the Rio de Santa Cruz, the Trinidad swung southward in the teeth of a howling polar storm. The men once more knew the acute discomforts and suffering of sailing in this terrible region, and their desire grew more intense to steer eastward to the balmy isles of the Spiceries. On the succeeding day, however, the wind abated and the weather even seemed to give a hint of spring. The sea was a shallow green, and they sailed close to the low, barren coastline, which ran westward at first and then turned southward. The Trinidad investigated briefly two large river mouths which soon proved shallow and of short length. Then the coast slanted sharply southeast, and at about a hundred miles from Rio de Santa Cruz, at 52½° S. latitude, it ended abruptly in a broad, sandy headland, which Magellan named the Cape of the Ten Thousand Virgins in honor of St. Ursula, upon whose day, October 21st, it was discovered. After they had sailed beyond the great cape, Magellan was surprised to see that it masked quite a large, deep bay, with a wide entrance. On the other, or south side of the opening, was another cape which he called *Cabo de Espiritu Santo,* or Cape of the Holy Ghost. Beyond the bay, he could see in the far background a range of snow-covered peaks, the first he had seen for years. Since the water of this bay was light green and hence was assumed to be shallow, the navigating officers questioned the need to spend time exploring it. The wind was favorable to continuing southward, the fleet was making a fast run, and it seemed too bad to lose the first really good southerly gale they had had. He hesitated, for it might take some days to explore such a large bay, and he knew his officers would be impatient to keep moving southward. He hove to and signaled for a conference. The three captains, Barbosa, Serrano, and Mesquita, and their pilots, all clambered aboard the *capitana.* Although they were all Portuguese and, except for Estevan Gomes, supporters of Magellan, they unanimously opposed wasting valuable time on searching this bay. They argued that the background of high mountains proved that there could be no transcontinental passage there. Magellan discerned to his dismay that all six of them had lost any interest in finding the *paso* and were avid to enrich themselves by a quick eastward trip to Maluco. The Captain General, on hearing their negative arguments, and perceiving their resolution, altered his procedure. His judgment was so superior to that of the men with whom he was debating that he felt it useless to argue farther. Apart from his conviction that a *paso* existed and could be found, and apart also from his firm resolution to carry out his commitment to the King, he was farsighted enough to realize that, if they yielded to this temptation, the political sponsors of the three late Spanish captains would inevitably demand his head and probably the heads of Barbosa and Serrano. No matter how valuable the spices they might bring back from Maluco to Spain via the Cape of Good Hope, his enemies would destroy him. Only after carrying out the declared objectives of the expedition would it be safe for him to return to Spain. Although this common-sense consideration of personal safety influenced Magellan somewhat, an exalted sense of spiritual election had now taken firm hold of him. He had become a zealot.

Magellan closed the discussion by peremptorily issuing a set of sailing instructions. He ordered Captain Mesquita to take the San Antonio, in company with Captain Serrano in the Concepción, and to sail straight through the bay and try to find an outlet to the west. He, on the Trinidad, would take Captain Barbosa on the Victoria and search along the southerly and northerly shores of the bay. He set the fleet's rendezvous inside the headland for five days later.

The captains and the pilots emerged from the cabin of the Captain General much dissatisfied. They stood in a group on the deck and grumbled openly, for they were resentful at having been called into conference to express their views and then receiving an order contrary to their suggestions. Captains John Serrano and Duarte Barbosa, the close friends and relatives of Magellan, who had always enthusiastically supported him, seemed now almost as irritated as the pilots, Carvalho and Gomes, who all along had been opposed to a continuance of the southern course.

For Magellan, although his will had prevailed, the attitude of his lieutenants was ominous. In case of mishap, he might well find himself deposed by the vote of his own compatriots. The four vessels had, at his insistence, barely sailed between the two capes, when the steady breeze from the north was succeeded by a sudden tempest from the east that drove all the ships far into the shallow bay. The Trinidad and the Victoria were able to run north, furl sail and cast anchor behind the shelter of the Cape of the Virgins. From that temporarily safe anchorage, the Captain General helplessly watched the San Antonio and the Concepción being blown by the full fury of the storm into the very bay where, against their own judgment, they had been ordered to enter. Peering through the spindrift, he watched the frantic attempts of the two ships, as they tried every trick of seamanship, to delay being driven toward the breakers ahead of them.

Only a rag of sail showed on each vessel. They seemed hopelessly cut off from further maneuvering by a long, rocky point that projected out into the raging bay. Yet, by some miracle of currents or of tide-rip, they managed to round the surf-buried, daggerlike promontory and again were sent driving toward the white line of breakers whose bellowing roar Magellan seemed to hear over the chorus of the storm, the pounding of the bare spars, the whip of the cordage, and the noise of the lunging waves. The gale was so intense that, even in their lee shelter, the anchors of the Trinidad and of the Victoria began to drag, so both vessels had to hoist storm sails and run through the entrance into the open sea. Then, in the smother of spray and rain, Magellan lost sight of the Victoria. For two days the Trinidad rolled and pitched in the storm, its waist deck awash and its pumps thumping to offset the constant leakage into the hold through the battered hatches and gun ports. Magellan feared the Trinidad could not keep afloat. If it came through, he felt it would be the only survivor of the armada. He thought of the Concepción and of the San Antonio as already lost, with a great part of the fleet's provisions. It would now be impossible to keep up his search for the *paso,* and they would not even have enough supplies for the eastward voyage to the Indies around the Cape of Good Hope. With a single ship and scanty provisions, he could hope to accomplish no more than to return to Spain. Then his mood changed, and he vowed grimly that, come what might, as long as the Trinidad remained afloat, he would stay in command and continue his quest for the *paso,* the westward route to Maluco.

On the second day the storm died down. When visibility had returned, the lookout called out that he could see the Victoria hull down on the horizon. The next morning, the consort rejoined the *capitana,* and both vessels steered westward toward the Cape of the Virgins. At dusk they again cast anchor under the lee of the promontory. Magellan issued orders for both ships to sail inshore next morning under soundings and to skirt the coast of the bay in search of any vestiges of the lost *naos.* At dawn, just as they were weighing anchor, the lookout reported a column of smoke deep in the bay, and Magellan headed southwest for it, hoping to find survivors who were signalling for rescue. After rounding the rocky peninsula behind which the San Antonio and Concepción had disappeared almost a week before, Magellan heard the hail from the lookout, "A Sail! A Sail!" and then the correction, "Two Sails! Two Sails!" In a moment, the San Antonio and the Concepción could be seen coming from the west, bowling along, all sails set, with a brisk, fair wind.

Magellan observed that both were dressed with gala bunting and flying every gay standard they had. As they neared the *capitana,* smoke puffed from each; the sound of their salutes reverberated across the bay and echoed from the cliffs astern. He could imagine but one cause for the blossoming of the multicolored flags and for this exuberant expenditure of gunpowder. They must have encountered the *paso!* Everyone aboard the *capitana* went wild with delight. The reaction was so swift that the men's emotions swept them away. Some fell on their knees in prayer, others indulged in every sort of grimace and gesture, and the younger *grumetes* took to mauling one another and wrestling on the deck to express their relief. Magellan was trembling as he crossed himself and bent his head in thanksgiving.

The San Antonio came alongside and luffed. Captain Alvaro de Mesquita, his face shining in excitement, deferentially shouted, "Hail my Captain General! I have the honor to report the discovery of the *paso.* It is a narrow, deep strait, with a heavy tidal flow, and we penetrated over a hundred miles before turning back!" In a few moments, Serrano, Mesquita, Guerra, and Gomes all came aboard the *capitana* to be surrounded and embraced by their exultant comrades. Barbosa hurriedly rowed over from the Victoria and hugged the Captain General at the impromptu council which was held in the grand cabin. The discoverers reported how, after tacking frantically in the storm and exhausting every maneuver to escape the lee shore, the two ships had been miraculously swept around the promontory by a strong current and then had been again blown helplessly by the gale toward the breakers. Suddenly they saw a narrow passage, like the mouth of a river, ahead of them in the surf, and managed to steer into it. Driven on by the wind and swept ahead by a rushing flood tide, they raced through these narrows into a wide lake. Still driven by the storm, they were carried west for some hours, across this lake into another narrow passage, although now the current had reversed, and what appeared to be a great ebb tide came rushing at them. They debouched from this second strait into a broad body of water that stretched far toward the setting sun, and, excited and triumphant, they had boldly sailed across this to where it discharged into several westward channels.

They entered one of these and observed that it bore the marks of a forty foot tidal drop along its precipitous shores. Taught by their previous disillusionment when they had assumed the Rio de Solis to be the *paso,* this time they made continuous tests of the water in the channel they were following westward to see if its saltiness decreased as they left the Atlantic behind them. They found, however, that it continued to be real sea brine throughout. Another lesson which they had learned was to check the comparative flow of the ebb and flood tides to see if the ebb was the stronger, as it would be if augmented by the outflow of a river's current. Their observations, however, showed that the flood tides from the Atlantic each time seemed as strong as the ebb or even stronger; hence they were sure there must be an outlet westward. Frequent soundings indicated a deep channel without sand banks or shallows, and every test and check convinced the pilots that this was a genuine strait which undoubtedly opened out in some great westward body of water, probably the Great South Sea itself. They had seized upon a change of wind and raced back to Magellan with the news.

The previously rebellious officers freely admitted their error and gave the Captain General full credit for his perspicacity. He used the occasion to re-establish his authority, finding it politic to assert a foreknowledge of the *paso's* existence and location. Don Antonio wrote, "Had it not been for the Captain General, we would not have found that strait, for we all thought and said it was closed on all sides. But he himself knew full well where to sail to find the well-hidden strait, which he had seen depicted on a map in the treasury of the King of Portugal, which was made by that excellent man, Martin of Bohemia. He therefore sent the two ships, the San Antonio and the Concepción to discover what was inside the cape of the bay." The statement that Ferdinand Magellan had known of the precise location of the strait at 53° S. latitude is contrary to our belief that he really had been by no means sure of its location, nor indeed, even certain of its existence. His desperate probing of the entire littoral southward from 35° S. latitude makes this evident. But the previous skeptics now meekly accepted his assertion of prescience and felicitated him upon his foresight and wisdom.

Magellan resolved to take advantage of this propitious moment to hold another council to win the support of his officers for his proposal to thread the *paso* and sail boldly across the western waters to Maluco. He held an impromptu meeting then and there. To his dismay, all the officers followed their previous selfish preference for taking no chances and making their fortunes by sailing eastward to Maluco. They argued that, although the *paso* had now been discovered, the fleet needed to be reprovisioned before undertaking a long westward voyage of exploration. They urged Magellan to go to meet Francisco Serrano at Ternate not by the unknown westward route, but by the safe, quick, eastward one, and bring back a rich cargo via the Cape of Good Hope to Spain. Then they could with good grace refit and revictual and, with a seaworthy fleet, sail directly from Spain for the *paso,* traverse it, and cross the Great South Sea westward to Maluco. Each captain reported a dangerous shortage of provisions and supplies, and the pressing need for a complete overhauling of his ship after over a year of tropical and Antarctic storms. The council ended in the same manner as the previous one, except that the Captain General was now in a dominant rather than a defiant position with them and could afford to be more conciliatory and persuasive. He was unyielding in his resolve to continue westward in spite of untrustworthy tackle, unseaworthy hulls, and a lack of food. He ended his speech with the passionate words: "Even if we have to eat the leather wrappings on the masts and yards, I will still go on to discover what I have promised Our Lord the King, and I trust that God will aid us and give us good fortune."

The council accepted his dictum, although with evident reluctance, all except Estevan Gomes, who stubbornly continued to argue until the Captain General abruptly announced the council was over. Gomes returned to the San Antonio audibly muttering that Magellan would cause all of them to die of scurvy and starvation. His openly rebellious attitude was overlooked by Magellan, who felt he could ignore his opposition, based as it was on jealousy.

At dawn, the *Armada de Maluco* ceremoniously fired a broadside and, in single file, led by the Concepción, entered the gateway of the *paso.* When they had passed from the narrow entrance-strait into the wider inner bay, the lookout reported a cluster of habitations on the southern shore. Magellan signalled the fleet to anchor and sent the Trinidad's armed longboat under Espinosa to reconnoiter.

The landing party were excited at the prospect of visiting the first village they had entered since leaving Santa Lucia six months before. No doubt they exchanged jocular speculations and guffaws about the native maidens awaiting them. As they reached the beach, a great cloud of sea birds rose from a stranded, hulking object, and an overpowering stench arose from the decaying body of a whale. Few of the men had ever been close to one of these gigantic monsters, and they gaped at the dimensions of the mammoth creature. Leaving the carcass and marching three miles inland, in cautious defensive formation, they ascended a barren hill to the supposed village. To their disappointment, the structures proved to be not native huts, but thatched barrows, each raised on posts five feet from the ground, and containing partly mummified Indian remains. These had been smoked over a fire, treated with bitumen, and encased in shrouds made of the sewn skins of the albatross. The height of these men had been between six feet and six feet, six inches. Some were decked out with head-dresses of sea birds' feathers fastened to meshed skullcaps made with the flexible sinews of seals, and some had necklaces of sharks' teeth and of seashells strung upon seal sinews. They had obsidian knives, long wooden spears hardened by fire, and war clubs made of knobby wood, studded with sharks' teeth. There were no domestic vessels either of pottery or basket weave, but each corpse had with it a little piece of chipped flint, together with a vein of iron ore in a hunk of granite. By striking one against the other a spark was generated quite as good as that procured by European flint and steel. In this respect, these people were more advanced than the Guarani Indians of Santa Lucia or the Patagonians of Saint Julian. Except for these graves, there was no evidence that the land had ever been inhabited. The undulating prairie, with its sandy soil and scattered patches of grass, stretched away to the horizon without a trace of life, either human or animal. Not even a wisp of smoke could be seen. Only the group of cadavers, their rude biers shakily supported by irregular sticks, gave testimony that somewhere near there must be men. It was an eerie spot, and the superstitious mariners gladly left it to return to their ships.

The flotilla resumed its course and soon reached a large island which bisected the strait. The Captain General directed the San Antonio to explore the southeastern channel that opened up before them, while he continued along the western strait with the other ships. The edges of the strait, instead of being walled by the barren cliffs that had bordered the entrance to the *paso,* were now covered with herbage, and behind were mountainous slopes covered by a forest of beeches and other deciduous hardwood trees, with an occasional hemlock or grove of pines, through which waterfalls leaped down to the channel. Don Antonio reflected the relief and jubilation of the armada when he wrote, "I believe that there is not a more beautiful or better strait in the world than that one." After proceeding westward all day, Magellan, finding the channel too deep for anchoring, moored the *naos* to the shore at the mouth of a little river which he called the River of Sardines, because of the shoals of silvery little fish that crowded into it. There were many experienced sardine fishermen among the sailors, and they soon were at work with their nets, catching, expertly preserving, and packing the tiny fish in casks.

Magellan found the moorings effective at this harbor, in spite of the rushing tides, although he would be at the mercy of a sudden southeast or southwest gale. Rather than endanger the *naos* in exploring a dangerous and wholly unknown channel, he sent Espinosa in the Trinidad's longboat to try and follow the strait to the sea. Before dusk on the fourth day after the longboat's departure, Magellan heard shots to the westward, and the lookout announced the return of the batel, which soon appeared, foaming along against the tide, the oarsmen throwing themselves into their strokes with great good will. The two serpentines of the boat were being fired alternately, and Espinosa was standing in the bow madly waving an improvised banner attached to a lance. When they got within a bowshot of the *capitana,* he shouted excitedly, "We've found it! We've found it! The Great South Sea! The Great South Sea!"

Pandemonium broke loose. The fishermen hauling the seines let them drop into the tide, the coopers who were working on the barrels drummed loudly for joy on their casks, and everyone aboard the ships leaped to the shrouds and to the bulwarks and cheered wildly. The longboat pulled alongside, and her men began to babble of a great promontory that jutted out in a boundless blue ocean. Don Antonio said, "The Captain General wept for joy and called that cape *Deseado* (which means the desired)."

Espinosa had had a dangerous and difficult voyage in the launch and had been fortunate in getting back to the ship. After leaving the Bay of Sardines, he had found the western part of the strait, a bleak, desolate waterway through a cleft between two barren shores which were made of rocks riven and piled up by volcanic and seismic convulsions. There were no suitable beaches on which to spend the night, no safe anchorage, and the crew had to pass the four nights cramped in the open boat and exposed to incessant rainfall. The winds had been tempestuous, shifting continually, so that the boat several times was almost driven against the sharp rocks. The forty-foot tides which rushed westward met the immense Pacific swells rolling eastward and caused a turbulent sea, and, when the great waves crashed against the precipices, they created backwashes that added confusion to the waters. One wild squall almost drove the boat completely outside the strait into the Great South Sea. The men had to labor at the oars continuously to avoid shipwreck. On one shore of the narrow strait a strong current would be foaming eastward, while on the opposite shore an equally strong current would be rushing westward; when the two met, whirlpools and vast eddies occurred. None of the seamen had ever experienced such conflicting currents, and they were amazed to find, at the very time the powerful tide was setting westward, that right down the center of the strait rushed a deep, strong current flowing eastward. It was a grave report Espinosa made to the gathering of the pilots, a report that made the Captain General feel apprehensive, despite his resolve to continue.

Now that the way actually was clear to the Great South Sea and the reality of the *paso* had been completely established, Magellan turned his attention to his next problem, that of subsistence for the voyage. He pushed the work of catching sardines and of shooting with bow and arrow the thousands of sea birds that preyed upon the shoals of fish. He announced that as soon as the San Antonio returned from the task of exploring the southern passageways, the armada would set sail. A week passed, and the San Antonio did not return. The Captain General left the *alguacil* and his marines with the longboat to protect the working

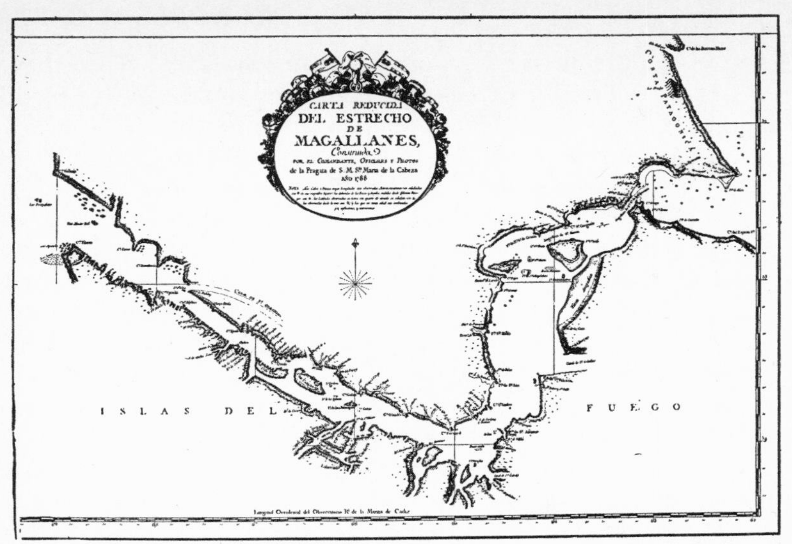

Engraving from "Ultimo Viage al Estrecho de Magallanes," 1788

THE STRAIT OF MAGELLAN

Engraving from de Bry's "Peregrinationes," 1619

MAGELLAN'S LANDFALL AT GUAM

squad who were preparing the provisions ashore, and he turned eastward with the three ships to seek the missing consort. He searched eastward in every direction through the maze of dangerous tidal canals, looked for smoke signals, and continually fired signal cannon; there was no trace of the missing San Antonio. The worried commander then planted a large cross high at one cape, with a letter to Captain Mesquita in an earthen pot beneath it, and raised conspicuous banners with similar messages on two islets at prominent intersections of the waterway. Everyone was anxious about the fate of the missing men and worried about the sufferings of the survivors of any shipwreck; none suspected that the San Antonio might have deserted, although this frightening thought did secretly occur to Magellan. At last, after running a hundred hazards in the search and being more than once on the brink of disaster, after even sailing back out into the Atlantic and swinging back again into the strait, he had to give up the search in desperation.

Some of the sailors began to whisper that there were supernatural reasons for the mysterious disappearance of the San Antonio; the crews were becoming uneasy and fearful. The Captain General was shaken by the loss of his largest ship with a good proportion of his men and a great part of his supplies, but he still clung to the hope that the San Antonio had been blown out to sea and would return. When he finally gave up this hope, he called upon the astrologer, Andres de San Martin, to solve the mystery. After a careful horoscope and nightlong study of the celestial spheres, the soothsayer announced that there had been a mutiny aboard, that the captain was wounded and a prisoner, and that the San Antonio had sailed back to Spain. Magellan accepted this as the probable though very unpalatable explanation. He wondered if Gomes had sailed back to pick up marooned Juan de Cartagena. In any event his enemies would calumniate him at home and do all possible to destroy Don Charles's faith in him. It was a disturbing thought and made it more necessary than ever to bring back the record of great accomplishments to Spain. He now was paying for a second time for his confidence in Alvaro de Mesquita, whom he had repeatedly warned against their common kinsman, Estevan Gomes. He upbraided himself for having reinstated Mesquita in command of the San Antonio, reflecting bitterly that he should have learned his lesson when, at Port Saint Julian, his cousin had disastrously disregarded his admonitions. His inherent resiliency in the face of reverses came to his aid, and Magellan led his two smaller consorts back to a little bay east of the River of Sardines where there was a good, sandy bottom for safe anchorage. There he saw to it that as many fish and birds as possible were preserved in preparation for their voyage.

Magellan then called for a combined inventory of the supplies and food of all three ships, and when Barbosa and Serrano brought their lists, and the totals were added up, he stared at the figures in consternation. The San Antonio had taken away so much of the food that it looked like madness to continue on the voyage. He did not mince words with Barbosa and Serrano, but privately admitted to them that their venture had now become a desperate gamble. He agreed that ordinarily the sensible thing would be to go back to Spain for supplies, but he convinced them that, with Gomes and Guerra in Spain ahead of them, it would be certain suicide to return and fall into the power of the vindictive Fonseca. They had no choice but to sail out into the unknown ocean without sufficient food. The two captains agreed not to divulge the shortages to the other officers, but to adopt a cheerful attitude, proclaiming that all barriers now were passed and that the road to ease and plenty lay before them.

Despite his perplexities, Magellan must now have had a sense of freedom he had not felt since leaving. His stores were pitifully small, but at last he could sleep without half expecting to be awakened by a knife at his throat. He must have been relieved to be rid of Gomes and Guerra, although the cost was much too high. He still had del Cano and Antonio de Coca with him, but he would keep them apart, under scrutiny, and he did not fear them.

On the day after the return of the squadron to the River of Sardines, while most of the crew were ashore engaged in the work of preserving and packing the bountiful catch of fish, the lookout sounded the alarm and called the attention of Ferdinand Magellan to the approach of a large bark canoe paddled by half a dozen naked Indians. A spiral of smoke showed that the glowing embers of their permanent camp fire were preserved and transported in the bottom of the canoe. Magellan judged they had seen the swarms of sea birds in the sky above the river mouth and had correctly read the sign that the sardines were spawning; they were hastening to join in the feasting. The fleet was hidden from their view, and the screaming and cawing of the army of sea birds prevented their hearing the shouts of the sailors and the tapping of the *toneleros'* hammers as they made the barrels ready for the salted fish. He ordered the *alguacil* to take the longboat, with rowers and guards, and quietly lie hidden at the edge of the river until he could get behind the Indians and cut them off. Then if they could not be lured peaceably by offers of red cloth, mirrors, and tinkling bells, he could make them captives. In a few moments the canoe came to the harbor and, stopping, drifted idly, the thunderstruck natives staring openmouthed at the spectacle of the strange ships with their great hulls, tall masts, and cordage. As the longboat approached, they all knelt in reverence, their brows upon their hands in the bottom of the canoe, rendering homage to the white deities, the first such beings they had ever seen. While the aborigines prostrated themselves, the *alguacil* prudently gathered up the harpoons and paddles, flicked the flint knives from the sinew girdles, and towed the canoe alongside the Trinidad, where all gathered at the rail.

Gently encouraging them to go aboard, he led them to the Captain General, who received them kindly and gave a mirror to the chief, a bell to the other brave, and a metal comb to each of the four women. They were stalwart, well formed savages, the chief about six feet, six inches in height; he must have weighed about two hundred and fifty pounds. He was copper colored, with red and white rings painted on his face and stripes of red down his thighs and legs, and absolutely naked; the women wore filthy seal skins about their waists. There bodies were not hairy, but they all had heads of long, coarse hair bound up by a thong. Their leathery skins were smeared with fish oil which gave out a repellent odor. Magellan noted how sleet had formed upon the naked, pendulous breasts of a young woman suckling an infant, and that the mother made no attempt to brush off a film of frozen spray which encased the child's bare back. The fish oil apparently protected them. The women wore necklaces made either of perforated shells or of seals' teeth, and in one case of the horny rings of the seagull's scaly legs. The savages accepted some cooked fish and tore voraciously at several roast ducks, but it was evident that they preferred their food raw.

Magellan watched with interest the interchange of signs whereby Carvalho and Enrique de Malacca, the fleet's interpreters, strove to reach the dull intelligence which shone dimly through the great black eyes of the mute Indians. They soon established a workable sign language and asked if there was game to be hunted on the uplands. The chief indicated that his people ate only mussels, sea birds, and fish, and he did not show any conception of game hunting on the pampas beyond the cliffs. When the question was put to him, however, as to whether warlike Indians were to be encountered inland, there could be no doubt of his having comprehended the inquiry. His expressive pantomine portrayed fear as he conveyed the idea of skin-clad, ferocious giants who were irresistible in combat. He sprang about the deck in various poses, his ordinarily impassive features becoming vivacious and displaying the emotions of aggressor and victim as he acted each part in turn. It was apparent that these fishing Indians remained on the shores of the strait, and that they were afraid of the Patagonians of the uplands.

The friendly visitors gorged themselves upon the food given them, and shortly afterward all six adults and three little children were asleep, uncovered and prone upon the water-soaked, hard deck, with the fine sleet forming a frozen glaze upon their bodies. The Spaniards had lifted their ingeniously made bark canoe on deck, and the paddles, harpoons, and knives were piled in a corner at the break of the forecastle. When the short Antarctic night had passed, however, neither the Indians nor their canoe were to be seen. Despite the watch on deck and the guards on shore, no man had heard nor seen them leave. Their disappearance caused uneasiness to the superstitious sailors, who at once began to imagine them to be spirits. Magellan thought of the squadron's vulnerability to a night attack by foes of such stealth. He feared they might come back in force or that a horde of Patagonian giants might drop down upon them from the cliffs.

He at once had Espinosa establish stronger outposts of guards, and he gave orders to hurry the work of provisioning, but it appeared that it would require at least two days longer to cure all the fish and flesh by smoke and salt. Therefore Espinosa and Carvalho approached Magellan with the suggestion that a hunting party be sent out after guanacos and antas, as the antelopes were called such as they had hunted on the inland prairies behind the Rio Santa Cruz. Magellan was opposed to risking any of his force in an inland excursion and perhaps thereby calling the attention of the Patagonians to the presence of the ships. Espinosa argued how much it would mean to the expedition to have a dozen fat guanacos to salt down, and he made so many promises of caution that at last the Captain General consented to a limited excursion.

The hunting party found small game to be plentiful and shot prairie hens as well as a large, bustard-like game bird. They bagged many rabbits and cavies, little rodents something like prairie dogs. Once a flock of rheas, or Patagonian ostriches, strutted by, well out of bowshot. The Spaniards had learned at Rio Santa Cruz that they could stalk them only from ambush, and therefore no attention was paid the giant birds. Many traces of antelope and guanaco were observed but, although the breeze was blowing toward the hunters, and hence was favorable, they came upon none of them. Espinosa became uneasy at this absence of game and feared it meant that Patagonian hunting parties were somewhere about. He therefore brought the men back to the ships without having encountered either any large game or any native inhabitants.

Before sailing, Magellan took a politic step to forestall later criticism and even persecution by the *Casa de Antillas.* Anticipating such action against him, he began to bolster his own future defense by favorable documentary evidence. Consequently, he issued a formal, official proclamation, drawn up by the Trinidad's clerk and signed and sealed in due form by the ship's notary on November 21, 1520. It is headed: "Written in the Canal of All Saints at 53° of south latitude, before the Island of Isleo." One original copy was addressed to Duarte Barbosa as Captain of the Victoria, as well as to the pilots, the master, and the countermaster under him. A replica was addressed to Captain Serrano and to his officers on the Concepción. The document stated frankly that the Captain General understood that these officers considered it a grave matter that he was determined to go forward on the voyage and that they felt that the time left in the favorable season for Antarctic navigation was too short for him to undertake it.

The Captain General then proceeded to say that, perhaps because of the execution of Captains Mendoza and Quesada and the marooning of Captain Cartagena, the present officers of the fleet might be afraid to express their judgment in opposition to his own. He went on to reassure them, asserting that he was one who sought the free advice and fearless counsel of his officers. He emphasized that it was their obligation to advise and help him in compliance with their solemn oath of dutiful service to His Majesty the Emperor. He reserved to himself the final decision, but asked that each of the eight officers immediately give his individual counsel in writing.

All the officers presumably gave their advice as requested. Only the text of the reply of Andres de San Martin, the fleet astrologer, has been preserved. It is one of the very few such documents of the armada which have survived. Under the date of November 22, 1520, San Martin said he approved of continuing the exploration of the *paso* for sixty days, until the middle of January, 1521, and then, with the winter storms approaching, he thought it would be prudent to load up with water and firewood and return to Spain. He said he did not believe it possible to reach Maluco westward through the *paso* which they then were exploring, but did not explain why he took this negative position. He was definitely opposed to Magellan's proposal to go as far south as 75°, because of the polar storms and frigid temperature. He also, surprisingly, disapproved of the plan to sail east to Maluco via the Cape of Good Hope, because of the shortage of food for such a long cruise as well as the wintry seas in the South Atlantic and Indian Ocean at the southern latitudes in which they would have to sail to avoid the Portuguese. Although the ships were intrinsically good, he said, their spars and rigging, particularly on the Victoria, were worn, the men were fatigued and weak, and many were sick. He was opposed to what was apparently Magellan's practice, navigating during the night, which was only of four or five hours duration at that season of the year in the Antarctic. He criticized this, not so much because of the risk in navigating, but because of the loss of sleep to the tired sailors.

This report of Andres de San Martin makes no constructive suggestions and could have been anything but inspiring to the perplexed commander in chief. If the expressions from the others of his staff were equally dispirited, and one can assume that they were, Magellan must have received but little encouragement in carrying on his perilous and difficult program. Moreover, such reports would be anything but helpful to him in defending himself later in Spain, in case the armada should fail to return in triumph.

At all events, he had ascertained the state of his officers' morale and knew their temper; he decided that the dispirited men would be tractable and would obediently follow his commands.

On the following day, November 23rd, the Captain General officially acknowledged the memoranda from his officers and announced his own unswerving decision. He swore by the habit of the Knights of Santiago which he wore that he would continue the voyage into the Great South Sea. He expressed confidence in the Divine Providence which had safely brought them to the *paso,* and he avowed his faith that God would conduct them successfully to the realization of their hopes.

Therefore, the next morning Magellan ordered the anchors raised, and, with the *capitana* leading, the three little ships sailed cautiously down the narrow, cliff-bordered channel. Here the gales unpredictably shifted their direction, and the mighty tides rushed at a speed far faster than that which any of the ships could muster, even in a stiff breeze. Magellan's steadfast belief in Divine guidance was bolstered by this difficult passage, which they made quite uneventfully; he thought it seemed as though the ships were guided and sheltered by a miraculous pilot.

After leaving the River of Sardines, he could find no safe anchorage and so went steadily onward. In the two short nights of the passage, he saw numerous fires of Indian encampments, which flickered all along the southern shores, so he gave the land the name it has retained, *Tierra de los Fuegos,* or the land of fires. In the daytime he could see no traces of the shy natives whose bivouacs were identified in the dark by their fires. He could plainly hear the roar of faraway seas beating upon a rocky coast, and he surmised that the land south of them was a large island. He kept along the narrow channel already explored by the longboat, and on November 28th, after two days of steady passage westward, they left behind the difficult strait which Magellan had named "Strait of All Saints," although posterity was to give it a different name, his own.

As they reached the western exit of the strait, Magellan saw the rocky headland of which Espinosa had told him jutting out into the ocean on the port bow. He had already named it Cape Deseado, or the wished-for cape. It was the wished-for landmark beyond which now stretched the Great South Sea, the limitless, blue ocean to which Magellan gave the name it still bears, *Mar Pacifico,* or Pacific Ocean.

CHAPTER XVIII

THE PACIFIC OCEAN

FERDINAND MAGELLAN thought that the passage of the *Armada de Maluco* from the *paso* into the Great South Sea should be marked by an appropriate ceremony. By dramatizing its importance, which he himself felt deeply, he hoped to spur the spirit of his reluctant officers and stimulate the fortitude of the sailors, who had been disturbed by the desertion of the San Antonio. And perhaps even more, he wished all to express their thankfulness to the Providence that had sustained them during the trials of the past year and had led them through so many perils not only to discover the *paso,* but actually to sail through it safely. How could any remain faint-hearted and unmoved at such a moment?

The three *naos* in single file cleared the northern promontory, plunging and rolling in the wild sea where the tide which rushed from the straits encountered the great eastward-surging swells. The *capitana* signaled the Victoria and the Concepción to draw up in close formation. Padre Valderrama, in festival vestments, stood high on the poop of the Trinidad and raised a large brass crucifix as he invoked the grace of Our Lady of Victory, the Patroness of the armada. It was the feast day of St. Andrew the Apostle, and an appeal was also made for his favor.

The Captain General and the fleet's company all knelt, and the priest bestowed a benediction upon the little flotilla, and upon the unknown sea into which they were venturing. All joined in chanting the *Te Deum,* and the earnest voices from the other two ships reached Magellan above the surge of the waves and the cries of the sea birds circling above. Then the Captain General held erect his silken banner of command bearing the lions and castles of Castile. All three ships broke out their bunting, and each thundered a broadside in homage to the Great South Sea. The startled sea-fowl flew high in the sky, with shrill cries, and the ships were wreathed in billows of black, sulphurous smoke which trailed to leeward. At the end of the ceremony, Magellan turned to the officers on the quarter-deck and said: "Gentlemen, we now are steering into waters where no ship has sailed before. May we always find them as peaceful as they are this morning. In this hope I shall name this sea the *Mar Pacifico.*" At noon Magellan took the sun as usual; the fleet was at 52° S. latitude. Therefore Cape Deseado, at the Pacific exit of the straits, was in exactly the same latitude as the Cape of the Virgins at the Atlantic entrance.

Even though it was summer, the air was chilly, for the frigid zone was near. The crews felt the cold keenly, so Magellan gave orders to turn sharply and steer as nearly due north as possible; as the wind was from the northwest, he kept well away from the lee coast. On December 2nd, they encountered winds from the southwest and were picked up by a favorable northward-flowing current that aided the steady gale to carry the ships along at a good speed. For over two weeks they followed the northerly route with the wind abeam in a smooth sea. The weather was clear and the temperature gradually became mild, like that of Andalusia in springtime. The sea was alive with strange fish, and the men trailed baited lines in the wake of the ships. Having little work to do, they spent lazy hours betting on the sea swallows, as they called the flying fish, and whether or not they would be snapped up by the large bonitos who followed their shadows, as they soared desperately above the waves before they landed back in the brine.

At about 42° S. latitude, Magellan discerned the promontory of Cape Tres Montes; thereafter they kept the brown, mountainous coastal range in sight. Therefore modern Chile ranks him as its discoverer. The somewhat conjectural charts which he had brought showed the unknown West Coast of South America meeting the eastward-jutting shores of Asia at a latitude of about 35° S.; he continued on his northward course, seeking the supposed point of juncture, until they reached 32° S. latitude. On December 18th, seeing no sign of the nearness of the coast of Asia, he steered away from the continent on his starboard and struck a course northwest in the hope of reaching Asia on this line. Had he chanced to adopt this northwest route a few days earlier, he would have reached the large island of Juan Fernandez, where he could have taken on water, wood, and some food. As it was, he barely missed the two little islets which lie to the east of it. If he had taken a northwest course even earlier, he would have sighted Easter Island, and from there on would have encountered a series of archipelagos that would have provided a continuous supply of victuals and water. However, the stumpy masts of his little ships were so near sea level that the lookouts in the crows' nests were not high enough to pick up the islands that lay just over the horizon. Even if they had had some form of telescope, which they did not, it could not have helped them in this case.

Magellan now had a steady, strong wind astern, and, with the sails once set, there was little for the crew to do except search the horizon and imagine that every low-lying cloud was land. The smoked fish and seafowl from the straits supplied ample rations, and the water from the River of Sardines was still palatable. But now that the weather was pleasant and the hardships had disappeared, tempers became testy and there were frequent quarrels. With light duties and no discomfort, friendliness was succeeded by fretfulness, and there was boasting and sneering. The Gallegos and Basques resented the assumption of superiority by the Castilians, and the French and Flemings, being northerners, banded together against the southerners, the Iberians and Italians.

However, the jarring factions were in accord on one subject, that the Isles of Spice were just over the horizon. They agreed that soon they would be at Ternate, loading the ships with the mace, cinnamon, cloves, and nutmegs that Francisco Serrano had accumulated for them. Then it would be up with the sails and across the Atlantic to Spain, with everyone's fortune made. One moonlit evening some of the men began to calculate the value of the cargo of spices that could be stowed aboard the Trinidad, once they reached Maluco. So many *quintals* of cloves would be worth so many ducats, and so many *fanegas* of nutmegs, so much. Then they began to estimate the *quintalada*, or share, of each man. Each *grumete* was entitled to a single *quintal* of cargo space; a *marinero*, two quintals; a *lombardero*, ten *quintals;* a pilot, twenty *quintals;* and the Captain General's share was forty *quintals*. They began to argue about their individual rights to larger shares. The argument became heated, and taunts succeeded logic. A knife was drawn and a man badly gashed before Espinosa and his marines could intervene.

To divert them, Magellan had Master Andrew of Bristol, the English constable of the *bombarderos*, give gun drills daily. He also had *Alguacil* Espinosa practice the crew in repelling boarders and in defending the forecastle from mock attack from the waist deck. But the men went about the drills half-heartedly, and even the rope's end hardly quickened them. They fumbled at the routine, and the lackluster eyes and shambling movements showed that this was due to malnutrition.

In the cooking arrangements of the Trinidad there were three distinct messes. All were rationed, and there was no favoritism as to size in the small portions doled out. No one any longer had wine, the staple of the Mediterranean sailor's diet which was more missed than anything else. However, the nature of the food differed. The officers' larder still had garlic, figs, and raisins left. The marines' steward also had garlic on hand, but the pantry of the forecastle had only ship biscuit, salted fish, and smoked sea birds. Consequently, without calculation, the officers and the men-at-arms had the benefit of antiscorbutics which maintained their health somewhat better than did the common sailor's diet. Had the effect of diet on scurvy been known, an equitable distribution of the garlic would have been made; as it was, the *marineros* were weakened, while the guards retained somewhat more vigor. However, everyone was debilitated by the meager diet, and before long the small rations were cut in half. Unless someone managed to catch a fish or hook a shark, a man did not receive enough to still the normal complaint of an empty stomach.

Now the blistering sun of the equator blazed down upon the fleet every day. The improperly smoked penguin meat, of which there were many barrels, spoiled in the tropical heat and bred long, fat, white worms, disgusting to look at, which crawled everywhere about the ship. The worms ate woolen clothing and leather, and their pincer jaws gnawed into the hull of the ship itself. The water in the casks turned yellow, became alive, and stank, so that to drink it one had to hold one's nostrils. Everyone tried to keep to windward of the hold, for the odor of the bilge became overpowering, and the air beneath the deck was suffocating. The listless men no longer could be forced to drill, but lay moodily about the deck.

The first victim of scurvy was a Brazilian stowaway, referred to in the official records only as "the Indian from the Land of Verzin"; he was quickly followed by the giant Patagonian called Juan Gigante. Both these South Americans had been favorites of Don Antonio, who spent much time learning their tongues in order to prepare the glossaries of the Guarani and Patagonian languages which he later brought back to the Signory of Venice.

Although the Europeans resisted malnutrition better than the two Indians, their health began to deteriorate rapidly, and soon the strain became pronounced. According to all Magellan's charts, the armada should by now have crossed the Great South Sea. What if the old legends were true and it was really an endless sea? Now they had passed the point where they could turn back, for the supply of food would not suffice for the return voyage. In any case, they could not double back against the vigorous west wind. Each day was like the last. The monotony of the days and of the unending gale astern told on the nerves of all aboard. The same clear horizon, the same unclouded, blazing sky, the same blue and white waves, and astern the two other little *naos*, met their gaze each day; and the same hunger ached in every man's stomach. Never, in all the African or Asian experience of any of the veteran navigators aboard, had any voyage lasted as much as a month without landfall. The compasses began acting queerly, and the older common seamen worried when they learned of it; the Captain General ordered the pilots to reinforce the needles' magnetism with their loadstones. The men also were superstitiously fearful of the two hitherto unknown galaxies of stars which are now known as the Magellanic clouds; these had first appeared high in the firmament after the armada had entered the Pacific. The astrologer, Andres de San Martin, was besieged by nervous inquiries about their import, and he had to admit his ignorance of their celestial influence, whether malign or benign.

Don Antonio had pinned his faith upon the charts. He wrote in his journal, "We changed our course to west by south, in order that we might approach nearer to the land of Cape Gaticara shown on our charts." He comments sarcastically. "That Cape, with the pardon of cosmographers, for they have not seen it, is not found where it is imagined to be."

At last Magellan threw the charts aside. It was clear they were worse than useless, and that the renowned geographers who had drawn them up were scholarly humbugs. Day after day, week after week, he peered ahead for land. Again and again a cloud formation or a mirage deceived him.

After two months of sailing, on St. Paul's day, January 24, 1521, Magellan descried a brilliant green patch diffused over the surface of some low-hanging white clouds. From his experience in eastern seas, he was sure the phenomenon was the reflection of sunlight on the waters of a shallow lagoon on an island at some distance. Soon the call "Land ho!" rang out. An island could now be seen far ahead, just under the green reflection. Everyone was galvanized into new life; eyes shone, lips smiled, and there was a sudden outburst of horseplay and practical joking. As they drew near, Magellan could see no signs of habitation; there were only sea birds and a growth of verdant bushes, but no trees. The leadsmen taking soundings from the bows kept reporting no bottom, and hence, although the ships had the anchors ready, they could not let them go. With the fresh wind and a strong set of current, the squadron could not maneuver into a position where Magellan dared launch a boat to go ashore; unanchored, the ships might be swept past the island and be unable to recover the boat. For a few moments it looked as if they were going to be as much tantalized as if the island were a pure mirage. Just as they gave up hope of landing, the Trinidad's leadsman shouted that he had found shallows; the Captain General had anchors dropped and sails furled at once, and the consorts followed suit. The Trinidad's longboat dashed into the breakers and got through safely; the men clambered out, capering and scampering like children on the sandy beach.

The island, named St. Paul's Island because it was the saint's feast day, was a rounded atoll made up of the circular walls of the crater of a submerged volcano. On the inner side, the emerald color of the lagoon was so vivid that its reflection made the breasts of white sea birds hovering over its surface seem green. Don Antonio was captivated by the contrast between the cobalt blue of the encircling ocean, the white of the tumbling surf, and the green of the interior lagoon. The windward shore of the island was a mass of tumbled coral rocks shattered by the constant impact of the surf. The landing party found these rocks alive with crabs and the waters offshore swarming with brilliantly colored fish. In the breakers, grayish sharks darted like dim shadows within the flanks of the waves. The hungry men expertly hooked sharks and other large fish off the reef and netted a number of small fish in the shallow lagoon.

There was no firewood to be had, for the only growth was a stunted bush with glossy leaves like a magnolia shrub and yielded no worthwhile fuel. Magellan had wood brought ashore and drying racks erected. The sharks' flesh was cut into strips, thoroughly smoked, and salted away in casks, and similar treatment was given the carcasses of numerous large gray gulls, or goonies.

The island was densely populated by sea birds. Evidently none of them had ever seen men before, and they made no attempt to escape when the sailors walked up to them. Nests were everywhere, and the eggs provided a variety of dishes for the famished men. There was much experimentation with roasting, broiling, and stewing the various water fowl, including black terns, white love birds, wingless rails, sea eagles, goonies, and pirate birds.

Duarte Barbosa showed the men how to locate nests of turtle eggs buried in the sand and taught them to hunt, in the shallow water of the lagoon near the shore, the edible sea slugs, or *bêches de mer,* used by the Chinese for making soup. Magellan ordered as many as possible collected, split open, cleaned, and smoked for consumption at sea.

By digging shallow wells, they obtained brackish water which seemed to be rain water stored in the sand, much less salty than the sea water. The failure to find fresh water was a serious disappointment, as each one had been rationed to a cup a day of the stinking fluid left in the casks. Magellan ordered the foul barrels brought ashore and scalded with boiling, brackish water. The casks had hardly been cleansed before a rain squall bore down upon the island. The men hastily spread out sails to catch the downpour, and an ample supply of sweet rain water was funneled into the ready containers.

Two months had passed since the armada sailed out of the strait into the Pacific, and until now there had been no opportunity for a conference between the Captain General and the officers of the other two vessels. Soon after they reached the island, therefore, he called a council to discuss the problems that faced them. They had no precedents to go by, the geographic guides they had relied upon had proved worthless, and they were without any certainty as to their position. They had, of course, identified many of the planets and constellations, but this did not help them much in their navigating, for the extant estimates of the pilots show them to have been very far off in their calculations.

During the four days they were on St. Paul, the navigators tried to ascertain its longitude, or east-west position on the globe. Magellan knew, from his own experience, the distance from Malacca westward to the Cape of Good Hope, and he could make a fair guess as to the distance across the Atlantic from the Cape of Good Hope to the Straits of Magellan. He therefore knew the approximate distance from Malacca westward around the world via the Cape of Good Hope to St. Paul's Island in the Pacific, where they now were. The difference between this known distance and the world's circumference would represent the distance they still had to sail to reach Malacca. The difficulty, of course, was that nobody had yet traveled clear around the world, so the best estimate could only be a guess. Magellan, like most of the astronomers of his day, much underestimated the size of the globe, and he therefore miscalculated the distance the armada yet had to sail from St. Paul's Island to reach the East Indies. He probably calculated St. Paul's latitude, or north-south position, correctly; apparently it was about 15° south of the equator, but since its longitude was not ascertained we cannot identify it today.

The discovery of St. Paul had banished the secret terror of an unending waste of waters which had possessed Magellan for a fortnight. He felt confident that from now on they would encounter other similar islands which would supply seafood and bird flesh, and that certainly fruits and greenstuffs would be found to cure the scurvy. There was less than a month's supply of food on hand, but with frequent landfalls that would do.

It was probably at this council at St. Paul's that Magellan divulged his determination to sail to the Philippines first, there to establish a safe Spanish base of operations, before entering the area about Maluco patroled by Portuguese ships. There is no doubt that the archipelago he had discovered on his secret eastern voyage from Malacca, about 1512, was the Philippines. The course he steered after leaving St. Paul and his subsequent statements and movements bear out the conviction that he meant to plant the flag of Spain on the Philippines and then operate from there. He apparently intended to make Francisco Serrano's King of Ternate, who still, so far as he knew, was independent of Portugal, a vassal of the Emperor, and to establish a fortified trading post at Ternate. The course he set was far to the north of the known latitude of Maluco, telling us as plainly as words his intention to seek the Philippines first.

By the fourth day at St. Paul, they had barreled much smoked shark meat, fish, and the carcasses of many birds. Magellan judged it time to weigh anchor, and the armada continued on its westward route. The crews had relished the abundance of diet afforded by the island and had benefited by the recreation, but since they secured no vegetables nor fruits, the change did not improve their health as much as Magellan had hoped. During the first two weeks after leaving St. Paul, a spirit of optimism prevailed in the three ships, no doubt due to fresh water and good food. In this fortnight they sailed two hundred leagues north-northwest with a sustained following wind. The pilots' observations showed them to be at 10°15′ S. latitude when they perceived at dawn, just ahead of them, another island similar to St. Paul.

As the ships drew near, the excited crews saw it to be an uninhabited atoll, with much herbage, and swarming with birds. The most comforting sight to Magellan was that of heavy clusters of coconuts, which he could see upon the tops of the nodding palms. This would mean the banishment of scurvy. As they neared the windward reef, the leadsmen taking soundings kept chanting that they found no bottom; the ships divided and passed to each side of the island, casting the lead anxiously and hurriedly. When the vessels united at leeward, having circled the atoll, and still the leadsmen could reach no bottom, fear gripped every heart. Magellan had the Trinidad hastily drop sail, followed by its consorts, and all three continued feverishly to sound the depths, while the crews stood tensely ready to drop anchor at the signal.

When there still were no soundings, consternation spread through the armada. Could it be possible they could not land? The ships had now drifted well beyond where there was any reasonable hope of finding bottom, but the leadsmen continued stubbornly to sound. Magellan hastily conferred across the waters with the captains on the other two ships as to the advisability of launching all batels to try to tow the *capitana* back. But time and distance had now slipped past. It would be a desperate move to send the longboats back alone, for even though the sails of the ships were furled, their high superstructure, both fore and aft, caught the wind almost like sails. The men on the batels would never be able to land, load with coconuts, and overtake the fleet. The armada was unable to sail back to the island against the wind and current. This could be attempted only by sailing a triangular course, and it was decided not to lose days of time in making the effort.

Magellan was confident that the westward crossing of the Great South Sea must by now be almost completed, and he expected to reach other islands in a short time. He gave the unattained island a name on his chart, Sharks' Island. Its longitude is unknown and we cannot identify it, but perhaps it was the islet we now know as Caroline Island.

On February 13th, after leaving Sharks' Island in the wake, the *capitana* changed the course to northwest; we calculate that Magellan crossed the Equator at about the longitude of 160° W. of Greenwich. He thereby missed finding Christmas Island and Jarvis Island, where he could have procured ample supplies. He must have passed very near the Marshall, Gilbert, and Mulgraves archipelagoes without sighting a single island. We do not know if the little flotilla sailed in close formation or in single file, but one wonders why the three *naos* did not spread fanwise across the sea, keeping barely in touch with one another. However, the fear that a storm might separate them under those circumstances probably led the three frightened commanders to keep close together.

The voyage became more and more terrible. Under the heat of the Equator, almost all the crew and many of the men-at-arms were down with scurvy. Stricken men lay groaning wherever there was a bit of shade, and those still on their feet tottered and staggered. The sick had such swollen joints that they shrieked when they had to move a hand or foot. Ulcers broke out all over their bodies. Their gums were puffed out and their teeth were covered by the pulpy growth; when they tried to eat, their teeth loosened in the sockets and fell out. Their palates became so enlarged and sore that men died of starvation rather than swallow what food was available. The fetid breath of the sufferers was almost unbearable, and this, together with the putrifying odors from the bilge, made the ship's atmosphere nauseating even to those hitherto inured to it.

In this crisis, Don Antonio says Ferdinand Magellan set an example to all his officers. Never complaining, never despairing, he would each day take his observations, study the chart, and scan the horizon in the expectation of seeing a cloudy shape. Many a time his hopes rose, only to be abandoned sadly when a vague mass proved to be but a cloud. The ship's barber, who acted as physician, succumbed, exhausted by his unselfish efforts to relieve the sick. Now the medical responsibility on the Trinidad devolved largely upon Magellan himself, aided by Don Antonio, Cristóbal Rabelo, and Padre Valderrama. They were among the few who were not sick. They were weak and emaciated from undernourishment, but not stricken with the dreadful scurvy.

In the dim light of dawn Magellan would start on his rounds. His first task was to give a sip of water to each of the sufferers and help them relieve their bodily needs. It was then, at dawn, he would find those to whom he could be of no further earthly aid. He carefully saved the personal trinkets of a dead sailor for his family, and, after Padre Valderrama had said a brief prayer, they would drop the corpse overside without ceremony. Each dawn the sharks which followed the ship clustered expectantly about the lee quarter.

The next chore of the medical corps was to make some sort of broth for those sufferers who could not swallow solids. As long as some shark and bird meat from St. Paul was left, they were able to make a fair soup by combining the rations of all the patients and adding their portions of ship's biscuit. When the supply was exhausted, Don Antonio offered to any *grumete* who would bring him a rat to use for making broth the equivalent of half a year's pay. He also paid well for any fish that was caught, although some of the men refused to accept money. However, there in mid-ocean the catch was scanty, although dozens of baited lines and several drag nets were kept oversides night and day. No sea birds were seen. There was no life but the two other ships—all else was steely sea, leaden sky, and brazen sun and moon.

When there was no longer any fish nor meat for the broth, Magellan collected the stony fragments of biscuits that were the leavings of the bread casks, stained yellow with the urine of rats, and had these crumbs pounded into powder, being careful to include all the maggots, as these might contain some nourishment. Some casks in the hold had once held raisins, honey, and preserved quinces; he had the enriched, sweet slivers of wood cut from the inside of these barrels. He also scraped the inside of empty pork barrels with a knife and added the greasy sawdust to the pitiful mess, moistening it with hot water and pretending bravely to the patients that they were being fed a gruel.

Next he had the rawhide wrapping which encased the mainyard, to protect it from chafing against the shrouds, cut from the spar. It had been exposed to the sun and wind for two years and was as hard as wood, but after it was trailed overboard for three days it became softened. It was then boiled in water, cut into bits, and grilled upon embers. Only those without scurvy could chew upon it, but the Captain General doled out this tough ration to such few able bodied men as were able to gain sustenance from it.

The death-rate increased. Padre Valderrama heard the confession of each gasping sufferer and gave him the last rites of the Church. Don Antonio wrote the poor wretch's farewell message to his parents, wife, or sweetheart in his notebook. He gathered up in a cloth the few coins, the medal or holy relic, or the jackknife that the man wanted preserved and sent back to a hill village in Italy, a cabin in the Basque mountains, or a fisherman's hut in Brittany. The little packages all were duly labeled and put in Don Antonio's chest. (Later, from Seville, he piously sent these keepsakes to their scattered destinations by the hands of wandering friars.)

Magellan gave humble thanks to the Almighty for the good trade wind that so steadily continued to blow them westward, and he implored the continued intercession of the Holy Mother of God to avert any storms or calms, either of which would have put an end to all their sufferings. Even a brisk gale would have caused the loss of their canvas, for there were not half a dozen men now able to struggle with a billowing sail or pull on a straining sheet. The weather continued good, and the ships sailed on and on with their starving, dying crews. No land showed on the empty horizon.

On February 24, 1521, the log shows that the armada had reached 12° N. latitude; on February 27th, the position was 13° N. latitude, the course was altered from northwest to west-northwest, and on the same day was changed to due west. Magellan was desperately trying to find the Philippines.

At last, on March 5, 1521, there was absolutely nothing left to eat. Twenty-five men in the fleet were so weakened by scurvy and hunger that they could not stand, but lay helpless on the decks. Nineteen members of the company had been buried at sea, dead of scurvy. Those who had escaped the acute attacks of the disease were so weakened by starvation that they had to cling to the rail or rigging as they lurched about, and some crawled on their hands and knees to save themselves from falling. The hallucinations of seeing land increased, and the cry of "Land ho!" sounded feebly at intervals all during the day. Nobody any longer paid it any attention.

At dusk, the Captain General sent a *grumete* named Navarro to the crow's nest to look ahead for reefs, for by now the armada no longer hove to at night, in spite of the danger of driving ahead in the darkness in an unknown ocean. The crews lacked the strength and the will to haul upon the heavy sails twice daily, and Magellan had fatalistically decided to run whatever risk there might be. Moreover, he knew that in their desperate situation they could not afford to lose the fifty or sixty miles of westing progress which the nightly run represented.

When young Navarro had laboriously climbed to the crow's nest at the masthead, he peered across the sea and thought he saw a dim, low-lying cloud on the horizon. In the twilight it looked convincingly like an island, but he could not be sure; the darkness closed in and he lost it to view. When he came down upon the deck, he mentioned his vivid impression. His statement was listened to with skepticism, and one of the men told Navarro feelingly that he gladly would give him the gold ring he wore if they saw land in the morning. Several others made similar pledges. The canny sailor extended the conversation and secured additional promises of jewelry from others of the circle about him.

At the first break of day, Navarro climbed the ratlines to the main top. Sure enough, far ahead on the starboard was a mountain peak. He could hardly doubt it, but he held his peace and waited impatiently as the false dawn disappeared and darkness again reigned. Shortly the sky again lightened, and he saw clearly a land mass with a high mountain. Twice he wet his lips and swallowed, twice he tried to cry out, and only a squawk came. Then he mastered himself and, with tears running down his cheeks and in a queer, cracking voice that was not his own, he screamed, "Praise God! Praise God! Land! Land! Land! Land!" Then he burst out in a fit of weeping.

Below him on the deck there were raucous shouts, shrill laughter, and yells. Dying men tottered to the rail, men previously too weak to walk clambered up the shrouds like monkeys. Someone touched off the lombard that was kept loaded on the poop as an emergency signal. Minutes later there were answering flashes and loud booms from the Victoria and the

Concepción, and the standard of Castile was hoisted on each ship. Everyone was drunk with joy, laughing, leaping, hugging his neighbor, thumping him on the back. Men who had not spoken to each other for weeks exchanged friendly grins. Magellan, standing aloft on the poop deck, smiled through his tears like an indulgent father. Father Valderrama raised the Cross, and the ship's company wept unashamedly as they intoned the *Laudate Domine.* The men crowded about Navarro, the sailor who had first seen land, and insisted on carrying out their half jocular promises of reward to him. So many pieces of jewelry were pressed upon the simple sailor that Gines de Mafra, the pilot, records that their total value must have amounted to a hundred ducats, about fifteen hundred dollars today, and a snug fortune at that time.

At noon, while they were sailing directly for the peak, a larger, low island was seen on the port bow; it was nearer, so the course was changed for it. By sunset the men could see that it was heavily wooded and had high, red cliffs. Several waterfalls which dashed down the rocks into the sea made the thirsty men lick their lips. As the armada drew near, the wind died away. It was a night of moonlight, so the sails were not struck, but the flotilla barely moved. All night the fleet lay almost motionless, and at dawn they coasted along until the watchers crowding the rail sighted a break in the cliffs and saw a little bay between the shoulders of the highlands. They could make out a number of canoes drawn up on its sandy beach, while back from the shore a row of thatched houses on stilts was visible.

Never had any port looked so welcome. Magellan felt friendly to the whole world, but particularly to the unknown people in that little settlement. However, he had his responsibilities, so he ordered the *alguacil* to arm as many marines as were fit for duty. He also ordered the cannon to be loaded and the lombardiers with lighted fuses to stand by. The *capitana* entered the harbor while the other two ships hove to outside the bar. The lead showed good soundings, and Magellan decided to anchor. It was an open question whether there were men aboard with enough vigor to drop the sails quickly at the word of command. The Captain General decided to station his strongest men at the anchor, and he solved the question of the sails by ordering the master and countermaster to be ready with axes. At his signal, they cut the halyards, and the heavy canvas came down on the run. The anchor was let go, and the ship lay with its broadside pointing to the village.

The launching of the skiff was the next problem for the enfeebled men, trembling with weakness, but after much straining and several mishaps the boat was clumsily shoved over the side. It hit the water with a great splash, but fortunately did not fill and sink. Before the landing party could man it to get ashore, dozens of native sailing canoes came dashing up. They were a new type of canoe to the Europeans, dugouts hollowed out of a tree trunk with a large wooden outrigger floating parallel to the canoe and lashed to two smaller cross spars which held it in place. Each had a lateen sail, made of broad dried banana or palm leaves stitched together, and was manned by four men. They used round-bladed paddles with a carved handle which extended to a long, tapering point, so that it might be used as a harpoon. The boatmen showed their dexterity by circling the Trinidad, darting about and crossing one another's path in all directions. Although the breeze was very light, they turned and changed course as swiftly as Bedouin cavalrymen in a review.

At a signal, half a dozen dugouts suddenly converged upon the Trinidad and came alongside. The natives swarmed aboard in a manner disconcerting to Magellan. They were stalwart warriors, in prime physical condition, their muscles rippling beneath their light tan skin. Each was naked except for a belt of decorated tapa cloth about his waist, and into this was thrust a stone knife with the handle wrapped in birdskin. They carried light, concave shields about five feet by three, formed of several pieces of wood joined with rattan lashings. These were painted with geometric designs in black and red and bore tufts of human hair at intervals. Their only missile weapons were spears of chestnut, about ten feet long, with four long barbed edges carved out of the shaft just behind a tip of obsidian, flint, or a sharp fish bone. Some of the spears were serrated slashing weapons, with jagged edges made of small triangular shark's teeth firmly lashed to the shaft by sinews through pierced holes in the base of the teeth. Besides his spear, each man had a light war club carved of chestnut, stained black, with the handle wrapped in a multicolored basket weave.

They wore no ornaments except a single strip of bright tapa cloth drawn about the forehead to keep their long brown hair out of their eyes. They were not tattooed or disfigured, but had high cheek bones, straight noses, thin lips, and brown eyes. Fearless in bearing, the islanders showed no feeling of inferiority to the white men, and, after scrutinizing them and the details of the ship, they commenced what was no less than a wholesale looting of everything portable. They picked up hatchets, pails, ladles, knives, or anything within reach. They had never seen metals before and were especially fascinated by objects of steel, which they smelt, licked, tapped, and scratched.

As more and more canoes came alongside, the Captain General became alarmed and had himself quickly armored, ordering Don Antonio and such others as were strong enough to do so to hurry and do likewise. He stationed the *alguacil* and his marines on the poop deck and had several small cannon trained on the waist. Such natives as were on the poop deck were now ordered off by the *alguacil* with friendly but firm gestures. They started to obey good humoredly, but took with them to the waist deck whatever they had appropriated. Magellan then called to the sailors to reclaim their belongings, but the natives showed indignation when asked to surrender their prizes and refused to give them up. When the feeble, sick sailors attempted to seize them, the powerful savages contemptuously shoved them aside. In the struggle, one of the crew fell to the deck and, in his weakened condition, lay there helpless. The savages seemed much amused, and one of them arrogantly kicked the fallen man. Magellan shouted to his men on the waist deck to withdraw quickly to the forecastle and poop, as he was going to open fire upon the intruders.

As one of the *grumetes* started up the steps to the quarter-deck, a tall, muscular chief laughingly seized him by the shoulder, spun him around, and flung him headlong against the bulwark. Then, with a shout of derision, he thrust out his foot and tripped another who was hurrying to leave the waist. The Captain General nodded to Espinosa, who aimed his crossbow and loosed the shaft. The feathered butt appeared protruding from the chief's chest. He plucked the arrow out with a wrench and dumbly inspected its crimson head, while the dark arterial blood spurted from his wound. As he looked vacantly at the strange missile, he collapsed, while his stupefied companions gazed uncomprehending upon his extinction. Magellan gave a command, and half a dozen crossbows twanged. At such short range every shot was effective, and the deck was covered with writhing, moaning natives. The others disappeared over the side in a flash, but the lateen-sailed craft that fled back to shore bore with them the Trinidad's skiff, the savages having cut the painter and stolen the boat even in their moment of retreat. Magellan was amazed at their presence of mind in the face of their surprise, and he realized they would be formidable foes.

The men-at-arms impetuously rushed down the stairs from the quarter-deck and started to dispatch the wounded with their halberds, but the Captain General shouted that they were to be spared and made prisoners, as he wanted to question them. The marines were too excited to hear the command and butchered all but one slightly wounded warrior, whom Espinosa managed to save.

Magellan was greatly disturbed by this outbreak and realized that, since blood had been shed, he would be unable to barter for food with the natives. Yet he could not blame himself for having ordered the arrows shot. The situation had almost got out of hand, and he felt that nothing but prompt action had saved the crew from being massacred. He was by nature and by training inclined to conciliation, but he also had learned from experience to watch for cunning and treachery.

We now know that the Chamorros of Guam were, in their confident ignorance and their calm assumption of pre-eminent property rights, more to be feared than if they had been a wily and malicious people. Magellan called the Chamorros *ladrones,* or thieves, and named Guam the Island of Thieves, but he did not, of course, know their ethnic background. They were descended from a group of light-colored Polynesian sea wanderers who at some distant period had landed upon the Mariana archipelago. They conquered the black, wooly haired Melanesian dwellers in the islands but, instead of massacring them, made them helots. The warriors who came aboard the Trinidad were of this privileged caste, taught by their priests that they were the chosen sons of the immortal gods and entitled to enjoy the earth and all its fruits.

When they first saw the white men, they thought they must be supernatural visitors, and, although some of the boldest of the chiefs came out in their canoes to greet them, they did so with reverence. The vigorous savages respected only physical strength, and they found the great ships manned by a few feeble men who could barely stand and move about, while many others lay helpless on the deck, disfigured by their disease. Their sense of racial superiority reasserted itself, and they showed scorn for the pale weaklings. They saw many tempting novelties which they appropriated, not as thieves, but as children would grasp such things without knowing their nature or use.

After the canoes drew away, Ferdinand Magellan stood despairingly surveying the bloody scene. The landfall had turned out badly, and he did not know how to right the disaster. It was terrible to be so near vegetables, fruit, and water, and to be unable to relieve his men. The islanders had brought no provisions at all aboard with them. He must at once get food for his crew, and now, of course, it would have somehow to be obtained by force, costly though that might be.

The Captain General decided not to attempt to make a landing so late in the day, despite the need to retrieve the priceless skiff. He did not dare spend the night near the shore, and so, with aching labor, the Trinidad's anchor was weighed and the *trinqueta* unfurled to the land breeze that came at dusk. The three ships stood out to sea and lay on and off the bay all night. At dawn they stood in again, and, sailing in single line, with the leadsmen in the bows taking soundings, skirted the inner bay; each ship in turn discharged a broadside into the village. There were screams from the terrified inhabitants, who could be seen running for the interior. Magellan then led a landing party of sixty men in the three batels, and, as soon as he set foot ashore, he fell upon his knees and gave thanks to the Almighty. Then he and all the famished men hurried to the bank of a little river where they dipped their helmets and drank. The artillery fire had driven away all the villagers, and, although no bodies were found, there was much blood in evidence. Magellan left nothing to chance, but stationed a dozen crossbowmen on each of the two promontories that flanked the bay and kept a dozen in reserve with the boats on the beach, while he directed a small group in the hurried but orderly pillaging of the village. He was unable to prevent the starved raiders from gulping down some of the food instead of carrying it to the beach. An abundance of coconuts, rice, yams, and bananas was found in the large community storehouse, and many baskets of them were gathered from individual huts. Several dozen pigs and some hundreds of chickens were secured, and a number of the ships' casks were filled with water from the river.

The native warriors had been so cowed by the gunfire that they made no attempt to harass the retiring raiders. The three batels rowed triumphantly back to the ships, loaded with food and water, and towing behind them the unharmed skiff of the Trinidad.

No sooner were the provisions and water casks taken on board than the Captain General, fearing a night attack, raised the anchors and sailed hastily away from the unfriendly port. His caution in putting to sea was justified by the sight of a swarm of lateen-sailed dugouts which, to his surprise, now followed them out of the bay. The Spaniards thought they had destroyed all canoes, but evidently the natives must have kept a number up the river, out of sight from the beach. They sailed in their swift outriggers ahead of and around the slow *naos,* even impudently passing between the Trinidad and its laboring batel, which had been too heavy for the weak seamen to hoist back on deck and was being towed. When the hostile flotilla was reinforced by a number of other canoes which sailed out from various points along the coast, the Captain General had the cannon loaded with small stones and held ready, but he took no action. The frustrated natives showed their hatred by gibes and grimaces, but they could do no harm, for they possessed neither slings nor bows and evidently were averse to hurling away their carved, decorated spears. They showered the decks with filth and with small stones, but Magellan ordered that no answering demonstration be made.

The armada cruised cautiously into the night, with only the *trinquetes* hoisted. The iron pots bubbled with savory stews of chicken, rice, and pork. Everyone who was able gorged on baked yams and bananas, which Don Antonio called long figs. Enrique the Malay baked a breadfruit whole over the embers and mixed its starchy contents with the milk of the coconut to make a pudding which was easily absorbed by the sick men; it did them more good than any medicine. Some, however, were too far gone to be able to assimilate food, and one of these was the able Constable of the *lombarderos,* Master Andrew of Bristol, the only Englishman in the armada.

Although the booty from Guam had saved the armada from starvation, it would be consumed in a few days, and once again there would be no food aboard the ships. The Captain General therefore immediately led the way to the nearby island now called Rota. No sooner had the anchors plunged into the water of a little bay than several outrigger canoes bearing armed warriors paddled up near the fleet. The circumspection with which they held their distance was evidence that the punishment inflicted at Guam had been reported to Rota. Fortunately they had kept one Chamorro prisoner, and he was made to understand what they wanted and act as interpreter. He called to the canoes that the white, supernatural visitors desired to purchase some fruits, nuts, and chickens from them, and that for these stores they would receive treasures of fabulous worth, knives and hatchets for shipbuilding infinitely better than anything they knew. He said the white men promised to do no harm to the island, and he asked that some principal chiefs come to visit the *capitana* and arrange the transactions.

The scouts in the canoes listened intently to the message and called back a number of questions. Then they raced their dugouts toward shore, balancing them so that the heavy wooden outriggers which were useful in sailing were entirely out of the water and did not impede their progress in paddling.

About noon, a larger ship, made by building a platform across two canoes, and bearing a grass hut on its deck, shoved off from the beach. Its lateen sails quickly brought it near, and Magellan observed that the painted prow of each of its pontoons rose high in the air and was carved into the shape of sharks' heads, with shells for eyes and real sharks' teeth. As it drew alongside, a conch shell was blown as a horn and there was a tattoo of drums. Three men nimbly came aboard. They evidently were priests, but it was impossible to tell their age or to identify their features, for each one wore a mask made of coconut shell pierced for the eyes and nose, with a grinning row of shark's teeth, and topped by a great wig of human hair dyed crimson. They wore short cloaks of yellow and red feathers. One had a large ivory whale tooth as a pendant from his neck. Another had a collar formed of the tusks of boars, from which was suspended a little leather bag, and the third carried, mounted on a staff, the wooden figure of a little idol. Each had attached, above his right knee, a human skull in which pebbles rattled as he walked, and each bore painted coconut-shell rattles with human thighbones as handles.

The Captain General had Enrique and the Chamorro prisoner display the goods to be offered in trade, and explain the ratio of exchange for specific fruits, vegetables, swine, and poultry. He intentionally made lavish offers to insure getting the precious provisions quickly, for he thought the roadstead would be dangerous in case of storm, and he also wanted to get to sea to avoid a surprise attack. He conveyed to his visitors his intention of sailing that same night and was able to cut short the usual native chaffering. Before long the large boat went back to shore for the provisions, and by dusk the entire transaction had been completed.

Magellan had felt unhappy about the slaughter of the chiefs aboard the Trinidad and the bombardment of the village of Umatac. Unavoidable though these bloody actions had been, he particularly regretted them because he realized that the archipelago would probably fall within his own future province as Governor of the Pacific. Guam would probably become an important port of call, a base for his ships on their voyages to and from Maluco through the *paso*. He foresaw that Guam might eventually hold the same important relation to the Spanish oriental empire as Mozambique in East Africa held to Portuguese India. Therefore it was essential to erase, if possible, the bad impression created by his first visit. He tried to win the good will of the three priestly visitors by giving them handsome presents when they left the Trinidad. He especially rewarded the prisoner from Guam with gifts which to him were almost regal and released him from captivity. The gratified Chamorro, after accepting all the gifts, asked to be allowed to accompany the expedition. As he would be of considerable value as an interpreter, the Captain General welcomed his services and entered him on the rolls in that capacity.

On March 9, 1521, as the evening star rose over the forested shore and the first watch was called for the night, the *Armada de Maluco* set out to sea with a westerly wind. Before long the Isle of Rota had faded away in the moonlight. The fleet sailed on a west-southwest course for a week and passed numerous small, forested islands. The Captain General did not wish to lose time by stopping nor to risk encounters with other unfriendly islanders. The sick men had responded to the curative effects of fresh victuals and had benefited from the general spirit of elation of the crew. The sailors boasted that their achievements to date had been epochal, for they had not only found and traversed the *paso* about which the scholars of Europe had debated for decades, but they had also discovered and crossed the legendary Great South Sea and would, without doubt, very soon confound the world by reaching the Spiceries.

Ferdinand Magellan was no longer followed by scowls, but was treated with deference by all. He responded to the change in atmosphere, threw off his grim aspect, and became expansive and affable. His comrades recognized that in the future their leader would take his place as one of the high dignitaries of the Empire, secure in honors, offices, and possessions, and that his comrades could look forward to participating in the magnificent rewards which the Emperor would bestow upon him.

Almost all the crewmen and officers were still suffering from the frightful aftermath of scurvy, and some remained crippled, with swollen joints, loosened teeth, and lingering body sores. Nevertheless, so great was the rebound of their spirits that again there were squabbles over their comparative shares in the spoils to be taken at Maluco.

At 11° N. latitude, Ferdinand Magellan sighted a cape which proved to be the extremity of a large island. This was on March 16, 1521, the day of St. Lazarus, and according to his custom he named it the Island of St. Lazarus. It was, in fact, the southern end of the Island of Samar, and Magellan had again discovered the Philippine Islands. He had apparently come upon the same archipelago, on his secret voyage from Malacca in 1512, from the opposite or South China Sea side, at the same latitude of 11° N., perhaps at the Calamian Island group or the Isle of Mindoro. Since he reached the Philippines the second time *from the opposite direction,* it is evident that he was the first man ever to complete the circumnavigation of the globe.

CHAPTER XIX

THE PHILIPPINES

THE little fleet followed the coast of the large island of Samar on a southwest course for some time. Then Magellan turned south; as the waters were full of shoals, he thought it best to anchor for the night off the small island of Suluan. Next morning he continued on the southerly course, and at dusk they anchored in a sheltered bay at the wooded island of Homonhon, in Leyte Gulf about eleven miles south of Samar. At dawn he sent an exploring party ashore. After some hours the party returned, reporting the island to be about ten miles by five in extent, quite uninhabited, but with abandoned taro and rice fields and groves of coconut and breadfruit trees. Since they were soon to enter the zone of Maluco and perhaps encounter a Portuguese armada there, Magellan decided it would be well to stop in this safe harbor to repair the hulls and rigging and give the invalids a chance to recuperate. His first care was to anchor in protected positions, for he knew the danger of typhoons in this area. Then he set the men to building an encampment consisting of a stockade on a bluff, with a battery that commanded the port, and tents in a pleasant grove for the sick men. Magellan made it a practice to visit each sick man every morning without fail, giving each sufferer an orange and pouring a cupful of fresh coconut milk for him. Don Antonio says that this personal attention on the part of the Captain General did much to help the invalids recover. Squads of the able-bodied were assigned to careen the ships and repair the spars and rigging. The remainder of the company were given liberty ashore to hunt, fish, or wander at will about the island.

Omatu, the Chamorro from Guam, told them which plants and fruits were edible and which poisonous. He was of particular help in selecting greens for salads for the sick, and prepared a beneficial gruel called poi from the taro root. He brought them such unknown fruits as the mangosteen, the mango, and the papaya, as well as the custard-apple which they nicknamed "bull's heart." He located an old plantation, on the far side of the island, and from it kept the patients amply supplied with bananas and coconuts. Don Antonio, in his journal, enthusiastically described the general utility of the coconut palm. A few trees grown in a back yard, he asserted, would supply a household with the equivalents of butter, vinegar, wine, oil, bread, and milk, besides providing cordage, thatch, utensils, and other useful items.

Many of the sailors gravitated to the shore and called upon Omatu to help them fish and hunt mollusks. He led them thigh-deep out on the reef to spear rock cod and demonstrated how to pin down the seven-foot Moray eel that lies in ambush in the corals, ready to tear off a man's leg with one bite of its sawlike teeth. He also taught them how to slash away the grasping tentacles of the octopus.

The Spaniards had been on the island two days when, on Monday, March 18, 1521, the lookout reported the approach of a canoe carrying ten armed men. They proved friendly, but neither Enrique nor Omatu was able to converse with them except by signs. They were light in color, muscular, and had long black hair, glossy with coconut oil, which they also used as a body ointment. Their gums and teeth were stained dark red from chewing betel nut. As a gesture of courtesy, they offered the sailors some of the betel, and, although the Spaniards were repelled by the constant spitting, Magellan pretended to partake with gusto. He was elated to observe the prevalence of this habit, for it seemed to him definite evidence that they were approaching the East Indies.

Three days later, the chief who ruled the area arrived. He was a dignified, elderly man, and Magellan greeted him with ceremony. His face was tattooed, and he wore no clothes except a skirt made of woven cloth resembling cotton and adorned by a tasselled fringe of silk. The presence of silk was evidence to Magellan of trading contact with the Orient. His weapons, instead of being made of bone or flint, were fashioned of a bronze metal with a high tin content. This was the first time any of the aborigines they had met on the entire voyage had possessed any metal. He wore earrings, armlets, and bracelets, all of gold, and his shield, javelin and dagger were gold-encrusted. The Spaniards became excited at this, but Magellan cautioned them to act indifferent toward gold, as if it were of no value to them.

When they asked him questions about spices, in sign language, the chief was unable to understand what they meant. However, he was able to explain that the island on which they found themselves was called

Homonhon; it and the island from which he came, called Suluan, were part of an immense archipelago stretching north for hundreds of miles. In describing the immense group, the old chief conveyed to Magellan in pantomime that they once had all been part of a single piece of inhabited land which a kindly giant had carried upon his shoulders. This patient giant finally grew indignant at the constant quarrels of the ungrateful men he was serving so unselfishly, so he flung his burden into the sea. It broke into seven thousand fragments which became the islands that lay ahead of them.

Magellan was deeply moved to learn that he had discovered such a vast realm for King Charles, a realm of which he himself would be *Adelantado,* or Governor. Under the terms of his contract with the crown, he would be entitled to claim two of the best islands for himself and his heirs forever, as lord donatory.

Don Antonio had a narrow escape on the morning of the last day at the island. Alone aboard the Trinidad, instead of being ashore with most of the company, he was idly fishing over the side when he had to jump up on the wet bulwark to pull in a catch, but he slipped on the slimy surface and fell overboard. He was half drowned, he says, when he managed to clutch a rope dangling from the ship. However, he could not get up the side and had to cling to the rope for some time before anyone heard his shouts and came to his rescue. It would have been strange had he been drowned in a quiet harbor, from an anchored ship, after living through the tempests of two oceans. He writes, "I was saved not, I believe, through my own merits, but through the mercy of that font of charity, the most Blessed Virgin Mary."

Ten days on Homonhon, where they rested lazily or bathed in the shark-free waters inside the reef, and were nourished by suitable food, restored most of the scurvy sufferers to health. When the armada set sail again, on the afternoon of March 25, 1521, it was once more manned by a vigorous complement, ready to work the ships and fight if necessary.

The fleet followed a west-southwest course, sailing only by day and taking frequent soundings. Threading narrow channels swept by swift currents, they passed four large, forested islands. The course carried the flotilla through the Surigao channel into the large Sea of Mindanao. On the third night, while anchored, they saw a large bonfire to the north. At dawn on March 28, 1521, they sailed toward the small island where they had seen the fire, off which they anchored. A small boat carrying eight men put out from shore and warily hovered near them.

Enrique hailed them with an invitation to come aboard, and, to Magellan's immense delight, he was answered in his native tongue. For Magellan this was a moment of fulfillment. These men spoke the Malay tongue of Enrique, the *lingua franca* of the East Indies. It was indisputable proof that his geographic theory had been sound, and that by sailing due west from Spain he really had reached the Orient. A rapid exchange ensued, Enrique trying to persuade the natives to trust the bearded white men and come aboard. He described the rich gifts they could expect, but the natives remained suspicious.

Enrique then tried to tempt them to visit the ship by putting some trade goods on a plank and floating it to them. They lifted up the offerings and, after calling their thanks, sailed rapidly toward a large island about ten miles to port. About three hours passed when a flat, broad-beamed *balanghai,* or barge, with a single square sail, drew near. Under a roof of nipa thatch, a dignitary reclined on mats with a number of attendants about him. Enrique again engaged in fluent conversation, and Magellan himself was able to recognize and translate some bits of the Malay for the benefit of those about him.

The island was called Limassawa, and its *datu,* or ruler, Rajah Colambu, was the individual occupying the barge. He had decided to come out himself and see the strange ships, but he declined to approach nearer, keeping just out of range of a thrown spear, not realizing that the strangers could reach him if they wished with missiles of which he was ignorant.

The Malays put a small raft overside and sent it with the current to the Trinidad. It bore fruit, vegetables, nuts, and a large earthenware pot of palm wine. There also were dishes of cooked rice, roast pork, and stewed fowl, which, to the surprise of the Europeans, were in large jars of white Chinese porcelain decorated with colored floral designs. These were of a common Canton type familiar to Magellan, and he examined them eagerly, for they confirmed the linguistic evidence of their being in the Orient. Now he was sure he had actually circumnavigated the globe.

The men of the armada loaded the raft with trade gifts and shoved it back to the Rajah. In the meantime, Enrique had answered a volley of questions across the water to the Malays, who had not drawn any nearer. He gave them an account of the long voyage from Spain, dwelt upon the omnipotence of the Emperor Charles, and elaborated upon the wondrous navigating instruments and invincible weapons which they could see if they came aboard. At last the cautious potentate agreed to send two emissaries to investigate. A canoe brought them alongside, and they were welcomed with ceremony. The Captain General received them in due state, wearing a velvet cloak and plumed hat, seated in a crimson armchair. They were fascinated by the globes, compasses, and hourglasses which Enrique exhibited to them. Then a Spanish man-at-arms in full panoply was shown them, and in a mock fight several others attacked him with swords and spears to awe the visitors with the invulnerability of the white man's armor. The envoys were then loaded with presents and sent overside with a cordial invitation to return. Before they left, they presented a case of preserved ginger and a bar of gold to the Captain General from the Rajah. Magellan accepted the ginger, but thought it politic to decline the metal, pretending a complete lack of interest in gold. Gines de Mafra wrote that, although the Captain General tactfully appeared to disprize the gold, in reality he was radiant at the sight of it, and said triumphantly to those about him: "I am now in the land I hoped to reach!" These words appear to us to be additional evidence that Ferdinand Magellan had had the gold-bearing Philippines as his goal.

The Rajah had by now become reassured as to the good faith of the white men, for he himself came aboard from the barge, followed by all his suite. The Captain General embraced him and seated him in a violet-colored armchair beside his own, ceremoniously robing him in a red and yellow bathrobe and a Turkish fez. After some hours of polite palaver, the Rajah suggested that Ferdinand Magellan and he perform the Malay ritual of *Cassi Cassi,* the blood ceremony of friendship wherein each tastes a few drops of the other's blood; the two men thereby became sworn blood brothers. As a parting gift, the Captain General gave the Rajah bolts of various colored cloth, pieces of fine linen, a handsome necklace of carved coral beads, and a small compass. They quitted each other in high spirits, and the Rajah insisted on taking Don Antonio and Enrique, the interpreter, ashore with him to show them his court.

This visit to the native village gave both Don Antonio and Enrique some qualms of conscience as Catholics, for it occured upon Good Friday, and the Rajah pressed them to partake of a dish of pork, rice, and gravy, flavored with ginger, which they felt they could not refuse to accept. The Rajah pledged them in so many drinks of palm wine that all three reached a high state of conviviality, and Don Antonio reports that Enrique finally succumbed entirely and became thoroughly drunk. When temperate Don Antonio returned to the Trinidad, he confessed to the Chaplain that he not only had eaten meat on Good Friday, but had committed the cardinal sins of gluttony and drunkenness.

It was on this night, too, March 28, 1521, that Antonio de Coca, scion of the Fonsecas and sole survivor of the Captains' Cabal, died and was buried at sea.

The squadron moved up close to the island, anchored in front of the town, and remained there for a week. A brother of Rajah Colambu, who ruled a large district known as the State of Calagan on the great neighboring island of Mindanao, now came to visit him and to participate in trading with the Europeans. This *Datu* Siaui not only wore many gold ornaments and had gold-mounted weapons, but he had three little spots of gold, spaced like a triangle, mounted in each front tooth, so that when he smiled his whole mouth glittered. He told the Spaniards that in his home all the household utensils were of gold, and he sent a canoe back for some of the precious metal for trading purposes. The canoe returned with a woven fiber sack filled with nuggets the size of hen's eggs, which he exchanged on an even basis, pound for pound, for iron. The Captain General repeatedly cautioned the men not to show their eagerness to get the gold, for only thus could they maintain its established trading parity with iron. Magellan himself, as a matter of policy, declined politely the second offer of a gift of a bar of gold, saying, to the mystification of the Rajah, that he already had more gold than he wanted.

The people of Limassawa proved very friendly, and the whites mingled with them without any fear of treachery. On Easter Sunday a solemn High Mass was celebrated ashore, with a salute of six guns from the ships at the moment of the Elevation of the Host. The natives were pagans, not Mohammedans, and were much edified by the religious ceremony; many expressed a desire to become Christians. Magellan erected a large cross, surmounted by a gilded crown of wood, on a high hill beyond the town, and formally took possession for Spain of the entire archipelago, which he called the Islands of St. Lazarus.

A council of his officers was now called by the Captain General to discuss further plans. Captains Serrano and Duarte Barbosa, along with all the other officers, emphasized that their explicit orders had been to go directly to the Spiceries and then sail back for Spain. They urged that this course should be followed. Serrano spoke feelingly of their being anxiously awaited in Ternate by Magellan's comrade, his brother, Francisco Serrano, who had acccumulated an immensely valuable cargo of spices for them, and he begged that they should not delay in reaching Ternate as quickly as possible. Ferdinand Magellan, while agreeing in principle, seems to have divulged to them that, although the discovery of so vast a group of islands had not been visualized by the King when the official, public instructions to the fleet had been issued, there had nevertheless been a secret understanding on the subject. He had privately informed His Majesty of the existence of an archipelago which he had discovered at latitude 10° N., and the King had authorized it as an objective. Magellan pointed out to his officers that the archipelago was more extensive than any previously known to Europeans, apparently greater than the Canaries, Madeira, the Azores, and the Cape Verdes combined. He was sure it was their duty to explore it more thoroughly, so as to acquaint the King with the details of his new possessions, and in order that the Crown might make formal announcement of their annexation. He had learned from Rajah Colambu that the island of Cebu, the most populous and the richest of all, lay only a few days' sail away, and it would be desirable to visit the ruler of this civilized community and secure his submission to King Charles. He asked how it would appear in Spain if they had to report they had been within a week's sail of this great province, but had not taken time to visit it. After further discussion, Magellan's views prevailed, as always. It was voted to push on for Cebu, but to make only a short stay there and then head directly for Maluco. As Don Antonio's journal ominously notes, obviously *post factum,* "The Captain General determined to go to Cebu, for so did his unhappy fate will."

Rajah Colambu had become so attached to his blood-brother Magellan that he offered to pilot the armada to Cebu and facilitate peaceful negotiations with its Rajah. The Captain General accepted his offer, and, finding that Colambu's departure was being delayed by the necessity of completing the rice harvest before setting forth, he sent ashore a hundred men from the crew to aid in gathering it. The energetic Spaniards entered with zest into the work of harvesting and completed in two days what would have taken the natives a week to accomplish. However, now the Malays insisted upon holding their time-honored harvest festival before the Rajah's departure. The Spaniards participated in this with the same wholehearted spirit as in the work, and what started as a feast, with singing and dancing, ended, as might have been expected, in a drunken orgy. The entire community became intoxicated with palm wine and the excitement of saying farewell to their white friends. Many of the crew were scattered for some days in outlying huts, and the Captain General had to send armed parties to search for the delinquents. Finally, however, the last reveler was dragged aboard, and the men set to work at the capstans and brought up the anchors. On April 3, 1521, preceded by the happy-go-lucky Rajah in a long galley, the little fleet broke out its canvas, fired a farewell broadside, and left the friendly town. Their route lay northwest through the Canigao channel until they neared the Camote Islands, and then they turned southwest toward Cebu.

They sailed past many picturesque islands, through narrow, tree-lined channels. On the second night, the breeze being favorable and the waterway open, the squadron sailed ahead in the moonlight and so outdistanced the guiding galley that the next day they had to ride at anchor, waiting for the Malays to catch up. The Rajah Colambu was so much impressed by the navigating skill of the Spaniards in being able to follow the course without his aid that he came aboard the *capitana* to stay, ordering his galley to follow behind.

As they skirted the Isle of Cebu, they were struck by the great number of large villages they saw all along the shore. The houses were built on stilts at the water's edge, and from the shoreline of each village there generally was a geometric pattern of fishweirs staked out to a considerable distance. Many outrigger craft with bright-colored cotton sails, called *prahus,* gathered about the Spanish ships and followed them in procession. None was allowed to come alongside, however, for it had been decided to treat first with the Rajah of Cebu in formal fashion. Therefore they would not accept any advances from his subjects or lesser officials, except as his authorized delegates.

When, on April 7, 1521, the fleet entered Cebu harbor, Magellan was overjoyed to see a large Chinese junk at anchor there. The appearance of this trader from Cathay showed that they were near Maluco. Don Antonio and Enrique were immediately sent ashore in a small boat with presents for the Rajah and a formal greeting from the Captain General. As they drew near the shore, they saw that the long, rickety bamboo wharf was crowded with the curious populace. Just as Don Antonio was about to clamber up the ladder to the dock, the ships fired a thunderous broadside in salute, and the crowd of natives, panic stricken, fled into the town, leaving the pier deserted. Cebu was a large city with wide streets laid out at right angles. The royal residence stood in an open plot opposite the landing place, and upon reaching it they were at once conducted into the presence of the Rajah. He was a short, fat, brown man, seated on a divan of grass rugs, and he apparently had not been perturbed by the thunder of the broadside. He wore a yellow silk turban and a loin cloth. His face was broad, with high cheekbones and a flat nose, and was tattooed with purple and red geometric patterns that extended to his torso. He wore gold earrings and a necklace of large pearls, and his thick fingers were bedecked with jewelled gold rings. He was sucking palm wine through a reed from a flowered porcelain jar, and occasionally selected and ate a turtle's egg from a decorated Chinese lacquer bowl on a cushion by his side. A double row of chiefs, wearing silk turbans of varied colors, hempen vests decorated with beads, shells, or sequins of copper, and white cotton kilts that reached from waist to knee, stood behind him. They had beaded cloth belts embroidered with silk, and in these were thrust copper daggers, or krisses, with wavy blades and bone hilts mounted with gold.

Standing directly behind the Rajah was a man of lighter complexion than the others, whose features looked Arabian. His turban, vest, and broad sash were of silk, and he wore cotton trousers and cloth shoes, whereas the Malay chiefs with whom he was grouped were barelegged. Enrique recognized him at once to be an Arab trader, probably from the Kingdom of Siam, and assumed him to be the owner of the junk in the harbor.

Don Antonio and Enrique made a grave obeisance, and Enrique informed the Rajah that their master was a subject of the Emperor of Europe, the greatest King on earth, and had been sent on a voyage to seek spices from the Isle of Maluco. He explained that the squadron had stopped at Limassawa for provisions, and, hearing there of the wealth and importance of the Rajah of Cebu, they had come to offer him the friendship of their great ruler and to trade their merchandise for food-stuffs.

The Rajah listened in impassive silence. When Don Antonio presented him with two handsome Venetian glass beakers decorated in gilt, he glanced at them and set them to one side without comment, although Don Antonio thought he could perceive a gleam of appreciation in his eyes. The Rajah, still silent, reached for an oblong box of bronze inlaid with silver and helped himself to a chew of betel nut. He chewed upon this, and reflected for a moment, then said affably that the visitors were welcome, but that of course they would have to pay the usual charges collected from any ships entering the port.

Enrique had been well coached by Magellan, so he answered firmly that his master, the Captain General, the representative of the great Emperor, would not expect even to be asked to submit to any commercial charges. The Rajah replied suavely that no exceptions could be made. He pointed out the Arab as another foreigner who had just arrived with a trading cargo, and who, although an annual visitor, had to conform to this rule. In accordance with his instructions, Enrique said stiffly and coldly, "My master offers you peace, but if you ask for war, it is all one with him. Although a peaceful man, he will brook no affronts to the dignity of his lord, the Emperor." The Rajah frowned at these audacious words and half rose from his cushion. There was a general growl from the chiefs about him, and Don Antonio heard a disquieting rattle of wooden scabbards. Although unable to understand the exchange of words, he was alarmed at the resentful expression of the Rajah, but nevertheless tried to preserve a resolute appearance. Enrique was relieved, Don Antonio writes, to hear the Siamese trader say audibly to the Rajah that these were the same white men who had conquered Calicut, Goa, and Malacca. "Provoke them and they are terrible in their wrath, but deal with them peaceably and they will trade fairly, and you will greatly benefit thereby," said the trader. The Rajah sank back on his cushion, swallowed a couple of times, and had recourse to his betel nut. He composed himself, smiled, and said amicably that he would refer the question to his council for deliberation and would advise them in two days of his decision.

Enrique then respectfully remarked that he could not help but understand the words of the merchant, for they had been spoken in his native tongue. He hoped the Rajah would not think him rude if he pointed out that the white men described by the merchant as having performed such great exploits in the Indies were Portuguese, a European people inferior in warlike strength to the Spaniards, whose King was also Emperor of all Europe and whose enmity was even more to be feared than that of the Portuguese. Having thus turned the situation to his advantage, Enrique recited the friendly and ceremonious message to the Rajah which the

Captain General had dictated to him, and which Don Antonio quotes in full. It was composed in altruistic terms and conveyed Magellan's honorable intentions toward the islanders.

Don Antonio reports that the Rajah seemed favorably impressed by this declaration of friendly purpose. He says that *el Moro,* or the moor, as he called the Arab, explained the thought behind Enrique's message and elaborated upon it. Don Antonio was relieved that the influential Siamese trader apparently was not unfavorable to their mission, and he judged that he must have had friendly relations with the European merchants at Malacca.

The Rajah dismissed them with a show of polite consideration and promised to send his answer to the Captain General, at the same time ordering that the envoys be served with refreshments before they withdrew. Immediately slaves placed many porcelain platters of meat before them, and poured palm wine from jars.

Shortly after their return aboard ship, a boat came alongside bearing large hampers of rice and baskets of oranges, lemons, and bananas, a gift from the Rajah. The next morning Rajah Colambu, who was on very friendly terms with the Rajah of Cebu, went ashore and informed his brother potentate of the satisfactory relations he himself had with the Spaniards.

Don Antonio details the various interchanges between the Captain General and the Rajah. Suffice it to say that these resulted in the establishment of cordial relations and the offer of the Rajah to become a Christian and a vassal of the Emperor.

In the meantime, the commercial aims of the expedition had not been neglected. A store was set up in a large house on the beach, a quantity of merchandise was transferred ashore, counters were set up, scales hung, and a schedule of exchange decided upon. Leon de Ezpeleta, the purser of the Trinidad, was put in charge and was assisted by the pursers of the other ships. The *Casa de Antillas* had strict rules regarding all trading done by its ship captains, and detailed records had to be kept. Magellan therefore instructed the accountant and the notary on each ship to supervise the transactions of the purser of their vessel. It was the rule that, once a ship came back to Seville, the funds and cargo were embargoed until the auditors of the *Casa* had made a careful check of all the books, and the captain was held accountable for every *maravedi.* Magellan was well aware that he would be subjected to an unusually strict audit. Not only the *Casa de Antillas,* but also the banking syndicate represented by Cristóbal de Haro, would require an accounting of the large investment confided to his care. Accordingly he took pains to see that every formality was observed and that accurate records were kept.

The inhabitants of these islands were accustomed to the use of weights and measures. Don Antonio describes their scales as similar to those used at the European fairs, and he says the natives were fair in trade. Although the Spaniards wanted gold and pearls, they pretended to be reluctant to accept gold in exchange for iron and bronze. There was little else the natives had to offer beyond goats, fowl, coconuts, ginger, rice, sugar cane, fruit, and palm wine. The only native handicraft, apart from woven hempen cloth and embroidery, was the manufacture of cast bronze utensils and ornaments. There were several small foundries at Cebu, with two or three workers each, where they cast in bronze by the "lost wax" method. A few items were also hammered or stamped out of sheet bronze. The Spaniards acquired some specimens of this bronze work to take back to Spain, such as mortars and pestles, rice measures, hand gongs, lamps, wine bowls and flagons, and inlaid boxes for betel. However, once a representative group of samples was secured, no more of this primitive bronze work was desired. Thereafter, the Spanish traders accepted gold with pretended reluctance, since it was supposedly the only marketable commodity that the natives had left to offer. On this basis a considerable amount of gold was traded for iron, and Don Antonio says that the rate of exchange was ten pieces of gold (worth fifteen ducats) for fourteen pounds of iron, or in modern times about sixteen dollars in gold for a pound of iron.

Don Antonio's journal recounts that a transformation now came over the leader of the armada, and these commercial operations became quite secondary. Magellan, whose sense of his God-given mission was always profound, became obsessed with a fervent missionary zeal. The sincerity and fanaticism of his purpose soon infected many of the other Spaniards, and the diary now reflected Don Antonio's preoccupation with proselyting among the natives. The Captain General, Don Antonio, Cristóbal Rabelo, and Padre Valderrama devoted themselves untiringly to the saving of pagan souls. Don Antonio quotes many of the homilies that Magellan delivered so earnestly to the people of Cebu, in which he seems to have been quite carried away by his own eloquence.

Don Antonio had presumably been sent by the Signory of Venice to observe and report on the possibilities for a spice trade directly between Spain and Maluco, an assignment which must have been very agreeable to his natural interest in the commercial side of the undertaking. Venice had never been active in converting either pagans or Moslems, but had always respected the creeds of all peoples, so he was completely inexperienced in the practice or theory of the kind of crusade for conversions that now occupied his leader's mind. Perhaps it was a combination of two factors that swayed him, a kind of nervous reaction in himself after the terrible dangers of the voyage, and the novelty of undertaking now to spread Christianity. At any rate, Don Antonio no longer gave thought to the spice trade, but seemed as obsessed as Magellan with Christianizing the pagans of Cebu.

As for the acquisition of gold from the natives, Magellan's two captains by no means neglected their opportunities. Both Duarte Barbosa and John Serrano disregarded the strict prohibition of private trading which Magellan had promulgated, now that their leader's whole attention was turned toward heaven rather than the market place. These two had once been closely associated in business in India, both were mercantile-minded, and they apparently carried on a surreptitious trade in gold and in pearls behind Magellan's back.

The formal christening of *Datu* Humabon, Rajah of Cebu, whose conversion had just been made, now occupied the minds of the Christian enthusiasts. The last difficult problem was solved when Magellan tolerantly overlooked the doctrine of monogamy. He succeeded in prevailing upon Padre Valderrama not to press the point, but to baptize the ruler and his plural wives at the same time. The ceremony, according to Don Antonio, was made as impressive as possible. The costumes of the participants were breath-taking, and there was a parade, with banners and bands, and with the strictest protocol governing who went before whom. The pagan idols were destroyed in a supreme act of renunciation by the natives, and a Christian altar was erected. Finally occurred the solemn military Mass, followed by the baptism of the Rajah, of his queens, and of his relatives and courtiers.

After the main ceremony, the populace formed in long lines for baptism, mothers leading their children and carrying infants. At last the exhausted priest, weighed down by his heavy, stiff vestments, could no longer even mutter the holy ritual. He had no strength left to raise his arms in blessing, and in the late afternoon thousands of would-be converts had to be turned away. For the balance of the week, the devoted Padre worked every day administering the holy rites, until at last he triumphantly announced that most of the subjects of the Rajah had become duly accepted children of the Holy Church.

Magellan was filled with elation at the successful demonstration that civilized Christianity could be brought to the heathen in the manner prescribed by its founder, preaching love and charity and peaceful brotherhood. He well might feel triumphant, for he had gained the salvation of many souls, in addition to securing for Don Charles the willing fealty of a populous province whose very existence had hitherto been unknown to Europe. Padre Valderrama was in ecstasy with all the conversions. The proselyting dream of Ferdinand Magellan did indeed take permanent form, for to this day the people of these islands number millions of Catholics and constitute the only Christian commonwealth in all Asia.

Magellan now concentrated upon consolidating his Christian kingdom. He learned that some of the caciques, or chiefs, of outlying villages, had failed to desert their idols, and he at once summoned them before him. In the presence of the Christian King, as he now styled the Rajah, he demanded the immediate surrender of the wooden idols for destruction. He threatened the caciques with death, and their villages with fire, should they persist in their idolatry. Despite Magellan's previous fair words, this amounted to forced conversion, a practice by no means uncommon even up to recent times, and certainly more the rule than the exception in the sixteenth century. He had several old women arrested and punished for concealing figures of their heathen gods, and he upbraided the Christian King for retaining some household images.

Ferdinand Magellan, Padre Valderrama, Cristóbal Rabelo, and Don Antonio were so engrossed in preaching the principles of upright Christian behavior that they were the last to know what was going on at the same time behind the Captain General's back. Magellan's two captains and many of their followers were, in fact, engaging in loose and drunken behavior ashore, even going so far as to raid the harems of the chiefs by force. Although the extent of their disgraceful nocturnal excesses was by tacit conspiracy hidden from Magellan, his native converts knew and were scandalized. It finally became impossible to keep Duarte Barbosa's absence on a spree from his knowledge, and, just as once before, he had to arrest and shackle his incorrigible friend in order to bring him back to sobriety. This time he felt himself forced to demote Barbosa from command and to entrust the captaincy of the Victoria to the dependable but inexperienced Cristóbal Rabelo.

The visit of the Christian armada to Cebu had now degenerated into a saturnalia completely incompatible with the high pretensions of its Christian commander. As we have seen, the armada was mostly manned by very youthful sailors, and the Captain General himself was only forty-one. The men had had no female companionship since leaving Brazil sixteen months before, and when they were given unlimited shore leave in the sensuous environment of polygamous Cebu, their reactions were inevitable. It was the native custom for only married women to wear clothing; the maidens' innocent nudity was a further cause of demoralization to the seamen. The young sailors had been reared in the prurient belief that human nakedness was sinful, and now they ran wild. Just as in Brazil, a lad who had a jackknife or a few iron fishhooks to trade could obtain all the feminine companionship he wished.

Magellan attempted to curb this license by invoking the wrath of the Church. He had Padre Valderrama assemble the crew and denounce it as a mortal sin for any Christian man to hold intercourse with a pagan woman. The result of this sermon was paradoxical. The simple and forthright sailors became ardent apostles of Christianity and artlessly baptized any women with whom they proposed to have intercourse; they thereby joyously furthered the Christianizing of the populace. Don Antonio says that the native women preferred the white men to the native males as lovers. The women's preference for the more vigorous Europeans deeply wounded the pride of the Filipino chieftains, and quite naturally aroused their jealousy. Relations between the two races were rapidly reaching an explosive pitch, but Magellan, in his ecstatic state of religious fervor, remained oblivious of the imminent crisis.

The practical veterans of the fleet, Serrano, Barbosa, Carvalho, and others who had dealt at arms' length with dozens of native potentates, all were disturbed by the state of religious exaltation in which Magellan had become enveloped. They thought his indulgent and sympathetic attitude toward the Filipinos complete folly. This cynicism of the leaders was natural and reflected the viewpoint of their caste. They all had been trained in the Iberian school of colonial administration, and their attitude toward weaker populations was as pitiless as that of da Gama, Albuquerque, Cortes, and Pizarro. Had any one of them been Captain General at Cebu, slavery would have been the lot of the natives rather than the clasped hand of Christian brotherhood. They resented Magellan's altruistic attitude, his apostasy toward his own militant class, and also his neglect of mercantile considerations. Magellan was, perhaps, not wholly ahead of his own day in his kindliness toward the Filipinos, for his policy was that advocated by las Casas in the Spanish colonies and by Francis Xavier in the Portuguese territories; they, however, were priests, and he was a man of the sword. His captains considered that he was yielding to the influence of Padre Valderrama, and thought he would do better to listen to their own realistic counsel.

After the *Datu* Humabon had been baptized in the name of Rajah Charles, the Captain General thereafter formally referred to him as the Christian King. This was evidence of Magellan's far-reaching intention to establish him as ruler of the extensive Archipelago of St. Lazarus (as Magellan had named these islands) in the name of his suzerain, the Emperor Charles; Magellan had gone so far as to offer to sustain him in this hegemony. The Rajah now informed the Captain General that some of the chiefs on the Island of Cebu and many on the nearby islands had refused to accept his rule, saying they were as good as he. They also declined to abandon their old religion. The Captain General called a convocation of all the chiefs in Cebu and announced that any man who refused to acknowledge the sovereignty of the Christian King would be killed and his possessions confiscated. He also insisted again that all the chiefs should at once become Christians, destroy the old shrines, and burn their idols. His threat cowed the chiefs, and they all agreed to conform to his dictum.

There was, however, one powerful cacique who did not attend the meeting, but who sent word to the Christian King that he would not abandon the old religion and would wage war on any chief who did so. This rebel was Cacique Cilapulapu, whose district was on the Island of Mactan, directly across the channel from Cebu and forming one side of its harbor. On learning of his defiance, Magellan sent a detachment of marines under Espinosa to burn Cilapulapu's capital, the town of Bulaia. The town was sacked and the women all ravished before the torch was applied. The Captain General then sent a peremptory demand that Cilapulapu render homage to the Christian King, as ruling for the Emperor Charles. He also demanded that the rebel chief immediately pay a tribute, the amount of which was fixed in certain quantities of swine, goats, fowl, rice, and coconuts, in accordance with native precedents in such cases. The recalcitrant chieftain agreed to pay tribute, but offered to send only about two-thirds of the quantities demanded. Magellan thereupon decided to make an example of him, in order to establish the prestige of the Spaniards and support the authority of the Christian King.

He called a council of his officers and informed them of his intention. All his lieutenants, led by John Serrano, urged him not to intervene in civil wars nor to take on the responsibilities of the Rajah Humabon. They pointed out that not only was this contrary to the best colonial tradition of Spain and Portugal, but in their case they had been sent not to colonize, and not to do missionary work, but simply and solely to find the western route to Maluco and to bring back spices to Spain. They referred to the royal orders, which particularly forbade any deviation from the limited duties assigned to them. They strongly reminded the Captain General that, in the previous council, held on April 3, 1521, at Limassawa, they had unanimously presented the same facts and arguments, but that he himself had vetoed them. He had proposed that they cruise up as far as Cebu merely in order to acquaint themselves with the features of the archipelago, so that they might report back to Don Charles regarding its possibilities. They remarked that they had now been at Cebu three weeks and had accomplished many unforeseen things, but they all vigorously urged that the armada should disengage itself from any further commitments there and proceed at once to keep its rendezvous with Francisco Serrano at Ternate. They knew that they were less than a fortnight's easy sail from Ternate, for they had learned, presumably from the Siamese trader, Cristóbal the Moor, the route to the Spice Islands. Don Antonio writes, "We heard of Maluco while at Cebu."

Magellan stubbornly vetoed the proposal for an immediate departure, and he not only announced his intention of punishing Cacique Cilapulapu, but also his determination to command the punitive expedition himself. This statement was received with dismay. The officers immediately objected that the King's express command ordered the Captain General to stay with the fleet, rather than to go ashore, and it was especially against orders that he should engage in any such hazardous enterprise. They brought out that it was a basic principle of both the Portuguese and Spanish governments that fleet commanders should not risk their persons ashore. Duarte Barbosa reminded Ferdinand of the loss in South Africa of his former chief, Viceroy Francisco de Almeida, who had incautiously exposed himself. He spoke of the massacre of Magellan's predecessor, Captain Juan Dias de Solis, who also had risked his person with a landing party.

The Captain General was practically convinced that it would be best for him not to accompany the landing party when someone, perhaps del Cano, insinuated with sly malice that he had reached the age when he should no longer participate in hand-to-hand combat. The Captain General, stung by the sneer, swung back to his original intention of leading the foray in person.

Although Magellan had proposed to discipline Cilapulapu as a policy measure, he now began to assume that the project was a religious one; he would punish the defiant pagan for having sacrilegiously denounced Christ and for having proclaimed his intention of persecuting the Christian converts.

The officers had hardly recovered from their first shock when the Captain General announced decisively that he would not permit any of them to accompany him in the attack on Cilapulapu, that he would not let Espinosa or the men-at-arms take part in it, and that he would allow only volunteers to share with him in the undertaking. In terms of religious exaltation, he affirmed that he would depend upon the Cross of Christ and the support of his Patroness, Our Lady of Victory, to win the battle for him. He then abruptly dismissed the council, leaving his associates dumfounded at his condition, which they considered to be a state of religious hysteria.

Magellan's next steps are almost incredible for a veteran of so many amphibious raids in East Africa, India, Morocco, and Malaya. No one knew better than he the importance of the element of surprise and the need for painstaking preparation of the task force as well as close study of the terrain to be assaulted. Obsessed as he now was with his idea of being a soldier of Christ who would be made irresistible by Divine aid, Magellan not only neglected the most elementary precautions, but in fact took steps which would certainly insure defeat to any foray not counting upon a miracle to give it victory.

Instead of keeping his plan secret, he invited the people of the town of Cebu to be witnesses of the exploit. The Christian King offered to assist him with a thousand veteran warriors, but the Captain General not only loftily declined the offer, but explicitly forbade the Christian King to intervene in the fight. Crown Prince Cilumai then came to Magellan privately and disclosed that he planned to land secretly on Mactan with a contingent of his own, to take the enemy in the rear after the Spaniards had engaged them, but the Captain General dissuaded him from doing this and instead invited him to be a spectator of the battle.

That night, a son of the Cacique Zula, who ruled over half of Mactan and was an enemy of Cilapulapu, came in a canoe to the Trinidad, ostensibly to deliver two goats as part of his father's tribute. He brought a message to Magellan from Cacique Zula that he would cooperate by attacking Cilapulapu by land when Magellan invaded the island. Magellan rebuffed the offer, stating that he needed no help to punish the rebel, but would do so with his own men.

The Captain General then announced that he would make the attack that very night, but instead of instructing the *alguacil,* Gonzalo Gomes de Espinosa, to lead his disciplined marines under their sergeants, he reiterated that he did not desire any of the officers, but only wished to take volunteers from among the men, twenty from each ship.

Accordingly the *alguacil* and his fighters felt piqued and did not volunteer. At midnight, a motley contingent of stewards, *grumetes*, cabin boys, and *sobresalientes* assembled. They were armored with corselets and helmets, but were not supplied with greaves or leg armor. In addition to swords and lances, they were given harquebuses and crossbows, although many of them were not experts in the handling of these complicated arms. The sixty volunteers filled three batels. The row to the beach was very short, and they arrived three hours before dawn. Twenty or thirty *balanghais* bearing spectators, including the Christian King, the Crown Prince, and some of the Christianized chiefs, accompanied the three attacking boats and ranged themselves behind them, not to participate in the attack, but to observe the Christian victory.

Instead of attacking at once, Magellan sent Cristóbal the Moor ashore with a message to Cilapulapu that, if he would obey the Emperor Charles, recognize the Christian King as his Sovereign, and pay his tribute to the Captain General, he would consider him as a friend; but if he wished otherwise, he should see how the Spanish lances could wound. Cilapulapu replied defiantly that if the Spaniards had lances, his men also had lances of bamboo, as well as stakes hardened with fire. He naively requested that the Captain General not attack at once, but wait until morning, as he would then have more men to oppose him. Magellan took this as a ruse to get him to attack in the darkness, which would have been advantageous to the defenders because they had dug pitfalls in front of their position. The Christian King counseled the Captain General to wait until daylight, he again asked permission to join him with a thousand men, and again his offer was declined.

The absence of planning began to make itself felt as the cramped volunteers were kept crowded and uncomfortable in the longboats for three long hours, shivering in the chill from the river and tortured by night insects. When dawn came, Magellan ordered the boats forward, but it was found that the entire distance between the batels and the shore was filled with coral reefs and the craft could not proceed. The tide was at ebb, and only with a full tide could the boats have got the men to shore. As it was, they had to leap overboard in their heavy armor and stumble waist-deep over concealed reefs for the distance of two good bowshots. Forty-eight men were led ashore, and eleven were left behind to serve the bombards, although it soon appeared that the range was too long for fire from the cannon to reach the shore. Consequently the landing party had no artillery coverage.

A preliminary heavy bombardment would have been feasible, for the three ships were anchored in the stream only three miles down and one of them could easily have moved up into position within half an hour; its broadsides could have given the attackers a protective barrage. However, Captains Serrano and Barbosa were sulking in their cabins, obeying orders that they were to have nothing to do with the operation, and faithful Espinosa and his men-at-arms stayed behind, having been told they were not needed.

When the already tired and partly dispirited volunteers landed, they found waiting to receive them a native army variously estimated at from fifteen hundred to six thousand trained warriors. These were divided into three divisions, drawn up in a crescent so that they could easily surround the little Spanish force from three sides. There were a series of three parallel trenches between the beach and the town. Cilapulapu and his bodyguard were posted behind these, so that they were not only beyond the range of the bombards, but also beyond effective reach of the small arms.

The Spaniards advanced to the edge of the first ditch and opened fire, but their bullets and crossbow bolts were so spent by the distance that they hardly penetrated the light shields of the Filipinos. The harquebuses were a novel weapon, still in an experimental stage of development, and to handle them required training which was lacking in this instance. The enemy had at first been frightened by the noise of their discharge, but when they found that the balls were harmless, they lost their fear. The firing of a crossbow in battle required skill, and these excellent combat weapons were of but little use to the untrained attackers. When Magellan realized the ineffectiveness of his fire and recognized that he was rapidly exhausting his store of powder and of arrows, Don Antonio says he called again and again, "Cease fire! Cease fire!" But the excited volunteers gave no heed to his command. The company had not been drilled, and there were no subalterns or noncommissioned officers to repeat the orders or to see that they were carried out. Magellan was almost alone in attempting to

Engraving from de Bry's "Peregrinationes," 1599

MAGELLAN'S LANDING AT CEBU

Engraving from de Bry's "Peregrinationes," 1595

THE FATAL BATTLE OF MACTAN

direct a mob of demoralized men. His only aides were Don Antonio, a foreigner, and Cristóbal Rabelo, an inexperienced youth, neither of whom had any prestige with the fighters. Had the *alguacil* and his *merinos* been there, they would undoubtedly have saved the day.

Magellan saw that it was useless to continue fighting at such long range. He ordered his men to close with the enemy, for, with their armor and superior steel weapons, he thought they could defeat them in combat. To carry out his order, it was necessary for them to cross the three lines of deep trenches, sliding down the bank of each trench and then clambering up the slippery opposite side, a difficult feat under the weight of heavy armor and carrying a lance and a bulky harquebus or crossbow. The enemy did not dispute the crossing of the trenches, since they were perfectly willing to have the Spaniards walk into their trap; the trenches would be serious barriers to a retreat. After the last trench had been traversed, Magellan arranged his muddy, tired men in battle formation and proceeded against the enemy, who had retreated to a position in the village. As the Spaniards advanced against them, the Filipinos retreated, and Magellan realized that they were trying to draw him inland away from the range of the ship artillery, should the fleet come to his support. Therefore he ordered Cristóbal Rabelo to take a squad and set fire to the village, while he drew back to the edge of the nearest trench.

When the Spaniards attempted to carry out this order, the Filipinos immediately rushed forward and cut off Cristóbal Rabelo and his young comrade Juan de la Torre, the son-in-law of John Serrano. Despite their armor and their brave defense, the mass of attackers overwhelmed the young Spaniards and quickly killed them with their spears.

Both these brave young men were favorites of Magellan, and both seem to have been related to him. To see them thus abruptly cut down by the massed enemy frightened the inexperienced soldiers, and the shock seems to have brought Magellan to his senses. For the first time he apparently realized his predicament in face of the large and effective native force. At all events, he ordered his men to withdraw to the boats.

The Filipinos were greatly encouraged by their success in the village, and, as soon as the Spaniards began to retreat, they charged them with spears, but were repulsed. Magellan handled the withdrawal through the ditches in his usual skillful manner. He divided his vastly outnumbered force into two lines; one line kept the enemy at bay until the other had slid, wallowed, and crawled across the ditch and taken a position on the opposite side. From there, the second line covered the retirement of the first with their arrows. This tactic was successfully repeated three times, although the enemy kept up an incessant attack throughout. When the entire body had finally extricated itself from the third trench and was retreating in good order toward the beach, the natives sent strong forces at a run around both their flanks with the intention of intercepting them before they could reach the boats. When the raw, undisciplined sailors saw they were in danger of being cut off from the sea, they broke ranks and raced in panic for the shore, every man for himself. Magellan tried to rally them, but they paid no attention to him. He was left with Don Antonio, Enrique, and six other men, including the supernumerary Anton de Escovar, the foreign *lombardero* Filiberto, two sailors, and two stewards. These devoted men stayed with him, instead of fleeing with the others.

While the nine Spaniards, fighting desperately, were holding their ground, a poisoned arrow struck Magellan in his unarmored leg. He plucked it out and continued to fight where he was, although for safety's sake he should then have retreated. Don Antonio says that the Captain General stayed back purposely in order to prevent the enemy from cutting off the fugitives, many of whom were wounded and could retreat but slowly through the water. Don Antonio wrote, "When they wounded him, he turned back many times to see if they were all in the boats. Had it not been for that unfortunate Captain, not a single one of us would have been saved, for while he was fighting, the others retired to the boats."

As soon as Magellan was satisfied that his men had escaped, he commenced to give ground, but his wounded leg was already very lame, and he was able to retreat but slowly. Those with him picked him up and, covering him as well as they could with their shields, carried him down the beach and into the sea. By this time they were beset by so many of the enemy that they could no longer continue their retreat, but had to put Magellan down and defend him there, standing up to their knees in water, hoping for help from the boats. The Filipinos in fury concentrated their attack on Magellan. Twice they knocked off his hemlet, and twice his defenders were able to replace it. They now were under a shower of spears, and even of stones and sod. Don Antonio says that the Filipinos would pick up the same spear and throw it four or six times.

This terrible fight continued for a full hour, while forty armored Spaniards sat in the boats a hundred yards away. Our Lady of Victory had not intervened, and not one man dared come to Magellan's relief. Finally some of the Christianized natives could stand idly by no longer, and heroically advanced to attempt to bring him off. Just as the rescue party neared the little group, now cut down to five, the Spaniards in one of the boats discharged a culverin at the shore. They had aimed it so badly that, instead of reaching the enemy, the shrapnel charge of small stones and bullets struck the rescuing squad of friendly Filipinos in the rear, killing four of them and dispersing the others. The spectators looked on as if mesmerized.

At this juncture, Magellan was wounded in the face by a spear, but valiantly killed his attacker with his lance. As the Filipino fell, the lance remained in his body and was wrenched from Magellan's hand. His lance gone, Magellan tried to draw his sword, but could only get it half way out of the scabbard; he had been wounded in his sword arm with a bamboo spear, and he could not control his muscles.

When the natives saw that Magellan was defenseless, they rushed upon him. Only Don Antonio, Enrique, Filiberto, and Escobar were left to try to cover him with their shields. His other four defenders had already given their lives. The heavy onslaught pushed the wounded and weakened warriors to one side. A Filipino slashed beneath their shields with a long scimitar and cut Magellan on his unarmored left leg, so that he fell face downward into the water. Then Don Antonio says, "They all rushed upon him with iron and bamboo spears, and with their cutlasses, until they killed our mirror, our light and comfort, and our true guide." He continues: "Thereupon, beholding him dead, we, being wounded, retreated as best we could to the boats, which were already pulling off."

It was finished. The earthly destiny of Ferdinand Magellan had led him to voyage around the whole world to his death, and his last weeks of religious exaltation seem to have been almost premonitory. It was as if the reward of earthly riches he had striven for so hard and long was not worth the having to him; once it was in his grasp, his whole being turned away from it, toward the realms of the spirit.

A great career was over, but life went on. His little fleet had to carry on somehow. If, with the death of Ferdinand Magellan, Spain's chance of acquiring Maluco, of establishing an Empire in the Orient, and of making the Pacific Ocean a Castilian Lake also died, what of that? The Philippine Islands remained Christian, as Magellan had hoped. His name is immortalized by his *paso* and by the constellation that shines down upon the ocean which he opened up to the western world.

And we can but repeat Don Antonio's prayer uttered to the Grand Master of Rhodes: "I hope that the fame of so noble a Captain will not be effaced in our time."

CHAPTER XX

AFTERMATH

THE demoralized Spanish volunteers, huddled in the longboats, saw Magellan go down and watched in horror as the crowding natives plunged their spears into his submerged body. Panic seized the Spaniards, and they started to row away, paying no attention to the four survivors who by now were trying desperately to escape. The enemy, too, seemed to have forgotten them in their savage triumph at felling Magellan. The four were sorely wounded, and their armor and weapons hampered them unbearably as they struggled breast-deep in the water, stumbling over the coral reefs and shouting to their comrades to wait. A few in the boats, seeing their plight, held back the rowers until the exhausted fugitives reached them and were pulled aboard.

As the three longboats drew away, the victors pursued them in canoes. Some of the faster native craft maneuvered to cut off the slow batels, but at this point the Christian King sent out his force of a thousand warriors in balangays to provide protection. Rajah Humabon himself followed the longboats, weeping unashamedly for the loss of Magellan as he helped lift the four wounded men aboard the Trinidad.

That afternoon the crews of the armada chose Duarte Barbosa their new Captain General, and the Christian King immediately came to assure him of his support. In the atmosphere of shock and sorrow, one of their first thoughts was to recover Magellan's body and give him Christian burial. After a hurried discussion, Barbosa agreed to let Rajah Humabon go to *Datu* Cilapulapu with a proposal to ransom the body of the fallen commander by payment of a treasure in copper and iron, instead of taking any initiative to restore Spanish prestige by strong action. Duarte Barbosa, with his years of experience in Portuguese explorations and battles, well knew that, properly armed and organized and with artillery support, the Europeans had invariably prevailed, even over native forces astronomically greater in number than themselves. Yet he could not muster the courage nor the resourcefulness to strike a hard blow, which would have been the only means of saving the day. Rajah Humabon meekly went upon his errand, and the cacique rejected his offer with a cutting reply.

Barbosa now weakly began to treat Rajah Humabon as an ally to whom he looked for protection and advice. This only served to confuse the Rajah and undermine his already waning faith in Spanish invincibility. The Rajah cannot have had much personal respect for the new Spanish leader in any case, for Duarte's profligate conduct throughout their stay had been common gossip. Without doubt, the depraved life he had led for many years had destroyed most of his early powers and promise, and the crews of the armada could hardly have selected one less fitted to command.

The Christian King had already begun to doubt the wisdom of continuing his fealty to the Spanish Emperor when he received a conciliatory message from Cilapulapu. Until recently, he had been on cordial terms with the cacique, whose sister was one of his principal wives. Now the cacique urged him to turn against the Spaniards and offered to help him punish them as the desecrators of their ancient altars and the violators of their harems. If Humabon refused, the cacique threatened to form an alliance against him with all the other chiefs, and to punish him along with the Spaniards. It was obvious to the Rajah that, if the Spaniards did not immediately destroy Cilapulapu, he himself would have little choice but to join with him. The Spaniards might themselves get away, but he, the Christian King, would be left to face the other chiefs and would most certainly be overthrown.

Cilapulapu's military reputation had been high in the archipelago even before his defeat of Magellan, and he now assumed the role of national champion and found confederates on every side. The native priests blessed his patriotic boldness and pledged the intervention of the gods on his side to help him attack and destroy the impious foreigners. Cilapulapu had captured many steel swords, halberds, lances, crossbows, harquebuses, helmets, and corselets, and he had the suits of armor that had been worn by Cristóbal Rabelo, Juan de la Torre, and Magellan himself. The cacique's pressure upon Humabon grew more and more insistent.

In the meanwhile, the four wounded men lay in a cabin on board the Trinidad, and at dawn Barbosa visited them. The supernumerary, Anton de Escovar, obviously was past hope, and was soon to expire. The lombardier, Filiberto, was mortally hurt. Don Antonio also appeared doomed, for his entire body was swollen due to a poisoned arrow which had entered his face. Enrique was less seriously wounded in body, but more hurt in spirit than anyone else in the armada, prostrated by the death of one who had been a comrade rather than a master and whom he had loved with single-hearted devotion. He had been treated for his wound, and was the only one of the four who had regained consciousness.

Barbosa examined Enrique's wound and decided it was not serious, so he brusquely ordered him to return to duty. He needed the service of Enrique as envoy and interpreter. Enrique, however, turned his face toward the wall and lay as if in a stupor, ignoring Barbosa's command.

A wave of fury mounted in Barbosa. He had hated the slave in the past, for he had never forgiven nor forgotten the righteous scorn with which Enrique had looked upon him when he had twice failed in his duty to Magellan and had had to be brought to his senses by stern punishment. Now he was the Captain General himself, and he meant to show the wretched slave his place.

Twice he commanded Enrique to get up and return to duty, and got no response. He leaned over the prostrate figure and shook it, then dealt it several cruel blows. Enrique did not lift a hand even to cover his face. Beside himself with rage, Barbosa kicked the slave savagely, shouting at him venomously between accesses of violence. He said that Enrique might be counting upon having been manumitted by Magellan's will, but he wasn't freed yet, and he, Barbosa, would see to it that he wasn't in the future. Lady Beatriz Magellan would keep him in slavery, and Barbosa would see to it his future life in Seville would be no bed of roses.

Then Barbosa, having vented his animosity, resumed his attitude of official authority. He sternly gave Enrique his choice, as a member of the crew, of getting up and obeying his orders at once, or being flogged for disobedience. Enrique recognized the familiar voice of naval discipline, and, with murder in his heart, got up, took his orders, and morosely went ashore to deliver a communication from Barbosa to the Christian King. He felt a searing hatred toward Barbosa for yesterday's failure to aid Magellan in his extremity, and held both Barbosa and Serrano to be traitors and murderers in letting Magellan be overcome. He felt no obligation at all toward these white men; his fidelity had belonged to Magellan alone.

The Christian King was in an agony of indecision when Enrique, who had in the past often acted as emissary between his master and the King, came to him bearing a message from Barbosa. It had been due in no small part to Enrique's ardor that Humabon had become the Christian King, so now he was astonished when Enrique warned him against Barbosa's duplicity and urged him to take advantage of the demoralization of the armada to seize the ships and become master of their armament and treasure.

Rajah Humabon's position resembled somewhat that of Enrique. In the beginning, it was force or the threat of force that caused him to swear fealty to the Spanish Emperor and to renounce his own religion. There is no doubt that the sincerity of Magellan had won the trust of his blood-brother, the Filipino ruler; but Humabon, like Enrique, had been more swayed by his regard for Magellan than by any love of the Spaniards, although he had been awed at their apparent strength. The Rajah, too, had observed the excesses of the foreigners, and knew that nothing could be more at variance than the preaching of Magellan and the practice of Barbosa. Now that Magellan was gone and the much-vaunted strength of the Spanish seemed to have evaporated, his animosity toward Duarte Barbosa predisposed him to listen sympathetically to Enrique's advice.

Moreover, the fiasco of the attack upon Cilapulapu had destroyed the prestige of the Spaniards with the Christian King. That their firearms had been ineffective was shown by comparing the losses of the two sides. The *Datu* had lost fifteen men, while the Spaniards had left behind them twenty armored dead. Humabon could not forget the spectacle of the steel-clad foreigners as they threw away their harquebuses and crossbows and fled for their lives, chased by the naked warriors of the *Datu.*

While the Rajah and Enrique were still discussing the matter, one of the lesser caciques hurried in to report a surprise move by the Spaniards. They had loaded their longboats with all the merchandise from the warehouse and had conveyed it back to the ships. This evidence of Barbosa's lack of confidence in him lent confirmation to Enrique's warning to the Rajah, and rid him of any lingering sense of responsibility he may have had toward the whites.

Enrique and the Rajah were now agreed to turn upon Barbosa, and the Rajah remembered a circumstance which could be used to trap him. Soon after the Spaniards had arrived, the Rajah had proposed to send to the Emperor Charles, as a token of fealty, a magnificent set of native regalia. He had shown Magellan a store of handsome rubies, diamonds, and pearls, together with several nuggets of gold, which he proposed to have wrought in the native fashion. This he had done, and he now displayed the completed set to Enrique. They determined to invite Barbosa and the other officers to attend a farewell banquet ashore to receive these symbols of tribute for the Emperor.

Barbosa was delighted with the idea of carrying this costly gift back to Emperor Charles, foreseeing advantage to himself from it, so he accepted the Rajah's invitation. Distrust, however, was expressed by his associates when he issued the order for them to attend the banquet. Serrano, who had been elected second-in-command, was loud in his misgivings and even wanted to hold back just as the party was ready to go. The two intimates were already jealous of one another, and Barbosa sneeringly accused Serrano of being afraid. Serrano retorted haughtily, "In order that you may not think this, Señor Duarte Barbosa, I shall be the first to go!" Thereupon he leaped into the longboat.

All the leading Spaniards were of the party, unarmored and in gala attire, and the ships were left without any senior officers. Don Antonio was the only aristocrat unable to leave his pallet, for his wounds were not healed, and undoubtedly his absence was a secret relief to Enrique.

A short time after the shore party had disappeared from view, those on the ships saw Gonzalo Gomez de Espinosa and Juan Lopes Carvalho hurry back to the wharf. The two men jumped into a skiff and rowed out to the fleet.

Barbosa and his comrades, Espinosa said, had showed no distrust at the banquet table, but at once had begun to drink quantities of palm wine and make advances to the women. Espinosa remained suspicious, and when he saw one of the chief's relatives whom Padre Valderrama had miraculously cured of an illness come up to the priest and draw him away from the table, his fears were confirmed. He and Carvalho got up and hurried back to the pier.

Espinosa had barely finished his story when the alarmed crew heard shouts and cries from the town. Espinosa, on the Trinidad, ordered the ship to action, while Carvalho did the same on the Victoria and shouted to Juan Sebastian del Cano, who had not been invited ashore, to put the Concepción in a state of defense. They cut the anchor cables, not daring to take time to pull up the anchors, and hoisted the sails. The Trinidad led the other two ships down the channel, and each poured a broadside into the town.

At that moment, the Victoria was hailed by John Serrano, who had been brought to the pier by a group of natives. His weapons and outer clothing had been taken from him, and his hands were bound. He called to Carvalho that the natives were going to butcher him then and there unless the bombardment was immediately discontinued.

Carvalho asked him what had become of the rest of the company, and he answered that they had all been murdered except Padre Valderrama and Enrique. He himself had persuaded his captors to ransom him for some bars of copper and two small serpentine cannon, and he begged Carvalho to send these articles ashore immediately and save his life. There was some colloquy as to how the exchange was to be made, since neither side trusted the other, and the Spaniards feared to venture too near. In the midst of the discussion, Carvalho suddenly turned cool to the whole proposal, Don Antonio says, because he realized that Serrano would become Captain General.

Don Antonio wrote: "He begged us earnestly to redeem him with some of the merchandise; but Juan Carvalho, his boon companion (Carvalho and Serrano, blood-brothers, were sworn to fraternity), and others would not allow the boat to go ashore, so they might remain masters of the ships. But although John Serrano wept and asked us not to set sail so quickly, for they would kill him, and said he prayed God to ask his soul of Juan Carvalho his comrade, in the day of judgment, we immediately departed. I do not know whether he is dead or alive."

Later, the general belief in Spain was that Serrano, having been spared the massacre because of his age, probably was kept a captive. Instructions to the commanders of later *Armadas de Maluco* all contained the specific order to attempt to ransom him. When Hernando Cortes, in 1527, sent a fleet from Mexico to Maluco to rescue the survivors of Magellan's expedition, the commander was given a letter to the Rajah of Cebu asking the release of Captain John Serrano.

The bitter denunciation of Carvalho by John Serrano was the last message that ever reached Spain from the thirty-eight missing men. It is not known if there were any survivors, nor is there any record of the subsequent career of Enrique. Two Portuguese writers reported from China that eight of Magellan's men were said to have been brought there as slaves. The lives of some skilled artisans among the Spaniards might well have been spared by Humabon, who could have sold them to the slave trader Cristóbal the Moor for the Chinese market, where their skills would command a good price.

The Subsequent Voyage

It was on May 1, 1521, that the armada fled from Cebu, escaping the hostile balangays which followed them at first. Once safely away, the leaderless crew selected the veteran pilot Juan Lopes Carvalho to command and pilot the fleet back to Spain, mistakenly believing him to possess the requisite technical navigating knowledge. The men also decided to abandon the Concepción, and therefore transferred its cargo and crew to the other two ships and burned it. There were one hundred and eight men left now, all on the Trinidad and the Victoria.

Captain General Carvalho had not enough education to be able to decipher Magellan's plan of the voyage, and had no idea how to guide the armada either to Maluco or back to Spain. For three months, he blindly steered the two ships on a meandering piratical cruise in the Sulu and South China seas, robbing and sinking any Malay *prahus,* Arab merchant ships, and Chinese junks he encountered. He commanded in true pirate-captain's style from Magellan's state cabin, where he maintained a harem

Etching presented to the author by Francisco Perfeito de Magalhães e Menezes, Conde de Alvellos

The Arrival of the Trinidad and Victoria in Maluco

of three unfortunate, high-caste Moslem women whom he had captured.

The scandalized crew at length deposed Carvalho and elected Gonzalo Gomez de Espinosa as Captain General. The honest and able marine, though he was illiterate and no navigator, at once restored discipline, discontinued the attacks on merchant shipping, and showed his customary common sense by working his way from island to island toward Maluco, inquiring the course at ports where he stopped to get supplies and from ships he encountered.

For four months Espinosa led them through the Sulu and Celebes seas and down Molucca Passage, until, on November 8, 1521, he finally arrived at Maluco. It had been twenty-six months since their departure from Spain, and nearly seven since the death of Magellan. In Maluco, Espinosa learned that Francisco Serrano and his ally, the King of Ternate, both were dead of poison, that Serrano's hoard of spices had been dissipated, and that the Portuguese were now in possession of the Island of Ternate. Espinosa at once led his two ships to the Island of Tidore, where he made an alliance with the King and persuaded him to swear allegiance to the Emperor Charles. He built a fortress with artillery there for the King, in order to permit him to command the harbor, and left a gun crew with him. He also built a warehouse, where he stored all his unsold copper, iron, and trade goods, and appointed a factor and an accountant. Then he loaded his two ships with spices and prepared to take advantage of the westward monsoon to sail back to Spain via the Cape of Good Hope.

Juan Sebastian del Cano

At the last minute, a mishap delayed the Trinidad's sailing, and Espinosa sent the Victoria ahead with a crew of forty-seven men under the command of Juan Sebastian del Cano. Del Cano followed the well-known Portuguese route, but kept to the south of their path. He did not have the respect of his men, there were mutinies and desertions en route, and Don Antonio, who writes a detailed account of the harrowing return voyage, significantly does not once mention the name of del Cano.

On September 8, 1522, the Victoria dropped anchor in Seville, just three years after it had sailed from there. Don Antonio and seventeen other emaciated survivors marched barefoot with lighted candles through the streets of Triana to give thanks at Ferdinand Magellan's favorite shrine of Our Lady of Victory.

Juan Sebastian del Cano had circumnavigated the globe. He brought back spices worth forty-five thousand ducats (about six hundred and seventy-five thousand dollars) which were turned over to Cristóbal de Haro and which more than paid for all the costs of both the ships and the cargo for the *Armada de Maluco*. As usual, the mariners who accomplished this great achievement received little reward, and the families of the men whose lives were lost got nothing at all. For propaganda purposes, the Emperor made the most of the exploit of circumnavigation. He had del Cano acclaimed as the circumnavigator, endowed him with a pretentious coat of arms, and gave him a handsome pension. However, perhaps because of Don Antonio's confidential report to him, Don Charles refused del Cano's petition to be made a Knight of Santiago, as Magellan had been. He also quietly rejected several other pleas from del Cano for favors.

Cristóbal de Haro was taken in by the plaudits, or perhaps he simply found it politic to join them, and therefore he had del Cano appointed chief pilot of the second *Armada de Maluco*. Del Cano suffered catastrophic losses when he tried to duplicate the achievement of Magellan in the *paso*. Worn out by a task too immense for his powers, he collapsed and died at sea.

Gonzalo Espinosa

Meanwhile, Gonzalo Espinosa, after sending the Victoria westward under del Cano, proceeded to repair the Trinidad. By the time the repairs were done, the monsoon had changed and he could not follow the Victoria around the Cape of Good Hope. Therefore he tried to bring his rich cargo eastward across the Pacific to Panama. He made the Ladrones Islands, and in seeking an easterly wind sailed so far north into the China Sea that the men suffered from the cold off the coast of Japan. Although he was of great heart and courage, Espinosa lacked knowledge of celestial navigation, and at last, with his crew of fifty-three reduced to twenty, he returned to Maluco and surrendered the Trinidad to the Portuguese at Ternate.

It was not until 1526 that the Portuguese released Espinosa and let him return to Spain. He was welcomed by Don Charles, who overlooked his humble birth and lack of education, created him a nobleman, and gave him a substantial pension. In 1529 he was promoted to a high post in the Spanish Navy. These rewards by the discerning Emperor were richly deserved, for Magellan's faithful *alguacil* emerges from the history of the *Armada de Maluco* as its most steadfast and competent officer.

Cristóbal de Haro

Cristóbal de Haro had been overjoyed when the Victoria returned with its profitable cargo, and was elated that there had proved to be a real *Paso de Maluco* in Spanish waters, just as Magellan had said. He at once persuaded the Emperor to carry out Fonseca's plan and establish a *Casa de Especierias,* or department of oriental trade, a counterpart of the *Casa de Antillas* which was located at Coruna and was completely under De Haro's control.

Cristóbal de Haro outfitted three successive *Armadas de Maluco* and managed to get reinforcements to the small Spanish garrison that Espinosa had left at Tidore. The little band there had also been augmented by aid sent from Mexico by Hernando Cortes, and they heroically held out against continuous Portuguese attacks. The plans of Cristóbal de Haro and of Jakob Fugger seemed certain of fulfillment, and Spain, and indirectly, Venice, appeared about to enjoy a goodly share of the spice trade. The Spaniards at Tidore had already seriously damaged Portugal's control of the trade, and Jakob Fugger seemed to have defeated the Medici in the global economic battle. The Florentines, however, now cleverly turned the tables on him by the use of his own favorite weapon, bribery. They used their gold to buy Jakob Fugger's own creation, the Holy Roman Emperor himself.

Don Charles

To Don Charles, after the death of Magellan, the adventure of Maluco lost its knightly glamor, and his interest waned. The Fuggers had obviously made the whole enterprise into a mercantile undertaking, in which he was not interested. In 1529, Don Charles was in great need of cash for his military campaign, and he therefore accepted, from the Portuguese King, the huge sum of three hundred and fifty thousand ducats (about five million dollars) to repudiate his claims to the sovereignty of Maluco. The negotiations between Don Charles and his brother-in-law, Dom John III, were carried on so secretly that even the alert Cristóbal de Haro was taken by surprise, and although he and Jakob Fugger protested and tried to stop the transaction, they were too late. The Florentines, who had provided Dom John with the money, never made a better bargain, and they quickly got back their purchase price.

The Spanish people were angry at this abandonment of their rights, and the Cortes of Castile indignantly refused to confirm the tentative treaty. But Don Charles held to his bargain and forbade de Haro and Fugger to send out the large, carefully equipped fifth *Armada de Maluco,* which had been prepared to hold Maluco against all Portuguese attacks. The Emperor ordered the *Casa de Especierias* to be closed, and this completely finished the whole great operation.

De Haro sued the Crown for his personal losses and, clever politician that he was, won his case, probably by bribery, and was compensated in full. The Fuggers tried to follow suit, but suffered from the anti-foreign resentment which then gripped Spain and were given short shrift by the courts, not regaining a penny of their great speculation. Cristóbal de Haro continued to carry on his prosperous trading business at his headquarters at Burgos, with various departments conducted by his sons, both legitimate and natural.

Bishop Fonseca

Soon after the death of Magellan, Bishop Juan Rodríguez de Fonseca had lost all influence in matters pertaining to Maluco. In 1522, when he had reached the peak of his power and was the dominant politician in Spain, he determined to appropriate for his bastard daughter's husband the governorship of the recently conquered Empire of the Aztecs, and in doing so to destroy Hernando Cortes. The father of Cortes, aided by a young relative, a lawyer, managed to call the plight of Cortes to the attention of the Holy Father in Rome, none other than Don Charles's former tutor, Adrian, now Pope Adrian VI. No one was better acquainted than he with the many and various rascalities of the Bishop of Burgos. His Holiness set up a Court of Inquiry and forced the hypocritical, venal churchman to attend. The evidence of forgeries, of substitutions of documents, and of suppressions of reports was overwhelming. The Pope discharged Fonseca from his offices of state and ruled that he was to have nothing further to do with the Indies; His Holiness sent a transcript of the evidence to the Emperor, who confirmed the verdict.

Fonseca had already been greatly affected by the marooning of Juan de Cartagena, and his sudden fall from power so shocked him that he lay at death's door in Toro for some months. He recovered, however, refused to resign his lucrative Bishopric of Burgos, and passed the rest of his life in study and in scholarly controversies; he no longer enjoyed any political influence.

Don Antonio

After Don Antonio Lombardo, whose real name was Ser Antonio Francesco Pigafetta, had disembarked in Seville, he accompanied del Cano to Valladolid to make a report to the Emperor, with whom he had an audience in Barcelona in 1519. He wrote in his journal, "I presented to his sacred Majesty, Don Carlos, neither gold nor silver, but things very highly esteemed by such a sovereign. Among other things, I gave him a book, written by my hand, concerning all the matters that had occurred from day to day during our voyage."

Don Antonio had now become a personage of consequence. He was the only person of rank and education to survive the voyage of circumnavigation, and therefore was sought after on all sides. His first duty was to report to the Doge and Signory of Venice, who had sent him on the expedition as unofficial observer. He was closeted with the Doge for many hours, and then he gave to a convocation of the Council of Ten, of the Senate Committee on the Spice Trade, and of the former Select Committee on Relations with Egypt, a circumstantial report on the economic and maritime features of the Philippines and of the East Indies. It was the first time that the Venetian Senators had heard at first hand a factual description of conditions in mystery-shrouded Maluco, whose tangy produce had been, as they said, "the milk and nutriment of the greatness of Venice."

In August, 1524, the Venetian Senate gave Don Antonio a copyright to print and publish his journal in Venice, but he never took advantage of this privilege. In the meanwhile, as he awaited his copyright, he had brought out a printed work on celestial navigation which made a noteworthy contribution to the science of the day.

Don Antonio's journal of the voyage of the *Armada de Maluco* complemented the great book of Duarte Barbosa's prime, which he had finished in 1516 but which was then available only in manuscript. Barbosa had described the geography and economy of the peoples of the perimeter of the Indian Ocean and of its many great gulfs as far as Malacca. Don Antonio's journal carried on from there down through the Philippines, Borneo, and the spiceries, as far as Timor. His work was by no means as profound as was the carefully written book of Duarte Barbosa, since Don Antonio had had to write much from hearsay and had picked up most of his information at random from oriental mariners and Chinese, Arab, and Malay traders whom he encountered in the course of the erratic wanderings of the Victoria. His account was of intense interest, however, for it was the only source available of knowledge concerning the extensive Indonesian area so important to European chancellories, counting houses, and universities.

Don Antonio was a keen observer and made faithful note of all that he saw and heard. He recounted fables as well as facts, and perhaps assumed that the distinction would be perceptible to his sophisticated readers. He himself had witnessed such astounding revelations and had encountered so many hitherto undreamed-of prodigies that he was credulous in accepting some of the legends recited to him. The editions of his manuscript which have been preserved are only expurgated copies, circumspectly written at the command of royal personages inimical to Don Charles, and Don Antonio had already had to excise much from his account that might offend the mighty monarch himself. It may be presumed that Don Antonio artfully gave place in his narrative to those otherwise inexplicable fairy tales so as to entertain his royal readers without putting himself in jeopardy with the Emperor.

Don Antonio was, in 1523, undoubtedly the most lionized personage in Christendom. John III of Portugal, the successor to Manuel and brother-in-law and maritime rival to the Emperor, commanded his presence and queried him particularly about the navigational and commercial aspects of the Far Indies. Then Queen Louise, Regent of France, who was at the hub of a brilliant circle of intellectuals and likewise a foe of the Emperor, ordered him to come to France, and not only to recite to her his tale of the wonders of the East, but also to have his journal copied for her.

In December, 1523, the erudite Medici Pope, Clement, at the axis of the diplomatic whirl between Francis I and Don Charles, also summoned Don Antonio to report to him in person, and later, in writing. Astronomers, geographers, botanists, ethnographers, and philologians all recognized Don Antonio as an authority and clamored for his time.

Don Antonio became sated with attention and decided to forsake the world and its vanities. Yet even when he approached the Grand Master of the Knights Hospitaller of St. John of Jerusalem, Philippe de Villers de l'Isle Adam, and sought admission to his ascetic order, he was once again asked for a copy of his journal. This last manuscript has survived, and it is the basis of our history of the great voyage.

In October, 1524, Don Antonio took the vows and assumed the robe, and in 1530 he accompanied the Grand Master to Malta when that island was bestowed upon the Order by Charles V. In 1536, Don Antonio Lombardo, or Ser Antonio Francesco Pigafetta, a Patrician of Venice and Knight of Rhodes, gave his life fighting in defense of Malta against a Turkish attack.

Magellan's Heirs

The Lady Beatriz, sorrowful at the stillbirth of her second child, followed in September, 1521, by the death of little Rodrigo, Magellan's heir, died in March, 1522, six months before the returning Victoria brought official notice of Magellan's death. Old Dom Diogo fought valiantly in the courts to defend the good name of his dead son-in-law, as well as to assert his own rights, but the opposition was all-powerful and the cause was hopeless.

Later Evaluations

In Europe, the memory of Magellan was execrated on all sides. The deserters, Gomes and Guerra, in order to exculpate themselves, maligned him when the San Antonio reached port. Cristóbal de Haro, of course, supported the diatribes of his son, Geronimo Guerra. The Fonsecas, still in power and deeply resentful at the fate of their sons, Juan de Cartagena and Antonio de Coca, joined in the chorus of malediction. When the Victoria at last returned, del Cano, who had been implicated in the mutiny, not only corroborated all that Magellan's detractors had already alleged, but circulated new slanders against him. Don Antonio himself found it necessary to excise from his journal all accounts of the mutinies and desertions, for the influence of Magellan's traducers at court was too strong to withstand. When Dom Diogo Barbosa and his son entered suit against the state for the lawful share of the valuable cargo of the Victoria that was due to Magellan's estate, the counsel for the Crown did not scruple to cite the detractions of Magellan's foes as proof of his failure to carry out his obligations under the contract, thus attempting to invalidate the contract and to discharge the royal treasury of any obligation to his heirs. Ferdinand Magellan had kept detailed records of every incident of the voyage, but these records never came to light, for del Cano and his confederates had destroyed all they could lay their hands on in Magellan's cabin, in order to get rid of any evidence against themselves.

In Portugal, the memory of Ferdinand Magellan was excoriated by almost all writers because of Dom Manuel's hatred of him and the mighty blow he had struck against the Portuguese Oriental Empire.

From our perspective in time, we see that, although Magellan's epic voyage of circumnavigation was ostensibly an imperialistic episode in the political struggle between the royal houses of Spain and Portugal, the chancelleries of Europe were well aware that, beneath the royal banners and the sails painted with religious symbols, the venture was commercial.

The armada captained by Magellan bore the flag of Spain, but its inspiration stemmed from the Rialto at Venice and from the spice emporium of Alexandria, both seeking to regain commercial advantage from Portugal, as well as from the countinghouse in Augsburg whose influence reached into every corner of the world. The disguised object of the cruise was to restore to the Republic of Venice and to the Hanseatic League their grip upon the industrial and mercantile economy of Europe through restoring their monopoly of oriental trade. Behind the scenes, the sponsor of the venture was the capitalist, Jakob Fugger of Augsburg, banker for both the Doge of Venice and the King of Spain. Magellan himself can hardly have been unaware of these currents of international commercial rivalry, and they certainly bore some relation to his own chivalric and daring motivation.

With the passage of time, men everywhere began to realize the great contributions Magellan had made to science. He settled the question of the sphericity of the world and of the habitability of the Antipodes. His circumnavigation solved the problem of the globe's linear circumference and of the length of a degree of longitude, and made innumerable additions to the world's navigational and geographic knowledge, including the recognition of the calendar's loss of a day on the westerly girdling of the globe.

Magellan is remembered by the place names which still survive along the coasts of Brazil, Uruguay, the Argentine, and Chile. The "Great South Sea" which he discovered is no longer called on the charts, as it once was, "Mare Magellicum," but his researches are honored by all astronomers in the title of the constellation known as the Magellanic Clouds. And Magellan's name is familiar to every schoolboy because of the historic strait which he discovered.

The results of his missionary efforts and of his statesmanship likewise have survived. The Spanish realm of the Philippines which he founded did, in fact, endure for almost four centuries; and when, a half century after Magellan's death, his successor landed at Cebu, he found reverenced in the pagan temple the little wooden statue of the Virgin and Child that Magellan had given to the Christian Queen. Today his archipelago is still Catholic, and the Commonwealth of the Philippines is the sole Christian nation in all Asia.

In these latter days, historians have learned that Ferdinand Magellan was not only a master navigator and scientific explorer, but that he was a man of noble character, great daring, and knightly ideals. Thus, belatedly, Antonio Pigafetta's prayer has been answered, that "the fame of so noble a captain will not be effaced in our time."

APPENDIX

1. LACK OF CERTAINTY AS TO INCIDENTS IN MAGELLAN'S LIFE

Many of the activities ascribed by historians to Ferdinand Magellan during his earlier years are based upon conjecture.

Few of these accounts were written by contemporaries, and there is little concerning his life prior to his entry into Spain that can be asserted with any certainty.

The Conde de Alvellos informed me that the name of Ferdinand was so common in his family in the sixteenth century that during the time of the Circumnavigator's service in the Orient there were, in all, seven Ferdinand Magellans in the forces of Dom Manuel in Asia and Africa. Hence, he averred, it has been impossible to be sure which Ferdinand Magellan is meant in some of the references in the chronicles.

I have accepted the Conde de Alvellos' selection of the personal genealogy and coat of arms of Ferdinand Magellan instead of those preferred by certain other historians.

I also have been guided by members of the Magellan family in fixing upon Ponte da Barca as his birthplace instead of Amaranthe or Porto, or Sabrosa, all of which claim the honor. Earlier historians, including Guillemard, agreed upon Sabrosa as Magellan's place of nativity. Although when I visited Sabrosa I was shown some interesting local evidence to substantiate Guillemard's claim, I feel that the exposure by Professor José Maria de Queiroz Velloso of the forgery of the so-called "First Will" of Magellan has eliminated serious consideration of Sabrosa as Magellan's birthplace.

There also is considerable doubt about the validity of facts concerning his brothers-in-arms. Francisco and Juan Rodríguez Serrano and Duarte Barbosa. The Vicomte de Lagoa identifies seven Juan Serranos as having been engaged in Portuguese India or in East Africa at the time Magellan's comrade won distinction there. Although Duarte Barbosa was definitely reported to have been killed in the massacre at Cebu in 1520, nevertheless, a few years later, a Duarte Barbosa, with somewhat the same characteristics, turned up on the Malabar Coast and has been identified by some historians as the same person. The Vicomte de Lagoa cites a letter of the Portuguese consul in Seville dated 1519 as evidence that Duarte was the nephew and not the son of Diogo Barbosa, as he generally has been described. I found in the Archives further evidence of this and have so treated him, although it is quite possible that he was Diogo's natural son and hence styled his nephew.

In like manner there can be adduced contradictory dates and details about many of the principal happenings of the period. This baffling situation is recognized by the contemporary Portuguese historians, who have conducted painstaking research into the archives of the reigns of Dom John II and of Dom Manuel and have found discrepancies in some of the generally accepted ancient histories of the era.

Few authentic official records of late medieval and early renaissance Portugal have survived to modern times. The early crown archives were kept in the *Torre do Tombo* in Lisbon, and almost all of these were cleared out and destroyed by royal order in 1459. Again in 1525 Dom Manuel commanded that all the documents in the State archives be scrapped excepting certain outstanding ones which were copied into a compilation known as *Leitura Nova,* completed in 1529.

During the interlude of Spanish rule of Portugal in the sixteenth century, many historic documents were removed by authorization of Don Philip II from the *Torre do Tombo* to the royal Spanish archives in Simancas and in Seville. During this period the maintenance of Portuguese state records was neglected and the condition of the files became chaotic.

In 1634 an official inventory disclosed much pilfering of vital statistics of the realm, which had for a long time been practically without any guardianship.

In 1755 the great earthquake utterly destroyed the repository of the national records, the *Torre do Tombo,* although the name of the tower is still used to describe the national archives.

In the Napoleonic wars, during which the Portuguese royal family and most of the nobility emigrated to Brazil, a vast number of family archives were lost.

In the civil war of 1842, many of the valuable private family libraries were destroyed when the manor houses of the aristocracy were burned.

The early kings habitually deposited a duplicate of each important document with the convents for safe keeping. Many of these monastic hoards of charters and titles survived until 1843, and constituted the major archives of the nation. But in that year an anticlerical government suppressed over four hundred and eighty religious houses in Portugal and closed the convents, ejected their inmates, and threw away the contents of their precious libraries or sold them as waste material. So little consideration was paid to the old documents that only a moiety of these priceless accumulations was salvaged and deposited in the files of the *Torre do Tombo* in Lisbon.

There is, nevertheless, still a mass of ancient records in various centers of Portugal which have never even been carefully inspected, much less catalogued, and there are said to be innumerable such documents at present mouldering in bundles and rapidly deteriorating. Perhaps among these unedited papers there will someday be discovered evidence that will clear up some of the uncertainties about the life and background of Ferdinand Magellan.

At the present time, however, most of the authoritative records concerning Magellan are those in the *Archivo de Indias* in Seville, many of which are listed in the note in the appendix.

2. THE COMPLEMENT OF A ROYAL SPANISH SHIP IN 1520

It was unusual, in 1520, that the captain should be an expert in navigation, as was Ferdinand Magellan or John Serrano. A captain was usually an aristocrat who was ignorant of seamanship, as were Captains Cartagena, Mendoza, and Quesada. He was actually the military commander, responsible for discipline and over-all control, and had little to do with navigation. The captain was expected to act as a just but stern parent to the men. He might have culprits flogged to the point of collapse, but he was always solicitous for the comfort of the sick and wounded. Although he held aloof from the crew, his bearing and character were reflected in the spirit of the ship, and his personal courage and his prowess in combat were the measure of the craft's effectiveness in action.

The officer second in authority to the captain was the *maestre,* or master. He was necessarily familiar with celestial navigation, but ordinarily left the navigation of the ship to the pilot. On a merchant ship, the *maestre* was in charge of the cargo and of all commercial details.

The third in command was the pilot. He was responsible for the navigation of the ship, and his tools were the astrolabe, the quadrant, the compass, the hourglasses, and supplementary nautical instruments. It was his duty to prick the location of the ship upon the chart; and he also had to attempt to forecast the weather. It was his particular province to watch over the rudder and the foremast, which were the two indispensable elements of the ship's equipment. The pilot had a deputy who relieved him on duty. On every clear day, the pilot and his deputy took the sun's altitude with the astrolabe, and at night they measured the height of the North Star or, when their voyage took them below the equator, of the Southern Cross.

Fourth in authority was the *contra-maestre,* or boatswain, who was the executive officer of the ship and was personally in command of the crew. Among the qualifications for the job were reading and writing, for the boatswain had to keep a record of the receipt and delivery of the freight. He was in charge of the stevedoring and the stowing of the cargo, and was particularly charged to guard against fire. The *contra-maestre* did not sit at the captain's table, but presided over the mess of the petty officers and seamen.

Fifth in the ship's hierarchy was the master-at-arms, or *alguacil,* who was assistant to the *contra-maestre* and administered punishment under the captain's orders. He had under him a group of guards who acted as the ship's police force. His subordinate officers or sergeants were called *merinos.* He devoted much time in good weather to drilling his men. He divided his marines into combat groups which were entrusted with the defense of the various sections of the fore- and aftercastles and of the decks. The master-at-arms also made certain units of his command responsible for fire prevention during action, and for repairs to the running gear in battle. It was his duty to see that the longboat and yawl were kept secure and in good condition, and he was responsible for the supply of wood and water. He saw to it that the decks were clear and clean and that the ropes, cables, and spare spars and sails were properly stowed and available.

Next in authority was the *despensero,* the head steward, in charge of the hardtack and all comestibles. He gave out the rations and conserved the supply of water.

Next came the ship's carpenter, who was a master of his craft. An expert boatwright, he could replace any wooden element that entered into the composition of the ship. In the course of a voyage lasting from one to three years, subject to the hazards of war and weather, there was no telling when it might be necessary for the carpenter to make repairs. Often he had to improvise substitutions for vital elements of the vessel.

Next to him was the *calafate,* or calker, also a technician, who kept the hull tight and maintained the pumps in good order. An opening of the seams while at sea could be fatal, hence his responsibility for the safety of the ship was very great. When the vessel was beached and careened for cleaning, it was the *calafate* and his crew who removed the barnacles and marine growth, and calked the seams and coated the hull with tar.

The ship's barber, although ranking low in the chain of command of the ship's complement, nevertheless was a man of education and of professional attainments. He was the ship's physician and surgeon and was responsible for such hygiene as was practiced. His standing is evidenced by the privilege he enjoyed of sharing the captain's mess along with the *maestre* and the pilot.

The *condestable,* or constable of the *bombarderos,* was a highly-paid expert artilleryman, generally of German or Flemish nationality. He not only had charge of the ship's ordnance, but also acted as armorer and guarded the powder from water and fire. His personal expertness in naval gunnery had to compensate for the lack of precision of the crude muzzle-loading cannon then used, and such firing accuracy as might be attained was to be attributed to his individual gun sighting. The constable took every opportunity to perfect his gun crews in the serving of the pieces, and held gun drills whenever the weather permitted.

The crew of a large *caravel de armada,* or *nao,* was composed of about thirty *marineros,* or first-class seamen of considerable experience and some practical knowledge of simple navigation, and about twenty-four *grumetes,* or common seamen, who performed the heavier manual work.

There were also about eighteen apprentices who were known as pages. Some of these ship's boys were the personal stewards for the captain, *maestre,* and pilot, and the rest cleaned decks, served at mess, and in general did the menial work. Watching the *ampolletas,* or hourglasses, and reversing them at the proper time, was among the pages' duties. A page sang the morning and the evening hymns, and every night in good weather one of the pages had to read aloud to the crew a portion of Christian doctrine. Many of the pages were sons or relatives of the ships' officers or of the seamen, and they were considered apprentices who would in due course advance to posts of responsibility. They made an important contribution to the life aboard ship.

Two detailed rosters of the complement of Magellan's armada are available, as will be seen in the transcriptions from the *Archivo General de Indias* given in this appendix.

3. THE OFFENSIVE ARMAMENT OF MAGELLAN'S FLEET

The broadside artillery of the Trinidad comprised about twenty muzzle-loading brass or iron carronades called bombards, which discharged round stones as projectiles and were fired by the application of a flame to the touch hole. The record shows that, in addition to the usual batteries, the armada was supplied with three extra heavy bombards which were acquired in Bilbao, although we do not know the vessels on which they were installed.

The auxiliary artillery for use on the decks and fighting tops of the fleet consisted of three *pasamuros* or carronades, fifty-eight smaller pieces called culverins, and seven falconets, or light cannon.

In addition to the above naval guns, the fleet carried a number of brass serpentines, artillery pieces so small in size as to be portable, but which could discharge a devastating load of pebbles, nails, and pieces of scrap iron. These were effective at short range from the longboats in small-craft action or against defenders massed on a beach to oppose a landing party.

The record shows that three tons of gunpowder, several tons of stone cannon balls, and a supply of balls of iron, together with sets of molds and tools for casting iron and lead projectiles, were taken aboard to serve the artillery.

For offensive small arms, the locker was stored with a thousand long lances, fencible arms which could also be thrown as spears. For use at close quarters there were two hundred pikes and a number of halberds, two-handed shafted weapons bearing the head of a spear and the blade of a battle-ax. Of missiles to be thrown by hand, there were ninety-five dozen darts and ten dozen steel-headed javelins, and there also were sixty windlass crossbars with three hundred and sixty dozens of arrows. Besides all the above orthodox individual weapons, such as had been in use in naval warfare for many centuries, Magellan managed to secure from the *Casa de Antillas* fifty matchlock harquebuses. This firearm was an innovation which had recently been very successfully used by the Turks and was just beginning to be introduced in some of the more modern European armies.

These harquebuses were muzzle-loading muskets, fired by applying a lighted fuse to a powder priming in the breech pan which, when ignited, exploded the charge of powder in the chamber. The weapon was so heavy that the harquebusier had to carry a crutch on which to support the barrel of his ponderous firearm when sighting and discharging it. As it took him some time to reload, he generally was accompanied by a crossbowman who fought alongside him to protect him while recharging his piece. The inventory of the arms closet lists one hundred and fifty yards of matchlock fuse and fifty powder flasks for the harquebuses, as well as ten dozen skeins of wire for the crossbows.

4. PHILIPPA OF LANCASTER

The modern American reader is puzzled that Portuguese historians have in general given so little attention to the great Englishwoman who was the ancestor not only of the dynasty of Avis, but of the destiny of the Portuguese Empire itself.

The atmosphere in which elegant, exquisitely cultured Philippa was imperiously foisted upon her evasive and reluctant spouse was one of secret resentment by the Portuguese nobility toward their supercilious English allies. This deep-seated hostility had its origin in the conduct of the English soldiery in the previous expedition of 1381 under the Earl of Cambridge.

These pitiless mercenaries of the White Companies, so graphically reincarnated by Conan Doyle, lived off the countryside of Portugal and desolated the land just as they had previously done in hapless France.

The Portuguese chronicler gallantly describes Philippa as beautiful, which she was not, and as the King's junior, which is in doubt, and as the Lady of the King's choice, whose hand he sought in a knightly manner, which he did not.

Having thus played the gentleman toward this Englishwoman of such statesmanlike and masterful parts, the court chronicler proceeds to immure her, cloistered in her bower, among her Portuguese ladies in waiting, devoting her days wholly to prayer and to acts of devotion. Her saintly round of litanies and vigils and fasts is described as having been only interrupted at regular intervals by her withdrawal for the brief period necessary for the bearing of the ten children whom she dutifully presented to her Lord the King.

Later Portuguese historians of the nineteenth and twentieth centuries seem to have been content to praise Dom John himself for many of his wife's great contributions to her adopted land. This is due not only to an understandable assertion of Portuguese nationalism, but also to the natural feeling of exasperation aroused in many Lusitanian breasts by the lordly attitude toward a weaker and commercially exploited ally which was exhibited by the English, particularly during the complacent Victorian and Edwardian periods.

5. ALJUBARROTA

The Portuguese chronicle describes the Battle of Aljubarrota as the routing of an overwhelming horde of invading Spaniards by the knightly prowess of a small body of patriots. In reality, Aljubarrota was one of the decisive engagements of the Hundred Years' War between France and England, both of which had substantial levies engaged in this battle. For the Portuguese it was in reality a civil conflict; the greater part of the chivalry of Portugal fought in this battle on the side of Castile, and these dissident Portuguese knights probably outnumbered their countrymen in the winning army of Dom John.

One hypothetical reconstruction of the battle has been made from the confused and contradictory accounts of the tactics employed. In this military analysis it is assumed that the French men-at-arms, estimated in the thousands, charged with the same gallic impetuosity that had cost France the fields of Creçy and Poitiers, and later was to cost her Agincourt and Pavia. The heedless French horsemen left their flanks wholly exposed to the murderous volley of clothyard arrows of the English veteran longbowmen (also estimated in the thousands), the charging war-horses sank down helplessly, and a bloody debacle of the Castilian forces ensued.

But in the Portuguese chronicle, the English archers are given little mention and no credit for the victory.

6. JUAN DE SOLIS

The record of service under the *Casa de Antillas* of Ferdinand Magellan's predecessor, Juan de Solis, was notably parallel to Magellan's. The similarity of their experiences is worthy of particular note by students of the life of Magellan, as it may shed light upon obscure details of Magellan's career.

De Solis, like Magellan, was a Portuguese navigator with long experience in the Orient who felt aggrieved by the denial of his claims upon the Crown and who therefore left Portugal and entered the Spanish service.

In 1508, de Solis was given command of a Spanish squadron with instructions to sail west through the Spanish zone and seek a strait to the north of Veragua that would lead from the Caribbean Sea to Maluco or the Spiceries. The detailed letter of instructions to de Solis from King Ferdinand is quite like the one which Charles later addressed to Ferdinand Magellan. Evidently the boy king patterned his own letter to Magellan upon that written a decade earlier to de Solis by his grandfather, a copy of which probably was given to Charles by Fonseca.

Moreover, de Solis, as a Portuguese, had, like Magellan, to submit to sharing his command with a native Spaniard, Vincent Yañez Pinzon. Pinzon was given independent authority as Vedor or Inspector General, just as later the Spaniard Juan de Cartagena was placed in an identical post of coeval authority with Magellan. This dual command resulted in friction between the Portuguese Captain General de Solis and the Spanish Vedor Pinzon, just as it later did between Magellan and Cartagena.

When the de Solis squadron returned to Seville in March, 1509, its lack of success was blamed wholly upon the Portuguese, de Solis, who was thrown into prison, while the Spaniard, Pinzon, was commended by the *Casa de Antillas* and rewarded with a sum of money.

In 1512, when the news reached Spain that the Portuguese had captured Malacca, de Solis, who had been released from prison, assured Fonseca that Malacca lay four-hundred leagues within the Spanish zone and that Maluco hence was in the Spanish rather than the Portuguese zone. A similar assertion later was made to Fonseca by Magellan.

Fonseca therefore decided to send de Solis on an eastward (not westward) expedition to Maluco. He gave him command of a fleet of three small vessels and ordered him to double the Cape of Good Hope and to visit Ceylon, Sumatra, and Malacca, and then to sail to the Spiceries and take possession of Maluco in the name of the King of Spain.

Fonseca at that time secured for de Solis from the King a contract similar to that later granted to Ferdinand Magellan. This stipulated that de Solis would be made *Adelantado,* or Governor, of the islands discovered by him, and he was promised, as was Magellan, that this office would be made hereditary.

A most interesting development then took place in that Fonseca extorted from de Solis a secret partnership agreement whereby the Bishop was conceded a half share in any future gains by de Solis. It is our belief that it was the rejection by Magellan of such a surreptitious proposition from Fonseca that caused the feud between them.

The parallel continued in that Fonseca had the King make de Solis a Knight Commander of the Order of Santiago, just as he later had Charles confer the same honor on Ferdinand Magellan.

Then the Portuguese ambassador, Vasconcelos, proceeded to practice bribery and sabotage to delay the sailing. In March, 1513, he even attempted to persuade de Solis to abandon the undertaking and to return to Portugal, just as his successors, Ambassador da Costa and Consul Alvarez, likewise tried to seduce Magellan from his duty to King Charles. The similarity ends there, however, because in September, 1513, Portuguese Dom Manuel did coerce the Spaniard, Don Ferdinand, into cancelling the voyage just as Captain General de Solis was about to sail.

However, in 1513, after Balboa had announced to Spain his discovery of the Great South Sea at Darien, Fonseca sent de Solis with two small boats westward for Maluco.

This time, strangely enough, the expedition appears to have been secretly financed by Cristóbal de Haro, who was, however, still in Lisbon and still in favor with the Portuguese King.

De Solis returned via Portuguese Madeira in October, 1514, and is believed to have reported secretly to de Haro that he had found the *paso*. He had in fact only discovered the Plate River, up which he had sailed for sixty miles.

De Solis now interested Diogo Barbosa of Seville in a project to sail westward to Maluco through his newly discovered *paso* (Rio de la Plata), and Fonseca no doubt was his hidden partner. King Ferdinand gave his quiet approval to this undertaking but took pains to emphasize publicly that it was a private speculation and not a royal venture.

Fonseca again insisted that Portuguese de Solis submit to the control of a Spanish Vedor and a Spanish Comptroller, just as he later imposed similar native officials upon Portuguese Magellan.

The Portuguese consul in Seville was so successful in his efforts at sabotage that when de Solis's armada of three vessels weighed anchor to sail, one of the ships suddenly developed a leak and went to the bottom. King Ferdinand was indignant at this Portuguese outrage and personally advanced the funds to purchase another vessel, and the fleet finally got away from the port of San Lucar in October, 1515.

The similarity of the careers of the two great Portuguese navigators persisted to a tragic end. De Solis, like Magellan, disregarded the written instructions to stay aboard his command and imprudently went ashore with a strong landing party to meet his end at the hands of a miserable rabble of half-armed barbarians.

7. DOM MANUEL THE FORTUNATE

King Manuel's treatment of Ferdinand Magellan was quite in keeping with his characteristic harshness toward the soldiers and sailors to whom he owed so much. His was a complicated nature, and his salient faults were his extravagant indulgence toward the sycophants who flattered him and his shameless ingratitude toward the heroic adventurers who made him "Lord of the Commerce and Navigation of India, Ethiopia and Persia." Manuel's record in this regard is quite consistent. He failed suitably to reward loyal Bartholomew Dias, who first rounded the Cape of Good Hope. He ignored the claims of Vasco da Gama, pioneer of the sea route to India, who finally in his exasperation decided to emigrate to Spain and made the same request of the King that later was made by Ferdinand Magellan, that he be given permission to enter the service of a foreign prince. Dom Manuel gave no recognition to Pedro Alvarez Cabral, discoverer of Brazil. He repudiated his Viceroy, Francisco d'Almeida, who saved his oriental establishment from destruction by Egypt and Venice. Almeida also, like Magellan and da Gama, planned to enter the Spanish service because of Manuel's ingratitude. He was completely heartless toward Affonso d'Albuquerque, who created for him a splendid empire. One of his more callous acts of ingratitude was to the simple knight, Duarte Pacheco, a scientific navigator, military genius, and accomplished scholar. Dom Manuel first acclaimed Pacheco a national champion for his heroic exploits in India and sent laudatory letters to all the courts of Europe extolling his martial achievements. He honored Pacheco by walking beside him through the streets of Lisbon in a triumphal procession; and then before long he let him rot in the prison in which he had been thrown on false charges. Manuel allowed the hero's destitute grandchildren to become objects of public charity.

Dom Manuel was niggardly, not only with his captains, but also with the ill paid, maltreated common soldiers and mariners who endured much in his name. He even defrauded them of their prize money and of the tiny pensions which had been promised them, and he made no provision at all for their widows and children. The porches of the churches within sight of Manuel's sumptuous palace, with all its pomp and pageantry, were crowded with armless and sightless veterans of great victories in India who had to beg for a crust to keep alive. This ingratitude was the principal flaw in Dom Manuel's character.

His heartlessness toward the explorers who were engaged in making Portugal great may have sprung from an inner sense of frustration and jealousy toward men of martial daring, for he himself was a palace king, rather than a warrior king. He had spent his boyhood as a hostage in Spain without expectation of becoming heir to the throne, and although he had been proficient at sports, he had received no military training. His predecessors on Portugal's throne had been men of war, and most of his royal contemporaries wore armor and risked their lives on the battlefield. Charles of Spain, Francis of France, Henry of England, and Sulieman of Turkey earned distinction as knights and soldiers. Although Dom Manuel on several occasions talked valorously of donning his helmet and taking ship against the Moors in Africa, he never carried out his threat to do so, and during his whole reign he never risked his person in the field of battle. The bitter gibe of Francis I of France deriding Manuel as the "Grocer King" doubtless had stung him deeply. Manuel was, in fact, an oddity to his fellow monarchs of Europe; he had no mistresses, maintained no harems, and his court lacked the conventional nursery for royal bastards. He lived in continence with his wife and brought up a large family of children to whom he was in general a devoted parent. He was a particularly pious Catholic who on holy days was not content to attend Mass at one church but would attend services at several in succession. Nevertheless he shared the belief in astrology that was typical of his day and maintained astrologers at his court whom he consulted in regard to any steps of importance.

Dom Manuel was a lanky, gregarious fellow, who loved horses and hunting and outdoor sports. He loved dancing, gayety, and horseplay, was abstemious in drink but was fond of the table, and habitually had music at his meals. He had an orderly, businesslike mind, and was a competent executive, directing the numerous departments of state without becoming submerged in petty routine. He disposed daily of a great mass of work. Although easily flattered, he was a keen judge of ability in his subordinates. A most extraordinary feature of his reign is the inexhaustible number of able admirals and administrators upon whom he could call. It was his deliberate policy to check and humble any servant who attained great distinction and to avoid giving him such further employment as would enhance his prestige.

As a comptroller, Manuel never succeeded in getting an over-all grasp of his complicated fiscal budget. He overestimated the extent of his income, vast though it was, and floundered in a welter of uncontrolled expenditures. Each year he operated his government on a mounting deficit which, before his death, began to impair the solvency of the empire. He was extravagant when prudent economy was in order, and penurious when royal munificence would have been appropriate.

Dom Manuel immobilized much of his revenue from India by a stupendous program of construction of public and ecclesiastical buildings. He strove to rival in two decades what had been gradually built in other European countries during the course of two centuries. He built a large and much needed hospital in Lisbon, and erected five royal palaces, thirteen monasteries, and eight large churches in Portugal alone, as well as a number of government edifices and churches in India, North and East Africa, and in Brazil. Architecture was his consuming artistic interest, and he imported foreign artists and artisans; he particularly favored several English and Irish builders of the Gothic school. He invented the so-called Manoelesque style of carved stone decoration with which he embellished his structures.

Manuel reformed the Portuguese courts of law, revised the statutes, purged the ranks of the nobility of many impostors, and corrected scandalous conditions in some lax Portuguese convents. He restored and preserved national monuments. His historians did extensive research in the state archives and composed a history of previous reigns. He built numerous roads, canals, and bridges, and improved and fortified harbors in Portugal, Africa and India. Except for returned adventurers from the Orient whom he treated ungratefully, his subjects felt little cause for complaint. His extensive program of public improvements created a demand for labor, already in very short supply, and his discovery of the rich fishing grounds off Newfoundland did much to reduce the cost of living for the lower classes. Dom Manuel barred the entry of the inquisition into Portugal during his reign, and he favored those Jews who adopted Christianity and became *conversos*. He gave them valuable trading privileges in Brazil and on the West Coast of Africa and extended other mercantile privileges to them, despite the opposition of his Florentine bankers.

He acted as his own foreign minister, maintaining embassies of unprecedented magnificence at all important courts, where his vigilant diplomats worked to prevent foreign interests from poaching in his West African, Brazilian, and Oriental waters.

Manuel's ambition was to unite Egypt and Arabia to his Indian realm, so that the Portuguese Empire would stretch from the Mediterranean to the China Sea. The King spent the rest of his life trying to create an alliance of Christian monarchs to war against Turkey, to stamp out Mohammedanism, and incidentally to bring about the creation of the Portuguese Empire of his dreams, but the Pope was his only sincere coadjutor in this plan of a Christian crusade. North African conquest became his monomania, and he threw away in Moroccan adventures the Indian revenues which would have paid rich dividends reinvested in his oriental establishment.

In 1517, at the age of fifty-one, the King was saddened by the death in childbirth of thirty-five year old Queen Mary, and publicly announced his intention of abdicating the throne in favor of his son, Crown Prince John. Dom Manuel meant to pass his later years in retirement in the southern province of the Algarve. Prince John, in his exuberance at the prospect of early accession, made some comment about his father which courtiers repeated to the King. Stung by his son's lack of appreciation, the King abandoned his plan to abdicate and announced his intention of marrying his son's fiancée, Eleanor, aged twenty, the sister of Charles of Spain. Disregarding her tearful resistance, he carried out his intention in a private marriage. The young people had become genuinely enamored, and the breaking-off of their engagement and Eleanor's subsequent forced marriage to the King could not be expected to cool their ardor. All the court, with the exception of her aging spouse, knew that the Queen's bed was free to her former betrothed, who was now her stepson. None dared open the King's eyes, and the courtiers laughed in their sleeves at this scandalous result of his heartless behavior.

Although Dom Manuel's own death was preceded by that of Ferdinand Magellan, the King died in ignorance of that happening. He was still tortured by anxiety as to the outcome of his former vassal's bold threat against his sovereign interests.

8. JUAN RODRIGUEZ DE FONSECA

Bishop Las Casas tersely sums up the character of Bishop Fonseca by stating, "He was more of a business man than a Bishop."

Washington Irving commented upon the surprising fact that Spanish historians had consistently refrained from relating the important activities and predominant influence of Juan Rodríguez de Fonseca during the reigns of Ferdinand and Isabella and during the early reign of Charles V. He ascribes this to a conspiracy of silence due to shame that one of the highest prelates could have practiced such venality and nepotism in the same period in the history of the Church in Spain which was made glorious by the careers of some of her most saintly and illustrious bishops.

It must be recognized that the mask of hypocrisy was torn from the face of Fonseca by none other than the Holy Father himself, and that the crimes imputed to him in this history are those for which he was condemned by the Pope in his report to the absent Emperor concerning Fonseca's malpractices.

It is difficult for an American to reconcile the worldly activities of the churchmen of Juan de Fonseca's day with their sacred titles of Bishop or Cardinal. Vested with awesome sanctity, they also, without surrender of claim to priestly veneration, filled the roles now played in modern society by politician, diplomat, and businessman. The name "bishop" not only signified that the bearer was a holder of holy office, but also implied rank. The clergy were not only the spiritual shepherds of the flock, but likewise the guardians of its material interests. A bishop was a consecrated magnate of worldly interest and rich domains, who quite properly inhabited a palace and was served by a retinue. Spain was then largely governed by seven archbishops and forty bishops, independent local lords of their dioceses under feudal tenure from the Crown.

In Juan Rodríguez de Fonseca's time the clergy dominated politics not only in the Spanish Peninsula but in all Christendom. Many Cabinet ministers of western Europe were prelates, among them Cardinal Wolsey in England, Cardinal Amboise in France, Cardinal de' Medici in Tuscany, Cardinal Ximenes in Spain, and Cardinal Adrian in Flanders. Much of Germany was governed by archbishops who were princes in their own right, and even the Holy Father, as ruler of the Papal States, was a temporal sovereign. The marvel is not that under such a system there were so many unprincipled Spanish churchmen, but rather that there were so many conscientious ones. Yet many of Fonseca's clerical associates were sincerely devout, and some of them attained a degree of spirituality perhaps unequaled since that time.

In medieval Spain the administration of mundane affairs by the clergy had the tacit consent of society, for it preserved a workable system in a country that was not only perpetually on the defensive against Moorish invaders, but also was so sunk in civil warfare that most of the population were kept under arms, on guard against one another. The only gristmills and smithies that were not burned in forays from neighboring districts, the only orchards and vineyards not laid waste, and the only flocks and herds not driven off by marauders, were those protected by the Church. The weaker members of society, fatherless children, widows, and the aged, placed their affairs in the hands of the Church as their only refuge. The Spanish monasteries carried on work nowadays assigned not only to hospitals, orphanages, schools, libraries, and museums, but also that of modern safe deposit and trust companies.

The Church had become the monopolist of much of Spain's revenues and privileges, and it might seem at first glance that the clergy had appropriated from the landowning aristocracy the management of the economy of the country. The reverse, however, was true, for the feudal nobility in reality had obtained control of almost all the material wealth of Spain by filling the main positions of the Church. It became the rule that only the sons and daughters of hidalgos like the Fonsecas could be made abbots of rich monasteries or abbesses of equally wealthy nunneries.

The prelates of Spain not only were fiscal trustees of the national economy, but also, along with the Jews and the lawyers from the walled free cities, they constituted the *letrados,* the lettered class of the kingdom. These *letrados* filled the parliaments that wrote the statutes and supplied the judges who interpreted the law. The clerical *letrados* shared the government with the grandees, who, despite their lofty lineage and resounding titles, were generally illiterate, and well born *letrados* like Fonseca became the statesmen of Spain.

Soon after the death of Magellan, Bishop Juan Rodríguez de Fonseca lost all influence in matters pertaining to Maluco. In 1522, when he had reached the peak of his power and was the dominant politician in Spain, he determined to appropriate for his bastard daughter's husband the governorship of the recently conquered empire of the Aztecs, and in doing so to destroy Hernando Cortes. The father of Cortes, aided by a young lawyer, a relative, managed to call the plight of Cortes to the attention of the Holy Father in Rome, none other than Don Charles's former tutor, Adrian, now Pope Adrian VI; no one was better acquainted than he with the rascalities of the Bishop of Burgos. His Holiness set up a court of inquiry and forced the hypocritical churchman to attend. The evidence of forgeries, substitution of documents, and suppression of reports was overwhelming. The Pope discharged Fonseca from his various offices of state and ruled he was to have nothing further to do with the Indies, and His Holiness sent a transcript of the evidence to the Emperor, who confirmed the verdict.

Fonseca had already been greatly affected by the marooning of Cartagena and his sudden fall from power so shocked him that he lay at death's door in Toro for some months. However, he recovered, refused to resign his lucrative Bishopric of Burgos, and passed the rest of his life in study and in scholarly controversies, but he no longer enjoyed any political influence.

During all the years in which Juan de Fonseca filled a succession of important bishoprics, he made little pretense of assuming any responsibility for carrying out either his priestly or his governmental obligations to the dioceses dependent upon him. He drew the revenues from his sinecures without moving his own office from the *Casa de Antillas* in Seville or giving up the least of his lay activities. The archives of Burgos show vigorous complaints by businessmen concerning his neglect of important local matters that urgently needed his authorization before any action could be taken. Secure in royal favor and conscious of his great wealth, Fonseca arrogantly ignored those who were without influence. However, he was never too busy with Church or State affairs to neglect his own pecuniary interests, and he devoted much time to lawsuits defending his usurpations of fiscal privileges.

In the strenuous period of Castilian civil strife in which we have shown his active participation, Fonseca characteristically sought relaxation from the crudities of political brigandage by indulging his private taste for architecture. He gave commissions to artists brought from Italy and Flanders, thus spending much of the wealth that he had extorted from the persecuted Jews, wrung from the enslaved Indians, and confiscated from the plunder of the conquistadors. He spent large sums in rebuilding and decorating churches in Coca, Alaejos, and Toro. In Toro, the shell of a large hospital which he donated still stands. He extensively reconstructed the family castles, strengthening them as strongholds and embellishing them as palaces. The ruined castle at Coca, with its unique terra cotta exterior decoration, is a masterpiece of massive monumental design.

Many of the ecclesiastical sculptures that still survive in Old Castile can be traced to his princely munificence, and may be identified by his signature, for Fonseca always had carved on all his creations the blazon of the many-pointed Fonseca stars of the family coat of arms. He also had these characteristic Fonseca stars woven into the handsome tapestries that he had executed in Flanders for the chapter room in the cathedral at Palencia. Chubby, playful little Italian cherubs were used in addition to the Fonseca stars to identify the handiwork created by his order.

We see a symbol of Fonseca's career in the series of contorted, writhing stone figures of slaves which act as caryatids to support the graceful mezzanine gallery of the courtyard of the handsome Fonseca palace that he built in Salamanca in 1515. For it was upon the necks of exploited and suffering men that Juan Rodríguez de Fonseca, Lord Bishop of Burgos, erected the edifice of his worldly glory.

In the cathedral of Palencia there is a small oil portrait of Fonseca in the beautiful *retablo* of the altar of Our Lady of Compassion. It shows him at the age of fifty-five, in his full powers. Suave, swarthy features, full sensual lips, an understanding gaze in large eyes under a pensive brow, and a martial, muscular frame mark the masterful, predatory aristocrat. Cynical, sophisticated, self-confident, and pitiless, he appears a subtle lord of the Renaissance, with much of the soldier and none of the saint.

In the gallery of the Archives of the Indies in Seville, there is a representation of a bureaucratic Juan Rodríguez de Fonseca, the maritime entrepreneur, in the kneeling group in the painting known as the *Virgin de los Mareantes* done for the *Casa de Antillas* by Alexandro Fernandez. Sculptured over a side entrance of the Cathedral of Burgos is an impudently self-righteous, life-size figure of the Bishop of Burgos, a portly Pharisee in full canonicals, kneeling unctuously before an enthroned Virgin who beams gentle approval, while the Christ Child, held in her arms, extends his little hands toward him.

However, Fonseca received no flattery from the talented sculptor of his magnificent sepulcher on the altar of the family church at Coca. The consummately chiseled countenance of his life-size recumbent figure in alabaster is strikingly executed, apparently copied from a death mask. It eloquently, and perhaps vindictively, conveys in the pinched, chapfallen features something of the avarice and miserliness that marred the character of this prince of materialists.

Every Saturday in the year in the Cathedral of Palencia, at the altar of *Nuestra Señora de la Compassion,* a Requiem Mass for the repose of the soul of Juan Rodríguez de Fonseca is still celebrated, endowed in perpetuity by his will.

The shadows of more than four centuries have obscured the memory of Fonseca's sins and successes, and vicissitudes to come may yet erase the surviving sculptured memorials which he bequeathed to posterity. However, the name of Juan Rodríguez de Fonseca, Bishop of Burgos, is still preserved in the majestic Gulf of Fonseca, in the Pacific Ocean.

9. CORRUPTION AT THE PORT OF SEVILLE

Most of the difficulties experienced by Ferdinand Magellan on his great voyage were directly traceable to the frauds perpetrated by the ship chandlers of Seville, who were protected in their heartless malpractices by Sebastian Alvarez, the Portuguese Consul.

The discontent of the crews, culminating in the mutiny at Bay Saint Julian, the desertion of the San Antonio, and the travail of the Pacific passage, are directly traceable to the short rations necessitated by the concealed shortages brought about by the Portuguese saboteur. The staff of the *Casa de Antillas* was corrupt from top to bottom. Ever since it had been founded in 1503 by Bishop Fonseca, the ships' stores department of the organization had thrived on short weights and false counts, and had learned to outwit even the most careful and exacting ship's stewards and officers.

The record for rascality of the Sevillian ship chandlers was notorious. It required the utmost vigilance on the part of a ship's officers not only to prevent the making of inferior substitutions, but to prevent withdrawal of the stores even after suitable goods had actually been delivered on shipboard. It was common practice for the dealers to plant accomplices in the crew who would operate aboard ship just before dawn, when vigilance was slack. At that hour they would send back ashore valuable items of cargo that had been received and receipted during the previous day. Such thieves always deserted the ship before it sailed. They were then hidden from the ship's search officers and protected by the corrupt harbor police.

The audacious frauds practiced by the Sevillian port officials even upon the King's forces are illustrated by something that occurred about this time. An important royal expedition against the caribs in the West Indies had been readied at Seville by the *Casa de Antillas.* Vigorous, hardy mounts had been called for to carry the heavily armored cavaliers through the difficult tropical terrain, and special care had been taken by the commander of the expedition to secure, at a premium price, young Andalusion horses of mettle and stamina. Just before the fleet sailed, an official parade was staged in Seville at which the spirited performance of these chargers was admired by the spectators. Immediately after the review, at nightfall, the men-at-arms were sent aboard the transport with their arms and horse-tackle, and the war horses were turned over to the port official entrusted with the technical job of getting them aboard the *taforeia* or horse-carrier, and seeing them snugly stalled for their hazardous passage. The cavaliers were not allowed to intrude upon this horse-loading operation. No torches were permitted below deck on the *taforeia,* and it was not until next day, when the fleet was well out to sea, that it was discovered that the magnificent young horses had never been put aboard. They had been replaced in the darkness by worn-out nags which had been brought to Seville by gipsy horse traders to sell cheaply to the local bull ring. These poor, aged hacks were quite useless for the arduous cavalry work upon which the success of the expedition had depended. Yet highly treasonous as was the fraud, which obviously was due to official connivance at the port, none of the perpetrators was ever brought to trial.

It was because of this chronically corrupt situation that Magellan and de Haro insisted on personally inspecting all stores delivered to the ships, but despite their vigilance the Portuguese Consul outwitted them and the fleet sailed with less than half its supposed rations aboard.

10. CLAIMANTS FOR INHERITANCE OF MAGELLAN'S ESTATE

Rodrigo de Magellan, the infant son of Ferdinand Magellan, died in September, 1521, five months after his father's death. The only other child had been stillborn. Doña Beatriz Barbosa de Magallanes survived her son and her husband, but she died in March, 1522, before the return of the ship Victoria in September, 1522, with official notice of Magellan's death.

Therefore Diogo Barbosa and his son Jaime entered suit as heirs-at-law for a share in the proceeds of the sale of the spice cargo of the Victoria. A favorable decision was rendered on July 17, 1525, but in the meantime Diogo Barbosa had died, and Jaime Barbosa lacked the means and the influence to enforce a settlement.

Neither Ferdinand Magellan's brother, Diogo de Sousa, nor his sister, Isabel, wife of Dom John da Silva Telles, Lord of the *Casa Pereira de Sabrosa,* made any attempt to qualify as heirs under his will.

In April, 1563, Donha do Prado de Magalhaes, who claimed to be a niece of Ferdinand Magellan, entered an unsuccessful suit to be declared his heiress.

In July, 1568, a first cousin, Lorenzo de Magallanes of Jerez, Spain, made a vigorous and sustained attempt to qualify as heir to Ferdinand Magellan. He claimed his share to be worth eighty thousand ducats, plus accrued interest for over half a century which brought the amount involved to the equivalent of over one and a half million dollars. The Crown fought the suit aggressively, the legal costs were ruinous, and Lorenzo died penniless before establishing a valid claim.

In 1796, suit was entered in the Spanish courts for the sum due the estate of Ferdinand Magellan under the terms of the original contract made by the Crown with Ferdinand Magellan and Ruy Faleiro in 1518. With accrued interest for two hundred and seventy-five years the amount of the claim was enormous. The alleged heir was Antonio da Silva Castel Branco, who was a nephew of the Prime Minister, Manuel Godoy, Duke of Alcudia, and Principe de la Paz. Covering documents placed in evidence by the claimant included an alleged will of Ferdinand Magellan dated 1505. These instruments have since been shown to be forgeries. The overwhelming influence of Manuel Godoy obtained a sympathetic reception of the claim by the Courts but a favorable decision was averted because of his removal from power by Napoleon Bonaparte.

11. CRISTOBAL DE HARO'S SUBSEQUENT ARMADAS DE MALUCO

After the return of the Victoria in September, 1522, the plot of Bishop Fonseca and of Cristóbal de Haro took definite form, and in 1522 their soaring hopes reached their zenith.

This was when Don Charles issued a formal order in which, in triumphant terms, he announced a definite program to maintain the sovereign rights he claimed in Maluco. He laid down a broad general policy which proposed the occupation and colonization of the Spiceries and was in tenor a defiance of Portugal's assertion of rights to them. In this proclamation Don Charles expressed the confident expectation that the Trinidad would soon arrive with a cargo of spices in the wake of the Victoria.

He announced that in 1521 a second expedition of seven caravels had already sailed from Mexico across the Pacific bound for Maluco under the command of Don Gil Gonzalez de Avila. This assertion was somewhat premature, as the expeditionary plan to which it referred was delayed in execution.

In the same document the King authorized the establishment of a colonial bureau independent of the *Casa de Antillas*, which he chartered as the *Casa de Especierias*, to be domiciled in the Atlantic port of Coruña in the province of Galicia.

This first general order was quickly followed by others which gave complete control of the new *casa* in Coruña to Cristóbal de Haro as its factor. A contract under the royal seal was then executed by the Crown with Cristóbal de Haro in which the King particularly pledged his royal faith and word "that de Haro would be given the exclusive privilege of financing the next four expeditions (if any) to Maluco." De Haro was promised compensation in this contract in case the King for any reason decided against sending all four projected armadas to Maluco.

Moreover de Haro was given the monopoly of the domestic sale of spices in all Spain, with the privilege of fixing the legal prices at which they were to be sold.

His ships were to be exempted from the usual port charges, and his importations were to be free of customs duties and of municipal and provincial taxes. The financial share of the Crown in the returns was limited to a mere twenty per cent instead of the customary forty per cent which de Haro previously had had to pay to the Crown of Portugal.

The fact that one of the principal signers for the King was Archbishop Juan Rodríguez de Fonseca goes far to explain why its terms were so generous to Cristóbal de Haro.

Once the monopoly was firmly assured, Cristóbal de Haro hurried to send forward a strong armada to follow up the achievements of Magellan's expedition.

There were, however, almost as many delays experienced in Coruña in building this fleet as Magellan and de Haro had met in preparing the first *Armada de Maluco* of Magellan. It is not known how much of this was due to Portuguese sabotage.

It was not until July 24, 1525, that the second *Armada de Maluco* of seven carefully outfitted ships finally set sail from Coruña under the command of Don Garcia Jofre de Loaisa, Knight of Rhodes, with Juan Sebastian del Cano as Pilot Major. The Fuggers had invested ten thousand ducats in trade goods, besides which Cristóbal de Haro had personally invested twelve hundred thousand *maravedis* in the cargo.

Del Cano's blunders serve to emphasize the superior seamanship of his predecessor, Ferdinand Magellan. He could not find the mouth of the strait and mistook the Rio Santa Cruz to be the *paso*. His losses in trying to navigate the strait were catastrophic, and both he and Loaisa died from overwork and worry shortly after they reached the Pacific. A single caravel got through to Tidore. Of the four hundred and fifty men of this fleet, eight survivors were returned from Maluco to Spain by the Portuguese in 1536.

On April 3, 1526, a supporting fleet of four caravels sailed; this constituted the third *Armada de Maluco,* which de Haro had permitted to be financed by a syndicate of bankers of Seville. Sebastian Cabot, Pilot Major of Castile, was Captain General, and Martin Mendes, the former accountant of Magellan's Victoria, went as second-in-command. Cabot was close to Cristóbal de Haro, who had financed his famous voyage to Labrador from England two decades earlier in 1497. The failure of this third *Armada de Maluco* again underlined the great seamanship of Ferdinand Magellan. Sebastian Cabot lost his *capitana* and all its valuable cargo by bad navigation off the coast of Brazil, and, after spending some time in the Rio de la Plata seeking rumored gold and silver mines, he returned to Spain. He was publicly accused of having tarried at the Rio de la Plata because he was afraid to face the perils of the passage of Magellan's *paso*.

On October 31, 1527, the long-planned Mexican expedition finally sailed from Aguatanejo, Mexico. One caravel arrived at Tidore, reinforced the Spanish garrison there, and made two efforts to return to Mexico via the Pacific with a rich cargo, but finally had to surrender to the Portuguese in Maluco. Neither Cristóbal de Haro nor Jakob Fugger had any financial interest in this armada, which was financed by Hernando Cortes as a charge against the Crown revenues in Mexico. Don Charles himself had consistently pushed the launching of such a fleet from America. It appears to have represented an attempt by Cortes, archenemy of the faction formerly headed by Bishop Fonseca, to seize control of the Spanish share of the spice trade from Cristóbal de Haro.

In 1525, eight *naos* especially designed for the passage of the *paso* and the crossing of the Pacific were launched at Coruña. These made up the fifth *Armada de Maluco,* under the command of Dom Simon de Alcazaba, a Portuguese navigator with a background somewhat like that of Ferdinand Magellan. The Crown invested six thousand gold pesos in the construction of the ships, but the expedition otherwise was financed by the Fuggers and by Cristóbal de Haro. This fifth armada was designed to carry sufficient forces to garrison the Spiceries and to hold control of the Archipelago for Spain. The high ambitions of Cristóbal de Haro were crushed when, on April 22, 1529, Don Charles, distracted by financial worries, suddenly signed the Treaty of Zaragoza whereby he sold the sovereignty of Maluco to his brother-in-law of Portugal for three hundred and fifty thousand gold ducats. This treaty met with the indignant disapproval of the Cortes of Castile, which exercised its constitutional rights and refused to ratify it. The King, however, made it effective by prohibiting any further trading with Maluco and forbade any Spanish vessel to sail in Oriental waters. Thereby Don Charles not only deserted de Haro and the Fuggers, but also abandoned the little band of loyal subjects, some of them survivors of Magellan's expedition, who still held out in Maluco, where they maintained the Emperor's claim to sovereignty and guarded a treasure awaiting transport to Spain.

After the Emperor had ordered the *Casa de Especierias* liquidated, Cristóbal de Haro sued the Crown under his contract for his losses and, clever politician that he was, won his case, probably by bribery. He continued to carry on his prosperous trading business from his headquarters in Burgos and from his branch in Antwerp.

The Fuggers tried for twenty years to obtain reimbursement in the Spanish courts for their huge investment in the King's armadas, but they were harshly treated as aliens by the Spanish tribunals and were repaid not a *maravedi* of their speculation.

12. TRANSCRIPTION OF RECORDS FROM THE ARCHIVO GENERAL DE INDIAS, SEVILLE

Most of the known documents pertaining to the expedition of Ferdinand Magellan are in the *Archivo General de Indias* in Seville. Some of the information regarding Magellan's undertaking has been gathered from the files on the four subsequent royal *Armadas de Maluco*. The official character of all these merchant adventures to the Spiceries necessitated the issuance of Crown charters and orders and the legal maintenance of detailed records, some of which have been preserved in the state archives.

Much additional light on Magellan's fleet is derived from court records of litigation. The numerous mishaps which befell the Spanish voyagers to the East Indies resulted in many court actions against the Crown on the part of heirs for wages and also by the underwriters for reimbursement for capital invested.

King Charles V in 1529 sold Castile's claim to sovereignty over the spice isles to his brother-in-law, the King of Portugal, for five million dollars in cash, and forbade all further Spanish trade with the Spiceries.

He made no provision for compensation for his subjects, the mariners, shipowners, and merchants whose interests were unfavorably affected. The Cortes of Castile disapproved of the transaction and refused to confirm the treaty.

This encouraged Cristóbal de Haro, the Fuggers, and other participants in the expeditions to petition the Crown to allocate to them part of the money paid by Portugal. When the claims were ignored they sought relief in the Courts.

I was given generous assistance in Seville by the staff of the *Archivo* under the direction of the Secretary, Don Diego Bermudez Camacho, who literally inundated me with documents. I found that research in the *Archivo* required experience and expert knowledge, and therefore I accepted the offer of Dr. Manuel Hidalgo Nieto, Professor of History at the University of Seville, an authority in the field of the history of Spanish finance and commerce in Flanders and in the Indies, to direct the research for me.

I append below a memorandum of his notes from the *Archivo General de Indias* of Seville and from the *Biblioteca de la Real Academia Gallega* in Coruña, which were abstracted for me from the original documents or from authentic records by Dr. Manuel Hidalgo Nieto.

Professor Hidalgo's memoranda were typed for me in the *Archivo* by his secretary, Senorita Angelina Lopez, under the supervision of Dr. Adele Kibre, the American paleographer, who was kind enough to edit them for me.

These notes, which are in the original vernacular, have been bound by me in five volumes, and the items most pertinent to the history of Ferdinand Magellan have been selected for classification in this appendix. I shall be glad to furnish photostats of these typed notes to any historians or students who may request them.

List of Transcriptions from Records in the Archivo General de Indias, Seville

(Note: The date of each document, its identification in the archives, its subject matter, and the number of typed pages, are given in that order for each entry.)

1494, *Patronato Legajo 1 Ramo 6,* text of the original treaty of Tordesillas, 17 pp.

1518, *Patronato Legajo 34 Ramo 2,* letter from Ferdinand Magellan to Don Charles regarding the riot on the docks at Triana, 5 pp.

1519, *Patronato Real Legajo 34 Ramo 6,* Armada de Magellanes, roster of the fleet showing a complement of 239 persons, 7 pp.

1519–1522, *Patronato Legajo 34 Ramo 11,* record of the deaths of 103 members of Magellan's Armada de Maluco, 12 pp.

1519, *Patronato Legajo 34 Ramo 9,* letter to Don Charles from the pilots of the Armada de Maluco asking an increase in salaries, 2 pp.

1519, *Patronato Leg. 34 Ramo 6 2ª Carpeta,* testimony of Ferdinand Magellan before a notary that it has been impossible to recruit native Castilians for the crew and that it is necessary to enlist aliens, 18 pp.

1520, *Patronato Legajo 34 Ramo 25,* account of payments made by Cristóbal de Haro at San Lucar de Barrameda for the Armada de Maluco, 10 pp.

1520, *Papeles de Justicia Legajo 943,* Casa de Antillas, report of Juan Lopez de Rescalde of transfer of wine and wheat from the Casa de Antillas to Coruña by order of Bishop Fonseca, 2 pp.

1521, *Patronato Real Legajo 34 Ramo 18,* fragment of a letter from John Lopez de Rescalde, to Bishop Fonseca regarding the disagreements between Magellan and Cartagena; the arrest of Cartagena and the mutiny at Bay St. Julian, 7 pp.

1521, *Patronato Legajo 34 Ramo 15,* fragment from a letter of John Lopez de Rescalde to Bishop Fonseca concerning the punishment of the mutineers at Bay St. Julian, 4 pp.

1521, *Patronato Legajo 34 Ramo 17,* proceedings of the naval court of inquiry held in Bay St. Julian and giving the formal findings on the mutiny, 18 pp.

1521, *Patronato Legajo 34 Ramo 14,* report to the King from Juan Lopez de Rescalde, factor of Casa de Antillas, which discredits Magellan and endorses the acts of the de Haro–Fonseca clique, 5 pp.

1522, *Portada del Documento Contaduria Legajo 427 No. 11,* record of the spices brought back from Maluco in the Victoria and turned over to Cristóbal de Haro, 5 pp.

1522, *Patronato Legajo 34 Ramo 19,* testimony of Juan Sebastian del Cano concerning the mutiny at Bay St. Julian and the desertion by the San Antonio, 16 pp.

1522, *Seccion 2° Contaduria Legajo 427,* copy of a royal order insuring to Cristóbal de Haro the monopoly of drugs and spices from Maluco, 5 pp.

1522, *Patronato Real Legajo 40 Doc. 6 Pieza 1ª,* evidence in the "Suit of the Fuggers against the Crown," 2 pp.

1522, *Patronato 40 No. 6 Pieza 1ª,* charter of Casa de Especieria in Coruña and Declaration of Broad General Policy regarding Maluco and Colonization thereof, 22 pp.

1522, *Patronato Legajo 34 Ramo 20,* roll of the crew of the Trinidad who died in the Orient under command of Captain General Espinosa, 4 pp.

1522, *Patronato Legajo 34 Ramo 4,* a roster of the fleet's complement, Armada de Magallanes, 59 pp.

1523, *Patronato Legajo 34 Ramo 22,* letter to King Charles from Ruy Faleiro, 2 pp.

1525, *Portada del Documento #1, Contaduria Legajo 2,* Armada of Simon de Alcazaba, the King appropriates 25,000 gold pesos for the use of Cristóbal de Haro, 5 pp.

1525, *Contaduria Legajo 427,* charge for victuals supplied by Cristóbal de Haro to the shipwrights at Coruña, 13 pp.

1526, *Patronato Real Legajo 40 Doc. #6,* exclusive charter by Crown to Jakob Fugger, Bartholomew Welser, and Cristóbal de Haro, 7 pp.

1526, *Papeles de Justicia Legajo 943,* receipt for funds from Cristóbal de Haro to Juan de Aranda, 2 pp.

1526, *Portada del Documento # 12, Contaduria Legajo 427,* report to the King from Casa de Antillas of the gold turned over to Cristóbal de Haro, Factor of the Casa de Especieria, 5 pp.

1526, *Patronato Real 43 Document 1 #2,* royal order to Hernando Cortes, Captain General of New Spain, to send an armada to Maluco to seek the survivors of the expeditions of Magellan, Loaysa and Cabot, 3 pp.

1526, *Patronato Real 43 Ramo 3 #2,* order from King Charles to Sebastian Cabot, whom he supposed to be in Maluco, 2 pp.

1526, *Patronato Real 43 Ramo 2 Dec. 2,* royal order to Louis Ponce de Leon in New Spain to help Hernando Cortes dispatch a fleet quickly to Maluco, 2 pp.

1526, *Patronato Real Legajo 40 Dec. 6, Folio 39–40,* Pieza Primera, evidence in the suit of Fugger & Nephew against the Crown.

1526, *Patronato Legajo 34 Ramo 24,* deposition that Captain General Espinosa and others were being held in prison in Lisbon, 2 pp.

1526, *Patronato Legajo 34 Ramo 26,* two court petitions from a cleric for an Oriental bishopric as a reward for aid to the Spanish cause in the East, 9 pp.

1526, *Patronato Legajo 34 Ramo 25,* accounting of Cristóbal de Haro for the spices he received in the Victoria, 7 pp.

1527, *Patronato Real 43 Ramo 10 #2,* fragment—testimony of a member of Saavedra's expedition from Mexico, 2 pp.

1527, *Patronato Real 43 Doc. 4 #2,* log and rutter of a nao sent by Cortes to investigate a suitable sailing course from Mexico westward toward Maluco, 6 pp.

1527, *Patronato Real 43 Ramo 5 #2,* instructions by Hernando Cortes to Captain General Saavedra of the expedition to Maluco, 38 pp.

1527, *Patronato Legajo 34 Ramo 16,* report to Casa de Especieria by Captain General Gonzalo Gomez de Espinosa upon his return to Spain, 2 pp.

1527, *Patronato Legajo 34 Ramo 27,* testimony of survivors from Maluco of the Capitana Trinidad, 38 pp.

1528, *#3 Contaduria Legajo 2,* decisions of the Council of the Indies as to reimbursement to Cristóbal de Haro for his investment in the Armadas de Maluco, 4 pp.

1528, *Patronato Legajo 34 Ramo 28,* Armada de Maluco of Simon de Alcazaba which was built and rigged in Coruña, claim for payment of Ruy de Souto, Master Shipbuilder in Coruña, 11 pp.

1529, *Patronato Real 43 Ramo 7 #2,* royal order that Hernando Cortes be repaid for his expenses in sending an armada to Maluco, 2 pp.

1529, *Patronato Legajo 35 Ramo 2,* petition to Crown to pay Captain General Gomez Gonzalo de Espinosa annual pension granted by the King, 35 pp.

1529, *Patronato Legajo 35 Ramo 3,* claim by Pedro de Sotomayor for share in the proceeds from spices of the Victoria, 10 pp.

1530, *Contaduria Legajo 2,* royal order to Cristóbal de Haro to pay claim of Master Antonio of Antwerp, lombardero of the nao San Graviel, 2 pp.

1532, *Patronato Real 43 Ramo 8 #2,* claim for reimbursement of Don Hernando Cortes, Marques del Valle for cost of the expedition sent to Maluco, 87 pp.

1533, *Patronato Legajo 35 Ramo 5,* suit against Cristóbal de Haro by Commander Francisco de Valenzuela, 44 pp.

1533, *Patronato Legajo 35 Ramo 6,* claim by the heirs of Martin Mendez, Contador of the Victoria, 69 pp.

1534, *Portada del Documento #7, Contaduria Legajo 427,* claim upon the Crown by Cristóbal de Haro for time spent in outfitting the Armadas de Maluco, 2 pp.

1534, *Patronato Real 43 Ramo 9 #2,* account of the expedition sent by Hernando Cortes under Saavedra to Maluco, 15 pp.

1534, *Patronato Real 43 Ramo 11 Doc. 2,* second report of the voyage of Saavedra to Maluco from Mexico, 27 pp.

1534, *Patronato Legajo 35 Ramo 8,* petition in the name of widows of three mariners of the Trinidad, 4 pp.

1534, *Patronato Legajo 35 Ramo 7,* suit brought by widow of Captain Juan Rodríguez Serrano against Cristóbal de Haro, 14 pp.

1534, *Contaduria Legajo 2 #9,* lien upon salaries and quintaladas of Magellan's crews in favor of Monastery of la Victoria in Seville, 2 pp.

1537, *Portado del Documento #4, Contaduria Legajo 2,* claim of heirs of Juan de Cartagena upon Cristóbal de Haro, for reimbursement for his investment, 4 pp.

1537, *Patronato Legajo 36 Ramo #11 Piezas 1–2–3–4–5,* claim of the widow of Juan Rodríguez, marinero on the Trinidad, 66 pp.

1538, *Patronato Legajo 35 Ramo 9, Documents #3 to 12 inclusive, Documents 15, 17, 18, 21, 22,* claim of Cristóbal de Haro against the Crown, 161 pp.

1538, *Patronato Real 43 #12 #2,* claim of Francisco Granado, scrivener in the ship of Saavedra, 4 pp.

1538, *Patronato Legajo 35 Ramo 1,* claim for pay of Captain General Gomez de Espinosa, 10 pp.

1538, *Patronato Legajo 35 Ramo 9,* suit of Cristóbal de Haro against the Crown for reimbursement for the sums invested by him in the Armadas de Maluco, 101 pp.

1538, *Patronato Legajo 34 Ramo 23,* court decisions in the suit of Cristóbal de Haro against the Crown, 4 pp.

1540–1559, *Patronato Legajo 35 Ramo 4,* suit for arrears of pay of Domingo de Barruti, scrivener of the Trinidad, 53 pp.

1544, *Patronato Real Legajo 40 Ramo 6 Pieza Z,* suit of heirs of Jakob Fugger against the Crown, 22 pp.

1546, *Legajo 36 Ramo 3,* claim for wages and quintaladas due Martin de Magallanes, sobresaliente on the Concepcion and on the Victoria, 95 pp.

1547, *Patronato Legajo 36 Ramo 4,* suit by widow of Francisco Ruiz of Moguer, Mariner on Concepcion and on Trinidad, 36 pp.

1547, *Patronato Legajo 36 Ramo 5,* suit by the heirs of Sebastian Garcia, marinero on the Concepcion and on the Trinidad, 51 pp.

1549, *Patronato Legajo 36 Ramo 6,* claim of widow of Alonso Hernandez, seaman on the Santiago and on the Trinidad, 31 pp.

1552, *Patronato Legajo 36 Ramo 7,* suit by sister of Pero Garcia, seaman on the Santiago and on the Trinidad, and on the Victoria, 60 pp.

1568, *Patronato Legajo 36 Ramo 8,* suit of Lorenzo de Magallanes of Jerez, Spain, against the Crown as heir to Ferdinand Magellan, 68 pp.

BIBLIOGRAPHY

SEVERAL comprehensive and scholarly bibliographies have recently been published which are generally available. They are to be found in the following:

William B. Greenlee: *A Descriptive Bibliography of the History of Portugal,* Hispanic American Historical Review, Vol. XX No. 3, August, 1940.
Henry R. Hart: *Sea Road to the Indies,* New York, 1950.
Charles B. Nowell: *History of Portugal,* New York, 1952.
Boise Penrose: *Travel and Discovery in the Renaissance,* Cambridge, Mass., 1952.

Consequently the author has restricted the present bibliography to books in his own possession.

The author is aware that, although there are in the United States several outstanding collections of manuscripts and books concerning the Age of Discovery which are second to none, nevertheless there are some American centers of culture in which but few publications concerning Portuguese and Spanish exploration (particularly in Africa and the Orient) are available. Therefore the author will undertake to furnish photostatic excerpts from the works in his possession to interested persons to whom the originals may not be obtainable.

The bibliography is divided into sections according to subject matter, and entries are listed chronologically within each section. Titles marked with an asterisk are either of less scholarly interest or bear only indirectly on Magellan's period.

1. *Historical Background of Magellan*

Agostinho Rebello da Costa, *Cidade do Porto,* Porto, 1789.
*J. Buchan Telfer, R.N. (translator), *Travels of Johann Schiltberger 1396–1427,* London, 1879.
Edward Luther Stevenson, *Portolan Charts,* New York, 1911.

Hamy Collection, *Portolan Charts,* New York, 1912.
E. Prestage, *Chronicles of Fernão Lopes,* Watford, 1928.
*R. M. Pidal, *The Cid and His Spain,* London, 1934.
*K. M. E. Murray, *Constitutional History of the Cinque Ports,* Manchester, 1935.
George E. Nunn, *The Diplomacy Concerning the Discovery of America,* Jenkintown, Pennsylvania, 1948.
António Caetano do Amaral, *Legislacão e Costumes de Portugal,* Porto, 1949.
A. de Magalhães Basto, *Crónica de Cinco Reis de Portugal,* Porto, 1949.
Frei António Brandão, *Crónica do Dom Henrique e Donha Teresa,* Porto, 1949.
———, *Crónicas de Dom Sancho I e Dom Afonso II,* Porto, 1949.
———, *Crónicas de Dom Sancho II e Dom Afonso III,* Porto, 1949.
P. Avelino de Jesus da Costa, *Codices Medievais,* Braga, 1949.
Fernão Lopes, *Crónica de Dom João I,* 2 vols., Porto, 1949.
D. Francisco Manuel de Melo, *Dom Teódosio II,* Porto, 1949.
Rui de Pina, *Crónica de Dom Dinis,* Porto, 1949.
P. Avelino de Jesus da Costa, S. *Martinho de Dume,* Braga, 1950.
Conde de Vila Franca, *D. João I e Aliança Inglesa,* Lisbon, 1950.
J. Huizinga, *The Waning of the Middle Ages,* London, 1950.
Marcello Caetano, *A Administração Municipal de Lisboa 1179–1380,* Lisbon, 1951.
*A. R. Lewis, *Naval Power and Trade in the Mediterranean (500–1100),* Princeton, 1951.
*E. F. Jacob, *The Later Middle Ages,* Oxford, 1951.
Elaine Sanceau, *Dom João II,* Porto, 1952.
F. B. Embid, *Arquitectura Portuguesa Manuelina,* Seville, no date.

2. *Ferdinand Magellan*

F. H. H. Guillemard, *Life of Ferdinand Magellan,* New York, 1890.
Blair and Robertson, *History of the Philippine Islands,* 14 vols., Cleveland, 1903.
Antonio Pigafetta (J. A. Robertson, editor), *Magellan's Voyage around the World,* 3 vols., Cleveland, 1906.
Jean Denucé, *La Question des Moluques et la première circumnavigation du globe,* Brussels, 1911.
*Ramón de Manjarres, *Conmemoraçion de Magallanes,* Seville, 1919.
Conde de Alvellos, *O Brazão dos Magalhães,* Porto, 1924.
Arthur Sturges Hildebrand, *Ferdinand Magellan,* New York, 1924.
E. F. Benson, *Ferdinand Magellan,* London, 1929.
George E. Nunn, *Origin of the Strait of Anian Concept,* Philadelphia, 1929.
*J. A. Brendon, *Ferdinand Magellan,* London, 1929.
George E. Nunn, *The Columbus and Magellan Concepts of South America,* Glenside, 1932.

Queiroz Velloso, *A Naturalidade de Fernão de Magalhães,* Rio de Janeiro, 1936.
Stefan Zweig, *Conqueror of the Seas,* New York, 1938.
———, *Fernão de Magalhães,* Rio de Janeiro, 1938.
Visconde de Lagôa, *Fernão de Magalhãis,* 2 vols., Lisbon, 1938.
*Pedro Correia de Marques, *Homenagem a Fernão de Magalhães,* Lisbon, 1942.
Carlos Amoretti, *Primer Viaje en Torno del Globo,* Buenos Aires, 1943.
*Rudolph Baumgardt, *Magellan,* Paris, 1943.
P. Mártir de Anglería (1530), *Décadas del Nuevo Mundo,* Buenos Aires, 1944.
*Léonce Peillard, *Magellan, mon maître,* Mesnil, 1948.

Juvenile books

*George M. Towle, *Magellan,* New York, 1880.
*Agnes Danforth Hewes, *Spice and the Devil's Cave,* New York, 1938.
*Louise Andrews Kent, *He Went with Magellan,* Boston, 1943.

3. *The Atlantic Ocean and West Africa*

Giovanni Battista Ramusio, *Delle Navigationi et Viaggi,* 3 vols., Venice, 1554.
Samuel Purchas, *Purchas, his Pilgrimage,* London, 1613.
William Bozman, *The Coast of Guinea; Gold, Slaves and Ivory,* London, 1705.
D. Miguel de Barrios, *Descripçion de las Islas del Mar Atlantico,* Madrid, 1793.
George Glas, *Discovery of the Canary Islands,* London, 1794.
R. H. Major, *Conquest of the Canarians,* London, 1872.
*Hugh McN. Dyer, R.N., *The West Coast of Africa,* London, 1876.
R. H. Major, *Discoveries of Prince Henry the Navigator,* London, 1877.
C. R. Beazley, *Prince Henry the Navigator,* New York, 1894.
*Rev. Carl Christian Reindorf, *History of the Gold Coast,* Basel, 1895.
Gomes Eannes de Azurara, *Discovery and Conquest of Guinea,* 2 vols., London, 1896.
Leo Africanus (trans. John Pory, 1600), *Africa 1491–1552,* London, 1896.
*Rasmus B. Anderson, *The Flateyjarbok of 10th Century Icelandic Discovery of America,* Copenhagen, 1906.
Virginia de Castro e Almeida, *Discoveries of Henry the Navigator,* London, 1906.
Sir Clements Markham, *Guanches of Tenerife,* London, 1907.
*A. W. Cardinall, *Bibliography of the Gold Coast,* Accra, 1931.
Richard Jobson, *The Golden Trade of the Aethiopians (1620),* London, 1932.
Edgar Prestage, *Portuguese Pioneers,* London, 1933.

G. R. Crone, *The Voyages of Cadamosto,* London, 1937.
Duarte Pacheco Pereira, *Esmeraldo de Situ Orbis,* London, 1937.
Samuel Eliot Morison, *Portuguese Voyages to America in the 15th Century,* Cambridge, Mass., 1940.
J. W. Blake, *Europeans in West Africa* (1450–1560), 2 vols., London, 1942.
Costa Brochado, *Infante Dom Henrique,* Lisbon, 1942.
Elaine Sanceau, *Henry the Navigator,* New York, 1947.
Alberto Iria, *O Algarve no Descobrimento da Guiné,* Lisbon, 1947.
*Tom Marvel, *The New Congo,* New York, 1948.
António J. Dias Dinis, *Gomes Eanes de Zurara,* Lisbon, 1949.
V. Fernandes, *La Côte occidentale d'Afrique (1506),* Bissau, 1951.

4. *East Africa*

Luys del Marmol Caravaial, *Descripçion General de Affrica,* 2 vols., Granada, 1573.
William Vincent, *Periplus of the Erythrean Sea,* 2 vols., London, 1800.
*W. F. W. Owen, R.N., *Narrative of Voyages to Africa, Arabia and Madagascar,* 2 vols., London, 1833.
*(English Commission), *Steam to India via the Red Sea,* London, 1838.
*Lieut. Barnard, R.N., *Three Years Cruise in the Mozambique Channel,* London, 1848.
*R. S. Whiteway, *Portuguese Expedition to Abyssinia* (1541), London, 1902.
*Jules Toutain, *Economic Life of the Ancient World,* London, 1930.
*Stanley Rogers, *The Indian Ocean,* London, 1932.
Rev. Sidney R. Welch, *Europe's Discovery of South Africa,* Capetown, 1935.
Pêro Pais, *Historia da Etiópia,* 3 vols., Lisbon, 1938.
Armando Cortesão, *Descobrimento do Preste João,* Lisbon, 1938.
Eric Axelson, *South-East Africa, 1488–1530,* Aberdeen, 1940.
Elaine Sanceau, *Preste João,* Porto, 1944.
Rev. Sidney R. Welch, *South Africa under King Manuel 1495–1521,* Capetown, 1946.
W. W. Hyde, *Ancient Greek Mariners,* New York, 1947.
Rev. Sidney R. Welch, *South Africa under John III—1521,* Capetown, 1948.
*W. B. Fisher, *The Middle East,* London, 1948.
*António Mendes Corrêa, *Ultramar Português Síntese da Africa,* Lisbon, 1949.
*Comte Moura-Braz, *Moçambique,* Lisbon, 1950.
*Cyrus Townsend Brady, Jr., *Commerce and Conquest in East Africa,* Salem, 1950.
S. R. Welch, *Africa do Sul sob Manuel,* Lisbon, 1950.
A. Kammerer, *La Découverte de Madagascar par les Portugais,* Lisbon, 1950.

5. *Portuguese Asia*

Fray Antonio e San Roman, *História General de la Yndia Oriental,* Valladolid, 1603.
Giovanni Battista Ramusio, *Delle Navigationi et Viaggi,* 3 vols., Venice, 1604.
Manuel de Faria y Sousa, *Portuguese Asia,* 3 vols., London, 1695.
J. Knox, *New Collection of Voyages and Discoveries,* 7 vols., London, 1767.
Abbé Raynal, *Europeans in the East and West Indies,* 8 vols., London, 1783.
Anonymous, *Os Portuguezes em Africa, Asia, América e Oceana,* 5 vols., Lisbon, 1849.
Sir J. E. Tennent, *Christianity in Ceylon,* London, 1850.
R. H. Major, *India in the 15th Century,* London, 1857.
John W. Jones, *Travels of Ludovico di Varthema, 1503–08,* London, 1863.
Walter de Gray Birch, *Commentaries of Afonso Dalboquerque,* London, 1875.
A. C. Burnell, *Voyage of Van Linschoten to the East Indies* (*1583*), 2 vols., London, 1885.
Edward Grey, *Travels of Pietro Della Valle in India* (*1614*), 2 vols., London, 1892.
Rev. A. J. D. D'Orsey, *Portuguese Missions in Asia and Africa,* London, 1893.
Mansel Longworth Dames, *Book of Duarte Barbosa,* 2 vols., London, 1898.
*Wm. F. Sinclair, *Travels of Pedro Teixeira* (*1586*), London, 1902.
H. Morse Stephens, *Albuquerque,* Oxford, 1897.
*John Fryer, *East India and Persia* (*1672*), 3 vols., London, 1909.
Garcia da Orta, *Simples and Drugs of India* (*1563*), London, 1913.
*Hendrik van Loon, *Dutch Navigators,* New York, 1916.
Sir Richard Carnac Temple, *Itinerary of Ludóvico di Varthema* (*1502*), London, 1928.
K. M. Panikkar, *Malabar and the Portuguese,* Bombay, 1929.
*P. Fernão Guerreiro, S.J., *Coisas Que Fizeram A Companhia de Jesus* (*1600*), Coimbra, 1930.
P. E. Pieris, *Portugal in Ceylon 1505–1658,* Cambridge, 1937.
*C. N. Parkinson, *Trade in the Eastern Seas,* Cambridge, 1937.
*Sir William Foster, *Voyages of Lancaster to E. India* (*1591*), London, 1940.
Costa Brochado, *Afonso de Albuquerque,* Lisbon, 1943.
João de Barros, *Década I, Livro IV,* Porto, 1945.
K. M. Panikkar, *India and the Indian Ocean,* London, 1945.
Augusto Reis Machado, *Duarte Barbosa,* Lisbon, 1946.
*António da Silva Rêgo, *História das Missões do Oriente* (*1499–1543*), 2 vols., Lisbon, 1947.
*Alberto da Silva Correia, *Colonização Portuguesa na India,* Lisbon, 1948.

Elaine Sanceau, *O Caminho da India,* Porto, 1948.
*———, *Dom João de Castro,* Porto, 1949.
António Baião, *Diário da Viagem de Vasco da Gama,* 2 vols., Porto, 1949.
Manuel de Faria e Sousa, *Asia Portuguesa* (trans. from Spanish into Portuguese), 6 vols., Porto, 1949.
Henry H. Hart, *Sea Road to the Indies,* New York, 1950.
*José Moreira Campos, *Grande Capitão André Furtado de Mendonça,* Lisbon, 1951.
W. B. Greenlee, *Víagem de Cabral,* Porto, 1952.
F. M. da Luz, *Fortalezas da India,* Coimbra, 1952.
*J. C. Neves, *D. Pedro Mascarenhas,* Lisbon, 1952.

6. *Malacca*

Bartolomé Leonardo de Argensola, *Conquista de las Islas Malucas,* Madrid, 1609.
Fray Marcello de Ribadeneyra, *História de los Reynos de Cuchinchina, Malaca, etc.,* Barcelona, 1613.
*Capt. Pasfield Oliver, R.A., *Voyage of François Leguat (1693),* 2 vols., London, 1891.
Henry Cogan, *Voyages of Ferdinand Mendez Pinto,* London, 1891.
Armando Cortesão, *The Book of Francisco Rodrígues,* London, 1904.
*William Foster, *Journal of John Jourdain (1608),* Cambridge, 1905.
*H. B. Morse, *Chronicles of East India Company (China), 1635,* 4 vols., Cambridge, 1926.
Fray Sebastien Manríque, *Travels (1629),* London, 1927.
*Fryke (1690) and Schweitzer (1675), *Voyages to the East Indies,* London, 1929.
*Sir William Foster, *Voyage of Thomas Best to the East Indies (1612),* London, 1934.
*———, *Voyage of Nicholas Downton to the East Indies (1614),* London, 1939.
*Maurice Collis, *The Land of the Great Image,* New York, 1943.
Armando Cortesão, *The Suma Oriental of Tomé Pires,* 2 vols., London, 1944.
Luis Silveira, *Itinerário de Sebastião Manrique (1628),* 2 vols., Lisbon, 1946.
Visconde de Lagôa, *Peregrinacão de Fernão Mendes Pinto,* Lisbon, 1947.
Maurice Collis, *The Grand Peregrination,* London, 1949.
Eduardo Brazão, *Relações Diplomáticas de Portugal Com a China (1516),* Lisbon, 1949.
*Luna de Oliveira, *Timor—Na História de Portugal,* Lisbon, 1949.

7. *Brazil, Patagonia, and the Western Atlantic*

*Capt. A. de Ulloa, *Journey through South America,* London, 1760.
Joaquim M. de Macedo, *Chorography of Brazil,* Leipzig, 1873.

*Dionísio de Alsedo y Herrera, *Piraterías Ingleses en la América Española,* Madrid, 1883.
Justin Winsor, *History of America,* 8 vols., Cambridge, Mass., 1889.
Sir Clements R. Markham, *Letters of Amerigo Vespucci,* London, 1894.
Henry Harrissé, *John and Sebastian Cabot,* London, 1896.
*E. Heawood, *Geographical Discovery,* Cambridge, 1912.
Carlos Malheiro Dias, *História da Colonização Portuguesa do Brasil,* 3 vols., Rio de Janeiro, 1920.
*Doctor Nicholas Monardes, *Joyefull Newes out of the Newe Founde World (1574),* 2 vols., London, 1925.
Nellis M. Crouse, *In Quest of the Western Ocean,* New York, 1928.
*I. A. Wright, *English Voyages to the Caribbean (1527),* London, 1929.
*J. N. L. Baker, *Geographical Discovery,* London, 1931.
*Symposium, *New Spain and the West,* 2 vols., Los Angeles, 1932.
*G. P. Insh, *The Company of Scotland and the Indies,* New York, 1932.
*Constantino Bayle, S.J., *España en Indias,* Vitoría, 1934.
William B. Greenlee, *Voyage of Cabral to Brazil and India,* London, 1938.
Gabriel Soares de Sousa, *Tratado Descriptivo do Brasil em 1587,* Rio de Janeiro, 1938.
*G. Barroso, *Brasil na Lenda,* São Paulo, 1941.
Antonio de Espinosa, *Description of the West Indies,* Smithsonian Institution, Washington, 1942.
Frederick J. Pohl, *Amerigo Vespucci, Pilot Major,* New York, 1944.
George E. Nunn, *The La Cosa Map and the Cabot Voyages,* Jenkintown, Pennsylvania, 1946.
Damião Peres, *Américo Vespúcio Expedição de 1501–2,* Porto, 1949.

8. *Strait of Magellan*

Don Antonio de Cordova, *Ultimo Viage al Estrecho de Magallanes,* Madrid, 1788.
British Admiralty, *Strait of Magellan,* London, 1790.
Siegmund Günther, *Martin Behaim,* Bamberg, 1890.
Sir Clements R. Markham, *Sarmiento's Voyages to the Straits of Magellan,* London, 1895.
Charles Darwin, *Journal of Researches,* New York, 1896.
Sir Clements R. Markham, *Early Spanish Voyages to the Straits of Magellan,* London, 1911.
Zelia Nuttall, *New Light on Drake,* London, 1914.
P. Constantino Bayle, S.J., *El Descubrimiento del Estrecho de Magallanes,* 2 vols., Madrid, 1920.

9. *Pacific Isles*

Giovanni Battista Ramusio, *Delle Navigationi et Viaggi,* Venice, 1604.
Fray Marcello de Ribadeneyra, *Historia de los Reynos de China,* Barcelona, 1613.

Richard Walter, *Voyage Round the World by George Anson,* London, 1750.
Juan de la Concepción, *Historia General de Philipinas,* Vol. I., Manila, 1788.
*Compilation, *Missionary Voyages to the South Pacific Islands,* London, 1799.
*Don Vicente Barrantes, *Guerras Piráticas de Filipinas,* Madrid, 1878.
*J. Foreman, *The Philippine Islands,* London, 1899.
*Ramon Reyes Lala, *The Philippine Islands,* New York, 1899.
*Government Report, *Report of the Philippine Commission to the President, Vols. I–IV,* Washington, 1900.
*Compañía de Jesús, *El Archipiélago Filipino, Vol. I,* Washington, 1900.
*Lord Amherst of Hackney, *The Discovery of the Solomon Islands, 1568,* 2 vols., London, 1901.
*War Dept., *The Philippine Islands,* Washington, 1902.
*T. H. P. de Tavera, *Biblioteca Filipina,* Washington, 1903.
*Blair and Robertson, *History of the Philippine Islands,* 14 vols., Cleveland, 1903.
*Gen. J. P. Sanger, U.S.A., *Philippine Geography, History and Population,* Washington, 1905.
Najeeb M. Saleeby, *Moro History, Law and Religion,* Manila, 1905.
*J. A. J. de Villiers, *East and West Indian Mirror, Voyage of Joris Van Spielbergen, 1614–17,* London, 1906.
*B. G. Corney, *Discovery of Easter Island (1722),* Cambridge, 1908.
*William Churchill, *Polynesian Wanderings,* Washington, 1911.
*Dean C. Worcester, *The Philippines, Past and Present,* New York, 1914.
*Austin Craig, *The Former Philippines,* New York, 1917.
*H. Morse Stephens, *Pacific Ocean in History,* New York, 1917.
Richard Walter, *Anson's Voyage Round the World (1740),* London, 1929.
*P. H. Buck, *Vikings of the Sunrise,* New York, 1937.
*C. McK. Parr, *Over and Above Our Pacific,* New York, 1941.
*W. Cameron Forbes, *The Philippine Islands,* Cambridge, Mass., 1945.
*Instituto Histórico de Marina, *Viajes y Descubrimientos en el Mar Pacifico,* 5 vols., Madrid, 1943–47.
*Horacio de la Costa, S.J., *Development of Native Clergy in the Philippines,* Manila, 1947.

10. *Sailing Ship Construction*

J. J. Welch, R.N., *Naval Architecture,* London, 1893.
E. G. Fishbourne, R.N., *Naval Architecture,* London, 1896.
M. Oppenheim, *English Naval Accounts (1485),* London, 1896.
Alfred Spont, *English Naval Records (1512),* London, 1897.
David Hannay, *Sea Trader,* London, 1912.
Gervasio de Artíñano, *La Arquitectura Naval Española en Madera,* Madrid, 1920.
Henry B. Culver, *Old Ships,* New York, 1924.
R. Morton Nance, *Sailing-Ship Models,* London, 1924.

Hawthorne Daniel, *Ships,* New York, 1925.
E. Keble Chatterton, *Ship-Models,* London, 1928.
Hendrik van Loon, *Ships and How They Sailed,* New York, 1935.
Enciclopedia Pela Imagem, *Os Navios,* Porto, 1940.
———, *Caravelas, Naus e Galés de Portugal,* Porto, 1940.

11. *Navigation of Sailing Ships*

Pedro de Syria, *Arte de la Verdadera Navegacion,* Valencia, 1602.
V. Tofiño de San Miguel, *Derrotero de las Costas de España,* Madrid, 1789.
J. M. Gilliss, U.S.N., *U.S. Astronomical Expedition to the Southern Hemisphere,* Washington, 1855.
A. G. Findlay, *Sailing Directory for the Ethiopic or South Atlantic Ocean,* London, 1875.
Henry Raper, R.N., *The Practice of Navigation,* London, 1892.
Gabriel Ferrand, *Instructions nautiques et routiers arabes (XV siecle),* Paris, 1921.
A. Fontoura da Costa, *La Science nautique des Portugais (1500),* Lisbon, 1941.
Diego Garcia de Palacio, *Instruccion Naútica Para Navegar* (1597), Madrid, 1944.
Salvador Garcia Franco, *Arte y Ciencia de Navegar,* 2 vols., Madrid, 1947.
Armando Cortesão, *A Ciência Naútica e o Renascimento,* Lisbon, 1949.
G. F. Hourani, *Arab Seafaring in the Indian Ocean,* Princeton, 1951.
Almirante Gago Coutinho, *A Naútica dos Descobrimentos,* 2 vols., Oporto, 1952.

12. *Christopher Columbus*

Don Ferdinand Columbus, *Life and Actions of Admiral Christopher Columbus,* London, 1673.
Washington Irving, *Life of Christopher Columbus,* New York, 1840.
Bartolomé de las Casas, *História de las Indias,* 5 vols., Madrid, 1875.
*Anonymous, *Los Restos de Cristoval Colon,* Seville, 1878.
*C. P. Mackie, *With the Admiral of the Ocean Sea,* Chicago, 1891.
Paul Leicester Ford, *Writings of Columbus,* New York, 1892.
Emilio Castelar, *Descubrimiento de América,* Madrid, 1892.
Richard H. Clarke, *Old and New Lights on Columbus,* New York, 1893.
J. M. Asensio y Toledo, *Cristóbal Colón,* 2 vols., Barcelona, *c.* 1900.
Henry Vignaud, *Toscanelli and Columbus,* London, 1902.
Filson Young, *Christopher Columbus,* 2 vols., London, 1906.
Henry Vignaud, *Columbian Tradition and Astronomer Toscanelli's Part,* London, 1920.
*Wm. Giles Nash, *True History of the Discovery of America,* London, 1924.
Van Wyck Brooks, *Journal of the First Voyage to America,* London, *c.* 1930.
H. H. Houben, *Christopher Columbus,* London, 1935.

Salvador de Madariaga, *Vida del Muy Magnífico Señor Don Cristóbal Colón,* Buenos Aires, 1940.
Samuel Eliot Morison, *Admiral of the Ocean Sea,* Boston, 1942.

13. *Jakob Fugger and Cristóbal de Haro*

Dr. Richard Ehrenberg, *Das Zeitalter der Fugger,* 2 vols., Jena, 1896.
Richard Hakluyt, *Principal Navigations, Voyages and Discoveries of the English Nation,* 12 vols., Glasgow, 1903.
*H. Gordon Selfridge, *The Romance of Commerce,* London, 1918.
C. H. Haring, *Trade and Navigation between Spain and the Indies,* London, 1918.
*Victor von Klarwill, *Fugger News Letters,* 2 vols., New York, 1925.
*A. B. Kerr, *Jacques Cœur,* London, 1927.
Dr. Richard Ehrenberg, *Capital and Finance in the Renaissance, a Study of the Fuggers and their Connections,* London, 1928.
J. Strieder, *Jacob Fugger the Rich,* New York, 1931.
Laetitia Lyell (introduction) assisted by Frank D. Watney, clk. to the Mercers' Co., *Acts of Court of the Mercers' Company 1453–1527,* Cambridge, 1936.
Eileen Power, *The Wool Trade in English Medieval History,* Oxford, 1941.
German Arciniegas, *Germans in the Conquest of America,* New York, 1943.
Götz, Freiherr von Pölnitz, *Jakob Fugger, Kaiser, Kirche und Kapital in der oberdeutschen Renaissance,* Tübingen, 1949.
———, *Jakob Fugger: Quellen und Erläuterungen,* Tübingen, 1951.
E. F. Jacob, *Study of the Later Middle Ages,* Oxford, 1951.
M. Postan and E. E. Rich, editors, (planned by the late Sir John Clapham and the late Eileen Power), *The Cambridge Economic History of Europe, Vol. II, Trade and Industry in the Middle Ages,* Cambridge, 1952.
Ciba Co. of Basel, Switzerland, *Medieval and Renaissance Industries,* a series of brochures, especially: 1. *Medieval Dyeing;* 4. *Purple;* 7. *Scarlet;* 39. *Madder and Turkey Red;* 85. *Indigo;* 10. *Trade Routes and Dye Markets in the Middle Ages;* 27. *The Textile Trades in Medieval Florence;* 13. *Guild Emblems and their Significance;* 49. *Flax and Hemp;* 80. *Lucchese Silks;* 29. *Venetian Silks;* 14. *Cloth-Making in Flanders;* 48. *The History of the Textile Crafts in Holland;* 47. *Cloth Merchants of the Renaissance as Patrons of Art;* 64. *Cotton and Cotton Trade in the Middle Ages;* 20. *The Development of the Textile Crafts in Spain;* 65. *The Cloth Trade and the Fairs of Champagne;* 19. *The Exchange;* 62. *Swiss Fairs and Markets in the Middle Ages.*

14. *Juan Rodríguez de Fonseca*

Antonio de Leon, *Confirmaciones Reales de las Indias,* Madrid, 1630.
Antonio de Solis, *Conquest of Mexico,* 2 vols., London, 1753.
Esprit Flechier, *Cardenal Ximenez de Cisneros,* Madrid, 1773.

Bernal Diaz del Castillo, *Conquest of Mexico,* 2 vols., London, 1803.
Washington Irving, *Life of Christopher Columbus,* New York, 1840.
Wm. H. Prescott, *History of the Reign of Ferdinand and Isabella,* 3 vols., Philadelphia, 1873.
———, *Conquest of Mexico,* 3 vols., Philadelphia, 1874.
Bartolomé de las Casas, *História de las Indias,* Madrid, 1875.
R. del Solar, *Casa de Contratación,* Seville, 1890.
Clements R. Markham, *Proceedings of Pedrarias Dávila,* London, 1895.
Duque de Alba, *Correspondencia de Gutierre Gomez de Fuensalida,* Madrid, 1907.
Antonio de Solis, *Conquista de Méjico,* Paris, 1908.
*Rafael Sabatini, *Torquemada and the Spanish Inquisition,* London, 1913.
C. H. Haring, *Trade between Spain and the Indies,* Cambridge, 1918.
Conde de Cedillo, *El Cardenal Cisneros,* 3 vols., Madrid, 1921.
*Henry Charles Lea, *History of the Inquisition of Spain,* 4 vols., London, 1922.
*———, *Inquisition in the Spanish Dependencies,* London, 1922.
Don Antonio C. Chapado, *Datas Históricos de la Ciudad de Toro,* Toro, 1923.
H. L. Seaver, *The Great Revolt in Castile,* Cambridge, Mass., 1928.
*C. E. Chapman, *Colonial Hispanic America,* New York, 1933.
Juan Dantin Cereceda, *Exploradores y Conquistadores de Indias,* Madrid, 1934.
Luciano Serrano, O.S.B., *El Obispado de Burgos,* 3 vols., Madrid, 1936.
Pedro Mártir de Anglería, *Décadas del Nuevo Mundo,* Buenos Aires, 1944.
*Salvador de Madariaga, *Rise of the Spanish American Empire,* London, 1947.
*William Thomas Walsh, *Personajes de la Inquisición,* Madrid, 1948.
F. Casas, *El Real Monasterio de Sancti Spiritus,* Toro, 1950.

15. *Venice in the Time of Magellan*

* W. D. Howells, *Venetian Life,* New York, 1867.
W. Carew Hazlitt, *The Venetian Republic,* 2 vols., London, 1900.
*George B. McClellan, *The Oligarchy of Venice,* Boston, 1904.
Pompeo Molmenti, *Venice,* 6 vols., Chicago, 1907.
*Alexander Robertson, *Venetian Discourses,* London, 1907.
Alethea Wiel, *Navy of Venice,* London, 1910.
*Laura M. Ragg, *Crises in Venetian History,* New York, 1928.
*H. H. Powers, *Venice and its Art,* New York, 1930.
Jules Sottas, *Messageries maritimes de Venise,* Paris, 1938.

16. *Charles V*

*Sir William Stirling-Maxwell, *Don John of Austria,* London, 1883.
William Robertson, *History of the Reign of the Emperor Charles V,* Philadelphia, 1875.

F. de Laiglesia, *Estudios Históricos* 1515–55, Madrid, 1908.
Edward Armstrong, *The Emperor Charles V*, 2 vols., London, 1929.
D. B. Wyndham Lewis, *Charles of Europe*, New York, 1931.
Karl Brandi, *The Emperor Charles V*, London, 1939.
E. G. Ontiveros, *Política Norteafricana de Carlos I*, Madrid, 1950.

17. *History of Spain*

John de Mariana, *General History of Spain*, London, 1699.
R. P. Duchesne, S.J., *Compendio de la Historía de España*, 2 vols., Madrid, 1764.
Henrique Flórez, *Memorias de las Reynas Catolicas*, Madrid, 1770.
*Robert Watson, *History of Philip III*, London, 1793.
*———, *History of Philip II*, London, 1794.
J. A. Condé, *The Arabs in Spain*, 3 vols., London, 1850.
D. V. Gebhardt, *História de España y de sus Indias*, 7 vols., Barcelona, 1864.
Wm. H. Prescott, *History of Ferdinand and Isabella*, Philadelphia, 1873.
*———, *History of Philip II*, Philadelphia, 1875.
*M. G. Imaz, *Príncipe Don Juan*, Amsterdam, 1890.
*H. C. Lea, *Moriscos of Spain*, London, 1901.
*Albert F. Calvert, *Spanish Arms and Armor*, London, 1907.
*B. Whishaw, *Arabic Spain*, London, 1912.
Rafael Altamira y Creves, *História de España*, 4 vols., Barcelona, 1913.
*———, *Civilización Española*, Madrid, 1915.
R. B. Merriman, *Spanish Empire*, 4 vols., New York, 1918.
Chas. E. Chapman, *History of Spain*, New York, 1922.
*Salvador de Madariaga, *Spain*, London, 1930.
H. J. Chaytor, *History of Aragon and Catalonia*, London, 1933.
Augustín Blánquez Fraile, *História de España*, Barcelona, 1936.
Pedro Mártir de Anglería, *Décadas del Nuevo Mundo*, Buenos Aires, 1944.
Julian Paz, *Archivo General de Simancas (Flanders, 1506)*, Madrid, 1946.
*R. M. Pidal, *The Spaniards in their History*, London, 1950.
M. Sarasola, *Vizcaya y Los Reyes Católicos*, Madrid, 1950.
A. de la Torre, *Documentos de los Reyes Católicos*, Barcelona, 1951.
J. V. Vives, *Fernando el Católico*, Madrid, 1952.

18. *History of Portugal*

Edward Blount, *Historie of Portugall*, London, 1600.
Manuel de Faria y Sousa, *Epitome de las Histórias Portuguesas*, Madrid, 1628.
Emanuel de Faria y Sousa (trans. Capt. John Stevens), *History of Portugal*, London, 1698.
Lequien de la Neufville, *Histoire général e de Portugal*, 2 vols., Paris, 1700.
Joseph François Lefitau, S.J., *Histoire des découvertes et conquestes des Portugais*, 2 vols., Paris, 1733.

Jerome Osorio (trans. James Gibbs), *History of the Portuguese,* London, 1752.

Richard Francis Burton (trans.), *Os Lusiadas,* 2 vols., London, 1880.

———, *Camoens,* London, 1881.

*F. Gribble, *Royal House of Portugal,* London, 1915.

Alexandre Herculano, *Inquisition in Portugal,* San Francisco, 1926.

J. D. M. Ford, *Letters of John III of Portugal, 1521,* Cambridge, Mass., 1931.

———, *Letters of the Court of John III of Portugal,* Cambridge, Mass., 1933.

António Baião, *Historia da Expansão Portuguesa No Mundo,* 3 vols., Lisbon, 1937.

*Virginia de Castro e Almeida, *Itinéraire historique du Portugal,* Lisbon, 1940.

*Enciclopedia Pela Imagem, *Castellos Portuguezes,* Porto, 1940.

H. V. Livermore, *History of Portugal,* Cambridge, 1947.

*Charles David Ley, *Portuguese Voyages 1498–1663,* London, 1947.

Damião de Góis, *Opúsculos Históricos,* Porto, 1949.

António Galvão, *Tratado dos Descobrimentos,* Porto, 1949.

Leonard Bacon (trans.), *The Lusiads,* New York, 1950.

*J. Gentil da Silva, *Estudos de História Portuguesa,* Lisbon, 1950.

*J. L. de Azevedo, *O Messianismo de Portugal,* Porto, 1950.

*A. de J. da Costa, *Relacões de D. Afonso V,* Braga, 1952.

Elaine Sanceau, *Dom João II,* Porto, 1952.

C. B. Nowell, *History of Portugal,* New York, 1952.

Boies Penrose, *Travel and Discovery in the Renaissance,* Cambridge, Mass., 1952.

INDEX

ABOUT THE AUTHOR

CHARLES MCKEW PARR has devoted a decade to the writing of *So Noble a Captain.* But they were not years spent as a recluse in a library. They were years crowded with the activities that have made him a successful businessman, politician, and farmer. He was born in Baltimore in 1884 of a family that settled in Maryland in Lord Baltimore's day. He attended Boys' Latin School and then went to West Point. But deafness disqualified him for military life, and he entered upon a business career which has taken him all over the world. Eventually he became chairman of the board of the Parr Electric Company, and the Parr Marine and Export Company, and a governor of the National Association of Electrical Distributors.

During World War I he took time out from business to serve as a Trade Advisor with the War Trade Board, as a Special Assistant to the Secretary of State, and as a foreign agent in Spain. During World War II Mr. Parr served as a dollar-a-year man with two Washington agencies.

Because he believes strongly that business men should participate in government instead of criticizing it, he entered local politics and served as a Representative and as a Senator in the Connecticut State Legislature. In several instances he was nominated by both the Republican and Democratic parties in his district.

He owns a farm in Chester, Connecticut, where he raises Southdown sheep, prize Leghorns, geese, and ducks. And here he has planted trees, thousands of them, to make his swamps useful, and to improve the land in the state he loves and serves. He rides over his small farm not in an automobile but on a horse (named Magellan). His extensive library is housed in an old box shop which has been in his wife's family since pre-Revolutionary days. The books are in many languages, of which Mr. Parr reads at least seven. Even the prayer book he carries to church on Sunday may be in Latin or Greek, Spanish or Portuguese. He was forty when he started to study classical Greek and he subsequently named all the Swiss dairy goats on his farm after characters from Homer.

His correspondence is enormous, for he has received the help of scholars all over the world in his researches on Magellan. His activities in one day may range from a study for a new local jail, to a directors' meeting of the chamber of commerce, a Rotary luncheon, the supervision of his grandsons' boxing lessons, the writing of a legislative report for his local newspaper column, and a conference with a county supervisor of foster homes for children.

He has a passion for details, a boundless vitality, and an intense interest in people, whether they live today or lived in the past. These are the traits that he has brought to his long study of Magellan. They have enabled Mr. Parr to understand and interpret the great forces of commerce and politics which exploited Magellan's personal integrity and imagination and made possible the great accomplishments of the period about which he has written.

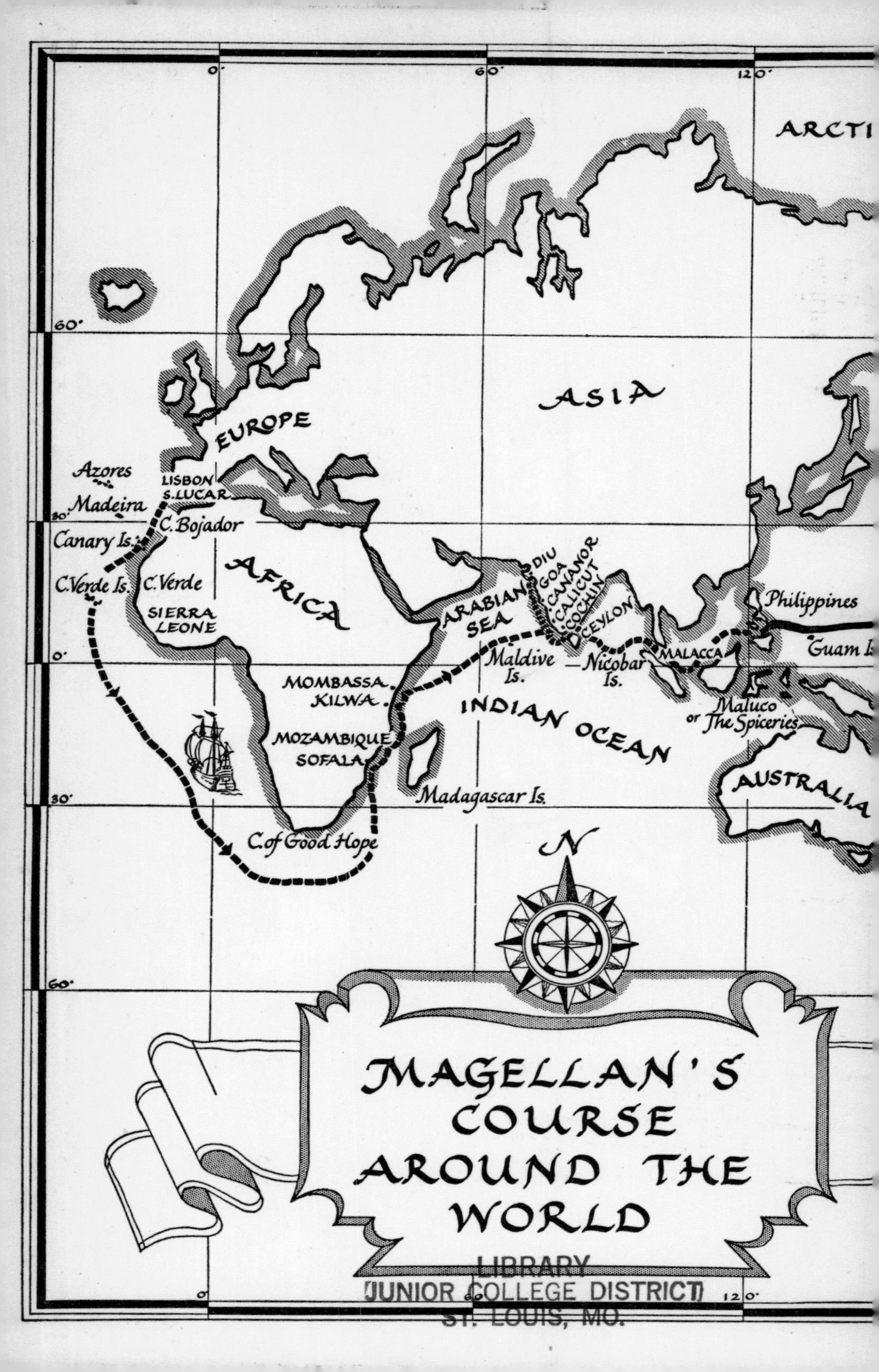

ARCTI
ASIA
EUROPE
Azores
Madeira
LISBON
S.LUCAR
C. Bojador
Canary Is.
AFRICA
C. Verde Is.
C. Verde
SIERRA
LEONE
ARABIAN
SEA
DIU
GOA
CANANOR
CALICUT
COCHIN
CEYLON
Philippines
Guam Is.
Maldive
Is.
Nicobar
Is.
MALACCA
MOMBASSA
KILWA
INDIAN OCEAN
Maluco
or The Spiceries
MOZAMBIQUE
SOFALA
AUSTRALIA
Madagascar Is.
C. of Good Hope
N
MAGELLAN'S
COURSE
AROUND THE
WORLD
0°
60°
120°
30°